D0849295

AFRICAN HISTORICAL DICTIONARIES
Edited by Jon Woronoff

1. *Cameroon,* by Victor T. LeVine and Roger P. Nye. 1974. Out of print. See No. 48.
2. *The Congo,* 2nd ed., by Virginia Thompson and Richard Adloff. 1984. Out of print. See No. 69.
3. *Swaziland,* by John J. Grotpeter. 1975.
4. *The Gambia,* 2nd ed., by Harry A. Gailey. 1987.
5. *Botswana,* by Richard P. Stevens. 1975. Out of print. See No. 70.
6. *Somalia,* by Margaret F. Castagno. 1975.
7. *Benin [Dahomey],* 2nd ed., by Samuel Decalo. 1987. Out of print. See No. 61.
8. *Burundi,* by Warren Weinstein. 1976.
9. *Togo,* 3rd ed., by Samuel Decalo. 1996.
10. *Lesotho,* by Gordon Haliburton. 1977.
11. *Mali,* 3rd ed., by Pascal James Imperato. 1996.
12. *Sierra Leone,* by Cyril Patrick Foray. 1977.
13. *Chad,* 2nd ed., by Samuel Decalo. 1987.
14. *Upper Volta,* by Daniel Miles McFarland. 1978.
15. *Tanzania,* by Laura S. Kurtz. 1978.
16. *Guinea,* 3rd ed., by Thomas O'Toole with Ibrahima Bah-Lalya. 1995.
17. *Sudan,* by John Voll. 1978. Out of print. See No. 53.
18. *Rhodesia/Zimbabwe,* by R. Kent Rasmussen. 1979. Out of print. See No. 46.
19. *Zambia,* by John J. Grotpeter. 1979.
20. *Niger,* 3rd ed., by Samuel Decalo. 1996.
21. *Equatorial Guinea,* 2nd ed., by Max Liniger-Goumaz. 1988.
22. *Guinea-Bissau,* 2nd ed., by Richard Lobban and Joshua Forrest. 1988.
23. *Senegal,* by Lucie G. Colvin. 1981. Out of print. See No. 65.
24. *Morocco,* by William Spencer. 1980. Out of print. See. No. 71.
25. *Malawi,* by Cynthia A. Crosby. 1980. Out of print. See No. 54.
26. *Angola,* by Phyllis Martin. 1980. Out of print. See No. 52.
27. *The Central African Republic,* by Pierre Kalck. 1980. Out of print. See No. 51.
28. *Algeria,* by Alf Andrew Heggoy. 1981. Out of print. See No. 66.
29. *Kenya,* by Bethwell A. Ogot. 1981.
30. *Gabon,* by David E. Gardinier. 1981. Out of print. See No. 58.
31. *Mauritania,* by Alfred G. Gerteiny. 1981. Out of print. See No. 68.

64. *Uganda,* by M. Louise Pirouet. 1995.
65. *Senegal,* 2nd ed., by Andrew F. Clark and Lucie Colvin Phillips. 1994.
66. *Algeria,* 2nd ed., by Phillip Chiviges Naylor and Alf Andrew Heggoy. 1994.
67. *Egypt,* 2nd ed., by Arthur Goldschmidt, Jr. 1994.
68. *Mauritania,* by Anthony G. Pazzanita. 1996.
69. *Congo,* 3rd ed., by Samuel Decalo, Virginia Thompson, and Richard Adloff. 1996.
70. *Botswana,* 3rd ed., by Jeff Ramsay, Barry Morton, and Fred Morton. 1996.
71. *Morocco,* 2nd ed., by Thomas K. Park. 1996.
72. *Tanzania,* 2nd ed., by Thomas P. Ofcansky and Rodger Yeager. 1997.
73. *Burundi,* by Ellen K. Eggers, 1997.

HISTORICAL DICTIONARY OF CHAD

Third Edition

by
SAMUEL DECALO

African Historical Dictionaries, No. 13

The Scarecrow Press, Inc.
Lanham, Md., & London

SCARECROW PRESS, INC.

Published in the United States of America
by Scarecrow Press, Inc.
4720 Boston Way
Lanham, Maryland 20706

4 Pleydell Gardens, Folkestone
Kent CT20 2DN, England

Second edition published by Scarecrow Press, Inc., Metuchen, N.J., & London, 1987.

British Cataloguing-in-Publication Information Available

Library of Congress Cataloging-in-Publication Data

Decalo, Samuel.
    Historical dictionary of Chad / Samuel Decalo.—3rd ed.
        p.   cm. — (African historical dictionaries ; no. 13)
    Includes bibliographical references and index.
    ISBN 0-8108-3253-4 (alk. paper)
    1. Chad—History—Dictionaries.   I. Title.   II. Series.
DT546.457.D4   1997
967.43′003—dc21   96-38910
                                                              CIP

ISBN 0-8108–3253-4 (cloth : alk. paper)

♾ ™ The paper used in this publication meets the minimum requirements of American National Standard for Information Sciences—Permanence of Paper for Printed Library Materials, ANSI Z39.48—1984. Manufactured in the United States of America.

To
Ruth and Niv

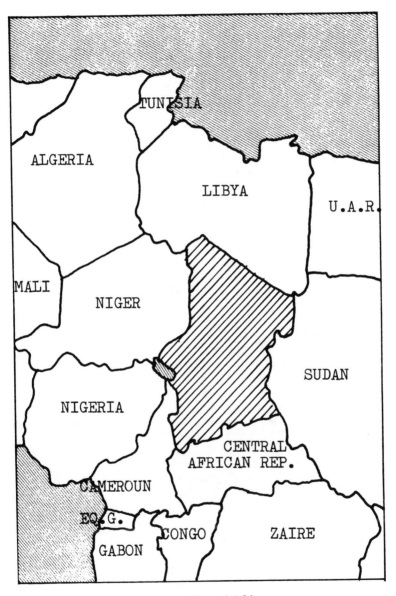

Chad and Central Africa

Contents

Maps and Tables

Maps

Tables

Acknowledgments

The author wishes to acknowledge the generous financial support of the University Research Committee of the University of Natal, without which this third edition would not have been feasible.

Editor's Foreword

In Chad, although there may be less fighting now, the underlying friction continues. In addition to personal, more than ideological, quarrels among various potential leaders—many of them warlords, others representatives of different ethnic groups and regions—there is now a further element: Religious divisions, between a northern Islamic cluster and a more animist or Christian south, are being exacerbated by the rise of Islamic fundamentalism, domestic and imported. Even if foreign intervention is no longer as blatant as in the days when Libya openly took sides with certain groups while France and the United States backed others, opposing forces do find support and bases in neighboring countries.

To outsiders, the interminable quarreling and fighting make little sense. To the inhabitants of Chad, whether some and not others of the many factions and formations come out on top is sometimes a matter of life and death, and often of political and economic advantage. Hence if foreigners wish to make sense of the struggle (and avoid foolish mistakes), they should take a much closer look at the realities of Chad—ethnic, religious, geographic, economic, and political. They should also pause to study the region's history, in which many of today's currents already have very deep roots. This may not help anyone to "solve" the problems of Chad, but at least the problems will be better understood.

That is the purpose of this *Historical Dictionary of Chad*. More than any other source book on the country, it provides information on significant persons, places, events, and institutions. It sheds light on the economy, society, and culture. Above all it examines Chad's history—not only the more recent history from the time of independence but also that of earlier periods, including colonial and precolonial times. Given the present state of turmoil, certainly persons are more important than institutions, and the presentation of important politicians, soldiers, and others is particularly useful. The chronology puts much of the history and its actors in context. The list of abbreviations and acronyms, itself a valuable reference source, makes it easier to trace the historical narrative. And the extensive bibliography is precious in indicating further sources of information.

This is now the third edition of the Chad volume. It is larger and more complete than ever. Given the countless changes that have intervened over the past decade, it was again a great challenge for any observer to get hold of the basic facts and work out a comprehensible analysis. This has been done again by Samuel Decalo, author of the first two editions and a specialist on francophone Africa and military regimes. Currently professor of political science at the University of Natal, he has lectured and written broadly on these subjects. He is also an old hand at historical dictionaries, having produced volumes on Benin, Congo-Brazzaville, Niger, and Togo as well as Chad.

Jon Woronoff
Series Editor

A Note on Spelling

Many of Chad's ethnic groups and some of the country's regions and geographical formations are spelled differently in English and in French, including the name of the country itself—Tchad in French. In most cases the French practice has been followed in this Dictionary since most of the literature one is likely to encounter is in that language. Often the more common variations in spelling are easy to recognize anyhow, as with Kanouri-Kanuri, Kenembou-Kanembu, Ouadai-Wadai, Ouled Sliman–Awlad Sulayman, Kouka-Kuka, Boudouma-Buduma and Bagirmi-Baghirmi-Baguirmi. In a few instances where confusion might arise (Ouadai-Wadai) cross-references link up the different variations of the same term or name.

The "Cultural Revolution" and authenticity drives during the last five years of the Tombalbaye era resulted in the changing of various place-names (Fort-Lamy to N'Djamena; Fort-Archambault to Sarh) and individual given names. Since most of the better known Chadian personalities covered in this dictionary already had a Muslim or other non-Christian name, the edict on name changes has had a much lesser impact in Chad than in some other countries enacting similar policies of authenticity. To avoid confusion in instances where name changes have occurred, the old given name is also listed in parentheses at the head of the entry. In a few instances individuals have opted for a complete transformation of both given and family name. In these cases the individual is listed under the new name with a cross-reference under the old name.

Finally, for the thorny issue of transliteration of Arabic names—especially pressing with the eclipse of Sara power in 1978 and the appearance on the national scene of an increasing number of personalities with Arab names—I must offer a sincere apology to linguistic purists for my opting to follow the spelling most commonly encountered in the social science literature and Chad official documentation rather than a possibly more linguistically correct variant that might, however, serve to confuse the average reader of this Dictionary.

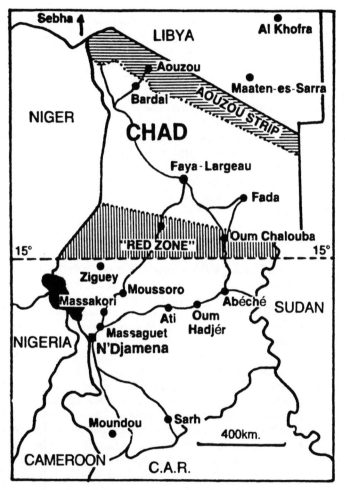

"Red Zone" and Aouzou Strip, 1984 (reprinted by permission from *West Africa* [London], September 24, 1985)

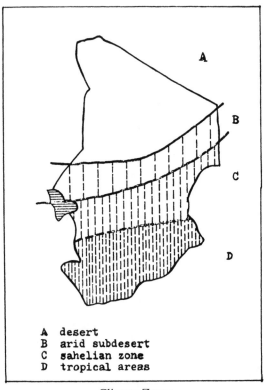

A desert
B arid subdesert
C sahelian zone
D tropical areas

Climate Zones

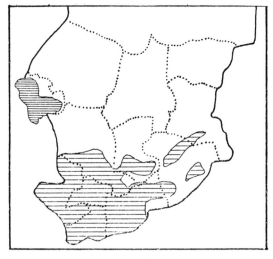

Cotton-Growing Areas

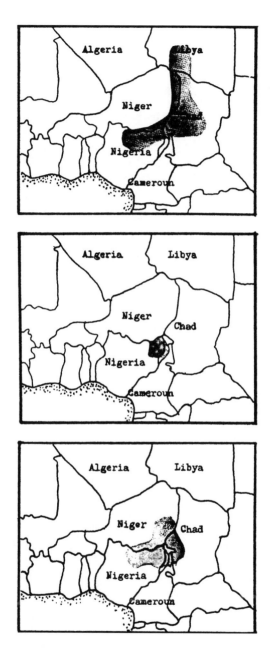

Kanem-Bornu Empire in 1300, 1450, and 1600 (top to bottom), following the empire's dimensions as outlined in Y. Urvoy's *Histoire de l'Empire du Bornou*, Paris, Librairie Larose, 1949.

Table 1. Demography

Préfectures	Area (sq km)	Population	Density (per sq km)
Batha	88,800	431,000	4.9
Biltine	46,850	216,000	4.6
Borkou-Ennedi-Tibesti	600,350	109,000	0.2
Chari-Baguirmi	82,910	844,000	10.2
Guera	58,950	254,000	4.3
Kanem	114,520	245,000	2.1
Lac	22,320	165,000	7.4
Logone Occidental	8,695	365,000	42.0
Logone Oriental	28,035	377,000	13.4
Mayo-Kebbi	30,105	852,000	28.3
Moyen Chari	45,180	646,000	14.3
Ouaddai	76,240	422,000	5.5
Salamat	63,000	131,000	2.1
Tandjilé	18,045	371,000	20.6
Total	1,284,000	5,428,000	4.2

Table 2. Ethnic Breakdown, 1964

1. *Southern Sedentary Groups*	1,139,000	34.2%
Sara	800,000	24.0
Mboum, Laka	112,000	3.4
Moundang	90,000	2.7
Toubouri	75,000	2.2
Massa (Banana)	50,000	1.5
Others	12,000	0.4
2. *Sedentary and Seminomadic Groups of the Sahel*	902,000	26.8%
Maba	170,000	5.0
Bulala, Kuka	80,000	2.5
Haddad	100,000	3.0
Daju	65,000	2.0
Massalit	48,000	1.5
Moubi	25,000	0.8
Zaghawa, Bideyat	40,000	1.2
Hadjeray	87,000	2.6
Kanembu	60,000	1.8
Buduma	20,000	0.6
Kotoko	7,000	0.2
Barma	35,000	1.1
Massalat	23,000	0.7
Others	142,000	3.7
3. *Nomadic Groups*	613,650	18.0%
Toubou	121,650	3.9
Arabs	460,000	14.0
Fulani	32,000	0.1
4. *Other Groups*	645,350	19.5
TOTAL	3,300,000	100%

Table 3. Principal Crops

	1990	1991	1992
Wheat	2	3	2
Rice	66	118	52
Maize	29	48	91
Millet	168	226	295
Sorghum	280	286	379
Other cereals	57	131	96
Potatoes	18	18	18
Sweet potatoes	46	46	46
Cassava	330	330	330
Yams	240	240	240
Taro	9	9	9
Dry beans	42	42	42
Other pulses	18	18	18
Groundnuts	108	97	147
Sesame seed	12	9	14
Cottonseed	98	104	110
Cotton	60	69	70
Dry onions	14	14	14
Other vegetables	60	60	60
Dates	32	32	32
Mangoes	32	32	32
Other fruit	50	51	52
Sugar cane	340	370	400

In 1,000 tons. More recent figures not available.

Table 4. Gross Domestic Product, 1992

GDP in billions CFAF	333.0
of which agricultural	144.7
of which services	114.7
of which manufacturing	52.5
of which industry	18.1

Table 5. Public Finances

	1989	1990	1991	1992	1993
Revenue	28.8	31.6	33.7	31.4	30.7
Expenditure	105.0	107.7	99.8	96.4	89.0
Deficit	76.2	76.1	66.1	65.0	58.3

In billions of CFAF

Table 6. Balance of Trade, 1988–1993

	1988	1989	1990	1991	1992	1993
Exports	146	155	230	194	182	136
Imports	228	240	259	250	243	201
Deficit	82	85	29	56	61	65

In millions of U.S. dollars

Table 7. Main Trade Partners, 1993

Exports to:		Imports from:	
Portugal	36	France	44
Germany	14	Cameroon	21
France	9	Nigeria	9
Morocco	5	United States	6
Taiwan	4	Japan	3

In percentage of global trade

Table 8. Cotton Production, 1989/90 versus 1993/94

1989/90	151.1 seed	48.3 lint
1993/94	100.0 seed	40.0 lint

In 1,000 tons

Abbreviations and Acronyms

AACT	Association des Anciens Combattants du Tchad
ACCT	Agence de Coopération Culturelle et Technique
ACTUS	Action Tchadienne pour l'Unité et le Socialisme
ADS	Action Démocratique et Sociale
ADT	Alliance pour la Démocratie au Tchad
AEF	Afrique Equatoriale Française
AET	Association des Enfants du Tchad
AID	(U.S.) Agency for International Development
ALN	Armée de Libération Nationale
AMT	Association des Métis du Tchad
ANC	Alliance Nationale pour le Changement
ANDD	Alliance Nationale pour Démocratie et Développement
ANDR	Alliance Nationale pour la Démocratie et le Renouveau
ANI	Armée Nationale Intégrée
ANS	Agence Nationale de Sécurité
ANT	Armée Nationale Tchadienne
APPD	Alliance des Partis Politiques pour la Démocratie
ASETF	Association des Stagiaires et Elèves Tchadiens en France
AST	Action Sociale Tchadienne
ATEC	Agence Transéquatoriale des Communications
ATP	Agence Tchadienne de Presse
ATUS	Action Tchadienne pour l'Unité et le Socialisme
BAM	Bureau des Affaires Musulmanes
BATAL	Banque Tchado-Arabe-Libyenne pour le Commerce Extérieur et le Développement
BCEAC	Banque Centrale des Etats de l'Afrique Equatoriale et du Cameroun
BCTD	Banque Tchadienne de Crédit et de Dépôts
BDEAC	Banque de Développement des Etats d'Afrique Centrale
BDT	Banque de Développement du Tchad

BDT	Bloc Démocratique Tchadien
BEAC	Banque des Etats de l'Afrique Centrale
B.E.T.	Borkou-Ennedi-Tibesti
BGT	Boissons et Glacières du Tchad
BIAT	Banque Internationale pour l'Afrique au Tchad
BICI	Banque Internationale pour le Commerce et l'Industrie du Tchad
BT	Bloc Tchadien
BTCD	Banque Tchadienne de Crédit et de Dépôts
BTDT	Bloc des Travailleurs Démocrates Tchadiens
CAC	Comité d'Action et de Coordination
CAC/CDR	Comité d'Action et de Concertation du Comité d'Action Révolutionnaire
C.A.R.	Central African Republic
CBLT	Commission du Bassin du Lac Tchad
CCAIT	Chambre de Commerce, de l'Agriculture et d'Industrie de la République du Tchad
CCCE	Caisse Centrale de Coopération Economique
CCCI	Compagnie Coloniale Commerciale et Industrielle (Guinea)
CCDFMI	Conseil Central pour la Défense des Forces Mobiles d'Intervention
CCER	Centre de Coordination et d'Exploitation du Renseignement
CCFAN	Conseil de Commandement des Forces Armées du Nord
CCFOM	Caisse Centrale de la France d'Outre-Mer
CDC	Caisse des Dépôts et Consignations
CDN	Commission de Défense Nationale
CDR	Conseil Démocratique de la Révolution
CDS	Comité de Défense et de Sécurité
CEEAC	Communauté Economique des Etats d'Afrique Centrale
CEP	Commission d'Enquête Parlementaire
CFA	Communauté Financière Africaine
CFAF	CFA franc (currency)
CFCO	Chemin de Fer du Congo-Océan
CFD	Caisse Française de Développement
CGTO	Commandement des Groupements des Troupes Offensives
CIA	(U.S.) Central Intelligence Agency
CILSS	Comité Inter-Etats de Lutte contre la Sécheresse dans le Sahel
CLTT	Confédération Libre des Travailleurs du Tchad

CMIAP	Comité Militaire Inter-Armée Provisoire
CMPA	Centre de Modernisation des Produits Animaux
CN	Conférence Nationale
CNC	Conseil National Consultatif
CNDS	Convention Nationale Démocratique et Sociale
CNL	Conseil National de la Libération
CNR	Conseil National de Redressement
CNR	Conseil National de la Révolution
CNSD	Convention Socio-Démocrate Tchadienne
CNT	Comité du Nord du Tchad
CNU	Conseil National d'Union
COMAL	Constructions Métalliques du Tchad
COPAC	Collective des Partis pour le Changement
COPOFAN	Comités Populaires des Forces Armées du Nord
CORPORTCHAD	Sociéte des Transporteurs Tchadiens
Cotonfran	Sociéte Cotonnière Franco-Tchadienne
Cotontchad	Sociéte Cotonnière du Tchad
CPD	Convention pour le Progrés et le Développement
CPP	Concertation des Partis Politiques
CPR	Conseil Provisoire de la Révolution
CPS	Comité Permanent du Sud
CPT	Conseil du Peuple Tchadien
CRCR	Centre de Recherches et de la Coordination des Renseignements
CRN	Commission de Réconciliation
CSM	Conseil Supérieur Militaire du Tchad
CSNPD	Comité de Sursaut National pour la Paix et la Démocratie
CSPC	Caisse de Stabilisation des Prix du Coton
CSR	Conseil Suprême de la Révolution
CST	Conseil Supérieur de la Transition
CTS	Compagnies Tchadiennes de Sécurité
CTT	Coopérative des Transporteurs Tchadiens
DDS	Direction de la Documentation et de la Sécurité
EC	European Community
EDF	European Development Fund (also FED)
EDT	Etudes et Documents Tchadiens
ENA	Ecole Nationale d'Administration
ENAD	Entente pour une Alternative Démocratique
Entente	Entente pour l'Application de la Loi-Cadre
ERDIC	Entente Républicaine pour la Défense des Intérêts Communs

FAC	Fonds d'Aide et de Coopération
FAC	Front d'Action Commune
FACP	Front d'Action Commune Provisoire
FACT	Front d'Action Civique du Tchad
FAIDT	Front d'Action pour l'Instauration de la Démocratie au Tchad
FAN	Forces Armées du Nord
FANT	Forces Armées Nationales Tchadiennes
FAO	Food and Agriculture Organization
FAO	Forces Armées Occidentales
FAP	Forces Armées Populaires
FAP	Forces Armées du Peuple
FAR	Front des Forces d'Action pour la République
FARF	Forces Armées de la République Fédérale
FAT	Forces Armées Tchadiennes
FCD	Forum pour le Changement Démocratique
FCSMR	Fonds Communs des Sociétés Mutuelles Rurales
FDAR	Fonds de Développement et d'Action Rurale
FDT	Front Démocratique du Tchad
FEANF	Fédération des Etudiants de l'Afrique Noire en France
FED	Fonds Européens de Développement (also EDF)
FESAC	Fondation de l'Enseignement Supérieur en Afrique Centrale
FIDES	Fonds d'Investissement pour le Développement Economique et Social des Territoires d'Outre-Mer
FLDT	Front de Libération Démocratique Tchadienne
FLT	Front de Libération du Tchad
FNT	Front National Tchadien
FOD	Forum d'Opposition Démocratique
FPL	Forces Populaires de Libération
FPLT	Front Populaire de Libération du Tchad
FPRT	Forces Populaires Révolutionnaires Tchadiennes
FPST	Front Patriotique de Salut Tchadien
FROLINAT	Front de Libération Nationale
FU	Forces Unifi
FUS	Front Uni de Sud
GDP	Groupe des Démocrates et Patriotes
GIRT	Groupement des Indépendants et Ruraux Tchadiens
GMT	Grands Moulins du Tchad
GOFAT	Groupe des Officiers des Forces Armées Tchadiennes

GPN	Gouvernement de Paix Nationale
GSN	Gouvernement de Salut National
GUNT	Gouvernement d'Union Nationale de Transition
ICJ	International Court of Justice
IEZVAC	Institut d'Enseignement Zootechnique et Vétérinaire d'Afrique Centrale
IHEOM	Institut des Hautes Etudes d'Outre-Mer
IIAP	Institut International de l'Administration Publique
ILO	International Labor Organization
IMF	International Monetary Fund
INSE	Institut National des Sciences de l'Education
INSH	Institut National des Sciences Humaines
INTSH	Institut National Tchadien pour les Sciences Humaines
IPN	Institut Pédagogique National
JEPPT	Jeunesse du Parti Progressiste Tchadien
LTDH	Ligue Tchadienne de Droits de l'Homme
MCT	Manufacture de Cigarettes du Tchad
MDD	Mouvement pour la Démocratie et le Développement
MDRT	Mouvement Démocratique de la Rénovation Tchadienne
MDST	Mouvement Démocratique et Socialiste du Tchad
MDT	Mouvement Démocratique Tchadien
MESAN	Mouvement d'Emancipation Sociale de l'Afrique Noire
MJT	Mouvement de la Jeunesse Tchadienne
MNLT	Mouvement National de Libération du Tchad
MNRCS	Mouvement National pour la Révolution Culturelle et Sociale
MNRT	Mouvement National de Réforme Tchadienne
MOSANAT	Mouvement de Salut National du Tchad
MPDT	Mouvement pour la Paix et le Développement au Tchad
MPLT	Mouvement pour la Libération du Tchad
MPN	Mouvement Patriotique National
MPS	Mouvement Populaire du Salut
MPT	Mouvement du Peuple Tchadien
MPT	Mouvement Populaire Tchadien
MRA	Mission de Réforme Administrative
MRPT	Mouvement Révolutionnaire du Peuple Tchadien
MRT	Mouvement Révolutionnaire Tchadien
MSA	Mouvement Socialiste Africain

MUDT	Mouvement pour l'Unité et la Démocratie au Tchad
NSCKN	Nouvelle Sociéte Commerciale de Kouilou-Nairi
OAMCE	Organisation Africaine et Malgache de Coopération Economique
OAU	Organization of African Unity
OCAMM	Organisation Commune Africaine, Malgache, et Mauritienne
OCRS	Organisation Commune des Régions Sahariennes
OFUNIR	Organisation des Femmes de l'Union Nationale pour l'Indépendance et la Révolution
OLAFRIC	Compagnie Huilière Africaine
OLTFI	Organisation de Libération du Tchad du Fascisme et de l'Impérialisme
OMVSD	Office de la Mise en Valeur du Sategui-Deressia
ONDR	Office National de Développement Rural
ORSTOM	Office de la Recherche Scientifique et Technique Outre-Mer
OTEF	Office Tchadien d'Etudes Ferroviaires
PAPJS	Parti Africain pour la Paix et la Justice Sociale
PCA	Poste de Contrôle Administratif
PCT	Parti Communiste Tchadien
PLD	Parti pour les Libertés et le Développement
PLUS	Parti Libéral pour l'Unité et la Solidarité
PNA	Parti National Africain
PPT	Parti Progressiste Tchadien
PRODEL	Société Frigorifique des Produits des Eleveurs Tchadiens
PRSNT	Parti Républicain pour le Salut National du Tchad
PSIT	Parti Socialiste Indépendant du Tchad
PSK	Parti Socialiste Koulamalliste
PST	Parti Socialiste du Tchad
RDA	Rassemblement Démocratique Africain
RDOT	Régiment de Défense Opérationnelle du Territoire
RDP	Rassemblement pour la Démocratie et le Progrès
RFP	Rassemblement des Forces Patriotiques
RIAOM	Régiment Inter-Armes d'Outre-Mer
RNDP	Rassemblement National Démocratique Populaire
RNT	Radio Nationale Tchadienne
RNT	Rassemblement Nationaliste Tchadien
RPF	Rassemblement du Peuple Français

RPPT	Regroupement des Partis Politiques du Tchad
RPT	Rassemblement du Peuple Tchadien
RRT	Rassemblement Révolutionnaire Tchadien
RUDT	Rassemblement pour l'Unité et la Démocratie au Tchad
SALT	Société Agricole Logone-Tchad
SAT	Syndicat Autonome du Tchad
SCBET	Société Commerciale de Borkou-Ennedi-Tibesti
SCKN	Société Commerciale de Kouilou-Niari
SEMA	Secteurs Expérimentaux de Modernisation Agricole
SEMAB	Secteur Expérimental de Modernisation Agricole de Bongor
SEMABLE	Secteur Expérimental de Modernisation Agricole du Blé
SEMALK	Secteur Expérimental de Modernisation Agricole de Laï et Kélo
SESUCHARI	Société d'Etudes Sucrières du Tchad
SHT	Société Hôtelière du Tchad
SIMAT	Société Industrielle de Matériel Agricole du Tchad
SIVIT	Société Industrielle de Viande du Tchad
SMA	Secteurs de Modernisation Agricole
SODELAC	Société pour le Développement de la Région du Lac
SOLT	Société Oléagineux du Logone-Tchad
SOMAT	Société du Matériel Agricole du Tchad
SONACOT	Société Nationale de Commercialisation du Tchad
SONASUT	Société Nationale Sucrière du Tchad
SOSUTCHAD	Société Sucrerie du Tchad
SOTERA	Société Tchadienne d'Exploitation de Ressources Animales
SRDR	Secteurs Régionaux de Développement Rural
STC	Société Tchadienne de Crédit
STEE	Société Tchadienne d'Energie Electrique
STI	Société Tchadienne d'Investissement
STT	Société Textile du Tchad
STT	Syndicat de Travailleurs du Tchad
UAM	Union Africaine et Malgache
UDE	Union Douanière Equatoriale
UDEAC	Union Douanière et Economique d'Afrique Centrale
UDIT	Union Démocratique Indépendante du Tchad

UDPT	Union Démocratique pour le Progrès du Tchad
UDR	Union pour la Démocratie et la République
UDSR	Union Démocratique et Socialiste de la Résistance
UDT	Union Démocratique du Tchad
UEAC	Union des Etats de l'Afrique Centrale
UFD	Union des Forces Démocratiques
UFK	Union Franco-Kanembou
UGFT	Union Générale des Fils du Tchad
UIDIC	Union Indépendante pour la Défense des Intérêts Communaux
UL	Union Logonaise
UN	Union Nationale
UN	United Nations
UNATRAT	Union Nationale des Travailleurs du Tchad
UND	Union Nationale Démocratique
UNDP	Union Nationale pour la Démocratie et le Progrès
UNDR	Union Nationale pour le Développement et le Renouveau
UNESCO	United Nations Educational, Scientific, and Cultural Organization
UNIR	Union Nationale pour l'Indépendance et la Révolution
Uniroute	Union Routière Centre-Africaine
UNT	Union Nationale Tchadienne
UNTT	Union Nationale des Travailleurs Tchadiens
UPFT	Union Progressiste Franco-Tchadienne
UPT	Union pour le Progrès du Tchad
URAC	Union des Républiques de l'Afrique Centrale
URD	Union pour le Renouveau et la Démocratie
URPT	Union Républicaine et Progressiste du Tchad
URT	Union Républicaine du Tchad
UST	Union des Syndicats du Tchad
UST	Union Socialiste Tchadienne
UT	Union Tchadienne

Selected Chronology

November 1901– December 1902	The three Franco-Senoussi battles for Bir Alali; Franco-Senoussi skirmishes go on until 1920
1905–1909	Franco-German colonial boundaries delimited
April 20, 1907	Battle of Ain Galakka
1908–1909	Turkish outposts reestablished in Tibesti with Teda cooperation
June 13, 1909	Abéché occupied by France, and Sultan Acyl elevated to the throne
1909–1912	Abéché reoccupied and Ouadai pacified after a general revolt
January 15, 1910	Afrique Equatoriale Française (AEF) federation established
November 4, 1911	Franco-German treaty on mutual exchange of territory affects Chad's boundaries
June 5, 1912	Sultan Acyl deposed in Abéché; no new sultans appointed until 1934
November 27, 1913	Borkou pacified by Colonel Emmanel Largeau; Ain Galakka retaken by France; Turkey withdraws from Tibesti
1913, 1916–1918	Major famines and epidemics in Ouadai wipe out 60 percent of the population
1914–1916	Conquest of Cameroon
1915–1918	Teda revolt (under Turkish flag) against France; temporary French withdrawal from Tibesti (1917)
April 12, 1916	Chad detached from Oubangui-Chari
November 1917	Kub Kub massacres in Abéché
1920	First civilian administrator of Chad appointed (previously military officers headed the administration); the derde of the Toubou submits to French rule and the pacification of B.E.T. is complete
November 11, 1929	Tibesti is detached from the Afrique Occidentale Française (AOF) federation (and Niger) and definitively linked to Chad and the AEF federation
January 1930	The "new" Awlad Sulayman wave arrives in Chad from Libya
August 16, 1940	Under Governor Félix Eboué Chad becomes the first territory to declare for the Gaullist Free French cause; Eboué subsequently promoted to head the AEF
1946	Gabriel Lisette founds the Parti Progressiste Tchadien (PPT)
1952	Bébalem riots and other unrest in Sara regions
March 1957	Major PPT electoral victory

May 15, 1957	Council of Government formed by Lisette
November 28, 1958	Proclamation of the Republic of Chad
June 16, 1959	Period of political instability and of provisional governments (including governments of Gountchomé Sahoulba and Ahmed Koulamallah) ends with the rise of the François Tombalbaye government
January 30, 1960	All remaining Muslim opposition parties join to form the Parti National Africain (PNA)
August 4, 1960	Lisette purged while on a visit to Israel and barred from reentering Chad; later all Europeans are barred from Chadian politics
August 11, 1960	Proclamation of Independence
March 1960	"Unity Congress" of Abéché, in which a single party—the Union pour le Progrès du Tchad (UPT)—is formed
January 20, 1962	One-party system established as all parties except the PPT are banned
April 14, 1962	Presidential system established in Chad
March 26, 1963	The National Assembly is dissolved and a major purge of political opponents begins
September 1963	Major riots in Fort-Lamy after the arrest of the top Muslim leadership of the country, including Koulamallah
June 4, 1964	One-party system officially legitimated via a constitutional amendment
January 23, 1965	French military forces formally evacuate B.E.T. garrisons, five years after Chad's independence
September 2, 1965	Bardai incidents
October 1965	The bloody Mangalmé tax riots erupt, marking the onset of the civil war in Chad
November 19, 1965	Major anti-Tombalbaye plot discovered, leading to the arrest of three ministers and the vice president of the National Assembly
January 1, 1966	Union Douanière et Economique d'Afrique (UDEAC) formed with Chad a member
June 23, 1966	Official founding date of Front de Libération Nationale (FROLINAT)
April 2, 1968	Union des Etats de l'Afrique Centrale (UEAC) is founded with Chad a member
April 28, 1968	Chad withdraws from the UDEAC
May 1968	Secret "Galopin Report" on Chadian maladministration of B.E.T.

July 29, 1968	Constituent Congress of the PPT youth wing, the JEPPT; formal beginning of the "Cultural Revolution"
August 28, 1968	Tombalbaye calls on French troops to assist in quelling Toubou rebellion in the north
April 1969	The French Mission de Réforme Administrative (MRA) is dispatched to Chad to overhaul the local administration
September 26, 1969	Increase in chiefly powers and reinstatement of sultans decreed as part of the MRA recommendations for the restoration of order in the country
June 18, 1970	Major amnesty of political prisoners
April 19–22, 1971	Major amnesty of political prisoners
August 27, 1971	Guerrilla-attempted coup in N'Djamena
November 29–30, 1971	Student strikes in Chad
June 5, 1972	Guerrilla-attempted coup in N'Djamena
December 1972	Chad-Libya rapprochement, leading to Chad's break with Israel and de facto renunciation of the Aouzou region to Libya
June 1973	"Black Sheep" plot revealed, leading to the arrest of Félix Malloum, Kalthouma Guembang, and others
August 27–30, 1973	PPT Congress of N'Djamena; dissolution of the PPT and its replacement by the Mouvement National pour la Révolution Culturelle et Sociale (MNRCS)
April 21, 1974	Françoise Claustre captured in B.E.T. by FROLINAT troops
August 27, 1974	Opération Agriculture launched by Tombalbaye
March 23, 1975	Arrests of senior military officers connected with an anti-Tombalbaye plot
April 4, 1975	Execution of Major Galopin by FROLINAT
April 13, 1975	Coup d'état in which Tombalbaye is killed; Malloum becomes head of state
May 13, 1975	Formation of 18-man provisional government
August 15, 1975	Return from Libyan self-exile of the derde of the Toubou
February 18, 1976	Hissène Habré attack on Faya-Largeau
April 15, 1976	Grenade attack in N'Djamena on Malloum and other officials celebrating the first anniversary of the 1975 coup
October 18, 1976	Habré ousted from Forces Armées du Nord (FAN) by Goukouni

January 29, 1977	Françoise Claustre released by Goukouni in Tripoli, Libya
March 31, 1977	Attempted coup in which Lt. Colonel Ali Dabio dies defending the Presidential Palace
January 22, 1978	Malloum-Habré negotiations in Khartoum, Sudan
February 23–27, 1978	Cease-fire talks under Libyan aegis lead to the Sabha Agreement; despite the agreement, Goukouni continues his attacks on the central government
August 25, 1978	Malloum-Habré accord announced
August 29, 1978	Habré assumes the premiership under Malloum's presidency as a new constitutional charter is announced
February 12, 1979	Malloum-Habré tug-of-war leads to an attempted coup by Habré in N'Djamena; the Chadian army is routed, leading to the eventual entry of Goukouni into N'Djamena
March 6, 1979	Anti-Muslim programs erupt in the south, following earlier mass exodus of Sara from the capital
March 16, 1979	First round of Kano peace talks (Kano I)
March 23, 1979	Provisional State Council set up in N'Djamena
April 29, 1979	Gouvernement d'Union Nationale de Transition (GUNT) administration under Lol Mahamat Choua, with Goukouni and Habré in key posts
November 10, 1979	New GUNT government, including representatives of existing 11 factions
March 21, 1980	Civil war erupts in N'Djamena after a Goukouni-Habré falling-out; N'Djamena becomes a ghost city as most inhabitants flee to Cameroon
June 15, 1980	Chad-Libya defense agreement signed
December 15, 1980	Aided by Libyan forces, Goukouni routs Habré from N'Djamena
January 6, 1981	Chad-Libya merger announced; the ill-defined proposal triggers CIA support for Habré, who is regrouping in the east
October 29, 1981	Goukouni is pressured to request withdrawal of Libyan troops in exchange for protection from Organization of African Unity (OAU) force
November 19, 1981	Abéché falls to Habré units following the withdrawal of Libyan troops
November 15–27, 1981	Zaire/Senegal units of OAU force arrive but refuse to stem Habré's assaults
January 7, 1982	Faya-Largeau falls to Habré troops
February 1982	Mangalmé and Oum-Hadjer fall to Habré units

May 8, 1982	Declaration of N'Djamena; new provisional government is set up
June 7, 1982	N'Djamena falls to Habré; Goukouni flees to B.E.T.
July 19, 1982	Acyl dies in an accident (years later revealed as an assassination)
August 7, 1982	Sarh falls to dissident Forces Armées Tchadiennes (FAT) troops allied with Habré
September 4, 1982	Moundou falls to dissident FAT troops aided by FAN units; Kamougoué flees to B.E.T. via Cameroon
September 29, 1982	New Acte Fondamental proclaimed
October 21, 1982	Habré sworn in as president of Chad
October 28, 1982	Goukouni announces the creation in Bardai of a Gouvernement de Salut National (GSN) pledged to the ouster of Habré
January 7, 1983	Unified Forces Armées Nationales Tchadiennes (FANT) set up
April 18, 1983	Chad-Nigeria border clashes on Lake Chad, May 1983; Goukouni counter offensive, supported by Libya, commences in B.E.T.
June 23, 1983	Faya-Largeau falls to Goukouni
July 10, 1983	Abéché falls to Goukouni but is later retaken by FAN troops personally led by Habré
July 1983	U.S.-French airlift of materiel to N'Djamena
August 3, 1983	France, nudged by the U.S., begins Opération Manta, creating a "Red Zone" limiting Goukouni's advance southward
September 1983	FAN atrocities in the southern préfectures spawn southern liberation movements from bases in the C.A.R.
June 3, 1984	GUNT squads based in the south attack Tandjilé and Mayo-Kebbi prefectural offices
September 17, 1984	France and Libya reach an accord for a simultaneous withdrawal of troops from Chad
June 1985	Some 1,000 "*codos*," formerly fighting Habré in the south, rally to the regime
December 1985	General Djibril Djogo is reconciled with Habré and joins the government
August 1986	GUNT splits, with Acheikh Ibn Oumar taking command; it continues to fall apart as fighting takes place between various factions
January 2, 1987	Fada liberated by Habré, with Libya suffering heavy losses

January 4, 1987	Libyan air raid on Arada, south of the 16th parallel
January 7, 1987	After the violation of the 16th parallel, Libyan forces in Ouadi-Doum are bombed by the French
February 1987	In reprisal for French attacks on Libyan positions, a Libyan bomber harmlessly drops bombs over N'Djamena
February 14, 1987	One of GUNT's major figures, Colonel Kamougoué, rallies to Habré
March 20, 1987	Libyans defeated by Chadian forces at Bir Kora
March 22, 1987	A 3,000-man Libyan column advancing on Fada from its base in Ouadi-Doum is routed by Chadian forces; later Ouadi-Doum itself is taken, with crushing losses
March 27, 1987	Faya falls without a fight to Habré's armies
July 1987	The alienation of the Hadjeray leads to the creation of the Mouvement de Salut National du Tchad (MOSANAT) rebellion against Habré in Guéra
August 8, 1987	Surprise Chadian attack on Aouzou ousts Libya from the outpost they had controlled for 14 years
August 27, 1987	Aided by air power (which France refused to provide to Habré), Libya recaptures Aouzou
August 1987	Libyan losses in B.E.T. include some 5,000 troops dead or captured, 315 tanks, and 51 aircraft, many of which are seized intact
September 5, 1987	Chadian attack at Libyan airbase Maaten-es-Sarra, 160 kilometers (100 miles) within Libya, destroys 22 planes
September 8, 1987	Two Libyan Tupolev-22 bombers fly over N'-Djamena; one downed by France
September 11, 1987	Libya's defeats by Chad trigger agreement to an OAU cease-fire
December 1987	Hadjero Senoussi rallies to Habré
February–June 1988	Several additional groups rally to Habré, including the CDR, MRPT, FAO, FDT, FAP, FPRT
June 1988	Acheikh Ibn Oumar arrested in Tripoli
September 1988	Diplomatic links between Chad and Libya reestablished
November 2, 1988	GUNT ceases to exist
November 21, 1988	Libyan Islamic Legion column from Sudan clashes with Chadian troops; further battles take place later
April 1, 1989	Defection of the Zaghawa, including Hassan Djamouss, Ibrahim Itno, and Idriss Déby, who flee to Darfur, Sudan, pursued by Habré's troops

May 3, 1989	Acheikh Ibn Oumar, rallying to Habré, is appointed foreign minister
August 4, 1989	Première Armée Volcan dissolves itself and rallies to Habré
August 1989	Chief of Staff Colonel Worimi captured by Déby's insurgents and taken to Darfur; Libya tries to buy him from Déby in order to trade him for 2,000 Libyan POWs in N'Djamena
August 31, 1989	Chad-Libya peace accord signed, stipulating the submission of the issue of sovereignty over Aouzou Strip to the International Court of Justice
September 20, 1989	A UTA Paris-bound jet explodes in the Sahara after refueling in N'Djamena; several groups claim responsibility
October 1989	Habré forces suffer heavy losses invading 320 kilometers (200 miles) into Sudan to rescue the wounded Worimi; further assaults within Darfur, with conflicting reports about mutual losses
February 2, 1990	A new opposition party, the Rassemblement du Peuple Tchadien (RPT), is formed
June 21, 1990	Amnesty International claims that Habré has been executing large numbers of Déby followers and Zaghawa in general
July 8, 1990	Chad's first elections since 1962 take place, with 436 candidates competing for 123 assembly seats
September 14, 1990	Habré sends his entire fighting armed forces into Sudan to crush Déby's insurgency
November 18, 1990	Major assault by Déby against the Chadian army; by the end of the month he emerges victorious
November 25, 1990	Habré comes to the front to spur his troops to victory; a daring and bloody Déby ambush nearly captures him and leaves many of his prime lieutenants dead
December 1, 1990	Habré flees to Cameroon, after ordering 320 political prisoners executed and emptying the treasury of its last US$28 million cash reserves; Déby enters Abéché, which is not defended by the government
December 2, 1990	Déby enters the undefended N'Djamena
December 4, 1990	Déby is installed as president of Chad by his party, the Mouvement Populaire du Salut (MPS)
December 8, 1990	Promptly repaying his debt to Libya, Déby orders all Libyan POWs freed, the closure of anti-Libya contra-bases in Chad, and the expulsion of 700 anti-Qaddafi rebels

January 17, 1991	Déby institutes compulsory military service
February 11–14, 1991	Déby's first state visits, to Libya, France, and Nigeria
February 14, 1991	First clash with Déby's regime as students strike for their stipends; Déby bans public assembly
May 18, 1991	Goukouni visits N'Djamena for talks with Déby; Déby promises a national conference followed by elections in May 1992
June 1991	Complaints mount about the integration of too many of Habré's former henchmen and of Zaghawa into the MPS party and government
September 5, 1991	Security agreement signed with Libya; France begins phasing out of its armed forces in Chad
September 18, 1991	Series of assaults on military bases in Bardai by pro-Habré units
October 13, 1991	Preemptive Déby strike against his former key ally and main lieutenant, Maldoum Bada Abbas; 60 executions in N'Djamena
December 24, 1991	Fierce fighting erupts in the Lake Chad area as pro-Habré forces try a push on N'Djamena, 140 kilometers (85 miles) to the south; Bol, the regional capital, falls briefly into insurgent hands; France delays the phasing out of its forces
January 8–9, 1992	New wave of arrests and executions of former sympathizers of Habré
January 25, 1992	Abbas released from prison, allegedly rehabilitated and chastened
February 4, 1992	New pro-Habré Mouvement pour la Démocratie et le Développement (MDD) assault repulsed back into Cameroon
February 11, 1992	The vice president of the Chad League for Human Rights is assassinated in N'Djamena, allegedly by Déby loyalists; strikes and demonstrations erupt; additional Sara military units join the southern rebellion led by Lt. Moise Nodji Ketté
February 21, 1992	Intramilitary fighting erupts in N'Djamena
March 1992	Falling-out of Déby and some ethnic Zaghawa supporters
April 1992	Famine grips parts of southern Chad
April 22, 1992	Zaghawa armed units, including tanks, clash around the Presidential Palace with loyalist troops
May 22, 1992	Government of Prime Minister Joseph Yodoyman inaugurated

May 24–June 5, 1992	Series of clashes in the Lake Chad area with Habré's MDD supporters
May 25, 1992	Labor unrest over back-pay; Commission of Inquiry reports that 40,000 people had been murdered under the Habré regime
May 26, 1992	Rassemblement National Démocratique Populaire (RNDP) alliance of parties formed against government of Yodoyman, pressing for the convening of a national conference
June 12, 1992	Despite a peace accord signed with Sara secessionists in the south, the rebellion continues
June 18, 1992	Attempted coup by Colonel Abbas Yacoub Kotti; when it fails, he flees to the west to mount a rebellion against Déby
August 17, 1992	Chad army reprisals for separatist guerrilla warfare in the south lead to the slaughter of 150 civilians in Doba; the chief of staff is dismissed
October 5, 1992	One-month strike by the trade union federation begins; as the strike continues, Déby arrests the leadership on November 4
December 1, 1992	Second Goukouni visit to N'Djamena
January 15, 1993	Conférence Nationale begins in N'Djamena with the participation of 750 delegates
January 23, 1993	Lt. Ketté's Comité de Sursaut National pour la Paix et la Démocratie (CSNPD) units attack government forces from the C.A.R.
February 1993	Heavy fighting in the Lake Chad area
March–April 1993	Garde Républicaine massacres in southern Chad; charges are made of "religious cleansing"
April 6, 1993	Dr. Fidèle Moungar, a southern physician, is elected prime minister by the Conférence Nationale
May 1993	Amnesty International accuses Déby of 500 summary executions since 1990
June 10, 1993	The Conseil Supérieur de la Transition (CST) refuses to ratify a general cooperation agreement signed with Libya in November 1992
January 24, 1994	Attack on Abéché garrison by Front National Tchadien (FNT) elements; retaliatory atrocities by the Garde Républicaine follow
February 1994	The International Court of Justice in The Hague confirms Chad's sovereignty over the Aouzou Strip; a six-month civil service strike begins

April 3, 1994	Tombalbaye is "rehabilitated" in accord with a decision of the Conférence Nationale; his property, originally confiscated, is returned to his heirs, and his body (buried in Faya) is exhumed and reburied in his home town
April 4, 1994	The CST extends the transitional phase in Chad by one year, thus postponing multiparty elections; these are later postponed further to April 1996
May 1994	Fighting along Lake Chad continues; Garde Républicaine atrocities along the C.A.R. border
May 30, 1994	Under the supervision of UN observers, Libyan troops withdraw from Aouzou after 21 years of occupation
June 24, 1994	CSNPD continues pounding government troops in the south
July 1, 1994	Civil service strike ends with a promise of back-pay, a 10 percent pay hike, and the doubling of minimum wages
August 4, 1994	Negotiations with Captain Ketté in Bangui; on August 10 the CSNPD renounces the rebellion; Ketté is promoted to lieutenant colonel and joins the cabinet; several hundred of his men join the Chadian army, and the Garde Républicaine withdraws from the south
August 6, 1994	The Chad League of Human Rights again criticizes the lack of human rights in Chad, insecurity in N'Djamena, and the brutality and autonomy of the Garde Républicaine
September 14, 1994	Mahamat Garfa, a former cabinet minister and chief of staff, flees N'Djamena with 300 troops to join the rebellion in the east
November 7, 1994	Leaflets distributed by fundamentalist Muslims in Abéché call on foreigners, Chadian citizens as well as expatriates, to leave Ouadai, or else face the fate of Westerners in Algeria and Egypt
January 25, 1995	A draft constitution is ready for a referendum
February 3, 1995	Agreement reached to connect the Doba oil fields, now recognized as much larger than originally assumed, by pipeline with Kribi in Cameroon
February 12– March 9, 1995	Census takes place in preparation for presidential and parliamentary elections; the elections are postponed in April due to the inadequacies of the census; Moungar's government falls over the fi-

	asco, and Koibla Djimasta, a Déby supporter, is elected premier
June 2, 1995	Troops ransack the premises of N'Djamena's main independent newspaper, beat up staff, and arrest the editor and a journalist, for writing that the armed forces were acting as an occupation force in southern Chad
June 14, 1995	A planned march in downtown N'Djamena protesting Déby's "retreat from the democratic process" is banned because it had not secured the necessary permission
July 3, 1995	The entire Bureau of the provisional legislature is indicted for corruption; Abbas Ali of the CSDS party is elected president of the CST
September 10, 1995	The editor of *N'Djaména-Hebdo,* also an assembly member and presidental candidate, is arrested; the Concertation des Partis Politiques (CPP) alliance of parties announces a boycott of Chad's institutions unless he is released and the head of the notorious Agence Nationale de Sécurité (ANS) secret police is dismissed

Introduction

Africa's fifth largest political entity, former French Equatorial Africa's largest component part both in area and in population, and two and a half times the size of France (her former colonial master), Chad is one of the continent's lesser known or understood countries. Located near the geographical center of Africa and, in the past, at the crossroads of many important caravan trails, Chad's 1,284,000 square kilometers (495,700 square miles) of landlocked territory straddle the traditional north-south, east-west continental divide lines. In 1995 the population was estimated to number over 6.5 million, though the country has never had a complete national census, with projections stemming largely from a 1964 survey.

Chad's population growth is relatively low because of poor diet, diseases, and the major devastating droughts and famines that afflicted the area in the 1970s and 1980s, all of which lowered life expectancy to 31 years. The population is an aggregate of sedentary and nomadic, Sudanic, Saharan, and sub-Saharan ethnic groups, representing a mix of languages and cultures numerous even for Africa. The diversity in forms of socioeconomic organization and political hierarchy represented in traditional Chadian life are such that to the Sara of the south, for example (as also to the Teda of the far north), details of court life in the former Ouadai and Bornu kingdoms of the Sahelian belt are so alien as to be incomprehensible, while to the Abéché (Ouadai) resident the anarchic, decentralized political life of the Sara or the intense individualism of the Teda are similarly totally alien and unacceptable.

The degree of ethnic, sociocultural, and religious variety found in Chad underscores the role of the area as a transition zone—between the Sahara, the Sahel, and the tropical rain forests as well as between the Muslim north and east and the animist and Black African south—and as the crossroads of cultural interaction and ethnic migrations. The vastness of the country, its general impoverishment, and the existing historic interethnic animosities (of great intensity and long duration) have all entrenched feelings of ethnic, cultural, and regional exclusiveness; and these have been greatly aggravated by nearly two decades of north-south civil war and 17 years of brutal northern rule. Indeed the physical integrity of the country itself is currently somewhat in question, with a federalist, even secessionist, drive increasingly voiced by southern leaders. It is thus no

1

coincidence that scholars approaching the study of Chad tend to compartmentalize their focus along geographical lines to the detriment of a unified approach of the country's history, ethnology, or geography.

The Land and the People

Extending from north to south for more than 1,600 kilometers (1,000 miles) (from lat. 23.5° to 7.5° N) and for up to 800 kilometers (500 miles) from east to west, Chad is bounded in the north by Libya (which in 1972 militarily annexed the Aouzou Strip, relinquishing it only in 1994), in the west by Niger, Nigeria, and Cameroon, in the south by the Central African Republic (the former Oubangui-Chari), and in the east by Sudan. The huge territory has no railroads at all and only poor unpaved tracks, many greatly decayed by neglect and decades of civil war and unrest. All of Chad's main urban centers—which are isolated from one another for up to six months each year due to torrential rains that transform the countryside into impassable swamplands—are far from the coast. N'Djamena, the capital (the former Fort-Lamy), is 1,126 kilometers (700 miles) from the coast, with goods traveling 1,920 to 2,970 kilometers (1,190 to 1,840 miles) to reach the city by several different routes. Abéché, the former imperial capital of Ouadai, is 1,653 kilometers (1,025 miles) from the Red Sea ports of Sudan, and Faya-Largeau, capital of the Borkou-Ennedi-Tibesti (B.E.T.) Préfecture in the north, is 2,550 kilometers (1,580 miles) from Libya's Tripoli. (See COMMUNICATIONS.)

The country is topographically a gigantic basin surrounded on three sides by intermittent mountain ranges. Lake Chad—until circa 500 B.C. a large (350,000 square kilometers or 135,000 square miles) inland sea stretching into Tibesti (and visited by Carthaginian merchants) and probably connected to the Nile valley—is the most dominant feature of the basin. The freshwater lake's surface area has periodically contracted and expanded in the contemporary era, varying from 8,000 to 25,000 square kilometers (3,000 to 9,600 square miles). During the Sahel drought of the 1970s the lake area could be crossed on foot in the Niger-Chad direction, with the receding waters transforming lake ports (e.g., N'Guigmi) in Niger into desert outposts. The lake is also Chad's lowest elevation (245 meters or 750 feet above sea level), with most of the country sloping upward in all directions from the basin. The highest point in Chad is the dead volcanic peak of Emi Koussi (3,414 meters or 11,200 feet) in the Tibesti volcanic massif (where large numbers of prehistoric rock drawings exist), which is also the highest point in the Sahara desert. The entire northern half of Chad is a rugged, extremely sparsely populated, arid desert (with the occasional oasis) sloping gently northward from Lake Chad to the Tibesti massif and the Ennedi sandstone plateau. The rest of the country is flat savannaland, progressively more humid to the south, bonded in the east by the Ouadai Mountains (which continue

across the border in Sudan's Darfur province), in the south by the Oubangui plateau of the Central African Republic, and along Nigeria and
Cameroon by the Adamaoua and Mandara mountain ranges.

The only year-round rivers in Chad—the Chari, the Logone, and their
tributaries—flow from the southeast, join at N'Djamena, and empty at
Lake Chad. The 1,200-kilometer (745-mile) Chari is formed by the
Gribingui, the Bamingui, and the Bahr Sara and is later joined by the Bahr
Salamat. The 970-kilometer (600-mile) Logone, which for part of its
course constitutes the Chad-Cameroon border, is formed by the Pendé
and M'Béré Rivers and has a very much more modest waterflow. Though
parts of their courses are navigable at all times (e.g., N'Djamena–Lake
Chad) and other segments are navigable for part of the year (e.g., the
Chari between N'Djamena and Sarh), the river system does not appreciably alleviate Chad's communications problems (due to its north-south
flow into an inland sea) and is used mostly for minor local trading purposes. On the other hand, the abundant fish resources in Chad's rivers and
annually inundated plains provide the populations in the south with a major protein-rich source of subsistence. Indeed, smoked and/or dried fish
segments (*banda*) from Chad's rivers are a particularly appreciated deli-
cacy in neighboring countries, where they are traded by local merchants.

Within Chad there are wide climatic variations and different rainfall
and vegetation patterns, all a function of Chad's wide latitudinal range.
In the wet tropical south (e.g., Sarh), where the majority of the population lives and where the country's prime cash crop—cotton—is cultivated, up to 1220 millimeters (48 inches) of rain fall annually during the
May–October wet season; in the Sahelian belt (e.g., N'Djamena)—and
prior to the series of droughts—annual rainfall rarely exceeds 300 to 800
millimeters (12 to 31 inches), most falling between June and September;
and in the northern B.E.T. precipitation is rare (a recorded average of 25
millimeters (1 inch) per year in Faya-Largeau), though the Saharan
peaks are often covered with frost and even some snow.

The country's vegetation is sparse, except in the occasional palm and
date oases, though sand dunes are not as prevalent as farther to the north
and west (in Niger, Libya, or Algeria). In the semiarid transitional Sahel
zone, thorn-bush vegetation slowly gives way in the south to the typical
savanna grasslands, and farther to the south tall grasslands and wooded
areas predominate. The southern areas also have an abundant and varie-
gated wildlife, with the Zakouma National Park being one of the world's
greatest reserves, though surprisingly very little known abroad.

Chad's main urban centers—where most of the modern economy is located—are N'Djamena (with a population estimated at 650,000 in 1993)
and Sarh (120,000), both modern towns tracing their origins to foundation at the turn of the century by the French colonizers. Of Chad's other
towns—Moundou (114,000), Abéché (85,000), Kélo (30,000), Bongor

(20,000), Doba (18,000), Pala (14,000), and Koumra (13,000)—only Abéché had a significant precolonial population; indeed, at the time of the French entry into the region, Abéché was by far the largest urban center, though French occupation and severe repression, accompanied by droughts, famines, and diseases, gravely depleted the population during the 1912–1918 period.

The ravages of nearly three decades of civil war or regional rebellion (only recently over, though pockets of rebellion still exist), along with the intense intranorthern tug-of-war for the capital between 1978 and 1982, altered many population demographics in the country. In 1980, for example, the bulk of N'Djamena's population fled to safety across the river to Cameroon, escaping the cross fire in the capital. The massive exodus of the Sara from the northern préfectures and N'Djamena likewise transformed Moundou, Bongor, and Doba, among others, from small though vibrant regional centers into sprawling metropolitan refugee centers, in some cases quadrupling the pre-1978 population estimates. With the stabilization of power in the hands of Hissène Habré in 1982 a modest inflow of personnel from the south took place, but many southerners remained in the south, and they were joined by others fleeing the atrocities in N'Djamena by the successor Idriss Déby regime. In the mid-1990s a further (though smaller) Sara disengagement from the east (Ouadai) took place as fundamentalist Muslim groups mounted a drive to purify the region from "infidels," calling on all non-Muslims to leave Ouadai or face the consequences. At the same time the capital, N'Djamena, increasingly began to be populated by former nomadic eastern and northern groups, previously gravitating more towards Abéché or Faya.

Even more problematic—and the cause of considerable concern in southern Chad, with demographic repercussions impossible to even estimate—is the fact that under northern political overlordship (since 1982) there has been a steady migration of peoples and livestock from the sparsely populated, drier, northern and eastern préfectures to the already well-populated, wetter, southern ones. The groups migrating are pastoral, Muslim, and northern, and they have mixed poorly with the indigenous Sara agricultural peoples, most of whom are either Christian or animist. Serious interethnic and interdenominational violence has taken place in many localities in the south, though it has hardly been mentioned in the official press or become known abroad. Most of it has been initiated by the incoming migrants, much of it against animist centers or sites. These increasing tensions in the south, on top of the brutal demeanor of Déby's Garde Républicaine (composed solidly of ethnic kinsmen) adds fuel to the separatist drive, which has been given major economic viability by the coming on-line in the 1990s of the large oil deposits at Doba.

Chad's population is roughly 50 percent Muslim (many of whom were originally only nominally so but are becoming radicalized by fundamentalist influences from Sudan), 43 percent animist, and 7 percent Christian (see RELIGION). More than one-half of the population lives in the southern 10 percent of the country, with most of the rest living in the central préfectures, and they speak over 110 languages and/or dialects. Arabic ("Chadic Arabic") is the lingua franca of the Sahara-Sahel regions, with Sara playing the same role in the south. With the rise of Habré in 1982 the official languages of Chad were defined as French and Arabic; Sara elements have protested in vain for the equal recognition of their language as an official one.

The various languages may be divided into 12 linguistic groups. The most important of these are: (1) the Sara-Baguirmi group, spoken by nearly 2 million people in southern Chad, (2) the Chado-Hamitic, a Chadic group that is related to the Hausa language; (3) the Moundang-Toubouri group, spoken by over half a million people in southwestern Chad; (4) the Kanembu-Zaghawa (Nilo-Saharan) group, spoken in central and northern Chad, mostly by nomadic clans; and (5) the Maba linguistic group, spoken in eastern Chad in Biltine and Ouadaï. As noted, Arabic in several dialects is also widely spoken or understood by Arab clans in Chad and by Muslim groups in the center and the north of the country. (See LINGUISTIC GROUPS.)

The large number of linguistic families reflects the variety of ethnic groups in the country. There are several ways of classifying these, the most common of which (apart from linguistic affiliation) is according to geographic location and form of settlement (nomadic/sedentary). The dominant group in the highly populated south (frequently referred to as *Tchad-utile*)—and indeed in the entire country—is the Sara constellation of clans that number over 2 million people, followed far behind by the Mboum, the Laka, the Moundang, and the Toubouri. In the center of the country are found the Maba (principal founding group of the Ouadaï kingdom) and the Daju (or Dadjo), the Barma (of the Baguirmi kingdom), the Buduma (of Lake Chad's islands and archipelago), the Kotoko (of Sao origins), the Hadjeray (known for their *margai* spirit cult), the Kanembu, the Kanuri, and the Tunjur as well as a large number of other sedentary or nomadic groups. Among the nomadic clans are numerous Arab fragments maintaining various transhumance patterns, their total number coming to over half a million. Also notable among the nomads are the proudly aloof and independent Toubou of B.E.T., who are divided into two major branches and numerous clans, and who spearheaded the ultimately successful anti-N'Djamena revolt in the 1960s and 1970s. Reflecting this heterogeneous population, Radio Tchad broadcasts its programs in nine different languages (French, Arabic, Sara, Toubouri, Massa, Gorane, Moundang, Fulani, and Kanembu), even though *Infotchad* (published by the Ministry of Information), Chad's only local newspaper during the Tombalbaye era, was only issued in French and had a circulation of barely 1,000.

The various groups are divided on a variety of issues, including religion—the south being essentially animist or Christian with the rest of the country predominantly Muslim—and social organization and hierarchy—with the Sara living mostly in autonomous villages with weak traditional chiefs, as opposed to the powerful and expansionist and quasi-sacred kingdoms of Baguirmi, Ouadai, and Kanem-Bornu in the Sahelian belt. The clash of these different ways of life has bred deep interethnic animosities. Historic friction has existed among the three kingdoms and their indigenous populations as a result of centuries of competition for primacy in the region and concomitant wars and raids against each other, and deeper resentments became entrenched among the southern populations because of a long history of brutal raids by northern armies for slaves that were then shipped to Egypt and Libya. The rise in political dominance in the 1950s of the more populous and advanced south strongly exacerbated these interethnic animosities essentially by disaffecting peoples of the Muslim north and east, who had been accustomed to thinking of southerners as slave material and not as political masters. In like manner the northern victory in the civil war in 1978 triggered panic and a massive disengagement from the "new" Chad in southern Sara areas, a development compounded by the brutality of both Habré's and Déby's reigns.

The entry of French authority into the region was greeted, as elsewhere in Africa, in different manners by various segments of the population. To the Barma and other ethnic groups associated with the Baguirmi kingdom, the French were military allies that had joined hands with them in defeating the Rabahist power that had twice razed Massenya, the capital, and ravaged the countryside for slaves; to the Sara, the French were saviors, since the French presence rapidly put to an end the various slave razzias from the northern kingdoms; to the xenophobic, Muslim, and Senoussi-leaning Maba of Ouadai, France was an infidel colonial power imposing its alien force (via the puppet Sultan Acyl) over a proud kingdom hitherto unvanquished. The French conquest of Equatorial Africa also put to an end Turkish halfhearted dreams for a Central African role (see TURKEY) while pitching French power against two competing colonial influences in the area—Rabah's personal empire in the Sahelian belt, and the Senoussi de facto religious stranglehold extending from Kufra (in the Fezzan) into all of B.E.T. and parts of Kanem.

The differential modes of reaction to France determined to a significant degree the way in which each ethnic group was to accommodate itself to the reality of French domination of the country. The Turks withdrew completely from B.E.T. and were later ousted from Libya by Italy; the Senoussi valiantly mounted a series of military raids against French troops (with Toubou and Tuareg help) before also withdrawing from their B.E.T. *zawayas* by 1920. The Toubou withdrew from all contact with the "aliens," and their individualism was respected by French officers so long as law and order were maintained in the desert regions. The Maba, who had long gravitated more to the north and east than toward the west and N'Djamena, continued in their passive resistance to the intrusion of Western and Christian influences in Ouadai and in their acute xenophobia and suspicion (which had been noted by Gustav Nachtigal over 40 years earlier), and they rapidly fell behind the rest of the colony on most indicators of modernization. Indeed, only the southern populations—hitherto despised and downtrodden—fully availed themselves of the very meager educational and commercial opportunities that opened up with the onset of colonial rule, to advance slowly upward within the modern economy and administration created in Chad. (An indication of the extreme slowness of socioeconomic modernization in Chad is provided in part by the educational figures [see EDUCATION] and by the fact that the first two indigenous physicians obtained their degrees only in 1962.) Consequently, the country's first intellectuals, scholars, and professionals tended to be southerners, and their modest numbers continued to grow at the expense of other groups. Even in the 1960s Abéché's population resisted sending children to the local Lycée Franco-Arabe (the only one) despite the fact that both in intent and in curriculum the school had been set up by the French to appease and satisfy local Muslim sensitivities regarding the possible "contamination" of their children in a "Western" school. All of these factors, coupled with the rapid development of cotton in the southern regions as the mainstay of the Chadian economy (see the section on the economy below), assured the growth of major educational, economic, and political disparities among the various regions of the country to the further detriment of unity and nation building.

Historical Background

For a country so isolated from the outside world and so little known today, a surprising amount is known about Chad's history over the ages. Apart from the tantalizing insights archaeologists are gleaning about the prehistoric lush and populated nature of Chad's B.E.T. (where thousands of cave drawings of tropical animals, as well as fish harpoons, have been found), Lake Chad, the crossroads of many civilizations, has always been associated with the legendary Sao. Allegedly migrating from the Nile valley (and reputed to be of giant stature), the Sao set up a series of walled settlements, practiced divine kingship in a hierarchical political system, and left behind remarkable art treasures before disappearing as a distinct ethnic group under the onslaught of Kanem-Bornu conquests and intermarriage that were to spawn the Kotoko, Buduma, and Kanuri ethnic groups.

Much of the history of the great kingdoms of the Sahelian belt is the story of the foundation, expansion, and mutual conflicts of Kanem-Bornu,

Baguirmi, and Ouadai. The first and most powerful of these three monarchies was Kanem-Bornu. Originally founded in the ninth century as a
small Zaghawa principality near Mao in Kanem (and through intermarriage giving rise to the Kanembu), the dominant Sefuwa Magumi dynasty,
which had adopted Islam in the eleventh century, was eventually ousted
from power around 1384–1388 by the Bulala and displaced westward.
There their new kingdom, Bornu, struck deep roots and by the sixteenth
century controlled a huge empire. Prospering from the trans-Saharan caravan trade, Bornuan power slowly declined in succeeding centuries and
was challenged by the Fulani in the first decade of the nineteenth century.
Crumbling under renascent Fulani power and their jihad (which stripped
Bornu of its western and northern dependencies), the reigning *mai* of
Bornu appealed for help to Shaikh Muhammad al-Amin, a Kanemi scholar
and warrior. Al-Kanemi, as he become known, helped to contain Fulani
power but also slowly established his own parallel dynasty in Bornu.
In 1846 his son, Umar, formally abolished the 1,000-year-old Sefuwa
Magumi dynasty. Barely 40 years later Bornu finally collapsed before the
Sudanese slave raider Rabah, who contested French authority in the Chad
region and perished in the Battle of Kousseri in 1900.

The histories of Baguirmi and Ouadai are more modest, if no less fas-
cinating. Both kingdoms were originally founded by small ethnic groups
from outside that imposed themselves over the local populace. Ouadai
was originally a Tunjur (from Darfur, in Sudan) possession, and Baguirmi
was founded by a Kinga clan (among others) descending from the eastern mountains. Around 1630 the Tunjur were displaced by Abd-el-
Kerim (the founder of the indigenous Maba dynasty), and migrating to
the west, they (briefly) toppled the Bulala in Kanem. Ouadai was to become the most powerful state in eastern Chad, sending military expeditions against both Darfur in the east and Bornu and Kanem in the west,
while periodically raiding the south for slaves for the caravans to the
northern slave markets. In the nineteenth century Bornu's decline in the
west and ethnic upheavals in the Fezzan-B.E.T. areas brought to a standstill trade over the Bornu-Fezzan caravan trails and shifted the trade patterns to the east, to Ouadai, which greatly enhanced the latter's power
and wealth. In contrast, Baguirmi, founded early in the sixteenth century,
was only for short periods completely autonomous from either Bornu or
Ouadai, between which it was precariously squeezed and to whom it frequently paid tribute. Like Bornu, Baguirmi fell to Rabah toward the end
of the nineteenth century. Ouadai, on the other hand, was not directly invaded by Rabahist forces, though its southern dependencies were detached from it and administered by one of Rabah's allies, Mohamed-es-
Senoussi, until his death at the hands of the French in 1911.

Despite important differences among them, all three kingdoms were
established sacred Sudanic monarchies benefiting (in different degrees)

from their control over the southern termini of the trans-Saharan caravan trails and their ability to raid the southern populations for slaves so needed in the north. All three countries were expansionist (though since they relied on cavalry, they rarely penetrated or controlled areas in the deep southern tsetse-infested grasslands); all three possessed and imported firearms (Bornu some cannons also), maintained contact with the Maghreb and even with the Ottoman court, and had economies solidly anchored in the slave trade. Finally, all three were at least tacitly Muslim, though in reality Islam did not strike deep roots among the rural masses until near the twentieth century.

Paradoxically, at the turn of the century the region that was to become Chad was contested not so much by the European colonial powers (essentially Britain and France, with the latter's excess caution and fear of the former's costing her Bornu and other populated areas of Nigeria) as by other forces in the area. Rabah's aspirations for a personal slave empire in the region have already been noted. He had married his daughter to the emir of Sokoto and was preparing for a major advance upon Kano (and possibly Zinder and Damergou) when he was diverted from these plans by the necessity of punishing Baguirmi, which had applied for French protection. Rabah's pretensions in the region were given serious attention by both Britain and France, and the latter considered him the main obstacle to French influence in Central Africa.

Simultaneously, in the north, the scattered Turkish outposts in Tibesti and Borkou (frequently including only Toubou tribesmen fighting under the Ottoman flag) also contested the entry of French authority into the region. Ottoman influence was later supplanted entirely by Senoussi ambitions for the extension of the dar-al-Islam into the south. The Sanusiya sent emissaries to various local kingdoms (such as Zinder, Ouadai, Aïr) in an effort to forge a united anti-French (actually anti-Christian) front, and their efforts continued into the second decade of the twentieth century. In reality France's major "colonial" competitor in the Sahara and Sahel was the Sanusiya order operating out of their B.E.T. and Kufra headquarters. Only savage skirmishes and pitched Franco-Senoussi desert battles conquered the north for France, and then in part due to the fall of Libya to Italy, which forced the Sanusiya to reevaluate its priorities in light of the greater Christian threat from the coast. By 1920 France was master of Chad; in that year civilian rule finally replaced military rule in the territory except in B.E.T., where French military administration continued until 1965, five years after the independence of Chad.

The Colonial Era and Independence

French colonial rule did not bring about great socioeconomic advances in Chad, which today has the second lowest gross national product in

Africa. Indeed, Chad was very much neglected once it was finally conquered, especially since administrative appointments to French Equatorial Africa (AEF) in general (and Chad in particular) were the least attractive and desirable postings and were frequently assigned either to novice colonial administrators or to derelict officials as a sign of demotion and/or punishment. Many of those posted to AEF were the dregs of the French colonial civil service. Because of this, and because of the extremely high attrition rates, in 1928, for example, fully 42 percent of Chad's administrative districts were unstaffed by French personnel. However, in that year the entire educational system in the country included only 3,431 pupils; as late as 1933 there were only 18 qualified teachers in Chad, and the largest school (in Fort-Lamy) had only three grades with 135 students (see EDUCATION).

Even after the Second World War and the onset of the post-1944 Brazzaville Conference reforms and policies of liberalization and democratization of colonial rule, Chad's advances were extremely modest in comparison with those of other French colonies, especially in the French West Africa (AOF) federation. In education, for example, the first high school in Chad was set up only after the Second World War, and in 1958 there were still only three in the entire country. Likewise, though recognizing the serious obstacles to systematic infrastructure-building in Chad, 60 years of French rule left behind hardly any paved roads, only a very rudimentary modern economy, and little knowledge of the true mining potentials of the territory. (Indeed, only in the middle and late 1930s were several areas of the B.E.T. for the first time explored and cursorily mapped, and only in 1960 to 1962 was a more serious effort mounted.)

The cultivation of cotton was imposed upon the southern populations (so that they might pay the poll tax and that the colony might start paying its keep) as early as 1928, coupled with the establishment of an all-powerful purchasing-ginning monopoly (Cotonfran, later Cotontchad). Yet, though cotton rapidly became the mainstay of the economy and Chad became the top cotton producer of the CFA franc zone (see COTTON), the low producer prices paid out, the artificial enhancement of chiefly powers in which this resulted (see CORDES DE CHEFS), initial local opposition to the planting of nonsubsistence "colonial" crops (though cotton was indigenous to the area), and administrative abuses of authority all assured that anti-French sentiment developed in the southern Sara areas, which had in the past been so well disposed to France's *civilisatrice* role.

Following the end of the Second World War and the onset of political activities in the colony, the local French administration actively cooperated with local expatriate and chiefly elites (the latter mostly though not exclusively Muslim and non-Sara) to keep the Sara "radicals" out of positions of political power. Thus, notwithstanding the rise to political prominence in Sara regions of Gabriel Lisette—only recently arrived in Chad as a colonial administrator—as head of the Parti Progressiste Tchadien (PPT) and a leader of the interterritorial Rassemblement Démocratique Africain (RDA), both Lisette and the PPT were for all practical purposes shut out of power until 1957. The entire 1945–1957 political era is the story of the tug-of-war between, on the one hand, the largely southern progressive militants (Lisette, Tombalbaye, Toura Gaba, etc.), and on the other, the chiefly elitist political alliances overtly or covertly supported by French expatriate commercial interests and the local French administration. The balance finally tilted against the latter with the enactment of the 1956 Loi-Cadre (Enabling Act), which, through the grant of universal franchise (and proper electoral weight to the more populous south), led to the increasingly large PPT victories of the 1957–1959 years.

The final shift in the balance of power between the two competing blocs in Chad also dislodged Lisette (the true architect of the PPT victories), partly because of the aggravating (to the Muslims) nature of his expatriate origins but also because of François Tombalbaye's political ambitions. The country thus emerged at independence under the leadership of Tombalbaye, who rapidly forged a (temporary) voluntary single political alliance between the PPT and remnants of the Muslim parties— the Union pour le Progrès du Tchad (UPT), formed in March 1961— which compressed under its roof most of the political giants of the country. The fruits of victory and absolute power proved to be too sweet to share, however, and soon the PPT's unilateral actions within the UPT led to the alliance's breakup and the eventual ban on all other political parties in Chad.

The Economy

Chad is one of Africa's poorest countries and one of 25 classified by the United Nations as the least developed in the world. The country's geographical location—far from the coast and subject to the vagaries of climate, which can determine survival or disaster—greatly limits its potential for socioeconomic development. Though this began to change in the 1970s when oil was first discovered both in Kanem and in larger quantities in the south, near Doba, the bleak picture remains of a country always susceptible to catastrophes due to geography and ecology.

The principal crops grown in Chad are millet, sorghum, manioc, rice, and wheat, mostly for the subsistence economy, and peanuts and cotton for the cash economy. North of the 10th parallel the absence of tsetse flies allows extensive stockbreeding, especially in the Kanem, Batha, Chari-Baguirmi, and Ouadai Préfectures, though Chad's herds were decimated in the Sahel drought of the 1970s. Fishing in Chad's annually overflowing rivers and in Lake Chad is also a major economic activity, especially for the Kotoko and the Buduma; the latter also produce up to three rich wheat harvests in the fertile alluvial-soil polders of Lake Chad. In the drier eastern préfectures stockbreeding was for a while supplemented by the collection of gum arabic from the acacia trees, though output drastically declined as a result of the drought and later as a consequence of unsettled conditions, while in the far northern B.E.T. the daily economy is based on a mix of raising camels and sheep (milk products predominate in the diet) and tending desert palm and/or vegetable gardens.

Cotton, indigenous to the region but only since 1928 produced for the export market, is the mainstay of the Chadian economy. Indeed, in one way or another, cotton dominates all aspects and branches of productive labor and industry in Chad. Apart from accounting for up to 80 percent of Chad's export earnings and occupying the productive efforts of one-half of the peasant population, the processing of cotton provides employment for over 75 percent of all industrial labor in the country and is the mainstay and impetus of the tertiary service sector while sustaining the country's trucking industry, which would completely collapse without the lucrative contracts for the transport of the cotton crop. Notwithstanding its extremely important role in Chad, cotton production has been under intense pressure in the country because of low global producer prices and the high cost of transporting Chad's output. Indeed, during the 1980s Cotontchad's entire infrastructure was scaled down, with many ginning plants closed and many workers laid off. The 1990s have seen both peaks of production and troughs as planters have reacted to the rise and fall of prices fixed by the government.

Until the Sahel droughts, Chad's extensive livestock population (and especially its cattle herds, estimated at 4.5 million) constituted the country's second most important economic resource, despite the fact that much of the trade in cattle does not enter the modern money economy. Until the droughts, which destroyed nearly one-third of Chad's herds, sales of cattle (on the hoof) tended to be conducted through traditional channels, with the herds being smuggled across the border into Nigeria and the Central African Republic. What livestock does reach the local modern sector barely suffices to provide the needs of Chad's three (later, only two) refrigerated meat-processing plants, which once had ambitious hopes of servicing the cattle-poor, meat-hungry markets of Zaire, Gabon, and Congo/Brazzaville. Still, livestock production accounts for some 13 percent of Chad's gross domestic product and is engaged in by some 40 percent of the labor force. As a result of the droughts of the 1970s and 1980s, but also because political power has been captured by northern leaders, much of Chad's cattle herd has shifted to the south, to the Mayo-Kebbi and Moyen-Chari regions, causing some of the societal tensions mentioned earlier.

Sugar growing and processing came of age in the late 1970s, when considerable foreign (mostly French) funds helped to develop a 6,000-

hectare (14,280-acre) plantation of irrigated cane fields and a refining plant at Banda with the capacity to process 30,000 tons of raw sugar. National sugar self-sufficiency was attained in the mid-1990s, though export possibilities for this low-cost, high-bulk commodity are meager.

Until 1974 the only mineral exported in any appreciable quantity was natron, widely used among the traditional population as low-grade salt for human and animal consumption. However, the bulkiness of the commodity, its relatively low price and the increasing availability of cheap high-grade commercial salt have dried up the demand for Chadian natron, long a staple import in northern Nigeria, reducing age-old natron-extraction activities around Lake Chad and Borkou. In like manner the disrupted patterns of transhumance in Ouadai-Biltine (caused by both droughts and unrest) have brought a dramatic decline in gum-arabic collection. Despite major governmental increases in producer prices, few nomadic clans have been willing to shift back to their old patterns to resume the collection of gum arabic.

Though traces of uranium, gold, bauxite, and several other ores have been detected in Chad, their extractive potentials have not been seriously studied, largely because of the vast known difficulties and costs of importing processing machinery into the country and evacuating output to the coast and on to Europe. On the other hand, in the mid-1970s oil deposits were detected at several sites (see OIL), and the minor Kanem deposits were tapped, themselves enough to satisfy 80 percent of the country's oil needs. The discovery of much large deposits in the south, near Doba, transformed the entire picture, however, and in 1995 plans were drawn up for the laying of a pipeline connecting the deposits with the Atlantic coast via Cameroon.

Even so, Chad's prospects for even limited economic development are inextricably linked with the problem of ameliorating the country's extremely poor communications system and breaking away from the country's acute isolation from world markets (see COMMUNICATIONS). Hence any future extension of the trans-Cameroonian railroad to some point in Chad (Moundou, Bongor)—discussed for decades—would greatly assist in the creation of some of the most minimal conditions needed for the country's development. Though no new decisions have been reached on this issue, the fact that significant oil resources are to be exploited in the country vastly increases the chances of some solution's being found to Chad's geographic isolation. This would immediately and most dramatically reduce transportation costs—currently inordinately high—making both Chad's cotton more competitive abroad and further exploration for exploitable mineral wealth more attractive to foreign consortia.

All of these considerations only serve to underscore the economic reasons for Chad's acute dependence upon French and other foreign fiscal largesse. With the Chadian administrative budget in deficit without external funds, the developmental budget either nonexistent or in whole a function of French-EC-UN contributions, exports in some years covering only 20 percent of imports, and the fragile economy highly susceptible to the uncontrollable vagaries of climate and rainfall in one of the harshest environments in Africa, it is not difficult to perceive the reasons for the pessimism among many economists regarding Chad's future. Yet all of these notwithstanding, rich mineral resources are either known to exist or are suspected of being buried in Chad's inhospitable B.E.T. regions, as in neighboring Niger, which in the 1980s transformed its equally desolate Aïr regions into the world's fifth largest uranium mines. The central tsetse-free plains can continue to provide pasture for immense cattle herds, while major agrarian strides can be undertaken in the south. If all of these natural resources are tapped, and if indigenous oil deposits turn out to be as substantial as envisaged, the long-term economic future of Chad need not be as bleak as past projections have indicated.

Post-independence Politics: Southern Hegemony

Since independence the political evolution of Chad has been marked by institutional decay, a period of increasing concentration of absolute power in the hands of President Tombalbaye, continuous purges of real and suspected political opponents, insensitive mismanagement of the country leading to the Toubou and Maba rebellions in the north and the east, and—just prior to the 1975 coup d'état that was to cut short Tombalbaye's reign as well as his life—increasing cultural repression and the launching of ambitious labor-intensive economic projects as part of Tombalbaye's "authenticity" and "Cultural Revolution" drives.

Tombalbaye's consolidation of power in Chad resulted in several waves of massive purges, arrests, and expulsions from the country of a large array of indigenous politicians. Some, such as Lisette and Ahmed Kotoko, were expelled on the grounds of their being "nonnationals" (even though some had lived in Chad all their adult lives). Others, such as the veteran Toura Gaba, Baba Hassane, and Abo Nassour, were imprisoned for varying periods of time, allegedly for subversive activities, later to be released and reintegrated at the highest levels of the political hierarchy. Still others, such as Jean Baptiste, Silas Selingar, and Marcel Lallia, were killed while under detention, and some (considered the dauphins or heirs apparent to the president) fell from grace because of their own ambitions or excessive greed, or because of Tombalbaye's fears of political maneuvering within the cabinet. Certainly there was no absence of real intrigues, plots, and attempted coups; Tombalbaye's claim that he had survived more plots than any other African leader may indeed have been valid, though the causes of the plotting may be disputed. In the process, however, Chad's constitution and political structures decayed through abuses of power or rule by decree (such as the unilateral 1963 dismissal and the 1975 prolongation of the National Assembly, the instituting of a one-party system, and so on).

Crass government mismanagement of the provinces—in part a function of the huge developmental needs of Chad, the poor training of civil servants in general, and existing interethnic tensions throughout the country—led in the mid-1960s to the Mangalmé tax riots and the Bardai incidents, which marked the onset of the popular rebellion in the east and the north. Though the regime in N'Djamena for some time denied that the incidents had occurred (and later played down their importance or causes), the then-secret "Galopin Report" (named after the French captain who authored it) revealed the personal and administrative callousness of southern personnel, civilian as well as military, posted in the B.E.T. following France's withdrawal from the region in 1965. Observers in Mangalmé similarly traced the causes of the bloody riots to the illegal doubling and trebling of taxes levied on the population by corrupt government officials. Though occurring at different times and in widely separated regions, the two eruptions rapidly sparked off further riots and rebellions until most of the central, eastern, and northern areas of Chad were in revolt, unsafe to travelers outside the immediate periphery of a few urban centers (such as Abéché, Faya-Largeau), which themselves were also under constant rebel pressure.

By mid-1968 the situation in Chad was quite serious—not so much because of the organization, strength, tactics, or numbers of the rebel forces as because of the weakness of the central government in N'Djamena, the vastness of the territory that had to be pacified or patrolled, and the extremely poor quality of the Chadian armed forces. After a great deal of hesitation the regime appealed to France for help in accord with the provisions stipulated in existing Franco-Chadian treaties. The military and administrative cooperation extended by France came under very vocal attack both in Paris (by the Left), and in Arab countries that had given the Front de Libération Nationale (FROLINAT) and the Front de Libération du Tchad (FLT) an operational base from which to launch their attacks on government forces in Chad.

The French military reentry into Chad, limited though it was, and despite some reverses in the field, was sufficient to defeat the main body of Toubou and Maba guerrillas and to push the remnants into isolated geographic pockets within which they could be contained by the retrained and rearmed Chadian army. Meanwhile, the much more important Mission de Réforme Administrative (MRA) pushed through (at times against Tombalbaye's wishes but with strong French insistence) a series of reforms in the traditional authority framework that tended to erase some of the deeper grievances that had given sustenance to the revolt. The most important of these reforms—apart from the rigorous screening, retraining, reassignment, and selective dismissal of incompetent/corrupt civil servants whose activities had aggravated the strife—was the reinstallment, with enhanced rights, of Chad's traditional chiefs, and especially the major sultans of the Sahel belt kingdoms and chiefdoms, who for several years had been deprived of their customary rights in taxation and local administration of justice. (After the 1975 coup, they were again demoted.)

The two-pronged military and administrative-reform approach to quelling the Chadian rebellions was so successful (though Libyan restraints on FROLINAT in exchange for Tombalbaye's acceptance of the never-ratified Mussolini-Laval border rectification was also a consideration) that by the time the 1975 coup erupted, much of the discontent in the country had shifted to the south. There the "Cultural Revolution" decreed by Tombalbaye (always very influenced by Zaire's President Mobutu Sese Seko) had spawned two quite unpopular programs: Opération Agriculture (or Opération Coton), which set unattainable labor-intensive cotton production targets, and compulsory Yondo initiation ceremonies. The former significantly disrupted the modern economy by its (unscheduled) costs of mobilizing the large numbers of often urban and inexperienced "volunteers" and transporting them to open up virgin territory to cotton cultivation. The Yondo initiation rites, while satisfying Sara traditional elements, were anathema to most modern urban Chadians as well as to Christians and had gained the country worldwide notoriety from the publicity of the brutal torture and murder of Christians who refused to undertake the rites.

The coup that toppled Tombalbaye on April 13, 1975, came shortly after a number of officers of the armed forces had been arrested in connection with a plot to overthrow him. Following the coup, which resulted in several deaths, including that of Tombalbaye himself, and in which non-Chadian elements played a role (see GOURVENAC, CAMILLE), the army set up the Conseil Supérieur Militaire (CSM) under the chairmanship of General Félix Malloum. Political prisoners were released shortly afterward, some of Tombalbaye's associates were arrested, and inquiries began on corruption and mismanagement of resources (a large cache of U.S. dollars was discovered in the dead president's home, possibly part of Libya's bribe for the Aouzou Strip), missing and presumed murdered political prisoners, and selected aspects of the now-defunct "Cultural Revolution." The new regime immediately called for an end to the civil rebellion and promised to respect the legitimate grievances and sensitivities of the populations that had risen up in arms.

Though FROLINAT, always quite divorced in reality from the guerrilla forces fighting in the field under its banner, rejected Malloum's call for a national reconciliation, the new regime scored several dramatic successes and one major failure. Large numbers of rebel elements from the east (in the past more engaged in brigandage than in guerrilla warfare) "rallied" to N'Djamena (many of these were promptly integrated into the central armed forces), while the derde of the Toubou acquiesced to return from self-exile in Libya and called upon Toubou elements to stop fighting. The one major failure of the CSM was the refusal of the Habré-Goukouni armed faction in Tibesti to heed the call for a reconciliation with N'Djamena. Indeed, despite the fact that in terms of level of fighting Chad had been quite tranquil for some time (compared to previous years), the rebellion obtained its widest international coverage when their forces attacked Bardai in mid-1974 and captured a number of Europeans, including Christian Staewan, cousin of West Germany's president, and French archaeologist Françoise Claustre. Though Germany promptly ransomed its hostage (flying in and out of Habré's hideout without Chad's approval and provoking a diplomatic break in relations), drawn-out negotiations between France and the rebel leaders brought Franco-Chadian relations to the breaking point (all French troops were ordered out of the country) without any concrete results, the CSM's appeals notwithstanding. Only with the falling-out of Habré and Goukouni in 1976 was Mrs. Claustre finally released.

The North in Power

By 1977 the CSM had expanded its base of support—hitherto mostly military—to include in the cabinet a number of civilians. The conservative/conservationist nature of the 1975 coup was by now clear, since hardly any of the tarnished figures of the Tombalbaye era had been prosecuted, and indeed, many were once again inside the periphery of the power hierarchy in N'Djamena.

By 1977, however, the military picture was rapidly deteriorating. The temporary lull in the fighting in Tibesti was shattered by a resurgence of armed incursions by Goukouni's units, now better armed, increasingly with sophisticated weapons, and battling a badly demoralized Chadian army unwilling to die for the wastelands of B.E.T. Goukouni was by now, moreover, the undisputed leader of the rebellion, having earlier dislodged the armchair revolutionary Dr. Abba Siddick from his usurped chairmanship of FROLINAT. More recently Goukouni had ousted Habré from coleadership of the Second Liberation Army, following continual policy clashes sharpened by a fundamental division over the advisability of relying on Libya for military aid and over the future of Mrs. Claustre, now in her third year of captivity.

As the Malloum government began to crumble under the constant military hammering from the north—with entire army units deserting or joining the rebellion—Malloum attempted a desperate ploy. In a crassly opportunistic move, Habré, in the political wilderness with his 500-odd warriors, was invited to become prime minister. The move was intended to underscore concretely the sincerity of the military's commitment to national reconciliation and power sharing, but it was too little, too late, and was aimed at the wrong personality. The move alienated many with its abject opportunism, dispirited and further disillusioned troops in the field by the spectacle of their former archenemy transformed into nominal chief of staff, and in any case brought into the government fold the one leader with little influence, at the time, over the course of the rebellion, and commanding only some 500 troops.

The marriage of convenience was, moreover, a farce from its inception. Malloum never truly intended to share meaningful power within the new bicephalous executive that was set up, and in fact he was deeply suspicious of every move undertaken by his new premier. Habré's innate aggressiveness and attempted policy initiatives, on the other hand, were stunted by the double-talk prevalent in Malloum circles and the illusion of power the post conveyed but did not contain. In February 1979 fighting erupted in the capital, and the Chadian army garrison was routed by Habré's men; they were saved from either massacre or captivity by a humiliating protective cordon thrown around them by French troops in the capital. As the tug-of-war dragged on, Goukouni marched into N'Djamena, having demolished all residual resistance, capturing up to one-third of the entire Chadian army.

As at the conclusion of other civil wars, victory (of the north, in Chad's case) did not usher in tranquility but rather a major falling-out of the victorious factions over the spoils of victory. A series of peace talks in Nigeria (itself flexing impressive diplomatic muscle to protect its northern interests) coincided with armed clashes in N'Djamena, until finally a wall-to-wall coalition was hammered out, giving each of the 11 factions a degree of cabinet representation. Within the Gouvernement d'Union Nationale de Transition (GUNT), headed by Goukouni, the defeated south was given quasi parity with Colonel Wadal Abdelkader Kamougoué, now the de facto strongman of the south, as vice president, while Habré had to be content with the key defense portfolio.

The GUNT experiment lasted for three years but was shaky from the outset. The fundamental problem was that few of the factions were committed to unity. The social glue, artificial or otherwise, that had bound Chad together since the colonial days had dissolved during the civil strife. No community of interests existed now, nor was there a leader powerful enough to impose himself on the others—certainly not Goukouni, magnanimous to the south (by leaving it untouched by central government, virtually a state within a state) but otherwise revealed as a moody, morose, temperamental, and ineffective leader and administrator. Habré was suspected by all and accepted by few and was in any case soon to bolt from the union. Ahmat Acyl, another rebel leader and now the foreign minister, was widely suspected of being Libya's puppet; and Kamougoué, who with part of the Chadian army and gendarmerie intact could have swung his weight behind one or another of the northern contenders and assured his victory, preferred to adopt a noncommitted (though in principle pro-Goukouni) stance, hoping the northern internecine struggle might create an opportunity for a resurgent southern role.

As a result of some of these contradictory and centripetal stances, an early falling-out between Goukouni and Habré developed into a titanic and destructive battle for the control of N'Djamena. As the city was slowly pounded to rubble, with Kamougoué opportunistically firing at both sides, much of the population of N'Djamena fled across the river to Kousseri, Cameroon. Unable to defeat his rival, Goukouni appealed for Libyan combat support, and on December 15, 1980, facing imminent attack by advancing Libyan troops, Habré fled the capital.

The entry of Libya into the internal imbroglio—at the behest of the de facto government of Chad—was received with deep reservations in many quarters that turned into a deeper enmity against Goukouni following an ill-defined Treaty of Union initiated by Goukouni and Muammar Qaddafi in Tripoli. Though it was not known at the time, the fate of GUNT was sealed. Massive CIA-funded materiel started arriving in Habré's bases in the east, and with these eventually came the stunning counteroffensive toward the capital. Goukouni, tricked into requesting the ouster of his Libyan ally in return for Organization of African Unity (OAU) contingents, found the OAU force both ineffectual and incapable of stemming Habré's advance. On June 7, 1982, it was Goukouni's turn to flee N'Djamena to regroup in his B.E.T. redoubt, to attempt a counterattack a year latter. Today, with hindsight, after the murderous Habré and Déby eras, most southern leaders view Goukouni's two years in office with some nostalgia.

The Habré Years

Within three months of Habré's rise to power the southern préfectures—hitherto islands of tranquility untouched by northern authority during the Goukouni years—fell to rule by the Forces Armées du Nord (FAN). A revolt within Kamougoué's camp over his separatist course, but sharpened by considerations of personal advancement under Habré and intra-south ethnic competitions (Ngambayé Mbaï), delivered the préfectures to N'Djamena. Kamougoué himself, wounded, slipped into exile, assisted by a Belgian priest, to resurface in B.E.T.—together with other southern officers, such as General Djogo—as a Goukouni lieutenant. From there the long trek back to N'Djamena began, this time for Goukouni, until by mid-1983 Abéché itself briefly fell to the new rebels, thought it was to be reconquered by Habré.

It was within this context (yet another tilt in the decade-old seesawing between Habré and Goukouni) that French force of arms intervened on

Habré's side. A "Red Zone" interdiction line was declared along the 15th parallel (later the 16th), patrolled by French troops and air squadrons, setting the southern limit to Goukouni's advance that would be tolerated by France. Though a Franco-Libyan agreement in September 1984 led to a mutual withdrawal of foreign troops from Chad, France discovered that it had been tricked and it returned its troops, and the delicate stalemate perpetuated itself.

As the fighting died out in the north, Habré turned his attention to the seething south, which had been antagonized by the wave of repression by his troops upon their initial entry into the area, and which was virtually in a state of open revolt under the "*codos*" (from "commandos") of Colonel Guérinan Kottiga. A new "national" political party was set up—the Union Nationale pour l'Indépendance et la Révolution (UNIR)—with six southerners among its 15 Executive Bureau members; southerners were also given half of the cabinet ministries, including some choice posts. The rebellion in the south continued, however, with both mass atrocities committed by Habré's forces and numerous refugees fleeing to the Central African Republic. The growing alienation of the south from N'Djamena brought some talk of creating a Sara Republic of Logone (together with Sara areas in the C.A.R.), but strong contrary French counsel and lack of military muscle prevented any concrete moves in that direction.

Ultimately Sara and other southern political and military leaders were bought off by Habré's offers of patronage and high office. Even most of the *codo* units were enticed to lay down their arms in 1985 by generous offers of financial remuneration and integration into the Chadian army. At the same time, Habré's forces of repression dealt harshly with any dissent that nevertheless developed. A series of skirmishes with Goukouni's and Libyan forces in B.E.T. in 1986 resulted in new French reinforcements (code-named Opération Epervier) as well as additional supplies of U.S. arms. By that time, moreover, the GUNT alliance-in-exile was virtually defunct. Goukouni was largely isolated, had clashed with his Libyan allies, and was allegedly even negotiating with N'Djamena. The collapse of GUNT produced a steady stream of military leaders rallying to N'Djamena, each of whom was accommodated in the power hierarchy. Djogo, for example, was made minister of justice; Kamougoué became minister of agriculture; and Acheikh Ibn Oumar, who in the mid-1980s briefly headed the strongest GUNT faction, was appointed foreign minister.

By 1987 Habré felt strong enough to move against Libya's armies in B.E.T., an issue that had always separated him from Goukouni. A bold January offensive that led to the March 1987 capture of the important Libyan base at Ouadi-Doum, with much war booty, triggered a massive Libyan withdrawal from all their positions south of the long-held Aouzou Strip. In August 1987 Habré seized Aouzou itself, dealing Libya a stunning reverse, though Chadian troops had to be withdrawn in the face of heavy Libyan air attacks and the unwillingness of France to provide Habré with air cover. Chad then invaded Libya itself, attacking and demolishing the large Maaten-es-Sarra airbase.

During these stunning defeats Libya lost such huge amounts of war materiel, including state-of-the-art Soviet jets and helicopters, that arms purchasing missions had to be dispatched to Brazil and other suppliers to seek immediate replenishments. Several thousand Libyan troops were also captured, including senior officers. Several hundred of these were organized in CIA camps in the outskirts of N'Djamena as an anti-Qaddafi counterforce, while others languished in POW camps until December 1990, when Habré was ousted and the camps were closed down. Libya's humiliation in Chad and the Chadian incursion into Libya proper finally persuaded Qaddafi to recognize Habré's leadership in N'Djamena and begin negotiations on the resolution of the issue of the sovereignty of the disputed Aouzou Strip. The matter was eventually handed over for adjudication by the International Court of Justice in The Hague, and in 1994 the court ruled in favor of Chad, leading to the final withdrawal of all Libyan troops from Chad.

Paradoxically, as Habré consolidated his support among former GUNT enemies, he alienated and drove into rebellion the eastern Hadjeray, who had supported his original bid for power against Goukouni; later, in the late 1980s, he further alienated the (also eastern) Zaghawa—both key allies, since Habré's own kinsmen, the Daza branch of the Toubou, were not very numerous. More important, among the Zaghawa who fled N'Djamena in 1989 to seek sanctuary in Sudan were the two former chiefs of staff (Djamouss and Déby), who as architects of the victories against Libya were regarded abroad as military geniuses.

The reasons for this falling-out of former allies were numerous. Habré's vindictive and brutal character resulted in numerous arrests and killings (40,000, it was claimed after his ouster), which created both ethnic and individual blood vendettas. Habré's suspicious nature and the force-oriented nature of politics in Chad seemed to encourage brute force as a simple solution to complex problems. Many in the original northern alliance also viewed politics as a winner-take-all equation and resented sharing power with formerly powerless GUNT leaders drifting into N'Djamena to secure key offices; some also had personal ambitions thwarted either by Habré's policies of spreading patronage to southerners, or by his suspicions.

With the defection of Déby (a badly wounded Djamouss was captured and killed in prison), Habré's reign suffered its first major reverse. That Habré realized the importance of immediately trying to destroy Déby's forthcoming military challenge was obvious from the urgency with which he assembled his choicest troops and dispatched them into action, including in several daring forays deep into Sudan. There, in Darfur, Déby was recruiting and training a new army from among ethnic Zaghawa of non-Chad origins; he had also joined hands with the Hadjeray rebellion (led by Maldoum Abbas, who was to march victoriously into N'Djamena with Déby); and he was receiving heavy financial and military support from Libya, anxious to avenge itself against Habré.

Despite prior pitched battles, in November 1990 Déby's forces (numbering 2,000) emerged from their bases in Sudan and engaged Habré's pre-positioned troops in Ouadai. In the ensuing battles Habré's forces were shattered despite the assistance of U.S. Hercules-30 supply planes (allegedly piloted by Zaireans), Israeli mercenaries, and a host of other advantages, not least of which was a much larger fighting force. Many of Habré's lieutenants, a veritable Who's Who of the former FAN army, were killed in the battles. On December 1, 1990, Déby and Abbas drove unopposed across the breadth of Chad into N'Djamena to become the new warlords of Chad. The day before, Habré fled Chad for Cameroon on a Zairean passport and with all the country's foreign exchange, after ordering the execution of some 300 political prisoners who were being held in cells in the Presidential Palace.

Among Déby's very first acts in office was to honor a commitment to release all Libyan POWs and disband the CIA bases and to pledge to install a democratic system. The first he was to implement immediately; the second is yet to come. Déby's regime to date has been marked by the same system of elite patronage, the same brutal excesses, the same falling-out with former comrades-in-arms, and the same attempted seizures of power that marked the Habré regime. An ethnic Zaghawa (many non-Chadian) Garde Républicaine replaced Habré's disbanded ethnic Daza Garde Présidentielle as the regime's key force of repression. It has conducted massacres in the south, much as Habré's forces had, evoking in turn rebellion and talk of secession. Individual assassinations have taken place, as well as summary executions, for supporting Habré's comeback efforts. Arrests and detentions without trial are routine. The editors and reporters of the sole independent newspaper in N'Djamena are periodically arrested and harassed—for "libelous" articles about the excesses of the regime. As in Habré's days, a political police and secret service—with different names but with some of the same key personnel—engage in much the same brutalities and abuses of human rights, though quantitatively Déby's regime is less murderous as well as more forgiving. And as in Habré's days, sporadic rebellions have flared up in the east and in the south, with remnants of Habré's forces—denied bases in Sudan and Libya—twice attempting a comeback from Niger in the Lake Chad region, while a new southern rebellion emerged, led by Lt. Ketté of the CSNPD and based in the Central African Republic. (Ketté rallied to the regime in 1993 after being promoted by Déby to lieutenant colonel, having part of his force integrated into the Chadian army, and having a seat granted to the CSNPD in the interim legislature.) Overall, the telling fact remains that in the preceding two decades 400,000 Chadians died, from both drought and civil strife.

Under pressure from France and external donor agents Déby convened a national conference in January 1993 with the participation of some 800 delegates, including Goukouni, who was to return to his permanent domicile in Algeria. Tombalbaye (whose son has emerged as a political force in Chad) was "rehabilitated"; his body was exhumed from its burial site in the distant Faya and reburied in his home village. A host of resolutions and recommendations came out of the conference, which in April set up a 57-member interim legislature, the Conseil Supérieur de la Transition (CST), under Prime Minister Fidèle Moungar, a southerner. Parliamentary and presidential elections were pledged to take place within 12 months, only to be annually postponed on a variety of technicalities.

Political parties, of which some 30 initially emerged, further proliferated as fluid alliances formed and reformed; at last count some 60 parties existed or had been founded since the political space for them had been created. Though several have distinct platforms—a number call for a federal system; one for the recognition of Sara as a third official language; two (from the east) for the eradication of all vestiges of French in the country—many are hardly distinguishable from one another, being primarily personal machines. And though most have strongly pressed for democratization and the normalization of political life, it is difficult not to conclude that quite a few groups are not unhappy with a situation that gives them status, a measure of power, and a source of patronage. Needless to say, Déby—whose 1989 "liberation movement" was transformed into the Mouvement Populaire du Salut (MPS) party—is not overly anxious to spur normalization, aware of his minority status and the general antinortherner feelings in the country as a whole.

What the future holds for Chad is very difficult to foretell at this stage. As of late 1995 most of the country was secure and at peace (though a potentially explosive religious fundamentalism in Ouadai is on the rise), and even Habré's die-hard loyalists (and minor associated groups) in Niger and in Chad's Lac Préfecture are relatively quiet. The trade unions have been demonstrating on and off for a variety of bread-and-butter issues, at times for months on end, but everyone knows that there is precious little money in the treasury and that Chad is the kind of country where a governmental paralysis threatens nothing. France has taken a backseat in much of the political bickering in N'Djamena. Paris seems to savor its current disengagement from the 30-year Chadian morass (most French troops are finally out of the country) and is well aware that, Déby's flaws notwithstanding, there is no better leader waiting in the southern "democratic" wings. Quite possibly the country is destined, at least for the time being, to be ruled by a northern autocracy—which has constantly shown its fighting mettle—sharing a measure of power with the south. In the longer run, however, the twin questions of religious fundamentalism in the east and the constant encroachments of pastoralists on cultivators raise the specter of possible additional troubles in this troubled land.

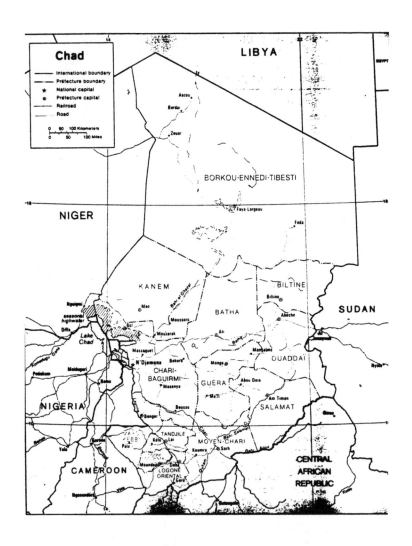

Chad

International boundary
Préfecture boundary
★ National capital
◉ Préfecture capital
Railroad
Road

0   50   100 Kilometers
0   50   100 Miles

LIBYA

EGYPT

Aozou

Bardaï

Zouar

BORKOU-ENNEDI-TIBESTI

NIGER

Faya-Largeau

Fada

KANEM

Bahr el Ghazal

BILTINE

Nguigmi

seasonal highwater

Mao

Moussoro

BATHA

Biltine

Abéché

SUDAN

Diffa

Lake Chad

Bol

Mouzarak

Ati

Bahr

Mangalmé

Massaguet

Bokoro

Mongo

OUADDAÏ

Komadugu

Gana

N'Djamena

CHARI-BAGUIRMI

Massenya

GUÉRA

Abou Deïa

Am Djarass

Nyala

Potiskum

Maiduguri

Melfi

Am Timan

SALAMAT

Bama

NIGERIA

Bousso

Bongor

Haraze

Benoue

Logone

TANDJILE

Bahr Salamat

Bahr Azoum

Yola

Barola

Pala

LOG. OCC.

Kélo

Laï

MOYEN-CHARI

Bahr Aouk

CENTRAL

Koumra

Sarh

AFRICAN

Moundou

Doba

REPUBLIC

Kebbi

CAMEROON

LOGONE ORIENTAL

Goré

Ngaoundéré

Vina

Nana

The Dictionary

ABAKAR, MAHAMAT HASSAN. Magistrate at the N'Djamena court, and first deputy state prosecutor. Abakar was appointed by Idriss Déby (q.v.) in 1990 to investigate and prepare a report on former president Hissène Habré's (q.v.) human rights violations and abuses of power. His report was issued in May 1992, documenting some 40,000 deaths directly attributed to the previous president.

ABAKAR, HISSEIN HASSAN. Imam of the Grande Mosquée of N'Djamena, and hence an extremely influential Muslim leader in Chad.

ABATCHA, IBRAHIM (1938–1968). Founder of the Front de Libération Nationale (FROLINAT) (q.v.) and its first major leader and field commander, Abatcha was killed in action in 1968 by government troops. Born in N'Djamena of Bornuan origins, Abatcha worked in a variety of positions (including in the SCLN firm), becoming a militant trade unionist. Imprisoned for one year by the French administration prior to independence, he was again briefly imprisoned in 1962 by François Tombalbaye (q.v.). He then left Chad to reside in Ghana, Egypt, and Sudan (1963–65), where he developed his Marxist leanings. Opting for armed struggle against the Tombalbaye regime, Abatcha received military training in Ghana and later in North Korea. Subsequently, while in Khartoum, he formed FROLINAT from exiled remnants of the Union Nationale Tchadienne (UNT) (q.v.) and the militantly Muslim Union Générale des Fils du Tchad (UGFT) (q.v.) under the leadership of Hassan Ahmed Moussa (q.v.). Though the two ideologically ill-fitted groups were to split up shortly thereafter, Abatcha retained the new name for his movement and, reentering Chad early in 1966, began guerrilla hit-and-run attacks against Chadian forces, especially in Ouadai. He was killed during one of these actions in March 1968. Abatcha was succeeded as active field commander by Abdel Hadj Issaka (q.v.), who was later deserted by his followers, with political control of FROLINAT being captured by Dr. Abba Siddick (q.v.).

ABATTOIR FRIGORIFIQUE DE FARCHA. N'Djamena's suburban slaughterhouse and freezing plant, set up in August 1958 to process beef supplies for local consumption and to service the strong need for fresh meat in neighboring countries. The French Prodel company had a majority interest in the Farcha plant. Early very optimistic expectations of vastly increased exports and concomitant state revenues never materialized despite high prices for meat abroad. Though the plant doubled its output between 1967 and 1971 (from 7,884 to 15,148 tons of processed meat), production fell to 7,971 tons in 1973. The decline was the composite result of the closure to Chad of the large Zaire market (which had purchased 8,466 tons in 1971), supply and transport problems consequent to the growing internal rebellion in Chad, decimation of cattle herds as a result of the Sahel drought, and the preference of cattleherders to sell their herds illicitly for higher prices in neighboring countries (especially Nigeria). At its peak of production the N'Djamena plant slaughtered 70,000 head of cattle per year, or roughly one-half of the cattle exported on the hoof by local merchants. (A similar ambitious plant in Sarh, the Abattoir Sarh, produced meat for local consumption before shutting down in 1972 for several years under similar pressures.) Damaged in the heavy fighting in N'Djamena (1978–82) the Farcha slaughterhouse was closed down until it could be rehabilitated. The slump in the livestock and fresh meat market only slowly turned around in the 1990s. Exports of fresh meat from Chad's slaughterhouses have been virtually nil, as cattleraisers continue to sell their herds illicitly abroad. See also CATTLE.

ABBA, MAHAMAT SEID (1935–). Early FROLINAT leader, born in 1935 in Yao and educated locally and in Paris in public administration, Abba served in the Chadian administration in a variety of capacities in Ati, Fada, and Mayo-Kebbi. Attracted to Ahmed Koulamallah's (q.v.) Mouvement Socialiste Africain (MSA), Abba, a party militant, later cofounded the Union Nationale Tchadienne (UNT) (q.v.) party in Kanem. As the new party's secretary-general between 1958 and 1963, Abba was a contemporary ally of Ibrahim Abatcha (q.v.), the founder of FROLINAT. Imprisoned for his antigovernment grassroots activities in 1963 (while Abatcha succeeded in fleeing abroad, where he founded FROLINAT), Abba was sentenced to 20 years in prison. He received amnesty from President Tombalbaye (q.v.) in 1971, was coopted into the Parti Progressiste Tchadien (PPT) Political Bureau and appointed PPT National Assembly deputy. Abba spurned these empty honors and flew to Tripoli, Libya, to claim a leadership role in the FROLINAT executive. Shunted aside by the wily Abba Siddick (q.v.)—who nevertheless made him vice president of the Conseil de la Révolution—Abba withdrew to Chad's eastern préfectures to raise a force of loyalists in an armed struggle against N'Djamena. With the fall of the capital, Abba was invited to participate in the Kano I peace talks. He was not initially given a post in the April 1979 GUNT (q.v.) government. Only after joining with other similarly slighted rebel leaders in forming the FACP (q.v.) grouping was Abba integrated into Goukouni's (q.v.) November 1979 wall-to-wall cabinet and appointed minister of interior. Retaining control of his small force—at the time going under the name FROLINAT-Fondamental (q.v.)—the ouster of the Goukouni regime by Hissène Habré (q.v.) in mid-1982 resulted in Abba's going into self-exile in Sudan. There he joined the Medela (q.v.) sponsored pro-Sudan MPNL grouping while participating in the Goukouni government-in-exile, the Gouvernement de Salut National (GSN) (q.v.). He personally participated in the GUNT armed offensive on Faya-Largeau, bringing with him a force of several hundred warriors, and was part of the clique that stayed with Goukouni's GUNT through 1985, when like most others he rallied to N'Djamena. Remnants of his force that remained in Sudan joined in the rebellion of Idriss Déby (q.v.) in 1989, and some came back to N'Djamena when Déby emerged victorious in 1990. However, a segment remained in opposition to N'Djamena into the mid-1990s.

ABBALA see ARABS

ABBAS, CHETTI ALI. Founding member in 1991 of the Rassemblement pour la Démocratie et le Progrès (RDF) (q.v.) party in opposition to Idriss Déby (q.v.). Abbas fled to northern Chad in January 1992 to avoid arrest in one of Déby's swoops on opposition leaders.

ABBAS, MALDOUM BADA (Colonel) (1952–). Minister of justice. Formerly the much more powerful and very close Idriss Déby (q.v.) lieutenant, key minister of interior, vice president of the Mouvement Populaire du Salut (MPS) governing party, and de facto number two person of the regime. A Hadjeray (q.v.), Abbas was originally part of the Goukouni-Habré revolt in B.E.T., though he sided with Hissène Habré (q.v.). When Habré occupied N'Djamena in 1982 Abbas was sent to France to attend a staff officers college. Commissioned a lieutenant shortly thereafter, he was appointed military prefect of Guéra, where he served until 1984. Progressively estranged by Habré's at times brutal mass purge of his Hadjeray (q.v.) entourage from the government after Idriss Miskine's (q.v.) assassination by poisoning in 1983, Abbas deserted the regime in 1986 and began a Hadjeray rebellion in Guéra in December of that year. His movement was called the Mouvement de Salut National du Tchad (MOSANAT). Further mass arrests of Hadjeray by Habré in 1987 (as well as the killing of Abbas's brother, Hamed Lamine), drove Abbas and his followers to Darfur, Sudan, where he formed an alliance with remnants of Abdelkadir Yacine's FROLINAT-Originel (qq.v.), Seid's Première Armée Volcan (qq.v.), and Libya's Islamic Legion (q.v.), which were at the time based there. When Habré's vicious purge moved on to affect the Zaghawa (q.v.) ethnic group—which led to another flight to Sudan of former close Habré lieutenants, including Idriss Déby (q.v.), one of the military architects of Habré's victories in B.E.T.—Abbas merged his rebellion with Déby's, and they jointly waged war against Habré. At the head of a large contingent of Hadjeray troops (including many nonnationals recruited in Sudan) as well as Zaghawa supporting Déby, Abbas participated in Opération Rezzou (q.v.), which crushed Habré's armies in Ouadai and without further opposition brought Déby and Abbas victorious into N'Djamena on December 2, 1990.

Though appointed to Chad's most important posts, Abbas felt that he and his Hadjeray warriors (including thousands of nonnationals) deserved much more, since numerically they had been by far the backbone of Déby's assault on N'Djamena. Boisterous and bombastic, Abbas unilaterally allocated to himself one of the two presidential palaces in N'Djamena and maintained a large (1,000-man), rowdy private Hadjeray force at his side. Increasingly a threat to Déby, and, indeed, considering himself coequal to the latter, Abbas was especially irked by the elimination of the position of MPS vice president that he occupied. He was arrested on October 13, 1991, on the pretext of an attempted coup d'état, preceded by an assault on a N'Djamena armory. Though the media gave credence to this story, Abbas was in reality framed, and thus the Hadjeray's growing self-assertion in N'Djamena was thwarted. Though a rebellion at Abbas's behest promptly broke out in Hadjeray areas in Guéra, Abbas was soon reconciled with Déby and, much chastened, was rehabilitated and released in January 1992, when he was appointed to the provisional council of the Republic. He was appointed minister of justice in 1995.

ABBAS, YOUSUF SALEH. Vice president of the Conférence Nationale (q.v.) of 1993 and member of the subsequent National Assembly. Abbas had been a GUNT (q.v.) aide of Goukouni (q.v.), and when the national convention was convened in 1993 was a candidate for the chairmanship, being elected as one of the two vice presidents alongside Adoum Hel-Bongo (q.v.), who became chairman.

ABDALLAH, AHMED (1933–1971). Former deputy to the National Assembly and ringleader of a 1971 attempted coup d'état. Parliamentary deputy since December 22, 1963, and former president of Chad's influential veterans association—the Association des Anciens Combattants due Tchad (AACT) (q.v.)—Abdallah lost his assembly seat in a 1967 purge. He then became an employee of ASECNA (an air insurance firm) and a clandestine government provocateur (though in reality he was allied with anti-Tombalbaye forces). In his former capacity he kept tabs for Tombalbaye on the links between cabinet ministers and FROLINAT (q.v.). In August 1971 Abdallah was involved in a plot to discredit former opposition members who had rallied to the government and had been integrated into high-level posts; shortly thereafter he was one of the ringleaders of the August 27 attempted coup that was sponsored by Libya. (See COUP [AT-TEMPTED] OF AUGUST 27, 1971.) Arrested consequent to revelations that his original accusations had been false, Abdallah was killed during interrogation.

ABD-EL-KADER (1880?–1950). Former chef de canton of Teda Ouria in the Borkou. Loyal to the Sanusiya (q.v.), Abd-el-Kader maintained secret contact with the order of Libya and with the Axis powers in North Africa during the Second World War. He was deposed for his anti-French activities in 1946, to be succeeded by his nephew Orjo as traditional ruler of the canton.

ABDELKADER, CHARLES. Former diplomat and educator. A teacher by profession, with training in public administration, Abdelkader served as Chad's delegate to UNESCO in Paris and in 1972 was appointed director of the Centre de Documentation Pédagogique at the Ministry of Education. In 1977 Abdelkader moved from Chad to Nigeria.

ABD-EL-KERIM. Legendary leader of the Maba (q.v.) uprising early in the seventeenth century that unseated the Tunjur (q.v.) dynasty, founded Wara (q.v.), and set up the Ouadai kingdom (q.v.). Abd-el-Kerim's dynasty ruled in Ouadai until 1915, when it was ousted by the French. Of Sudanic origin (his father came from a Jalali family from an area north of Khartoum and migrated to Maba country), Abd-el-Kerim was the governor of a province under the ruling Tunjur dynasty. According to some accounts, he became disaffected by the non-Muslim mannerisms and practices of the Tunjur and mounted the popular upheaval that ousted the dynasty from Ouadai. (Other versions give a more prosaic account of his motivations.) The date of the rebellion is subject to some controversy, being placed either (according to Heinrich Barth [q.v.]) in 1611 or (according to Gustav Nachtigal [q.v.]) in 1635. The capital of the new kingdom was then relocated to Wara, and for some time Ouadai paid tribute both to Darfur (q.v.) — the parent state of the Tunjur, currently in Sudan — and to the Kanem-Bornu Empire (q.v.) to the west.

ABDELKRIM, NADJO. Former head of the Forces Populaires Révolutionnaires Tchadiennes (FPRT), which was reconciled with Habré in 1988.

ABDERAHIM, DJALAL (1917–). Former cabinet minister. Born in 1917 in Am-Timan in the Salamat, and a merchant by profession, Abderahim established himself in N'Djamena. He was an early member of the pre-independence conservative UDT (q.v.) party but was unsuccessful in his first attempt to win an assembly seat. In the mid-1950s he became the treasurer of the AST (q.v.) party and in 1957 was elected to the assembly as deputy from Batha (q.v.). Shortly thereafter he joined the faction that was to become GIRT (q.v.)—which favored cooperation with Gabriel Lisette (q.v.) and the latter's Parti Progressiste Tchadien (PPT) (q.v.)—and was reelected to the assembly in 1959. In the assembly he served as president of the Economic Affairs Committee and later as vice president of the assembly. In December 1958 he was brought into Lisette's provisional government as minister of planning and tourism and—having officially defected to the PPT—served in the subsequent provisional governments as minister of cooperation. In August 1960, consequent to Lisette's own purge from the party, Abderahim was dropped from the cabinet, though he retained his assembly seat and the vice presidency. In November 1965 he ran afoul of the regime and was arrested for allegedly plotting against Tombalbaye. Following his June 1970 amnesty he retired from public life.

ABDERAHMANE, ABOUBAKER. Early head of the Third Liberation Army (q.v.) of FROLINAT. Of Kanembu origins, Abderahmane became disenchanted with FROLINAT (q.v.), of which he was a regional leader. In May 1977 he formally dropped out of the movement, rebelling against its domination by Toubou (q.v.) elements and concerns. After a period of exile in Nigeria during which he gained military, political, and manpower backing, Abderahmane reappeared in the Chadian political scene at the head of a small force operating in the vicinity of Bol near Lake Chad (qq.v.). This small force was grandiosely called the Third Army. Despite the fact that it had never been of consequence in the struggle against François Tombalbaye (q.v.), the force scored several propaganda coups that brought it publicity. Among these was the raid on the camp of the Continental Oil Company in Kanem, then prospecting for oil. This, plus the strong backing of Nigeria, gained the group a seat in the Kano I 1979 peace conference. The new GUNT (q.v.) regime in N'Djamena totally excluded Abderahmane from the division of the spoils of war, triggering Nigeria's withdrawal from the peacekeeping force. Internal schisms subsequently tore apart the Third Liberation Army. Abderahmane was for sometime presumed dead—killed by his own men over his overly close alliance with Nigeria—but he surfaced mysteriously at the Lagos I meeting (May 27, 1979), claiming that he had been under arrest by his own lieutenants. The internal split in his formation could not be healed, however, with the rump of the group falling under the sway of Lol Mahamat Choua (q.v.) and, later, Moussa Medela (q.v.).

ABDOULAYE, MAHAMAT. Leader of the post-1992 northern political party, the Mouvement pour la Paix et le Développement au Tchad (MPDT).

ABDOULAYE KINDJA, TIMOTHEE (1938–). Former director of the Abattoir Frigorifique de Farcha (AFF) (q.v.). Born in Adré on April 21, 1938, Abdoulaye Kindja served first as Inspector of Stock Hygiene, and later as Stockbreeding Controller. In April 1969 he was appointed deputy director (later director) of the AFF. In 1977 he was moved to head a division in the Ministry of Stockbreeding.

ABDOUSSALAM, IBRAHIM. Early de facto head of the Mouvement pour la Libération du Tchad (MPLT) (q.v.) in Kanem between 1982, when he rose to power, and 1986. Abdoussalam emerged in his leadership role after the demotion of Batram Adoum, the former head and other faction leader, for "serious errors committed in Sudan." Little is known about Abdoussalam except that he is himself from Kanem.

ABECHE. Chad's fourth largest city with 85,000 inhabitants, up dramatically from 30,000 two decades ago. Abéché also is the administrative headquarters of the Ouadai Préfecture and the former imperial capital of the powerful Ouadai kingdom (q.v.). Situated on a large undulating plateau at the edge of several mountain ranges, including the foothills of Darfur, Abéché was a small inconsequential village until 1850, when it was chosen to replace the beleaguered Wara (q.v.) as capital of the kingdom of Ouadai. Consequently the town rapidly became a major trade entrepôt and the southern terminus of the trans-Saharan caravan trails. (This latter development occurred due to the shift eastward of the trails when the Fezzan-Bornu route became unsafe in the nineteenth century [see CARAVAN ROUTES].) Also developing into a major transit center on the west-east pilgrim route to Mecca, Abéché at the time of the French intrusion in the area was Chad's largest urban center with a population of 28,000. Following the French occupation, the heavy-handed colonial policies (which included the imposition of staggeringly high taxes and massacres of the elite—see KUB KUB MASSACRE) greatly antagonized the population, which dispersed into the countryside. The major epidemics of 1913–1917 further diminished the declining city, whose population plummeted to 6,000 in 1919. Since then the population has slowly increased, though Abéché was not able to keep pace with the new "colonial" towns of Fort-Lamy (N'Djamena), Fort-Archambault (Sarh), or Moundou (currently ahead of it in population), which either did not exist or were minuscule settlements at the height of Abéché's imperial splendor. In the center of the town there is an important and highly picturesque Hausa (q.v.) *zariba* (q.v.) that assists pilgrims on their way to Mecca. As late as 1976 the town still had very few schools (most parents preferring to send their children to Koranic schools) and very rudimentary municipal services.

With a population traditionally suspicious of and opposed to all outside and especially Christian influences, Abéché's socioeconomic modernization has seriously lagged behind that of other cities, as has the development of the entire préfecture of Ouadai. The town itself is Chad's most picturesque, extremely oriental in appearance with its minarets, narrow and winding cobbled streets, nomadic traffic, and run-down structures, including the palace of Sultans Doudmourah and Ali Silek. Politically, Abéché overwhelmingly supported the various traditional Muslim chiefly parties that sprang up in the post-1945 era in Chad, and their political elimination after 1962 drove Ouadai's population and leaders to support FROLINAT (q.v.) and other anti-N'Djamena movements. Never truly reconciled to being ruled from the west by elites from former subject peoples (southerners in general, and the Sara in particular), the region remained highly unsettled and volatile even in the best of times. Between 1966 and 1970 land communications with N'Djamena were as often as not totally disrupted by the rebellion in the eastern part of Chad, and with the collapse of central authority in N'Djamena and the triumph of FROLINAT, Abéché changed hands a number of times. It was held by Goukouni, Habré, Acyl (qq.v.) as well as by Libyan forces; again by Goukouni, when much of the population deserted the nearly destroyed town; and then reconquered by Habré. The town fell to Déby in late November 1990, signaling the end of Habré's rule.

Even after the rise of Déby, the town and its garrison have been attacked by several rebel forces operating in the area. Strong fundamentalist religious influence from Sudan, toward which the region has always gravitated, started to be felt in 1993. A number of tracts have been disseminated in recent years calling for Muslims to adopt greater orthodoxy and warning all southerners (who predominate in administrative capacities) to leave the region lest they suffer the fate of foreigners in Algeria.

ABESHR see ABECHE

ABO NASSOUR, ABDOULAYE SABRE (1927–1983). One of Chad's most prominent politicians, opposition leader, former minister of interior and president of the National Assembly. Born in 1927 in Kapka (Biltine), the son of Kapka's sultan (abo = prince), Abo Nassour served for some time as the influential secretary of the sultan of the Zaghawa (q.v.) in Ouadai before becoming engaged in the politics of his home region. He rapidly became the most prominent of the Ouadaian leaders of the conservative and chiefly Action Sociale Tchadienne (AST) (q.v.) party and was elected deputy of the Territorial Assembly from Ouadai in 1952. In later elections (1957, 1959, and 1962) he was reelected on the UDIT (q.v.) ticket.

In the assembly Abo Nassour was the most influential non-Sara leader and a very powerful Muslim political broker. He served in a variety of parliamentary posts, including secretary of the assembly Bureau (1957–58) and chairman of several assembly committees. Abo Nassour was first brought into Chad's cabinet in December 1958 as minister of cooperation (serving through February 1959), and he then occupied a succession of other ministerial postings through 1963: minister of economics and finance, February–March 1959; minister of finance, March–June 1959; minister of interior, April 1960–May 1962; minister of the civil service, May 1962–August 1962; and minister of state, August 1962–August 1963. In the roundup of Muslim opposition leaders in mid-1963 Abo Nassour was one of the prominent politicians to be arrested, imprisoned, and sentenced to death for plotting against the regime. He benefited from the amnesty of November 1969, and as a token of the reconciliation of President François Tombalbaye (q.v.) with Muslim Chad, Abo Nassour was fully rehabilitated, reintegrated into the PPT (q.v.) party's hierarchy, elected to the National Assembly, voted in as the assembly's president (1970–1975), and appointed to the PTT's Political Bureau. However, it was Abo Nassour who was chosen to be Tombalbaye's personal envoy to offer reconciliation to the self-exiled derde (q.v.) of the Toubou (q.v.) in Libya, though Abo Nassour was not successful in his task of convincing the titular leader of the Toubou to return, thus helping to quell the revolt in B.E.T. (q.v.). Following the abolition of the PPT in favor of the "new" MNRCS (q.v.) party, Abo Nassour was elected to this party's Executive Committee and continued in his various government functions until the coup d'état of 1975.

Despite his period in prison under Tombalbaye, Abo Nassour was never a FROLINAT (q.v.) member. Indeed, a prime opportunist, he was the FROLINAT's most detested politician after Tombalbaye. After the 1975 coup d'état Abo Nassour was one of the few in Tombalbaye's cabinet to be imprisoned for corruption. After the victory of the north in the civil war Abo Nassour was totally eclipsed politically, and with the rise of Hissène Habré (q.v.) in 1982 he was arrested by the DDS (q.v.) and killed.

ABOUDEIA. Souspréfecture with administrative headquarters in the village of the same name; part of the Salamat Préfecture. The souspréfecture encompasses 16,000 square kilometers (6,200 square miles), with an estimated population of 30,000.

ABSAKINE, ALI. Chad's minister of the armed forces, a newly created post in 1995. Of Bulala (q.v.) chiefly origins, Absakine has been one of Déby's prime allies and was originally appointed minister of defense in May 1994.

ABSAKINE, OUMAR (1927–). Traditional leader of the Bulala (q.v.) of Yao (q.v.). Born in Yao in 1927, of the ruling lineage, Absakine became a member of the conservative AST (q.v.) alliance that dominated early Chadian politics. He was elected territorial councillor from Batha (q.v.) on the AST ticket and served in that capacity through 1958. In 1959 he was reelected to the National Assembly as a PPT (q.v.) member and served for three years as the secretary of the assembly Bureau (1960–63). Since 1963 he has not played a political role. As sultan of the Bulala, he was one of the traditional leaders who had their powers whittled down by President François Tombalbaye's (q.v.) antichiefly edicts, though later his traditional rights were restored at the recommendation of the French Mission de Réforme Administrative (MRA) (q.v.).

ACHEIKH IBN OUMAR, SAYYID (1951–). Former foreign minister, and key rebel leader. More properly, and in his early days, known as As-Saykh Ibn Omar, Acheikh emerged as the leader of the Conseil Démocratique de la Révolution (CDR) (q.v.) after the Ahmat Acyl's (q.v.) death on July 19, 1982. An Arab from Batha, born in 1951, Acheikh came into prominence as one of Acyl's prime military lieutenants. He participated in the post–Kano I GUNT (q.v.) governments, first as deputy secretary-general (April–November 1979), then briefly as minister of labor and education, and in July 1981 as minister of education. Following Hissène Habré's (q.v.) triumphant march into N'Djamena, Acyl and Acheikh allied their forces with Kamougoué's (q.v.) FAT (q.v.) and jointly resisted Habré's push southward. With the victory of FAN (q.v.), the battered CDR forces withdrew to the east, to Salamat and Biltine, their main power base. Acheikh, who had succeeded to CDR leadership when Acyl died in an accident (or was assassinated by Habré agents, as was later alleged) in July 1982, was integrated into Goukouni's (q.v.) GUNT government-in-exile as minister of defense. He was dropped from that post in mid-1984 when he and the CDR began to manifest separatist tendencies, related to Goukouni's lukewarm relations with Libya, and was detained by Goukouni for nearly a year until he agreed to sign the Cotonou agreement that formed a coalition of opposition groups. In 1986, after his release, he rebelled against Goukouni and set up a neo-GUNT front, the Front Patriotique Tchadien (FPT), and operated against the Habré regime from his normal base in Sudan. He was later successful in ousting Goukouni from the GUNT leadership, and he himself became head of the organization. As he made a tour of sympathetic African countries he was in turn deposed from the leadership of his own CDR by some of his lieutenants (such as Secretary-General Rakhis Manani, who replaced him), who argued that Acheikh's own split with Goukouni had allowed Habré to reconquer most of northern Chad.

As Libya grew tired of supporting the rebels in the north, especially after its own defeat at the hands of Habré, Acheikh made peace with N'Djamena in November 1988. Since at the time he commanded the largest armed force ranged against Habré, and the last main one, he was integrated into the government in a senior post, as minister of foreign affairs, the duties of which he assumed in March 1989. When Habré was ousted by Idriss Déby (q.v.) in December 1990 Acheikh was dropped from the cabinet but was appointed special presidential adviser. Progressively less militant and devoting more of his time to writing articles and pamphlets, in 1993 Acheikh left N'Djamena for self-exile in Burkina Faso and Paris.

ACTE FONDAMENTAL, SEPTEMBER 29, 1982. Fundamental Charter, or Constitution, decreed after Hissène Habré's (q.v.) assumption of power in N'Djamena. The Acte posited Chad as an indivisible lay republic, with a head of state and a national consultative council appointed by him until a new National Assembly could be elected. The Acte was valid until December 1989, when a new constitution was ratified, allegedly by 99.4 percent of the population. (See also CONSTITUTIONS.)

ACTION DEMOCRATIQUE ET SOCIALE (ADS). Chadian political ticket formed to compete in the 1951 French National Assembly first electoral college elections (see DOUBLE ELECTORAL COLLEGE). The ADS—under its leader, René Malbrant (q.v.)—was an affiliate of France's Rassemblement du Peuple Français (RPF) (q.v.) and was linked with the second electoral college Chadian party, the Union Démocratique du Tchad (UDT) (q.v.).

ACTION SOCIALE TCHADIENNE (AST). Successor to the conservative UDT (q.v.) party, renamed following Jean Baptiste's (q.v.) 1953 desertion from the UDT to form his own UDIT (q.v.) party. Aligned with France's Rassemblement du Peuple Français (q.v.) party (as was the UDT), the AST was largely a chiefly, Muslim, and conservative alliance for the preservation of traditional and European power against the "radical" upstarts of the south, the PPT (q.v.). Powerful especially in Ouadai, Batha, and Mayo-Kebbi, the AST — like the UDT — was rent by personal rivalries and splits, the most important of which was the 1957 creation of the Groupement des Indépendants et Ruraux Tchadiens (GIRT) (q.v.), composed of elements inclined to cooperate with the southern-dominated PPT coalition that was then slowly ascending to power. Just prior to the 1957 territorial elections, the PPT alliance — ERDIC (q.v.) — offered the AST 20 of the 65 assembly seats at stake if the party would join in a common electoral ticket. The AST leadership refused the offer, and the party was subsequently badly trounced in the elections when it gained only eight seats (compared to the GIRT's nine). Increasingly weakened by internal schisms and defections, the AST formed an electoral alliance the same year with Ahmed Koulamallah's (q.v.) Mouvement Socialiste Africain (MSA) (q.v.) and with the Union Démocratique Independante du Tchad (UDIT) (q.v.) named Union Socialiste Tchadienne (UST) (q.v.), which was successful in the partial elections in Chari-Baguirmi. The UST coalition in the National Assembly then held 26 seats to the 36 of the PPT alliance — then called the Entente (q.v.) — and suddenly acquired a majority in January 1959, when the GIRT deserted the Entente, joined the UST — renamed Mouvement Populaire Tchadien (q.v.) — leading to the collapse of the Gabriel Lisette (q.v.) provisional government (see PROVISIONAL GOVERNMENTS) and the creation of the short-lived MPT (q.v.) government, in which key AST members participated. Koulamallah's opportunistic defection from the latter Gountchomé Sahoulba (q.v.) government resulted in its demise and the creation of an equally short-lived Koulamallist administration before the situation stabilized under François Tombalbaye (q.v.) and the PPT. For all practical purposes the AST party disappeared with the creation of the UST alliance, though an AST faction continued to exist informally throughout the entire span of the UST, MPT, and later, the PNA (q.v.) parties. Among the prominent leaders of the AST were a number of Frenchmen — such as René Malbrant (q.v.), who was Chad's representative in Paris until his death in 1962 — forced to join one of the African parties with the abolition of the double electoral college (q.v.) system in the mid-1950s.

ACTION TCHADIENNE POUR L'UNITE ET LE SOCIALISME (ACTUS). Originally a small opposition group that joined in the anti-

Goukouni, anti-Habré (qq.v.) formation, the Rassemblement des Forces Patriotiques (RFP) (q.v.), in August 1984. It later fell under the political sway of Fidèle Moungar (q.v.), who was to be one of Idriss Déby's interim prime ministers.

ACYL, ADOUM (1964–1993). CDR (q.v.) leader, close ally of Yacoub Abbas Kotti (q.v.); both were killed for their anti-Déby activities on October 21, 1993.

ACYL, AHMAT (1944–1982). Military head of the Volcan Army (q.v.), the Conseil Démocratique de la Révolution (CDR) (q.v.), and former civil administrator and National Assembly deputy during the Tombalbaye (q.v.) era. An Arab born in 1944 in Djedda (Batha) to the Djatné Arab tribe, and on his mother's side coming from the superior chiefs of the Rachid, Acyl was educated locally (Abéché, Fort-Lamy) and abroad (Marseille). He graduated in 1966 as second lieutenant in health services and returned to Chad early the following year, when he was appointed deputy prefect of Guéra, and in 1969 deputy prefect of Logone Occidental. In December of the same year he was elected deputy of the National Assembly, serving as rapporteur of the assembly's Foreign Affairs Committee. Secretly a FROLINAT (q.v.) sympathizer, Acyl formally joined the revolt in 1971 and fled to Libya, where he was not acceptable to, nor taken seriously by Dr. Abba Siddick (q.v.), titular head of the movement. Consequently Acyl joined the Volcan Army (q.v.) and participated in some of the battles against government forces in Salamat, Biltine, and Ouadai, sharing power with Adoum Dana (q.v.). He subsequently won a power tug-of-war with Mohamed Baghalani (q.v.) and became head of the faction of the eastern First Liberation Army (q.v.), which refused to lay down its arms after the 1974 truce that took out of the rebellion the Moubi tribesmen. Acyl led the Volcan Army into a merger with the Forces Armées du Peuple (FAP), though retaining its power base, independence, supply sources, and external headquarters in Tripoli, Libya.

Increasingly regarded as no more than a puppet of Libya—which he was not—Acyl was not invited to join the Kano I peace talks. After Kano II, in which he did participate, together with all rebel leaders who had been excluded in the first round, he was left out of the new GUNT (q.v.) government and consequently joined the alternative Libyan-sponsored FACP (q.v.). Ultimately integrated into GUNT (November 1979), he served in the cabinet as minister of foreign affairs. Despite his "pro-Libya" label, he was essentially loyal to Goukouni (q.v.) to the end. After joining the GUNT coalition, his faction was renamed Conseil Démocratique de la Révolution (CDR). Acyl was always regarded by Hissène Habré (q.v.) as a major competitor for power, a threat

largely because of his popularity and power base in Biltine, his willing-
ness to deal reasonably with the defeated southern factions, and his consuming ambitions. In late 1981 Acyl unsuccessfully tried to eliminate
his main political/factional rival in the east—Mahamat Abba—in the
process depleting his military resources and indirectly allowing Habré
to gain the upper hand in his military assault on GUNT. With the fall of
N'Djamena to the Habré troops, Acyl withdrew to his eastern bastion
and concluded an alliance with Colonel Kamougoué's FAT (qq.v.), honored by his successor—Acheikh Ibn Oumar—in the joint FAT-CDR
resistance to Habré's southern assault. Acyl allegedly died in an accident in Laï on July 19, 1982, when he was hit by his own airplane's
propeller while retrieving his shoe from the ground. Persistent alternate
rumors have it that in reality he was murdered by "The Vultures" a
clandestine Habré Garde Présidentielle (q.v.) unit under Ismail Bal
(q.v.). Acyl was buried in Moundou.

ACYL, SULTAN OF OUADAI. French puppet sultan in Ouadai during
the early years of the occupation of the kingdom. A nephew of the
reigning Sultan Ali, Acyl fled Abéché to avoid being blinded by the
court, as was the custom at each royal succession with all male members of the royal lineages. He then cooperated with the advancing
French forces, hoping to come to power with their help. The French
alternated between supporting and rejecting his claims, but in 1908 he
was recalled from self-imposed exile and made sultan of Ouadai when
French troops entered Abéché. He was toppled in 1912 and exiled to
Laï (q.v.) after reneging on his pledges to France and following a
Kodoy (q.v.) uprising in Ouadai that presaged the major disturbances
of 1912–18. See also OUADAI KINGDOM.

ADELMOLLA, MOHAMMED SALEH. Secretary of information of
FROLINAT (q.v.) between 1966 and the fall of N'Djamena in 1979.
A member of the original secret committee of the Cairo student section of the Association des Fils du Tchad, Adelmolla participated in
the founding of FROLINAT and became an Abba Siddick (q.v.) loyalist. Temporarily in the political wilderness after Siddick's eclipse in
1977, Adelmolla returned to N'Djamena in 1979 to continue serving as
Siddick's information and liaison officer within Siddick's FROLINAT-
Originel (q.v.).

ADMINISTRATIVE ORGANIZATION. In the post–Second World
War but pre-independence era, Chad was divided into a (varying)
number of *régions* (q.v.) or *départements* (q.v.), which were in turn
subdivided into *districts* (q.v.) that encompassed a number of *cantons*

(q.v.). In 1950, for example, there were the following nine départements, with headquarters in the urban centers in parentheses:

Chari-Baguirmi (Fort-Lamy)   Ouadai (Abéché)
Kanem (Mao)   B.E.T. (Largeau)
Mayo-Kebbi (Bangor)   Batha (Ati)
Salamat (Am-Timan)   Logone (Moundou)
Moyen-Chari (Fort Archambault)

These départements were divided into 39 districts and six *postes de contrôle administratif* (PCA) (q.v.), each encompassing a number of cantons, which in turn grouped a number of villages or nomadic encampments. Even before independence the number of départements was increased to 11, consequent to either regional demands for greater administrative autonomy or political pressures. Thus in 1956 the 10th département—Guéra—was established, and in 1956 Biltine was set up as a département separate from Ouadai, under which it had previously been administered.

On February 13, 1960, the nomenclature of Chad's administrative units was changed, with the former régions/départements becoming *préfectures* and the former districts becoming *souspréfectures*. At the headquarters of the préfecture is the office of the prefect, who was to be assisted in his duties by an elected Conseil de Préfecture (q.v.); in each souspréfecture resides a subprefect responsible for his region to the prefecture headquarters.

The number of administrative units slowly climbed upward after independence. In 1962 the southern préfecture of Logone was divided into three separate units—Logone Oriental, Logone Occidental, and Tandjilé—in part due to the region's very high population density, necessitating administrative autonomy on the local level, but also in order to combat Gabriel Lisette's (q.v.) popularity (purged in 1960 but still a factor) in the region. Later, the Lac Préfecture was carved out of Kanem. Currently Chad has 14 préfectures, 54 souspréfectures, 27 postes administratifs, and 458 cantons. The préfectures are as follows (see also entries for each):

1. Chari-Baguirmi (HQ in N'Djamena). Souspréfectures of N'Djamena, Bokoro, Bousso, Massakory, Massenya. Administrative posts of Moïto, N'Gama, Massaguet, Dourbali.

2. Batha (HQ in Ati). Souspréfectures of Ati, Ouadi-Rime, Oum-Hadjer. Administrative posts in Mangalmé, Harazé-Djombo, and Assinet.

3. B.E.T. (HQ in Faya). Souspréfectures of Borkou, Ennedi, and Tibesti.

4. Guéra (HQ in Mongo). Souspréfectures of Mongo, Bitkine, and Melfi.

5. Kanem (HQ in Mao). Souspréfectures of Mao, Moussoro, Nord-Kanem. Administrative posts in Sallal, Rig-Rig, and Michemiré.

6. Lac (HQ in Bol). Souspréfectures of Bol, Ngouri. Administrative posts in Baga-Sola and Doum-Doum.

7. Logone Occidental (HQ in Moundou). Souspréfectures of Moundou, Beinamar, Bénoyé. Administrative post in Krim-Krim.

8. Logone Oriental (HQ in Doba). Souspréfectures of Doba, Baï-bokoum, Bébédjia, Goré. Administrative posts in Bessao, Doualat, and Larmanaye.

9. Mayo-Kebbi (HQ in Bongor). Souspréfectures of Bongor, Fianga, Gounou-Gaya, Léré, Pala. Administrative posts in Guélendeng, Binder, Gagal, and Torrock.

10. Moyen-Chari (HQ in Sarh). Souspréfectures of Sarh, Koumra, Kyabé, Maro, Moïssala. Administrative posts in Korbol, Bédaya, Bébiondo, Békamba, Goundi, and Dembo.

11. Ouadai (HQ in Abéché). Souspréfectures of Abéché-rural, Abéché-nomade, Adré, Am Dam, Goz-Beïda.

12. Salamat (HQ in Am-Timan). Souspréfectures of Am-Timan, Aboudeia, Harazé-Mangueigné.

13. Tandjilé (HQ in Laï). Souspréfectures of Laï and Kélo. Administrative post in Béré.

14. Biltine (HQ in Biltine). Souspréfectures of Biltine, Am-Zoer, Arada, Guéreda, and Iriba.

Chad also has nine municipalities—communes de plein exercise (q.v.)—governed by elected municipal councils. These are: N'Djamena, Abéché, Bongor, Doba, Sarh, Koumra, Laï, Moundou, and Pala (qq.v.).

ADMINISTRATIVE REFORM MISSION see MISSION DE REFORME ADMINISTRATIVE (MRA).

ADOUM, JUSTIN (1938–). Educator. Born in Laï on January 13, 1938, and one of the first Chadians to secure higher education, Adoum joined the Ministry of Education in 1967 as director of secondary and technical education. In 1970 he was promoted to the post of secretary-general of the Ministry of National Education. After the fall of N'Djamena, Adoum relocated to Moundou.

ADOUM, MAHAMAT ALI. Diplomat and former foreign minister. Adoum has served in a variety of diplomatic postings, but he was in particular Chad's long-term ambassador (1981–1991) to the United States and the United Nations. In 1991 he was appointed by Déby as ambassador to Libya, returning to Chad in May 20, 1992, to join the cabinet as minister of foreign affairs, serving until the Conférence Nationale (q.v.) government of April 1993 was set up.

ADOUM, MELFI (1918–1975). Former long-term National Assembly deputy of the Parti Progressiste Tchadien (PPT) (q.v.). Born in Melfi on November 5, 1918, and a male nurse by profession, Adoum was an early member of the AST (q.v.) party in Chari-Baguirmi and was elected to the National Assembly as AST deputy in May 1959. In 1960 he switched allegiances to the PPT and was reelected as a Tombalbaye (q.v.) loyalist through 1972. He survived over the years a number of purges of both party and assembly.

ADOUM, NGARADOUMRI BOURKOU. Deputy of the 1990 National Assembly and one of its four vice presidents. Mrs. Adoum was elected to the national assembly in July 1990 and served for six months until the collapse of Hissène Habré's (q.v.) regime and the dissolution of the structures he set up.

ADOUM, SIMON PIERRE (1936–). Diplomat and administrator. Born in Mao on August 10, 1936, and educated locally and in France at the Institut des Hautes Etudes d'Outre-Mer (IHEOM), Adoum joined the Chadian civil service in 1961 and was appointed subprefect of Doba. Later the same year he was transferred to Sarh as deputy prefect (October 1961–June 1962), following which he also served as subprefect of Moïssala (July–October 1962) and of Moundou (March–May 1965). From 1965 he was with the Foreign Ministry, serving as First Councillor at the Chadian Embassy in the USSR until 1972. He then returned to N'Djamena and was President François Tombalbaye's (q.v.) chef de cabinet for political affairs until the 1975 coup d'état. Since then Adoum has continued his career with a string of appointments with the regional administration. He is currently prefect of Moyen-Chari.

ADRE. Small border village in the Ouadai Préfecture and also the administrative headquarters of a souspréfecture of the same name. Adré is the main official crossing point into Sudan from Chad and on the main road leading to Al-Junaynah, much frequented by pilgrims en route to Mecca. The Chad-Sudan border region has been highly insecure since the mid-1960s, first because of the anti-N'Djamena rebellion by the Maba (q.v.) and other eastern ethnic groups, and later as the result of a succession of opposition groups seeking refuge in Sudan and raiding across the border into Chad. In the most recent case it was Idriss Déby (q.v.), currently president, who fled to Darfur in Sudan, to return in December 1990 as warlord of the country. The frontier has been officially closed on numerous occasions as Chad has tried to force Sudan to desist from overt or covert support for opposition elements residing in its territory. The souspréfecture covers a territory of 13,000 square kilometers (5,000 square miles), with a population of 135,000.

AFONO, TCHARI MAINA. Former rebel leader and one of Goukouni's (q.v.) GUNT (q.v.) cabinet ministers. After the rise to power of Hissène Habré (q.v.) in 1982, Afono fled to Maiduguri, Nigeria, and helped to raise an anti-Habré armed force that was part of the Forces Armées Occidentales (FAO) (q.v.). Afono was reconciled with Habré in January 1988, when he returned to N'Djamena. With the rise to power of the Idriss Déby (q.v.) regime, he served twice in the cabinet, first between May 1992 and October 1992 as secretary of state for labor and the civil service, and between October 1992 and the new Conférence Nationale (q.v.) government of April 1993 as secretary of state for interior.

AFRIQUE EQUATORIALE FRANÇAISE (AEF). French Equatorial Africa was one of France's two colonial African federations, encompassing the territories of Moyen Congo, Oubangui-Chari, Chad, and Gabon. (The former two became at independence Congo/Brazzaville and the Central African Republic.) The federation existed from 1910 to 1958, when it was dissolved, though with different administrative constituent parts throughout its history. When originally set up in 1910 Chad was part of a much larger Oubangui-Chari-Tchad colony, which was broken up in 1916. (AEF thus had only three colonies up to 1916.) In 1934, for reasons of economy, the entire AEF "stopped" being a federation and became a single colony, with its constituent parts transformed into administrative *régions* (subdivided into *départements*), all (except for Congo) under one governor based in Bangui. Because of the numerous administrative problems this arrangement raised with little actual reduction in costs, the formula was discarded very rapidly, and AEF "regained" its former federal status. In like manner, various régions and districts within each constituent colony in AEF have freely been detached or attached to other colonies over the years. Indeed, Tibesti (q.v.) was at one time part of Niger—and hence not even in the AEF federation but rather in France's second colonial federation, Afrique Occidentale Française (AOF)—and was only attached to Chad on February 18, 1930. Parts of southern Chad (the *circonscriptions* of Moyen-Chari and Logone) were transferred to Oubangui-Chari on December 31, 1925, and on December 31, 1933, the Fort-Archambault and Koumra districts were similarly detached from Chad and placed under the administrative authority of Bangui. (This in essence placed much of the Sara areas outside the Chad colony.) Most of these areas were reattached to Chad in 1937. Despite intermittent efforts to the contrary, AEF has always been highly centralized. In Brazzaville, the administrative capital of the federation, the French governor-general of AEF (directly responsible for the federation to the minister of colonies in Paris) was assisted by a Council of Government composed of the heads of the military and civil services and four other members nominated for two-year periods by the governor-general. After the Second World War there was also a Grand Council of AEF, composed of five delegates from each of the four constituent colonies, elected by their territorial assemblies. Each territory had its own governor, who was responsible to the AEF governor-general in Brazzaville, and a territorial assembly with limited deliberative powers that were only very slowly augmented in scope, until the 1956–1958 period brought internal autonomy to each colony.

AGANAYE, ADOUM (1920–). Early leading political figure, former cabinet minister, and diplomat. Born November 15, 1920, in N'Djamena and trained as an educator, Aganayé worked as a teacher, school director, and inspector of schools between 1939 and 1960, serving in Am-Timan (1939–42). Fort-Archambault (1942–44), Ati (1944–46), Moussoro (1951–55), Fort-Lamy (1955–58), and Bongor (1958–60). Between 1946 and 1951 Aganayé was a member of the AEF Grand Council in Brazzaville and independent deputy from Batha to the Counseil Représentatif (q.v.) in Fort-Lamy. Cofounder with Ahmed Koulamallah (q.v.) of the Parti Socialiste Indépendant du Tchad (PSIT) (q.v.), Aganayé clashed with his volatile partner on a number of occasions and was finally expelled from PSIT for "promoting schisms" in the party. He was defeated in his 1952 bid for reelection to the Territorial Assembly and in his 1956 race in Fort-Lamy's mayoralty elections.

During this time he was an important leader in the Parti Progressiste Tchadien (PPT) (q.v.) coalitions (ERDIC, Entente, etc.) becoming in due time a full-fledged PPT member. During the era of Chad's three provisional governments (q.v.), Aganayé served as minister of health (December 1958–February 1959) and as minister of labor (February 1959–March 1959), following which he was shunted into diplomatic duties by the emergent François Tombalbaye (q.v.) administration. After a few months (September–December 1960) as ambassador to the United Nations, Aganayé was appointed ambassador to Germany in 1961 and in 1964 was reassigned to represent Chad in Benelux, a position he held through 1970. Concurrently between 1961 and 1970 he served as ambassador to the EC as well. In May 1971 Aganayé was repatriated and brought into Tombalbaye's government as minister of transport, replacing Abdoulaye Lamana (q.v.) in August 1971 as president of Air Tchad. He fell afoul of the regime in mid-1973 in the wake of a major purge of potential antiadministration officials following the guerrilla attack on N'Djamena. Aganayé is currently in retirement.

AGENCE DE COOPERATION CULTURELLE ET TECHNIQUE (ACCT). International organization set up in Niamey, Niger, in 1970 to unite all francophone-francophile states. The organization includes most of former French and Belgian Africa, selected French-speaking states in the Middle East, the Maghreb, and Asia, former French territories (Seychelles, Dominica, Mauritius), and Belgium, Canada, Luxembourg, New Brunswick, and Quebec. Organized as a cultural organization, most of its activities have been in the domain of technical assistance.

AGENCE NATIONALE DE SECURITE (ANS). Infamous paramilitary unit under Idriss Déby's (q.v.) direct control. The ANS was the successor of the CRCR (q.v.) after the Conférence Nationale (q.v.) called for its dissolution. The CRCR in turn had been but a continuation (even with some of the same personnel) of the DDS (q.v.) of Hissène Habré's (q.v.) days. It is a brutal force of political suppression of Déby's opponents and of repression of society. In one recent instance, for example, it was involved in the attack on N'Djamena's sole independent newspaper, *N'Djaména-Hebdo,* in 1995.

AGENCE TRANSEQUATORIALE DES COMMUNICATIONS (ATEC). Interstate organization founded by the four members of the Union Douanière Equatoriale (UDE) (q.v.) on July 15, 1959, to regulate and coordinate interstate communications, including the Chemin de Fer Congo-Océan (CFCO), the riverine and ocean ports of Pointe-Noire, Bangui, and Brazzaville, and the Oubangui-Congo river transport network that serves traffic from Chad and the Central African Republic. Until Congo/Brazzaville's progressive disengagement and final rupture from ATEC, the organization exercised its competence in these areas via an administrative council of 12 members representing all four countries and including all four ministers of transport.

AGUID. Title of the main military commanders of the ancient Ouadai kingdom. Two of the most important commanders—of which there were many—were the *aguids* of the eastern provinces and of the western provinces.

AHAMAT, KINDER (1945–). Jurist and public prosecutor. Born in Sarh on July 17, 1945, and educated there (1952–57) and in Abéché and N'Djamena (1958–62), Ahamat studied law at the Institut International d'Administration Publique (IIAP) in Paris (1970–72) and was appointed state attorney in Abéché in 1972. He served as public prosecutor until the collapse of civil authority in the east in 1979, when he relocated to N'Djamena.

AIN GALAKKA. Desert oasis in Tibesti (q.v.) and former Senoussi (see SANUSIYA) *zawaya* (q.v.) and Turkish military outpost that changed hands a number of times during the French conquest of the B.E.T. regions of Chad. First occupied by the French in 1907—when the famous Sidi Muhammad al-Barrani (q.v.) was killed in the fighting—the post was retaken by Turko-Senoussi forces, only to fall again to the French in 1913. The oasis has a number of date plantations, many planted during the Turkish occupation of the region. (See also TURKEY.)

AIN GALAKKA ASSOCIATION. A quasi-secret association set up by Hissène Habré (q.v.) during the latter part of his presidency, bringing together Toubou (q.v.) kinsmen in N'Djamena from the region of Ain Galakka in the north in order to examine policies that could benefit the region, allow Habré (who also came from there) to retain control, and appoint personnel from the region to control positions. The association was disbanded when Habré was ousted in 1990.

AIR AFRIQUE AFFAIR. Early in 1972 President François Tombalbaye (q.v.) announced that Chad would withdraw from Air Afrique—francophone Africa's multinational airline and one of the few serving N'Djamena—and that he himself would resign as OCAMM (q.v.) chairman. The twin moves were a retaliation against the decision to relocate the airline's regional headquarters (for Equatorial Africa) from Douala, Cameroon, to Libreville, Gabon, following Cameroon's withdrawal from the airline. Tombalbaye had previously campaigned strongly for the relocation of the headquarters of Air Afrique to N'Djamena and had also complained that of the airline's 217 local employees not one top post was held by a Chadian. Moreover, the original decision to base a pilots' school in N'Djamena had been rescinded, with the school finally being erected in Dakar, Senegal. Following Tombalbaye's announcements, official notice was served to Air Afrique's then director general, Cheikh Fall, of Chad's withdrawal from the airline, and negotiations were begun with Air Zaïre and other regional African airlines to assure air services into Chad. In September 1972 a six-month delay in Chad's withdrawal was announced, and the withdrawal was rescinded in December. To justify the volte-face and the obvious failure of Tombalbaye's pressure ploy, it was announced that Tombalbaye had been misled and misadvised on the crisis with Air Afrique by his longtime associate, Secretary of State Antoine Bangui (q.v.), who was consequently dismissed.

AIR TCHAD. Chad's national airline, a joint venture between the French UTA airline (34 percent) and the government of Chad. Created in 1966, Air Tchad originally operated one DC-4, two DC-3s, and one Beechcraft Baron 58. The airline serviced several urban centers, and at the height of the civil strife, both in the 1970s and in the 1980s, it was the only means of communications between the capital and outlying regions. It carries roughly 20,000 passengers a year and up to 2,000 tons of freight. Surprisingly, throughout the turbulence in N'Djamena, Air Tchad has been one of the very few state enterprises not losing money. It currently operates a 19-seat Twin Otter and a 40-seat Fokker 27, both in the process of being phased out for new aircraft.

AL-. Definitive article preceding many Arabic names. Often ignored in alphabetization.

AL-AMIN, MUHAMMAD see AL-KANEMI, MUHAMMAD AL-AMIN; KANEM-BORNU EMPIRE

AL-BARRANI, SIDI MUHAMMAD (?–1907). Principal Kanem lieutenant of al-Sayyid Muhammad al-Mahdi (q.v.), son of the Grand Sanusi (see SANUSIYA) and foremost Senoussi missionary in the Sahara. In 1896 al-Barrani founded the Bir Alali (q.v.) Senoussi *zawaya* (q.v.) in Kanem and was a zealous proselytizer of the sect in northern Chad. He died in the fighting against the French colonial forces in Ain Galakka (q.v.) in 1907.

ALHABO, MAHAMAT AHMAT. Minister of finance and computerization. Alhabo, a technocrat, first joined the cabinet in April 1993, having been elected to it by the Conférence Nationale (q.v.), and served as minister of posts. He was dropped in a cabinet shuffle in May 1994 but reappeared in his current post in 1995.

ALHAJI. One who has performed the *hajj* (q.v.). Since the title carries with it the connotation of piety and status, and commands respect, pilgrims who have performed the *hajj* are in great demand to officiate at religious ceremonies and to head Koranic schools. Many of these, however, have not truly completed the *hajj*. The plural of Alhaji is Alhazai.

ALHAMDOU, ISSAKA RAMAT. Longtime GUNT (q.v.) spokesman to the EC countries, based in in Brussels. Chargé d'affaires at the Chadian Embassy in Paris between 1978 and 1982, Alhamdou lost his post with the collapse of the GUNT government in 1982. He promptly declared continued allegiance to Goukouni (q.v.) and became his external spokesman in Paris and Brussels. In February 1990, after the rise of the Idriss Déby (q.v.) government in N'Djamena, Alhamdou organized a new political party, the Rassemblement Nationaliste Tchadien (RNT) (q.v.).

ALI (KING OF BORNU, 1654–1684) (?–c1684). Son of Umar, who repulsed multiple pressures from the south (Kwararefa) and the north (the Tuareg) as well as an internal rebellion. The kingdom was so secure in his lifetime that Ali embarked on three lengthy pilgrimages to Mecca. Though he established a number of large mosques and other centers of study, famines eventually ravaged the kingdom, destroying most of his achievements.

ALI, ABBAS (1955–). President of the Conseil Supérieur de la Transition (CST) (q.v.) provisional legislature of Chad. A career diplomat and a member of the CSDT (q.v.) political party, Ali was elevated to the post of president in July 1995 when the entire CST Bureau was indicted for corruption and forced to resign.

ALI, ABDALLAH MAHAMAT (Colonel). Ambassador to France. A former director general of the insurance company STAR, Ali is Idriss Déby's (q.v.) cousin. In 1989 he joined Déby in Sudan in his assault on the presidency of Habré and participated in the fighting that led to victory and the conquest of N'Djamena in December 1990. He then headed Déby's armies during the pro-Habré Kanembu (q.v.) rebellions and fighting in the Lake Chad region. Having had his own family killed in the rebellion, Ali sent in secret agents to capture Goukouni Guet (q.v.), leader of the MDD (q.v.) rebellion, in Borno State, Nigeria, and kept Guet under constant torture in his N'Djamena cellar. Ali was dismissed from his command over the armed forces after the massacres by his troops at Doba (q.v.) in the south raised an outcry. He was then appointed foreign minister in February 1991, performed various other duties for the regime, and in 1995 became ambassador to France.

ALI, TAHIROU AL-HADJ. Deputy to the 1990 (Habré) National Assembly and one of its four vice presidents. Ali had been a deputy as early as 1962 and later served in François Tombalbaye's (q.v.) administration as an ambassador. On his return to Chad he rejoined the Chari-Baguirmi regional administration. He was elected from the Bousso district (of which he was head) in July 1990. After the National Assembly was dissolved following Habré's ouster Ali continued with his administrative career until joining the Conférence Nationale (q.v.) in 1993.

ALI GAJI (KING OF BORNU, 1470–1503) (?–c1503). Regarded as one of Kanem-Bornu's (q.v.) three great *mais* (q.v.). He personally ended the strife and residue of instability consequent to the split in the Sefuwa (q.v.) dynasty. Ali Gaji crushed the Bulala (q.v.), who had forced the kingdom's relocation from Kanem to Bornu in the fourteenth century under Umar Ibn Idriss (q.v.). Under his aegis the new permanent capital at Birni Ngazargamo (q.v.) was established close enough to the Hausa tributary states to control them but far enough away to be out of immediate danger in case of a rebellion. Ali Gaji's role was thus that of the reconsolidator of the ravaged kingdom following its ouster from Kanem.

ALIFA. From the Arabic *khalifa,* used not so much in the religious sense (i.e., "successor" or head of the Muslim community) but as designated deputy or surrogate ruler. Also, title of the ruler of Kanem, the representative of the *mai* (q.v.) of Bornu (q.v.).

ALIFA OF KANEM. Originally the Kanem-Bornu Empire's (q.v.) viceroy and *mai* (q.v.) representative in Mao (q.v.) for Kanem (q.v.). The title was established after Kanem was reconquered from the Tunjur (q.v.) invaders early in the eighteenth century by an army dispatched from Bornu, whose leader (a Hausa slave, see DALATAWA) was designated Khalifa (Alifa, q.v.) of Kanem. With Bornu's gradual decline in power Kanem became a tributary of the expanding Ouadai kingdom (q.v.) and later was ravaged by the Awlad Sulayman (q.v.) invasions from the north in the nineteenth century. The original dynasty still survives in Mao, however, though the Alifa was reduced by the French to the status of a mere chef de canton. During the François Tombalbaye (q.v.) era the Alifa (see DOUBA ALIFA, MAHAMAT) was a major pillar of the regime in exchange for his retention of an iron quasi-feudal administration in Kanem.

ALIMI, AHMAD (?–1808). *Mai* (q.v.) of the Kanem-Bornu Empire (q.v.) at the time of the Fulani (q.v.) invasions. Crushing a rebellion of his Fulani province of Deya that had gone over to the jihad of Uthman dan Fodio, Ahmad Alimi was unseated in turn and his capital sacked. He entered into a famous correspondence with Uthman dan Fodio in an effort to prove the inequity of a Fulani jihad on a sister Muslim state. Old and blind, Ahmad Alimi abdicated in favor of his son Dunama, but the succession was regarded as improper, setting the stage for factionalism and the usurpation of power by Muhammad al-Amin al-Kanemi (q.v.).

ALINGUE, JEAN BAWOYEU (1937–). Former prime minister of Chad. Born on August 18, 1937, in Ndrai-Ngalo in Tandjilé, and a Christian, Alingué is largely self-educated (though trained in Paris in accounting). Alingué (who is often also referred to by his other name, Bawoyeu) entered government service in 1953 as a clerk in Fort-Lamy's city treasury, becoming city controller in 1958. In 1960 and 1961 he attended the National Treasury School in Paris, following which he became treasury inspector and adviser to the director of public accounts (1960–1964). In 1966 he became treasurer general of Chad, a position he held until 1973, when he was appointed ambassador to the United States, Canada, and the United Nations. In 1977 he was shifted to head the Chadian embassy in France, serving in Paris until 1979. He then returned to Chad and became a refugee in the south, founding the Rassemblement pour l'Unité et la Démocratie au Tchad (RUDT) (q.v.), which took a line distinct from both Hissène Habré's and Goukouni's (qq.v.). In 1982 he was briefly tapped by Goukouni to be his minister of finance, fleeing for France with the entry of Habré's troops in the capital. He remained in Paris until 1985, when he established another grouping, the Front Démocratique du Tchad (FDT) (q.v.). Reconciled with Habré, Alingué returned to N'Djamena and in 1986 was appointed vice president of the Conseil National Consultatif (q.v.). President of the constitutional committee in 1988, Alingué played a major role in the drafting of the Constitution of 1989. In the subsequent elections Alingué was elected to Chad's new National Assembly as a deputy from Habré's UNIR (q.v.) party, and a month later, in August 1990, he was elected president of the assembly. By that time Habré's regime was crumbling under the onslaught of Idriss Déby (q.v.), and when Habré fled N'Djamena in December 1990 Alingué became briefly acting president of Chad. Why Alingué cooperated with Habré has been the subject of some speculation, since his own nephew (and allegedly some other members of his family) had been murdered by Habré's nephew, Korei Guini (q.v.), who was then head of the security services.

Alingué was integrated into Déby's government in December 1990 as minister of agriculture and in March 1991 was appointed prime minister of Chad. He provided Chad with a lackluster leadership until replaced in 1992 by Joseph Yodoyman (q.v.). In 1992 Alingué cofounded another party, the Union pour la Démocratie et la République (UDR) (q.v.), which was recognized in mid-1992 and given participation in the national conference the following year.

ALIO, KADRE (1922–1966). Important early Chadian deputy and early casualty of the civil war in Chad. A civil administrator of chiefly origin, Alio was elected deputy on the UDT (q.v.) party label in 1947, and was reelected in 1952 from Batha-Salamat. He was killed by guerrillas in 1966 during the upsurge of violence in the eastern préfectures.

AL-KANEMI, MUHAMMAD AL-AMIN (1778–1837). Popular name for Muhammad al-Amin, a Kanembu (q.v.) scholar and warrior (whose father had been a famous teacher in the Fezzan and in Kanem), who at the time of the Fulani (q.v.) invasions of the Kanem-Bornu Empire (q.v.) was invited to help the reigning *mai* (q.v.), eventually founding his own dynasty there, which still survives in contemporary Bornu in Nigeria. Born in the Fezzan (q.v.) and studying religion in Tripoli (Libya), al-Kanemi acquired fame as a *mallam* (q.v.) in Kanem and Bornu, where he taught religion, especially in the Ngala region, where he married the local *mai's* daughter. When called upon to help repulse the Fulani invasions al-Kanemi mobilized a large force of Kanembu spearmen and Shoa Arab (q.v.) cavalry and twice drove back the Fulani assaults (in 1808 and 1813), though not without the inevitable permanent loss of Bornu's western provinces. He was rewarded for his efforts by a large fiefdom in his home area. In 1814 he shifted the decaying empire's capital from Birni Ngazargamo (q.v.)—which had been razed by the Fulani—to Kukawa (q.v.). Involved in helping the new *mai* ascend to power, al-Kanemi rapidly became the de facto ruler of the country, though he allowed the *mais* to remain as nominal and symbolic kings. During his reign he instituted a variety of reforms, placed great emphasis upon Islam and Sharia law, and tried to establish peaceful relations with the powerful Fulani to the west. (He corresponded with the Fulani rulers, arguing that the jihad they had mounted should not be aimed against neighboring Muslim states such as Bornu.) During al-Kanemi's reign as well as during that of his son, Umar al-Kanemi (q.v.), most of the local Magumi (q.v.) nobility lost their important state positions to al-Kanemi's followers, many of whom were Shoa Arabs. Al-Kanemi, one of Africa's most interesting personalities, died in 1837. His son, Umar, abolished the archaic Sefuwa (q.v.) Magumi dynasty in 1846. The al-Kanemi dynasty lives on today through the (Nigerian) Shehu of Bornu, Umar Abubakar Garbai el-Kanemi, whose capital (since 1907) is at Yerwa. (See also BORNU; KANEM-BORNU EMPIRE.)

AL-KANEMI, UMAR IBN MUHAMMAD (?–1881). Son of Muhammad al-Amin al-Kanemi (q.v.), he succeeded his father in 1837 as de facto ruler of Bornu (q.v.) and demolished the parallel but nominal Sefuwa (q.v.) Magumi (q.v.) dynasty in 1846. Umar's friction with the Sefuwa *mai* (q.v.)—who was attempting to reassert his traditional role and powers as supreme ruler of Bornu—was complicated by a powerful challenge to Bornuan might from the expanding and aggressive Ouadai kingdom (q.v.) in the east, which had spread to control Baguirmi (q.v.) and Kanem (q.v.), both previously Bornuan tributary states. In an effort to dislodge the al-Kanemi dynasty, the Bornuan *mai* solicited the help of Ouadai, the Ouadaian troops entered Bornu while Umar was subjugating the Tuareg (q.v.) in Zinder (currently in Niger). Though the Ouadai forces plundered the Bornuan capital of Kukawa (q.v.), they retreated when Umar's armies returned from the Tuareg campaigns. In retaliation for the *mai's* treachery, the Sefuwa dynasty was abolished and the *mai* and others of his dynasty were executed. Umar was briefly deposed in favor of his brother but was later restored to power. He died in 1881. The al-Kanemi dynasty still survives in the form of the current Shehu of Bornu, Umar Abubakar Garbai el-Kanemi, in Nigeria.

ALKHALI, HISSEIN (1948–1979). Former secretary of state for foreign affairs and a Hissène Habré (q.v.) loyalist and FAN (q.v.) leader. Born in Ati in 1948, Alkhali obtained a diploma in administration, following which he continued his studies in Paris (1972–73, and again in 1975). In 1974 he was appointed to a senior post in the Chadian civil service and in 1977 became head of a division in the Ministry of Commerce and Industry. After the integration of Habré in General Félix Malloum's (q.v.) cabinet, Alkhali was elevated to the post of secretary of state for agriculture and on September 6, 1978, was shifted to head Foreign Affairs. Alkhali was killed during the intense interfactional fighting in N'Djamena on March 6, 1979.

ALKHALI, RAMAT. A political leader of the MPLT (q.v.). Alkhali served in Goukouni's (q.v.) cabinet as minister of transport from November 1979 to July 1981.

ALLAFI, NGOLABAYE (Colonel) (1945–1983). Former commander in chief of the Armée Nationale Intégrée (ANI) (q.v.), charged with setting up a "national" army after Goukouni's (q.v.) victory in the civil war in 1979. Nothing came of the ambitious project, since each faction, including the defeated FAT (q.v.), insisted on keeping control and command over its own troops and materiel in the continuous jockeying for better position vis-à-vis the other factions in N'Djamena. Thus at no time did Allafi command more than a few hundred troops. Allafi was notoriously unpopular in B.E.T. and personally repugnant to many elements of FAN (q.v.). As a junior and inexperienced lieutenant, he had been appointed subprefect of Bardai after the Bardai incidents of 1965 (q.v.), replacing Lt. Samuel Rodai (q.v.). Not only did he not soothe tempers in the area, but he also continued the heavy-handed and arbitrary policies of his predecessor, directly contributing to the civil rebellion in the north. In 1976 Allafi, now a captain, was appointed commander of the National and Nomadic Guard. Twice promoted, he was picked by Goukouni to serve as commander of the ANI after the fall of N'Djamena. After the collapse of the GUNT (q.v.) regime Allafi retreated to his southern hometown, and in July 1982 he was incorrectly reported killed in inter-FAT skirmishes. It was later revealed that he had been executed by FAN troops on October 24, 1983, after Hissène Habré's (q.v.) conquest of the southern préfectures, following a summary trial for his administrative blunders in Bardai in 1965.

ALLAHOU TAHER, LIMANE (1934–).Magistrate and early president of the National Assembly.

ALLAMI-MI, AHMAD. Long-term ambassador to France during Hissène Habré's (q.v.) rule. A diplomat serving as chargé d' affaires in Paris during 1979 and 1980, Allami-Mi was downgraded and reassigned other duties by President Goukouni (q.v) in 1980. Refusing to return to N'Djamena, Allami-Mi promptly declared his allegiance to Goukoun's protagonist, Hissène Habré, becoming Habré's external spokesman in Paris. With Habré's rise to power in 1982, Allami-Mi was appointed ambassador to France, and he retained that post until 1990 when Habré was ousted in N'Djamena by Idriss Déby (q.v.).

ALLATCHIMI, ALLENGA (1920–). Head of the Doza canton in Borkou. Of the traditional ruling family and chief royal clan, Allatchimi succeeded his father (Allatchi Yassoubmi) as head of the Doza canton in 1955. An important Toubou (q.v.) ruler, Allatchimi resides in his capital, Son, an oasis barely 3 kilometers from Faya-Largeau. Because of his proximity to central authority, Allatchimi played an ambivalent role vis-à-vis N'Djamena during the civil war.

ALLIANCE DES PARTIS POLITIQUES POUR LA DEMOCRATIE (APPD). Successor to ENAD (q.v.), a grouping of eight small opposition parties that was formed in N'Djamena in July 1994. In November 1994 APPD gave way to COPAC (q.v.).

ALLIANCE NATIONALE POUR DEMOCRATIE ET DEVELOPPE-MENT (ANDD). Opposition political party formed and recognized by the Idriss Déby (q.v.) regime in mid-1992.

ALLIANCE NATIONALE POUR LA DEMOCRATIE ET LE RENOU-
VEAU (ANDR). Political party formed by Joseph Yodoyman (q.v.),
who was soon to become prime minister of Chad, in December 1992.

ALLIANCE NATIONALE POUR LE CHANGEMENT (ANC). Political party headed by Yacoub A. Goukouni, formed in 1993 with, inter
alia, a nationalist linguistic plank.

ALLIANCE POUR LA DEMOCRATIE AU TCHAD (ADT). Opposi-
tion political party, first formed in Paris in 1992, and headed by Tidjani Thiam (q.v.), the former GUNT (q.v.) foreign minister.

AL-MAHDI, AL-SAYYID MUHAMMAD. Son of the founder of the
Sanusiya (q.v.) religious order, he expanded the sect into Chad's
B.E.T. and Kanem in the nineteenth century.

AL-SANUSI, AL-SAYYID MUHAMMAD BIN ALI AL-KHATTABI.
Founder of the Sanusiya (q.v.) religious order that spilled into Chad
from Libya.

AM DAM. Souspréfecture with headquarters in the village of the same
name, part of the préfecture of Ouadai. The souspréfecture encompasses a territory of 24,000 square kilometers (9,200 square miles),
with a population of 47,000, giving it a very low population density.

AM KAMEL. Important, well-known, and very populated quarter of
Abéché (q.v.), the quarter of the sultan and once also of the *Aguid*
(q.v.) el-Diaatne. Currently most of the population is a mixture of descendants of the sultan's families, Turks, Maba, and Misirié.

AM-SINENE. Northern suburb of N'Djamena and a favorite burial site
for victims of Hissène Habré's notorious DDE (q.v.). When Idriss
Déby (q.v.) rose to power, the site continued to be used by his CRCR
(q.v.) and later ANS (q.v.).

AM-TIMAN. Small urban center of 3,500 people and the administrative
headquarters of the Salamat Préfecture and the Am-Timan souspréfecture. The latter covers 20,000 square kilometers (7,700 square miles) and
has a largely seminomadic Arab population (see SALAMAT ARABS)
with the low population density of 2.0 per square kilometer. One important source of earnings throughout the region (constituting over one-third
of the earnings of the population) is fishing in the various tributaries of
the Salamat River. Am-Timan is connected by dirt roads, impassable in

the rainy season, with Melfi and Abéché (via Mangalmé), among others. (See also SALAMAT PREFECTURE.)

AMANE, IDRISS MAHAMAT. FROLINAT (q.v.) commander and briefly minister of information. A guerrilla leader from Ennedi, Amane succeeded Adoum Abou Haggar (q.v.) after the latter's execution in Tripoli, Libya, in 1974. As overall commander of the rebellion in Ennedi, Amane sided with his patron, Dr. Abba Siddick (q.v.), during Siddick's power tug-of-war with Goukouni. Losing control of FROL-INAT in 1977, the Siddick faction was renamed FROLINAT-Originel. Amane briefly served as minister of information in the GUNT (q.v.) coalition government of July 1981.

AMANE ABRAM, IDRISS MAHAMAT. Former minister of posts and telecommunications. A technocrat who formerly occupied a variety of top administrative positions, including the directorship of the Chadian broadcasting system, Amane Abram was appointed to the cabinet in 1973 and was retained by the Félix Malloum (q.v.) military administration until the fall of N'Djamena in 1978.

AMBADI, ABBAS MAHAMAT. Head of the Parti Libéral pour l'Unité et la Solidarité (PLUS) (q.v.), formed and recognized in 1993, and since 1995 minister of commerce and industrial promotion.

AMICALE DE LA JEUNESSE TCHADIENNE. Youth organization established in 1952 by Ahmed Koulamallah (q.v.) in an effort to develop grassroots support for his political ambitions, socialist credentials, and Parti Socialiste Indépendant du Tchad (PSIT) (q.v.). The organization was largely moribund.

AMICALE DES BORNOUANS. Socioeconomic grouping, later politically oriented, established in 1951 by predominantly Kanuri (q.v.) elements in Chad in support of the programs of Ahmed Koulamallah (q.v.) and of his political ambitions in competition with the French-supported Kanuri ethnic chief (*chef de race*).

ANAKAZA. Ethnic group in Borkou, long headed by their traditional rules, Mahamat Jimemi (q.v.). Composed of some two dozen clans, some traditionally servile, the Anakaza are part of the Daza (q.v.) subgroup of the Toubou (q.v.). Highly unruly, beset by blood feuds, cleavages, and personal animosities, the Anakaza were regarded by the French colonial administration as virtually ungovernable. Found in a wide arc from Faya-Largeau (q.v.) to Kirdimi and nomadizing the region from Oum Chalouba (q.v.) to the Djourab and Mortcha, many clans trace their origins to Oum Chalouba and their common ancestry to Bouttou, to arrive in Borkou 12 generations ago. Other clans have links with the Bideyat (q.v.). In the more contemporary era the Anakaza have been the prime source of support of Hissène Habré (q.v.), their best-known kinsman. The Daza are one of the two main Toubou clans, the other being the Teda, which is Goukouni's (q.v.) clan, explaining to some extent the tug-of-war of the two leaders in the contemporary era.

ANGATA YOSKOIMI (1890?–1980). Leader of the Gaeda Hajer (Arna, q.v.) subclan in Ennedi. With his traditional headquarters in Ouargala, some 100 kilometers (60 miles) southwest of Fada, Angata Yoskoimi—who was always on bad terms with the French colonial administration—was the de facto warlord of Ennedi. Powerful, rich, and with herds of hundreds of camels, Angata Yoskoimi's predecessors had been acknowledged suzerains of Ennedi, collecting tribute from the Toubou (q.v.) on behalf of the Ouadai Empire (q.v.).

AOUZOU. Small military outpost in the extreme north of Tibesti (q.v.) some 820 kilometers (490 miles) from Faya (q.v.) and 90 kilometers (55 miles) from Bardai. The Aouzou Strip, an area of territory up to 160 kilometers (100 miles) deep along the entire 1,600-kilometer (1,000-mile) Chadian border with Libya, was under Libyan military occupation (having been formally annexed in 1975 and strongly protected by garrisons, surface-to-air missiles, and air bases both in the strip and in the adjacent Libyan desert. The occupation of the 115,000 square kilometer (45,000 square mile) strip was the result of Libya's contention of the validity of the unratified Mussolini-Laval boundary agreement (q.v.). Libya's interest in the strip was due to rumors that the area was rich in uranium and other mineral ores. Contrary to original expectations, no mineral resources were found in the Aouzou Strip.

Though Libya's contentions were disputed by Chad, Libya presented documentation that former president François Tombalbaye (q.v.) ceded the strip to Libya in 1972 in exchange for Libya's withdrawal of support for Abba Siddick and his Tripoli-based FROLINAT (q.v.) and 23 billion CFA francs in cash. (The latter either never reached Tombalbaye, or the Chadian treasury.) In the late 1970s the Aouzou Strip was heavily fortified by the Libyan regime (which moved into the area its forward military air bases), and the entire area served as the springboard for the successive interventions in Chad between 1978 and 1986 by Libya and the Libya-supported GUNT (q.v.), which at one time controlled large parts of B.E.T. and even Abéché. Starting in December 1986 Hissène Habré (q.v.), who had never been willing to permit Libya's encroachment on his desert wastelands (including his hometown) to become permanent, mounted a series of masterful assaults against Libyan and GUNT military encampments in B.E.T. that rapidly brought much of the area under effective Chadian control. Faya, for example, fell to central control without a shot fired. A massive amount of heavy materiel (including tanks and aircraft) was destroyed or fell into Chadian hands, and thousands of Libyan prisoners of war were taken. On August 8, 1987, Chad mounted, with tacit U.S. prodding, a surprise attack on Aouzou itself (which had now been occupied by Libya for 14 years). The attack was successful, leading to the capture and/or destruction of further large amounts of war materiel. France's fear of a Libyan retaliation led it to deny Habré air cover, however, and Chadian forces had to withdraw from Aouzou on August 28 under heavy Libyan air bombardment. On September 5, Chad's army mounted a stunning attack deep into Libya on the strategically crucial Maaten-es-Sarra airbase and completely destroyed it. This blow finally convinced Libya's Muammar Qaddafi to accede to Chad's insistence that the dispute be presented to the International Court of Justice (ICJ) in The Hague for resolution. In February 1994 the ICJ decreed that the territory fell under Chad's sovereignty, and in May a UN observer team supervised the withdrawal of Libyan troops from the Aouzou Strip after an occupation of 21 years.

ARABI-EL-GONI (1920–1973). Influential veteran assembly deputy and politician from Ouadai. Born in Abéché in October 1920, working in his early years as an interpreter in Mongo, Arabi-el-Goni began his political career in 1947 at the age of 27 when he was elected to the Conseil Représentatif (q.v.) as deputy from Batha-Salamat on the Union Démocratique du Tchad (UDT) (q.v.) ticket. Rapidly becoming one of the party's most important leaders, Arabi-el-Goni continued to serve as an assembly deputy until his death, though he rallied to the country's majority party—the Parti Progressiste Tchadien (PPT) (q.v.)—in 1962. From 1947 to 1957 he also served as councillor of Afrique Equatoriale Française (q.v.), and from 1951 to 1959 he was Chad's deputy to the French National Assembly on the conservative RPF (q.v.)—later AST (q.v.)—ticket. A powerful figure in Ouadai and Abéché, though not overly popular in the mid-1960s due to his opportunistic support of the François Tombalbaye (q.v.) regime, Arabi-el-Goni was ambushed and shot by rebel elements in the vicinity of his hometown on October 21, 1973. He died in N'Djamena two days later. In the last few years of his life he had served as vice president of the National Assembly and president of its Education Committee.

ARABS. Throughout Chad there are large numbers of Arab tribes and subtribes, most nomadic or seminomadic, some sedentary, that, despite centuries of intermarriage or contact with their neighbors, still retain distinct Arab customs and characteristics and use the Arabic language.

Though there has not been a population census since 1964, official projections from that census, which had the Arabs at 32 percent of the population, yield a current estimate of roughly 2 million people.

The Arabs are collectively referred to by the Kanembu (q.v.) and the Kotoko (q.v.) as Shoa (q.v.); they are called Sua by the Barma (q.v.) and Aramka by the Maba (q.v.) of Ouadai. In all instances the various Arab clans are sharply differentiated from the Awlad Sulayman (q.v.) and the Tunjur (q.v.). Chad's Arab clans may be divided into two broad groups according to their main occupation as *abbala* (camel herders) and *baggara* (cattle raisers), and they are referred to as such in their localities. Mostly seminomadic, the Arab clans arrived in Chad in several waves during the period from the fourteenth century to the latter half of the nineteenth century. They are currently found in a broad arc from east to west, usually south of the central B.E.T. massif and north of the semitropical Sara country, in the regions of the former large kingdoms of Kanem-Bornu, Baguirmi, and Ouadai (qq.v.) More precisely, they are rarely found south of the 10th parallel, are limited in the north by the Sahara and by the Teda (q.v.) and the Daza (q.v.) in B.E.T. (q.v.), and are found throughout the area from the Nile valley in Sudan to Bornu in Nigeria, intermingled with the various sedentary groups in their localities.

The northern *abbala* Arabs have remained much purer than the more southern *baggara* clans. All groups are internally split into a large number of small clans that form the primary basis of allegiance. Chad's Arabs can also be divided into two broad categories (again leaving apart the Awlad Sulayman and the Tunjur) according to their genealogical traditions and original point of entry into Chad:

1. The Djoheina. These are groups that arrived from the Nile valley in the Sudan between the fourteenth and nineteenth centuries, claiming descent from Abdallah el-Djoheini. Tribes belonging to this lineage grouping form the majority of the Arabs in Chad (463,000 according to the 1964 census) and are also found extensively in Sudan, in Darfur (q.v.), and in Bornu. Among the Chadian clans tracing their descent to el-Djoheina are the Salamat Arabs (q.v.), the Beni Hemat, Ouled Rachid (q.v.), Misirié (q.v.), and Mahamid (q.v.), all of whom may be further subdivided into smaller groupings.

2. The Hassauna. These are groups tracing their descent from Hassan el-Gharbi and arriving in Chad from the north, also between the fourteenth and nineteenth centuries. Numerically a minority (25,000 in 1964), the Hassauna Arab clans are found especially in the west, in Kanem.

The two other major groups, usually treated separately from the previous ones, are the Awlad Sulayman (also Ouled Sliman) and the Tunjur. The Awlad Sulayman (in 1964 estimated at 3,800) arrived in Chad from Libya between 1840 and 1850, having been pushed southward by local events (see TURKEY). There were two waves of migration, one of which was violent and during which parts of Kanem were ravaged. Most of the Awlad Sulayman are found in Nigeria, though some remain in Kanem. The Tunjur are of Sudanic origins; after a period of rule over Ouadai they were displaced by an internal upheaval (see ABD-EL-KERIM) and, migrating westward, established a short-lived hegemony in Kanem, where they were later vanquished again. The Tunjur are currently found in small numbers both in Ouadai and in Kanem near Mondo.

In the precolonial era all Arab clans were attached in one way or another to one of the local kingdoms, paying an annual tribute and dispatching military units in time of war. They are mostly pastoralists and their lives revolve around their herding activities. The northern *abbala* annually travel 2,000 kilometers (1,200 miles) from pasture to pasture. Further south the availability of more plentiful water supplies makes the migratory distances for the *baggara* Arabs much shorter, with agricultural activities playing a small, secondary role. Except for the Awlad Sulayman and a few Ouadai clans that belong to the Sanusiya (q.v.) order, most of Chad's Arabs belong to the Tidjaniya (q.v.); the nomadic groups are much more devout and have several marabout orders of their own. Some of these groups have shifted their transhumance patterns further to the south to avoid the droughts of the 1970s and 1980s, which has brought them into friction with the largely sedentary and agrarian southern populations.

The various groups speak around 30 Arab dialects in Chad, and their numerical preponderance and economic role (as traders of their pastoral products) has made Chadic Arabic (as the dialects are called, or Turku or Tourkou) a lingua franca.

ARADA. Officially designated "nomadic" souspréfecture in the préfecture of Biltine. Headquartered in the village of the same name (population 650), the souspréfecture covers a territory of 18,000 square kilometers (7,000 square miles), with a population of 30,000, giving it a low population density. During Chad's lengthy civil wars, the region—even in the best of times relatively lawless and beset by clan warfare, banditry, and brigandage—was especially unsettled and a no-man's-land of total anarchy. Its population is ethnically very diverse but includes large numbers of Mahamid (q.v.).

ARCHAEOLOGY. Within the territorial confines of Chad are some of the most important archaeological sites in Africa, few of which have been thoroughly studied and many of which are presumed to be as yet undiscovered. Some of the oldest sites are found in the northern préfecture of B.E.T., whose important rock paintings were first seen and reported by Heinrich Barth (q.v.) in 1851. In Borkou and Tibesti the paintings and engravings are from 5000–2000 B.C., depicting simple hunting scenes and providing evidence of the region's former tropical climate and abundance of water. In Ennedi there are more paintings than engravings, most dating to before 3,000 B.C. They are found in over 500 grottos (currently known) that were first discovered in 1930 by French officers. Chad's southern archaeological sites are of more recent date, from 500 B.C. and later, the most important ones being the Sao (q.v.) sites from which important relics have been recovered, especially at Dal and Tado. Sao lost-wax methods of bronze-casting and the elongated features of their artwork have attracted scholarly attention.

Relics of prehistoric elephants have been discovered north of N'Djamena in the semidesert regions, and it is now quite accepted that in the past rivers used to flow from the Tibesti massif to form extensive though shallow lakes around which large populations were found and tropical life abounded. Numerous bone harpoons and cave drawings depicting prehistoric tropical animals have been found north of Faya-Largeau. Equally well confirmed is the fact that as late as 500 B.C. merchants from Carthage used to travel to Tibesti to trade with the populations there. Moreover, in 1957 discoveries in Ounianga Kebir (see OUNIANGA LAKES) of Aterian artifacts seem to confirm Leakey's hypothesis of the common origins of the North African and the East and Central African Sangoan cultures, while evidence mounts of a riverine link in the past between the Nile and the Niger Rivers, with Lake Chad (q.v.) as a modern-day remnant of the former huge sea in that region. The study of Chad's distant past is thus slowly clarifying many aspects of contemporary questions.

ARMED FORCES. One can really talk meaningfully about "Chad's" armed forces only for the period between independence and N'Djamena's fall to FROLINAT (q.v.) in 1979. Since then, despite the existence of the "Chadian" armed forces, the reality has been that: (1) From 1979 and throughout the civil war each of the factions retained its armed forces—under a variety of names—with attempts at unifying all the forces into a national force remaining in the realm of rhetoric or theory. (2) After the end of the national tug-of-war for power, both Hissène Habré (1982–1990), and Idriss Déby (since 1990) (qq.v), have integrated into "Chad's" armed forces all existing formations of the reconciled regional warlords—creating, however, a *nonfighting* army, with both keeping their own key ethnic armed units separate, autonomous, and with sole operational capability. (3) At all times significant formations of armed personnel have remained at the periphery of the state in armed conflict with the central government, though since 1994 conditions have stabilized considerably. Chad's "nonfighting army" has usually stayed in its barracks or on garrison duties. All the armed conflicts between the country's central protagonists—Goukouni (q.v.), Habré, Déby—and even the earlier conflicts, during the civil war between the north and the south that determined the fate of Chad, have been between opposing armed forces of no more than 4,000 troops on each side. Déby captured "Chad" in December 1990, for example, when he engaged Habré's (larger) forces with an army of 2,000.

In mid-1995 Chad still had an army of roughly (the number is an "official secret") 50,000 troops (one soldier per 120 people, one of Africa's highest ratios—in one of the continent's poorest countries) that consumes up to 40 percent of the national budget. After the blistering military defeats Chad dealt to Libya in 1986 and 1987, the country was by far the largest recipient of military aid from France as well as from the United States, and was one of only a few states in Africa in which the CIA had ongoing military clandestine missions. The Chadian army to this day has an extraordinarily high proportion of officers (10,000, or one of every five armed men) and noncommissioned officers (NCOs) (20,000)—a function both of self-promotion of rebelling units and of the kinds of inducements both Habré and Déby have offered to wean them back.

Today Déby controls Chad primarily via his Garde Républicaine (q.v.), much as Habré did before him with the Garde Présidentielle (q.v.), both of which are essentially ethnic armies. Under Déby the Zaghawa are the key ethnic group sustaining him, and they predominate in the Garde Républicaine; under Habré it was the Anakaza, a branch of the Daza subdivision of the Toubou. Ancillary paramilitary secret police units, the DDS under Habré, the CRCR and later ANS (qq.v.) under Déby, provide the urban terror/torture and liquidation arm of N'Djamena that controls or intimidates the modern sector. Under both Habré and Déby "Chad's" large unassimilated and untrustworthy army was not committed to any particular military task.

The large expansion in the armed forces began to take place when N'Djamena fell to the north. Until 1979 Chad's armed forces were composed of four different structures, the Garde Nationale (q.v.), the Sûreté Nationale (q.v.), the Gendarmerie Nationale (q.v.), and the regular army. The minister of interior (until the 1975 coup under the close supervision of President François Tombalbaye [q.v.]) directed the first two security forces, and the minister of defense and veteran affairs (between April 1973 and 1979) directed the latter two. The Garde Nationale was a quasi-military civil guard with special units for the control of the northern nomadic areas; the Sûreté Nationale was charged with border patrol, crime prevention, and the protection of the presidency, and it also had units working in nomadic areas as well as lightly armed infantry companies; the Gendarmerie Nationale was responsible for regular police duties, and the main component of the armed forces, the army, was primarily responsible for defense of the territorial integrity of Chad.

The regular army's strength in 1973 was 3,500 men in the infantry and 200 in a small air force. The infantry was divided into four battalions (previously there had only been two), one paratrooper company, and a camel corps (the mostly Toubou *Méharistes*) headquartered in Moussoro in the north. The army's equipment included armed scout cars and 60 mm and 81 mm mortars. The air force, rarely operational due to budgetary constraints and the high cost of airplane fuel, and until 1975 heavily staffed by French personnel, consisted of three C-47 medium transport planes, three light transport planes, and one helicopter, all serviced at the local French airbase of N'Djamena. There was also a minuscule navy on Lake Chad. The onset of the civil war saw the slight augmentation of these forces when in 1975 two additional paratroop companies were trained in Zaire and the infantry battalions were strengthened, leading to an armed force of 4,200. Even in those years, however, 30 to 33 percent of Chad's budget was allocated to the country's security forces, 10 percent of which went to the costly air force.

Despite a great deal of effort and money expended on Chad's armed forces, the various contingents were poorly trained, underweaponed, lacking in mobility and stamina, and divided into competitive commands that sparked off interarm grievances, some of which led to the coup of April 13, 1975 (q.v.). In the last few years of the Tombalbaye regime, moreover, traumatized by their near-defeat at the hands of the rebels, torn asunder by Tombalbaye's policy of playing off one branch of the armed forces against the other, and highly demoralized by the large number of arrests among the senior ranks of the officer corps, Chad's armed forces could not be considered to be effective structures, especially since they were detested in the countryside for their enforcement of the government's unpopular taxation policies.

Despite the precolonial warrior tradition of several ethnic groups in the area that became Chad, only the Sara (q.v.) and related groups (with no such precolonial proclivities) tended to join the French colonial forces in any numbers, primarily for the regular pay and upward mobility they afforded. At independence this southern predominance in the armed forces was perpetuated by the southern elite in power and by a continued resistance of other ethnic groups to a military career. (There were only two Arabs in Chad's officer corps, for example, both junior lieutenants.) Consequently in the 1970s there were an estimated

15,000 mostly Sara veterans of the French colonial armies in Chad (some having fought with General Philippe Leclerc [q.v.] in Libya) drawing French pensions and organized in the once influential veterans association, the Association des Anciens Combattants du Tchad (AACT) (q.v.).

Shortly after independence, under French officers and NCOs, the first units of Chad's regular army were created, encompassing at the outset barely 200 troops. This figure was only very slowly augmented over the years; in 1964 the force still numbered only 500 troops, with a defense budget of 447.5 million CFA francs. The major expansion and reorganization of the Chadian security forces began around 1965–66, following the rout of various army and gendarmerie units by rebel forces (see REBELLIONS) and especially after the Zouar (q.v.) garrison was overwhelmed by Toubou (q.v.) warriors. By 1968 Chad's armed forces were on the verge of collapse (despite their augmentation), and rebel forces controlled large areas of the country, effectively disrupting any regular communications between N'Djamena and other centers in the east and the north. It was at this stage that French troops were brought into the country to bolster the Chadian army as well as to retrain it. In effect, however, this was but an escalation of France's military role in Chad, since between 250 and 800 officers and NCOs had all along served in a variety of technical, advisory, and command capacities. Moreover, the northern préfecture of B.E.T. (q.v.) had remained under French military control for five years following Chad's independence. The initial French military assistance was rapidly terminated, though some time later a more sustained, powerful, and active force was brought in (see FRANCE, FORCES IN CHAD) to help quell the continuing rebellion, and French military assistance was linked with a revamping of the administrative practices that had helped to spark off the upheaval (see MISSION DE REFORME ADMINISTRATIVE). It was only in 1975, however, that the military's budget jumped to 3,472.3 million CFA francs and the force size expanded beyond 4,000 men.

The army headquarters at that time was in Camp Koufra (q.v.) in downtown N'Djamena, and the important French airbase and camp were in the suburbs of the city. Other major garrisons existed in Mongo and in Faya-Largeau as well as elsewhere. Though relatively cohesive in terms of ethnic composition, the strong element of the Mbaï (q.v.) Sara (q.v.) subgroup in the army had caused friction and resentments among other Sara groups. Army spirits had flagged as a result of President Tombalbaye's public disdain of the army (due to its reverses on the battlefield) and his policies of playing off the army against the gendarmerie, which was quasi-equal in strength but better armed and equipped. These classic divide-and-rule tactics were a result of Tombalbaye's increasing insecurity in office. The interarm tensions he set loose by his policies were greatly exacerbated by the elevation to a position of preeminence of the Compagnies Tchadiennes de Sécurité (CTS) (q.v.) in all matters relating to the security of the capital and the presidency. Despite this tactic and purges of senior army and gendarmerie officers from 1972 to 1975—and quite probably because of these actions—both armed hierarchies joined in the 1975 coup against Tombalbaye. The gendarmerie was somewhat divided on the matter, though it quickly rallied to the insurgents, with only the local CTS units offering any serious, though temporary, resistance to the coup. The latter were later disbanded. (See COUP OF APRIL 13, 1975.)

On April 3, 1975, shortly before the coup, several senior officers were arrested, including Colonel Djimé (q.v.) and Major Kottiga (q.v.)—the commander and the deputy commander of the gendarmerie—and General Djogo (q.v.), the head of Tombalbaye's military cabinet. These arrests were part of a series of purges of the upper echelons of the security forces that had previously brought about the arrests of two preceding chiefs of staff—Generals Doumro and Malloum (qq.v.)—and other personnel. Following the coup all the arrested officers were reinstated in the army and integrated at the highest levels of the military junta ruling the country; General Malloum was made head of state, with the force commanders of the Chadian security forces being: Major Ali Dabio (q.v.), army chief of staff; Major Kottiga, commander of the gendarmerie, Major Gouemourou (q.v.) as his deputy, and Lt. Ngarbaroum (q.v.) as director of the Sûreté. In mid-1976 a major reorganization of the top command of the Chadian armed forces returned the gendarmerie to Colonel Djimé, and Major Gouemourou became head of the armed forces, while Lt. Ngarbaroum was retained in his post. (See also COMMISSION DE DEFENSE NATIONALE.)

The victory of the north in the "first" (north-south) civil war resulted in a large number of southern prisoners of war, who were for long not released, causing the prime complaint of southern leaders in the post-1979 era. The southern armies, Forces Armée Tchadiennes (FAT) (q.v.), withdrew to the southern préfectures with what remained of the central army's materiel, and Colonel Kamougoué (q.v.), head of the gendarmerie, emerged as the region's strongman, displacing his superior, General Djogo, who withdrew with some 550 regular troops to Sarh. (He was later to join Goukouni [q.v.] in B.E.T., becoming his chief of staff, after he had been ousted by his troops.) The new semiautonomous administration of the south became the Kamougoué-headed Comité Permanent du Sud (CPS) (q.v.) based in Moundou (now swollen by large numbers of refugees from N'Djamena) and in command of some 3,500 troops committed to the defense of the south at all costs. The idea of an independent "Republic of Logone" now also emerged—an all-Sara entity vaguely reminiscent of a period during the colonial era when the southern extremity of Chad had been attached administratively to the Central African Republic, where a large number of Sara elements reside.

The array of military power in 1982 stood at 4,000 FAT troops (divided between Djogo and Kamougoué and slowly becoming factionalized); 4,000 Forces Armées du Nord (FAN) (q.v.) troops (mostly in the east but by now heavily supplied by covert CIA deliveries); 4,000 ill-trained troops of the Forces Armées du Peuple (FAP) (q.v.) (mostly in the capital or in a holding line facing Habré's troops in the east); and an estimated 1,500 Conseil Démocratique de la Révolution (CDR) (q.v.) troops (strung out along several localities from N'Djamena to Ouadai, and hence weak in any locality). The "battles" for Chad were fought—to the extent that there was any fighting—by much smaller numbers, however, for at least 50 percent of each force was in essence performing garrison duty in its "own" core area or keeping its presence (for the GUNT [q.v.] allies) visible in the capital. Indeed, at no time during Habré's 1982 advance from the east to capture N'Djamena from Goukouni was there a pitched battle encompassing more than 2,000 troops.

With Habré's military victory over Goukouni and his entry into N'Djamena on June 7, 1982, dissident FAT elements revolted against Kamougoué's separatist policies and, with FAN aid, delivered the southern préfectures to the Habré administration. In this conflict, which for the first time united much of Chad behind one administration, Ahmat Acyl's CDR forces fought alongside those of Kamougoué. The defeated GUNT allies then withdrew from N'Djamena to regroup in B.E.T., whence came Goukouni's counteroffensives. These, assisted by Libyan ground and air power, brought GUNT armies (a composite of Goukouni's and Kamougoué's loyalists) into Abéché and Faya-Largeau, though Abéché had to be vacated shortly thereafter. The military situation was stabilized by the pouring into Chad of French money and materiel, followed by paratroop and air units of the French army. These established a sanitary cordon along the 15th (later 16th) parallel—the "Red Zone"—beyond which GUNT was warned any military forays or advances would lead to French retaliation. The warning, however, was really aimed against Libya, whose air cover and other direct support was committed to GUNT. Considerable U.S. materiel was also forthcoming, especially since it had been covert CIA aid (some US$10 million) that had allowed Habré to triumph over Goukouni in 1982 in the first place. Later even more sophisticated U.S. hardware arrived in N'Djamena (including 24 shoulder-fired Stinger missiles, seven launchers, and two Hercules transport planes) as well as 50 trainers, some for Habré's infamous secret service, as Habré was seen a useful ally vis-à-vis Libya. The battle lines now well defined, and a Habré-style Goukouni comeback and victory "forbidden," the two protagonists concentrated on opening up new "fronts" (as when GUNT commando units began attacks on southern targets from bases in the C.A.R.) or on retraining and expanding their armed forces.

The gendarmerie that had delivered to Habré the southern préfectures was meanwhile reorganized and replaced by a FAN-dominated Police Militaire. A new "national" army was also announced—Forces Armées Nationales Tchadiennes (FANT) (q.v.)—composed of a merger of Habré's FAN and selected elements of the dissident FAT force, under the command of a Habré lieutenant and with effective operational control of troops heavily weighted in favor of northerners. Though on paper "unified," FANT was in reality divided on a multiplicity of issues, and interethnic relations were bad. Not surprisingly, desertions were numerous, and in the south the force was regarded as an occupation army. The scattered atrocities that accompanied the original takeover of the south also swung the population (mostly Sara) against FANT, triggering a number of rebellions against N'Djamena and the emergence of southern liberation forces fighting N'Djamena's control.

Habré's reign relied exclusively on his forces of repression. These included: (1) The (in 1988) 3,600-strong Garde Présidentielle, which was essentially an ethnic force composed of his ethnic Daza Toubou kinsmen. (2) The Direction de la Documentation et de la Sécurité (DDS) (q.v.), a brutal political secret police, headed by a presidential cousin, Korei Guini (q.v.). The DDS was trained by the U.S. and had attached to it six French military intelligence officers. The DDS was responsible for up to 40,000 murders of civilian leaders during the Habré era (1982–1990), including Abo Nassour (q.v.), Colonel Allafi (q.v.), Saleh Gaba, and Dr. Wayne Ndem. (3) The elite Régiment de Défense Opérationnelle du Territoire (RDOT) (q.v.), based in the Dabut camp at the edge of N'Djamena, a mixed force of ex-GUNT desert warriors, ex–southern gendarmes, and some European mercenaries. The latter had been recruited for Habré by France's Direction Générale de Sécurité Extérieure (DGSE) and Bob Denard, the infamous mercenary, since 1983, and was trained by American and French military officers. (4) The Service d'Investigation Présidentielle, a spy network, directly attached to the presidency and headed for a while by Habré's first wife, Hadjé Fatime Habré and later by Mahamet Nouri (q.v.), an old Habré crony.

Overall, the array of armed power in Chad prior to Habré's massive victories in 1986 and 1987 included largely FANT and GUNT forces. FANT included a large force in the center of the country along the "Red Zone," another in N'Djamena guarding against a coup, and another performing garrison duty in the south, collectively comprising 15,000 troops. GUNT forces were variably estimated at around 4,000 to 6,000 troops, organized in mobile units in B.E.T. with a concentration in Faya-Largeau. GUNT forces were supported by a number of other smaller military formations and/or political fronts that included, inter alia, the several factions that broke off from the former CDR under Acheikh Ibn Oumar (q.v.), altogether some 3,000 in the east, and other units in the south, including some 500 operating out of C.A.R. bases and led by ex-FAT officers formerly loyal to either Colonel Kamougoué or to Dr. Facho Balaam (q.v.). Goukouni's strength, however, included significant numbers of vehicles, armor, tanks, surface-to-air rockets, and air cover from Libyan formations based in rear air-bases in Libya, in Aouzou, and also in Faya-Largeau. These, however, were taken away from Goukouni in 1987 when he broke with Libya, or lost in the Habré assaults of 1986/87.

The armed stalemate with GUNT/Libya was broken by Habré, who, prodded and armed by the CIA, began a series of brilliant attacks on GUNT and Libyan positions in B.E.T., including the large Ouadi-Doum base. (When the booty captured there, including some Soviet state-of-the-art materiel, was opened for inspection French officials were livid at discovering American officers already there.) In the process Habré succeeded in liberating Faya and most of B.E.T. An assault on Aouzou (q.v.) itself was also successful, though since France refused to provide air cover, fearing embroilment in a war with Libya, Habré was forced to withdraw his troops with serious casualties. However, Habré then mounted a stunning assault deep into Libya itself on the large rear air supply base of Maaten-es-Sarra, catching the Libyans completely unprepared. In the process additional war materiel fell into Habré's hands or was destroyed, and thousands of Libyan prisoners were taken. Included were 51 Soviet airplanes and helicopters (one of which was so new that CIA agents flew in to inspect it), over 300 tanks, and hundreds of armored vehicles. Libya's military reverses, GUNT's virtual collapse, and the loss of most of B.E.T. to Habré led to Libya's reluctant agreement to submit the Aouzou Strip controversy to the International Court of Justice (ICJ), and to a normalization of relations with Habré. (In 1994 the ICJ decreed in favor of Chad, and the strip finally reverted to Chad sovereignty.)

Though riding high after these victories, and beginning a process of quasi-civilianization, Habré had over the years progressively alienated many of the ethnic groups that had supported his assault on N'Djamena, starting with the Hadjeray. When his purges moved into the Zaghawa (q.v.) community, this led to the estrangement from the regime of key officers, including Chief of Staff Djamouss (q.v.), and Idriss Déby, the officer most responsible for the stunning victories over Libya in 1986 and 1987. Both fled to Sudan in 1989, and after recruiting an army of kinsmen, Déby began his military assault on Habré. The actual numbers of forces involved in the Habré-Déby tug-of-war, as at the time of the Habré-Goukouni struggle, were not significant. Déby had at his command 2,000 troops as well as between 2,000 and 4,000 irregulars, mostly nonnationals from Sudan. Against him Habré sent—and in one instance (until nearly captured in an ambush) tried personally to lead—two understrength battalions of his commandos (veterans of the B.E.T. fighting), transported to battle allegedly by Zairean pilots flying American Hercules C-130 airplanes. This force was augmented by some southern *"codos"* (q.v.) loyal to Colonel Kottiga (q.v.) and Captain Tokinon (q.v.)—who, not particularly committed to dying for a northern leader, were used mostly for guarding the flanks—and Habré's elite Presidential Security unit (led into battle by Israeli officers, some to die in the fighting) that primarily defended Habré when he made an effort to lead the troops. The total force defending "Chad" against Déby in November 1990 was around 6,000 troops, out of an army then estimated at over 28,000. (The armed forces, augmented over the years as various armed factions rallied to Habré and were integrated into the Chadian armed forces, stood at three operational infantry battalions of 400 men and 127 infantry companies of 100–150 per company.) After Déby emerged victorious in the battles near the Sudanese border, he entered Abéché unopposed and then drove, again unopposed, across the breadth of Chad into N'Djamena, which fell without a shot fired, though the capital was garrisoned by large numbers of "Chad's" national army. Remnants of Habré's presidential support forces and Garde Présidentielle fled to Cameroon and eventually reached Niger, where they currently reside. They have mounted several unsuccessful counterattacks against N'Djamena in the Lake Chad region.

As of mid-1995 the armed forces of Chad—renamed Armée Nationale Tchadienne (ANT) (q.v.) in January 1991—amounted to around 50,000 troops, including an air force of 200. There is also a paramilitary force of some 6,000 composed of the national military police and the territorial military police. There are also 800 in the Sûreté and 3,900 personnel in village militia. Air force equipment includes 14 helicopters (10 Alouette and four Puma; the state-of-the-art Soviet helicopter captured by Habré was bartered for more conventional materiel), the two Hercules C-130A transport planes, nine DC-3s, one DC-4, 10 assorted other craft, and PC-7 trainer planes. Some of these are inoperative. Chad's armor includes two Panhard ERC-90s and 40-odd AML-60/90 armored vehicles (part of a larger force partly destroyed or abandoned in the Habré-Déby fighting in Ouadai), ten 76 mm and 105 mm guns, 81 mm and 120 mm mortars, recoilless launchers, 20 mm and 30 mm antiaircraft guns, and some Milan antitank guided missiles. Most of the latter were used against Libya in the late 1980s. The troops are organized into three battalions, 16 infantry companies, three parachute companies plus two additional "independent" ones, one reconnaissance squadron, two camel reconnaissance squadrons, three nomad companies, one armored battalion, two artillery batteries, one transport company, and a large number of commando squads.

The regular armed forces have for several years been slated to be reduced drastically to 15,000, under intense pressure from the IMF and France and with the strong backing of the 1993 Conférence Nationale (q.v.). Most of the force is not a national "fighting army," as most of the units are neither militarily nor politically reliable. The army as a whole has not been used by Déby in his sorties against the intermittent attacks on his authority (by Habré elements and others) in the western Lake Chad region or in the east. Nevertheless, it is very difficult to trim the army, which includes 10,000 troops (according to other estimates as many as 15,000) that are Déby's sole power prop in the country. Considered, correctly, as Déby's "personal army," they include the Garde Républicaine, which includes thousands of non-Chadian Zaghawa who followed him from Sudan to Chad. The remaining troops in the Chad army are in essence various ethnic or personalist forces that renounced secession or rebellion in exchange for integration into the central government's payroll. Dismissing them would release armed soldiers into the countryside who would be likely to rekindle the secessionist flames, just as their leader would feel that their "contract" with Déby had been violated.

The Chadian armed forces have had an inordinately frequent succession of chiefs of staff, reflecting the reshuffling of leaders at the head of the state, deaths (in action as well as by assassination or execution), alienation from the regime, revolts, and the ad hoc promotions and demotions characteristic of the highly unsettled conditions in N'Djamena. Many of the chiefs of staff since 1979 have also been nonprofessionals, and most have had no prior formal military training. The current (1995) chief of staff took over when General Moussa Bechar Houno died in a car accident in July 1995 in Paris. The latter replaced Lt. Colonel Mahamat Garfa (q.v.) in May 1994, who had deserted Déby and fled to the east to mount a rebellion against N'Djamena. Prior to that there were Lt. Colonel Abbas Yacoub Kotti (q.v.), who packed the armed forces with non-Chadian (Sudanese) Zaghawa and was killed by the Garde Républicaine itself in October 1993. Kotti had replaced Lt. Colonel Abdallah Mahamat Ali (q.v.) in September 1992 after the Doba massacres in the South that had triggered an outcry for his ouster. Ali himself had been appointed chief of staff only in February 1992, and solely for successfully (and brutally) repulsing a Habré armed attempted comeback from the Lake Chad area. He replaced Major Loum Hinassou Laina (q.v.). Habré also had an inordinately high number of chiefs of staff during his tenure in power, including Idriss Déby himself, followed by Hassan Djamouss (q.v.), Allafoza Koni Worimi (q.v.) (who was captured by Déby but was rescued by Habré forces, half-dead, deep in Sudan), Adoum Yacoub (q.v.) (Worimi's deputy, who mounted the attack into Sudan to rescue Worimi), and Yosko Issaka (q.v.).

Déby's main military power props today are, as previously noted, the Garde Républicaine and the Agence Nationale de Sécurité (ANS). The Garde is a brutal force of repression that has been progressively built up from 1,500 troops in 1992 to some 9,000 by 1995. In structure and function it is a duplicate of Habré's Garde Présidentielle. The Garde Républicaine is mostly a Zaghawa force, and it falls directly and solely under Déby's authority. Some 7,000 of its troops are Sudanese Zaghawa who accompanied Déby from his battles against Habré in the east or who were subsequently recruited in Sudan. Most of them neither speak nor understand any Arabic or French, but their ethnic reliability is absolute. The Garde has been used in skirmishes with Habré forces in the Lake Chad area and against Lt. Ketté's (q.v.) southern rebels near the C.A.R. border. Its troops are posted throughout the country in small but powerful concentrations. The Garde acts brutally and with impunity, and it has been involved in dozens of grisly slaughters of civilians. When in mid-1995 *N'Djaména-Hebdo,* the country's main independent paper, referred to the Garde as an army of occupation, the Garde invaded its premises, beat up its editors and staff, and smashed its presses. A French force of 250 has been in N'Djamena, some since mid-1992, trying to train the unwieldy armed forces. The Garde has been cited by Amnesty International as responsible for over 1,500 civilian deaths and for targeting potentially threatening individuals for political assassinations. One of those killed in such a manner was Abbas Yacoub Kotti, head of the CDR in October 1993.

ARMEE DE LIBERATION NATIONALE (ALN). Formal name of Goukouni's (q.v.) armed forces after GUNT's (q.v.) ouster from N'Djamena by Hissène Habré (q.v.) in June 1982. After a period of consolidation in Tibesti the ALN began a counterattack that, aided by Libyan tactical and air/armor support (whose numbers were grossly exaggerated in the West), captured Faya-Largeau on June 24, 1983, and, briefly, Abéché. Overextended supply lines and Western support for Habré led to a repulse of the ALN back to its Tibesti redoubt. The nominal overall ALN commander was the southerner General Djibril Negué Djogo (q.v.). After Habré began his stunning attacks in 1986 and 1987 on the ALN/Libyan units in B.E.T., GUNT forces rapidly disintegrated, Goukouni was ousted from overall command by

Acheikh Ibn Oumar, and Djogo himself deserted to join Habré in N'Djamena. By 1988 the ALN no longer existed.

ARMEE NATIONALE INTEGREE (ANI). Name of the new "national" army formed—in theory—by the five military factions involved in the Goukouni-Habré coalition of 1980. Lt. Colonel Allafi (q.v.) was appointed commander in chief of the force in June 1981. Nothing came of the attempted integration of the competing armies of FAP, FAT, FAN, FAO, and CDR (qq.v.), since each faction was unwilling to cede military authority over its fighting force. At no time did ANI have operational control over more than 300 troops; only after the return to power of Hissène Habré (q.v.) in mid-1982 was a more concerted effort made to unite the armed might of the victorious coalition.

ARMEE NATIONALE TCHADIENNE (ANT). The name of Chad's armed forces after Idriss Déby (q.v.) captured supreme power in N'Djamena in December 1990. (See ARMED FORCES.)

ARNA. One of the most unruly of the Toubou clans, regarded by the French administration as no more than brigands and bandits. The Arna, long under the leadership of Angata Yoskoimi (q.v.), nomadize the frontier area between Chad and Niger, a territory very much outside the immediate control of either state.

ARRONDISSEMENT. Basic administrative unit in Chad. (See also ADMINISTRATIVE ORGANIZATION; POSTE DE CONTROLE ADMINISTRATIF.)

ARTINE, ADOUDOU. Prominent N'Djamena businessman who defeated the secretary-general of the UNIR (q.v.) party committee for N'Djamena in the July 1990 legislative elections. He withdrew from politics when Déby seized N'Djamena in December 1990.

AS-SAYKH IBN OMAR, SAYYID. Proper name of Sayyid Acheikh Ibn Oumar. Since he is widely referred to under the latter version, see the entry under ACHEIKH.

ASONGORI. Sedentary ethnic group residing west and north of the Masalit (q.v.) in Ouadai and Biltine Préfectures. Arriving from the east with Abd-el-Kerim (q.v.), they are similar to the Maba but speak a different eastern Sudanic dialect and rarely intermarry with the Maba.

ASSALI, DJIBRILE. Secretary-general of the Union des Syndicats du Tchad (UST) (q.v.) confederation of Chad's trade unions. He served as one of the two vice presidents of the Conférence Nationale (q.v.) in 1993.

ASSANE, ANDREAS (1944–). Educator and diplomat. Born in Bongor on April 10, 1944, Assane was trained as a teacher and taught for several years at a primary school in N'Djamena. Between 1965 and 1967 he was attached to the Ministry of Economics and later to the Ministry of Foreign Affairs. In January 1968 Assane was appointed second secretary at the Chadian embassy in France. In 1974 he was promoted to first secretary, but he lost his post with the victory of Goukouni in the civil war. He has since resided in Paris.

ASSANE DAINA, MICHEL (1936–). Senior civil servant. Born in Boda in 1936, Assane Daina joined the staff of the minister of youth in 1957, serving as the minister's personal secretary until 1959. In that year he was promoted to the post of chief de cabinet of the minister of interior and in 1960 moved to become Chad's director of information. In March 1962 Assane Daina briefly served as a National Assembly deputy (until March 1963), following which he was appointed head of Chad's Statistics Services (1963–1965). In 1965 he became director of documentation in the Ministry of Tourism and Information, serving until 1972, when he moved to the Ministry of Interior in a senior administrative capacity.

ASSEMBLEE CONSTITUANTE. Transitional name for Chad's Assemblée Territoriale, which transformed itself into a constituent assembly on November 26, 1958, proclaimed the Republic of Chad, and, adopting the Constitution of March 31, 1959, became the Assemblée Nationale (q.v.).

ASSEMBLEE NATIONALE. (1) Legislative organ of independent Chad that in 1958 replaced the Assemblée Constituante (q.v.) and the Assemblée Territoriale (q.v.). During the François Tombalbaye (q.v.) era there were three elections. On March 4, 1962, 85 deputies were elected to replace those elected in May 1959. The assembly was dissolved in September 1963 following the Fort-Lamy riots (q.v.) and political arrests, and on December 22, 1963, a new assembly of 75 deputies was elected (34 of whom were freshmen) under the presidency of Adoum Tchéré (q.v.). This assembly was dissolved on December 31, 1967, and only on December 14, 1969, were new elections held for an enlarged (105-deputy) assembly in which only 10 veterans of the former body were elected. The president of the 1969 assembly was Abo Nassour (q.v.). Following the coup of 1975 the Assemblée Nationale was dissolved; its term of office had been prolonged by decree to December

1975. No elections were held in Chad between 1969 and 1990, nor was there an elected legislature in Chad between 1975 and 1990.

(2) In the 1989–1990 constitutionalization of the Habré regime a new election was held in July 1990 (see ELECTIONS [LEGISLATIVE] OF JULY 8, 1990) and a new 65-seat Assemblée Nationale emerged. That assembly was itself disbanded shortly with the fall of Hissène Habré (q.v.) and the entry into N'Djamena of Idriss Déby's (q.v.) troops. A new Assemblée National based on new elections has been envisaged for several years.

ASSEMBLEE TERRITORIALE. Deliberative organ established in 1952 as successor to the Conseil Représentatif (q.v.) and precursor to the Assemblée Nationale (q.v.). Elected by a double electoral college (q.v.), the Assemblée Territoriale had 45 members, one-third of whom were elected by the first electoral college. Its president and first vice president were Europeans, and Bechir Sow (q.v.), the deputy from Kanem, was the second vice president. Among the prominent politicians of the future who sat in the Assemblée Territoriale were Arabi-el-Goni (q.v.), Marc Dounia (q.v.), Marcel Lallia (q.v.), the sultan of Mao, Ibrahim Babikir (q.v.), and Jules Pierre Toura Gaba (q.v.). In terms of political affiliations the assembly was composed of the conservative Union Démocratique du Tchad (q.v.) (allied with the RPF, q.v.)—24 seats—and the six members of the FACT (q.v.) coalition of progressives led by Gabriel Lisette (q.v.). Together with the 15 delegates chosen by the first (largely European) electoral college, expatriate, conservative, mercantile, traditional, and chiefly African interests predominated in the organ, holding 30 of the 45 seats. By 1957, however, the Parti Progressiste Tchadien (q.v.)—previously a member of FACT—was in ascendance, and by independence it was in control of the assembly.

ASSIMILATION POLICY. Underlying tenet of French colonial philosophy in Africa, which assumed the slow cultural assimilation of colonial populations. The status of *assimilé* or *évolué* was assigned to colonial subjects who had acquired the accoutrements of French culture—dress, education, religion, language, mannerisms, and so on—or had served with distinction in the colonial armies or in the French civil service. The status conferred the right to petition for French citizenship, a process so complex in actuality that only a few thousand in all of French Africa acquired it. The advantages of being classified an évolué and petitioning for citizenship included voting rights, governance under French civil and penal codes, and freedom from the onerous *indigénat* (q.v.) code and *corvée* labor.

The bedrock assumption of the assimilation policy was the unquestioned superiority of French (and Western) culture over all others and its suitability for all populations irrespective of geographic location. The policy was rarely, and then only halfheartedly, applied in Chad, as elsewhere in France's colonies.

In any case it was patently clear from the beginning that the French effort would not be even nominally successful in an area so deeply permeated with Muslim influences and anti-Western suspicions, especially in light of the extremely meager resources allocated to Chad for educational and other advances. "Assimilation" essentially worked only in the south among the Sara and other allied ethnic groups, and even there it was much more theory than reality.

ASSIMILE. An *assimilé* was a colonial subject who had assimilated the basic ingredients of all aspects of French culture and mannerisms or had served with distinction in the colonial armies or civil service. (See also ASSIMILATION POLICY; INDIGENAT.)

ASSOCIATION DES ANCIENS COMBATTANTS DU TCHAD (AACT). Chad's powerful veterans association pressure group, which is affiliated with the Union Fraternelle des Anciens Combattants. Among its former presidents and important administrators were: Ahmed Abdallah (q.v.), Jean-Charlot Bakouré (q.v.), and General Ngaro Doumro (q.v.). In light of the large numbers of Sara veterans of the French colonial armies (estimated around 15,000) some 500 million CFA francs is paid out by France every year in the form of pensions, disability benefits, and death compensations.

ASSOCIATION DES ENFANTS DU TCHAD (AET) see UNION GENERALE DES FILS DU TCHAD (UGFT)

ASSOCIATION DES METIS DU TCHAD (AMT). Short-lived organization grouping together mulatto elements in Chad. Founded by Jean Baptiste (q.v.), the powerful early opposition leader, himself of mixed parentage, from Ennedi. The AMT, which never had more than 150 members, was banned in 1962.

ASSOCIATION DES STAGIAIRES ET ELEVES TCHADIENS EN FRANCE (ASETF). Chadian students' association in France, formed in 1963. Composed of some 1,000 students in various French institutions, ASETF increasingly became radicalized and opposed to the rule of Tombalbaye in N'Djamena. In April 1973 violent demonstrations and a brief occupation of the Chadian embassy in Paris resulted in the mass revocation by the Chadian government of all student grants. Though the government in due course relented, relations between the regime in N'Djamena and the ASETF remained notoriously poor. A certain proportion of the student body was openly supporting FROLINAT (q.v.), while others rallied around opposition figures like Dr. Outel Bono (q.v.). Paradoxically, the victory of northern forces in the civil war virtually foreclosed the opportunities of new French-trained cadres for integration in the civil administration in Chad. Not only was that administration totally ravaged, defunct, and with empty coffers, but also most of the available posts were allocated to supporters of the victorious military factions. With the rise to power of Hissène Habré (q.v.) in 1982 the regime was hard-pressed to provide grants for its overseas students, preferring to use its powers of patronage to wean to its side veteran southern administrators rather than young ASETF graduates.

ATI. Administrative headquarters of the Batha Préfecture and of the Ati souspréfecture. The latter includes 95,000 inhabitants, roughly half of whom are Bulala (q.v.). Within the town of Ati (population 10,000) resides a small colony of the descendants of Muhammad el-Abid, brother of Ahmed es-Sherif (Grand Master of the Sanusiya [q.v.]), who retreated south into the region from Kufra (q.v.) when Italian troops advanced in southern Libya in the 1920s. The town is a bleak one some 445 kilometers (267 miles) from N'Djamena and 154 kilometers (92 miles) from Mongo, with communications frequently impossible due to the poor roads and the rainy season. On Lake Fitri (q.v.) is found Yao (q.v.), the capital of the small Bulala sultanate.

AUTHENTICITY see CULTURAL REVOLUTION; MOUVEMENT NATIONAL POUR LA REVOLUTION CULTURELLE ET SOCIALE (MNRCS); YONDO.

AWAT, MUKHTER NASSER (Dr.). Former left-wing leader of a small FROLINAT (q.v.) splinter movement, the Front Populaire de Libération du Tchad (FPLT) (q.v.). Awat had considerable influence among Chadian refugee communities, especially in Sudan.

AWLAD SULAYMAN (also OULED SLIMAN). An Arab tribe tracing its descent from Siliman (or Sulayman), a companion of the Prophet. The Awlad Sulayman are sharply differentiated by all other tribes from the rest of the Arab clans in Chad and are called Minimini or Wasili by the Kanembu (q.v.). They arrived in Chad from the north and were one of the last Arab groups to migrate into the region. Pushed southward by the expanding Turkish forces in the Fezzan (see TURKEY), one branch of the Awlad Sulayman swept into Kanem (q.v.) around 1842, ravaging the settlements in their path and disrupting the caravan routes (q.v.) in the region. (This forced the shift eastward of the principal routes, into Ouadai.) The Awlad Sulayman expansion was checked by the Tuareg (q.v.) in the west (in Niger) in 1855, and their remnants regrouped in Kanem. They later became devout Senoussi (see SANUSIYA) and fiercely resisted the entry of French colonial power into northern Chad. After their final defeat at the hands of the French in 1920, many of this branch migrated into Bornu in Nigeria.

The second branch of the Awlad Sulayman remained in the Fezzan until the late 1920s, when they too moved into Kanem under pressure from the Italian occupation forces in Libya. They are settled among the Daza (q.v.), with whom they intermarried, complicating efforts to estimate their numbers. Of the "older" branch that retained their ethnic individualism, there are only about 4,000 in Chad, nearly all of them in Kanem.

AZZA see HADDAD

-B-

BABA HASSANE, MAHAMAT SALEH ABOUDIGUENE (1933–). Former foreign minister and veteran politician with a checkered career. Born in Bongor (q.v.) (Mayo-Kebbi, q.v.) on January 25, 1933, and trained as an accountant, Baba Hassane's early years were undistinguished as he worked as clerk and bookkeeper with the French firm NSCKN (1949–51), the Banque Internationale pour l'Afrique Occidentale (1951–53), and the Mustapha Gademi company (1953–56). In 1956 he was elected to Fort-Lamy's municipal council and began his meteoric rise in politics. An important member of the Parti Progressiste Tchadien (PPT) (q.v.), Baba Hassane was elected the party's deputy to the assembly from Chari-Baguirmi (May 1959–March 1962) after a previous unsuccessful attempt on the UDSR (q.v.) ticket. Earlier, however, in May 1957, he had been appointed minister of social affairs, a post he held until December 1958, when he was appointed minister of animal husbandry (until February 1959), then minister of economics (until March 1959), and secretary of state to the presidency (March 1959–June 1960), all in Chad's pre-independence cabinets.

A member of the Political Bureau of the PPT since May 1959, Baba Hassane became minister of justice (June–August 1960) and then minister of economics and transport after independence (August 1960–March 1962), serving concurrently as minister-resident in Bongor. In 1963 he served as High Commissioner for the Plan. In that year Baba Hassane, a Muslim, was arrested for his alleged role in the March 1963 Fort-Lamy riots (q.v.). Tried and imprisoned, his sentence was suspended in January 1965, and he was posted to Chad's Planning Commission. In 1967 he was officially amnestied and appointed ambassador to Nigeria (1967–71) and, fully rehabilitated, was reintegrated into the PPT Political Bureau, made vice chairman of the PPT's Administrative Commission, and appointed foreign minister in May 1971. A ruthless, arrogant, and ambitious politician (though a tolerant Muslim), Baba Hassane—despite his earlier purge—was considered in many circles as a possible successor to Tombalbaye (q.v.). Partly because of this, he was downgraded in 1973 to head the Ministry of Tourism, Information, and Traditional Affairs, and shortly before the 1975 coup d'état he was again arrested and brought to trial for treason. After the coup he was promptly released from prison along with the other political prisoners of the Tombalbaye regime. His former ministerial activities having been scrutinized and apparently proven in order, Baba Hassane was appointed in July 1975 as political adviser to the Conseil Supérieur Militaire (q.v.), a post he held until the 1977 Malloum-Habré administration.

BABALAY, HASSANE (?–1936). Early leader of the Hausa (q.v.) community in Abéché after whom the local *zariba* (q.v.) is named (see ZARIBA BABALAY). Little is known about Babalay's early life except that he was born in the Kano emirate in Nigeria to a slaveholding family and that he made the pilgrimage to Mecca via the North African route. Later, on a second pilgrimage, he arrived in Ouadai during the reign of Sultan Yusuf (1883–1892) and settled in Abéché, working first for Fezzani merchants before branching off on his own. He prospered from the slave trade and from commerce with Fezzan. The local *zariba* was at the outset an extension of his own household and compound, enlarged to accommodate and cater to the needs of other pilgrims using the Ouadai route to Sudan and on to Mecca. It rapidly became a separate village in which Babalay ruled supreme. He is still spoken of with veneration for his piety and enterprise as well as his wealth. At the height of his power Babalay controlled a network of trading enterprises—administered by trusted lieutenants—radiating in all directions from Abéché. Babalay died in 1936, and though one of his sons took over his mercantile interests, the network collapsed, having been based on Babalay's personality and contacts.

BABALIA. Small Bulala (q.v.) ethnic sliver found north of N'Djamena, with their historic capital in Dal, currently in ruins. The Babalia have twice changed their language, most recently to Arabic.

BABAOYE, THIAM AHMAT. N'Djamena businessman, appointed vice president of the Ligue Tchadienne de Droits de l'Homme (q.v.)

in April 1992 after the assassination by Idriss Déby's (q.v.) agents of the previous incumbent.

BABIKIR, IBRAHIM. Early political aspirant. Descending from one of Rabah's (q.v.) principal lieutenants and by profession a postal agent, Babikir was elected to the French National Assembly (1946–52) on the Rassemblement du Peuple Français (RPF) (q.v.) ticket, concurrently serving as deputy to the Conseil Représentatif (q.v.) as a member of the Union Républicaine et Progressiste du Tchad (URPT) (q.v.). In the 1952 elections to the Territorial Assembly he ran on the Union Démocratique du Tchad (UDT) (q.v.) list but was defeated and then faded from the public eye.

BACHAR, FARIS. Leader of a segment of the FNT (q.v.) rebel opposition to the government of Idriss Déby (q.v.) that was not reconciled to N'Djamena. The group attacked the Chadian army garrison of Abéché on January 24, 1994, and has carried out a number of other attacks on government troops.

BAELE. Language spoken by the Zaghawa (q.v.) and Bideyat (q.v.) of Biltine, part of the Central Saharan linguistic group. (See also LINGUISTIC GROUPS.)

BAGGARA. Cattle-raising seminomads. (See also ARABS.)

BAGHALANI, MOHAMED (1927–1977). Militant fundamentalist FROLINAT (q.v.) leader and former head of the Volcan Army (q.v.). Of Jellaba (q.v.) origins and hence actually Sudanese, and a member of the UNT (q.v.), Baghalani fled to the Central African Republic after the massive anti-Muslim purges of 1963 in Fort-Lamy. In Bangui he met Abdel Hadj Issaka (q.v.), and after a soujourn in Sudan he began recruiting potential guerrillas among the Chadian refugees and students. It was in Sudan that he was himself recruited by Ibrahim Abatcha (q.v.), serving as courier and external link between Abatcha's troops and Sudan. With extensive contacts in Ouadai as well as Sudan, Baghalani was also a member of the Muslim Brotherhood and served as a counterweight to the alleged "atheist," Dr. Abba Siddick (q.v.), who emerged as the nominal leader of FROLINAT in Tripoli, Libya, after Abatcha's death in 1968. By virtue of his veteran status, Baghalani was part of the triumvirate that was supposed to govern FROLINAT until a new congress elected Abatcha's successor. Siddick succeeded, however, in disencumbering himself of his coleaders, and Baghalani (self-styled "General") was isolated in the east with only a small force paying allegiance to him. With Siddick's eclipse in 1976–77, Baghalani's Volcan Army, hitherto more engaged in sporadic pillaging than liberation struggle, became somewhat more influential and moved towards greater realignment with Goukouni's Forces Armées du Nord (FAN) (q.v.). This process was cut short by Baghalani's death in a traffic accident in Tripoli in March 1977.

BAGUIRMI KINGDOM. Barma (q.v.) kingdom centered on its capital of Massenya (q.v.), under nearly continuous military pressure from — and frequently tributary to — both the Kanem-Bornu Empire (q.v.) and the Ouadai kingdom (q.v.). Massenya was established around 1512 by Kukawa (q.v.), Kinga (q.v.), Barma, and Fulani (q.v.) elements, and shortly thereafter the nascent kingdom adopted Islam. Successor kings took the ancient title of *mbang* (q.v.) and expanded the kingdom to the south and the east. Baguirmi expanded in the seventeenth century, reached its apogee of power in the eighteenth, rapidly decayed in the nineteenth, succumbed to Rabah's (q.v.) onslaught in 1892, and requested French protection in 1897.

At the height of its power Baguirmi covered much of the territory of the contemporary Chari-Baguirmi Préfecture, loosely controlling parts of Guéra to the east and the Logone area to the west. Since its foundation, there have been 26 sultans on the throne, who during the colonial era were appointed as *chefs de canton,* nominally in charge of the heart of the former kingdom. The first sultan was Birni Bessé (1513–28); the seventh, Bourkomanda I (1631–61), is credited with the major expansion of the kingdom into Kanem. Around 1775 Baguirmi, on the basis of slave raids into the southern Sara (q.v.) areas and the supply of slaves to the north, began specializing in catering to the need for eunuchs in the Ottoman Empire. During the reign of Abder Rahman Guarang I, the 16th sultan, Baguirmi's decline began with a major assault by Ouadaian troops, who had been asked by Bornu to subdue the kingdom after it had renounced its customary tribute. Ouadai's official justification of the invasion was the decay of Islam in Baguirmi consequent to Guarang's incestuous marriage with his sister. The Baguirmi-Ouadai war resulted in the brutal pillage of Baguirmi, with nearly the entire dynasty being killed and some 20,000 inhabitants captured and sold into slavery. Baguirmi never recovered from the war, and subsequent *mbangs* were forced to pay tribute to both Ouadai and Bornu while periodically being raided by the former as well.

Baguirmi was again raided, and Massenya razed, when the Ouadaian tribute was renounced by Mohamad Abou Sekin (1858–77), and during the reign of Abder Rahman Guarang II (1883–1918) Baguirmi was invaded and destroyed by Rabah's forces (1892), after which Guarang requested France's protection from Emile Gentil (q.v.) (1897). In retaliation, Rabah moved against Massenya again and burned it to the ground. Guarang's forces then joined with the advancing French troops and participated in the Battle of Kousseri (q.v.), where Rabah was killed and his armies finally defeated (1900). Though Guarang was allowed to regain his throne, his powers were greatly reduced. His successor, Muhamad, was made *chef de canton* of the Massenya district, the core of the kingdom. In the post-independence era and as a result of the antichiefly policies of the Tombalbaye (q.v.) regime, the sultanate of Baguirmi—by now a somewhat nominal position, though still replete with traditional duties and respect—was abolished, together with some of the other sultanates. This policy was reversed on June 15, 1970, when the sultanate was reinstated with a new sultan consequent to the recommendations of the French Mission de Réforme Administrative (q.v.), which was searching for methods to popularize the central government in N'Djamena. The powers of the traditional sultan were again curtailed after the overthrow of the Tombalbaye regime in 1975.

Baguirmi was essentially a feudal monarchy. The kingdom was administratively organized around local chiefs ruling in the name of the *mbang*. In the capital strict protocol was observed, with a hierarchy of titled ministers in charge of specific functions. For example, the Mbarma, of noble free birth, was the First War Chief; the Patia, a slave, served as Second War Chief; and the Ngarmane was Chief of Eunuchs and in charge of the slave razzias in the south on the *mbang*'s treasury's account.

BAGUIRMI KINGDOM, KINGS OF. The following chronology is one of several, and there is some controversy regarding the precise years of each reign. The variations among suggested dates are of a small order though of major import to historians.

Birni Bessé (1513–28)
Lubatko (1528–40)
Malo (1540–61)
Abdaah (1561–1602)
Omar (1602–20)
Dalai (1620–31)
Bourkomanda I (1631–61)
Abderahman Woli
  (1661–70)
Dalo Birni (1670–76)
Abdel Kadri Woli
  (1676–1704)
Bar (1704–19)

Wanga (1719–34)
Bourkomanda Tad Lelé
  (1734–39)
Loel (1739–49)
Muhamad el-Amin (1749–84)
Abder Rahman Guarang I
  (1784–1806)
Ngarba-Bira (1806)
Bourkomanda (1806–46)
Abd el-Kedir (1846–58)
Mohamad Abou Sekin (1858–77)
Abder Rahman Guarang II
  (1883–1918)

BAHARINA. From the Arabic for "those of the Nile," a term applied to the forces of Zubayr Pasha (q.v.) and, at the outset, those of Rabah (q.v.) that invaded Chad from Sudan and pillaged the region in a broad slave-raiding sweep from east to west into Cameroon.

BAHR. Arabic for river. Most rivers in eastern and southern Chad are known under this prefix.

BAHR-EL-GHAZAL. In Arabic, "River of the Gazelle." Long, currently mostly dry riverbed and depression running in a northeastern direction through Kanem from the eastern side of Lake Chad to the Bodélé Depression (q.v.). In ancient times the Bahr-el-Ghazal was part of a much larger Lake Chad that included the Bodélé Depression and possibly connected the Nile and Benue River basins. Currently, during the rainy season the Bahr-el-Ghazal attracts many Fulani herdsmen and their cattle. Not to be confused with the province in Sudan with the same name or with the Nile affluent.

BAHR SALAMAT. Principal upper tributary to the Chari River (q.v.), itself receiving the waters of the Bahr Azoum, whose source is in Sudan. The river gives its name to the southern préfecture bordering the Central African Republic. (See also SALAMAT PREFECTURE.)

BAHR TINGA, CAMPEMENT see PARC NATIONAL DE ZAKOUMA

BAIBOKOUM. Souspréfecture in the Logone Orientale Préfecture with administrative headquarters in the village of the same name. It encompasses a territory of 13,000 square kilometers (5,000 square miles) and has a population of 80,000.

BAKHIT, MOHAMMED (1856–1916). Last independent sultan (1900–1916) of Daju (q.v.). His successors, regarded as sultans by their people, were "political agents" in the eyes of French colonial authorities.

BAKHIT, MUSTAPHA (1886–1946). Successor of Mohammed Bakhit (q.v.), who was his father. A French colonial soldier, he was appointed by the French as a political agent in Goz-Beida in 1917 shortly after the death of his father. Bakhit traveled to Mecca three times, and died of a heart attack in 1946. He was succeeded by his son, Abd el Kerim, in 1953, who himself died in March 1957.

BAKO, JOSEPH (1937–). Former secretary-general for foreign affairs. Born in N'Djamena on May 31, 1937, Bako was educated locally and in Paris, where he studied law and economics at the Institut des Hautes Etudes d'Outre-Mer (IHEOM) and the University of Paris. Upon his return to N'Djamena he was immediately appointed secretary-general for foreign affairs. He fell into eclipse following the 1975 coup d'état, when he was assigned to other duties.

BAKOURE, SOHOLLOT (JEAN CHARLOT) (1916–). Early radical trade union leader, longtime assembly deputy, traditional leader of the Sara-Kaba, and former chairman of the Mouvement National pour la Révolution Culturelle et Sociale (MNRCS) (q.v.) parliamentary party. Known until 1962 under his former name—Jean Charlot—and born in Kyabé (Moyen-Chari) of mixed racial parentage on August 16, 1916, Bakouré was trained in France as an agricultural technician. He served in the French colonial forces and was discharged with the rank of sergeant. A radical militant in the 1940s and 1950s, Bakouré was president of a branch of the CGT (Communist)–aligned Syndicat de Travailleurs du Tchad. In 1952 he was elected to the Chadian Territorial Assembly as deputy from Moyen-Chari and in 1956 he headed a list, BTDT (q.v.), in his effort to be elected to the French National Assembly from Chad. In November 1956 he also was elected to Fort-Lamy's municipal council and a year later was reelected deputy to the Territorial Assembly, having earlier joined the Parti Progressiste Tchadien (PPT) (q.v.). The assembly's long-standing president of the Finance Committee, Bakouré has also served on the Cotton Price Stabilization Committee and on the Veterans Administration Committee.

In 1959 he was Chad's delegate to France's Social and Economic Council. To further his political ambitions and avoid the fate of several other Chadians of mixed racial origin (and hence nationality) who were being expelled from Chad as "noncitizens" (see LISETTE, GABRIEL), Bakouré changed his name in 1961 and renounced his French citizenship. He was one of the very few assembly deputies to survive the various purges of the Tombalbaye (q.v.) era, and with the creation of the MNRCS in 1973, he was appointed to its Executive Committee. Bakouré also became Superior Chief of the Sara-Kaba in 1974. At the time of the 1975 coup d'état he still served in these posts and as president of the assembly's Finance Committee and the MNRCS Parliamentary Party. He was one of the few figures of the Tombalbaye regime to be arrested after the coup, but, like most, he was later released. He is no longer active politically.

BAL, ISMAIL. Former pro-Habré militant and prefect of Salamat. Bal acquired notoriety when he set up, within Hissène Habré's Garde Présidentielle (qq.v.) a unit nicknamed "The Vultures" that carried out a series of assassinations of Habré's enemies, including, allegedly, Ahmat Acyl (q.v.), head of the CDR (q.v.) in 1982, and Idriss Miskine (q.v.), Chad's foreign minister in 1984.

BALAAM, FACHO FAUSTIN (Dr.). Former rebel leader against Hissène Habré (q.v.) in southern Chad. A veterinarian/zoologist who obtained his training in Paris and who taught at the University of Dakar until 1975, Balaam remained in self-exile until 1981. He then returned to Chad and set up an integrationist party—the Union Nationale Démocratique (UND) (q.v.)—which was the only one at the time urging for a north-south reconciliation under President Goukouni (q.v.), though with a Marxist platform. The party was never very strong and was largely localized in Mayo-Kebbi. Later Balaam briefly served in Goukouni's GUNT (q.v.) cabinet as minister of transport and works (1981–82) before the fall of N'Djamena to Habré's troops. Withdrawing from the capital, Balaam remained loyal to Goukouni and served as his political adviser in Bardai and as external political spokesman for Goukouni's Gouvernement de Salut Nationale (q.v.). In 1984 Balaam, still nominally a member of GUNT, declared that the UND was totally opposed to the Habré presidency and neutral about the relative merits of a Goukouni or Kamougoué (q.v.) leadership. He then opened an active guerrilla front in the south, carried out from Sara bases in the Central African Republic. The UND's stated primary goal was to rid the Sara préfectures of the control of the Habré administration. On August 12, 1984, Balaam affiliated his UND to the newly created (also under his aegis) Rassemblement des Forces Patriotiques (RFP) (q.v.), which united some of the anti-GUNT and anti-Habré military and political formations in Chad. He cooperated with several other groups in the south, and when GUNT ceased to exist in 1988 he joined with three other opposition groups to form the Front Patriotique Tchadien (FPT) under the leadership of Acheikh Ibn Oumar (q.v.) of the CDR. A few months later Balaam was reconciled with Habré. Calling off his struggle, he returned to N'Djamena, where he was integrated into Habré's government as secretary of state for agriculture.

BALASSANE, MAMADIO. One of the leaders of the FROLINAT-Fondamental (q.v.) in the 1990s.

BANANA see MASSA

BANDA. Indigenous name for the very popular smoked fish segments prepared by the Hausa, Kotoko, and Bornuans in Chad and exported to Nigeria, Cameroon, and the Central African Republic. The fish is still prepared in its entirety in the traditional manner and is very popular abroad.

BANGUI. Capital of the Central African Republic and, previously, of the French colony of Oubangui-Chari. Much of Chad's imports and exports are still handled via Bangui. Exports, for example, are hauled by truck (via Sarh) and then loaded onto barges in Bangui to continue their journey down the Oubangui River (when the waters are high) to the Congo River (of which the Oubangui is an affluent) and to the port of Brazzaville. There they join the Congo-Océan railroad (see CHEMIN DE FER DU CONGO-OCEAN), which transports them to Pointe-Noire on the Atlantic coast for transshipment abroad. (See also COM-MUNICATIONS; RAILROADS.) Bangui was the site of several "peace negotiations" between the government of Idriss Déby (q.v.) and rebel Sara leaders, most notably Captain Ketté (q.v.), who in August 1994 renounced armed struggle and rallied to the government.

BANGUI, ANTOINE ROMBAYE (1932–). Important former politician and at one time François Tombalbaye's (q.v.) most trusted lieutenant and heir apparent. Born in Dabo on September 22, 1932, and trained as a teacher in the Central African Republic and at the Ecole Poly-technique in Grenoble, France, Bangui spent his early years in educa-tion. He served as primary school inspector and instructor at the Barthélémy Boganda Lycée in Bangui (C.A.R.) and at Chad's Collège de Bongor, where he taught physics and mathematics. After Chad's independence Bangui became head of a department at the Ministry of Education, rising to become minister of education (March–June 1962) and then minister of public works (1962–64). He was the only mem-ber of Tombalbaye's cabinet in 1963 to oppose the purge and impris-onment of Tombalbaye's main political competitor, Jules Pierre Toura Gaba (q.v.). As a consequence, in 1964 Bangui was temporarily dis-patched abroad on diplomatic duties as ambassador to Italy and West Germany (1964–66). Upon his return he was attached to the presi-dential office as secretary of state in charge of coordination. Bangui was a member of the Political Bureau of the reigning party, the PPT (q.v.), and his loyalty and indispensability to Tombalbaye—whose right-hand man he rapidly became—along with his ambitions, made him one of Chad's most influential politicians as well as heir apparent to Tombalbaye. Bangui's political career came to an abrupt end shortly after his January 1972 appointment as minister of planning. In a purge that stunned observers, Bangui was accused of a host of crimes, including misleading the president of Chad on the factors be-hind the Air Afrique affair (q.v.) and involvement in the plotting of the June 1972 guerrilla attack on N'Djamena (see COUP [AT-TEMPTED] OF JUNE 5, 1972). Bangui was then paraded with sev-eral other former high officials throughout the Sara areas in the south, where the crowds called for the imposition of the death penalty. He was partly rehabilitated prior to the 1975 coup d'état, when he was re-leased from prison, and some time later he was appointed ambassador to Romania. He then wrote two books, one on his experiences as a prisoner. At the end of his diplomatic appointment he remained overseas and joined UNESCO in 1983. Only in 1992 did he return to N'Djamena. He then set up a political party in the southern Sara regions. In May 1995 he was nearly beaten to death by Idriss Déby's Garde Républicaine (qq.v.) troops in Logone Occidentale.

BANQUE CENTRALE DES ETATS DE L'AFRIQUE EQUATORIALE ET DU CAMEROUN (BCEAC). Central bank of Chad, Gabon, Cameroon, the Central African Republic, and Congo/Brazzaville, all of which participate in a common monetary union and share a common currency (see COMMUNAUTE FINANCIERE AFRICAINE [CFA] FRANC) issued by the BCEAC. Originally the bank's headquarters was in Paris, with branch offices in all member countries. In November 1974 the foundation stone of the BCEAC's new headquarters in Africa—the relocation being forced upon the bank by member states—was laid in Yaoundé, Cameroon. Earlier, in April 1973, the bank had changed its name to Banque des Etats de l'Afrique Centrale (BEAC) (q.v.).

BANQUE DE DEVELOPPEMENT DES ETATS D'AFRIQUE CENTRALE (BDEAC). Developmental bank, set up after the April 30, 1976, agreement of the finance ministers of the UDEAC (q.v.) states, Chad, Kuwait, and the head of the African Development Bank. The new bank pledged to finance the UDEAC ten-year development plan with 50 percent of its resources to be devoted at all times to community projects. The bank's foundation stone was laid in Brazzaville on September 6, 1976. The bank's capital was set at 16,000 million CFA francs. The bank became operational in 1982.

BANQUE DE DEVELOPPEMENT DU TCHAD (BDT). Established on June 15, 1962, as successor of the Société Tchadienne de Crédit. The BDT's share-capital of 420 million CFA francs is subscribed to by the government, public institutions, the Caisse Centrale de Coopération Economique (CCCE) (q.v.)—via long-term loans—and the Banque des Etats de l'Afrique Centrale (BEAC) (q.v.). The BDT also controls the majority shares of the consortium that supports the Banque Tchadienne de Crédit et de Dépôts (BTCD) (q.v.), for long the only bank incorporated in Chad. The BDT's principal operations have been in the field of granting short-term agricultural credit and, to a lesser extent, medium-term loans to the industrial and construction sectors. By the mid-1970s the BDT was in an extremely precarious fiscal situation due to huge governmental arrears and was barely kept afloat on a month-to-month basis by CCCE loans and advance payments. Like most financial institutions, the BDT ceased operations in N'Djamena between 1978 and 1980, and completely closed down later, reopening in 1990.

BANQUE DES ETATS DE L'AFRIQUE CENTRALE (BEAC). Post–April 1973 name of the Banque Centrale des Etats de l'Afrique Equatoriale et du Cameroun (q.v.). The post-1976 headquarters of the bank is in Yaoundé, Cameroon.

BANQUE INTERNATIONALE POUR L'AFRIQUE AU TCHAD (BIAT). Currently a defunct bank, whose assets and liabilities were assumed by Banque Méridien BIAO. BIAT was also closed for two years in 1980.

BANQUE INTERNATIONALE POUR LE COMMERCE ET L'INDUSTRIE DU TCHAD (BICI). Currently inoperative bank that collapsed due to bad debts. It was a joint company with 40 percent Chad government equity, 29.4 percent Banque de Paris equity, and 30.6 percent participation on the part of SFOM.

BANQUE MERIDIEN BIAO TCHAD. Joint company, 51 percent owned by the Méridien BIAO group and 35 percent by the state, that succeeded the defunct Banque Internationale pour l'Afrique au Tchad (BIAT).

BANQUE TCHADIENNE DE CREDIT ET DE DEPOTS (BTCD). Joint company, originally 51 percent state-owned, founded with 440 million CFA francs in capital in 1963. The bank had its headquarters in N'Djamena and a branch in Moundou. With the collapse of the Félix Malloum (q.v.) administration in 1978 the N'Djamena center promptly closed down. It was subsequently reopened after the battles for N'Djamena, this time with only 40 percent state equity, 34 percent Crédit Lyonnais investment, and 26 percent Banque de Développement du Tchad (q.v.) participation. By 1991 the BTCD had accumulated 1.8 billion CFA francs of bad debts and was inoperative.

BANQUE TCHADO-ARABE-LIBYENNE POUR LE COMMERCE EXTERIEUR ET LE DEVELOPPEMENT (BATAL). Intermittently operational bank with 49 percent of its 250 million CFA francs capital contributed by the Chadian government, the rest by Libya. The bank's main purpose was to spur economic transactions between the two countries and to finance joint programs of technical cooperation. The bank was one of the concrete instances of financial largesse on the part of Libya after Chad's diplomatic break with Israel. Its activities were suspended in July 1977 and again in 1982, reflecting tensions between the two countries, and it never reopened.

BANU SAYF. A variant transliteration of Sefuwa (q.v.).

BAPTISTE, JEAN (1920–1964). Prominent Ouadai politician who played a major role in Chadian politics until the imposition of single-party rule in 1962 and his own arrest and execution. Little is known about his origins. Born either in Ennedi or in Salamat, a transporter by profession, and of mixed racial parentage, Baptiste entered politics via the conservative Muslim party, the Union Démocratique du Tchad (UDT) (q.v.), and became an important Ouadai political broker. His power base rested on Mahamat Jimemi (q.v.), chief of the Anakaza clan (q.v.); Allenga Allatchimi (q.v.), chief of the Gada, and Abidor. In 1952 he was elected the party's deputy to the Territorial Assembly from B.E.T. (q.v.) as well as UDT deputy to the AEF (q.v.) Grand Council in Brazzaville. He served as assembly deputy until his arrest in 1963, though as delegate of the Union Démocratique Indépendante du Tchad (UDIT) (q.v.), which he had cofounded in 1954 with the politically inclined French Governor Rogué. In 1956 he cooperated with Gabriel Lisette's (q.v.) PPT (q.v.) alliance — the ERDIC (q.v.) — in the elections for Fort-Lamy's municipal council and was elected Fourth Deputy Mayor; after Lisette's purge by his own party Baptiste succeeded to the mayoralty. A member also of the Entente (q.v.) coalition and minister of planning in Lisette's May 1957 government, Baptiste lost his ministry a year later when he deserted the Entente over a dispute regarding the Chadian delegates to the interterritorial Organisation Commune des Régions Sahariennes (OCRS) (q.v.).

His own candidacy having been rejected, Baptiste was incensed by the rejection also of his nominee, Allatchi Issa Allatchimi (q.v.). His absence from the ruling coalition was, however, brief. He soon returned as minister of economics in Lisette's provisional government of December 1958, and as minister of public works in the subsequent provisional Gountchomé Sahoulba (q.v.) government of February 1959. He was excluded from the next provisional government (see PROVISIONAL GOVERNMENTS) of Ahmed Koulamallah (q.v.) — despite its including practically every other prominent politician — because of his very bad relations with Koulamallah personally as well as with the Tidjaniya (q.v.) Muslim order (the largest in Chad), as Baptiste was president of the rival Wahhabi Muslim community. The animosity between the two politicians (which had surfaced years earlier) led to the collapse of the Koulamallah government and the reentry of Baptiste into the next government, the March 1959 provisional government of François Tombalbaye (q.v.) as minister of economics, tourism and health. In the next Tombalbaye government (June 1959) Baptiste emerged as minister of social affairs, health, and labor, but he was expelled from the cabinet in February 1960 when he helped forge the northern Muslim coalition, the Parti National Africain (PNA) (q.v.), of which he became executive president.

Baptiste then paradoxically became completely isolated in the PNA by his plea for cooperation with the PPT. Expelled from the party he had founded (for "treason") and unacceptable as an ally to the PPT due to his 1961 reneging on a pledge that there be only one (PNA-PPT) electoral list for the Fort-Lamy mayoral elections, Baptiste's insecure political position was underscored when he was stripped of the Fort-Lamy mayoralty and briefly arrested. He was released from prison but kept under police surveillance for possible opposition activities, and his Chadian citizenship was revoked on the grounds that only one of his parents had been a national. (The same tactics had been used by Tombalbaye to purge Lisette, Kotoko, and others.) Though Baptiste resisted his expulsion from Chad (noting that he had earlier renounced his French citizenship), he was again arrested in 1963 in the major swoop on Muslim non-PPT elements in the country (see FORT-LAMY RIOTS). Escorted to the B.E.T. (to the Ounianga Kebir region)—where most of those purged were to be incarcerated—Baptiste was killed there, possibly as early as 1964. (According to another version, Baptiste died in Fort-Archambault in 1964 after torture.) The government announced his death only in 1970 when former and future amnesty lists of those arrested did not list his name. (The regime then claimed that Baptiste had been killed, at his own request, by another prisoner, Silas Benoit Selingar [q.v.].) Baptiste had been a popular N'Djamena politician among the large Muslim and nonsouthern groups in the city (despite his opportunistic intrigues), and some of his supporters gravitated toward his son, René Baptiste (q.v.).

BAPTISTE, RENE. Jean Baptiste's (q.v.) son, also arrested in the 1963 swoop on anti-Tombalbaye elements. Released in the general amnesty of April 1971 shortly after the announcement that his father had been killed while in prison and allegedly at his own request. At the time of his arrest René Baptiste had been in high school. Though he did not exhibit political ambitions, he garnered some political support among former supporters of his father.

BARDAI. Small village, today of around 3,000 people, which is the administrative headquarters of the Tibesti souspréfecture in B.E.T. (q.v.) and which headquartered Ouaddaye Goukouni's (q.v.) post-1982 insurrection against Hissène Habré (q.v.). Bardai was also the scene of the 1974 guerrilla kidnapping of Françoise Claustre (q.v.).

The immediate vicinity of Bardai is one of volcanic craters, gorges, spectacular cliffs, and sulfuric deposits. A major tourist attraction—as is the entire B.E.T.—in settled times, Tibesti was the center of the Toubou rebellion of 1965 (see BARDAI INCIDENTS, 1965) and the center of the tug-of-war between N'Djamena and armed rebels, including Libyan troops, until 1994. Bardai is 735 kilometers (455 miles) from Faya-Largeau (q.v.), the administrative capital of the B.E.T., and 90 kilometers (55 miles) from Aouzou (q.v.). The village is not to be confused with the small center having a similar name on the Sudan-Ouadai border.

BARDAI INCIDENTS, 1965. The triggering cause of the Toubou (q.v.) rebellion in B.E.T. A beer-hall brawl during the night of September 2, 1965, resulted in the stabbing and death of a Chadian soldier. The southern subprefect, Lt. Samuel Rodai (q.v.), decreed a series of demeaning punitive measures, inter alia parading the entire village, many naked, and including the derde (q.v.) of the Toubou. Though the prefect of B.E.T., Colonel Odingar (q.v.), ordered the release of detained women and children and reversed some of Rodai's decrees, the damage was done. The derde slipped into exile in Libya, while his sons raised the banner of war. Rodai's replacement as subprefect, Lt. Ngolabaye Allafi (q.v.), was even more inept, and his crass actions further inflamed the situation.

BARMA. Indigenous name of the people of Baguirmi (see BAGUIRMI KINGDOM) who are called by the Massa (q.v.) *damakay* and pejoratively by the Kotoko (q.v.) *makwade* ("vultures"). Situated between the two powerful—and intermittently warring—neighbors, Bornu to the west and Ouadai to the east, the Barma kingdom of Baguirmi was under constant military pressure, paid tribute to one or the other of its neighbors (frequently to both), and finally collapsed under Rabah's (q.v.) slave-raiding onslaughts. The Barma are found around Massenya (q.v.)—the former kingdom's capital—along the Chari River (q.v.) in the vicinity of N'Djamena, and in Melfi, Madiago, and north of Mandjafa. The number of pure Barma is very small, estimated in 1964 (in the country's only census) to number around 35,000, and in 1994, 43,750, though a large number of other ethnic groups have become more or less assimilated with the Barma linguistically and culturally. These include Fulani, Kanuri, Sara, Massa, and Niellim (qq.v.) groups. The Barma language (*tar barma*) is different from Kanuri or Maba and has been classified by some as a language family including also the Kinga (q.v.) and Bulala (q.v.), though it has borrowed specialized terminologies from both Kanuri and Arabic. The Barma established their kingdom during the sixteenth century on land originally occupied by Massa and Sara elements, with a Kinga clan playing a major role or participating in the foundation of the original ruling dynasty. (The legends are somewhat contradictory.) The kingdom was soon converted to Islam under the influence of a Fulan *faki* (q.v.), though pre-Islamic practices and rites survive to this day. The Barma are mostly agriculturalists raising millet and sorghum, with peanuts and cotton as secondary crops.

BAROUM, BAJOGLO (JACQUES) (Dr.) (1932–). Physician and former foreign minister. Born in Laï on July 13, 1932, Baroum was educated in Bongor and Brazzaville, following which he studied medicine at Lyons and at the University of Paris (1953–1962). When he graduated in 1962 he became Chad's first indigenous doctor and upon his return to Chad was appointed chief medical officer at the pediatrics department in the Fort-Lamy Hospital (1962–64). Having been active while in France in the militant student organization, the Fédération des Etudiants de l'Afrique Noire en France (q.v.), Baroum became a member of the Political Bureau of the Parti Progressiste Tchadien (PPT) (q.v.) in 1963, and he became minister of health in January 1964. In November 1964 he was promoted to minister of foreign affairs, a post he held for seven years, through May 1971, when he was replaced by the rehabilitated Mahamat Saleh Baba Hassane (q.v.) and reassigned to head the Ministry of Public Health and Social Affairs. From March to October 1973 Baroum was also in charge of the Ministry of Finance. A capable doctor and administrator, Baroum's long tenure during one of Chad's most hectic political periods was a function of his avoidance at all costs of clique politics and his unswerving loyalty to François Tombalbaye (q.v.). (In this he may be contrasted with Dr. Outel Bono [q.v.], Chad's second doctor, who, similarly involved in a political career, suffered a radically different fate.) A relatively noncontroversial figure, Baroum served also as vice chairman of the PPT's Political and Institutional Committee. With the eclipse of the PPT in favor of the MNRCS (q.v.), Baroum became a member of the latter's Executive Committee. Following the coup d'état of 1975, Baroum returned to his medical career.

BARROUD, MAHAMAT ADOUM. Former cabinet minister and assembly deputy. The son of the sultan of Dar Tama, Barroud was one of the early members of the conservative chiefly party, the Union Démocratique du Tchad (UDT) (q.v.), and served as its deputy in the Territorial Assembly from 1952 to 1957, later serving briefly as minister of justice (January–November 1964) representing in the cabinet his native Ouadai. Barroud was arrested and imprisoned in November 1965 for allegedly plotting against François Tombalbaye's (q.v.) regime. He was released in the large amnesties of June 1969, and he served as counselor to Chad's Supreme Court before retiring.

BARTH, HEINRICH (1821–1861). Famous German explorer. Born in February 1821 and educated as a scholar in classics and linguistics, Barth toured North Africa from Tangier to Egypt between 1845 and 1847 and traveled up the Nile as far as Wadi Halfa and published accounts of his explorations. After his return to Germany he was invited by the British government, at the suggestion of expedition leader James Richardson (1809–1851), to join an upcoming expedition into Central Africa. The expedition started from Tripoli in 1850. After Richardson's death in 1851 Barth assumed the leadership, reaching Kukawa (q.v.), capital of Bornu (q.v.), in April 1851. With the assistance of Shehu Umar (see AL-KANEMI, UMAR IBN MUHAMMAD) Barth mounted expeditions to Baguirmi, Kanem, Logone, and the Adamawa region in Cameroon, though because of unsettled conditions he was unable to visit Ouadai. He returned to England in 1855. In 1857 and 1858 he published his five volumes on the regions he had explored; these were regarded as the epitome of scholarly research by fellow German explorer Gustav Nachtigal (q.v.), who visited some of the same areas 20 years later and was greatly aided by Barth's observations. Indeed, the wealth of data provided by Barth, including detailed linguistic studies, makes him the greatest of the nineteenth-century explorers of the western Sudan, and his works are classics for the study of Chad.

BATHA PREFECTURE. Préfecture in north-central Chad covering an area of 88,855 square kilometers (34,300 square miles), with a population of 431,000, giving it a population density of 4.9 per square kilometer. Batha is divided into three souspréfectures, Ati, Ouadi-Rime, and Oum-Hadjer, and has three *postes administratifs,* one of which was the scene of the violent Mangalmé tax riots (q.v.) in 1965 that essentially marked the beginning of the rebellion (q.v.) outside B.E.T. (q.v.). Throughout the 1980s parts of Batha have been under the sway of rebel anti-Habré and later anti-Déby armed groups, such as Abba Seid's First Army and Acheikh Ibn Oumar's CDR (q.v.).

The population of Batha is composed of Kukas, Bulalas, Salamat Arabs, Moubi, and Misirié Arabs (qq.v.), all of whom are Muslim. Local production includes cattle herding, with significant exports (on the hoof) to Nigeria and the Central African Republic, gum arabic (q.v.), and dried fish from Lake Fitri (q.v.), where Yao (q.v.), the capital of the Bulala sultanate, is located. Millet and groundnuts are also grown for local consumption. The Sahelian droughts of the 1970s devastated Batha's cattle herds, which had been the second largest in Chad after those of Kanem; many surviving herds had to be moved to the south or sold. Communications in and out of Batha are very poor in general and impossible in the rainy season. Ati (q.v.) is 311 kilometers (193 miles) from Abéché, 154 kilometers (95 miles) from Mongo, and 455

kilometers (282 miles) from N'Djamena. On most indicators the préfecture lags behind the more developed ones in Chad; the school attendance rate, for example, is barely 3.8 percent.

BATHA RIVER. Rising near Hadjer-Kamaran on the Sudan-Ouadai border region, the Batha River (frequently dry) flows westward through
central Ouadai and southern Batha to spill into Lake Fitri (q.v.) at Yao
(q.v.). Except in unusually wet seasons the Batha is more of a *wadi*
(q.v.) and is dry most of the year. The word *batha* in Arabic denotes
swampy areas, especially riverbeds.

BATTLE FOR N'DJAMENA. Sometimes referred to as the First, Second, or Third, to differentiate among the "First," March–December
1980, tug-of-war between Goukouni and Habré (qq.v.), the "Second"
(1982), a relatively short and incisive Habré advance on the capital,
and the "Third," in which Déby (q.v.) took the capital on December 2,
1990, unopposed after Habré had fled Chad. In the first battle, begun
by Habré with assaults on FAP (q.v.) forces, the nine-month conflict
resulted in Habré's defeat and containment in the far east of Chad.
Libyan troops, invited in by Goukouni's GUNT (q.v.) government,
played a crucial role. During the first two battles for N'Djamena most
of the town was destroyed and over 100,000 people fled into exile
across the river to Cameroon.

BATTLE OF KOUSSERI (1900) see KOUSSERI; RABAH

BAUCHE, SEID (1935–). Administrator and former cabinet minister.
Born in Goz-Beida in 1935 and educated locally and in France at the Institut des Hautes Etudes d'Outre-Mer (IHEOM), Bauche was appointed
subprefect of Batha in 1959 and served until 1965, when he became
deputy director of fiscal control in the central government. In November 1966 he was appointed prefect of Guéra and in August 1971 prefect
of Logone Orientale, a post he retained through the coup of 1975. He
was subsequently appointed by Hissène Habré (q.v.) in August 1987 as
his minister of livestock and rural hydraulics, and in April 1988 was
shifted to the post of minister of food security and disaster victims, remaining there until the rise of the Idriss Déby (q.v.) regime in 1990.

BAWOYEU, JEAN ALINGUE see ALINGUE, JEAN BAWOYEU.

BEADENGAR, DESSANDE (DESSANDE TOKOBE, PIERRE AL-
FRED) (1936–). Educator, former cabinet minister, and ambassador
to the United Nations. Born in Fort Sibut in the Central African Republic on March 28, 1936 (under the name of Dessande Tokobé),

Beadengar taught between 1958 and 1961 at a Fort Crampel (C.A.R.) primary school and later (1961–64) studied at the Auteuil Teachers Training College in Paris. He then continued teaching at Bambara (C.A.R.) and at Sarh and Koumra in southern Chad until appointed by President François Tombalbaye (q.v.) to head the Ministry of Information and Tourism (1968–73). In 1973 he was transferred to head the Ministry of Water and Forest Resources, Fisheries, and Wildlife, a post he held until the 1975 coup d'état. In August 1975 he was appointed by the Conseil Supérieur Militaire (CSM) (q.v.) as Chad's permanent representative to the United Nations, serving in that capacity until 1978.

BEADOUMRI, NANDONGAR (1950–). Diplomat. Born in 1950 in Kaba-Koutou in southern Chad and educated in Sahr (1964–70) and the Ecole Nationale d'Administration in N'Djamena (1972–74), Beadoumri assumed duties in the Ministry of Foreign Affairs in 1974, interrupted while he secured a diploma in Spain (1975–76) in African and Arab studies. In 1976 he was appointed first secretary to the Chadian embassy in Zaire and served in a similar capacity until the rise to power in 1982 of Hissène Habré (q.v.). He was then returned to Chad and was attached to the Ministry of Foreign Affairs as head of one of its sections.

BEASSOMAL, NADJITA YONHOMBEL (Colonel). Former commander of Chad's tiny air force. A southerner, Beassomal had been minister of economic affairs in the GUNT (q.v.) government-in-exile and inherited the Mouvement du Peuple Tchadien (MPT) (q.v.) originally set up by Colonel Kamougoué (q.v.) when the latter belatedly rallied to N'Djamena. When Idriss Déby (q.v.) fled N'Djamena to raise a force against Hissène Habré (q.v.), Beassomal joined the revolt on his side, and after Déby's victory in December 1990 he was appointed minister of information and later transferred to head the Ministry of State for Public Works and Transport. In December 1991 he was promoted to minister of defense and in October 1992 transferred to head the Ministry of Posts. He stayed in the government until the Conférence Nationale (q.v.) of 1993 selected its own cabinet.

BEBALEM RIOTS, 1952. One of the more prominent eruptions of anti-chiefly violence in southern Chad, in part consequent to the French administration's emphasis on cotton cultivation and the enhancement of the powers of chiefs—and the chiefs' potential for abuses of authority—toward this end. (See CHIEFS; COTTON.) The direct cause of the riots was the support of the Parti Progressiste Tchadien (PPT) (q.v.) for the 1952 Territorial Assembly election of the popular claimant to the chieftaincy of Bénoyé, who garnered most of the Bébalem votes. The candidate was defeated in the elections, however, and the population felt that this was yet another example of the connivance of the French administration with the local *chef de canton*. Mass attacks developed against the latter and other chiefs in the vicinity, detested due to their self-aggrandizement via the cotton *cordes de chefs* (q.v.) abuses. On April 16, 1952, troops had to be sent into Bébalem and Bénoyé to rescue the chiefs from the wrath of the villagers. There were many casualties among the peasants in the process.

BEBEDJIA. Souspréfecture with administrative headquarters in the village of the same name, in the préfecture of Logone Orientale.

BECHAR, MAHAMAT (1936–). Educator and former minister. Born in 1936 in Maho, a teacher by profession, Bechar served as an educational inspector before entering political life. Elected PPT (q.v.) deputy from Kanem in May 1959 and OCRS (q.v.) delegate of Chad, Bechar later fell afoul of François Tombalbaye (q.v.) and was shut out of political office. After the 1975 coup d'état he was brought into General Félix Malloum's (q.v.) cabinet as minister of agriculture (1975–76) and then of tourism (1976–77), but he was dropped with the rapprochement between Malloum and Hissène Habré (q.v.). He subsequently filled lower-level diplomatic and administrative duties until his early retirement.

BEDAYA. Important Sara initiation center for the Yondo (q.v.) rites, emphasized during the last few years of the François Tombalbaye (q.v.) era; also Tombalbaye's hometown. Bedaya is a *poste administratif* within the Koumra (q.v.) souspréfecture in Moyen-Chari.

BEDJOND. At times also known as Mbaï-Bédiondo (a name they reject) and Nangda, the Bedjond are a Sara subgroup of 45,000, localized around the Bédiondo and the neighboring cantons. They were a prime target for numerous devastating Fulani slave raids from the west.

BEGUY, GUEDAH DANIEL (1936–). Former labor inspector. Born in N'Djamena on June 4, 1936, and educated at home and abroad, Beguy obtained a diploma in labor law. He served as an instructor of labor law between 1959 and 1961 while attached to the Ministry of Interior as a labor inspector, and in 1964 he was appointed cultural and economic attaché at the Chadian embassy to the EC in Brussels. In 1973 he was repatriated to become director of the National Handicrafts Office in the Secretariat of Labor, Youth, and Sports, a post he held until 1978.

BEHIDI, JOSEPH (1945–1992). Former vice president of the Chadian human rights organization, the Ligue Tchadienne de Droits de l'Homme (q.v.). A lawyer with a degree from France, Behidi practiced in N'Djamena until the league was created in 1990, when he was elected its vice president. He was assassinated in N'Djamena on February 15, 1992, by elements of President Idriss Déby's Garde Républicaine (qq.v.). He had earlier defended the independent *N'Djaména-Hebdo* newspaper, which was exposing abuses of human rights, against charges of slander by two Garde officers.

BEINAMAR. Souspréfecture with administrative headquarters in the village of the same name, within the préfecture of Logone Occidentale.

BEL KACEM EL TUATI (1895?–1966). An Arab from Tuat who, after wanderings through the Fezzan and Borkou, finally settled in Faya-Largeau in 1943. Renowned and respected for his piety, religious knowledge, and fairness, Bel Kacem became a major mediator and peacemaker in the turbulent Toubou (q.v.) interclan strife. Often referred to as "Sidi," he mediated two highly volatile disputes: in 1946 after the death of Kirdimi, and in 1955 during an interclan feud in Libya. Throughout his life he subsisted on his modest vegetable plots and various offerings given him by the faithful.

BENI WAIL see HASSAUNA

BENOYE. Souspréfecture with administrative headquarters in the village of the same name in the préfecture of Logone Occidentale.

BEREMADJE, MADENGAR. Former minister of finance. A Sara of the Nar subgroup, Beremadjé served in the Ministry of Finance, rising to become director of the Treasury in 1972. Following the 1975 coup he was integrated in General Félix Malloum's (q.v.) cabinet as minister of finance, serving in that capacity until 1979. Beremadjé came back into prominence with the rise of Hissène Habré (q.v.) when he became secretary-general to the presidency. After Idriss Déby (q.v.) marched into N'Djamena, Beremadjé was appointed, effective January 1991, director general of finance.

BERI. Communal name of the Zaghawa (q.v.) and Bideyat (q.v.) ethnic groups. The latter two names are the Arab designations of the ethnic groups that refer to themselves as Beri. They live in close proximity to the Daza Toubou (qq.v.) and straddle also the Chad-Sudan border.

B.E.T. see BORKOU-ENNEDI-TIBESTI (B.E.T.) PREFECTURE

BEYASSOUM, SAMUEL (1941–). Magistrate, born in Bongor on December 19, 1941. With a degree from the Institut des Hautes Etudes d'Outre-Mer (IHEOM) in Paris, Beyassoum served as deputy attorney general of Chad in 1964 and 1965. From 1965 to 1969 he served as circuit judge in N'Djamena, Bongor, and Sarh, and in December 1969 he joined the Ministry of Education as director of cultural affairs. In 1972 Beyassoum returned to legal duties as circuit court judge in the southern préfectures.

BIDEYAT. A small (25,000) ethnic group subdivided into a number of clans in the Fada region in Ennedi (q.v.). Though living a pattern of life similar to that of the Daza (q.v.) branch of the Toubou (q.v.), the Bideyat strongly resent being confused with them. The language of the Bideyat (*Baélé*) is of different origin from that of the Toubou; there is some speculation that they are descendants of the pastoralists portrayed in the various cave drawings (q.v.) in Ennedi, or of Zaghawa (q.v.) origin, to whom they are closely related. "Bideyat" is an Arab appellation; the people refer to themselves as Beri (q.v.).

BIDI, NEATOBEI. Head of the Parti Africain pour la Paix et la Justice Sociale (PAPJS) (q.v.), a southern party that stands for federalism and greater regional autonomy.

BIDON, MAHAMAT SAKER. Former head of Hissène Habré's (q.v.) infamous Direction de la Documentation et de la Sécurité (DDS) (q.v.) secret police.

BILALA see BULALA

BILTINE PREFECTURE. Préfecture north of Ouadai, out of which it was carved in the mid-1950s. Biltine encompasses an area of 46,850 square kilometers (18,100 square miles) and has a population of 216,000, giving it a population density of 4.6 per square kilometer. Biltine is divided into the souspréfectures of Biltine (the town is also the administrative headquarters of the préfecture), Am-Zoer, Arada, Guéreda, and Iriba. The population of the Biltine is a mixture of Maba (q.v.), Zaghawa (q.v.), and other seminomadic groups that raise and export camels to Libya and cattle to Sudan and tend the acacia trees in the region that produces gum arabic (q.v.). The préfecture's school attendance rate is extremely low at 2.8 percent. The semidesert Biltine was hard hit by the Sahelian droughts in the 1970s and 1980s, which destituted many of its nomadic groups.

BIR ALALI. A Senoussi (see SANUSIYA) *zawaya* (q.v.) founded in 1896 by Sidi Muhammad al-Barrani (q.v.) as a deep outpost in Kanem.

Attacked by French forces in 1901 during the occupation of Chad, Bir Alali was finally conquered in January 1902, when a force of over 600 troops was necessary to wrestle it from its defenders. The outpost was reconquered on December 4, 1902, by a combined force of 3,000 Awlad Sulayman (q.v.), Toubou (q.v.), and Tuareg (q.v.), but it was retaken in bloody fighting the very next day.

BIRGOU. Name of the Tunjur (q.v.) state in Ouadai (q.v.) prior to the Maba uprising led by Abd-el-Kerim (q.v.) that expelled the Tunjur in 1611.

BIRKED. Important ethnic group in neighboring Darfur, Sudan, a segment of which resides west of Dar Sila in Chad. Virtually indistinguishable from the Daju (q.v.) and speaking a language practically identical to that of the Moubi (q.v.), their precise numbers in Chad have been difficult to assess.

BIRNI NGAZARGAMO. Capital of the powerful Bornu (q.v.) Empire. Founded around 1484 following the expulsion of the Sefuwa (q.v.) Magumi (q.v.) from Kanem and their relocation west of Lake Chad (see KANEM-BORNU EMPIRE). Birni Ngazargamo ("the walled fortress" in Hausa) remained Bornu's capital until 1814. In 1808 the town was conquered and razed by Fulani and Hausa elements revolting against Bornuan overlordship and as part of the widespread jihad in the region. After the fate of Bornu was stabilized by Muhammad al-Amin al-Kanemi (q.v.), the new capital of the kingdom, Kukawa (q.v.), was founded some distance away in 1814. Birni Ngazargamo was surrounded by a circular wall about two kilometers in diameter, and at the center of the town stood the *mai*'s (q.v.) palace. Little more is known about the appearance of the city, though some ruins still remain 177 kilometers (110 miles) northwest of Maiduguri in northern Nigeria.

BISSO, MAMADOU. Former director general of Chad's electricity and water board. Bisso was also a leader of the Rassemblement pour la Démocratie et le Progrès (RDP) (q.v.), an unauthorized party of Kanembu from the Lake Chad and Kanem regions. Bisso was himself a Kanembu. Since this was the area from which Hissène Habré (q.v.) mounted his armed assault against the Idriss Déby (q.v.) regime early in 1992, Bisso was one of 60 people arrested in N'Djamena in February 1992 by Déby's infamous CRCR (q.v.) secret police and executed on suspicion of being in alliance with Habré's insurrection and his MDD (q.v.) party. Most knowledgeable commentators claim that Bisso was not involved with Habré's MDD.

BITANGUI, LAURENT (1927–). High-level administrator. Born in Am-Timan on August 3, 1927, and educated locally and abroad, Bitangui served in several top-level positions in the François Tombalbaye (q.v.) administration. He was secretary-general of the National Assembly (1961–63), director of internal affairs in the Ministry of Interior (1963–67), Government General Delegate for N'Djamena (1964–71), and again director of Interior (1971–75).

BITKINE. Small town in the souspréfecture of the same name in the Guéra Préfecture. With a population of 4,000, Bitkine holds an important weekly market that draws purchasers from Sarh and herders from Ati.

BLACK SHEEP PLOT, 1973. An alleged political sorcery plot led by Mrs. Kalthouma Guembang (q.v.), head of the women's section of the ruling party, the Parti Progressiste Tchadien (PPT) (q.v.). Also involved in the plot were several military figures, including General Félix Malloum (q.v.). The plot was allegedly aimed at toppling President François Tombalbaye (q.v.) and involved sorcery and magic, taking the form of the burial alive of a black sheep and the casting of spells that were supposed to eject Tombalbaye from power. All those involved in the ceremony were arrested in June 1973 and, after some delay, were put on trial for the plot and for maintaining contact with FROLINAT (q.v.). When their trial resulted in what Tombalbaye felt were very short prison sentences, the plotters were about to be retried (on the grounds of "errors" on the part of the jurists) when the coup d'état of 1975 intervened. All the prisoners were then promptly released and Malloum was made head of state.

BLOC DEMOCRATIQUE TCHADIEN (BDT). Small political nucleus founded by Jean Charlot Bakouré (q.v.) that soon merged with the Parti Progressiste Tchadien (PPT) (q.v.). (See also POLITICAL PARTIES.)

BLOC DES TRAVAILLEURS DEMOCRATES TCHADIENS (BTDT). List for the 1956 French National Assembly elections headed by trade union militant Jean Charlot Bakouré (q.v.) and Ahmet Mahamat Saleh (q.v.), a former student at Al-Azhar. The radical platform of the BTDT evoked little mass response in Chad. The party obtained only 4,843 votes in the 1956 elections, compared to the 130,843 cast for Gabriel Lisette's (q.v.) Union Tchadienne (q.v.), with which the BTDT soon merged.

BLOC TCHADIEN (BT). Electoral list headed by Bechir Sow (q.v.) for the 1956 French National Assembly elections in the second electoral college. The conservative BT emerged from the splintering of the

Union Démocratique du Tchad (q.v.) and its transformation into the Action Sociale Tchadienne (q.v.). Very much an isolated, personalist, and small electoral ticket, the party fared poorly and Bechir Sow himself was defeated in his bid for reelection. The BT obtained the lowest number of votes and disappeared shortly thereafter.

BODELE DEPRESSION. Huge depression well below the level of Lake Chad, with which it is connected via the Bahr-el-Ghazal (q.v.) riverbed valley. The depression stretches from a tongue near Faya-Largeau (q.v.) in Tibesti (q.v.) and encompasses much of the Tibesti-Kanem border. The Neolithic times Lake Chad (then a large sea) covered a much larger area and flowed through the Bahr-el-Ghazal to the Bodélé depression and was probably also connected indirectly with the Nile basin system. As late as 500 B.C., merchants from ancient Carthage journeyed to this general area to trade with the then well-populated and much wetter region. (See also ARCHAEOLOGY; BAHR-EL-GHAZAL; LAKE CHAD.)

BOHIADI, BRUNO see DORALTA, DJIRAIBAYE

BOISSONS ET GLACIERES DU TCHAD (BGT). Private bottling company set up with French capital in 1971 in N'Djamena. Capitalized at 100 million CFA francs, the plant had an annual production capacity of 20,000 hl of soft drinks and ice. The facilities were badly damaged in the battles that raged in N'Djamena from 1978 to 1982. The plant was renamed in 1982 Boissons Gazeuses du Tchad.

BOKORO. Souspréfecture covering 17,000 square kilometers (6,560 square miles) with headquarters in the village with the same name, part of the préfecture of Chari-Baguirmi. Bokoro is also an important garrison town, 313 kilometers (194 miles) east of N'Djamena. Units from Bokoro were involved in the first attack on François Tombalbaye (q.v.) during the 1975 coup d'état. (See Coup of April 13, 1975.)

BOL. Administrative headquarters of the Lac Préfecture (q.v.) and its Bol souspréfecture. A small town of some 1,500 inhabitants on a peninsula in Lake Chad, Bol is populated mostly by Buduma (q.v.), Kanuri (q.v.), and Kanembu (q.v.). The region and town were captured several times by pro-Habré (q.v.) troops fighting the Déby (q.v.) government in N'Djamena in 1992.

BOLTOU. Common ancestor of many of the subclans of the Anakaza (q.v.) group of the Daza of Borkou.

BONGOR. Important southern town and the administrative headquarters of the Mayo-Kebbi Préfecture (q.v.) and the Bongor souspréfecture within it. The latter encompasses a territory of 11,500 square kilometers (4,400 square miles) and a population of 120,000. Around 20,000 of the souspréfecture's population live in Bongor proper (1994 estimates), making the town Chad's sixth largest urban center, after N'Djamena, Sarh, Moundou, Abéché, and Kélo. Formerly part of German Cameroon, Bongor is on the Logone River (q.v.), which links it with N'Djamena by barge for several months during the year. An important, vibrant, developing center, Bongor is some 300 kilometers (185 miles) from Moundou and 230 kilometers (143 miles) from N'Djamena. The souspréfecture is bounded on the east and west by the Chari and Logone Rivers, which carry alluvial soil that floods over part of the rainy season, making all travel impossible. Indeed, part of the préfecture is totally submerged between July and December. The first European to penetrate and explore the region was Heinrich Barth (q.v.) in 1852, followed in 1854 by Vogel and in 1872 by Gustav Nachtigal (q.v.). The region was not fully explored or delimited until 1910, partly because of the difficult communications in the region. The main groups in the district are various Sara (q.v.) clans (but overwhelmingly the Massa [q.v.]), and some Barma, Arabs, and Fulani (qq.v.). Bongor was the center of Gabriel Lisette's (q.v.) political base and a prime holdout against the north in the civil-military struggles from 1978 to 1982. It was finally delivered to Hissène Habré (q.v.) in August 1982, after the garrison refused to put up a fight against dissident FAT (q.v.) troops under Major Zamtato and Lt. Colonel Rodai (qq.v.), who had declared themselves in opposition to the separatist policies of Colonel Kamougoué (q.v.), the de facto strongman of the south. Following the entry of FAN (q.v.) troops into Bongor, a series of atrocities and settling of accounts greatly embittered the local population.

BONO, OUTEL (Dr.) (1934–1973). Prominent and vocal critic of President François Tombalbaye (q.v.). He was assassinated in a Paris street in 1973. Born in Fort-Archambault in 1934, Bono studied medicine in France, and when he set up his practice in Fort-Lamy in 1962 he was Chad's second indigenous doctor (the other was Dr. Baroum, q.v.). Earlier Bono had been a member of the Union Nationale Tchadienne (q.v.), precursor of FROLINAT (q.v.). Of Sara origins, and increasingly popular among the urban youth and intellectuals, Bono rapidly became leader of the Young Turks in the National Assembly and the PPT (q.v.) Political Bureau, to which he had been appointed shortly after his arrival from France. His uncautious criticism of the regime brought about his arrest in March 1963 (barely two months after he was integrated into the PPT) and in a secret trial before the Cour Criminelle Spéciale he was condemned to death for plotting the overthrow of Tombalbaye. International pressure secured the commuting of Bono's sentence to 15 years' imprisonment in January 1965 and his amnesty in August 1965. For a while avoiding politics, Bono worked as director of public health, attached also to Fort-Lamy's hospital. His notoriously poor relations with Tombalbaye brought about his second arrest in May 1969 for a strong vocal criticism of Chad's cotton policies (which benefited especially chiefs and officials but not farmers), the continued presence of French troops in Chad, the attempt to quell the rebellions (q.v.) in the country through military means, and Tombalbaye's "paranoiac" style of leadership. At his trial it was revealed that Bono had been in contact with Dr. Abba Siddick (q.v.) and other FROLINAT (q.v.) leaders, though Bono was definitely opposed to Siddick's attempt to impose FROLINAT's Muslim and socialist solution on Chad. He was categorized by Tombalbaye as "an element of disorder that should disappear to leave the country at peace." Sentenced to five years' imprisonment (his criticism had been open, at a public meeting in Fort-Lamy's Cultural Center), Bono was again soon amnestied but also placed under constant police surveillance. Though reappointed to his old medical posts, he left Chad in July 1972 allegedly to undertake refresher medical courses at the Sapetrière Hospital in Paris; in reality the trip was also intended to allow him further contact with FROLINAT (which did not lead to any mutual understandings, however) and the solidification of his political support abroad prior to the launching of a southern-based opposition movement to Tombalbaye. His popularity among students and intellectuals abroad still unabated, it was announced in mid-1973 that the Mouvement Démocratique de la Rénovation Tchadienne (MDRT) (q.v.) would be formally launched on August 27. The day before, Bono was intercepted in the Bastille area of Paris and assassinated. The murder, never fully solved, has usually been attributed to Tombalbaye agents, probably working with the tacit but unofficial support of the French secret service. Tombalbaye has claimed that internal MDRT splits had resulted in the killing, though early in 1975 Tombalbaye accused his longtime aide Georges Diguimbayé of the murder. The return of Bono's body to Chad was refused by the government, and he was buried in his French wife's hometown.

BONOSSOLA, MOUSTAPHA PHILLIPE (1918–1974). Former deputy, entrepreneur, and unionist. Born in Faya-Largeau on October 18, 1918, and originally a sanitary worker and male nurse, Bonossola became an important trader and union leader in Salamat. Director of the Fishermen's Cooperative in Salamat and Moyen-Chari, Bonossola won election to the National Assembly in 1957 and was reelected through 1969. In the assembly, he served as president of the Committee on Transport and Economics.

BORKOU. Central B.E.T. (q.v.) souspréfecture with administrative headquarters in Faya-Largeau (q.v.), and the capital of the préfecture. Covering an immense area of 250,000 square kilometers (96,500 square miles), with a population of 32,000, Borkou's population density is 0.1 per square kilometer, the second lowest in B.E.T. and in Chad. Though a desert—of great beauty and natural tourist potentials—where rain may not fall for 10 years at a time, subterranean water is frequently close to the surface, a fact utilized by its seminomadic Toubou (q.v.) population, some 7,000 of whom are Teda (q.v.), the rest Daza (q.v.). The region is swept for most of the year by violent dry northeasterly winds. Unsettled to this day, and unsafe since the Toubou rebellion began in the mid-1960s, Borkou was the crossing point for caravan routes (q.v.) connecting Libya with Ouadai. Occupied by French troops in 1913, Faya-Largeau was France's most important military base in B.E.T. and is still a major garrison town.

BORKOU-ENNEDI-TIBESTI (B.E.T.) PREFECTURE. Huge northern préfecture (usually referred to by its acronym) that encompasses fully half of Chad. Including 600,350 square kilometers (231,800 square miles) (much larger than Cameroon and roughly the size of the Central African Republic), B.E.T. is very sparsely populated with 110,000 people (density of 0.2 per square kilometer), most of whom are seminomadic Toubou (q.v.). Divided into three large souspréfectures—Borkou, Ennedi, and Tibesti—B.E.T. is the only part of Chad to have been under continuous military administration throughout the colonial era. Indeed, French forces did not vacate the area at Chad's independence but five years later (January 23, 1965), at which time Chadian forces and administrators took over. The latter's heavy-handed, corrupt, and inept administration—interacting with the proud, traditionally independent, and aggressive Toubou—is now acknowledged to have been the root cause of the Toubou rebellion that eventually led to northern-dominated regimes in N'Djamena.

    B.E.T. was the center of extensive prehistoric habitation at the edge of a previously much larger Lake Chad (q.v.). Cave drawings and engravings in the area (over 500 in Ennedi) depict tropical wildlife now extinct and ancient contact with peoples from the north (see ARCHAEOLOGY). B.E.T. was also the focal crossroads for several major trans-Saharan caravan routes (q.v.) connecting the Fezzan (Libya) with Kanem-Bornu (q.v.) and Ouadai (q.v.). Prior to the arrival of the French, the region had military outposts of the Sanusiya (q.v.) order, and later, small Turkish garrisons. (See also AIN GALAKKA; TURKEY.)

B.E.T. was only effectively occupied by France in 1913–14 and was not completely pacified until 1922. Its exploration and delineation lasted until 1936, and there are still some areas not fully mapped.

The huge territory (part of which had been attached to the Afrique Occidentale Française federation in the past) used to be administered from Faya-Largeau (q.v.) by a military prefect to whom were attached three subprefects for the constituent souspréfectures and some 100 civil servants, mostly from the south. The French never regarded B.E.T. as governable, due to the population's general unwillingness to come into contact with Western influence, and the colonial administration merely tried to keep the region peaceful, the caravan trails open, and the intermittent banditry within manageable proportions. Shortly after France handed over effective control of the area to Chadian administrators in 1965, a series of crude and overbearing actions by the latter resulted in the disaffection of the traditionally anarchic and highly independent Toubou and the onset of the rebellion that still simmers on. (See also BARDAI INCIDENTS, 1965; DERDE.) B.E.T. changed hands numerous times during the civil strife in Chad, but with the ouster of Libya from the region (and from Aouzou, q.v.), and Goukouni having renounced armed struggle in 1988, the region has been largely at peace, though still at a high level of "normal" unruliness.

Agriculturally the B.E.T. Préfecture is largely barren. It has some date and palm groves and vegetable gardens in the oases, with small herds of camels, sheep, and cattle being raised by the Toubou. Some salt mines (see NATRON) were formerly exploited extensively, but these are now of little importance. Existing tracks are constantly swept over by sandstorms and are in general very arduous to the uninitiated, especially given the huge distances involved. N'Djamena, for example, is 1090 kilometers (676 miles) from Faya-Largeau; from there, it is still 2550 kilometers (1580 miles) to Tripoli, 735 kilometers (456 miles) to Bardai (q.v.), and 410 kilometers (254 miles) to Fada (q.v.). The moonlike landscape of B.E.T. is breathtaking, though, and together with the cave paintings in the region serves as a magnet for the venturesome. Some of the world's wildest scenery is found in this part of Chad, which in more settled times could serve as a springboard for a major tourist industry.

BORNU. Former southernmost region of the Kanem Empire, Bornu became a powerful trading empire centered west of Lake Chad (currently in Nigeria) and dominating Kanem and the trade routes to the north. (See also CARAVAN ROUTES; FEZZAN-BORNU TRAIL; KANEM-BORNU EMPIRE.) Originating as a small Zaghawa (q.v.) principality in Kanem, the ruling dynasty—the Sefuwa (q.v.) Magumi (q.v.)—were expelled to the west in the fourteenth century by the Bulala (q.v.). There the new kingdom flourished, eventually to regain control over Kanem. Early in the nineteenth century Bornu began to crumble under the onslaught of the Fulani (q.v.) invasions but was saved by the leadership of Mohammad al-Amin al-Kanemi (q.v.) and of his son, Umar al-Kanemi (q.v.), who eventually eliminated the Sefuwa dynasty. Currently Bornu is an emirate in the North-East state of Nigeria. The Shehu (q.v.) resides in Yerwa.

BORORO. Nomadic Fulani (q.v.) who rarely stay more than a few days in one location. In the dry season they are found in Mayo-Kebbi (in the vicinity of Bongor), and with the onset of the rainy season they migrate to a region north of Lake Chad in Kanem. The Bororo rarely intermarry with other groups and they have largely remained impervious to outside influences.

BOUA. Aggressive ethnic group centered on their traditional capital at Korbol and patterned after the kingdom of Baguirmi (q.v.). Residing along the Chari River, the Boua utilized Baguirmi's decline to declare their suzerainty, setting up links with the Ouadai kingdom (q.v.) to the east. Their kingdom has a king list of 10 rulers; during Rabah's conquests in the region the Boua were not vanquished.

BOUKAR, ABDOU NANASBAYE (1934–). Diplomat. Born in 1934 and educated locally and at the Ecole Nationale d'Administration in Paris, Boukar was at the outset self-employed and later taught for a few years (1953–59) before beginning his diplomatic career. He undertook a diplomatic internship in Paris (1960), served as First Secretary at France's Consulate in Kano, Nigeria (1960–61), and was subsequently appointed Chad's ambassador to Nigeria (1961–64). In April 1964 he was transferred to New York, where he served as ambassador to the United States and representative to the United Nations (1964–68). For a short time later he served as executive secretary-general of the Union des Etats de l'Afrique Centrale (UEAC) (q.v.), and in 1969 he was appointed as Chad's ambassador to the Soviet Union. He served in that capacity until 1974, when he was repatriated to N'Djamena and appointed permanent secretary of the Ministry of Foreign Affairs. In 1979 he became minister of information but lost the post with the rise of the Hissène Habré (q.v.) regime.

BOUKAR, MALLOUM MAHAMAD. Coleader of the First Liberation Army (q.v.) under Mahamat Seid Abba (q.v.) until 1979, Boukar was one of the early "Cairo students" on the secret committee of 1965–66 that led to the establishment of FROLINAT (q.v.). In 1977 he headed the short-lived Conseil Provisoire de la Révolution (CPR) (q.v.) that confirmed Abba Siddick's (q.v.) ouster—and his replacement by Boukar—and the unification of the FROLINAT factions under Goukouni (q.v.).

BOUKAR, OUMAR. President of the Action pour le Renouveau du Tchad, a small political party founded in January 1993.

BOULE. National food in Chad. A farina cake served with a variety of sauces.

BOURDAMI, ABDERAHMANE (Captain) (1956–1990). Feared head of Hissène Habré's (q.v.) presidential security unit who died in the fighting against Idriss Déby's (q.v.) insurgency in eastern Chad in November 1990.

BOURKOU, LOUISE (1934–). Party militant. Born in Sarh on July 5, 1934, a schoolteacher by profession, Louise Bourkou was an early militant of the Parti Progressiste Tchadien (PPT) (q.v.) and a leader of the party's women's branch. In 1962 she was first elected deputy to the National Assembly and served as rapporteur of its Social Affairs Committee. Her mandate as deputy was one of the very few to be renewed in 1969, and she continued to serve in the assembly until the 1975 coup d'état.

BOUSSO. Souspréfecture covering 14,000 square kilometers (5,400 square miles), with some 20,000 people, with administrative headquarters in the village of the same name; part of the préfecture of Chari-Baguirmi (q.v.).

BRAHIM, MAHAMAT (1927–). Party militant. Born in 1927 in Isseirou of a chiefly family, Brahim joined the Kanem branch of the Parti Progressiste Tchadien (PPT) (q.v.) and was elected to the National Assembly in March 1957. There he served in a variety of posts, including as president of the assembly, and became one of the few deputies to last out the turbulent purges of the mid-1960s.

BRAHIM, YOUSSOUF. One of Goukouni's (q.v.) prime lieutenants in the 1970s. He disappeared in 1980 and is presumed to have been liquidated by the Libyans over the counsel he gave to Goukouni to avoid entanglement with Tripoli.

BRAHIM SEID, JOSEPH see SEID, JOSEPH BRAHIM

BRASSERIES DU LOGONE. Beer and soft-drinks factory founded in Moundou on January 14, 1965, with 800 million CFA francs private capital. The capacity of the plant was twice augmented, in 1971 and in 1986, to satisfy strong local demand.

BUDUMA. Large Yedina (q.v.) subgroup numbering around 23,000 and inhabiting the islands and peninsulas of Lake Chad in the Bol district (qq.v.). Their name derives from their ancestor Boulou, a Kanembu (q.v.) of Fulani (q.v.) origin and his Sao (q.v.) wife in the fifteenth century. The Buduma have remained isolated, of their own volition, from outside (and Islamic) influences and speak a language derived from Kotoko (q.v.) or ancient Sao. Their principal activity is fishing in distinctively styled pirogues and stockbreeding.

BULALA (also BILALA). Ethnic group of Arab ancestry that derives its name from the leader (Balal) of a segment of the Kanembu (q.v.) who organized to oppose the hold of the Sefuwa (q.v.) Magumi (q.v.) dynasty in Kanem, toppling it in 1356 and driving it into Bornu (q.v.) in 1380 and reigning in its place for some 120 years. Currently the Bulala are found in the vicinity of Lake Fitri (q.v.) around their capital of Yao (q.v.), though some elements are also found in Massakory, in the east in Oum-Hadjer, and as nomads among the Daza (q.v.), with whom they are at times confused. Intermixed also with the Kukawa (near Ati), Medogo, and other groups, the Bulala were estimated in the mid-1950s to number around 35,000, though with other clans with whom they have become assimilated they numbered 205,000. Following their brief reign in Kanem, the Bulala dynasty collapsed under the impact of the renascent Bornu Empire. They later suffered from inroads by Baguirmi, Ouadai, and the Tunjur and were eventually displaced primarily to the area around Yao, where they established a small sultanate. No longer speaking Kanembu but a local Kouka dialect, all remain fairly conversant with Arabic. The Bulala are essentially agricultural farmers raising millet, maize, and cotton. There is also some stockbreeding and fishing. Though nominally Muslim, the Bulala also practice a variety of pre-Islamic rites.

BURA-MABANG. Language of the Maba (q.v.) clans of Ouadai. (See also MABA.)

BUREAU DES AFFAIRES MUSULMANES. Department in the French administration under the overall direction of Military Intelligence and in charge, since 1927, of preparing reports on Islam in Chad. Among those that have remained secret are investigations of the distribution of popular support for the different orders, studies of the content of Muslim (Koranic) education, and so on. Most of the researchers in Chad were nonnationals, many from Algeria or other Maghrebian areas. Underlying this research was the French fear of the resurgence of an anti-French Muslim movement under some charismatic leader. Efforts were made by the administration to reinforce existing domestic interorder cleavages, to isolate Chadian Islam from outside influences, and to favor the pro-establishment Tidjaniya (q.v.) order.

-C-

CABOT, JEAN. Former vice-chancellor of the University of N'Djamena (q.v.) and former dean of the Vincennes Faculty of the Université de Paris and professor of geography at Chad's Collège de Bongor.

CAISSE CENTRALE DE COOPERATION ECONOMIQUE (CCCE). Official French agency through which French governmental aid to francophone Africa is channeled, banked, and administered. Successor to the Caisse Centrale de la France d'Outre-Mer (CCFOM), and itself later renamed the Caisse Française de Développement (CFD). As an example of the levels of funding Chad has secured, usually via Banque de Développement du Tchad (BDT) (q.v.) for infusion into government-approved projects, between 1960 and 1971 the sum of 68,119 million French francs was disbursed to Chad, and between 1989 and 1994 the sum of 12 billion CFA francs.

CAISSE CENTRALE DE LA FRANCE D'OUTRE-MER (CCFOM) see CAISSE CENTRALE DE COOPERATION ECONOMIQUE (CCCE)

CAISSE DE STABILISATION DES PRIX DU COTON (CSPC). Price stabilization fund for cotton. The organization fixes prices paid to Chad's producers, taking into account world market prices and the costs of collecting and exporting the produce. Profits or losses are shared jointly by the CSPC and Cotontchad (q.v.) according to percentages established in a complex formula.

CAISSE DES DEPOTS ET CONSIGNATIONS (CDC). Official French agency that serves as banker, administrator, and manager of francophone Africa's pension, national security, and other social welfare programs.

CAISSE FRANÇAISE DE DEVELOPPEMENT (CFD) see CAISSE CENTRALE DE COOPERATION ECONOMIQUE (CCCE).

CAMP KOUFRA. Important military headquarters in the center of N'Djamena.

CANTON. Basic administrative unit encompassing a number of villages. (See also ADMINISTRATIVE ORGANIZATION.)

CARAVAN ROUTES. Dating from remote antiquity, the trans-Saharan routes through Chad connect various points in the Maghreb with terminals on the other side of the Sahara desert. The rise and fall in the importance of these terminals has been directly related to the level of general security of the routes. As early as 1000 B.C. the trails were used by chariots and caravans making the voyage from the north with the ancient Carthaginians sending expeditions to control and monopolize the trans-Saharan trade. The Garamantian route (q.v.), linking Tripoli, Fezzan, and Bornu, was by far the most important, with traffic reaching its height during the sixteenth century as a consequence of the safety of the voyage that was secured by the powerful Bornu and Songhai Empires. With the destruction of Songhai in the 1590s by Morocco's el-Mansur and the slow decay in Bornuan power in the seventeenth century, the trail progressively became prey to marauding Tuareg (q.v.) and other groups. Until the 1820s the route nevertheless remained the most popular one due to the good relations between Tripoli and Bornu. The fall of the Karamanli dynasty (q.v.) in Tripoli and the decline of Bornu under the Fulani (q.v.) assaults brought about a total drying up of traffic and the shift of the caravan trails to the east. (Indeed the Tripoli-Bornu route was practically closed between 1830 and 1842.) In the nineteenth century the two most important trans-Saharan routes were those connecting Ghadames to Kano (to the west, reflecting the rise of the Fulani Empire) and the Cyrenaica-Kufra-Ouadai route that replaced the unsafe Tripoli-Bornu route. Though Ouadai had some difficulty maintaining the security of the trail in its immediate north, the conversion of the Awlad Sulayman and elements of the Toubou to the Sanusiya (qq.v.) order brought about a dramatic improvement, and the trail was extensively used until the French occupation of the region. Among the non-trans-Saharan trails in the region, the most important connected Sokoto or Kano to Kukawa (q.v.) and on to Goulfei (or other Kotoko [q.v.] centers on the Chari River) and via Massenya (q.v.) to Abéché. The most dangerous stretch on this trail was the much-disputed territory between the Baguirmi and Ouadai kingdoms, where local villages pillaged passing caravans. The route continued from Abéché to the Nile at Wad Medani (via Darfur, q.v.). From there routes branched off either to the north to Omdurman (Khartoum) or south to Suakin, or through Eritrea to Massawa, from which pilgrims (q.v.) could cross the Red Sea to Jedda in Saudi Arabia. (See also FEZZAN-BORNU TRAIL; GARMANTIAN ROUTE.)

CATHOLIC MISSIONS see CHRISTIAN MISSIONS

CATTLE. Until the Sahelian droughts of the 1970s and 1980s Chad had one of Black Africa's largest herds, estimated in 1972 at around 4.7 million head. Most of them of the zebu (q.v.) variety, some 85 percent of the herd was found in the Kanem, Chari-Baguirmi, Batha, and Ouadai Préfectures (qq.v.). Chad's livestock in general suffered less from the drought than hard-hit Niger and Mauritania, with much of the herd being evacuated to the south away from the worst areas of drought. Still, over 15 percent of Chad's cattle perished in the north in the 1970s and a similar percentage probably died from diseases contracted in the southern tsetse-infected regions. Many young and pregnant cattle were, moreover, sold to Nigeria in an effort to salvage at least some profits from the rapidly diminished herds. Currently the herd is estimated at around 4 million, after further losses in 1984 and 1985. Cattle exports have traditionally been Chad's second most important cash-economy activity, after cotton production. Between one-half and three-quarters of the cattle exported on the hoof do not appear in official figures, being driven (especially) north of Lake Chad via Rig Rig to Nigeria and Niger, where they are sold through traditional channels. Chadian border patrols have been inadequate in their efforts to redirect this trade through official channels. Thus in 1970 Chad "officially" exported 31,761 head of cattle, though the true figure probably stood in the vicinity of 150,000.

The size of the Chadian herds of cattle has sparked efforts to develop frozen meat exports to neighboring countries where the widespread presence of the tsetse fly has stultified meat production. Exports from the Abattoir Frigorifique de Farcha (q.v.) and similar plants in Sarh and Abéché were at the outset gratifying, but they rapidly declined. The N'Djamena plant, for example, exported 48 tons in 1948 and over 15,000 tons in 1971 before exports plummeted. The Abéché plant engaged in exports only between 1950 and 1958. The ambitious Sarh abattoir, which included a refrigerated slaughterhouse with a capacity for 36,000 head of cattle per year, a tannery, and a shoe factory, had to close down completely in 1971, and since it reopened it has operated significantly beneath capacity. Since 1990 its exports have been virtually nil, even though it had primarily been aimed at the export trade. Part of the problem has been the preference of cattle raisers to sell their stock illicitly for much higher prices than those offered by the government, and the disruption of communications as a consequence of the rebellion in Chad's cattle-raising préfectures. (See also LIVESTOCK.)

CENTRE DE COORDINATION ET D'EXPLOITATION DU RENSEIGNEMENT (CCER). Chad's intelligence division, formerly headed by a French national, Major Camille Gourvenac (q.v.), whose aid was of crucial importance for the success of the 1975 coup d'état. Little is known about the operations of the CCER, besides its normal secret-service functions. Gourvenac's immediate ouster was a specific condition demanded by Hissène Habré (q.v.) when invited to join the Félix Malloum (q.v.) administration in 1978.

CENTRE DE MODERNISATION DES PRODUITS ANIMAUX (CMPA). State organ set up in 1984, but existing in different forms previously, aimed at encouraging and marketing poultry and dairy farming. Though highly subsidized by the state, CMPA was unable to penetrate private purchasing networks and closed down in 1990.

CENTRE DE RECHERCHES ET DE LA COORDINATION DES REN-SEIGNEMENTS (CRCR). Idriss Déby's (q.v.) brutal secret police. Set up in May 1991 six months after Déby marched into N'Djamena, and including personnel of Hissène Habré's (q.v.) disbanded secret police, the DDS (q.v.), the CRCR was originally headed by veteran police inspector Abderaman Abou Moussa. The CRCR started from the outset a crackdown on former Habré sympathizers and power barons and then expanded it to include leaders of opposition groups as well. The arrests and killings were so brutal that when the Conférence Nationale (q.v.) convened in 1993, the disbanding of the CRCR was the subject of one of its resolutions. Déby implemented the disbanding of the CRCR, but a new organ, the Agence Nationale de Sécurité (ANS) (q.v.), sprang up in its place, much with the same mission and personnel.

CERDEGUA. One of the oldest established Teda clans in Tibesti, inhabiting an area north of Bardai, in the proximity of Zouia.

CFA FRANC see **COMMUNAUTE FINANCIERE AFRICAINE (CFA) FRANC**

CHAD BASIN COMMISSION see **COMMISSION DU BASSIN DU LAC TCHAD**

CHADALLAH, KAFINE (Lt. Colonel). Former deputy chief of staff during the early years of Idriss Déby's (q.v.) administration. Chadallah defected and went underground after the Abbas-Déby falling-out and resurfaced in Paris, where he has been since.

CHADITUDE see **CULTURAL REVOLUTION**

CHAMBRE DE COMMERCE, D'AGRICULTURE, ET D'INDUS-TRIE DE LA REPUBLIQUE DU TCHAD (CCAIT). Chamber of Commerce, founded in 1938 with headquarters in N'Djamena and branches in Sarh, Moundou, and Abéché.

CHAPELLE, JEAN (Colonel) (1905–). Former French colonial officer and administrator, author, and former deputy director of INTSH (q.v.). Born in 1905 in Sète, graduating from the elite Saint Cyr academy in 1927, Chapelle began his military career in Mauritania, Mali, Niger, and Chad. He spent 17 years in Chad, including five as prefect of B.E.T.

until independence. In 1963 he was appointed deputy director of INTSH and curator of the Musée National Tchadien. In the last four years before his departure in 1974 his post was localized but he remained as consultant. His writings on Chad's northern populations (especially the Toubou [q.v.]) are much acclaimed.

CHARI RIVER. Chad's principal north-flowing river, 1,200 kilometers (750 miles) long. Formed by the union of the Gribingui, the Bamingui, and the Bahr Sara (rising in the Central African Republic), the Chari forms its first delta at Sarh, where it receives the Bahr Salamat (q.v.). Fed by heavy rains in the Central African Republic and in Cameroon, the Chari is navigable between Sarh and N'Djamena between August and December (on occasion between July and February). Between June and November the Chari overflows its banks, inundating huge areas of land known locally as *yaéré*. Extensive fishing activities are then conducted by the various ethnic groups inhabiting the Chari basin, and this is the principal economic activity of the season. Between N'Djamena—where the Logone River (q.v.) joins the Chari—and Lake Chad, the Chari-Logone forms the Chad-Cameroon border and is navigable year-round. This section is an important riverine venue for the export of dried fish and natron.

CHARI-BAGUIRMI PREFECTURE. The préfecture encompasses an area of 82,910 square kilometers (32,012 square miles) and a population of 844,000, giving it a population density of 10.2 per square kilometer. (The préfecture's population has nearly doubled since the 1970s. It is divided into five souspréfectures (N'Djamena-rural, Bokoro, Bousso, Massakory, and Massenya), and its administrative headquarters is in N'Djamena. The préfecture essentially covers most of the former Baguirmi kingdom (q.v.). Its population is a mixture of Barma, Fulani, Arab, Kotoko, Tunjur, and Kanembu (qq.v.). Including as it does the capital of Chad, N'Djamena, the préfecture is the nerve center of the nation. Its main rural products are millet, fish, cattle (exported on the hoof illicitly to Nigeria), meat products, and groundnuts. Except for roads leading out of N'Djamena (which rapidly deteriorate within short distances from the capital), communications are very unreliable during the rainy season, though they tend to be maintained much better than in outlying préfectures. N'Djamena is also linked for varying periods of the season by river with Sarh and Bongor. Until the recent drought the préfecture had the third largest cattle herd in Chad. The rate of school attendance (22.6 percent) is median between the south and the north and east of the country. Part of the higher figure here is, however, a reflection of the vicinity to N'Djamena.

CHARI-LOGONE. Name of the stretch of the Chari (q.v.) and Logone (q.v.) Rivers that join the N'Djamena and jointly flow into Lake Chad (q.v.).

CHARLOT, JEAN see BAKOURE, SOHOLLOT

CHARTE FONDAMENTALE. Interim constitution that brought about the dissolution of the Conseil Supérieur Militaire (q.v.) of the Chad Army (under Félix Malloum [q.v.]) and the CCFAN of Hissène Habré (qq.v.). The August 25, 1978, charter set up a bicephalous executive (with Malloum as president and Habré as prime minister), a Conseil de Défense et de Sécurité (CDS) (q.v.) with equal CSM and CCFAN membership (eight each), and a consultative body of 16 representatives, from all préfectures, called the Conseil National d'Union (CNU) (q.v.). Feuding between Malloum and Habré led to the collapse of the government and the entry into the capital of the northern armies of Goukouni (q.v.).

CHEKNA. Actual name of the town currently carrying the name Massenya (q.v.), historical capital of the Baguirmi kingdom (q.v.) and administrative headquarters of the Chari-Baguirmi Préfecture.

CHEMIN DE FER DU CONGO-OCEAN (CFCO). Railroad entirely within the People's Republic of Congo, linking its capital, Brazzaville, with its Atlantic port of Pointe-Noire. The CFCO was built between 1922 and 1934 at great fiscal and human cost. Some 125,000 laborers worked on the line, with some 10 percent of them perishing in the process. Large numbers of Sara (q.v.) from Chad were pressed into *corvée* (q.v.) labor for its construction. The railroad currently carries around 3,150,000 tons of goods per year over its 515 kilometers (320 miles) of rails (including a 1962 spur). Sine 1969 it has been managed by the Agence Transcongolaise des Communications (ATEC). The line is extensively used by both the Central African Republic and Chad for the evacuation of their produce and the importation of their needs. Part of Chad's cotton crop and other southern-produced commodities are hauled by truck via Sarh to Bangui (qq.v.) and floated down the Oubangui River to Brazzaville for transshipment to Pointe-Noire. If the Trans-Cameroonian railroad (q.v.) is extended to Chad (as has been talked about for over a decade) the importance of the CFCO to Chad may dramatically decline.

CHIEF. There has always been a major distinction in Chad between the powerful northern chiefs and sultans—including those of Ouadai, Baguirmi, and Kanem (qq.v.)—and the chiefs in the south, especially in Sara areas. The latter have usually been of the village variety with few real powers. Until 1920 the French had no unified policy vis-à-vis traditional authority, though chiefs were routinely relied upon as surrogate rulers, especially in Muslim areas. In the 1930s some of the powers of the chiefs in southern areas were augmented, and new chiefs were imposed artificially, usually to provide better direction to the drive to spread cotton cultivation throughout the territory. This led to an artificial increase in chiefly authority in the south, abuses of power, and growing popular disaffection (see CORDES DE CHEFS). In 1946 some chiefs were removed from office by the colonial administration, and in 1954 a Territorial Assembly statute sought to impose major reforms in the area of chiefly authority, though it was not implemented and the goals were lost sight of. During the early years of political activity in Chad many chiefs sat in the various organs set up (including the Assemblée Territoriale, q.v.) and were leaders of their respective parties. This was especially true for the conservative formations in Chad, such as the Union Démocratique du Chad (UDC) (q.v.), of which as many as 50 percent of the assembly deputies were of chiefly origin. When the Parti Progressiste Tchadien (PPT) (q.v.) rose to power in the late 1950s—and despite the fact that several prominent chiefs supported the party—new reforms were passed, leading to the 1963 edict removing from chiefs the power to raise taxes and denying their former right to serve as traditional justice of the peace in their fiefdoms. The reforms caused major disaffection among the populations of the former kingdoms and added fuel to the anti-N'Djamena rebellion in the countryside in the middle and late 1960s. So unpopular was the policy of curtailing chiefly authority in the north and center of Chad that the reinstatement of the powers of the sultans was a prime recommendation of the Mission de Réforme Administrative (q.v.); on September 24, 1969, the sultans of Ouadai, Kanem, and Baguirmi were reinstated, bringing the policy toward chiefs full circle. This was promptly reversed, however, after the 1975 coup d'état—when chiefly powers were "abolished" by edict—and the whole issue became academic in the late 1970s with the utter collapse of central authority.

CHOUA, LOL MAHAMAT (1939–). Briefly Chad's head of government, and more recently mayor of N'Djamena and president of the Conseil Supérieur de la Transition (CST) (q.v.), the transitional nonelected legislature of Chad. A Kanemi Arab born in Mao on June 15, 1939, and a labor inspector after studies in France, Lol continued his studies between 1971 and 1973 and then joined the Caisse Nationale de Prévoyance Sociale in N'Djamena. (He was one of the very few Kanembu to have received higher education in France.) He held this post, with no commitment to the opposition, at the time of the fall of the capital to Goukouni's (q.v.) forces. Only then did he join the Third Liberation Army (q.v.) and shortly later succeeded to its leadership after the eclipse of Aboubaker Abderahmane (q.v.). At the 1979 Kano conference he was Nigeria's compromise candidate and became president of GUNT (q.v.) and head of state of Chad, with Goukouni as his minister of interior and Hissène Habré (q.v.) as minister of defense. He was very much regarded as a protégé of Habré, and when the latter won N'Djamena from Goukouni, Choua was rewarded with the Ministry of Transport in 1982 and later was appointed ambassador to the Soviet Union. He subsequently became mayor of N'Djamena, serving until 1992, when he was removed from office by Idriss Déby (q.v.). A founder of the Rassemblement pour la Démocratie et le Progrès (RDP) (q.v.) party, he fled N'Djamena in January 1992 to avoid arrest but returned to participate in the 1993 Conférence Nationale (q.v.), where he was elected president of the CST, serving until October 1994. He was then defeated for a fourth term by a Déby candidate, Bachar Gadaya.

CHRISTIAN MISSIONS. The majority of the Christian missions in Chad are concentrated in the southern préfectures. Protestant evangelists arrived in the area first, around 1920, and established themselves in Léré, Fort-Archambault, and Doba in 1925 and in Fort-Lamy in 1926. Their utilization of the Sangho (q.v.) language of the Central African Republic for proselytizing purposes led to the 1964 edict banning the language in Chad. Catholic missionaries arrived in Chad around 1929 via the Logone and Moyen-Chari, reaching Fort-Lamy only in 1946. Figures of Chad's religious distribution (see RELIGION) have always greatly overestimated the Christian population, for in Sara (q.v.) areas large numbers profess Christianity for outward prestige while in essence remaining tied to traditional religion. (The extent of this was attested to by the enthusiasm with which many seized upon the 1973 popularization of the Yondo [q.v.] rites in the south.) This dichotomy is best visible in the statistics of private (Christian) education in the country. In the 1965/66 school year Protestant schools had 1,380 students and Catholic schools 18,980. In that year private education in Chad accounted for 12.4 percent of total pupils, or 20,360 of 163,962 pupils, while in other parts of francophone Africa the ratio has been closer to 50 percent. (See also EDUCATION; RELIGION.) Subject to this qualification, then, the number of Christians in Chad is estimated at around 29 percent of the population. The Catholic population is organized into the metropolitan archdiocese of N'Djamena, and the suffragette dioceses of Moundou, Pala, and Sarh.

CITE DU 28 NOVEMBRE. The modernistic complex of villas built in 1971 for the use of the heads of state attending the N'Djamena OCAM meeting. Originally known as the Cité de l'OCAM, the complex was renamed in honor of Chad's independence. It was heavily damaged during the Battle for N'Djamena (q.v.) as well as earlier during the exchange of fire attending the 1975 coup d'état.

CIVIL SERVICE. The number of civil servants in Chad has continuously increased over the years, consuming between 50 and 60 percent of the national budget. In June 1965 their number stood at 7,089; in June 1968 there were 9,245; in June 1970 their number had gone up to 9,640; and in 1975 there were 12,500 people on the public payroll (then roughly one-half of salaried workers in the country, and a 76 percent increase in numbers between 1965 and 1975). One year after the coup—in April 1976—this figure (despite alleged "austerity cuts" by the new military regime) had jumped to 13,464, and by 1978 there were 15,000.

The fall of N'Djamena to northern forces in 1978 saw a massive exodus of southerners to the southern préfectures—where they swelled the rolls of the regional civil service. For all practical purposes the disengagement of the Sara (q.v.) from N'Djamena brought about the end of central administration. Salaries were not paid to those few who did remain in the capital (or to those largely unqualified northerners hired to replace them); indeed, the first salaries since 1978 were only paid in June 1981, and only sporadically until around 1984. Essential services (water, electricity, sanitation, etc.) also remained at a very primitive level in the northern part of the country and were only moderately better in the southern préfectures until around 1985.

With normalization in N'Djamena, most of the southern civil servants returned to the capital and were there augmented by many kin of the victorious armies of Hissène Habré (q.v.). The civil service payroll thus rapidly escalated, and the rolls were once again augmented when Idriss Déby (q.v.) came to power, as Zaghawa personnel began to enter in larger numbers into the civil service. Their figure has been more or less stable for several years at around 26,000, with their salaries consuming over one-half of the state budget. One of the insistent conditions of both the World Bank/IMF and France, which are heavily subsidizing the Chadian budget, is that the number of civil servants as well as of members of the armed forces be slashed by up to 40 percent. To date very little progress has been made on this front.

Since the onset of the turmoil in N'Djamena, and to this day, the civil service has been very demoralized by both its low salaries and its infrequent pay. As recently as mid-1994 the bulk of the civil service was still owed back-pay. During the ten-year civil war most had "parallel" jobs and were frequently not to be found in their offices or posts. As many as 15 percent are presumed to be phantom workers, their salaries picked up by administrative superiors. Since the rise of Déby a number of cuts in fringe benefits (15–25 percent) and wages (5–10 percent) as well as the imposition of an income tax were decreed, though most of these belt-tightening measures were canceled after the 50 percent devaluation of the CFA franc in 1994. These actions have brought about frequent union strikes and much labor tumult in N'Djamena, including a six-month strike in February 1994.

CLAUSTRE, FRANÇOISE (1937–). French archaeologist captured on April 21, 1974, in Tibesti (q.v.) by rebels led by Hissène Habré (q.v.). Her husband, Pierre, was held captive also after he went to Chad to try to secure her freedom in August 1975. In mid-1976, with the Claustres still in Habré's desert wilderness headquarters, the handling of the negotiations for her release by France brought Franco-Chadian relations to a nadir. In January 1977, after a falling-out between Habré and Goukouni (q.v.), the Claustres were released and brought to Tripoli, Libya, ending one of the most bizarre political kidnapping cases.

CODOS. From "Commandos." Groups that offered armed resistance to Hissène Habré's (q.v.) spread of authority south from N'Djamena after his victory over Goukouni (q.v.) in 1982. Under the command of Colonel Guérinan Kottiga (q.v.) in mid-1985, around 1,500 *codos* went over to the government, followed by Kottiga himself in March 1986. General Djogo (q.v.), who after the Battle for N'Djamena (q.v.) made his way to B.E.T. (together with some Chadian army troops) to join the GUNT (q.v.) government-in-exile, was also reconciled with Habré in December 1986.

COLLECTIVE DES PARTIS POUR LE CHANGEMENT (COPAC). Alliance of eight anti-Déby political parties set up in N'Djamena in mid-1994. Their spokesman was Abderahman Djasnabayé. The parties included those of former prime minister Dr. Fidèle Moungar (q.v.), former minister Adoum Moussa Seif (q.v.) and of Saleh Kebzabo (q.v.), owner of the independent *N'Djaména-Hebdo* newspaper.

LE COMBAT PROGRESSISTE. Early party newspaper. Established in 1957 as the monthly newspaper of the Parti Progressiste Tchadien (PPT) (q.v.), the paper was published irregularly for several years. Its director was Gabriel Lisette, with Jules Pierre Toura Gaba (qq.v.) as managing director.

COMITE D'ACTION ET DE CONCERTATION DU COMITE D'ACTION REVOLUTIONNAIRE (CAC/CDR). Eastern opposition group, originally part of the CDR (q.v.) that was reconciled to Hissène Habré's (q.v.) regime in 1988. Its leader was Mahamat Senoussi Khatir (q.v.).

COMITE D'ACTION ET DE COORDINATION (CAC). An anti-Libya faction of the CDR (q.v.) set up in 1984 that rallied to Hissène Habré (q.v.) in 1985.

COMITE DE SURSAUT NATIONAL POUR LA PAIX ET LA DEMOCRATIE (CSNPD). Southern rebel opposition to the regime of Idriss Déby (q.v.). Led by Lt. Ketté (later self-promoted captain) (q.v.) the group of maquis ambushed Chadian government troops in the southern préfectures from 1992 to 1994, escaping to the sanctuary of the Central African Republic. As a result of these assaults several retaliatory atrocities were committed by Déby's troops, as in Doba when 150 innocent civilians were slaughtered. A series of meetings in Bangui led to a cessation of hostilities in August 1994 with an agreement that the CSNPD would be recognized as a political party, its leader would be promoted (to colonel) and integrated into the government, and those of its men who wished (and 150 did) could join the Chadian armed forces.

COMITE DU NORD DU TCHAD (CNT). Ad hoc conservative grouping of Muslim leaders who addressed a letter of protest to Charles de Gaulle on March 14, 1967, criticizing the anti-Muslim policies of the N'Djamena government. The group was disbanded by the Chadian security services, and their efforts came to nought. Most of the Muslim leadership was by then in jail or in exile, and the rebellion was still far away.

COMITE INTER-ETATS DE LUTTE CONTRE LA SECHERESSE DANS LE SAHEL (CILSS). International organization grouping most of the Sahel states, aimed at studying drought, land erosion, and the encroaching desertification of the Sahel, as well as combating these conditions.

COMITE MILITAIRE INTER-ARMEE PROVISOIRE (CMIAP). Provisional joint alliance between the CCFAN of Goukouni and Habré (qq.v.) and the Baghalani Volcan Army (q.v.) aimed at reuniting the various FROLINAT (q.v.) groups after the 1972 split between Abba Siddick (q.v.) and Goukouni. Formed in October 1976 with eight members (four from each armed force) with Adoum Togoi (q.v.), chief of staff of the CCFAN, serving as president. The CMIAP remained mostly a paper structure.

COMITE NATIONAL DE REDRESSEMENT (CNR). Armed mostly Zaghawa (q.v.) irregulars, in opposition to the regime of Idriss Déby (q.v.) in N'Djamena after he liquidated their leader, Colonel Abbas Kotti (q.v.) in October 1993. The CNR participated alongside troops of the FNT (q.v.) in the January 1994 assault on the Chadian government garrison in Abéché, and has been active along the Sudan border. It is led by Hissein Kotti, brother of the liquidated Abbas Kotti.

COMITE PERMANENT DU SUD (CPS). Moundou-based joint military council through which the de facto government of Colonel Kamougoué governed the southern préfectures of Chad following the collapse of central authority in N'Djamena. The Comité was disbanded in 1982 when rebel FAT (q.v.) elements joined with Hissène Habré's FAN (qq.v.) forces to overthrow the de facto southern administration. The Comité operated very much as Kamougoué's personal advisory board rather than as a collegiate council, and allegations of Kamougoué's heavy-handedness—and fiscal improprieties—abounded. Nevertheless, the Comité was widely viewed as the sole legitimate authority in the south.

COMITE POUR LA RELANCE ECONOMIQUE. Committee established on January 23, 1976, charged with conducting a comprehensive analysis of Chad's economic situation and methods by which it may be improved. The committee was directly accountable to the president of the Conseil Supérieur Militaire (CSM) (q.v.) and was composed of seven members drawn from Chad's main economic sectors.

COMITES POPULAIRES DES FORCES ARMEES DU NORD (COPOFAN). Precursor to Hissène Habré's UNIR (qq.v.) party. An attempt was made to establish a series of such committees throughout the country with such names in 1983, shortly after Habré seized power from Goukouni (q.v.) in N'Djamena. The attempt was met with an abysmal response, and it was not until some of Habré's new southern allies told him the words "Nord" and "FAN" inspired hatred and fear that the effort was given up and the name of Habré's eventual political movement was changed to UNIR.

COMMANDEMENT DES GROUPEMENTS DES TROUPES OFFENSIVES (CGTO). Southern *codos* (q.v.) group under the control of Colonel Guérinan Kottiga (q.v.) that rallied to the regime of Hissène Habré (q.v.).

COMMISSION DE DEFENSE NATIONALE (CDN). Military organ created on May 28, 1976, as part of a general reorganization of the armed forces of Chad. Though the specific purposes of the CDN were not spelled out, all members of the CSM (q.v.) were automatically included in the CDN, with General Djibrile Djogo (q.v.) as secretary-general. The organ became inoperative in 1979.

COMMISSION D'ENQUETE PARLEMENTAIRE (CEP). Special parliamentary commission formed in 1973 with vast investigatory powers. Composed of six members under National Assembly President Abo Nassour (q.v.)—and directly responsible to President François

Tombalbaye (q.v.)—the commission's scope of inquiry was "redressing the abuses of certain technocrats" and ridding the country of embezzlement and corrupt practices. More often than not the CEP acted as the legitimating organ for the purge of technocrats opposed to Tombalbaye's leadership. Among high officials and intellectuals purged by the commission were Minister of Finance Elie Romba (accused of maladministration); Minister of Transport Adoum Aganayé (q.v.) (accused of embezzlement but not imprisoned for it); General Félix Malloum (q.v.) (originally accused of "administrative irregularities"); and many Ouadai Muslim leaders.

COMMISSION DE RECONCILIATION (CRN). A 12-man committee set up in May 1994 to try to resolve the southern rebellion of the CSNPD (q.v.) that was triggering Garde Républicaine (q.v.) retaliatory massacres. The committee had two delegates each from the government, the interim assembly CST (q.v.), the National Assembly, human rights groups, and from the country's legalized parties, plus four well-known personalities. It proceeded to the south in July and in due course achieved a reconciliation with Captain Ketté (q.v.), leader of the rebellion.

COMMISSION DU BASSIN DU LAC TCHAD (CBLT). Interstate organ for the mutual development and protection of the Lake Chad basin that covers some 200,000 square kilometers (77,220 square miles). The commission was founded on May 22, 1964, when a convention was signed following five previous meetings from March 1962 to April 1964. The participating states—Chad, Cameroon, Niger, and Nigeria—pledged that they would act to prevent policies or action likely to pollute the lake or drain its waters and would act to promote cooperation on projects affecting the basin. The commission is composed of eight delegates, two from each participating state, has a secretariat in N'Djamena, and is supposed to meet at least once a year. A proposal for the navigation of the lake and transportation across it was drawn up, and several other research projects were commissioned, including: (1) a 1966–69 UNESCO development of a scale model of the basin and all known underground water resources; (2) a 1967–70 FAO study on the waterways of the basin in which 17 international experts participated; and (3) feasibility studies financed by AID regarding the improvement of the N'Djamena-Maiduguri (Nigeria) road. The commission fell into lethargy in the mid-1970s, in part due to the intensification of the conflict in Chad. It held no meetings between 1976 and 1982, and in 1978 its headquarters were shifted to Maroua, Cameroon. Most of its goals have not been attained, and all its member states do what they will in their portion of the basin. Chad has accused Nigeria of diverting waters from Lake Chad, which in 1986 was declared a disaster zone. No progress took place on most issues through 1990, when a summit meeting of the CBLT called on outside donor nations to help preserve the lake by more bountiful donations.

COMMUNAUTE ECONOMIQUE DES ETATS D'AFRIQUE CENTRALE (CEEAC). Organization of 10 equatorial states, formed on October 17, 1983, and quasi-equivalent to the ECOWAS in West Africa. The grouping included the four states of the UDEAC (q.v.), Equatorial Guinea, São Tomé, Zaire, Rwanda, and Burundi. Chad temporarily walked out of the UDEAC during the Tombalbaye (q.v.) era.

COMMUNAUTE FINANCIERE AFRICAINE (CFA) FRANC. Common currency of the Communauté Financière Africaine, which includes all former territories of the colonial federations of France (the French West Africa and French Equatorial Africa federations) except for Mauritania and Guinea (which established their separate currencies) and including Madagascar and the former French League of Nations mandates of Togo and Cameroon. (Equatorial Guinea joined the grouping in 1984.) Established in 1946 as the Colonies Françaises d'Afrique franc, the currency's name was changed to its present one in 1962. Fully guaranteed by France and pegged to the French franc, into which it is freely convertible, CFA monetary reserves are held in Paris. The fiscal domination this gives to France has been the subject of various demands by francophone states that some of the monetary treaties be modified and reserves be transferred to Africa. Several measures in this direction took place in the 1970s, though they did not change the reality of the situation. Indeed, when France devalued the CFA-French franc ratio by 50 percent in 1994, it did so unilaterally.

COMMUNAUTE FRANÇAISE. Free association of autonomous republics set up with France's adoption of the constitution of the Fifth Republic. Within the community France retained jurisdiction over foreign affairs, defense, external communications, and fiscal and monetary matters. The structures set up originally for the community included an executive (the French president), assisted by an Executive Council (all heads of the associated republics and the French minister of community affairs), and a Senate, with representation from all the territories in proportion to their populations. Early in 1960 an amendment to the French constitution was promulgated allowing the associated republics to attain full independence while remaining in the community.

COMMUNES DE PLEIN EXERCISE. Legal status in Chad conferred upon municipalities. To acquire such a status a town must be able to

finance its own budget from local revenues. There are nine municipalities in Chad: N'Djamena (which received its status in 1919),
Abéché, Bongor, Doba, Sarh, Koumra, Laï, Moundou, and Pala
(which received their status in 1961). The municipalities have elected
councils of between 11 and 37 members, with the mayor elected from
the council members. The powers of the municipalities are always
subordinate to those of the local prefect.

COMMUNICATIONS. Chad's transportion communications are very
primitive and in an abysmal condition. Until 1985 there were no bridges
across the Chari River, and even the capital had no reliable access to
Kousseri, across the river in Cameroon. Crossings were by ferry, but
these have not been able to operate when droughts (as in the 1980s) have
drastically lowered the river's levels. In 1985 a pontoon bridge was constructed connecting N'Djamena with Kousseri, and a year later a similar bridge was built at Léré across the Mayo-Kebbi River.

Of Chad's 32,000 kilometers (19,840 miles) of roads only 500 kilometers (310 miles) were ever paved, and most of these are in such an
acute state of disrepair that the original asphalt has disappeared completely on many stretches. During the rainy season large parts of the
country are flooded and become completely isolated for up to six
months. Of the remaining roads only 7,300 kilometers (4,530 miles)
of dirt tracks are in any manner intermittently "maintained," while
24,000 kilometers (14,900 miles) of tracks receive no attention at any
time. Only 1,260 kilometers (780 miles) of the road system, moreover,
can be regarded—in the best of times—as "all-weather" roads. During the rainy season many Chadians who need to travel from N'Djamena to the southern parts of the country use Cameroon's paved road
system, despite the lengthy detours involved. Because of these problems of communications there are massive differences in the prices of
locally grown commodities from region to region. In the late 1980s,
for example, millet harvested in the south cost there 30 CFA francs for
a 2.5-kilogram bag, 150 CFA francs in N'Djamena, and 320 CFA
francs in Ouadai. The country also has only a modest number of tele-
phones (2,000 in N'Djamena and 500 throughout the rest of the country) and private vehicles.

Chad's location at the heart of Africa creates great difficulties for
its export and import trade, which must traverse huge distances. Chad
has access to the ocean ports via five routes, none of which is fully satisfactory and all of which add considerable cost to imports and exports. The routes are:

1. N'Djamena–Pointe-Noire (Congo/Brazzaville) via Sarh and
    Bangui by road and track (1200 kilometers, or 745 miles),

down the Oubangui and Congo Rivers by barge to Brazzaville (1260 kilometers, 780 miles), and on the Congo-Océan railroad (see CHEMIN DE FER DU CONGO-OCEAN) to Pointe-Noire (510 kilometers, 316 miles). The total distance to the Atlantic Ocean is 2,970 kilometers (1,841 miles). This route is one of the principal ones used by Chad. Its drawbacks are many. For example, the several transshipments involved are costly; the Oubangui River has in recent years been quite shallow, delaying exports at times for months; and the CFCO allows limited capacity in the downstream direction due to Congo's own needs. For these reasons a progressively larger proportion of Chad's trade has been channeled to other routes, and hopes are pinned on the extension of the Trans-Cameroonian railroad to the Chadian border.

2. N'Djamena-Douala (Cameroon) via N'Gouandéré (current terminal of the Trans-Cameroonian railroad) and on to Douala by railroad. The long stretch of track involved on this route and the length of the journey (1,800 kilometers, 1,116 miles) are the major drawbacks of this route. The extension of the Trans-Cameroonian railroad to the Chari River or to N'Djamena would greatly increase the attractiveness of this communications option, which is the fastest and the shortest to the Atlantic Ocean. This route has been used increasingly since the 1980s, even though in the 1970s the Nigerian route was favored, and today it is by far the most used. With the discovery of large amounts of oil in Chad and hence plans to build a pipeline via Cameroon to the coast, there has been renewed talk of extending the Trans-Cameroonian railroad to Chad.

3. N'Djamena-Lagos (Nigeria) via Maiduguri by road (240 kilometers, 149 miles) and on by rail to Lagos (1,680 kilometers, 1,041 miles) for a total of 1,920 kilometers (1,190 miles). Though this is shorter than the Cameroon route, Chadian exports are often shipped out of ports other than Lagos (lengthening the journey) due to the acute congestion in Lagos. Another major drawback is that the Nigerian railroad has little excess capacity at the height of the (Nigerian) groundnut evacuation season, and Nigerian goods receive preference. Still, this was a principal route used for much of Chad's imports and exports in the 1970s when exasperation with the constant problems caused a shift of most of Chad's exports and imports to the Cameroonian route.

4. The trans-Saharan route. This includes some 3,200 kilometers (1,984 miles) of ancient tracks to Tripoli, Libya. This route

has carried very little traffic in recent times, especially because of the prolonged period of unsettled conditions in Chad's B.E.T. Préfecture. Despite an offer in the 1970s by Libya to pave the entire section through B.E.T., the route has little importance for Chad.

5. N'Djamena–Abéché–Port Sudan (Sudan). This route crosses sections of eastern Chad intermittently occupied by rebel forces and always in a state of unrest. From Abéché the route continues to Al-Junaynah in Sudan—the future terminus of the Sudanese railroad, barely 20 kilometers (12 miles) from the border—and on to Port Sudan on the Red Sea. The Abéché–Port Sudan section is 1,653 kilometers (1,025 miles) long. This route is only of marginal interest to Chad and then only to areas in the east near Abéché. (See also CHEMIN DE FER DU CONGO-OCEAN; OFFICE TCHADIEN D'ETUDES FERROVIAIRES; TRANS-CAMEROONIAN RAILROAD.)

COMPAGNIE HUILIERE AFRICAINE (OLAFRIC). N'Djamena's groundnut oil mills, founded in 1955. The mills are supplied with groundnuts from the Chari-Baguirmi Préfecture and have a capacity of 800,000 liters per year. OLAFRIC's produce is mixed with oil from the cotton mills at Moundou, the Société des Oléagineux du Logone-Tchad (SOLT), to produce a mixture of 40 percent cotton oil and 60 percent groundnut oil. Production has always lagged behind capacity.

COMPAGNIES TCHADIENNES DE SECURITE (CTS). Former mobile police units that were, until the 1975 coup d'état, directly under President François Tombalbaye's (q.v.) control and greatly dreaded in the countryside. Created early in 1967—when they were structurally attached to the Sûreté Nationale (q.v.)—as an armed constabulary force (equipped with light mortars), the CTS was supposed to act as a border and antismuggling force. The CTS was progressively augmented to 750 men organized into three highly mobile companies, two of which operated in the east while one was stationed in N'Djamena. The latter company was increasingly used by Tombalbaye as his own guard against plots and attempted plots from within the armed forces and was feared and detested by the rest of Chad's security forces for its better equipment and preferential treatment (see ARMED FORCES). Until the coup, the force commander was Colonel Salebiani. The N'Djamena company of the CTS put up strong resistance to the assaulting units at the time of the 1975 coup and suffered heavy casualties, though some elements rallied to the insurgents. The CTS was subsequently disbanded.

CONCERTATION DES PARTIS POLITIQUES (CPP). An alliance of 40 of the then 46 anti-Déby political parties in Chad in early 1994, headed by former prime minister Alingué (q.v.). Eight others organized themselves later in the Entente (q.v.).

CONFEDERATION LIBRE DES TRAVAILLEURS DU TCHAD (CLTT). Small trade union that split away from the former monolithic UST (q.v.) after the collapse of the Hissène Habré (q.v.) regime. It has been at the forefront of strikes against the Idriss Déby (q.v.) regime over back-pay.

CONFERENCE NATIONALE. Chad's national conference, which took place at Diguel, in the outskirts of N'Djamena, from January 15 to April 7, 1993, with the participation of 750 delegates, including representatives of 32 political parties, 20 associations, and six rebel movements, and at a cost of US$4 million, which was fully borne by France and the United States. Among the notable figures at the conference was Goukouni (q.v.), who received a great deal of respect because of the basic decency of his administration after he won control of N'Djamena, with some talk even of his being a good compromise leader for the presidency. Adoum Maurice Hel-Bongo (q.v.) was elected chairman of the conference. After lengthy debates on procedures to bring speedy multiparty elections, the conference was surprisingly polarized on the issue of religion, with strong fundamentalist Muslim pressures emerging. Déby was retained as interim president until the elections, and a 57-member transitional legislature was elected, the Conseil Supérieur de la Transition (CST) (q.v.), with Lol Mahamat Choua (q.v.) as its president. Dr. Fidèle Moungar (q.v.), a physician, was appointed the new prime minister from a list of 16 hopefuls. The intermittent massacres in the south by Déby's Garde Républicaine were roundly condemned, and the conference enjoined the disbanding of the secret political police, the CRCR (q.v.). (It was indeed disbanded, but another structure, the ANS (q.v.), with identical functions and personnel, was established.)

CONGO FRANÇAIS. Name of the vast region in Equatorial Africa, with headquarters in Libreville (Gabon), of which Oubangui-Chari-Tchad (q.v.) was a constituent colony. Congo Français was formed as an administrative unit in 1906 and was replaced by the Afrique Equatoriale Française (AEF) (q.v.) federation in 1910.

CONSEIL CENTRAL POUR LA DEFENSE DES FORCES MOBILES D'INTERVENTION (CCDFMI). Armed units, formerly of the Chadian army, commanded by Major Pierre Tokinon (q.v.), that rallied to Hissène Habré's (q.v.) rule in 1988.

CONSEIL DE COMMANDEMENT DES FORCES ARMEES DU NORD (CCFAN). Formal executive body of the FAN (q.v.) headed by Hissène Habré (q.v.). In theory the CCFAN was the ultimate fount of power in Chad following Goukouni's (q.v.) ouster in 1982. The CCFAN had the authority—lodged in the constitution of September 29, 1982 (that it alone could amend)—to appoint as well as call to account the president of the republic. The CCFAN was originally formed in October 1972 as the Toubou (q.v.) political counterpart to FROLINAT (q.v.), then dominated by Abba Siddick (q.v.), and was co-led by Habré and Goukouni, with a council of the top Toubou commanders headed by Adoum Togoi (q.v.), the chief of staff. Following the Goukouni-Habré falling-out, Habré was expelled, together with his 300-odd Anakaza troops. Later the Goukouni-dominated FAN (and CCFAN) changed its name to Forces Armées Populaires (FAP) (q.v.) and the old name was reclaimed by Habré.

CONSEIL DE DEFENSE ET DE SECURITE (CDS). Short-lived joint CCFAN (q.v.) and CSM (q.v.) structure set up by the Charte Fondamentale (q.v.) of August 1978 at the time of the Malloum-Habré (qq.v.) joint leadership of Chad. In theory composed of eight representatives of each opposing group, the CDS meetings—prior to CDS dissolution consequent to the collapse of the alliance—were highly acrimonious and counterproductive.

CONSEIL DEMOCRATIQUE DE LA REVOLUTION (CDR). Name adopted in mid-1980 by the Volcan Army (q.v.) of Ahmat Acyl (q.v.) Pro-Libya and pro-Goukouni, the CDR operated in its traditional Biltine-Salamat redoubt, shutting out Habré (q.v.) in the east, though competing—at times very violently—with Mahamat Seid Abba (q.v.) and his military forces. Shut out from the Nigeria-sponsored peace meetings (see KANO MEETINGS), the CDR joined with four other excluded factions to form the anti-N'Djamena Front d'Action Commune Provisoire (FACP) (q.v.), which promptly resulted in their being invited to the expanded Kano II and Lagos I peace talks. The CDR's political head was Ahmat Acyl, with Chaibo Bicharo as his deputy. With Acyl's death in 1982, the leadership passed to Acheikh Ibn Oumar (q.v.). The CDR commanded some 2,000 troops in 1982, but the force was heavily reduced during the battles with Habré's troops in July 1982, when the CDR sided with Kamougoué's FAT (qq.v.) in an unsuccessful effort to prevent the fall of the southern préfectures to Habré.

Always suspect due to its "Libyan connection," including its headquarters in Tripoli (until the fall of N'Djamena), the CDR was in essence an integrationalist force, supporting Goukouni and GUNT (qq.v.). As most of GUNT's fighting forces were progressively reconciled with Habré, the CDR remained one of the few with a large number of troops that were not. In 1986, assisted by Libya, which temporarily arrested Goukouni, Acheikh declared Goukouni no longer head of GUNT, assumed the leadership himself, and for some time fought against Goukouni's FAP (q.v.). Based in Darfur (q.v.), near the provincial capital of El-Fasher, and supplied by Libya by air, the CDR was in the 1980s (before it split into three factions due to a power tug-of-war between Acheikh and the CDR secretary-general, Adoum Rakhis Manani [q.v.]) the best fighting force in Chad. After Libya's stunning defeat in the Habré assault on B.E.T., Acheikh aligned his faction of the CDR into a new neo-GUNT formation, the Front Patriotique Tchadien (FPT) (q.v.), though by 1988 he was negotiating with Habré for a return to N'Djamena. The reconciliation took place early in 1989: Acheikh was named foreign minister, and 800 of his troops were integrated into the Chadian army. Part of the CDR refused to follow Acheikh's reconciliation with N'Djamena, however, and continued the armed struggle. This faction, led by Manani, and more pro-Libyan, has been active in attacks on Chadian army garrisons in the Abéché region, together with the FPT. Another faction, also calling itself CDR and headed by Aboubakar Adzalo Barraka, briefly allied itself with Goukouni in the early 1990s as he tried to revive a "new" FROLINAT (q.v.) against Déby.

CONSEIL DU PEUPLE TCHADIEN (CPT). Small armed formation, headed by Yacob Hamed, that was allied for some time with Goukouni in the early 1990s as part of the latter's "new" FROLINAT (q.v.).

CONSEIL ECONOMIQUE ET SOCIAL. An advisory council with recommendatory authority over legislation in the social and economic areas. Stipulated by the April 1962 constitution, the council was not erected by decree until November–December 1966, and it held its first session in April 1967. Its 25 members, appointed to renewable two-year terms of office, are organized into three commissions: social affairs; agricultural affairs; and finance, transportation, tourism, and the economy. The membership of the council—which cannot include elected officials—includes several French businessmen, missionaries, and technical experts. The council was defunct between 1978 and 1983 due to unsettled conditions in N'Djamena.

CONSEIL NATIONAL CONSULTATIF (CNC). National Consultative Council set up by CCFAN (q.v.) decree in the constitution of September 29, 1982, following the rise to power of the Hissène Habré (q.v.) regime in N'Djamena. Membership in the council was incompatible with ministerial appointment. The body included 30 national councillors, with each préfecture, including the capital, represented by two such delegates, forming a quasi-consultative assembly, appointed and dismissed by the head of state, Habré. The CNC was dissolved early in 1990 prior to the July 1990 elections that produced an elected National Assembly.

CONSEIL NATIONAL DE LA LIBERATION (CNL). Fifteen-member national council set up in November 1984 as the supreme organ directing the struggle against the Hissène Habré (q.v.) regime in N' Djamena. Formed in Bardai, the council included Goukouni (q.v.) as its head, Acheikh Ibn Oumar (q.v.), Mohammed Ayet Said, Gary Mina, Wiry Kyr Tomar, and Major Najitayoun Bil. The council included seven of the 11 signatories of the 1979 Lagos peace agreement that led to the creation of the GUNT (q.v.) government, including the FAO, CDR, UND, FAB, and FAT (qq.v.). Splinters of these groups, however, declared for either Habré or Balaam (q.v.). (See, for example, RASSEMBLEMENT DES FORCES PATRIOTIQUES.)

CONSEIL NATIONAL DE LA REVOLUTION (CNR). Formally the supreme decision-making organ of FROLINAT (q.v.) during Abba Siddick's (q.v.) tenure. In reality the council hardly played any role, met rarely, and allowed its membership to atrophy. Following Siddick's ouster, efforts were made to revitalize the CNR by linking all dissident groups to it. In 1977, for example, a 31-man council was named to represent all factions, though unity did not emerge. The fall of N'Djamena made unity even more problematic, for now each faction was competing for a share of the spoils.

CONSEIL NATIONAL DE REDRESSEMENT (CNR). Liberation movement launched by supporters of Abbas Yacoub Kotti (q.v.), liquidated by Idriss Déby's (q.v.) regime in October 1993.

CONSEIL NATIONAL D'UNION (CNU). Short-lived—and in reality mostly on paper—16-man council representing all préfectures of Chad and N'Djamena, set up as part of the constitution of August 29, 1978, which led to the bicephalous Malloum-Habré (qq.v.) administration.

CONSEIL PROVISOIRE DE LA REVOLUTION (CPR). (1) Temporary and ad hoc committee set up after the 1977 Karangua meeting between FAN (q.v.) and Acyl's (q.v.) Volcan Army (q.v.). The meeting confirmed Abba Siddick's (q.v.) ouster from FROLINAT (q.v.) and aimed at unifying all the military forces under Goukouni (q.v.). The CPR was placed under the leadership of Malloum Mahamad Boukar (q.v.) and led to the creation the following year of the 31-man Conseil National de la Révolution (q.v.).

(2) Idriss Déby's (q.v.) 1991 interim consultative national assembly, which was set up pending elections. As in Habré's interim assembly before Déby's, representation was by region, though all delegates had to be members of Déby's party, the MPS (q.v.). The assembly was replaced by the Conférence Nationale (q.v.) of 1993, which selected another temporary body to act in that capacity until elections were held.

CONSEIL REPRESENTATIF. Chad's first colonial territorial assembly. Established throughout the AEF (q.v.) federation and French West Africa consequent to a 1946 decree, Chad's Conseil Représentatif had 30 members chosen from two electoral colleges (see DOUBLE ELECTORAL COLLEGE), 10 from the first (European) and 20 from the second (African) college. Following the first territorial elections (1947) the party makeup of the council was: from the second electoral college, 11 UDT (q.v.), two UPFT (q.v.), four URPT (q.v.), one PPT (q.v.), and two independents; from the first electoral college, five URT (q.v.) and five independents. The council was thus an extremely meek and powerless deliberative organ beholden to an alliance of conservative traditional chiefs and European merchants.

CONSEIL SUPERIEUR DE LA TRANSITION (CST). An interim deliberative national assembly of 57 members that emerged from the Conférence Nationale (q.v.) of 1993, to be in place until it scheduled national elections that would result in a regular assembly. Its president was Lol Mahamat Choua (q.v.). The CST's mandate was extended twice, since elections were originally assumed to take place in 1994. In July 1955 the entire bureau of the CST was indicted and removed for corruption, and Abbas Ali (q.v.), a leader of the CSDT party was appointed its president.

CONSEIL SUPERIEUR MILITAIRE DU TCHAD (CSM). The military ruling junta of Chad following the 1975 coup d'état. Members of the CSM, as rank-ordered by the regime, were (all of q.v.): General Malloum, president; Colonel Djimé, Lieutenant Mahmoud, Major Kamougoué, General Djogo, Captain Zakaria, Captain Roasngar, and Lieutenant Gouara Lassou. One senior military officer not on the CSM was General Doumro (q.v.). All members of the CSM were also cabinet ministers and held the most important portfolios. Four government commissions were set up shortly after the coup: public service; economic and social affairs; financial affairs; and military matters. The commissions included civilians but were all chaired by military officers. The CSM was dissolved following the adoption of the Charte Fondamentale (q.v.) of August 25, 1978. (See also COMMISSION DE DEFENSE NATIONALE; COUP OF APRIL 13, 1975; GROUPE DES OFFICIERS DES FORCES ARMEES TCHADIENNES.)

CONSEIL SUPREME DE LA REVOLUTION (CSR). A coordinating organ of seven factions actively battling the regime of Hissène Habré (q.v.) in 1985. Agreement was signed in Cotonou, Benin, on August 30, 1985, by Acheikh Ibn Oumar of the CDR (qq.v.); Oueddei Goukouni of the FAP (qq.v); and Colonel Wadal Abdelkader Kamougoué of the MPRT (qq.v.); Abdelkadir Yacine of the FROLINAT-Originel (qq.v.); Hadjero Senoussi of the FROLINAT-Fondamental (qq.v.); Mahamat Seid Abba (q.v.) of the First Army, and Dr. Facho Balaam of the RFP (qq.v.). The CSR was under the presidency of Goukouni, with Kamougoué as his vice president.

CONSEILS DE NOTABLES. Consultative organs decreed for the AEF (q.v.) territories on July 4, 1936. Previous decrees (in 1919 and 1925) had set up similar organs in French West Africa and in Cameroon. The councils were set up with between eight and 16 African traditional leaders and a few *évolués* (q.v.) under each French *chef de département*. Appointed for a term of three years and meeting at least once a year, the councils provided a forum for the consultation of the traditional chiefs in matters pertaining to taxation and *corvée* (q.v.) labor. In Chad the councils were in reality only set up during the Second World War and were very rapidly outdated by the 1944–46 reforms of Félix Eboué (q.v.) and the Brazzaville Conference. In 1954 the organs were officially renamed Conseils de Notables Régionaux du Tchad and were granted somewhat greater powers. At that time the councils included 167 members of whom 87 were either sultans or chiefs; the rest included 20 veterans and all 30 Territorial Assembly deputies from the second electoral college. (See also DOUBLE ELECTORAL COLLEGE.) In 1958 the councils, with a few changes, were renamed Conseils de Régions (q.v.) and in 1960, Conseils de Préfectures (q.v.).

CONSEILS DE NOTABLES REGIONAUX DU TCHAD see CONSEILS DE NOTABLES

CONSEILS DE PREFECTURES. Successor organs to the Conseils de Régions (q.v.) following the 1960 renaming of Chad's administrative units, and successor to the colonial era's Conseils de Notables (q.v.). The councils—significantly strengthened in the late 1960s along the lines proposed by the French Mission de Réforme Administrative (q.v.)—are composed of 10 to 30 members (depending on the préfecture's population) appointed by the minister of interior from lists submitted to him by the local prefect, who presides over the meetings. Since the 1969 reforms (see MISSION DE REFORME ADMINISTRATIVE) the most important sultans are statutory vice chairmen of the councils. Civil servants and elected officials are not eligible to sit on the councils, which are essentially bodies of traditional and socioeconomic leaders with deliberative authority over regional development matters, agriculture, and religion.

CONSEILS DE REGIONS. Successors to the Conseils de Notables (q.v.) and the Conseils de Notables Régionaux du Tchad, the councils were consultative organs established by decree on November 6, 1958, in every *région* in Chad. Council members were to be elected for five years by universal suffrage from local electoral districts in proportion to the population of each region (10 from regions with fewer than 100,000 people—B.E.T.—up to 50 from the most populous regions). The councils were granted limited powers on issues of local development and taxation. In 1960 they were renamed Conseils de Préfectures (q.v.) following the renaming of Chad's administrative units, and some time later the method of selecting members was changed.

CONSTITUTION RENOVEE. Name ("Changed Constitution") officially used to designate the Chadian constitution as amended by the National Assembly on June 5, 1964, legally making Chad a one-party (PPT, q.v.) state. (See also CONSTITUTIONS.)

CONSTITUTIONS. Chad has had eight constitutions and three major constitutional amendments. These were, in chronological order:

1. Constitution of March 31, 1959, creating a parliamentary system with an executive prime minister elected for five years and confirmed in office by the National Assembly. A Conseil Economique et Social (q.v.) was also named, though this organ was not set up until 1967.

2. Constitution of November 28, 1960. The "Independence" constitution created a quasi-presidential system with enhanced powers for the head of state.

3. Constitution of April 16, 1962, creating a presidential system in which the National Assembly, elected for five years on the basis of a single electoral list (see POLITICAL PARTIES) formed part of an electoral college (including also mayors, principal chiefs, municipal councillors, etc.) for the purpose of electing the president of the Republic. The president's term of office was increased to seven years.

4. Constitutional Law of December 29, 1965, which drastically modified the 1962 constitution by legally decreeing a one-party state.

5. Constitutional Law of February 7, 1967, which modified certain structural features of the constitution.

6. Constitution of November 1973, which was announced and ratified in record time, legalizing the demise of the PPT (q.v.) and its replacement by the MNRC (q.v.), and codifying the Cultural Revolution (q.v.).

7. Constitution of August 29, 1978, promulgated to accommodate Hissène Habré's (q.v.) integration into the Chadian government. A bicephalous executive was erected with Félix Malloum (q.v.) as president and Habré as his prime minister. Also set up was a 16-member civil-military Conseil National representing all préfectures and a Conseil de Défense et de Sécurité (CDS) (q.v.) with eight members each from CCFAN and CSM (qq.v.).

8. Declaration of N'Djamena, May 8, 1982; in essence a provisional constitution set up after difficult negotiations among the factions of GUNT (q.v.) at a time when the Habré forces were beginning their advance on N'Djamena. The declaration set up an executive president, Goukouni (q.v.), assisted by a 15-man policy steering organ (Council of State) presided by Kamougoué (q.v.), and on which all factions were represented by law. Members of the council could not serve on the cabinet, which was headed by Djidingar (q.v.) and responsible to the head of state.

9. Constitution of September 29, 1982; constitution of the FAN (q.v.), adopted after the fall of N'Djamena to Habré forces. The constitution set up a powerful executive president acting as head of state and of government, assisted by a council of ministers (cabinet) named by the Conseil de Commandement des Forces Armées du Nord (CCFAN) (q.v.). In case of high treason the head of state could be called to account for his acts by the CCFAN before an ad hoc CCFAN High Court to be set up for this purpose. Article 18 supplied a long list of areas on which the government under the president has prime responsibilities. The constitution also set up a Conseil National Consultatif (CNC) (q.v.), membership on which is incompatible with ministerial appointment. The 30 members of the CNC—two from each of Chad's préfectures and from the capital city—were appointed and dismissed by the president.

Constitutional amendments could only be passed by an absolute majority of the CCFAN, called in for that purpose.

10. Constitution of 1989. This was supposed to result in the constitutionalization of the Habré regime. It took place less than a year before Habré was ousted by Idriss Déby. The document, drafted by a committee in which Alingué (q.v.) (later prime minister) and Habré's deputy Mahamat Nouri (q.v.), played a major role, was ratified by a 99.4 percent vote on December 19, 1989. It had 200 articles and provided a presidential system in a secular state with both French and Arabic as national languages. There was also a National Assembly of deputies elected for five years, and elections were indeed held, from a single-party (Habré's) list. The constitution was abolished on December 2, 1990, when Déby seized N'Djamena, promising a new constitution within 30 months.

11. The Transitional Charter of the Conférence Nationale (q.v.) supposedly in force until April 1995, when a new constitution was supposed to be in place. The charter remained in place, however, since in 1994 the draft of the new constitution was not acceptable to most delegates at the CST (q.v.), who felt that it was dictatorial. An amended draft has not yet been ratified by referendum, nor—as of December 1995—were elections held, on a variety of pretexts, and hence normalization has been delayed.

CONTACT. Current affairs journal established in N'Djamena in mid-1989 by businessman Koulamallah Souradj. At the time it was the only privately owned periodical in the country.

CONVENTION NATIONALE DEMOCRATIQUE ET SOCIALE (CNDS). Political party headed by Adoum Moussa Seif (q.v.). The party has a strong antifederalist plank.

CONVENTION POUR LE PROGRES ET LE DEVELOPPEMENT (CPD). Political movement set up on February 4, 1992, headed by Adoum Hadjero Senoussi (q.v.), including several former rebel leaders recently returned from exile, and Seydou Sahoulba (q.v.). The movement tried, unsuccessfully, to mediate between Hissène Habré (q.v.) (then mounting a comeback attempt via the Lake Chad area) and Idriss Déby (q.v.).

CONVENTION SOCIO-DEMOCRATE TCHADIENNE (CNSD). Social-democratic party, one of several in Chad, headed by Younous

Ibeidou. It includes many former Habré (q.v.) supporters, including former housing minister Bilai Soubiane (q.v.). One of its leaders, Abbas Ali (q.v.), was elected president of the country's interim legislature, the Conseil Supérieur de la Transition (CST) (q.v.), in July 1995 when the CST's entire bureau was indicted for corruption.

COOPERATIVE DES TRANSPORTEURS TCHADIENS (CTT or CORPORTCHAD). Giant trucking cooperative formed in 1955 by a number of small transporters to challenge the lucrative monopoly of Union Routière Centre-Africaine (Uniroute) (q.v.)—later Unitchadienne (q.v.)—and especially its stranglehold over the cotton-hauling routes. In 1958 the CTT obtained part of Cotonfran's (q.v.) trucking routes, and between 1966 and 1972 the CTT and Unitchadienne shared equally these highly profitable contracts. Between 1972 and 1975 the CTT's share of Cotontchad's (q.v.) business was only 20 percent, and in 1975 the latter began its own cotton-evacuation program. Benefiting from government policy favoring the indigenous CTT via preferential freight allocations, the CTT has acquired a trucking quasi monopoly in many areas but at the expense of extremely high costs and waste in the absence of competition. It has been estimated, for example, that on the N'Djamena-Maiduguri (Nigeria) route (see COMMUNICATIONS), over which a significant percentage of Chad's exports and imports are hauled, prices could be reduced by 50 percent under a competitive system with no decline in quality of service or frequency. According to a May 1957 agreement between Chad and Nigeria 85 percent of all traffic between the two countries (actually between Nigerian border towns and N'Djamena) must be hauled in Chadian trucks. This has resulted in windfall profits for Chadian entrepreneurs and their political backers (many politicians invest their funds in trucks) since Chadian trucking rates are considerably higher than Nigerian rates. Moreover, during the Sahelian drought (and especially in 1973 and 1974) major stockpile bottlenecks of relief aid supplies developed in northern Nigeria as Chadian trucks could not cope with the huge volume of supplies donated. In 1969 the CTT owned 520 trucks with a capacity of 4,746 tons, more than twice the capacity of its rival, Unitchadienne. Together the two companies controlled about 85 percent of Chad's public transport, with the CTT itself controlling 65 percent of total traffic. The monopoly the cooperative has in Chad on all internal and external traffic continued into the 1990s. In 1991 CTT had 394 members, owned 620 trucks with a capacity of around 17,500 tons, as well as 108 tanker trucks for fuel transport with a capacity of 3,430 cubic meters. In an average year the cooperative transports some 160,000 tons of freight.

CORDES DE CHEFS. Village and regional chiefs' plots of land, usually 0.5 hectares (1.25 acres) in size (but some very much larger), forcibly cultivated by local farmers for the personal profit of the chief. The much abused and hated practice developed from the colonial imposition of cotton production quotas in the southern areas of Chad and the appointment of chiefs as general supervisors for the fulfillment of the allotments (in exchange for a 5 percent indemnity). In the process chiefly authority was artificially enhanced, and abuses of authority proliferated. Many chiefs—including those in non–cotton growing areas—added or established "*cordes*" of millet or of rice, which they forced the peasants to cultivate, leading to much friction and unrest. However, the chiefs' need to hire assistants to enforce the French cotton policies and quotas led to the proliferation of similar (smaller) plots for the account of the assistants. In the 1940s and 1950s some major abuses of authority were discovered. In 1954, for example, came the revelation that 90 percent of the cotton in the canton of Déli was being grown—with French tacit approval—for the private accounts of the local chief, Miadoum, and his assistants. Eruptions of antichiefly sentiments, violence, and the lynching of village chiefs became much more frequent after the Second World War, and anti-French feeling ran high. The practice was officially outlawed in 1955, though it continued in a more modest guise.

In parts of the country where cotton was not grown, similar abuses of authority developed with other crops, most notably date and palm plantations. In Kanem, where the Alifa's (q.v.) power was immense, right through the late 1960s his share of tenants' crops was upwards of one-third. Since neither the colonial power nor the Tombalbaye (q.v.) regime cared to antagonize the Alifa, peasants had only one option—emigration to other domains—and some groups did in fact relocate spontaneously.

CORTADELLAS, EDOUARD (General) (1913–). Former commander in chief of the joint Franco-Chadian forces assembled in 1969 to quell the rebellion in northern and eastern Chad. Born in Toulouse, France, on January 25, 1913, and seeing action in France, the Middle East, Indochina, and Algeria, Cortadellas was promoted to captain in 1942, major in 1951, lieutenant colonel in 1958, and colonel in 1968. A paratroop specialist, he was sent to N'Djamena to replace the first French commander (Brigadier Michel Arnaud) who was recalled to Paris at President François Tombalbaye's (q.v.) request after barely four months in Chad. Cortadellas—whose 24-year-old NCO son was killed early in 1971 in operations in northern Chad—completed his mission on September 1, 1972, when he retired from active duty. (See also ARMED FORCES; FRANCE, FORCES IN CHAD; REBELLIONS.)

CORVEE. Forced labor for purposes of infrastructure-building and porterage exacted in francophone Africa until the end of the Second World War as part of the *indigénat* (q.v.) code applicable to the non-*assimilé* (q.v.) population. In Chad large numbers of southern (Sara) farmers were recruited (often forcibly) for the construction of the Congo-Océan railroad (see CHEMIN DE FER DU CONGO-OCEAN) in what is now Congo-Brazzaville and for other communications infrastructures. Many workers died in the process, and there were several rebellions in 1929 and 1930 along the Chad–Central African Republic (at the time Oubangui-Chari) border, where labor was being impressed.

COTONFRAN see SOCIETE COTONNIERE FRANCOTCHAD-IENNE

COTONTCHAD see SOCIETE COTONNIERE DU TCHAD

COTTON. Chad's principal export, accounting for 80 percent of export revenues, the principal source of economic activity involving over 50 percent of Chad's farmers, and Chad's principal basis for light and service industries. Chad is the world's twelfth-ranking exporter of cotton and francophone Africa's (indeed the franc zone's) leader. Cotton has always been indigenous to the country, though its extensive cultivation dates from the onset of the colonial era when villagers were forced to plant it in excess of their immediate needs in order to pay their head taxes. With the appointment of village chiefs as the officials responsible for the cultivation of the cotton quotas, many abuses of power developed (see CORDES DE CHEFS). Chiefly authority in the south was artificially enhanced, where it had been only nominal, and cotton cultivation came to be equated with colonial rule. These factors contributed to the resistance in many areas to the spread or increase of acreage under cotton cultivation. Because of major transport costs, including the long haul overland and shipment to European centers, local producer prices have been consistently low (and official abuses high), working as a further disincentive for increased production. Today the bulk of Chad's cotton is purchased by Germany.

In 1929, a few years after the creation of Cotonfran (q.v.), cotton began to be grown in commercial quantities, with increasing tonnages, especially after the Second World War. (Production went up from 27,926 tons in 1946/47 to 80,645 tons in 1957/58.) The highest tonnage until 1975/76 occurred in 1968/69 (148,856 tons) with 1965–1975 production usually around 100,000 tons. In 1974 Opération Agriculture (q.v.) was launched by President François Tombalbaye (q.v.) with the goal of harvesting 750,000 tons of cotton by the

end of the year with the assistance of urban and rural "volunteers."
The wildly optimistic plan, cut short by a few months by the coup of
1975, caused major manpower dislocations and large expenditures,
with only minor long-term production benefits. The 1974/75 harvest

COTTON PRODUCTION, 1950, 1958, 1962–94 (in tons)

Year	Grain
1950/51	40,897
1958/59	65,976
1962/63	94,459
1963/64	104,907
1964/65	99,106
1965/66	86,827
1966/67	122,856
1967/68	102,033
1968/69	148,819
1969/70	117,035
1970/71	95,018
1971/72	108,802
1972/73	104,215
1973/74	115,069
1974/75	143,640
1975/76	174,062
1976/77	144,000
1977/78	110,000
1978/79	140,039
1979/80	86,000
1980/81	85,000
1981/82	71,000
1982/83	102,000
1983/84	150,000
1984/85	162,000
1985/86	123,000
1986/87	98,500
1987/88	90,000
1988/89	127,000
1989/90	150,000
1990/91	160,000
1991/92	174,000
1992/93	122,000
1993/94	80,000

was only 143,640 tons (a major improvement nonetheless), and fa-
vorable conditions raised production to 174,062 tons in 1975/76, an
all-time high. Production plummeted subsequently as a consequence

of the drought, population dislocations consequent to the fall of N'-Djamena to northern insurgents, and a switch to food crops. Cotton production made a dramatic comeback, however, in 1983/84, when Chad had its second-best (until then) harvest of 150,000 tons.

The price paid in Chad to producers has remained stable for long periods of time, irrespective of actual world prices. Thus, for 12 years (1958–1970) the producers' price was fixed at 26 CFA francs (around US$0.10) per kilogram (2.2 pounds), though the cost to farmers of cotton cultivation had increased significantly. (Fertilizer costs had gone up by 20 percent during this period, and significantly more since.) Prices were increased to 31 CFA francs in 1971, but this price increase has not motivated farmers to increase cotton cultivation, which, according to some scholars, is a "detested habit" acquired solely for the purpose of satisfying tax obligations. Government efforts to raise cotton production (upon which the modern sector depends so heavily) by increasing the head tax has had the reverse effect, sparking both tax rebellions and tax evasion, none of which the government can really control. (To pay his tax obligation, a farmer had to produce 5 kg in 1930, 21 kg in 1947 and 30 kg in 1970.) Only in the late 1970s were producer prices augmented seriously, to reach 80 CFA francs in 1983/84. The préfecture with the highest production of cotton has been Mayo-Kebbi—37,940 tons in 1972/73 or 36.4 percent of Chad's total production—followed by Logone Orientale and Moyen-Chari, each producing around 15 percent of Chad's total. Very little cotton is raised outside these areas—hence the designation of these Sara (q.v.) regions as "Tchad-utile" (q.v.), for they essentially pay for the administration of the entire country.

Cotton is usually planted between mid-June and mid-July over an area estimated at 300,000 hectares (741,000 acres) and involving actively 950,000 farmers. The cotton crop is harvested in November and December and is collected by Cotontchad (q.v.) (previously Cotonfran, q.v.) until 1975 with the assistance of Chad's two trucking monopolies, Unitchadienne (q.v.) and the Coopérative des Transporteurs Tchadiens (q.v.), to be processed in (originally) 24 ginning mills that employed 3,500 workers, prior to evacuation to transshipment points for European destinations. Yields have in general been low due to lack of irrigation or fertilizer and due to the utter neglect of the crop when the subsistence crops require attention. In 1984, for example, Chad's record-high yield of 836 kilograms per hectare was francophone Africa's second-lowest yield. The textile mills in Sarh (q.v.) process domestic cotton supplying two-thirds of Chad's needs, or 8 million meters of textiles.

In the past decade the level of cotton production has oscillated wildly, reaching an all-time high of 174,000 tons in 1991/92, but plunging only two years later to 80,000 tons. The reason for this has been the collapse of global cotton prices (by 50 percent from 1985 to 1987), which, coupled with the especially high cost of evacuating Chad's produce to Europe, did not make cotton cultivation a very attractive option for farmers. This also affected Cotontchad, which was on the verge of collapse in the mid-1980s. In 1986 Cotontchad was granted a US$47 million rescue package to restructure itself, and in 1992 the company was operating with leaner facilities, having at one point closed down over half its mills and dismissed some 50 percent of its labor force. (In the 1980s it was envisioned that Chad would have to cap cotton production at 100,000 tons in order to avoid excessive losses.) Though cotton prices have recovered since the late 1980s, major fluctuations in production accompany global market price changes. (See also SOCIETE COTONNIERE DU TCHAD; SOCIETE COTONNIERE FRANCO-TCHADIENNE.)

COUMATTEAU, MAURICE (1929–). Administrator and former cabinet minister. Born in Moundou on March 3, 1929, and trained in Paris at the Institut des Hautes Etudes d'Outre-Mer (IHEOM), Coumatteau first worked as a teacher (1952–57) before being appointed Gabriel Lisette's (q.v.) minister of youth (1957–59). In 1961, following François Tombalbaye's (q.v.) rise to power and the purge of Lisette, Coumatteau was appointed prefect of Ouadai and in 1963 inspector of administrative affairs in N'Djamena. He then served in a succession of high-level administrative posts, including as secretary of general education (1965), prefect of Kanem (1966), and prefect of Moyen-Chari (1967–69). In 1969 Coumatteau was appointed general director of the Société pour le Développement de la Région du Lac (SODELAC) (q.v.), and in 1973 he joined the Conseil Economique et Social (q.v.), holding both posts until the coup of 1975.

COUP (ATTEMPTED) OF AUGUST 27, 1971. Libyan-supported attempted attack against the regime of François Tombalbaye (q.v.), which took place early in the morning of August 27, 1971. The leader of the assault was Ahmed Abdallah (q.v.), a National Assembly deputy from Batha who later died in custody. His group unsuccessfully stormed N'Djamena's radio station prior to an alleged attempt to assassinate Tombalbaye. Following the attempted coup, Chad broke diplomatic relations with Libya, ruptured all air links, and issued an invitation to all anti-Qaddafi groups to establish themselves in N'Djamena. At the same time Tombalbaye laid territorial claims to Libya's Fezzan on the grounds of "historic rights." Libya retaliated by recognizing FROLINAT (q.v.) and Abba Siddick (q.v.) and officially offering him a Tripoli base against the N'Djamena regime. The Chad-Libya dispute was mediated by several African statesmen, and a reconciliation was brought about, with Libya renouncing support for FROLINAT and offering Chad a host of fiscal credits (only a few of which materialized) in exchange for Chad's diplomatic break with Israel and de facto acceptance of the territorial validity of the Mussolini-Laval boundary agreement (q.v.). (See also LIBYA.)

COUP (ATTEMPTED) OF JUNE 5, 1972. An alleged aborted coup, though properly speaking more of a guerrilla assault on N'Djamena's installations with the possible anticipation of the creation of an uprising leading to a coup. The attack on N'Djamena's airport and other locations was ineptly led by a former French army sergeant major turned Sarh restaurateur, Jean Claude Gentil. Having joined FROLINAT (q.v.) and convinced Abba Siddick (q.v.) of the coup potentials of an assault on N'Djamena, "Major General" Emile (his new name) led his 20-man group in the sabotage attempt against the airport, petrol storage tanks, and radio and power stations. Most members of the group were apprehended before too much damage could be done, and the assault was followed by a major government purge of figures suspected of links with FROLINAT. The purge developed into a general sweep of all elements suspected of harboring anti-Tombalbaye feelings, and some 1,000 people were allegedly arrested, including such top politicians as Marc Dounia (q.v.) and Antoine Bangui (q.v.).

COUP OF APRIL 13, 1975. Early morning coup d'état in which President François Tombalbaye (q.v.) was killed. Initiated by Lieutenant Dimtoloum (q.v.), who led his units from Bokoro, the force was joined in N'Djamena by some elements of the gendarmerie and other units for the assault upon the Presidential Palace at 5:00 A.M.. The insurgents were later joined by General Odingar (q.v.) and Captain Dabio (q.v.), with the former taking command of the assault, leading to its successful completion. There were numerous casualties among the security forces, segments of which resisted the attack fiercely. The coup d'état was to a significant extent assisted by the supportive role of Major Camille Gourvenac (q.v), the French expatriate secret service director. While the coup had a variety of motivations (see ARMED FORCES), it was in many ways a classic retaliatory action by the military elite against Tombalbaye, who had in the past several years purged the armed forces of many of their senior officers. In the new Conseil Supérieur Militaire du Tchad (CSM) (q.v.), set up after the coup d'état, General Félix Malloum (q.v.)—imprisoned by Tombalbaye since July 1973—was made chairman, and several other officers recently arrested and purged were integrated in the CSM and the government. The CSM appealed to all political exiles to return to Chad and called upon the rebel leaders in the north and the east to lay down their arms and to rally to the new regime. Though the rebellion did not die out, the CSM scored a major triumph when the derde (q.v.) of the Toubou (q.v.) returned from self-imposed exile in Libya. Paradoxically, however, political prisoners were not released for two weeks after the coup, and barely a dozen of Tombalbaye's ministers and officials were arrested for corrupt practices despite the massive fiscal irregularities of the former regime and CSM pledges to purge all those involved.

COUP (ATTEMPTED) OF MARCH 31, 1977. Armed assault, with the aid of the Garde Nomade (q.v.), on the Presidential Palace. Reflecting in part unresolved interarm tensions in the armed forces, the attack was repulsed, though with a number of casualties, including Lieutenant Colonel Dabio (q.v.).

COUP (ATTEMPTED) OF APRIL 1–2, 1989. Touted by Hissène Habré (q.v.) as an attempted coup by key Zaghawa (q.v.) lieutenants that helped sustain him in power, aimed inter alia at killing Acheikh Ibn Oumar (q.v.), though in reality a preemptive strike by Habré prior to a possible power-grab by the Zaghawa. Having alienated the Hadjeray (q.v.) in the mid-1980s through a series of purges, arrests, and misguided liquidations, Habré had in 1988 and 1989 begun a similar swath of destruction among his Zaghawa allies. Among those most disaffected were Hassan Djamouss (q.v.), the hero of the 1986–87 victory against Libya—whose brother-in-law Siddick Ali Fadoul (a secret police officer who was later killed in detention) had all five of his brothers arrested; Idriss Déby (q.v.), who accompanied Habré's victorious march into N'Djamena in 1982; and Minister of Interior Ibrahim Mahamat Itno (q.v.). On the night of April 1 the major Zaghawa leaders fled the capital toward Sudan, under hot pursuit by Habré's troops. Itno was captured and promptly killed; Djamouss was badly wounded and then was also killed. Déby survived to raise an army and oust Habré from power on December 2, 1990.

COUP (ATTEMPTED) OF OCTOBER 13, 1991. Spurious coup attempt claim by Idriss Déby (q.v.), used to eliminate the rising ambitions of a rival, Maldoum Bada Abbas (q.v.). The official story, still referred to in some analyses in the West, had it that Abbas (then technically the second most important person in the new Déby regime) and his Hadjeray (q.v.) supporters had raided an arms depot in N'Djamena prior to an assault on Déby over promotion grievances. There may have been an attack on the arms depot by rowdy elements of his entourage, but Abbas was not involved in a coup bid, though he was arrested and framed for mounting one. He was released from prison the following year, and in 1995 he was integrated into Déby's cabinet. (For more details, see ABBAS, MALDOUM BADA.)

COUR DE SURETE DE L'ETAT. State court set up by General Félix Malloum (q.v.) in October 1976 when Chad's Supreme Court (see COUR SUPREME) was closed down. The court was composed of eight members, civilian as well as military, and was specifically empowered to try capital offenses against the state. The court continued to meet throughout the Goukouni, Habré, and Déby (qq.v.) eras, acting functionally, together with the N'Djamena Court of Appeals, as the supreme court of Chad. A Supreme Court has never been reinstated, since to do so would open a venue for claims against the state itself as well as constitutional claims, neither of which any head of state has been willing to tolerate.

COUR SUPERIEURE DE JUSTICE. Not to be confused with the Cour Suprême du Tchad (q.v.), the Cour Supérieure de Justice was a special high tribunal set up in July 1972 to deal with cases of embezzlement (and general maladministration) by high government officials. Members of the court were elected by the National Assembly. Despite a great deal of fanfare greeting the creation of the court and pledges that it would root out corruption in high places, the court spent most of its time in purging President François Tombalbaye's (q.v.) real or imagined enemies, whether corrupt or not. The court, under a different name—Haute Cour—was resurrected in February 1985, again to root out corruption.

COUR SUPREME DU TCHAD. Chad's Supreme Court during the Tombalbaye (q.v.) era and resurrected in 1990 (not to be confused with the Cour Supérieure de Justice [q.v.]). The Cour Suprême was established on April 2, 1963, with five magistrates. Because of the acute shortage of trained legal personnel in Chad, all cases coming before the Cour Suprême were until 1967 referred to Paris, to the Appellate Court, as during colonial days. The court also sat as a high tribunal in cases involving treason, when its five magistrates were joined by a jury of 15 from the electoral college. Between 1963 and 1971 the president of the Cour Suprême was Hanoun Outman (q.v.); in 1971 the former minister of health, Pierre Djimé (q.v.), became its president. The Cour Suprême was closed down after the 1975 coup d'état, and it remained inoperative until Habré's 1990 constitution revived it. It then had three panels, one constitutional, one judicial, and one administrative and financial, and 15 magistrates. Between 1975 and 1990 N'Djamena's Court of Appeals served functionally as a supreme court, though without the title, except in more serious cases when the Cour de Sûreté d'Etat played the role of a supreme court.

CULTURAL REVOLUTION. A series of policies during the Tombalbaye (q.v.) era aimed at purging Chad of foreign and colonial practices and influences. Officially launched at the 1968 first congress of the JEPPT (q.v.)—the PPT's youth wing—the "Cultural Revolution" actually came into force only several years later, especially between 1972 and Tombalbaye's ouster. During this period the names of several towns were "Chadianized" (Fort-Lamy became N'Djamena; Fort-Archambault was renamed Sarh), street names and monuments were purged of colonial figures (except for Avenue Charles de Gaulle and the Félix Eboué monument in the capital), greeting terms were changed (e.g., "*compatriote*" instead of "*Monsieur*"), and government officials were required (at the pain of dismissal and possibly arrest) to drop their Christian names in favor of ethnic names. The Yondo (q.v.) initiation rites—or an equivalent—became quasi-obligatory for the Westernized population, at the inspiration of Dr. André Vixamar (q.v.), a Haitian. According to President Tombalbaye, the Yondo rites were the essence of *Tchaditude* or *authenticité* (other terms used for "Cultural Revolution"). His prescription that all Chadians undergo the rites led to many religious protests, and various expatriate missionary groups were subsequently expelled from the country. Indigenous priests were in particular singled out to undergo the rites, and many who refused were brutally tortured and killed (see YONDO). In some respects the rites may be viewed as an attempt by Tombalbaye and his aides to unite the southern elements in the country in face of the northern Muslim rebellion.

-D-

DABI, ABDERAHMANE. Secretary-general of the government, since June 1994, replacing Dono Horngar Neldita.

DABIO, ALI (Lt. Colonel) (?–1977). Chief of staff of Chad's army from August 1975 to March 1977, not well known until the 1975 coup d'état. He was promoted to major after the coup, having assisted the plotters at a critical juncture: he arrived at the scene of the fighting with a force of troops which, taken over under the direction of General Odingar (q.v.), the army commander, tipped the balance against troops resisting the assault on the Presidential Palace. In 1977 Dabio was promoted again, to lieutenant colonel, when his star seemed to be rising very rapidly. He died, however, on March 31, 1977, while repulsing an attack on the Presidential Palace.

DAGACHE, OKI MAHAMAT (Lt. Colonel). One of Idriss Déby's (q.v.) cronies, Dagache was appointed deputy director of the president's military cabinet in 1994.

DAI see DAYE

DAIDANSOU, KADAFI. Deputy secretary general of the government under Idriss Déby (q.v.), an administrative post, appointed in November 1991. In December the same year Daidansou was appointed secretary of state for foreign affairs, and in May 1992 he was appointed secretary of state for finance. He served until the Conférence Nationale (q.v.) in 1993 selected its own cabinet.

DAIDANSOU, RENE. A pastor who participated in the 1993 Conférence Nationale (q.v.), Daidansou was one of five candidates nominated for the chairmanship of the conference. Adoum Hel-Bongo (q.v.) was ultimately elected.

DAJU (also DADJO). A Sudanese ethnic group that for some time formed the reigning dynasty of Darfur (q.v.) and dominated Ouadai (q.v.) in the fifteenth century. Today both their numbers and their power are minimal. Estimates of Chad's Daju are particularly unreliable because of their current intermixture with the Maba (q.v.) and intermarriage with Arab elements and Hadjeray (q.v.) groups such as the Kinga (q.v.). Estimates range widely from slightly more than 6,000 (counting only the ethnically pure Am Dam Daju) to possibly some 100,000. They are currently found in Chad in Dar Sila (q.v.)—near Mongo (q.v.)—in Goz Beida, and in general north of the Guéra mountains and Abou Telfane. Calling themselves Koska, the Daju were chased out of Darfur in the sixteenth century by the Tunjur (q.v.), and they then split into two groups. They did not arrive at Dar Sila until a much later date (at the beginning of the eighteenth century), and in the vicinity of Mongo only in the nineteenth century. Since the eighteenth century most of the Daju have been under the domination of the Ouadai kingdom (q.v.). Though converted to Islam (and their Sudanic language rapidly replaced by Arabic), they retained many pre-Islamic beliefs and cults that are similar to those of the Kinga in the same general region. In Sudan's Darfur the Daju number 100,000 and are regarded as one of the oldest population groups in the region.

DALATAWA. Kanembu (q.v.)–Kanuri (q.v.) subgroup, found mostly in Mao (q.v.) in the Kanem Préfecture. The Dalatawa are the descendants of the Bornuan army sent in the mid–seventeenth century to expel the Tunjur (q.v.) invaders who had conquered Kanem, which was regarded as a Bornuan tributary state. The leader of the expeditionary force was a Hausa slave by the name of Dala Afuno (or Afno), and his descendants (named after him) still reign as customary chiefs and as the Alifas (q.v.) of Mao, the principal traditional leaders of Kanem.

DALMAIS, PAUL. Former archbishop of N'Djamena, replaced in 1981 by Charles Vandome.

DAMAYE, DANGBE LAOUBELE see DANGBE, LAOUBELE DAMAYE

DANA, ADOUM ABDULAHI. Former rebel leader based in Sudan, and interim head of the Volcan Army (q.v.) after the death of "General" Mohamed Baghalani (q.v.) in 1977. Widely regarded as "Sudan's man," Dana's military forays against N'Djamena's forces came from bases in Sudan. After the fall of N'Djamena to Goukouni (q.v.), the Volcan Army split into several factions, with Dana retaining a small force of 300 men and a larger group following Acyl's CDR (qq.v.). Not invited to attend the first Kano Meeting (q.v.) in 1979, he was invited to the second and joined Goukouni's November 1979 GUNT (q.v.) government as minister of public works. He was dropped from the cabinet in July 1981 due to his siding with Hissène Habré (q.v.) against Goukouni, but he patched up his differences with the latter and joined the Bardai-based GUNT government. Due to splits in the Volcan Army, Dana's own force was then often referred to as the First Volcan Army.

DANGALEAT. A Hadjeray (q.v.) ethnic group, probably of Nilotic origin.

DANGBE, LAOUBELE DAMAYE. Minister of health, appointed in April 1995. A former rector of the Faculty of Letters at the University of Chad, Dangbé participated in the 1993 Conférence Nationale as leader of a party, the Rassemblement du Peuple Tchadien (RPT) (q.v.).

DANSALA, BAMBE. Early Idriss Déby (q.v.) cabinet member. Dansala was appointed minister of rural development in March 1991, retaining his post through several shuffles until May 1992, when he was transferred to head the Ministry of Agriculture. He served in that capacity until the Conférence Nationale (q.v.) chose its own cabinet in 1993.

DAR. Arabic word for "home" or "realm," as in Darfur or Dar Sila— realm of the Fur or Sila.

DAR KOUTI. Former province and tributary state of the Ouadai kingdom (q.v.), currently partly within the Central African Republic. Dar Kouti was conquered in 1890 by Rabah (q.v.), who appointed Mohamed-es-Senoussi (q.v.) as sultan. Of a rival lineage, es-Senoussi remained loyal to Rabah. For a while, Dar Kouti's capital, N'Délé, became an important caravan stop on the southern slave and ivory route and a stop on the pilgrim route to Mecca. Resistance to the French penetration of the region was intense, and in 1911 the French decided to eliminate es-Senoussi's stronghold, which they did. Es-Senoussi was killed in the fighting and the sultanate was disbanded.

DAR ROUNGA. Former tributary state of the Ouadai kingdom (q.v.) south of Abéché (q.v.). Populated mostly by various Arab clans and a mixture of other ethnic groups, the area had previously been administered by the *aguid* (q.v.) of Salamat.

DAR SILA. Region in Ouadai where a Daju (q.v.) political entity still exists today. After the overthrow of the Daju (also Dadjo) dynasty in Darfur (q.v.), the reigning king, Ahmad al-Dadj, escaped to central Ouadai and set up a small principality in Dar Sila. The entity survived the upheaval of Abd-el-Kerim (q.v.) in Ouadai, and had 14 kings until full French sovereignty was exerted in 1916. Dar Sila was the southernmost sultanate constituting the boundary between acknowledged Darfur and Ouadai power. With its capital in the small village of Goz Beida, there are currently some 60,000 people living in the sultanate, of which 36,000 are Daju, 18,000 Arab nomads, and some 6,000 Sinyar. The kings of Dar Sila were: Ahmed al-Dadj, 1486–1508; Ibrahim, 1508–19; Adam, 1519–72; Hassaballah, 1572–1616; Habib, 1616–44; Chou'aib, 1644–64; Saleh, 1664–1703; Charaf, 1703–35; Issa Hadjar, 1735–79; Abd el-Kerim, 1779–1813; Abd el-Latif, 1813–51; El Hadj Bolad, 1851–79; Ishaq, 1879–1900; Bakhit, 1900–1916.

DARFUR. Region immediately east of Ouadai (q.v.) in Sudan, and center of several powerful kingdoms in the past; its capital is el-Fasher. The pre-eighteenth-century history of Darfur has not been fully documented, but there were three dynasties in the region: the Daju (q.v.), about whose ancient history little is known but whose dominion was centered to the south and east of the Jabal Marra mountains; the Tunjar (q.v.)—centered north of the Jabal Marra massif—who replaced the Daju and pushed a segment of them into Chad; and the Keira dynasty, which replaced the Tunjur in Darfur, though the Tunjur were to rule for another century in Ouadai. (See also BIRGOU; DAJU; OUADAI; TUNJUR.) Tradition maintains that the Daju came from the east and established their rule over the various tribes in Darfur during the twelfth and thirteenth centuries before being displaced (peacefully), for reasons still not fully clear, by the Tunjur. The origin of the Tunjur is also subject to several interpretations, but by the sixteenth century they ruled a large empire centered at Uri and Ayn Farah, stretching from Darfur to Dar Sila (q.v.) and including Ouadai (Birgou). Overthrown in Darfur by the Keira during the sixteenth century, a Tunjur dynasty continued its rule in Ouadai until the upheaval by Abd-el-Kerim (q.v.) in 1611 (or 1635). The new Maba (q.v.) state of Ouadai then continued paying tribute to Darfur until a series of inconclusive wars between them in the eighteenth century established the coequal status of the two. Given the balance of power that developed in the East, Ouadai's ambitions then swung to the west and south, while Darfur expanded mostly to the northeast eventually conquering the Kordofan plains, which it soon lost, however, to a joint Turco-Egyptian force in 1821. Though nominally converted to Islam as early as the seventeenth century, Islam only made serious inroads in Darfur in the late nineteenth century, following its conquest by Zubeir Pasha (q.v.) on November 2, 1874. Zubeir's deputy, Rabah (q.v.), later began his brutal slave-raiding conquest of Central Africa from Darfur. At the end of the nineteenth century the Darfur periphery was organized into a series of principalities in the Jabal Marra mountains ruled by members of the royal clans. After the overthrow of Zubeir Pasha's hegemony in the area and the defeat and death of Rabah (1900), Darfur—for some time in rapid decline—having fared poorly during the Mahdi's rule in Sudan, was not integrated into the new Sudanese territorial entity, largely due to its isolation and lack of importance. The region thus remained largely independent of European control (the French also were disinclined to launch their occupation from Ouadai, which itself was barely conquered) until the second decade of the twentieth century. In 1916, however, during the First World War, Sultan Ali Dinar (1898–1916) declared war against Great Britain, and his kingdom was consequently invaded and absorbed into Sudan. Darfur has always been extremely suspicious of foreigners, especially Christians, as was well documented by Gustav Nachtigal (q.v.) during his visit there in the latter part of the nineteenth century.

In the contemporary era Darfur has been (and remains today) a very unruly province in Sudan, virtually out of the control of the government in Khartoum. Apart from a few checkpoints, the border with Chad is utterly meaningless to quasi-nomadic ethnic groups that cross it periodically. Even the provincial capital, el-Fasher, is largely autonomous from Khartoum. The province has given refuge to numerous armed groups fleeing N'Djamena's control, who openly recruit armies from refugee groups there (as well as from Sudanese ethnic kinsmen) and mount attacks in Chad from bases in Darfur. Both

Hissène Habré (q.v.) and, more recently, Idriss Déby (q.v.) mounted their military assaults, which eventually brought them to power in Chad, from Darfur, with little interference from the official authorities, both provincial and national. Indeed, when Déby's armies conquered N'Djamena on December 2, 1990, they included thousands of non-Chadian Zaghawa (q.v.) and other Sudanese groups who spoke neither French nor Arabic. Libya—which played a major role in Chadian events between 1972 and at least 1988—also maintained a large and undisputed military presence in Darfur. Large units of Libya's (mostly nonindigenous) Islamic Legion (q.v.) were based in Darfur, as were numerous of Libya's military officers. During Déby's preparations for his assault on Habré in 1989 and 1990 a regular military air link existed between Kufra (q.v.) (in the Libyan desert) and el-Fasher, in Darfur.

DARSALLAH. First derde (q.v.) of the Teda (q.v.). Of the Tomaghera (q.v.) clan, Darsallah was the son of Kodor Fouri, common ancestor of the Tomaghera, Gounda, and Tarsoa clans, in the sixteenth century. Darsallah received his white turban (*kadmul* [q.v.], symbol of office) from the Tozoba, a tradition that has remained over the ages.

DASSERT, DJIBRINE (Colonel). Former chief of staff of Idriss Déby's (q.v.) forces during the assault on N'Djamena. A southerner, Dassert was an early supporter of Déby and was a cofounder of Déby's MPS (q.v.). On the entry of Déby's troops into N'Djamena, Dassert was rewarded by appointment as minister of defense in Déby's first government in 1990. However, as a southerner, he was rapidly marginalized by a host of demands by Déby's northern supporters, and he resigned from the government in November 1992 to join one of the opposition parties.

DAYE (also DAI). Small Sara ethnic group of about 60,000, found along the middle reaches of the Mandoul and in the Moïssala district. Though virtually assimilated into the wider Sara family of ethnic groups, the Daye dialect remains distinctly different.

DAZA. One of the two branches of the Toubou (q.v.) people in northern Chad, who call themselves Dazagada ("those who speak Dazaga"). The other branch, the Teda (q.v.) (or Tedagada), found farther west, in Tibesti, speak a very similar dialect, and both dialects are linked to the Kanuri (q.v.) language. The two branches have more often than not been extremely antagonistic to each other, with the Daza in particular holding the Teda in deep contempt. The Daza are called "Gorane" by the Arab populations in the region, a name that has paradoxically been used exclusively to refer to them in contemporary Western reports about Hissène Habré (q.v.), their most illustrious leader. The Daza are especially found in the Borkou and Ennedi regions of B.E.T. (q.v.) and in larger numbers in northern Kanem. They are divided into a variety of subgroups that nomadize specific valleys. Estimates of the numbers of Daza in northern Chad vary. They probably encompass 250,000 people, most of whom (200,000) are in Chad, primarily in Kanem (120,000), Borkou (40,000), and Ennedi (19,000). In the northern regions the Daza are mostly Senoussi (see SANUSIYA); in the south and in Kanem they belong to the Tidjaniya (q.v.) sect. (See also TOUBOU.) The Daza joined in the Toubou rebellion against N'Djamena in the mid-1960s, though they were polarized behind different leaders. Goukouni (q.v.) emerged as the leader of the Teda, while Habré gained the allegiance of the Anakaza (q.v.), the Daza subgroup of which he is a member.

DEBI. Turban in the Teda language, and better known in Chad specifically as *kadmul* (q.v.), the symbol of office of the derde (q.v.) of the Teda (q.v.).

DEBOUT, FRANÇOIS (1933–). Agricultural director and former National Assembly deputy. Born in 1933 in Ngandayé in Logone Occidentale, Debout has had a lifelong commitment to agricultural education. He occupied several such posts between 1953 and 1958, when he was selected for specialized training in France. Following his return to Chad he served as instructor of public works at the Agricultural School of Ba-Illi (where he had begun his own education) and was later appointed director of the Bekdo Experimental Farm (1964–69) and head of the Agricultural Sector of Biltine. In 1969 he was elected deputy to the National Assembly, and he remained in that organ until the 1975 coup.

DEBY, DAOUSSA. Powerful presidential aide to Idriss Déby, his brother.

DEBY, IDRISS (Lt. Colonel) (1952–). President of Chad since December 2, 1990, when his armed forces swept in from Darfur (q.v.) to defeat Hissène Habré's (q.v.) armies and capture N'Djamena. Of Zagahawa (q.v.) ethnicity and son of a destitute seminomadic herdsman in the Fada oasis (Ennedi), Déby seems to have been destined for a military career. He was lucky enough to have been selected for pilot training after cadet training in N'Djamena and in 1976 was sent to France where he obtained his wings. He returned to N'Djamena in 1978 to serve in the Malloum-Habré regime. As the tug-of-war between Malloum (q.v.) and

Habré broke out, and later between Goukouni (q.v.) and Habré, Déby sided with Habré and accompanied him into brief exile in Libya. Becoming his right-hand man and chief of staff, he brilliantly led Habré's FAN (q.v.) troops into N'Djamena on June 7, 1982, and into southern Chad the following month. Promoted to colonel and chief of staff, he followed his military successes in 1983 with action against Goukouni's and Libya's troops in Chad, and in 1985 he was sent to Paris to take the Ecole de Guerre's senior officers' staff course. He was replaced as chief of staff by Hassan Djamouss (q.v.), also a Zaghawa. On his return in 1986 he was attached to Habré's presidential office as a security and defense aide, and he headed the daring raid on Libya's Maaten-es-Sarra airbase that helped to convince Libya to sue for peace.

Notwithstanding this success, in April 1989, as Habré's paranoid swath of destruction decimated the Zaghawa who had originally sustained him, Déby was accused of plotting a coup. Déby and some of his Zaghawa colleagues fled N'Djamena, with Habré's troops in hot pursuit. Two of his close companions did not make it: Minister of Interior Ibrahim Mahamat Itno (q.v.) was captured while in N'Djamena and promptly executed, and Chief of Staff Djamouss was severely wounded during the flight, captured by Habré's troops, and also executed.

Déby managed to reach Darfur, Sudan, a secure base for his counterassault, and later went to Libya. Revealing to Muammar Qaddafi the full extent of official and covert (i.e., CIA) aid the United States had extended to Habré, Déby received Qaddafi's pledge of Libya's fiscal and military aid, in exchange for a promise to release all Libyan POWs still held in N'Djamena since the Chadian victory in B.E.T. in 1987. (Indeed, among Déby's first acts when he came to power in 1990 were to dismantle the CIA camps and to order all Libyan POWs freed.) In Darfur Déby founded the Front Patriotique du Salut Tchadien (FPST) (q.v.), later renamed the Mouvement Populaire du Salut (MPS) (q.v.), built up a large fighting force, and established links with other elements there opposing Habré. Among the groups that linked up with him were the Hadjeray MOSANAT (q.v.) of Lt. Maldoum Bada Abbas (q.v.), alienated earlier in the 1980s; remnants of the FROLINAT First Army of Mahamat Abba Seid (qq.v.); the unreconciled faction of the CDR (q.v.) under Dr. Moctar Moussa (q.v.); Mahamat Saleh (q.v.); Ousmane Gam (q.v.), Hassan Fadoul, and Djibrine Dassert (q.v.).

Since Habré had a healthy respect for the military capabilities of his former chief of staff, Chadian troops were on several occasions sent deep into Darfur to attack Déby's training camps. Déby simply withdrew deeper into Darfur, making occasional forays into Ouadai. (In one of these he captured Habré's chief of staff, Colonel Worimi (q.v.), who was later rescued by Chadian troops. In November 1990 Déby was ready and initiated Opération Rezzou (q.v.), which took place in eastern Chad near the Darfur border. There Déby's and Habré's troops met in several sharp battles. In one of these, which Habré personally directed, he was nearly captured. Déby scored several spectacular victories, and as Habré's armies scattered, leaving 1,700 dead (to Déby's 700 casualties), Déby took Abéché unopposed, and the next day, December 2, 1990, entered N'Djaména, again unopposed. Habré, having looted the treasury, slipped across the border into Niger with some 1,000 of his troops and DDS (q.v.) henchmen.

On December 4 Déby was inaugurated as head of state, promising democracy and a reign of law. He was to deliver none of these. His reign until recently has been only slightly less brutal or bloody than Habré's, and he has repeated many of the mistakes that Habré had committed before him. His regime has been characterized by massacres of innocent villagers in the south; arrests, liquidations, and "disappearances" of political leaders and other influentials; and intimidation of civic leaders, human rights advocates, and what few newspaper editors dared to criticize the activities of his security forces. Déby has also dragged his feet on the issue of democratization and multiparty elections. Thus, though a national conference took place in 1993 (see CONFERENCE NATIONALE) and elections were supposed to take place as early as 1994, they were postponed to 1995, and for one reason or another they are still scheduled to take place at some indeterminate time in the future. His main forces of repression are the 2,000-strong elite, nearly all-Zaghawa, Garde Républicaine (q.v.)—the functional equivalent of Habré's Daza (q.v.) Garde Présidentielle (q.v.), and the secret political police, the Agence Nationale de Sécurité (ANS) (q.v.). The latter is the successor of the CRCR (q.v.), disbanded at the express request of the Conférence Nationale due to its atrocities, but constituted with much the same purposes and personnel. (Many of the officers had also previously served in Habré's secret police force, the DDS.)

DECLARATION DE N'DJAMENA. In essence a provisional constitution adopted on May 8, 1982, by Goukouni's GUNT (qq.v.) government. The various factions of GUNT confirmed Goukouni as president of Chad, with Djidingar (q.v.) as prime minister, and divided 15 seats in the Council of State among the various groups. (See also CONSTITUTIONS.) Shortly later Goukouni was ousted by Hissène Habré (q.v.).

DELSIA SOUSSIA, ROBERT (1932–). Former minister of defense. Born in 1932 in Moulfoudayel (in the district of Fianga) and trained as a veterinarian nurse, Delsia Soussia was elected to the Territorial

Assembly as PPT (q.v.) delegate from Mayo-Kebbi on March 31, 1957, and was reelected in 1959 and 1962. In June 1959 he was brought into the cabinet as secretary of state for public works, and from April to August 1960 served as secretary of state for interior affairs. In August 1960 he was appointed minister of social affairs, and in March 1962 he was promoted to the key post of minister of national defense. His eclipse was equally swift; in 1964 Delsia Soussia—briefly considered as heir apparent to Tombalbaye (q.v.)—was downgraded to minister of state in charge of defense as Tombalbaye assumed greater personal control over the security forces of Chad, and in November of the same year Delsia Soussia lost all control over defense affairs when he was appointed minister delegate to the presidency, an advisory post without the control of a portfolio. In November 1965 he was arrested for allegedly plotting against Tombalbaye in a comeback effort, and was only rehabilitated in the major amnesties of 1969.

DEPARTEMENT. Temporary administrative unit into which Chad was divided prior to the Second World War. (See also ADMINISTRATIVE ORGANIZATION.)

DERDE. Teda (q.v.) title denoting chief of clan. When applied to the Teda as a whole, refers to the superior nonhereditary chief of the Tomaghera (q.v.) clan, who is chosen from the clan's three major families (the Erdindoga, Laindoga, and Aramidoga) by a council of notables of the Tozoba clan (from which previous derdes had been chosen). The derde is recognized as the spiritual head of all the Teda of Tibesti and is therefore the most important traditional leader in the north. The last fully independent derde was Shaffai Bogarmi, who ruled the Teda from 1894 until defeated by the French and driven into the Fezzan in 1914. In 1920 he returned to Tibesti, made his peace with the French and reassumed his traditional authority until his death in 1939. Prior to the French colonial era the derde had exacted tribute from all the desert oases and cultivators of palm trees in the Tibesti, as well as from trans-Saharan caravans, and he also received a percentage of the booty captured by his tribesmen in their various raids. His symbol of authority is the pre-Islamic *kadmul* (q.v.) green turban. The next derde after Shaffai Bogarmi, chosen in 1939, was Wodei Kichidemi (q.v.), who in 1975 returned to Zouar, his capital, after nine years in self-exile in Libya during the B.E.T. (q.v.) rebellion (see REBELLIONS) in which four of his five sons were killed. (Goukouni [q.v.], former president of Chad, and currently in similar self-exile in Libya and Algeria, is his last surviving son.) Kichidemi's immediate power was over his own Tomaghera, and to a lesser extent over the two other "noble" clans, the Gounda and the Arna; among the other Teda clans, which are highly autonomous, he had prestige but little authority. In 1966 President Tombalbaye (q.v.) — taking over direct control of B.E.T. from the French — withdrew the derde's customary judicial powers while at the same time the Chadian local administration greatly offended Toubou (q.v.) sensitivities by a series of high-handed measures and atrocities, all of which sparked the rebellion in the north and the derde's escape to Libya. As noted, he returned to Chad on August 14, 1975, shortly after the coup d'état that brought about Tombalbaye's death. He was given full military honors by the new military regime and was reinstated in office with his pre-1986 powers restored. Shortly later he called upon all Toubou rebels to lay down their arms, and when Goukouni ignored him, he disinherited him, naming Hissa Luli Ali Humé (q.v.) as successor derde of the Toubou. Kichidemi's reconciliation with N'Djamena was brief, however. By 1977 he was back in exile in Libya, where he died later that year.

DERRING, KOUMBAMBA (Captain). Former quartermaster general of the Chadian army. A Malloum (q.v.) (and later Kamougoué [q.v.]) loyalist, Derring was appointed director of trade and industry following the 1975 coup d'état and army quartermaster general in mid-1976. A Sara from the south, he was also one of the FAT (q.v.) cabinet ministers in the post–Kano II GUNT (q.v.) government, serving as minister of foreign affairs from April to November 1979. With the fall of the Sara south to FAN (q.v.) and rebel FAT elements, Derring was arrested in Kélo and was summarily executed.

DESSANDE TOKOBE, PIERRE ALFRED see BEADENGAR, DESSANDE

DEVELOPMENT PLANS. Between 1960 and 1964 Chad had no development or investment plans. An intermediate 1964–65 plan conducted basic research and studies, including inventories of potential resources, and mapped existing prospects for the economy. Following this the First Five-Year Plan (1966–70) was launched.

The First Five-Year Plan projected expenditures of 47,012 million CFA francs aimed at lessening Chad's dependence upon outside forces via (1) rapid agricultural development, (2) renovation of transport infrastructures, including roads and feeder roads, and (3) the training of agricultural cadres. Some 42.5 percent of the funds were earmarked for the productive sector, 33.5 percent for infrastructure, and 10.8 percent for training. The plan's goals were completely revised downward in 1969 when it was obvious that the projected targets were highly optimistic. Despite the massive scaling down of the plan, only 65 percent of the objectives were attained, expenditures reaching only 26,200 million CFA francs.

In 1971 the Second Five-Year Plan (1971–75) was launched, part of a master Ten-Year Plan (1971–80), the goal of which was the doubling of national revenue, with priority on exports, especially cotton, cattle, and sugar. The cotton target for 1975 was fixed at 200,000 tons, and when it became clear by 1974 that the target, though a realistic one, would probably not be attained, Opération Agriculture (q.v.) was launched by the Tombalbaye (q.v.) regime. Cattle projections, too, were directly affected for the worse by the Sahelian drought (see CATTLE; DROUGHT) and actually greatly decreased, while the projected expansion of sugar production was much lower than expected.

The Ten-Year Plan projected expenditures of 221,000 million CFA francs, with 79,700 million allocated for road construction, 57,000 million for railroads (the extension of the Trans-Cameroonian railroad; see COMMUNICATIONS), 24,300 million for agriculture, 13,200 million for stockbreeding, 10,200 million for industry, 10,000 million for education, and 4,200 million for water resources. The plan was drastically revised downward in 1975/76, with most of its goals reduced beyond recognition. It had originally been drafted with the assistance of teams from both the United Nations and the Fonds d'Aide et de Coopération (FAC) (q.v.).

With the fall of N'Djamena, first to Goukouni's forces and later to Habré's (qq.v.), economic activity, except in the south, came to a halt. Buildings and factories destroyed during the fighting remained for years in shambles, damaged and deserted. Over half of N'Djamena's population fled during the internecine fighting in N'Djamena at the time, and few of those who returned had adequate funds to rebuild businesses. Moreover, with Habré came a large number of Toubou (q.v.), Hadjeray (q.v.), and Zaghawa (q.v.) camp-followers, who ruthlessly took over choice properties without payment. Revenue sources for the central administration also shriveled. Even in 1984, fully 85 percent of Chad's budgetary revenues came from customs duties on imports. For all practical purposes "planning" of all sorts was at a standstill in Chad for nearly a decade. In 1985 an Interim 1986–1988 Development Plan was produced for a donors' meeting, but as it was unrealistic it never got off the ground. A new attempt, in 1987, produced the 1987–1989 Development Plan, aiming at a 1.2 percent growth in GDP, with emphasis on the rehabilitation of Cotontchad, which was suddenly piling up massive debts in the late 1980s. The program saved Cotontchad by restructuring it, but it was otherwise not very successful. The following year the fall of the Habré regime to Déby set development efforts back again. In 1993 the Déby regime finally produced its own 1993–1998 Five-Year Plan with the financial involvement of France, the World Bank, the African Development Bank, the European Development Fund, and Germany. The plan aimed at increasing the GDP by 5 percent per year, rehabilitating destroyed or inefficient projects, and studying the feasibility of the pipeline connecting Doba with the Atlantic coast via Cameroon.

DIALLO, ALI MUHAMMAD. Head of the Mouvement National de Réforme Tchadienne political party, formed in 1992.

DIAR, ALI DJALBOR. Minister of tourism, water, and forests, appointed in July 1984 and replaced two years later.

DIMTOLOUM (Major). The military officer who initiated the 1975 coup d'état that toppled President François Tombalbaye's (q.v.) regime. Then a lieutenant, Dimtoloum mounted the coup from the Bokoro barracks, driving into the capital and attacking the local gendarmerie depot. (See COUP OF APRIL 13, 1975.) His poorly armed troops were then joined by some elements of the local Compagnie Tchadienne de Sécurité (q.v.)—most of which resisted the attack for hours—and by units commanded by Captain (later promoted to lieutenant colonel) Ali Dabio (q.v.) and General Odingar (q.v.), both of whom had been surprised by the coup. Dimtoloum was promoted to captain after the coup d'état and assigned to duties in Kanem. In 1982 he resurfaced in Tandjilé, heading GUNT (q.v.) army squads attacking Habré (q.v.) militia units there.

DIRECTION DE LA DOCUMENTATION ET DE LA SECURITE (DDS). Hissène Habré's (q.v.) infamous secret political police, which has been accused of direct or indirect involvement in thousands of brutal murders. The DDS received much secret funding from the U.S. embassy in N'Djamena and training from CIA agents. In exchange Habré was more than happy to allow the CIA to run a "secret" (actually well-known) base in Am-Sinene (q.v.) in the northern suburbs of N'Djamena that trained a Libyan fifth column from some of the officers captured by Chad during its attacks on Libyan troops in B.E.T. and in Maaten-es-Sarra. (The base and the CIA's destabilization efforts were terminated early in 1991.) The base was paradoxically also the DDS's largest detention center for prisoners. The head of the DDS was Habré's first cousin, Korei Guini (q.v.), a particularly brutal and much feared officer, with wide authority to liquidate anyone he felt was a threat to the stability of the regime. Guini was also largely trained by the CIA, though the DDS was supported also by six military intelligence officers. Later, in 1990, Hamed Hallata (q.v.) assumed the post from Guini. The alienation from Habré of the Zaghawa military elite that eventually ousted him was largely because of the brutalities of Guini.

Numerous DDS officers and hundreds of its troops escaped N'Djamena with the fall of the capital to Idriss Déby (q.v.) on December 2, 1990. Many are found to this day in Niger's Lake Chad area (where they are referred to as the Khmer Rouge), from where they have made occasional forays into Chad. However, numerous middle-echelon DDS officers were integrated into Déby's own secret police, the CRCR (q.v.) and later the ANS (q.v.).

DISTRICTS. Pre-independence administrative units into which Chad was divided. Above the district level were the *régions* (q.v.). Following independence the districts were renamed *souspréfectures* (q.v.) and the régions became *préfectures* (q.v.). The number of districts in Chad varied over the years. In 1950, for example, the country was composed of nine régions, which were divided into 39 districts and six *postes de contrôle administratif* (q.v.), each of the local units further divided into *cantons* (q.v.) encompassing a number of villages. (See also ADMINISTRATIVE ORGANIZATION.)

DJABAYE, BRAHIM (1922–). Educator and former PPT (q.v.) militant. Born in 1922 in Odona-N'Garkassilé (near Abéché), Djabaye was a devout and dedicated Koranic school pupil who was selected to continue his education at Cairo's Al-Azhar University (1940–52). Upon his return to Chad in 1952 he joined the teaching staff of the Lycée Franco-Arabe in Abéché, teaching Arabic. A member of the PPT Steering Committee in Abéché, Djabaye was elected to the National Assembly in 1969, remaining in that post until the coup of 1975. He then resumed his teaching career until his retirement.

DJALABO, OTHMAN ABOUBAKAR see OTHMAN, DJALABO ABOUBAKAR

DJALAL, ABDERAHIM see ABDERAHIM, DJALAL

DJAMOUSS, HASSAN (1954–1989). Former chief of staff. Djamouss was born in Iriba, Biltine, in 1954 (though some sources list his birthdate as early as 1953 and as late as 1956) of mixed Hadjeray-Kanembu origins. He studied in the Ba-Illi agricultural technical school (1971–75), following which he served for one year with the Salamat agricultural sector and then in 1976 joined the national office for rural development. He joined in Hissène Habré's (q.v.) rebellion and became one of Habré's main lieutenants in FAN (q.v.). When Habré advanced and seized N'Djamena in 1982, Djamouss was at his side and was promptly appointed commissioner for the plan and national reconstruction. A few months later he was appointed minister of public works, mines, and petroleum, and in 1984 minister of the civil service. Djamouss was judged by Habré as a master strategist and was catapulted in 1985 to the post of chief of staff of the armed forces, replacing Idriss Déby (q.v.), who was dispatched to Paris for formal training at a military staff college. Djamouss then led the Chadian army in its stunning victories against Libyan forces in Tibesti (March 1987), Aouzou (August 1987), and deep into Libya against the major Maaten-es-Sarra airbase, which finally convinced the Libyans to extricate themselves from the Chadian morass before suffering even greater humiliation. Djamouss was referred to by one Western military analyst as one of "the greatest military geniuses since Rommel." Wounded in one of the battles that he personally led, Djamouss was evacuated to Paris for treatment and was later replaced as chief of staff by Yosko Issaka (q.v.), a former supporter of Goukouni (q.v.) of Daza ethnicity.

Though widely hailed as Chad's greatest hero, Djamouss was by 1987 increasingly unhappy with Habré's policies, which had already alienated most Hadjeray and were beginning to affect the loyalties of the Zaghawa as well. In 1989 the arrest of all five brothers of Djamouss's brother-in-law, Fadoul Siddick (q.v.), and Siddick's own liquidation, drove Djamouss into a conspiracy, which Habré nipped in the bud when he ordered a purge and arrest of many Zaghawa leaders, including Djamouss, Ibrahim Itno (q.v.), and Déby. The three and some of their military followers fled N'Djamena for Darfur (except for Itno, who was captured and killed before he could escape the capital) under hot pursuit by Habré's troops. Djamouss was later badly wounded in an ambush in Darfur and was captured and brought back to N'Djamena for interrogation by Habré. He was then executed in the Presidency, despite the official story that he died in hospital from his wounds. Déby continued the banner of rebellion and, linking up with the existing Hadjeray revolt, raised a strong Zaghawa-Hadjeray army that ousted Habré from power on December 2, 1990.

DJARI, NGAMA. Administrator and former cabinet minister, Djari was a prefect when Idriss Déby (q.v.) seized power and was brought into Déby's cabinet as secretary of state for security and the interior, serving from July 1992 to May 1992, when he returned to prefectural duties.

DJEMB EL-BAHR. Old N'Djamena quarter, once a major Hausa (q.v.) *zariba* (q.v.). The area is east of the market at the center of town.

DJEMB EL-GATO. N'Djamena quarter across from the town square. Originally populated by remnants of Rabah's (q.v.) lieutenants and followers brought to Fort-Lamy by the French, and by wealthy Ouadai merchants. Among the oldest quarters of the city.

DJERAKI, ZAID (1906–1969). Former Speaker of the National Assembly. Born in 1906 in Tchallo-Edeba, a prosperous merchant, Djeraki entered public life only in the 1950s, though he had been a major contributor of funds to the PPT (q.v.). In November 1956 he was elected municipal councillor of N'Djamena and in May 1959 PPT delegate from Guéra. In the assembly he was promptly elected vice president and later Speaker. Djeraki retired from public life in 1964.

DJERMA, MAHAMAT (1943–). Former mayor of N'Djamena. Born in Abéché on December 16, 1943, an administrator in the civil service by profession, Djerma was mayor of N'Djamena from 1973 to the 1975 coup d'état. A prominent PPT (q.v.) militant, Djerma was appointed despite his youth to the Executive Committee of the MNRCS (q.v.) in 1973 and served in that organ until its dissolution after the 1975 coup d'état. He then joined the FROLINAT (q.v.) rebellion to become a close Goukouni (q.v.) lieutenant and remained part of the opposition to the regimes in N'Djamena. In early 1991 he defected from the virtually defunct FROLINAT, and in mid-1992, after cofounding the Union Nationale (UN) (of which he became vice president) together with Abdoulaye Lamana (q.v.), he rallied to the regime of Idriss Déby (q.v.).

DJIBER, MAHAMAT. Former Tombalbaye (q.v.) prefect of B.E.T. (1971–77). Regarded as sympathetic to the rebellion, Djiber was integrated into Habré's FAN (qq.v.) council and held an administrative post in the office of the presidency until Habré was ousted from power.

DJIBRINE, PAUL (1933–). Former political leader and opposition figure. Born in Kim in 1933, and an agricultural worker by profession, Djibrine entered politics via his unionist activities when he created an autonomous union in Mayo-Kebbi in 1957, and in 1960 he won the mayoralty of Bongor. In 1957 he was also elected to the Territorial Assembly from Mayo-Kebbi, and for a few weeks (March 24–June 16, 1959) he was secretary of state in charge of planning. From June 1959 to March 1962 Djibrine served as President Tombalbaye's (q.v.) minister of civil service (for two months also of education). Dropped from his cabinet positions in mid-1962, Djibrine was briefly arrested, and again arrested in 1965 (while deputy mayor of Bongor), allegedly for plotting Tombalbaye's removal from power. He was imprisoned until a 1969 amnesty, at which time, partly rehabilitated, he was appointed counselor to Chad's Supreme Court, serving until the court was disbanded in 1975.

DJIDINGAR, DONO-NGARDOUM (MICHEL) (1928–). Veteran politician, former prime minister, and under Habré a cabinet minister. Born in 1928 in Donou-Manga (Logone) and the son of the *chef de canton* of Goulaye (Läi), Djidingar was raised as a farmer with little formal education. He has 10 wives and is the father of more than 30 children. Djidingar first achieved prominence when he became Logone's deputy to Chad's Territorial Assembly in March 1957. He remained in the assembly through December 1963. Between 1959 and 1961 he also represented Chad as senator to the French Community, following which he was integrated into François Tombalbaye's (q.v.) cabinet as minister of finance, the economy, posts, and telecommunications. Self-educated, a staunch party man, and good social mixer, Djidingar remained in the cabinet throughout the turbulent purges of the 1960s, in which many of Tombalbaye's former lieutenants disappeared from the national scene. In 1965 he lost control over the ministry of finance, which was set up as a separate ministry, though he retained the other responsibilities of his former portfolio. In April 1966 his ministry was enlarged to encompass also Public Works, and in May 1971 he was transferred to head the Ministry of Agriculture and Rural Development. In October 1973 he was again transferred, this time to head the Ministry of Stockbreeding. A member of the Political Bureau of the PPT (q.v.) and later the Executive Committee of the MNRCS (q.v.), Djidingar's easygoing and engaging personality and his veteran status on the cabinet have gained him a large variety of positions on the governing boards of organizations such as Air Afrique, the BCEAC (q.v.), the Société Hôtelière de l'Afrique Centrale, and others. He remained in the cabinet until the coup d'état of 1975, when he retired to his hometown, becoming its mayor. As one of the south's most powerful traditional leaders, he was invited back to N'Djamena to serve in the GUNT (q.v.) government of Goukouni (q.v.) as prime minister, and he served in that capacity from May 1982 to the fall of the capital to Hissène Habré (q.v.). He was one of the first to rally to Habré's rise to power, having founded the Rassemblement pour l'Unité et la Démocratie au Tchad (q.v.), which urged a north-south reconciliation while being anti-Kamougoué. (The party later merged with Habré's UNIR [q.v.].) He was retained by Habré first as minister without portfolio (to 1984) and then as minister of agriculture and rural development, as an "example" to other Sara leaders of Habre's intent to bring about national reconciliation and a multiethnic administration. Djidingar held that post until 1986, when he was appointed minister without portfolio, and in 1987 minister of state in the presidential office, being too important a southern leader to be dismissed.

DJIMASTA, KOIBLA. Prime minister of Chad. A former GUNT (q.v.) militant and member of the GUNT government, Djimasta was appointed minister of public health when Hissène Habré seized power in 1982. After Habré was ousted and Idriss Déby (q.v.) came to power, Djimasta joined Déby's cabinet in May 1992 as minister of interior, serving until October 1992. He then participated in the Conférence Nationale (q.v.) in 1993 (and from there was elected to the interim national assembly), as a moderate leader of the Union pour la Démocratie et la République (UDR) (q.v.) political party. In June 1994 Déby named Djimasta prime minister of Chad, replacing Nouradine Koumakoyé Kassiré (q.v.), and Djimasta was confirmed in that role by 36 of the 54 votes of the assembly.

DJIME, MAMARI NGAKINAR (Colonel) (1934–). Former vice president of the Conseil Supérieur Militaire (CSM) (q.v.), minister of interior and security in the post-1975 military regime, and former head of the gendarmerie. A Sara-Kaba, born in Sarh on March 19, 1934, Djimé was educated locally and at the Ecole Général Leclerc in Brazzaville (1948–52). In 1952 he joined the French colonial armies, serving in Pointe-Noire (Congo/Brazzaville) and later (with the rank of sergeant) in Tunisia and Algeria. He was repatriated in 1956, and in 1957 he attended the officer cadets academy in Brazzaville, and then from 1958 to 1960 the Frejus Officers' School in France (1958–60). Passed as second lieutenant, he then attended St. Maixient and returned to Chad in 1961, serving briefly in the gendarmerie. In 1962 Djimé was sent back to France for further courses at the Ecole Supérieure des Officiers de Gendarmerie, and upon his return to Fort-Lamy he was given command of Chad's gendarmerie. He was promoted to captain in 1965, and after further senior staff courses in Paris and Montpellier (1969–70), to major and force commander. In 1972 he was promoted to lieutenant colonel, and in 1975 to colonel. Shortly thereafter, and barely two weeks before the 1975 coup d'état, Colonel Djimé and several other key officers were arrested for a series of disturbances (including a fire) at N'Djamena's gendarmerie headquarters, since explained as an aborted coup. As Djimé was quite popular among the troops, his arrest—part of the third series of purges in the armed forces—was a definite spark that helped to set off the coup d'état two weeks later. After the coup he was reintegrated into the security forces of Chad and given the vice presidency of the CSM and the Ministry of Interior and Security, a key position. In mid-1976 he reassumed his command over the gendarmerie, taking over from Major Kottiga Guérinan, who in turn took over as minister of interior and security. Djimé was one of the strong figures of the military regime. Minister of state between 1976 and 1978, Djimé was appointed minister of defense in 1978 by Hissène Habré (q.v.), then prime minister. His appointment was extended by Goukouni (q.v.) in 1981, and he remained in office until N'Djamena fell to Habré in 1982. Djimé remained out of the limelight, and part of the time in France, until 1984, when he was recruited into supporting the newly formed FDT (q.v.) party of General Djogo (q.v.) that rallied to Habré in 1986.

DJIME, TOUGOU (PIERRE) (1933–). Former minister of interior, attorney general, and president of the Supreme Court. Born in Fort-Lamy on July 10, 1933, Djimé was educated in Sarh and completed his secondary and higher education in France. He graduated with a law degree from the University of Bordeaux in 1960 and studied until 1963 at the University of Paris. Appointed as a magistrate upon his return to Chad in 1964, Djimé was promoted to the post of N'Djamena attorney general in 1965. Early in 1967 he was brought into the Political Bureau of the reigning PPT (q.v.) party, and in mid-1968 he was brought into François Tombalbaye's (q.v.) cabinet as minister of health. He served in that capacity until May 1971, when he became president of the Supreme Court, a position he held until 1975, returning to magisterial duties in the N'Djamena appellate court after the 1975 coup abolished the Supreme Court (see COUR SUPREME). In 1990 he was appointed minister of interior.

DJIMRASENGAR, NADJILEM. Director of Radio Chad until May 1992. He was then dismissed when allegations linked him with the crimes of Habré's DDS (qq.v) secret police.

DJOGO, DJIBRIL NEGUE (General) (1932–). Minister under President Hissène Habré (q.v.) and former military head of the Goukouni Gouvernement de Salut National (GSN) (qq.v.) forces in B.E.T., former minister of health, labor, and social affairs, member of the Conseil Supérieur Militaire (CSM) (q.v.), and former GUNT (q.v.) vice president of Chad. Of Sara-Kaba origins and a Catholic, Djogo was born in 1932 and joined the French colonial forces at an early age, eventually serving as an instructor at the Ecole Général Leclerc in Brazzaville. He was then dispatched to attend officers' courses at Frejus and St. Maixient and obtained his paratroopers' insignia. He saw action in Algeria and was repatriated in 1962. He served briefly in Ouagadougou (Burkina Faso) on the U.A.M. Defense Committee with the rank of major, and after the committee's dissolution he returned to Chad as deputy chief of staff of the armed forces and commander of the First Infantry Battalion (1964). Involved in a dispute with the chief of staff, in 1965 Djogo was abruptly banished to remote and inhospitable Faya-Largeau (q.v.) in the B.E.T. (q.v.) with the rank of lieutenant colonel and as military prefect of B.E.T. (and commander of the Northern Sector Forces). His command of this most delicate and difficult post was, according to

French officers, distinguished, and he was regarded as the army's most competent officer. In 1967, just as abruptly as when he had been banished to B.E.T., Djogo was recalled to the capital and appointed commander of the gendarmerie. In July 1972 he was given political duties when he was appointed head of President Tombalbaye's (q.v.) military cabinet, a post he occupied until April 2, 1975, when he was arrested, along with several other military officers (he had also been arrested before, briefly, in 1972), in connection with rumors of a plot to overthrow Tombalbaye. Released after the coup that erupted two weeks later, Djogo was integrated into the CSM and appointed minister of finance. In mid-1976 he was transferred to head the Ministry of Health, Labor, and Social Affairs, having earlier relinquished the gendarmerie. An able and well-liked officer, Djogo was one of the key men in the military regime. With the departure from the scene of General Félix Malloum (q.v.)—a result of the northern victory in the civil war—Djogo became the most senior southern representative in the new GUNT (q.v.) government set up by Goukouni (q.v.) in N'Djamena. Politically weak, however, and challenged by his subordinate, Colonel Kamougoué (q.v.), Djogo soon ceded the vice presidency of GUNT to the latter and withdrew with the remainders of the badly tattered Chadian armed forces to Sarh. Kamougoué, now vice president, became the strongman of the south, ruling in Moundou, a quasi-autonomous Sara state within a state. With the ouster of the Goukouni regime in June 1982 and the August–September 1982 FAT (q.v.) revolt that delivered the southern préfectures to Hissène Habré (q.v.), both southern leaders (Djogo and Kamougoué) in due course found their way to Bardai, where Goukouni was regrouping for a counteroffensive. In this effort, however, the roles of the two southerners were reversed, with Djogo becoming the commander in chief of the Armée de Libération Nationale (q.v.) of the Goukouni GSN. He is credited with masterminding the successful offensive that brought Goukouni's forces into Faya-Largeau and (briefly) into Abéché. As a stalemate developed between GUNT forces and Habré's regime (supported by France and the United States), a number of leaders and factions seceded from GUNT, including Djogo, who in 1985 left B.E.T. for Paris. There he set up the Front Démocratique du Tchad (FDT) (q.v.) political party, which opposed both Goukouni and Habré, but in 1986 Habré enticed him into a reconciliation and invited him to N'Djamena, appointing him minister of justice and then minister of public works and transport in April 1988. He served in that capacity until Idriss Déby (q.v) marched into N'Djamena in December 1990, when he was retired.

DJOHEINA. Large group of seminomadic Arab clans claiming descent from Abdallah el-Djoheini and coming to Chad in waves from the Nile valley in the Sudan from the fourteenth to the nineteenth centuries. Found in a wide arc from Sudan to Bornu, component subgroups include the Salamat Arabs (q.v.), the Beni Hemat, Ouled Rachid (q.v.), Misirié (q.v.), and Mahamid (q.v.), all of whom are further subdivided into a large number of clans. In the 1964 census the Djoheina were estimated to include 349,000 of Chad's 371,000 Arabs. The current proportion has probably remained the same, though population estimates are much higher. (See also ARABS.)

DJOMIA, MBAINAUDO. Head of the southern party, the Mouvement Social pour la Démocratie au Tchad (q.v.), which stands, inter alia, for the recognition of Sara as the third language of Chad, alongside Arabic and French.

DJONDANG, ENOCH. President of the Ligue Tchadienne de Droits de l'Homme (q.v.) since 1990.

DJONKITO, JULIENNE. Former secretary of state for health. Mrs. Djonkito resigned from Idriss Déby's (q.v) cabinet in August 1992, the third appointee to do so, claiming that she had insufficient influence to perform her duties.

DJONOUMA, ABDOULAYE (1928–). Civil administrator and former cabinet minister. Born in Moïssala in Moyen-Chari on July 15, 1928, Djonouma was educated at Sarh, Brazzaville, and at the Institut des Hautes Etudes d'Outre-Mer (IHEOM) in Paris, where he obtained a degree in civil administration. Upon his return to Chad in 1964 he was appointed director of the Fonds de Développement et d'Action Rurale (q.v.) and also, in 1967, director of Rural Economy in the Ministry of Planning. Djonouma held these posts until 1971, when he joined the PPT (q.v.) Political Bureau and was simultaneously promoted into the cabinet as minister of planning. In October 1973 he was shifted to head the Ministry of Public Works and Territorial Development, a post he held until the 1975 coup d'état. In 1974 he also served on the Chad Committee for Drought Relief and grossly enriched himself from funds intended for the starving north. His activities enraged the donating Western powers, but François Tombalbaye (q.v.) refused to fire him, clashing with the United States in his defense. Djonouma was arrested after the 1975 coup d'état, but plans to place him on trial were aborted as the civil war crisis demanded unity.

DOBA. Capital of the Logone Orientale Préfecture and seventh largest city in Chad, with a population of around 20,000. Founded by Bedjond (q.v.) arriving from the east, Doba was a prime target of Fulani (q.v.)

slave-raiding expeditions right into the twentieth century. The city, always a vibrant one, dramatically expanded with the fall of N'Djamena to northern forces in 1978. The town fell to Hissène Habré (q.v.) troops on September 3, 1982. Doba is also the name of the main souspréfecture in Logone Orientale with administrative headquarters in the same town. The souspréfecture had an estimated population of over 100,000, many people having relocated following the 1978 fall of N'Djamena. It is in this region that Chad's main economic future lies, since abundant oil deposits have been discovered here, and an international accord for the construction of an oil pipeline to Cameroon was signed in 1994. Some of the worst abuses of the Déby regime have also happened here, in particular the August 1992 slaughter of 150 civilians in retaliation for the activities in the region of Lt. Ketté's (q.v.) opposition commandos.

DOGOUIA. Small picturesque "tourist" village 60 kilometers (37 miles) north of N'Djamena on the Chari River. Dogouia was the site of the November 1978 meeting of the heads of Chad's 11 warring factions, following which the GUNT (q.v.) government was set up. Later Dogouia was the headquarters for the Libyan armed forces that assisted Goukouni (q.v.) in ousting Habré's (q.v.) forces from the capital. After the Libyans left, Dogouia became a "secret" U.S. (CIA) military airbase. Halfway between Ouadi-Doum in northern Chad and the huge Yoko airbase in Cameroon, Dogouia presumably provided limited war cover for Habré's forces in their assault on Libya in B.E.T., and also support for various subversive U.S. activities within Libya, utilizing Libyan POWs captured in B.E.T. The base was evacuated after Idriss Déby (q.v.) came to power in December 1990.

DOMBAL, DJIMBAGUE. President of the Union des Syndicats du Tchad (UST) (q.v.) trade union confederation. He has been arrested a number of times in the Déby (q.v.) era (e.g., in November 1992) for his hard stand on the lengthy strikes mounted by the UST.

DONADJI, KEDEM. Minister of posts and telecommunications, appointed on June 8, 1995.

DONOUMANGA. Important regional trading center in the Laï souspréfecture, part of the southern Tandjilé Préfecture. The village encompasses some 3,000 farmers.

DORALTA, DJIRAIBAYE (BRUNO BOHIADI) (1922–). Former diplomat and cabinet minister. Born at Bekoy on December 12, 1922, and known until the "Cultural Revolution" (q.v.) as Bruno Bohiadi, Doralta was educated locally and at the Ecole Edouard-Renard in

Brazzaville, becoming an instructor in 1939. By 1964 he was inspector of primary education. He actively entered politics only in the mid-1950s and in May 1959 was elected PPT (q.v.) deputy to the Territorial Assembly from Moyen-Chari (through 1965), later becoming president of the assembly's Legislation and Defense Committee. In 1960, upon Chad's independence, he joined Chad's delegation to the United Nations, and when he returned he was elected mayor of Fort-Archambault (Sarh) in 1963. He remained mayor of Sarh and school inspector in the region until 1965. Doralta returned to diplomatic duties when he was appointed ambassador to the Soviet Union in 1966 and in 1969 to the United States and the UN. Returning to Chad in 1971, Doralta joined François Tombalbaye's (q.v.) cabinet for the first time as commissioner to the presidency in charge of planning and external aid. In November of the same year he was promoted to full ministerial rank as minister of education. Still not a member of the PPT inner circle, the Political Bureau, Doralta was further promoted in October 1973 when he was made minister of foreign affairs, a post he held until the coup d'état of 1975. Though he then served in a variety of other posts, he soon retired from public life.

DORE. Alternate name of the Toubouri (also Toupouri). Name of their mythical ancestor, whose contemporary descendant and current religious leader is known as the Ouankoulou.

DOUBA ALIFA, MAHAMAT (1929–). President Tombalbaye's (q.v.) powerful, much-feared, and venal Muslim minister of interior, one of the strongmen of the regime. Born on September 10, 1929, in Bousso, to the principal sultan of Chari-Baguirmi (q.v.), and eventually succeeding his father, Douba Alifa (see ALIFA) served as *chef de canton* of Bousso until 1959, when he actively joined national politics. In that year's elections he was elected to the National Assembly and was one of the very few deputies to survive in that post until 1975. In 1959 and 1960 he was the assembly's secretary, and from 1962 to 1968 the assembly's vice president. In 1968 Douba Alifa was brought into Tombalbaye's cabinet as minister of interior, becoming one of the strongmen of the administration and one of the most influential within the PPT (q.v.) Political Bureau. Implicated in April 1973 in massive embezzlement of relief aid for a local cholera epidemic, Douba Alifa was downgraded in October 1973 to the post of minister-delegate to the presidency in charge of relations with parliament and the MNRCS (q.v.) (which he held until the coup of 1975). After the coup he was accused of a host of fiscal and other irregularities while in office, but he was not brought to account because of the inherent weakness of the military regime, which feared the possible outbreak of a popular upheaval in Kanem if its dominant traditional leader were to be imprisoned—despite the fact that Douba Alifa had been throughout an arrogant feudal despot, cruel and insensitive to his peasantry, whom he taxed extremely heavily. In exchange for peace and stability in Douba Alifa's dominions, Tombalbaye largely left him alone, accountable to no one and regularly pocketing a large percentage of the funds collected on behalf of the central government. Indeed, during Tombalbaye's tenure there was no rebellion in Kanem–Chari-Baguirmi.

DOUBANGAR, JEROME (1934–). Administrator. Born on April 12, 1934, in Bodo and educated locally and at the Institut des Hautes Etudes d'Outre-Mer (IHEOM) in Paris, Doubangar was appointed after his studies as director of social and economic affairs at the Ministry for Foreign Affairs and, later, as an administrator with SODELAC (q.v.). In November 1966 he was appointed prefect of the Lac Préfecture (q.v.), a post he held until the coup d'état of 1975.

DOUBLE ELECTORAL COLLEGE. Electoral system set up in French colonial territories in August–September 1945, under which territorial representatives were elected from two separate electoral colleges, one composed of metropolitan citizens, and the second of Africans satisfying certain lower criteria. The system drastically discriminated against the electoral power of the African populations and was abolished in 1956. In the first election in Chad one deputy—René Malbrant—was chosen by a combined first electoral college of Chad and Oubangui-Chari, while the noncitizens of the second electoral college elected a French military officer—Baucheron de Boissoudy. (The second electoral college was then minute, with barely 8,000 voters.) For the 1947 elections for the Conseil Représentatif (q.v.), 10 deputies were elected by the first college and 20 by the second. (See also ASSEMBLEE TERRITORIALE; CONSEIL REPRESENTATIF; INDIGENAT.)

DOUKORE, ALI SALIM see SALIM, ALI DOUKORE

DOUMRO, NGARO NGUENABAYE (JACQUES) (General), (1919–). Chad's most senior officer and former minister of the civil service. Born in Sarh in 1919, Doumro joined the French colonial forces in 1938 and initially served with the Senegalese Artillery Regiment (as a private) before being reassigned to the Sixth Colonial Infantry Regiment, in which he served through 1961. He saw action during the Second World War and later in Algeria. In 1955 he was promoted to second lieutenant and in 1961 was repatriated to Chad with the rank of full lieutenant. He then rapidly rose up in the ranks to captain in 1962, to major and chief of staff in 1964, to colonel in 1965, and soon after, to brigadier general. A former president of the influential ex-servicemen's association, Doumro was brought into the PPT (q.v.) Political Bureau ("to represent the armed forces") in April 1971. (He had been hospitalized in Paris for some time in 1970.) Despite his impressive credentials and very rapid promotion up the officer hierarchy, Doumro was viewed in N'Djamena as the regime's straw man, and he lost control over the armed forces to the younger Colonel Félix Malloum (q.v.). The same year that he was brought into the PPT Political Bureau, Doumro was purged from the army in the aftermath of a clash between him and Tombalbaye (q.v.) regarding the politicization of the army (demanded by Tombalbaye) and the student upheavals in Chad and of Chadian students in Europe (see STUDENT UPHEAVAL OF 1971) in which the crowds chanted "Vive Doumro" and "The Army to power." He was placed under house arrest on December 27, 1971, and later cashiered from the armed forces, with Malloum becoming the acting chief of staff. Doumro's purge was the first in a series of political purges of the senior hierarchy of the armed forces that would contribute three and a half years later to the eruption of the 1975 coup d'état. Following the coup of April 1975 Doumro was brought into the military regime that was established; he was appointed minister of the civil service and labor, though he was not integrated into the ultimate decision-making hierarchy, the Conseil Supérieur Militaire (CSM) (q.v.). In mid-1976 he was relieved of his responsibility over labor, though not over the civil service, and in 1978 he was retired from the armed forces.

DOUNIA, MARC (1916–1979). Veteran politician and former minister of interior. Of chiefly origins, Dounia was born in Koumra on April 17, 1916, and trained as a sanitary assistant. He was an early member of the Parti Progressiste Tchadien (PPT) (q.v.) and in 1946 was elected to the AEF (q.v.) Council. Dounia was also a deputy to the Conseil Représentatif (q.v.) beginning in 1947, though he was defeated in his 1952 reelection bid before winning back his seat in 1957. He then remained a deputy of the Territorial Assembly until 1963, serving as the assembly's vice president, and then president, from 1959 to 1962. During this period he held several other posts, including mayor of Koumra and senator to the French Community (1959–61). Brought into François Tombalbaye's (q.v.) cabinet as secretary of state in January 1962, Dounia had a checkered career. He was promoted to the key post of minister of interior on May 4, 1962. Barely two years later, in January 1964, he was downgraded sharply to the post of secretary of state in charge of tourism, allegedly due to his undisguised presidential ambitions. In December 1965 Dounia—previously one of Tombalbaye's most trusted associates—was appointed minister-delegate to the presidency in charge of relations with parliament, only to be dropped from the cabinet late the following year; two years later Dounia was again back in the cabinet. He was purged after the guerrilla attack on N'Djameña (see COUP [ATTEMPTED] OF 1972), when, together with a large number of other politicians, he was accused of pro-FROLINAT (q.v.) sympathies. He was taken to his home region and paraded before the masses, acknowledging his guilt. Dounia was released from prison shortly after the 1975 coup d'état and died soon after.

DOUTOUM, ABDOULAYE. Former Habré (q.v.) cabinet minister. Doutoum was first brought into the cabinet as minister of transport and civil aviation in August 1987 and was later transferred to head the Ministry of Public Works and Housing. He was dismissed from Habré's cabinet in February 1990.

DOUTOUM, IBRAHIM (1933–). Former senator to the French Community. Born in 1933 in Madala and a merchant by profession, Doutoum was an early member of the UDIT (q.v.) party in Ouadai. He was elected on the party's ticket in March 1957 to become deputy to the Territorial Assembly and was reelected twice as Ouadai's representative. Doutoum served as Speaker of the assembly (1959–60) and secretary of the committee on foreign affairs and defense. In June 1959 he was elected Chad's senator to the French Community, serving in Paris until January 1961. Since the imposition of a single-party system in Chad, Doutoum has been largely involved in private economic activities.

DOUTOUM, MAHAMAT HABIB. Idriss Déby's (q.v.) personal choice for the post of secretary-general of the MPS (q.v.) party, and appointed in December 1990 as minister of livestock and animal resources. In March 1991 he was transferred to head the Ministry of Mines, Energy, and Water. In October 1992 he was again transferred, this time to head the Ministry of Trade, and served in that capacity until the Conférence Nationale (q.v.) in 1993 selected its own cabinet.

DROUGHTS. The Sahel has periodically been ravaged by persistent and debilitating droughts that leave immense destruction in their wake, triggering population and livestock dislocations and mass starvation and death. Some of these droughts have acquired indigenous names, and are recounted, in fear and awe, from generation to generation through oral tradition, serving historians as chronological reference points. The periodic (massive) variations in the size of Lake Chad are also indications of the effect of drought on the area. The 1968–1976 drought cut a devastating swath of destruction through much of Africa's Sahel zone and greatly damaged Chad's economy. (Later reports, however, indicated that the destruction was not as monumental as originally reported, and that at least part of the immense death toll had been more the result of population dislocations attending the civil war.) The drought was eventually broken in 1974–75, though rainfall patterns continued to be erratic for the next few years. 1974 was the sixth year of an extremely dry spell of weather, though later in the year torrential rains greatly complicated the relief distribution efforts throughout the country. The drought affected some two-thirds of Chad, bringing massive crop failures and the death of over 20 percent of the country's livestock. (See also CATTLE.) It was conservatively estimated that eight to ten years would be required for the economy to regain lost ground and for the country to replenish its previously sizable cattle herds. Agriculture was also hard-hit, since many farmers consumed their planting seed in order to survive, and only limited amounts of crops were planted. Moreover, most of the international relief aid supplies did not reach the affected regions in the north, center, and east (for political reasons, these being the Muslim areas under rebellion) but was diverted into the largely unaffected southern Sara regions (President Tombalbaye's [q.v.] source of political support); much of it actually reached the open market, where it was sold, having been "appropriated" by high officials, including, it has been alleged, the president's wife. Many political figures reaped small fortunes from their ownership of segments of the country's graft-ridden and inefficient transportation companies, whose price schedules are nearly double those in neighboring Nigeria. Major stockpiles of relief aid built up in Maiduguri and other Nigerian border areas, where they either rotted away or were slowly pilfered while Chadian trucks from the quasi monopoly Coopérative des Transporteurs Tchadiens (q.v.) tried to cope with the unprecedented traffic loads. The international scandals that erupted consequent to the administrative inefficiency and crass contempt for human misery in affected areas in Chad spilled into the world press and finally brought about Tombalbaye's reaction: the barring of U.S. and other relief aid into the country on a variety of pretexts (e.g., grain contamination, interference in domestic affairs, etc.). According to some French sources, the accusations against the president's wife were the final irritant, and the most important one. (After the coup, large bundles of currency were found in the dead president's domicile; estimates were never confirmed, since the money then disappeared, but there was upwards of US$1 million.) Whatever the validity of any specific accusation, there is little doubt that much damage was done and probably tens of thousands of lives were lost due to N'Djamena's maladministration of the world relief aid. Moreover, out of misplaced national pride, Chad was the last Sahelian country to declare a famine emergency and request drought aid, and the regime has consistently underestimated the seriousness of the situation in the countryside.

At the height of the drought, in June 1973, Lake Chad had shrunk to one-third of its normal size (see LAKE CHAD), and in certain places the large mudflats allowed easy land passage from Chad to Nigeria or Niger. The drought also brought about population and livestock dislocations; many of the large cattle herds were evacuated southward (where up to 10 percent perished in tsetse-infested areas) while many were sold in an undernourished, pregnant, or young state to Nigeria. Several seminomadic clans settled in refugee camps in urban cities in search of food. The onset of another period of low rainfall and crop destruction in 1976/77 dashed earlier hopes that the Sahelian drought had run its course. The inevitable tumult and administrative breakdowns associated with the power shift in N'Djamena consequent to the collapse of Sara power likewise complicated efforts to assess and repair the ravages of the drought. Moreover, hardly had the drought of the 1970s passed into memory when a second drought, accompanied by starvation and death, hit Chad, beginning in 1984; this one, coming on the heels of the previous drought, was in some ways more vicious, affecting for the first time the hitherto relatively immune areas in the southern préfectures. (See also FAMINES.)

DUNAMA (?–1820). Last *mai* (q.v.) of the 1,000-year-old Sefuwa (q.v.) dynasty of the Empire of Bornu (q.v.). Dunama ruled between 1808 and 1820, yielding power to al-Kanemi (q.v.). Succeeding his father, Ahmad Alimi, around 1808 subsequent to Uthman dan Fodio's military assaults, Dunama's rise to power factionalized the Bornuan court. Needing assistance in stemming the Fulani (q.v.) invasions, Dunama invited al-Kanemi in 1808 to head the Bornuan armies that in due course repulsed the Fulani. Al-Kanemi was again called in the next year and he became the power prop of the throne. Dunama was deposed in an internal court power-shuffle in 1809, but his successor— Muhammad Ngileruma, Dunama's uncle—was overthrown by al-Kanemi and Dunama was reinstated. Fearing the growing influence of his benefactor, Dunama tried to bring about al-Kanemi's eclipse. The plan backfired, leading to Dunama's own death and the de facto accession to power of al-Kanemi, though Dunama's son, Ibrahim, was retained for a while as the puppet *mai*.

DUNAMA DIBBALEMI (?–c. 1259). Sefuwa *mai* (qq.v.) of the Kanem kingdom at its apogee. He greatly expanded the domain of Kanem's authority, with a mighty cavalry force reputed to include 41,000 horses. His kingdom nevertheless disintegrated into a number of feuding entities, and central authority was eroded. Dunama Dibbalemi was also attacked by the nomadic Bulala (q.v.) in a quasi-religious revolt over the loss or violation of a sacred talisman. Eventually the revolt was to oust the Sefuwa Mugami (qq.v.) dynasty and force its relocation to Bornu. Dunama Dibbalemi is also credited with the establishment in Cairo of religious colleges for Kanemi students.

-E-

EBOUE, FELIX (1884–1944). Governor of Chad, governor-general of the AEF (q.v.) federation, and symbol of Gaullist resistance during the Second World War. Born in Cayenne (French Guyana) in 1884 of African descent, Eboué's career as a colonial administrator included service in Oubangui-Chari (the current C.A.R.), the Caribbean, where he was governor of Guadeloupe from 1936 to 1938, and Chad, where he was governor from 1938 to 1941. On August 26, 1940, Eboué was the first important governor to rally his colony to the side of the Free French of Charles de Gaulle—at a time when most were declaring for Vichy France or staying neutral. Providing a major psychological boost to the French resistance at its bleakest moment, Eboué evaded Vichy's efforts to neutralize his authority and was promptly rewarded by de Gaulle with the governorate-general of the entire AEF. He served in that post until he died in Cairo before the end of the war on May 17, 1944. His memory is honored in Chad, the former AEF countries, and in France with schools, hospitals, and streets named after him. His body is interred in the Pantheon in Paris. During Chad's "Cultural Revolution" (q.v.) Eboué's name was only one of two "foreign" names not expunged from the country, the other being de Gaulle's.

ECOLE NATIONALE D'ADMINISTRATION (ENA). Specialized institution set up in 1963 and fully operational by 1966 (when it had 55 students), training cadres for the government's departments of customs, finance, and foreign affairs. Directly or indirectly the ENA continued the educational bias favoring personnel from the southern préfectures (see EDUCATION). By 1970, for example, 10 years after independence, not a single student from Ouadai had been enrolled; in 1976, 85 percent of all graduates were of southern origin. This was to change after N'Djamena fell to northern leaders. The school was for long headed by the Frenchman Bernard Lanne, who also presented Chad's case on the Aouzou (q.v.) Strip to an OAU committee that was trying to arbitrate the dispute with Libya.

EDDEYMI, KINNIMI (Derde). Current derde (q.v.) of the Toubou (q.v.), elected according to traditional ceremony by the Tozoba clan and enthroned on April 21, 1979, at Kayouba near Sherda. Eddeymi belongs to the Arami branch, descendants of Moli, who had not possessed the derdeship for nearly a century. Eddeymi was elected derde at the death of the former derde, Wodei Kichidemi (q.v.), who had specifically disinherited his last surviving son, Goukouni (q.v.), for disregarding his 1975 call to end the military struggle against N'Djamena following the derde's reconciliation with General Félix Malloum (q.v.), who had just overthrown the Tombalbaye (q.v.) regime.

EDERGUIA. One of the oldest established Teda clans in Tibesti, though according to some the clan is of Bideyat (q.v.) origins and did not settle in Tibesti until the seventeenth century. During the enthronement of a new derde (q.v.), the Ederguia's seniority is recognized by exchanges of gifts, including camels for palm trees.

EDUCATION. Organized educational programs began very late in Chad (1920), essentially under private (missionary) stimulus, and the spread of education prior to independence was extremely slow. In 1921 there was only one school in Fort-Lamy with 50 to 60 students, and it was closed down for five to six months when its only teacher went to France on home leave. At the time, there were only 10 schools in the entire country, one in each *circonscription,* all staffed by former non-commissioned officers or civil servants without any formal training themselves, though with some firsthand knowledge of the Western world. By 1928 the total number of students in the entire colony was 3,431 in public schools and 6,000 in mission schools. By 1933 there were still only 18 trained teachers in the entire country, and the largest school, in Fort-Lamy, had three grades and 135 students, most non-Chadian, the children of the Senegalese *tirailleurs* the French forces brought with them into the territory.

Twenty years later total school attendance stood at 17,054, with the public institutions accounting for 13,920 pupils; of the remaining, 2,853 were in Catholic schools and 281 in Protestant schools. Private schools did not exist anywhere in the Muslim north or east. In 1965, for example, not a single one was to be found in all of B.E.T., Kanem, Lac, Batha, Biltine Préfectures; only in 1968 was one (with 25 pupils) established in Ouadai. Most of the Christian effort has been concentrated in Moyen-Chari, the Logones, and in Chari-Baguirmi and Mayo-Kebbi.

The education of girls has lagged behind even more seriously, including, to some extent, in southern districts. In 1951, for example, the total number of girls in primary schools was 424, increasing to 8,981 by independence in 1960 and 30,974 by 1965. Secondary schools have also been a very recent introduction in Chad's educational system. Indeed, the first in all of Chad was established in Fort-Lamy only after the end of the Second World War. Shortly before independence (in 1958) there were still no more than three in the entire colony, and only after the departure of the French did their number expand to 20, with at least one secondary school in each préfecture except Biltine, and with a few private secondary schools in the grand total. In 1970/71 the educational system was capped by the establishment of the University of N'Djamena.

The very low rates of school attendance in the Muslim areas have been due to opposition there to Western (seen as Christian or pagan) education. On the other hand, practically every village, even the smaller ones, has a local makeshift Koranic school, staffed by a *faki* (q.v.) or —in large centers—a more formally trained religious leader, which provides a modicum of general education in addition to literacy in Arabic and competence in religion, the prime objectives of education in the countryside. So deep has been the east's suspicion of Christians and their "contaminating habits" historically that in an effort to promote education in Abéché (one of the larger urban centers) the French had to devise a unique Franco-Arab secondary school hybrid (see LYCEE FRANCO-ARABE D'ABECHE), and even that was not particularly successful in attracting pupils. Moreover, the motivation behind this school was less to raise educational rates in the east (e.g., not a single school graduate in the entire district of Adré, with 100,000 population) than to counteract the "virulent" Islamic influences arriving from the north and east, seen as containing anti-French and anti-colonial messages. At independence Chad had 225 primary schools (35 of these were private), three secondary schools, and nine technical schools, with a grand total of 55,160 students, giving the country the very low school attendance rate of 11 percent. After independence, though, the school attendance figures rose rapidly. In 1968/69 it was estimated that 38.5 percent of all boys and 9.1 percent of all girls attended primary school, and in 1971/72 the overall scholarization rate had reached 22 percent, with the figure for some préfectures hovering around 75 percent. In that year there were 183,840 primary school students, 9,418 secondary school pupils, and the local university had just been opened. Despite these impressive advances Chad's expenditures on education have been the lowest of the UDEAC (q.v.) countries, and the rate of growth of education in Chad in the decade of 1964 to 1974 was lower even than that of the Central African Republic.

The civil war in Chad, and especially the breakdown of central authority in 1978, dealt a death blow to education in many parts of the country. Most schools, including the university, stopped operating, partly due to a total absence of funds for operating costs and salaries, and several of them were also heavily damaged and/or looted in the battles for the capital. Over 3,000 teachers deserted the profession.

Most of them southerners, they fled with the rise to power of the north in N'Djamena, abandoning a profession that led to starvation, often reverting to farming in their home village. In 1984 there was only one secondary school open in all of Chad, in N'Djamena, with classes of over 100. All pupils had by then lost three academic years due to the civil turbulence and the closure of schools.

It was several years before the educational establishment was back on its feet, a function of the fact that many schools, either destroyed in the fighting or looted by various military factions, received low budgetary priority. Also, many schoolteachers did not return to their posts, and hence the number of unqualified personnel in the educational system greatly increased in the 1980s. By 1987, though, most schools resumed teaching with full classes. In 1987/88 there were 306,042 primary school pupils in the country, 24,066 secondary school students, 3,976 students enrolled in technical or teacher training colleges, and 1,500 at the National University of N'Djamena. The figures improved in subsequent years, though they have yet to reach the levels attained before the civil war. In 1994, for example, 57 percent of the country's primary school-age children attended school, with 7 percent proceeding to secondary school. The vast majority of the pupils (especially at the secondary level) were, however, in the southern préfectures, where also girls' education very seriously lagged behind boys' education.

Primary School Enrollment, 1987

Préfecture	Pupils	Percentage of All School-Age Children
Batha	4,861	8.0
Biltine	4,401	14.5
B.E.T.	2,542	16.7
Chari-Baguirmi	39,440	33.4
Guéra	25,124	70.7
Kanem	4,898	14.6
Lac	2,441	10.6
Logone Occidental	35,852	70.0
Logone Oriental	43,414	82.1
Mayo-Kebbi	44,510	37.3
Moyen-Chari	64,789	71.6
Ouadai	7,653	13.0
Salamat	6,523	35.5
Tandjilé	19,954	37.6
Total	306,042	40.3

The erosion in standards of education, and the "lost" three years of the civil war era, however, had an invidious effect on examination passage rates. In 1994, 92 percent of high school students failed their intermediate exams, and 86 percent of them failed in their exams for entry to university. A series of trade union and teachers' strikes in 1992 and in subsequent years, continued to bring about the closure of the educational establishment, to the further detriment of standards in the country.

The figures in the table, though somewhat dated, provide some indication of levels of education in the country.

EID-EL-KEBIR. Muslim feast of the rams, commemorating Abraham's sacrifice.

ELECTIONS (LEGISLATIVE) OF JULY 8, 1990. These elections were the first in Chad since 1963 and were based on Hissène Habré's (q.v.) recently ratified constitution of 1989. A total of 436 candidates competed for the new National Assembly's 123 seats, from 60 constituencies, each electing one to five representatives, with all contenders running as "independents." Five seats were specifically reserved for women. The turnout was officially 56 percent of those eligible to vote. A number of prominent UNIR (q.v.) members were defeated in the elections, including Senoussi Wadak, the minister of national disasters, and three former (unelected) CNC (q.v.) delegates—Nadjita Ngororo, Bobekreo Tchimné, Doungous Kimto—who were defeated in the south by young civil servants and/or chiefs.

EMI KOUSSI. Highest mountain in the entire Sahara desert, located within the territorial confines of Chad. Of volcanic origin, Emi Koussi reaches a height of 3,414 meters (11,200 feet) in the Tibesti (q.v.) volcanic massif. Some 500 Teda (q.v.) live along its slopes. Emi Koussi is essentially a series of sharp overhanging cliffs, narrow gorges, and rugged foothills, all of which provide spectacular scenery.

ENNEDI. A vast souspréfecture of 180,000 square kilometers (69,500 square miles) in the B.E.T. (q.v.) Préfecture with administrative headquarters in Fada (q.v.). The population of the largely arid Ennedi (which, according to one observer is "one of the most beautiful deserts in the world") is estimated at around 42,000 (a population density of 0.2 per square kilometer), most of whom are seminomadic Toubou (q.v.) of the Daza (q.v.) branch, with a scattering of other clans and groups. A large number of grottos have been discovered in Ennedi containing ancient cave drawings. Although at the start of the 1950s some 40 sites were thought to exist, some 500 were discovered in 1956. (See ARCHAEOLOGY.) Ennedi is a series of plateaus in the eastern part of B.E.T., with a few low mountain ranges reaching to the

Basso peak of 1,450 meters (4,760 feet). The area was first mapped only in 1934, and it still has regions that have not been fully explored.

ENTENTE POUR L'APPLICATION DE LA LOI-CADRE (ENTENTE). Also known simply as the Entente, temporary 1957 name of the existing progressive PPT (q.v.) -led political formation, the Entente Républicaine pour la Défense des Intérêts Communaux (ERDIC) (q.v.). The coalition was composed of the PPT, UDIT (q.v.), PSIT (q.v.), and part of the AST (q.v.).

ENTENTE POUR UNE ALTERNATIVE DEMOCRATIQUE (ENAD). Political alliance, and supposed electoral compact, created in July 1994 by eight small parties that had not been invited to participate in the larger compact of 40 parties created earlier, the Concertation des Partis Politiques (CPP) (q.v.). In November 1994, after ENAD was formed, the Alliance des Partis Politiques pour la Démocratie (APPD) (q.v.) was created, and finally, the Collective des Partis pour le Changement (CO-PAC) (q.v.). Both formations, however, were much smaller than the CPP. (See also POLITICAL PARTIES.)

ENTENTE REPUBLICAINE POUR LA DEFENSE DES INTERETS COMMUNAUX (ERDIC). PPT (q.v.) -led and organized political alliance and electoral compact of the nontraditionalist parties and leaders in Chad, including the UDIT (q.v.) of Jean Baptiste (q.v.) and some segments of other parties. In the 1956 municipal elections of Fort-Lamy ERDIC scored a major (and its first) victory, obtaining 50 percent of the votes and 18 of the 33 seats, leaving six seats for the PSK (q.v.) and six for the AST (q.v.). ERDIC's majority went up to 21 when Ahmed Kotoko (q.v.) rallied his party (then called the RPDT) to the PPT coalition, as did three former AST members. The Entente—as ERDIC was equally well known (though there was a slight change in party composition)—maintained its cohesion despite a series of personality and ideological schisms within it, and in the March 1957 Territorial Assembly elections it was catapulted to power. The coalition that came to power at the time was composed of the PPT, UDIT, and PSIT (of Ahmed Kotoko), and with the cooperation of the GIRT (q.v.)—a former segment of the UDT (q.v.) that split off to help the PPT—the Entente formed the provisional government of December 1958. In January 1959 the GIRT shifted to the opposition, transforming the Entente's 39–26 assembly majority into a 34–31 minority and causing the collapse of Gabriel Lisette's (q.v) government. A series of unstable and short-lived governments then followed (see PROVISIONAL GOVERNMENTS) as each leader tried his luck in hammering out a temporary coalition, until the situation stabilized under François Tombalbaye (q.v.). By 1959/60 most non-PPT leaders had either joined the PPT or opted for the coalescing opposition, so that the "Entente," for all practical purposes, meant the PPT. Some time later the PPT entrenched itself in power, and by 1962 Chad was a de facto one-party state. (See also POLITICAL PARTIES.)

EPERVIER see OPERATION EPERVIER.

ETHNIC GROUPS: CLASSIFICATIONS. See Table 2, p. xix.

ETUDES ET DOCUMENTS TCHADIENS. Irregularly issued mimeographed publications of the INTSH (q.v.) research center. There are three series: general reports, historical and archival reports, and linguistic research. Also published are *Mémoires de l'INTSH,* the first issue of which came out in 1969.

EUROPEAN COMMUNITY (EC) ASSOCIATE MEMBER. Consequent to the Yaoundé conventions of 1963 and 1969 Chad has been an associate member of the EC, receiving preferential tariff treatments for its commodity exports and partaking of the community's technical assistance fund, the Fonds Européens de Développement (q.v.)

EUROPEAN DEVELOPMENT FUND see FONDS EUROPEENS DE DEVELOPPEMENT

EVOLUE see ASSIMILATION POLICY; ASSIMILE; INDIGENAT

-F-

FADA. The small (population 1,500) administrative headquarters of the vast desert Ennedi (q.v.) souspréfecture in the B.E.T. (q.v.) Préfecture. The village for a while had a small bungalow for tourists, and until the civil wars began, it was the starting point for trips to the famous Guelta d'Archei (q.v.) as well as various grottos containing cave engravings (see ARCHAEOLOGY). The entire B.E.T., however, became unsafe for travel with the onset of the 1966 rebellion and in fact was controlled until 1987 by Libyan troops. As Libya's southernmost stronghold, Fada was defended by a large force, 1,000 of whom were killed during Chad's stunning assaults on Libyan forces. A mid-March 3,000-man Libyan attack from Ouadi-Doum, 80 kilometers (50 miles) to the north, was routed, following which Chadian troops attacked Ouadi-Doum itself, capturing there a huge war booty. Fada is 410 kilometers (254 miles) from Faya (q.v.), the capital of the entire B.E.T., 645 kilometers (400 miles) from Abéché, and 80 kilometers (50 miles) from Guelta d'Archei.

FADIL, SALEH. Fierce chief of staff of the pro-Habré FANT (q.v.) faction of the MDD (q.v.) forces (at times referred as MDD-FANT) that invaded the Lake Chad region from Niger in 1991 in an attempt to overthrow the regime of Idriss Déby (q.v.). The force was dispersed by Déby's armies commanded by the brutal Colonel Ali (q.v.).

FADOUL, LAURENT (1919–1979). Former director of the Centre National de Nutrition. Born in Léré on November 15, 1919, and educated in public health, Fadoul became head of the Nutrition Center in July 1966, serving in that capacity until shortly before his death in 1979.

FADOUL, SIDDICK (1950–1987). One of the Fadoul family liquidated by Hissène Habré's (q.v.) security services, helping to trigger the Zaghawa (q.v.) defections from N'Djamena, including Idriss Déby (q.v.), eventually bringing down the regime of Habré.

FAKI. Arabic for scholar (especially one trained in jurisprudence) and also loosely applied to religious instructors in general. In Chad the term is usually applied to the Koranic school teachers or marabouts and the various Muslim learned men who move around the country (or are settled in specific localities), performing various functions at religious feasts and teaching youngsters the essentials of Arabic and the Koran. A major source of income for the *fokara* (plural) is the fabrication of lucky amulets.

FAMINES. Natural calamities (such as the prolonged catastrophic droughts of the 1970s) as well as economic repercussions of population dislocations (subsequent to wars, razzias, etc.) have periodically caused monumental famines in Chad. Some of these famines have received local names, such as *bongarondo, boromasi, mbalao, mogu-imamberi,* and so on. Their ravages have often been immense, though the better known famines are those of 1913–14 and 1916–18 in Ouadai, during which up to 60 percent of the kingdom's population perished (including from the attending epidemics). The drought and famines of the mid-1970s were also of monumental proportions, causing major population and livestock dislocations. Up to 30 percent of Chad's cattle were lost, and the country began to recuperate from the ravages only in 1978. For this reason the most recent drought (of 1984/85) was viewed with deep concern. Coming on the heels of the previous devastation, with few food reserves and superimposed upon a divided country in the midst of a civil war, large numbers of people were expected to die unless the international community responded with massive and immediate relief aid. This did not materialize, since the drought was relatively short-lived. (See also DROUGHTS.)

FAP-FROLINAT see FORCES ARMEES POPULAIRES

FARAH, MAHAMAT SEID. One of UNIR's (q.v.) leading organizers, and member of the party's executive committee. In December 1984 Farah presided over the opening of UNIR's first external branch, in Abidjan, Côte d'Ivoire.

FARCHA. Eastern suburb of N'Djamena in which are located the national veterinarian laboratories, the veterinary school (see IEZVAC), the Abattoir Frigorifique de Farcha (q.v.), and the important Farcha airbase.

FARRIS, MAHAMAT (1942–). Economist. Born on September 30, 1942, in Ati and educated at the Lycée Félix Eboué in N'Djamena and later in economics at the University of Montpellier in France (1962–69). After further banking studies Farris returned to Chad and was appointed secretary-general of the Banque de Développement du Tchad (q.v.) and Chadian deputy governor of the World Bank (1970–75). In 1976 he was transferred to head the Banque Tchadienne de Crédit et de Dépôts (q.v.) and after the fall of N'Djamena he went to work in France.

FAYA see FAYA-LARGEAU

FAYA-LARGEAU. Named Largeau during the colonial era (after the French military commander) and since known either as Faya (its original name) or Faya-Largeau (to avoid confusion), the town is the administrative headquarters of the B.E.T. (q.v.) Préfecture in northern Chad and of the constituent Borkou souspréfecture. Since its conquest by France, a major oasis serving as the military headquarters for troops patrolling the entire préfecture, Faya-Largeau is the largest urban center in the entire northern half of Chad and has had a population as large as 5,250. The town is 1,090 kilometers (676 miles) from N'Djamena, 2,550 kilometers (1,581 miles) from Tripoli, Libya, and 365 kilometers (226 miles) from Fada (q.v.). Within it formerly resided a large colony of Fezzani merchants that in more settled times acted as prime middlemen for the trade with Libya. Faya-Largeau is at the edge of the Bodélé depression (q.v.) and is surrounded on all sides by steep cliffs. The climate is extremely dry since a full decade can pass without a drop of rain falling; subterranean water is to be found, however, as in many parts of the desert, a few feet under the surface. North of the town are the three famous Ounianga lakes (q.v.) with different colored waters (blue, red, violet). Since the onset of the Toubou (q.v.) rebellions in 1966, Faya-Largeau has been attacked, seized, recaptured, and devastated by various military contenders, including Libya. The sprawling oasis town was captured by Goukouni's (q.v.) troops (on June 24, 1983), to be "liberated" by Habré's (q.v.) troops before falling again to a Goukouni force assisted by Libyan ground and air contingents. The town, largely destroyed by now, changed hands again when Habré's assaults in the north liberated most of B.E.T. After the peace accords with Libya, a rehabilitation of the town began, since there is no other locality that can better serve as administrative headquarters of Chad's vast northern region.

FECKOUA, LAOUKISSAM LAURENT (1944–). Former head of INTSH (q.v.). Born in 1944 in Mindaoré and educated in N'Djamena, Dakar, Abidjan, and Paris, Feckoua first served as technical adviser at the Ministry of Education and Cultural Affairs (1971–72) before being appointed permanent secretary of education and cultural affairs. In 1973 he was transferred to the directorship of Higher Education and Research, and in 1975 he became director of INTSH. With the fall of N'Djamena to Goukouni's (q.v.) forces, Feckoua was brought into the GUNT (q.v.) government as minister of planning and cooperation (November 1979), a post he held until the rise of the Habré (q.v.) regime in 1982.

FEDERATION DES ETUDIANTS DE L'AFRIQUE NOIRE EN FRANCE (FEANF). Militant union of francophone Africa's students in France, with branches in various university cities. Several of Chad's intellectuals have played a role in the FEANF during their studies in France, notably Dr. Bajoglo Baroum (q.v.). The FEANF-affiliated Chadian students (many from the south) were strongly against the Tombalbaye (q.v.) regime and supported its 1975 overthrow.

FELLATA see FULANI

FEZZAN-BORNU TRAIL. One of the oldest trans-Saharan caravan routes (q.v.) connecting Tripoli (Libya) via the Fezzan (southern Libya) to Bornu (q.v.), the old Garamantian route (q.v.). Though the flow of traffic fluctuated over the centuries (for details, see CARAVAN ROUTES), it was the most popular route until the 1820s, when unsettled conditions at both terminals (see BORNU; KARAMANLI DYNASTY) eroded its general security from banditry by Toubou and Tuareg (qq.v.) elements. The Fezzan-Bornu trail was then totally eclipsed by a more eastern route connecting Ouadai (the new power center in the region) with Benghazi.

FIANGA. Small souspréfecture with administrative headquarters in the village with the same name, part of the préfecture of Mayo-Kebbi. The souspréfecture encompasses 6,000 square kilometers (2,317 square miles) and a population of 80,000. The village is some 300 kilometers (186 miles) south of N'Djamena.

FIRST LIBERATION ARMY. Formal name adopted circa 1969 by several military groups operating in eastern Chad (including part of the former FLT [q.v.]) to distinguish themselves from the new guerrilla activity waged by the Toubou (q.v.) under Goukouni (q.v.) in the northern B.E.T. The First Liberation Army was in reality merely a coterie of warlords, loosely controlled by a fissiparous, faction-ridden leadership and engaged in hit-and-run tactics with little overall strategy, coordination, or long-term planning. Virtually all of its field commanders after Ibrahim Abatcha (q.v.) either were murdered, were "executed" by their men, or disappeared under mysterious circumstances. Beginning as a handful of ill-equipped student recruits led by seven North Korean–trained cadres (including Abatcha), the force grew to include several hundred men commanded by Abdel Hadj Issaka (killed), Djalabo Othman (killed), Adoum Abou Haggar (executed), and Idriss Mahamat Amane (overthrown) (qq.v.). Nominally under FROLINAT (q.v.) control as of the late 1960s (and specifically under Abba Siddick [q.v.]) part of the force—its Moubi (q.v.) component—made its peace with N'Djamena in 1974. The rest eventually followed Baghalani as the Volcan Army (q.v.) (also known as the Volcan Force), with Mahamat Abba's (q.v.) 1976 appearance on the scene further splitting the force. Briefly, and only nominally, integrated with the Second Liberation Army by Goukouni in 1977 (after Abba Siddick's eclipse), the separate components in the east waging war against N'Djamena (or against each other) have always maintained their independence and individuality. Most entities joined in the GUNT (q.v.) government of Goukouni, and after the latter's ouster from N'Djamena in 1982 allied in the struggle to regain the capital. In the 1980s, however, the First Army again split several times, over both personality cleavages but also over GUNT's overly tight relations with Libya. The main group was dominated by Ahmat Acyl (q.v.), and later Acheikh Ibn Oumar (q.v.), under the banner of the CDR (q.v.), which for some time became the largest, and ultimately the only, force continuing the struggle against Hissène Habré (q.v.). When Acheikh was finally reconciled with Habré and joined his government to become foreign minister, only a few small groups remained of the former First Liberation Army/Volcan Army, most based in Darfur.

FOCCART, JACQUES (1913–). France's former secretary-general to the presidency in charge of African and Malagasy affairs. Born on August 31, 1913, and raised in Guadeloupe, where his father was a landowner, Foccart joined the Resistance during the Second World War and emerged in its aftermath as a key administrator in the Fourth and Fifth French Republics. He capped his career as the architect and major policymaker of France's relations with its former colonial territories, as evidenced by his 14 years (1960–74) as secretary-general to the presidency in this sphere. An extremely powerful person in his domain, Foccart could make and break the weak unicrop African regimes by recommending or withdrawing French financial assistance. Feared and disliked in many circles, Foccart became the bête noire of the Tombalbaye (q.v.) regime in the early 1970s when the latter claimed—probably with a measure of truth—that Foccart was conspiring with Tombalbaye's opposition to bring an end to his presidency. In a major attack on Foccart, Tombalbaye personally called him "the sworn enemy of Chad" who wanted to bring about the splintering of the country and accused him (before an "anti-Foccart demonstration" of 100,000 in N'Djamena) of sponsoring 14 plots against the "security and happiness" of Chad. Consequently the Chadian National Assembly passed a resolution denouncing Foccart.

FODEIBU, OREZI. Former key political aide and secret police agent of Hissène Habré (q.v.) and later director of Chad's oil refining company. Fodeibu, who is a Kamadja, was removed from his post and arrested by the CRCR (q.v.) after the January 1992 attack from Lake Chad of residual Habré elements (the MDD, q.v.) trying to make a comeback.

FONDATION DE L'ENSEIGNEMENT SUPERIEUR EN AFRIQUE CENTRALE (FESAC). Joint higher education agency for the former French Equatorial Africa, created to continue the educational cooperation of the region during the colonial era. FESAC set up in December 1961 the Centre d'Enseignement Supérieur de Brazzaville with a law school and divisions of humanities and sciences; the center, for the use of nationals from all of the former French territories, was nationalized by Congo/Brazzaville in 1972. Until the creation in 1971 of the University of N'Djamena, the only higher education provided locally was through the Institut d'Enseignement Zootechnique et Vétérinaire d'Afrique Centrale (q.v.), created by FESAC on October 1, 1964. Other professional and technical schools in Chad include the Ecole Nationale d'Administration (q.v.), which opened in January 1965 as a two-year school, the Ecole Nationale des Adjoints Techniques (a four-year program of studies for technical staff in public works and agriculture), the Ecole Nationale d'Infirmiers, the Ecole Nationale de Service Social et d'Enseignement Ménager, the Centre National de Formation du Personnel de la Santé Publique, and the Ecole Nationale des Télécommunications.

FESAC—heavily dependent upon French fiscal and technical assistance—was administered by a council composed of delegates from member states. Apart from the Chad professional center, it sponsored two other technical schools: the Institut d'Etudes Agronomiques in Mbaiki, Central African Republic, and the Institut Polytechnique de Libreville in Gabon.

FONDS COMMUNS DES SOCIETES MUTUELLES RURALES (FCSMR). Predecessor of the Fonds de Développement et d'Action Rurale (FDAR) (q.v.).

FONDS D'AIDE ET DE COOPERATION (FAC). French development fund dispensing financial and technical assistance to former colonial territories, FAC is the successor, following the independence of much of Africa, of the Fonds d'Investissement pour le Développement Economique et Social des Territoires d'Outre-Mer (FIDES) (q.v.), and of the regional OCRS (q.v.) since 1963. Funds allocated to Chad between 1959 and the end of 1973 amounted to 314 million French francs.

FONDS DE DEVELOPPEMENT ET D'ACTION RURALE (FDAR). State organ set up in January 1965 to replace the Fonds Communs des Sociétés Mutuelles Rurales (q.v.) and aimed at the stimulation of agricultural production. Financed by injections of state capital (out of a small allocation from the *taxe civique* paid by all Chadians), the FDAR is primarily involved in the regulation and stabilization of agricultural produce, which it does through its monopoly over the purchase and sale of certain commodities and the encouragement of cooperative action aimed at higher productivity. The FDAR has held monopolies over the purchase of a wide variety of crops, including gum arabic (q.v.), granted in 1965, rice cultivation in Laï (detached from the competence of SEMALK [q.v.] in 1970), and others. FDAR is specifically forbidden to enter the market in crops or regions allocated to the SEMA (q.v.) structures. It maintains a warehouse in N'Djamena in which rice is stored and sold during the rainy season when prices frequently soar in the capital.

FONDS D'INVESTISSEMENT POUR LE DEVELOPPEMENT ECONOMIQUE ET SOCIAL DES TERRITOIRES D'OUTRE-MER (FIDES). Established on April 30, 1946, and the precursor of the contemporary Fonds d'Aide et de Coopération (q.v.), FIDES was the French development fund that dispensed economic and technical assistance to overseas colonies and associated territories. Between 1948 and 1959 the sum of 12,537 million CFA francs was disbursed to Chad in the form of grants and loans.

FONDS EUROPEENS DE DEVELOPPEMENT (FED). The European Development Fund is an agency of the European Community, with which most of Africa is linked via the Yaoundé treaties of 1963 and 1969. The FED dispenses the EC's economic and technical assistance to member and associate states. Chad received funds totalling US$84.1 million up to mid-1974. Much of the fiscal aid has gone into infrastructure building and, in particular, the construction of all-weather roads and airfields.

FORCES ARMEES DE LA REPUBLIQUE FEDERALE (FARF). One of seven small rebel groups operating in southern Chad in 1994, pressing for a federal division of authority. The FARF, which is led by Laokein Bardé Frisson (q.v.), broke off from CSNPD, the main southern forces, after the latter rallied to Idriss Déby (q.v.) in 1994 in exchange for integration into the Chadian national army and a post in the government for Lt. Ketté (promoted to colonel).

FORCES ARMEES DU NORD (FAN). Name coined in July 1969 in a congress of all military leaders fighting Tombalbaye (q.v.) in the northern préfectures. Also known as the Second Liberation Army (q.v.) (see also FIRST LIBERATION ARMY), the force was under the overall direction of Mahamat Ali Taher (q.v.). After Taher's death, FAN was headed by the Goukouni-Habré (qq.v.) team. Their falling-out in 1976 led to the name's being relinquished to Habré's group, with Goukouni's faction—after an alliance with Ahmat Acyl's (q.v.) Volcan Army (q.v.) (a segment of the First Liberation Army)—opting for the name Forces Armées Populaires (FAP) (q.v.). FAN's size varied from around 1,000 during the Goukouni-Habré leadership to over 5,000 at the time of N'Djamena's conquest by Habré in 1982. During the FAN-FAP tug-of-war in 1980 FAN was decimated, and with Habré's defeat remnants of the force retreated to Ouadai and Biltine. Following regroupment and secret funding and materiel from the U.S. CIA the force began its spectacular advance on N'Djamena, capturing the capital on June 7, 1982. The FAN then ceased to exist, officially being subsumed under the new national army set up in 1982, the Forces Armées Nationales Tchadiennes (FANT) (q.v.), which was a merger of FAN and FAT (q.v.). The core of FANT—its operational control, key officers, and commander in chief—remained, for the duration of the Habré era, ex-FAN men.

FORCES ARMEES DU PEUPLE (FAP). Not to be confused with the Forces Armées Populaires, which has the same acronym. Splinter group, headed by Ahmed Moussaye, reconciled with Habré (q.v.) in 1987.

FORCES ARMEES NATIONALES TCHADIENNES (FANT). New name for the allegedly national and unified armed forces of Chad following the ouster from N'Djamena of the GUNT (q.v.) government of Goukouni (q.v.) and the capture of the southern préfectures. FANT was supposedly a merger of Habré's FAN (q.v.) and the former dissident southern FAT (q.v.). In reality at least 50 percent of FAT refused to serve in FANT, with some elements joining their leader, Kamougoué (q.v.), in his alliance with Goukouni in B.E.T. Total FANT forces in 1986 allegedly numbered 22,000 troops, increasing to over 40,000 as various groups rallied to Habré in the late 1980s. However, at no time was this body an actual "fighting army." Indeed, when Habré sent all his available force in 1989 to the eastern frontier to try to stem Idriss Déby's (q.v.) invasion from Darfur, only his former ex-FAN desert warriors and additional elite forces participated in the battles. The bulk of FANT remained in N'Djamena, or in garrisons elsewhere, and did nothing to prevent Déby's unopposed entry into the capital on December 2, 1990.

FORCES ARMEES OCCIDENTALES (FAO). Originally referring to itself as FROLINAT's "Third Liberation Army" (q.v.) (the First and Second being along Chad's northern and eastern borders), and headed by Idriss Moustapha (q.v.), who was killed in June 1979, the FAO was active among the Kanemi in the Lac Préfecture. Following Moustapha's death two groups emerged, the MPLT (q.v.) of Aboubaker Abderahmane (q.v.), and an FAO now headed by Moussa Medela (q.v.). Further splits subsequently arose in the FAO, with one segment joining with Habré's (q.v.) fleeing loyalists (after Habré had been expelled from N'Djamena) to form the Mouvement pour la Démocratie et le Développement (MDD) (q.v.) to fight Idriss Déby (q.v.) in the Lake Chad area, and another segment, reconciled with N'Djamena, joining in the Conférence Nationale (q.v.) of 1993.

FORCES ARMEES POPULAIRES (FAP). Name of the merged forces of Goukouni (q.v.) (then known as FAN [q.v.]) and remnants of Ahmat Acyl's Volcan Army (qq.v.), part of the First Liberation Army (q.v.). The 1978 merger led to the unification of most of the anti-N'Djamena forces under Goukouni, the formal ouster of Abba Siddick (q.v.) from his former leadership of FROLINAT (q.v.), and the virtual isolation of Hissène Habré (q.v.), who then resumed the use of the name FAN for his own armed forces. The FAP scored major successes against N'Djamena and, utilizing the falling-out between General Félix Malloum (q.v.) and Habré (who had been enticed to join the government), moved into the capital unopposed in February 1979. An inevitable falling-out among members of the victorious alliance sapped the FAP's strength, and it remained an unruly, loosely commanded, undisciplined force. At the height of its strength it encompassed 7,000 men, though its operational strength was more in the vicinity of 4,000.

Though FAP had the tacit support of the southern autonomous FAT, the two major military forces remained apart, suspicious of each other, and with opposite goals. Consequently the FAN advance on N'Djamena—funded secretly by the U.S. CIA—was not to be checked. Tricked into ousting his major prop—the Libyan troops that had in the first instance allowed him to emerge triumphant against Habré in 1980—Goukouni and FAT proved incapable of stemming the Habré advance that seized N'Djamena on June 7, 1982.

The ousted FAP forces, joined by elements of the equally defeated FAT and CDR, regrouped in Bardai, and from there, with limited Libyan assistance, they counterattacked in 1984, seizing all of B.E.T. and briefly also Abéché. The FAP advance was blocked by Opération Manta (q.v.), mounted by France, which effectively partitioned the country between Habré and Goukouni. Over time Habré became the strongest, and FAP and Libyan forces were militarily ousted out from B.E.T., and the lengthy rebellion was more or less over.

FORCES ARMEES TCHADIENNES (FAT). Nucleus of the pre-1979 Sara-dominated central armed forces of Chad. After their defeat at the hands of Goukouni and Habré (qq.v.) and the fall of N'Djamena in 1979, remnants of the Chadian army—roughly 40 percent of its original strength (see ARMED FORCES)—withdrew to the southern préfectures under the leadership of General Djogo and Colonel Kamougoué (qq.v.). In the Choua (q.v.) government of April 1979 Djogo served as vice president and commander in chief (with Kamougoué in charge of some 600 gendarmes), but in the second GUNT (q.v.) government Djogo retired to Sarh to command the local garrison, and Kamougoué emerged as the de facto ruler of the southern quasi-autonomous préfectures, with the Comité Permanent du Sud governing from Moundou, and in command of some 2,500 gendarmes. The bulk of the Chadian army—captured during the northern assaults on N'Djamena—remained, however, in prisoner-of-war camps in Chari-Baguirmi.

Though Kamougoué was a member of the GUNT government and FAT was formally "unified" with the victorious FAN (q.v.) to form a new "national" army, FAT remained a distinct force. Its preoccupation lay primarily in governing and protecting the Sara préfectures while utilizing every opportunity to divide and erode the northern alliance in power in N'Djamena. Thus in the falling-out between Goukouni and Habré in 1980, FAT at times shelled both armed forces and, though committed to Goukouni, only minimally contributed to his defense. The same occurred again in 1982 when a resurgent Habré army mounted its assault on N'Djamena. Though this time FAT undertook a stronger commitment to Goukouni's GUNT government—by fielding troops in several disastrous battles that failed to stem the CIA-supported Habré—at no time was Kamougoué willing to leave the south undefended. This halfhearted support contributed to the defeat and ouster of Goukouni and further polarized opinion in the south.

Shortly after the fall of N'Djamena an internal split in FAT, triggered by personal competitiveness in the officer corps and abetted by inducements by Habré in N'Djamena, led to Kamougoué's ouster and the takeover of the south by FAN and dissident FAT elements. The leaders of the anti-Kamougoué uprising—Allafi, Rodai, Zamtato (qq.v.)—all received their reward from Habré, even as FAT was disbanded, and selected elements of it merged with the FAN armies in the new "national" FANT (q.v.) under a loyal Habré commander in chief. Djogo, Kamougoué, and other GUNT loyalists made their way to Bardaï in the north to join Goukouni in his counteroffensive that was to bring GUNT forces to the gates of Faya-Largeau and Abéché in mid-1984.

FORCES POPULAIRES DE LIBERATION (FPL). Name adopted by Mahamat Seid Abba (q.v.) for his small armed force, following the ejection of the GUNT (q.v.) government from N'Djamena by Hissène Habré in 1982.

FORCES POPULAIRES REVOLUTIONNAIRES TCHADIENNES (FPRT). Small armed group, reconciled with Habré (q.v.) in 1987, and headed by Nadjo Abdelkrim (q.v.).

FORCES UNIFI (FU). Army, gendarmerie, and police elements in the Sara southern préfectures, reorganized by Colonel Kamougoué (q.v.) after the fall of N'Djamena in 1979 and the withdrawal of all Sara troops from the capital. The FU was charged with the defense at all costs of the Sara homeland and with providing law-and-order services now that the central government was in "enemy" hands. In reality the force remained divided into its military (General Djogo, q.v.) and gendarmerie (Colonel Kamougoué) components, even as increasingly the name Forces Unifi was replaced by Forces Armées Tchadiennes (q.v.).

FOREIGN ASSISTANCE. Chad's principal sources of foreign aid have traditionally been France (through budget-balancing subsidies, the CCCE [q.v.], and the FAC [q.v.]), and the European Development Fund (Fonds Européens de Développement, FED [q.v.]). Since Chad's rupture with Israel (q.v.) in 1972—and most probably because of it—new capital assistance has been pledged to Chad from a variety of Arab countries not previously involved with the country. Among these was a US$12 million loan from Iraq, a 23.5 billion CFA francs loan from Libya (q.v.), and a 2 billion CFA francs grant from Libya, all pledged in 1973. In that year France maintained in Chad a task force of 723 technical assistants, of whom 350 were teachers. The upheavals in N'Djamena (1978–82) brought about the evacuation of all foreign personnel from the capital. Most of the technical assistants, however, had been all along concentrated in the southern préfectures, and since these were not affected by the evacuations, they remained in their posts.

After the entry of Habré into N'Djamena in 1982, important U.S. military aid began reaching the country. This was both to bolster Chad's resolve to recapture B.E.T. from Libyan (and GUNT, q.v.) forces, and a "price" for allowing anti-Libya CIA destabilizing operations out of bases near N'Djamena. France in turn provided armed might in restraining Libyan-GUNT advances south of the 16th parallel. (See OPERATION EPERVIER; OPERATION MANTA.) During the actual Chadian assault on Libya's forces in B.E.T. (and the raid on Maaten-es-Sarra in Libya) some limited aircover was provided by the United States since the French were fearful of becoming embroiled in a war with Libya.

FORT-ARCHAMBAULT. Pre-Tchaditude (q.v.) name for Sarh (q.v.). The town was named after a young French officer who died of disease there in 1896.

FORT-LAMY. Pre-Tchaditude (q.v.) name for N'Djamena (q.v.). Named after the commander of the French forces who died in the Battle of Kousseri (1900) against Rabah (q.v.).

FORT-LAMY RIOTS, 1963. A series of explosive popular riots in September 1963 in Fort-Lamy (but also in Am-Timan and a few other localities) that resulted in a number of deaths, estimated from 20 up to 500. The riots were sparked off by the arrest of Chad's major opposition leaders following a PNA (q.v.) strategy meeting (banned by law) at one of their homes. Among those arrested were the popular former mayor of Fort-Lamy, Jean Baptiste (q.v.), Djibrine Kherallah (q.v.), Baba Hassane (q.v.), and later, Ahmed Koulamallah (q.v.).

Crowds attempting to separate the arresting officials and those being arrested were fired upon, and according to some observers up to 100 were killed in Fort-Lamy in that encounter alone.

FORT-LAMY SULTANATE. Totally artificial sultanate (Fort-Lamy did not even exist prior to the arrival of the French), set up by the French with Sharif Muhammad Ijl at its head. Ijl had been one of Rabah's (q.v.) lieutenants, an Arab, and had been brought to Fort-Lamy from Dikwa (q.v.)

by Emile Gentil (q.v.), who named him at the outset chief of the town's Arab population. (Most of these had been either slave merchants or Rabahists.) In 1919 Ijl became *chef de canton,* with a palace of sorts in the Djemb el-Gato (q.v.) district. He ruled—without much power or prestige—as "sultan" of Fort-Lamy from 1912 on. By 1945 the artificiality of the sultanate was obvious to all and the utility of the structure practically nil; within the "sultanante" there were many ethnic chiefs (*chef de race*) with considerably more authority than the official sultan (especially the chief of the Kanuri and of the Hausa). The sultanate was consequently disbanded, though Ijl's son, Sharif Kasser, who had succeeded to the "throne," continued to style himself sultan of the city.

FORUM D'OPPOSITION DEMOCRATIQUE (FOD). Political alliance of 15 political parties set up in September 1992 and headed by Nouradine Koumakoyé Delwa Kassiré (q.v.), pressing for the convening of a national conference. When the conference was ultimately convened (see CONFERENCE NATIONALE), the alliance was defeated in the elections for the chairmanship of the conference by Adoum Maurice Hel-Bongo (q.v.). In November 1993 it renamed itself Forum pour le Changement Démocratique (FCD).

FORUM POUR LE CHANGEMENT DEMOCRATIQUE (FCD) see FORUM D'OPPOSITION DEMOCRATIQUE.

FRANC ZONE. Monetary transaction association formed by most of the territories once ruled by France, including the Communauté Financière Africaine (q.v.). National regional currencies, pegged to the French franc, are freely exchangeable and transferable within the france zone, under French fiscal control.

FRANCE, FORCES IN CHAD. Chad had always been a major base for France's colonial armies, including air personnel and equipment, one of three such bases in Africa. (The others are Diego Suarez and Dakar, Senegal.) Strategically located in Africa, Airbase 142 (N'Djamena) has been a major foreign installation of the French Air Force. French forces were also stationed in Chad (the Sixth Régiment Inter-Armes d'Outre-Mer (RIAOM) [q.v.], designated as the units available to help any state requesting military assistance under treaties with France), and until 1965 France's military control of B.E.T. (q.v.) similarly underscored the importance of the French military presence in Chad.

Until 1978 Chad's armed forces were also beefed up with up to 500 French officers and noncommissioned officers and this dependence on foreign advisers grew with the escalation of the rebellion in the country. The total number of French personnel in Chad has varied over the years. Apart from 30-odd mercenaries in critical posts (such as "Major" Gourvenac [q.v.] in the CCER [q.v.] until the 1975 expulsion of France's military presence in the country (an outcome of the Claustre [q.v.] fiasco) Chad's forces were usually augmented by between 300 and 500 French military advisers. At the height of France's military assistance in crushing the actual original rebellion (i.e., until 1980, when N'Djamena fell), some 2,000 additional troops were in the country, apart from personnel on the Mission de Réforme Administrative (MRS) (q.v.). Most of France's regular troops were of the Sixth RIAOM, augmented at one time by elements of the Third Régiment d'Infantrie de Marine. At that time the French forces in the country included: the MRA military personnel—529 officers and NCOs; the regular airbase RIAOM personnel—240 men; airbase reinforcements—385 men; troops fighting the rebels—two companies of the Foreign Legion and two companies of infantry—600 men; and miscellaneous temporary reinforcements of various strengths.

Though in the past French troops had been involved in combat duty as well, the return of a military presence in Chad after the fall of Tombalbaye (q.v.) was characterized by its supportive noncombat role. The troops, for example, were ordered not to take sides in the Malloum-Habré (qq.v.) falling-out (1978)—a fact that sealed the fate of the Sara-dominated military regime and led to Goukouni's (q.v.) triumphant entry into the capital. French troops were then withdrawn in 1979 and 1980 at the request of Goukouni's GUNT (q.v.) government (on the grounds that since the rebellion was over there was no need for military aid from the colonial power). Shortly thereafter, however, Goukouni's weakness vis-à-vis his rival, Habré, and France's continued neutrality resulted in Libya's being invited to assist GUNT in its tug-of-war with Habré. The increased Libyan role in Central African affairs, coupled with the ominous Treaty of Unification between the two countries, brought about world concern and secret CIA military support for Habré's comeback from the east. When Habré was ultimately successful and Goukouni and his allies were expelled to the B.E.T. desert regions, a renewed Goukouni-Libyan alliance threatened to sweep Goukouni back to power. Heeding Habré's call for military help, and strongly nudged by the Ronald Reagan administration, France returned military forces to Chad. Establishing a "Red Zone" (q.v.) south of which Goukouni's troops would not be allowed to proceed, France contained the conflict, in effect dividing the country in half. (See OPERATION MANTA.) In late 1984, facing domestic pressures to withdraw from the area and let the two warlords battle it out themselves, President François Mitterrand negotiated an agreement of mutual withdrawal with Libya's Muammar Qaddafi and withdrew most of France's 3,000-odd troops. Libya, however, had no intention of withdrawing, and in due course France was forced to reenter the arena. In February 1986 GUNT advances across the 16th parallel forced a French bombing of a Libyan airbase in northern Chad, with Libyan retaliation, and again the French forces were built up, launching Opération Epervier (q.v.), which included the stationing of French troops in Abéché (at the height of the emergency there were 2,700 in Chad), a radar station in Moussoro, and a number of French Mirage jets and Puma helicopters in Chad airbases, with backup personnel and aircraft in Gabon, Senegal, and the Central African Republic.

Habré by then, however, was much more swayed by U.S. advisers, and despite French counsel for caution, initiated the series of assaults on Libyan troops and bases in B.E.T. that ultimately brought about Libya's defeat and complete withdrawal. During this fighting French timidity prevented a more rapid Chadian victory, as France flatly refused to grant Chad's forces any air cover, and some of the advances (especially the conquest of Aouzou) had to be relinquished when the Libyans counterattacked. As the Libyan menace receded after its defeat at the hands of Chad, French forces were scaled down. And when Idriss Déby's armies descended into Ouadai to clash with Habré's armies, French officers were ordered to maintain strict neutrality. By mid-1992 Force Epervier was down to 700 troops, with Paris now seeing a fundamentalist Sudan rather than Libya as the main destabilizing agent in the region.

FRENCH EQUATORIAL AFRICA, GOVERNORS OF, 1886–1960.

Savorgnan de Brazza (1886–98)
de la Mothe (1898–1901)
Grodet (1901–04)
Gentil (1904–08)
Merlin (1908–17)
Angoulvant (1918–19)
Angagneur (1920–24)
Antonetti (1924–34)
Renard (1934–35)
Reste (1935–39)

Boisson (1939–40)
Husson (1940)
de Lerminat (1940)
Eboué (1940–44)
Bayardelle (1944–47)
Luizet (1947)
Cornut-Gentille (1947–51)
Ghauvet (1951–58)
Messmer (1958)
Bourges (1958–60)

FRENCH MILITARY ASSISTANCE see FRANCE, FORCES IN CHAD; REBELLIONS

FRENCH UNION. Structure established under the French constitution of October 1946 allowing a measure of representation to French colonial territories in the policy-making process of France. The French Union was composed of metropolitan France and its overseas territories, classified as Overseas Departments, Overseas Territories, Associated Territories, Protectorates, and Associated States. Chad, like most of France's possessions in Africa, fell under the heading of Overseas Territory. The Union had a president (the French president), a high council, and an assembly in which deputies from the various territories participated in the deliberations. The new provisions also allowed for African representation in the two houses of the French Parliament and in the Economic Council.

FRISSON, LAOKEIN BARDE. Military leader of the FARF (q.v.) rebel force fighting Idriss Déby's (q.v.) regime in southern Chad that broke away from the CSNPD (q.v.) when the latter rallied to Déby in 1994. FARF's goal is the establishment of a federal system.

FROLINAT see FRONT DE LIBERATION NATIONALE (FROLINAT)

FROLINAT-FONDAMENTAL. Splinter FROLINAT group, numbering no more than 300 members, that was founded in 1978 by Adoum Hadjero Senoussi (q.v.) following the ouster of Abba Siddick's (q.v.) leadership and the rise of Goukouni (q.v.) as leader of FROLINAT (q.v.). The movement formally deserted GUNT (q.v.) in December 1988. FROLINAT-Fondamental has been prone to splintering. For long its leader was Hadjero Senoussi, with Mahamat Nour al-Hassana as its secretary-general; more recently Mamadio Balassane (q.v.) emerged as its leader, rallying to the Déby (q.v.) regime in March 1991. Pro-Sudanese, pro-Islamic, and conservative, FROLINAT-Fondamental looks back to the early days of the rebellion against N'Djamena when the struggle was in part over religious and pan-Arab rights.

FROLINAT-ORIGINEL. Name adopted by Abba Siddick (q.v.) and his few followers after his loss of control over FROLINAT (q.v.) between 1974 and 1976. At first completely shunted aside in the division of spoils in N'Djamena, Siddick and some of his lieutenants were ultimately given posts in the GUNT (q.v.) government. And though Siddick vacillated, he eventually made his peace with Hissène Habré (q.v.) too—after Goukouni's ouster—and remained in the Chadian cabinet. His opportunism, however, led to a split in his own minuscule following, with only a minority staying with him. The majority moved to opposing Habré under their old name, and this group was now headed by Abdelkadir Yacine (q.v.).

FRONT D'ACTION CIVIQUE DU TCHAD (FACT). Early temporary coalition of Chad's progressive parties. Composed of the PPT, PSIT, UDSR (qq.v.), and independents, FACT was created in 1951 and was successful in the 1952 territorial elections in Chari-Baguirmi and Moyen-Chari, where it won all six seats, with the opposition traditionalist UDT (q.v.) gaining the 24 seats from the remaining districts. Prominent members of FACT included Marc Dounia, Gabriel Lisette, Ahmed Kotoko, Ahmed Koulamallah, Jules Pierre Toura Gaba, and Adoum Aganayé (qq.v.). The president of the coalition was Koulamallah, and Toura Gaba was secretary-general. The coalition fell apart right after the 1952 elections due to Koulamallah's unwillingness to accept second place to Lisette and his continuous differences with Kotoko.

FRONT D'ACTION COMMUNE (FAC) see **FRONT D'ACTION COMMUNE PROVISOIRE**

FRONT D'ACTION COMMUNE PROVISOIRE (FACP). Libyan-formed "shadow cabinet" set up on June 2, 1979, grouping all those who had failed to secure representation in Lol Mahamat Choua's (q.v.) GUNT (q.v.) cabinet of April 29, 1979. Among those excluded were Libya's then-ally Ahmat Acyl, Mahamat Seid Abba, Abba Siddick, and Adoum Abdulahi Dana (qq.v.). After the subsequent GUNT cabinet integrated the originally excluded personalities, FAC (minus "Provisoire") was transformed into an internal (to GUNT) caucusing faction, with Acyl as chairman, and loyalties neither to Habré nor to Goukouni (qq.v.). With the fall of N'Djamena to Habré in 1982 most of the FAC personalities escaped to raise the banner of rebellion that led them in 1984 to the conquest of the northern half of Chad.

FRONT D'ACTION POUR L'INSTAURATION DE LA DEMOCRATIE AU TCHAD (FAIDT). Small armed guerrilla band that sprang up in eastern Chad in late 1994 in opposition to the regime of Idriss Déby (q.v.).

FRONT DE LIBERATION DEMOCRATIQUE TCHADIENNE (FLDT). Temporary name of Adoum Hadjero Senoussi's (q.v.) formation in 1987.

FRONT DE LIBERATION DU TCHAD (FLT) (also known as FRONT DE LIBERATION NATIONALE TCHADIENNE; FRONT POUR LA LIBERATION DU TCHAD). Largely inactive rival organization to FROLINAT (q.v.), with which it should not be confused. Originating in the merger of the Union Générale des Fils du Tchad's (q.v.) political arm, the Mouvement National de Libération du Tchad (q.v.)—which was renamed the Front de Libération Nationale Tchadienne in 1966—and the radical Union Nationale Tchadienne of Ibrahim Abatcha (q.v.) that created FROLINAT, FLT was that segment of

FROLINAT that followed Hassan Ahmed Moussa (q.v.) out of the union. From its inception rather moribund as a guerrilla movement, and in general fearsome of actual combat and avoiding contact with Chadian forces, the FLT has operated out of its headquarters in Khartoum and bases along the Sudanese border, with occasional forays into Ouadai and Salamat. The FLT was essentially a regional Ouadaian group with mostly Maba ethnic and Sudanese external support whose early successes in the Biltine were not exploited due to poor organization, timid leadership, and unarticulated and hazy goals. In 1975 the Toubou derde's (qq.v.) return from Libya and rally to the new post-coup government in N'Djamena evoked Moussa's announcement from Khartoum that the FLT would similarly rally to the regime and renounce armed combat. The FLT was formally dissolved in April 1977. Other guerrilla groups in the east, some of which had either been in the FLT or had been erroneously lumped with it abroad, continued the anti-N'Djamena struggle.

FRONT DE LIBERATION NATIONALE (FROLINAT). Umbrella guerrilla movement in existence until 1977–78 that sprang up in opposition to the abuses of authority of President François Tombalbaye (q.v.). Not to be confused with the Front de Libération du Tchad (FLT). FROLINAT was originally formed in exile under a slightly different name in 1962 and was resurrected in a congress (though in reality, in a conclave of 24 delegates) on June 22, 1966, "on sacred recently liberated soil" (in reality, at Nyala, safely across the border in Sudan), as a union between Ibrahim Abatcha's (q.v.) radical Union Nationale Tchadienne (q.v.) and dissidents of the political arm of the ultraconservative (fundamentalist) Union Générale des Fils du Tchad (q.v.), the Mouvement National de Libération du Tchad of Hassan Ahmed Moussa (q.v.) (profiting from the fact that Moussa was at the time temporarily in jail in Khartoum), which was at the time affiliated with the Muslim Brotherhood. The first leader of the joint movement was Abatcha. Shortly after its creation the two groups fell apart, with Moussa abrogating the Nyala agreement upon his release from prison, and opting for the FLT name, while Abatcha and his followers retained the name of the movement. Abatcha himself was killed in operations against the government in Abéché in 1968. His death precipitated a major power struggle and falling-out among his lieutenants, especially between his North Korean–trained field chief of staff, Abdel Hadj Issaka (q.v.), who controlled a powerful force of rebels in the Salamat region, and a number of external contenders for the throne, including Dr. Abba Siddick (q.v.) (at the time only covertly a member), Mohamed Baghalani (q.v.), and Djalabo Aboubakar Othman (q.v.). A decision not to hold elections for a new secretary-general to succeed Abatcha benefited Siddick, who was able to shunt aside Baghalani (on the grounds of embezzlement of FROLINAT funds) and to bring about the liquidation of both Djalabo and Issaka. By 1969 Abba Siddick had acquired de facto political control over the FROLINAT external structure and become the best-known (indeed in the West, the only known) leader of the movement. The same year, having packed FROLINAT with his cronies, Siddick declared himself secretary-general of the organization, again in the absence of the requisite elections.

FROLINAT's headquarters was intermittently in Algiers and Tripoli, and it received financial and diplomatic support from both of those Arab governments. In September 1971 Libya recognized the movement as the "sole" representative of the Chadian people and sponsored several coup attempts against Tombalbaye's regime. These policies brought about a break in relations between the two countries, already cool in light of Libya's continuous military and fiscal support for FROLINAT. A reconciliation was effected over a year later following Chad's break with Israel and tacit renunciation of territory in the north (see MUSSOLINI-LAVAL BOUNDARY AGREEMENT); at the same time, Libya began to restrain FROLINAT's guerrilla efforts in the south and pledged important credits to N'Djamena. With Siddick's rise to power in remote Tripoli, relations between the political (i.e., external) arm of FROLINAT and its military (i.e., internal) fighting units rapidly deteriorated. Not only had FROLINAT only loosely—and Siddick not at all—controlled the actual guerrilla forces, but also several units completely rejected his leadership. Seen as a coward who never once entered the war zone, Siddick was rejected by others for his atheism and/or alleged Marxism. The Toubou (q.v.), who ultimately bore the brunt of the fight against N'Djamena, despised his opportunism in lauding their victories as "FROLINAT" successes while denying them both military and medical supplies. (Most of these commodities went to the eastern front, where groups more sympathetic to his leadership operated.)

In 1971 Goukouni (q.v.) broke completely with Siddick and formally set up his Second Liberation Army (q.v.) as a quasi-autonomous force, with the assistance of Mahamat Ali Taher (q.v.), a deputy of Ibrahim Abatcha, who became his right-hand man and military commander. (The First Liberation Army [q.v.], including non-Toubou ethnic elements, headed by Mahamat Seid Abba (q.v.) and leaning toward Sudan, operated in the East.) Goukouni's force was the precursor of FAN (q.v.) (under Goukouni and Habré [q.v.]); the eastern army was the precursor of the Volcan Army (q.v.) and later the CDR. In 1976 FROLINAT suffered another split when Mahamat Abba, a contemporary of Abatcha, was released from N'Djamena jails and came to

Tripoli to claim the mantle of leadership. When he too was shunted aside by Siddick, Abba withdrew to his eastern fiefdom, completing the splintering of the First Liberation Army.

Shortly thereafter Siddick was directly challenged by Goukouni and ousted from the leadership of the movement. Goukouni became titular head and merged the "political" and "military" arms within his FAN. For some time FAN continued to be referred to as FAN-FROLINAT, but for all practical purposes the FROLINAT label had been eclipsed. Those groups that did not join Goukouni coined various appellations utilizing the "FROLINAT" name, and several remain in use today. Siddick's very limited group, for example, called itself FROLINAT-Originel (q.v.) (in late 1984 it actually split into two, with two so-named groups in existence); other groups refer to themselves as FROLINAT-Orthodoxe, FROLINAT-Authentique, and so on. All are minute groupings, with very little influence or military might.

A new twist came on January 14, 1993, when Mahmoud Ali Mahmoud, a little-known die-hard FROLINAT militant, unilaterally declared himself the leader of the (more or less nonexistent) movement, and denied all former heads of FROLINAT (and specifically Goukouni, Mahamat Abba, Abba Siddick) the right of affiliation due to their lack of honesty and revolutionary sincerity.

FRONT DE LIBERATION NATIONALE TCHADIENNE see FRONT DE LIBERATION DU TCHAD

FRONT DEMOCRATIQUE DU TCHAD (FDT). Political movement set up in 1985 by Alingué (q.v.) before he joined Hissène Habré's (q.v.) government and merged his party with Habré's UNIR (q.v.). Among the cofounders were General Djogo, Colonel Djimé, Djibrine Hisseine Grinky, and Michel N'Gangbet (qq.v.).

FRONT DES FORCES D'ACTION POUR LA REPUBLIQUE (FAR). Political party set up in 1992 by N'Garledji Yarongar (q.v.) which participated in the Conférence Nationale (q.v.) of 1993.

FRONT NATIONAL AL-KHOUMI. Opposition group in the early 1970s led by Dr. Wahab in Nyala, Sudan. The group had little political impact, though it obtained some financial support from Chadians working or living in Sudan.

FRONT NATIONAL TCHADIEN (FNT). One of the few armed opposition groups active in Chad in the mid-1990s, though much of the movement rallied to N'Djamena between 1992 and 1994. The FNT was set up after the assassination of Abbas Yacoub Kotti (q.v.) and operates in Ouadai, partly out of bases in Darfur. In January 1994 it attacked and seized Abéché for a few hours before withdrawing. It was headed by Dr. Faris Bachar, who signed a peace accord in 1992 that was rejected by part of the movement. Two other segments rallied to N'Djamena, one in 1993 under Colonel Daoud, and another on October 12, 1994, under Mahamat Sabout Ali, but die-hard elements (by now only a few hundred warriors) still operated in Ouadai. The movement had slowly become a fundamentalist religious and separatist movement, demanding the liberation of Ouadai specifically and its transformation into an Islamic state.

FRONT PATRIOTIQUE DE SALUT TCHADIEN (FPST). Name of Idriss Déby's (q.v.) liberation armies during his struggle against Hissène Habré (q.v.). The political arm of the FPST was called the Mouvement Populaire du Salut (MPS), which remains Déby's political machine today.

FRONT POPULAIRE DE LIBERATION DU TCHAD (FPLT). Opposition splinter movement formed by Dr. Mukhtar Nasser Awat (q.v.) in the 1970s. Little-known within Chad, Awat was very popular in émigré and refugee communities in Sudan.

FRONT POUR LA LIBERATION DU TCHAD (FLT) see FRONT DE LIBERATION DU TCHAD (FLT)

FRONT UNI DU SUD (FUS). Secessionist movement set up after the Kano I talks that resulted in the withdrawal of southern army and gendarmerie forces to Sarh and Moundou. The "front" involved a number of civil and military leaders unwilling to submit to northern rule and was based in Moundou. The FUS gave way to the PRSNT (q.v.) in April 1979, led by Colonel Kamougoué (q.v.).

FULANI. Also known as Peul, Fellata, and as Bororo when nomadic. The Fulani are a Muslim people numbering over 9 million and found principally in West Africa in Nigeria, Niger, Mali, Cameroon, and Guinea, and in smaller concentrations in other countries, including Chad. Their history in Chad has been complex. They established themselves in Baguirmi at the end of the fifteenth century after the region was converted to Islam by the Fulani Oual Dede, who died in Ngar Dogo, near Chekna, on his way back from a pilgrimage to Mecca. His sons continued his preaching activities there, and the village became an important religious center and an attraction for Fulani from elsewhere. Fulani elements also seeped into Chad from Bornu, which, until the religious wars in the nineteenth century, dominated several of their principalities, and there has always been a steady and significant cross-Chad Fulani (and Hausa) pilgrimage to Mecca (see PILGRIMS), with many of these pilgrims settling on the route to provide services for their brethren. Other Fulani elements entered Chad from Cameroon (where there existed the Adamaoua Fulani sultanate) either peacefully or through localized wars of conquest. Currently found throughout Chad in small numbers and especially in Chari-Baguirmi and Mayo-Kebbi, the Fulani are great seminomadic pastoralists (see BORORO), though they are sometimes found as sedentary agriculturalists. Their numbers were estimated in 1984 at around 79,000, though they are undoubtedly more numerous. (For the Fulani attacks on Bornu see BORNU.)

FUNDAMENTAL CHARTER see CHARTE FONDAMENTALE

-G-

GADAYA, BACHAR MAHAMAT. President of Chad's Conseil Supérieur de la Transition (CST) (q.v.), replacing Lol Mahamat Choua (q.v.) in October 1994. Gadaya, who is from Guéra and a key member of the MPS (q.v.) political party, was Idriss Déby's (q.v.) personal choice for the post, and he replaced Choua, who had developed presidential ambitions.

GADDY, HAROUN. Idriss Déby's (q.v.) secretary of state for public corporations. A Hadjeray (q.v.), Gaddy had occupied the same post under Hissène Habré (q.v.), but was dropped from the cabinet in 1987 as part of Habré's purge of Hadjeray personnel.

GALOPIN, PIERRE (CAPTAIN). French officer serving with the French forces in Chad, whose secret report, the "Galopin Report," presented in May 1968, drew attention for the first time to the grave abuses of power by Chadian civilians and military men in the north and the role this played in provoking the rebellions in Toubou (q.v.) areas. The report emphasized the arbitrary nature of authority in B.E.T., the inflated and illegal taxes levied there (most of which were pocketed by the southern officers), the brutalization of the population and the major indignities imposed on tribal leaders and women. Galopin's report was kept secret for a number of years, though by the 1970s President François Tombalbaye (q.v.) began to acknowledge openly that the rebellion was to a large extent a consequence of maladministration by the central government. Paradoxically, Galopin—whose report had done so much to vindicate the righteousness of the Toubou rebellion—was captured in 1974 by FROLINAT (q.v.) forces in the north, tortured, and personally executed by Hissène Habré when he tried to negotiate the release from captivity of Mrs. Françoise Claustre (q.v.).

GAM, OUSMANE. Former president of Idriss Déby's (q.v.) interim national assembly in 1991 and 1992. A southerner who rallied to Idriss Déby (q.v.) and helped to institutionalize Déby's MPS (q.v.) political party after the latter seized N'Djamena, Gam lost his post after the 1993 Conférence Nationale (q.v.) elected its own head. He was then appointed government secretary-general.

GAMBAYE. Important Sara (q.v.) subgroup, better known as Ngambayé (q.v.).

GARAMANTIAN ROUTE. Caravan trail dating to antiquity and linking Tripoli via the Fezzan with Bornu. Control over trade moving across the trail constituted one of the major sources of wealth of ancient Carthage. Despite attempts to monopolize the route completely and to expand trade with the south, traffic was quite moderate until the introduction of the camel in the first century A.D. by Rome. (For the historical evolution of the trail, see CARAVAN ROUTES; FEZZAN-BORNU TRAIL.)

GARANDI, DIKOA (1939–). Educator and former cabinet minister. Born on October 4, 1939, in Fianga (Mayo-Kebbi), of Toubouri origins, Garandi was educated locally at Bongor, Fort-Lamy, and at Brazzaville, and he also studied at the University of Besançon, France. From 1963 to 1966 he was a mathematics instructor at a Fort-Lamy school and then entered François Tombalbaye's (q.v.) government as director of primary education at the Ministry of Education. In September 1967 he became secretary-general of education at the ministry, and in October 1968 he joined the cabinet as minister of education. He remained in the cabinet until December 1971, when he became head of Tombalbaye's presidential office staff, and in 1973 he was again appointed briefly to head the Ministry of Education. A member of the Executive Committee of the MNRCS (q.v.) between 1973 and 1975, Garandi was secretary-delegate in charge of Orientation, Organization, and Propaganda of the MNRCS and the "Cultural Revolution" (q.v.). Garandi reentered education during the turbulent period of the late 1970s and then left the country.

GARBA, SALIBOU. Minister of the civil service and labor since May 1994. A leader of the AND (q.v.) political party, Garba joined the cabinet in April 1993 after the Conférence Nationale (q.v.) as minister of mines and energy.

GARDE NATIONALE ET NOMADE. A quasi-military civil guard, administratively part of Chad's armed forces (q.v.), operating in the countryside and during the civil war guarding public buildings and officials and securing general law and order under the supervision of the minister of interior. Successor of the pre-independence Garde Territoriale (q.v.), the Garde Nationale et Nomade was composed of the nonmobile countryside Garde Nationale and the special units equipped to secure order in seminomadic areas, the Garde Nomade. The force was progressively strengthened from 2,000 personnel to 4,500 in 1973. Until the 1975 coup d'état the force was commanded by the French national Major Camille Gourvenac (q.v.), who played a critical role in securing the success of the coup. He was confirmed in his post by the new military regime, which also appointed him to several policy-making committees. Later Major Gouemourou (q.v.) was appointed commander of the force, and in mid-1976 Captain Allafi (q.v.) assumed command of the Garde. On March 31, 1977, a segment of the Guard was involved in an attempted coup in N'Djamena. After the attempt, the force was subordinated structurally to the regular army. The force—essentially a poorly trained one—was organized into 70-man units attached to the various préfectures to perform various duties under the local prefect. In N'Djamena the units assist other personnel in guarding public installations and public officials. The Garde Nomade was headquartered in the northern desert regions of Kanem. In August 1970 several hundred Moubi rebels (of the FLT, q.v.) rallied to the side of the government, and about 500 of them were recruited to augment the Garde. During the latter stages of the civil war the force suffered major attrition in strength through massive desertions, sometimes battalion-wide. Many of the troops deserting promptly switched sides, joining the rebels. Remaining troops were decimated during the siege of Faya-Largeau in 1978, and the force was completely disbanded after the fall of N'Djamena and the rise of northern power in the capital. Elements loyal to the south in this largely non-Sara force were merged with the FAT (q.v.) and the gendarmerie and participated in the defense of the Sara préfectures in subsequent clashes with Habré's (q.v.) troops. (See also ARMED FORCES.)

GARDE NOMADE. Section of the Garde Nationale et Nomade (q.v.), with specific responsibility for securing order in Chad's nomadic regions, which they patrolled continuously.

GARDE PRESIDENTIELLE. Hissène Habré's (q.v.) presidential security force, which was by far the strongest armed unit in the country. Composed exclusively of his ethnic Daza (q.v.) Toubou (q.v.) kinsmen and heavily armed, the Garde was the only unit trusted in combat, and at its height in 1988 included some 3,600 troops, headed by Mahamat Nouri (q.v.), a personal friend of Habré's. The Garde bore the brunt of the fighting with Idriss Déby's (q.v.) armies in November 1990, and many of its key officers fell in the battles. When the Garde was defeated, the road to N'Djamena was open for Déby, since the regular Chadian army (some 28,000 strong) was not a fighting force. Once Déby came to power, he institutionalized a similar ethnic force (though Zaghawa, his own ethnicity), the Garde Républicaine (q.v.).

GARDE REPUBLICAINE. Idriss Déby's (q.v.) main military prop and fighting force. A well-armed force of some 2,500 troops (originally only 1,500), nearly exclusively recruited from Déby's Zaghawa (q.v.) ethnic group, and with many Zaghawa nonnationals from Sudan. The force has been used to crush armed rebellions, including those in 1991 in the Lake Chad region and the revolt of the CSNPD (q.v.) in southern préfectures in 1993 and 1994, and it has done so in a brutal manner with numerous atrocities. The Garde has also been responsible for liquidations and intimidation of Déby's political opponents, real or potential, for example, assassinating in broad daylight the deputy head of the Chadian human rights league and destroying the printing presses of N'Djamena's sole independent newspaper. Garde members strut around N'Djamena demanding and taking free services, and in the southern préfectures they act as an occupation force. See also ARMED FORCES.

GARDE TERRITORIALE. Precursor, during the colonial era, of the Garde Nationale. (See GARDE NATIONALE ET NOMADE; also ARMED FORCES.)

GARFA, MAHAMAT (Colonel). Former chief of staff and cabinet minister. Formerly Idriss Déby's (q.v.) chief of staff, Garfa was demoted in May 1994 and appointed minister of mines and energy. On September 14, 1994, he defected from the regime and fled N'Djamena with several hundred troops personally loyal to him to join a revolt in eastern Chad.

GENDARMERIE NATIONALE. Formed shortly after independence and originally staffed by French officers and noncommissioned officers, most of the gendarmerie was composed of Sara (q.v.) veterans of France's colonial armies. Its original strength of 600 men in 1964 was greatly augmented after the onset of the civil rebellion in the country and reached 1,600 men in 1971 and nearly 4,000 in 1974. Until 1971 the force, directed by the minister of defense, was organized into 25-man mobile units trained in mob control and armed with light weapons, including automatic rifles. The units were normally dispersed in the countryside and especially in the southern préfectures where the threat of civil violence was low or nonexistent. Toward the end of the Tombalbaye (q.v.) era the gendarmerie's strength was augmented to make the structure equal in numbers to the militarily discredited army, but the gendarmerie was also better equipped and received preferential treatment—all factors that created interarm jealousies and competitions. Tombalbaye's divide-and-rule tactics and his preference for the gendarmerie backfired when on April 3, 1975, a conspiracy was aborted with the arrest of the gendarmerie's commander, Colonel Djimé (q.v.), and deputy commander, Major Kottiga Guérinan (q.v.). A relatively unknown officer, Captain Nguetbaye Kagbé, was promoted to head the force. At the time of the successful coup 10 days later, the gendarmerie hesitated briefly before joining with the insurgents to attack Tombalbaye's residence. Major Kottiga Guérinan was appointed the force's commander after the coup d'état, but in mid-1976 the command was returned to Colonel Djimé, and still later to Colonel Kamougoué (q.v.). With the fall of N'Djamena to Goukouni (q.v.), unscathed elements of the gendarmerie withdrew to the southern préfectures, establishing their de facto headquarters in Moundou. There, commanded by Kamougoué, who had become the strongman of the south, they formed the last defense line against the resurgent Muslim north. After the southern préfectures fell to Hissène Habré (q.v.) as well (August–September 1982), FAN (q.v.) officers took over command of the gendarmerie, and it was later completely revamped and transformed into a Police Militaire under solid northern control. (See also ARMED FORCES.)

GENTIL, EMILE (1866–1914). Explorer, military commander, and administrator. Born in Volmunster (Moselle), France, in 1866, Gentil had served with Brazza in the Upper Sangha (Central African Republic) prior to his arrival in Chad. From 1895 to 1898 he made his way up the Chari River (q.v.) to Lake Chad, and he extended France's protection to Baguirmi. Named French Commissioner in the Chari region in 1900, Gentil defeated Rabah (q.v.) at Kouno, linked his troops with those of Lamy and Foureau, and participated in the Battle of Kousseri (q.v.), in which Rabah was finally defeated and killed. Gentil was later named Commissioner to the French Congo. He died in Bordeaux in 1914.

GIRT see GROUPEMENT DES INDEPENDANTS ET RURAUX TCHADIENS

GLOS, NICOLAS DE (1911–1976). Colonial administrator and lay missionary. Born in Cannes on February 10, 1911, Glos served in the Free

French Movement during the Second World War, after which he joined the colonial administration in Brazzaville. He served in a variety of posts, including in the Central African Republic, and was prefect of the Guéra Préfecture in Chad in the 1950s. At independence he served for a while as a lay missionary in N'Djamena, and later as Jesuit director of instruction. He was also editor of the journal *Tchad et Culture*, which he built up into a respectable scholarly publication. He was killed in N'Djamena in a criminal incident.

GODIAN, LOUIS (1915–). Administrator and unionist, born in Bédiondo on June 21, 1915. By profession an accountant, Godian was the former president of the trade union of the civil employees of the AEF armed forces (during the colonial era) and treasurer of the AEF confederation of the CATC territorial unions. From 1963 to 1965 he served as permanent representative of Chad to Congo/Brazzaville and Gabon and from 1965 to 1969 as president of the Société Industrielle de Viande du Tchad (SIVIT), based in Sarh. He retired in 1975.

GOLBAI. Core social unit among the Lake clan of the Sara (q.v.) ethnic group, corresponding to the *tafourounda* of the Gambayé (q.v.). Composed of the nuclear family, which includes all brothers, married or unmarried, and unmarried sisters and their children. Their compound is surrounded by a straw enclosure and has total autonomy vis-à-vis all others. Each village in Sara country is composed of a number of such units. While war chiefs and land chiefs in the past had certain specific duties and rights, they were never the omnipotent leaders as in the Muslim country farther north, nor did they have the authority they later acquired as a consequence of colonial policies.

GOLBERT, JULES see NGOLBE, M'BAIDOUMINGA

GOLERE. King of the Moundang (q.v.) ethnic group, whose residence is in Léré (q.v.) in the Logone Orientale Préfecture.

GOLO, TOUSSOU (FRANÇOIS) (1939–). Educator, National Assembly deputy, and former secretary of state. Born in Bongor in 1939, Golo was educated locally and graduated from Bongor college with a teacher's certificate. After a year as director of Donomanga School (1960–61) Golo became secretary-general of the Bongor Municipal Council (1961–62) and in 1963 was elected to the National Assembly. He served as deputy for six years through 1969, following which he returned to education. In May 1971 he was brought into François Tombalbaye's (q.v.) cabinet as secretary of state for agriculture and animal husbandry, only then becoming an active PPT (q.v.) member.

In October 1973 he became secretary of state for public works, a post he occupied until the 1975 coup d'état. Since the coup he has been with the Bongor municipal administration.

GONI, MUKHTAR (?–1809). Leader of the Fulani (q.v.) jihad against the Bornu (q.v.) Empire. Residing in Deya, a Bornuan province, Goni joined the Fulani rebellion of Uthman dan Fodio and in 1808 personally led the armies that sacked Bornu's capital. Goni was killed in the subsequent liberation of the capital by al-Kanemi (q.v.) in 1809.

GOR. Mbaï subgroup of some importance. Previously known as the Mbaï-Doba (Gor is the name they call themselves), some 70,000 are to be found in the Logone Orientale and Moyen-Chari Préfectures. Their history has been replete with internal division, schism, and warfare as well as constant Baguirmi and Fulani (qq.v.) slave raids. Gor territory has seen much rural development and modernization, and despite their modest numbers, many Gor have reached senior posts in the government and armed forces—among them General Odingar, Antoine Bangui, and Joseph Brahim Seid (qq.v.).

GORAGA. Blood-price among the Toubou (q.v.) in the B.E.T. Still exacted in cases of murder, where the injured family has to be repaid either by the death of the murderer (or his parents) or through payment of about one dozen camels. Among the Kanembu (q.v.) it is called *dabbou* and amounts to fifty cattle.

GORALLAH, ROBERT. Union leader and president of the Union Nationale des Travailleurs Tchadiens (UNTT) (q.v.). Formerly attached to President Tombalbaye's (q.v.) presidential office staff, and in 1967 becoming a member of the Conseil Economique et Social (q.v.), Gorallah was appointed in January 1968 as president of Chad's newly unified trade union movement, Union Nationale des Travailleurs du Tchad (UNATRAT) (q.v.), and served until 1978.

GORANE. Pejorative Arab name for the Daza (q.v.) branch of the Toubou (q.v.) in Ennedi. Since Chad has a heavy Arab population, the Daza are widely referred to by this name. The Gorane (or Daza) constituted the bulk of Hissène Habré's (q.v.) armies and support.

GORE. Souspréfecture with administrative headquarters in the village of the same name, part of the southern préfecture of Logone Orientale.

GOTTINGAR, VALERY KAYA WHORR. Journalist and former director of Agence Tchadienne de Presse. Born in Sarh, educated locally and at a school for journalists in Paris, he served as editor in the Chadian Press Agency before becoming its director in January 1973. Since 1977 Gottingar has been with the Ministry of Information as head of a division.

GOUARA LASSOU (Captain) (1948–). Former minister of foreign affairs and for long Hissène Habré's (q.v.) number two man. A Moundang born in Torrola in Mayo-Kebbi in 1948 and educated at the Ecole Général Leclerc in Brazzaville (1961–65) and at the Bouar Military Academy (Central African Republic), Gouara Lassou graduated as a second lieutenant. He saw military service immediately in Bardai and served with units in Bokoro and Sarh. The coup of 1975 brought about his integration into the Conseil Militaire Supérieure (CMS) (q.v.) as minister of agriculture. A year later he was appointed minister of education, serving in that capacity during both the Malloum (q.v.) administration and the Malloum-Habré interregnum. Dedicated and efficient, he was retained in the cabinet during the Goukouni GUNT (qq.v.) administration as minister of the civil service, though he left the cabinet prior to the Habré counterattack on N'Djamena in 1982. He was reappointed to Habré's cabinet in 1982, briefly as minister of defense and then back to his former position as minister of education. A leftist, and personally loyal to Habré despite his southern origins, Gouara Lassou was promoted to the Ministry of Foreign Affairs in mid-1984 after Idriss Miskine (q.v.) was assassinated. Effectively the regime's number two man, he was also appointed as executive secretary of Habré's new political party, UNIR (q.v.). Despite his high status, Gouara Lassou remained a "southern outsider" to the more hardline northerners, at the same time being regarded as an ambitious upstart by the more veteran Sara politicians looking for a role in the Habré administration. As more former opponents of Habré came to be reconciled with N'Djamena, Gouara Lassou was transferred in 1989 from the Foreign Ministry (which was given to Acheikh Ibn Oumar, the last major holdout) and named minister of agriculture, though he was retained as UNIR's executive secretary. He lost his post with the rise of the Idriss Déby (q.v.) regime in 1990.

GOUEMOUROU, ADOUM (Lt. Colonel). Former head of Chad's armed forces. Gouemourou assumed command over the B.E.T. area activities against guerrillas, following the evacuation of French troops in 1972. He was appointed deputy chief of staff of the gendarmerie and head of the Chadian army after the 1975 coup d'état. He became chief of staff with Hissène Habré's (q.v.) entry into the Malloum (q.v.) government (replacing General Odingar [q.v.]) but retired from active service soon after.

GOUKOUNI, OUEDDEIMI (1947–). Former president of Chad (August 1979–June 1982) and head of the Gouvernement de Salut National (GSN) controlling B.E.T., and currently the only main former rebel leader not in N'Djamena. Fourth, last, and only surviving son of the derde (q.v.) of the Toubou (q.v.) in the 1970s, Wodei Kichidemi (q.v.), Goukouni was born in Zouar in 1947 and attended primary school in Bardai. He joined the civil administration in Faya-Largeau and, incensed by the Bardai incidents of 1965 (q.v.), he raised the banner of rebellion in Tibesti. Heading a small band of Toubou warriors loosely affiliated with FROLINAT (q.v.), his armed group was known as the Second Liberation Army (q.v.). Constantly clashing with FROLINAT's titular head, Abba Siddick (q.v.), over the latter's lack of support for the Toubou fighters—and several times under house arrest in Libya, Siddick's sponsor—Goukouni challenged Siddick's leadership, and together with Hissène Habré (q.v.) (who comes from a rival Toubou branch, the Daza [q.v.]) succeeded in ousting Siddick from FROLINAT, unifying some of the other rebel factions through their leadership of the CCFAN (q.v.).

In 1974 the capture of Mrs. Françoise Claustre (q.v.) brought the small band global notoriety. But personality differences, accentuated by their divergent views on how to conclude the kidnapping episode, ultimately led to a split and to Habré's ouster from FAN (q.v.) in 1976. Somewhat later Goukouni freed Mrs. Claustre. While Habré rallied to the regime in N'Djamena, accepting the premiership under General Félix Malloum (q.v.), Goukouni continued pounding the Chadian army in the north, steadily advancing on the capital. Finally, with Malloum and Habré deadlocked in a bloody conflict in N'Djamena, Goukouni marched into the capital. On March 23, 1979, as president of the Provisional Council of State, Goukouni was forced to accept a broadening of his governing coalition to include representation of all factions involved in the rebellion. Taking a backseat in the Nigerian-sponsored Lol Mahamat Choua (q.v.) government as minister of interior (April–August 1979), Goukouni then reassumed direct control as president of GUNT (q.v.). His perennial tug-of-war with Habré once again resulted in a rift that was fought out in a bloody and extremely destructive battle in the streets of N'Djamena, leading to the flight of much of the capital's population to Cameroon. (See BATTLE FOR N'DJAMENA.)

Plagued by lack of international recognition and the unwillingness of his reluctant southern allies—the FAT—to come wholeheartedly to his support, Goukouni invited Libyan troops into Chad to bolster his minority rule. Arriving in large numbers in May 1980, they rapidly contained the Habré rebellion, pushing his scattered troops to the far eastern provinces. (Some estimates have the number of Libyans in

Chad at the time at 30,000, possibly a very inflated figure.) Goukouni's actions and his subsequent weak leadership at the helm of Chad sealed his fate, as the CIA began subsidizing Habré's efforts at a comeback. Both trusting and naive diplomatically, Goukouni gave in to international demands that he expel his Libyan allies in exchange for a pledge for the stationing of an OAU force in Chad. The OAU force, however, provided no real buffer to the advancing Habré troops, and on June 7, 1982, Goukouni and his GUNT allies had to flee the capital.

Though a morose leader, he exhibited both humility and magnanimity after his conquest of N'Djamena, and he was later to obtain the grudging support of many of the southern leaders he had defeated—e.g., General Djogo (q.v.) and Colonel Kamougoué (q.v.)—who followed him into self-exile in B.E.T. (The southerner, General Djogo, was appointed commander in chief of the ANL [q.v.] armies.) Mending fences with Tripoli, Goukouni set up the Gouvernement de Salut National in Bardai and mounted an offensive (with Libyan tactical and military aid) that brought him into Abéché by mid-1983. Anxious U.S. proddings brought about the renewed entry of French troops into the country, who provided a buffer zone (the "Red Zone" [q.v.]) between the combatants along the 15th and later the 16th parallel. This line—which left all of B.E.T. to GUNT, and progressively to Libyan troops—was largely respected until 1986–87, despite occasional mutual forays.

In 1986 Goukouni broke with his Libyan allies. Relations between the Toubou and their erstwhile allies had all along been notoriously bad— with Goukouni himself again under house arrest and possibly the victim of an assassination attempt in Tripoli. This set off an anti-Libya revolt of his loyalist Teda (q.v.) clan warriors and enticed Habré to launch his military drives in B.E.T. that brought about a stunning series of defeats of Libya's forces and the capture of vast amounts of war materiel. Concurrent with these events, and for several years prior to them, several of Goukouni's main allies had deserted GUNT and made their peace with Habré. Goukouni himself had progressively lost control of FROLINAT, which split up into several segments in 1984. Indeed, by 1986 Goukouni was very much a leader without a movement, especially after Acheikh Ibn Oumar (q.v.) formally broke with Goukouni to set up, temporarily, a neo-GUNT movement, before himself rallying to Habré.

Largely a spent force since the mid-1980s, Goukouni was unable to get the jealous Habré to grant him any governmental role, despite negotiations between the two. He resided primarily in exile in Algiers. In June 1987 he formally recognized Habré's primacy in Chad, but even this did not suffice for Habré, aware of Goukouni's many—belated—friends in N'Djamena. Goukouni visited N'Djamena several times after the rise of the Idriss Déby (q.v.) regime in 1990 but, unlike other former rebel leaders, was not offered any serious governmental inducement to join the regime, much for the same reasons Habré had kept Goukouni at arm's length. In each instance he returned to his domicile in Algiers. During the 1993 Conférence Nationale (q.v.), which he attended, there was a visible groundswell of support for him on the part of many southern delegates, aware that Goukouni's 1980 presidency had been completely without vengeance, bloodshed, or rancor, the sole northerner to seize power and deal humanely with those he had defeated. But Goukouni's chances of rising to power democratically are today extremely slim, as he has no political machine in a Chad filled with presidential hopefuls and an Idriss Déby who has no intention of losing democratically the power that he has won by force of arms. Moreover, his Teda clan are numerically few, and relations with the other main Toubou branch—Habré's Daza—are bad.

GOULAYE. A major Sara (q.v.) subgroup in the Moyen-Chari Préfecture and found mostly in the Laï district. Numbering roughly 125,000, the Goulaye are the second largest Sara clan, after the Ngambayé, and one of the most affected by missionary efforts in the area.

GOULFEIL. Riverine town in Cameroon, site of an ancient Sao (q.v.) city-state. The name means "tired," referring to the founding clan that tired of wandering and settled on the site. The ruling dynasty included seven kings before an epidemic virtually decimated the town. Reestablished, Goulfeil had another 15 rulers before a Bulala lineage came to power, providing 43 more kings before the arrival of the French in the area. Goulfeil was surrounded by massive walls, crumbling remains of which still stand. It developed a high level of artistic accomplishment that is still being studied with interest.

GOUNDA. Second most noble Teda (q.v.) clan, after the Tomaghera (q.v.). The Gounda nomadize an area in Tibesti (Abo, Afafi), Fezzan (in Libya), and eastern Niger.

GOUNOU-GAYA. Souspréfecture with headquarters in the village with the same name, part of the préfecture of Mayo-Kebbi.

GOURVENAC, CAMILLE (Major) (1928–1978). French expatriate officer, commander of the Garde Nationale et Nomade (q.v.), and director of the Centre de Coordination et d'Exploitation du Renseignement (q.v.), Chad's secret service and military intelligence agency. During the Tombalbaye (q.v.) era one of the president's security and intelligence advisers. Gourvenac has been accused by critics of the torture of prisoners and of brutality. He played a key role in the events leading up to the 1975 coup d'état. Following the coup, Gourvenac—a prime opportunist—was reconfirmed in his posts and was appointed to the Military Commission of the new regime, the most important of the four created. Under personal contract to the Chadian government (and not part of France's technical assistance effort), Gourvenac's contract was terminated by Hissène Habré (q.v.) in 1978, and he died soon after. Gourvenac's dismissal was Habré's prime condition for entry into Félix Malloum's (q.v.) government.

GOUVERNEMENT DE PAIX NATIONALE (GPN). Bardai-based interim government-in-exile, set up in October 1982 by Goukouni (q.v.) after his expulsion by Hissène Habré (q.v.) from N'Djamena on June 7, 1982. It soon changed its name to Gouvernement de Salut National (q.v.).

GOUVERNEMENT DE SALUT NATIONAL (GSN). Bardai-based government-in-exile of Goukouni (q.v.) and elements expelled by Hissène Habré's (q.v.) victory in 1982 (formerly, though briefly, known as Gouvernement de Paix Nationale). Factions originally supporting Goukouni within the GSN included (all qq.v.) FAT (Kamougoué, Djogo), CDR (Acheikh Ibn Oumar), FAO (Moussa Medela), FPL (Mahamat Seid Abba), UND (Facho Balaam), Volcan Army (Adoum Dana), and FROLINAT-Originel (Abdelkadir Yacine). By late 1984, however, schisms had developed within each group, elements of which regrouped in other combinations.

GOUVERNEMENT D'UNION NATIONALE DE TRANSITION (GUNT). Provisional Government of National Unity set up after the victory of the north in the civil war. Headed by Goukouni (q.v.) (after a brief interregnum under Lol Mahamat Choua)[q.v.], GUNT was a coalition of 11 groups/factions that laboriously agreed to participate in the government of Chad after a series of meetings in Nigeria (see KANO MEETINGS) and at Dogouia (q.v.). Of the 21 original cabinet members, 10 were southerners, with Goukouni as president and Colonel Kamougoué (q.v.) as vice president. GUNT was never a cohesive government, even after the internal Goukouni-Habré tug-of-war resulted in Habré's (q.v.) defeat and retreat to the far eastern préfectures, from which he was to return, triumphant, two years later. At all times interfactional feuding and fighting was the norm, with the south participating in GUNT but not allowing northern troops or administrators into its self-governing territory. GUNT fell on June 7, 1982, when Habré's troops, secretly aided by the CIA, captured N'Djamena. GUNT, anxious for international legitimacy, had ousted its major military prop, Libyan troops, but their replacement, OAU units, refused to defend the regime. After the fall of N'Djamena,

Goukouni, Kamougoué, and other GUNT supporters withdrew to Bardai to set up the GSN (q.v.), which by mid-1984 reconquered most of B.E.T., with renewed Libyan aid.

The reentry of French troops into Chad on the side of Habré, and much-enhanced secret and not-so-secret U.S. military aid (aimed at destabilizing Libya) kept the balance of power along the 16th parallel, preventing a Goukouni/Libyan advance on N'Djamena. For some time Acheikh Ibn Oumar (q.v.), whose CDR (q.v.) had become the prime military force within GUNT, was its leader (having "expelled" Goukouni, who was also briefly arrested by Libya), or the leader of a so-called "neo-GUNT." (Acheikh's 1986 leadership saw GUNT group together the FAO, FROLINAT-Originel, MRP, FROLINAT-Fondamental, First Liberation Army, CDR, and UDN.) In 1986 Habré broke the tacit division of the country by attacking, defeating, and expelling Libyan and GUNT elements from much of B.E.T., following which GUNT—already crumbling due to defections—rapidly became an irrelevant force. Habré's victory over Libya saw the rallying to N'Djamena of many of the elements previously opposing it, and especially of Acheikh, who was rewarded with the Foreign Ministry. The falling-out between Habré and his most important ethnic allies, first the Hadjeray and then the Zaghawa (including Idriss Déby [q.v.]), was in due course to spell his doom, but both groups did not link up with the moribund GUNT. For a while Goukouni tried to revive both GUNT and FROLINAT, but within the context of a possible national reconciliation and the 1993 Conférence Nationale (q.v.), this was unrealistic.

GOVERNMENT OF CHAD (1995). Governance in Chad under Idriss Déby (q.v.) has been marked by constant shuffles and large cabinets. The following was the government as of mid-1995, including only key ministers.

Prime Minister	Koibla Djimasta
Armed Forces	Ali Absakine
Civil Service and Labor	Salibou Garba
Commerce and Industry	Abbas Mahamat Ambadi
Communications	Youssouf Mboudou Mbami
Culture, Youth, Sports	Mahamat Seid Fara
Environment and Tourism	Moïse Nodji Ketté
Finance	Mahamat Ahmat Alhabo
Foreign Affairs	Ahmat Abderahman Haggar
Interior	Mahamat Nouri
Justice	Maldoum Bada Abbas
Livestock and Water	Mahamat Nour Mallaye
Mines and Energy	Paul Mbainodoum

National Education	Nassour Waidou
Planning and Cooperation	Mariam Mahamat Nour
Public Health	Laoubelé Damaye Dangbé
Public Security	Noudjalbaye Ngaryanam
Public Works	Gali Gatta N'Gothe
Rural Development	Mahamat Adoum Kalapoum
Women's Promotion	Achta Selgué

GOVERNORATE. New name for Chad's circonscriptions as part of Tombalbaye's "Cultural Revolution" (qq.v.). The term was not widely used across the country and was dropped after the 1975 coup d'état.

GOVERNORS (MILITARY AND CIVILIAN) OF CHAD.

Destenave (1900–02)
Largeau (1902–04)
Gouraud (1904–06)
Largeau (1906–08)
Millot (1908–09)
Moll (1909–10)
Maillard (1910–11)
Largeau (1911–12)
Kirtzman (1912)
Briand (1912–13)
Largeau (1913–15)
Briand (1915–16)
Martelly (1916–18)
Ducarre (1918–20)
Lavit (1920–22)
Reste (1922–26)
De Coppet (1926–29)
Buhaut-Launay (1929–33)
Brunot (1933–34)
Dagain (1934–38)
Eboué (1938–41)
Lapie (1941–43)
Leclerc (1943)
Latrille (1943–44)
Rogué (1944–46)
Léger (1946)
Rogué (1946–49)
Le Layec (1949)
De Mauduit (1949–50)
Casamata (1950–51)

Hanin (1951)
Colombani (1951–56)
Troadec (1956–58)
Doustin (1958–60)

GOZ-BEIDA. Souspréfecture with administrative headquarters in the village of the same name, part of the préfecture of Ouadai. Goz-Beida encompasses 26,000 square kilometers (10,040 square miles) and has a population of 42,000.

GRANDE MOSQUEE. N'Djamena's main mosque, damaged in the civil war of 1980. Currently its imam is Hissein Hassan Abakar (q.v.).

GRANDS MOULINS DU TCHAD (GMT). Highly automated flour mills (employing only 17 people) established in N'Djamena in 1964 to process wheat raised on Lake Chad's polders (q.v.). Due to low producer prices paid by the government, much of Chad's wheat is smuggled into neighboring countries, and the mills have worked well below capacity. Much to Chad's embarrassment, wheat has had to be obtained from the World Food Programme in order to supply the raw material for the mills. GMT produces flour, biscuits, pasta, and cattle feed. The company was capitalized at 158 million CFA francs. GMT closed completely in 1980 due to the unsettled conditions in the country and never reopened since it was inherently unprofitable.

GRINKY, DJIBRINE HISSEINE. Former FAP (q.v.) leader who joined General Djogo's (q.v.) Front Démocratique du Tchad (q.v.) in 1986, and later that year rallied to Habré. Of mixed parentage (his father is Nigerian), Grinky was appointed to Habré's cabinet as minister of culture, youth, and sports but was under constant surveillance by the political police (and, indeed, was picked up twice) because it was believed that he had mixed loyalties.

GROUNDNUTS. Together with sorghum and millet, groundnuts (or peanuts) are one of the most important staple consumption crops grown in Chad. Only 3 to 5 percent of total production is a surplus available for the local oil mills, and since 1971 a decline in production of groundnuts has caused major raw-material supply problems for the mills. Groundnuts are grown in two basic zones: in the center-east of the country, where they are planted together with millet, with part of the harvest available for commercial sale; and in the southern préfectures, where they are grown together with sorghum, but where cotton is the prime cash crop. Chad's nuts cannot be economically exported to the world markets, and consequently most of the domestic surplus is ground into oil and by-products. Since November 1965 SONACOT (q.v.) has had a monopoly over the purchase of Chad's groundnuts.

GROUPE DES DEMOCRATES ET PATRIOTES (GDP). One of several names of the political party set up in Paris in 1984 by then ambassador to France Jean Bawoyeu Alingué (q.v.). The party took a position independent of both Habré and Goukouni (qq.v.).

GROUPE DES OFFICIERS DES FORCES ARMEES TCHADI-ENNES (GOFAT). Steering committee of the 1975–1978 military regime. Original title of what was to become the Conseil Supérieur Militaire (q.v.).

GROUPE DU AVRIL 1. Original name of Idriss Déby's (q.v.) revolt against Hissène Habré (q.v.) after he reached the sanctuary of Darfur. The date commemorated the break between the two leaders, formerly allies.

GROUPEMENT DES INDEPENDANTS ET RURAUX TCHADIENS (GIRT). A group of conservative and traditionalist AST (q.v.) dissidents that formed as a separate faction in 1956 on a cooperationist platform vis-à-vis the party of the south, the PPT (q.v.), and its political alliance, ERDIC (q.v.). The dissidents, led by Gountchomé Sahoulba (q.v.), formally constituted themselves as a separate party after the partial elections in Chari-Baguirmi in 1958 in which the Union Socialiste Tchadienne (UST) (q.v.) won over ERDIC. In the Territorial Assembly they played a pivotal role between the two opposing formations, since their eight votes could tilt the balance of power in either direction. Originally supporting the PPT coalition, the GIRT caused the downfall of the Gabriel Lisette (q.v.) provisional government by switching support to the UST on January 30, 1959. Sahoulba then formed a new provisional government (a UST-GIRT alliance called the MPT [q.v.]) which, lasting just 12 days, gave way to another provisional government by Ahmed Koulamallah (q.v.) and later to François Tombalbaye's (q.v.) provisional government. (see PROVISIONAL GOVERNMENTS.) The GIRT's opportunistic balancing role during this period brought about its own eclipse. In the May 1959 elections the party won only two seats, and in January 1960 the remnants of the party merged into the newly established opposition party, the PNA (q.v.).

GUARANG I, ABDER RAHMAN, KING (1784–1806) OF BAGUIRMI. Sixteenth *mai* (q.v.) of Baguirmi (q.v.) and one of the kingdom's more depraved and cruel rulers. Guarang's incestuous marriage to his sister was the official pretext seized by Ouadai to invade and raze much of Baguirmi. The bulk of the royal lineage was killed and some 20,000 Barma were captured and sold into slavery. Baguirmi, now a tributary to Ouadai, never recovered from the assault despite subsequent attempts to reassert itself, and it fell into decay.

GUARANG II, ABDER RAHMAN, KING (1883–1918) OF BAGUIRMI. Last independent *mai* (q.v.) of Baguirmi (q.v.). The 21st to ascend the throne, Guarang II inherited a very weak buffer kingdom between the mighty Bornu and Ouadai, having in the past been raided and/or been tributary to one or the other. In 1892 Rabah (q.v.) further eroded Baguirmi's autonomy. In due course the capital, Massenya, was twice razed. The appearance of French influence in the region was welcomed by Guarang, who promptly signed a protectorate treaty with France in 1897, helping with porters, supplies, and military formations to bring about the defeat of Rabahist power in the Battle of Kousseri (q.v.) in 1900.

GUELTA D'ARCHEI. Spectacular narrow canyon with red walls, peppered with baboon-inhabited caves and cool freshwater pools. This major tourist attraction is located 80 kilometers (50 miles) southeast of Fada (q.v.) in the Ennedi souspréfecture of B.E.T.

GUERA MOUNTAINS. A rugged range of mountains in the Mongo souspréfecture. Reaching a peak of 1,768 meters (5,800 feet), they are inhabited by Hadjeray (q.v.) clans who, though converted to Islam, still practice the *margai* (q.v.) cult.

GUERA PREFECTURE. With administrative headquarters in Mongo (q.v.), Guéra covers an area of 58,940 square kilometers (22,760 square miles) in central Chad and encompasses a mostly Hadjeray (q.v.) population of 255,000, giving it a population density of 4.3 per square kilometer. The préfecture is divided into three souspréfectures—Mongo, Bitkine (q.v.), and Melfi (q.v.)—and has an extremely picturesque landscape ranging from the rugged Guéra Mountains where the *margai* (q.v.) cult is still practiced to the wildlife Siniaka-Minia and Zakouma ranges (see RESERVE DE SINIAKA-MINIA; PARC NATIONAL DE ZAKOUMA). Guéra's great popularity as a tourist center (for those rugged few who knew of its beauties) was cut short by the civil rebellion that started in 1965 in the region and unsettled conditions that obtain virtually to this day.

Communications in the préfecture are poor. Dirt roads connect Mongo with N'Djamena (520 kilometers, or 322 miles), Abéché (372 kilometers, 231 miles), Ati (153 kilometers, 95 miles), and connect Melfi with Sarh (312 kilometers, 193 miles), but these are totally impassable between mid-July and mid-October during the rainy season.

The population produces some cotton for the cash economy as well as millet, sorghum, and groundnuts. In the precolonial era Guéra was under the suzerainty of the Ouadai kingdom (q.v.), and the latter's brutal periodic slave raids in the area evoked local petitions for French protection. The préfecture was prime guerrilla territory after the Mangalmé tax riots (q.v.) that marked the onset of Chad's civil wars, and it was the préfecture (and ethnic group) first disaffected by Habré's (q.v.) iron-fisted rule. Later, during the Déby reign, Guéra's Hadjeray again rebelled after the arrest of Maldoum Bada Abbas (q.v.), and though some of the rebels laid down their arms following the reconciliation between the two, a segment continued fighting through 1995.

GUEREDA. Souspréfecture with headquarters in the village of the same name, part of the préfecture of Biltine. Guereda lies 175 kilometers (109 miles) east of Biltine and encompasses a territory of 12,000 square kilometers (4,300 square miles) and a population of 36,000. The village, which has both a garrison and a customs post, was at the center of the "rebel" zone during the civil war in the 1970s.

GUERINAN, KOTTIGA see KOTTIGA, GUERINAN.

GUET, GOUKOUNI. Early and ferocious Goukouni military commander, of the Daza (q.v.) branch of the Toubou (q.v.), who assisted in the capture of N'Djamena in 1979. He followed Goukouni (q.v.), once ousted from power, to B.E.T. but rallied to Habré in 1987 and was appointed the latter's deputy chief of staff. Guet was subsequently sent for formal military training at Sandhurst, England, and was there when Habré's government fell. He returned to Chad to foment and lead the Kanembu revolt in the Lake Chad area during December 1991–January 1992 under the banner of the MDD-FANT (qq.v.), joining hands with remnants of the FAO (q.v.). After this effort failed, Guet moved to northern Central African Republic, together with Korei Guini (q.v.) and Orezi Fodeibu (q.v.), where he raised another army, of some 1,000 men, which was involved in raids on Batha and Ouadai. He then returned to northern Nigeria, where he was de facto MDD spokesman and organizer. Guet was kidnapped in Borno state by Chad secret agents sent in May 1992 at the express orders of then chief of staff Abdallah Mahamat Ali (q.v.), who had lost his family during the MDD rebellion in Kanem. Guet was kept in Ali's cellar in N'Djamena and regularly tortured, until Ali was demoted (for the brutality of his troops in the southern préfectures), when Guet was killed.

GUIAGOUSSOU, HISSEINE MAHAMAT (1938–). Administrator, born on June 28, 1938, in Moussoro. Guiagoussou served briefly as head of the Legislative Service (October 1960 to January 1961) and as deputy secretary-general of the National Assembly (January to June 1961) before departing for the United States, where he served from 1962 to 1965 as Second Secretary at the Chadian mission to the United Nations. From 1965 to 1975 he was head of the Foreign Ministry's Division of Organizations and International Affairs.

GUIDARI. Important regional market town in the Tandjilé Préfecture, part of the Laï souspréfecture. With a population of 2,500, Guidari has an important weekly market.

GUILADOUMA, ETIENNE (1938–). Youth leader, instructor, and National Assembly deputy. Born in December 1938 in Bébédjia to the former chef de canton of Kessely, Guiladouma was educated in Doba, Fort-Lamy, and at a Jesuit secondary school, completing his studies in Dakar, Senegal. A municipal councillor of Moundou and one of the founding members of the JEPPT (q.v.)—of which he was elected second vice president in its founding congress—Guiladouma was elected to the National Assembly in 1969 and served on it until its dissolution after the 1975 coup. He has not held public office since.

GUINASSOU, TAHER. Former key Habré (q.v.) aide and cabinet minister. Guinassou was Habré's FAN (q.v.) chief of staff, and after Habré seized N'Djamena, he joined the cabinet in the key position of minister of interior and security. He was Habré's personal representative at the aborted Addis Ababa January 1984 peace talks. In July 1984 Guinassou was transferred to assume the Ministry of Livestock and Rural Hydraulics, where he stayed until Habré's fall from power.

GUINI, KOREI. Habré's cousin and, during his reign, head of the fearsome and brutal DDS (q.v.) political police. After Habré's ouster from power in December 1990, Guini was involved in raising several armies in the Lake Chad region and in the Central African Republic, attempting to dislodge Idriss Déby (q.v.) from power.

GUM ARABIC. Secretion of the acacia tree that is used in the pharmaceutical and food industries. Sudan is the world's leading producer, supplying 46,000 tons yearly, 80 percent of the world supply. In Chad, regions producing gum arabic include Batha-Guéra, Biltine-Ouadai, and Lac-Kanem. Interest in the commodity arose only in 1953 and 1954 when a mission was sent to Sudan to study techniques of harvesting it, and since 1960 there have been methodic efforts to collect it. Production rose steadily from 56 tons (all from Biltine) in 1956/57 to 743 tons in 1964/65 (50 percent from Biltine) and 1,709 tons in 1969/70 (catapulting Chad to the fifth place in world production) but plummeted in subsequent years, largely due to the drought (which changed the migratory patterns of the nomads who harvest the crop) and the rebellion, which has made methodic upkeep and harvesting difficult. SONACOT (q.v.) has the monopoly over the purchase and marketing of gum arabic. In the 1960s the company paid 35 CFA francs per kilogram of gum arabic and sold it to foreign companies at 91 CFA francs. The price paid to producers was raised to 50 francs in the early 1970s, and in 1975 shortage of the commodity brought about another raise, to 70 francs. Though exports of gum arabic resumed in the 1980s, tonnages are quite modest.

GUNT see GOUVERNEMENT D'UNION NATIONALE DE TRANSITION

GURIA see YEDINA

-H-

HABRE, HISSENE (1942–). Former president of Chad. Born in 1942 in Faya-Largeau, the son of a desert shepherd of the Anakaza (q.v.) clan of the Daza (q.v.) or Gorane (q.v.) branch of the Toubou, Habré was educated locally and obtained employment as a clerk in the French army's Construction and Works Department in Faya-Largeau. Promoted by the French and by President Tombalbaye (q.v.)—both seeking loyal northerners—Habré was rapidly transformed into an administrator, first as deputy prefect of Moussoro (1963). He was then dispatched to Paris for formal higher training (at the elite Institut des Hautes Etudes d'Outre-Mer (IHEOM). Habré petitioned to continue his studies in Paris in law, but he was refused. He nevertheless persisted, and only returned to N'Djamena in 1971. Sent to Tripoli, Libya, on a secret mission to negotiate with FROLINAT's Abba Siddick (qq.v.), Habré promptly deserted and sought a senior post (allegedly deputy secretary general) with FROLINAT. Shunted aside by Siddick, Habré assumed the leadership of the CCFAN (q.v.) (1972–76), which was aimed at stepping up the pace of fighting in B.E.T. and shaking off Siddick's timid leadership. Coleader of the FAN (q.v.) force in Tibesti (along with Goukouni, then his ally), Habré and his warrior band scored a dramatic propaganda coup on April 21, 1974, with the capture in Bardai of several Europeans, including Mrs. Françoise Claustre (q.v.), an archaeologist (studying prehistoric tombs) and Christian Staewan, cousin of Germany's President Gustave Heinemann. The German government promptly paid the $823,000 ransom and met other FROLINAT demands (broadcasting a propaganda manifesto); as Chad's formal ally, the French government was unable to do so, and the "Claustre affair" dragged on for three years.

Habré's inclination to continue capitalizing on Claustre's captivity when Goukouni favored her unconditional release on humanitarian grounds drove the final wedge that split the duo apart in 1976. After a period in the political wilderness, with only 300 of his warriors with him, Habré made his peace with General Félix Malloum (q.v.) in N'-Djamena and joined him in August 1978 in a bicephalous executive on which he served as prime minister. Habré was suited neither by temper nor by ambition for sharing power, and he soon fell out with Malloum. As the two clashed violently in N'Djamena, Goukouni's troops demolished the remnants of the Chadian army and entered the capital.

Within the new array of power, the arrogant, aggressive, and ambitious Habré had to accept a secondary role as minister of defense. Unable to accept a secondary role to Goukouni (who was also from a rival Toubou clan), in March 1980 Habré rebelled, and bitter fighting erupted between his forces and those of GUNT (q.v.). In the process, which lasted some eight months, most of the capital was destroyed, its population fleeing across the river to Cameroon. Ultimately ousted by Libyan troops invited for that purpose by Goukouni, Habré regrouped in Biltine and in Darfur and, aided by heavy surreptitious CIA military aid, began his long trek back to N'Djamena and ultimate power. Allegedly a brilliant tactician, his defeat of his rival, Goukouni, in 1982, was more the result of the fragmentation of the GUNT alliance, the CIA infusions of money and materiel for his troops, and the fact that Goukouni had asked the Libyans to leave Chad, banking on OAU pledges to ensure the balance of power, which they did not. Seizing power on June 7, 1982, Habré continued on to conquer the southern préfectures with the aid of dissident Sara FAT (q.v.) commanders. The conquest was accompanied by a major settling of accounts, arbitrary arrests, and assassinations, which triggered for the first time the emergence of "liberation" movements in the south.

A counteroffensive by Goukouni in 1984 brought the entire B.E.T. Préfecture (half of the country) into rebel hands. The fact that Libya had reentered the civil war, siding with Goukouni, brought about the entry of French force (prodded by the U.S.) behind Habré and the stabilization of military lines along the 16th parallel. Habré has been judged "tough, efficient, intelligent" as well as "ruthless, uncompromising, egotistical." Seemingly contradictory, both assessments are true. When Habré is compared to Goukouni, however, the dramatic differences in the characters and leadership style of the two are striking. Habré's brutal reign (1982–1990) resulted in a forceful "unification" of the country that brought about many atrocities and some 40,000 deaths, mostly by his Garde Présidentielle (q.v.) and DDS (q.v.) secret police. Some 10,000 political prisoners were allegedly killed in secret prisons under and in the presidential compound alone. This pattern stands in stark contrast to Goukouni's magnanimous "hands-off" policy once he seized N'Djamena in 1980, which won converts in the defeated south and brought him southern allies later, when he was ousted, in his reconquest of B.E.T. in the mid-1980s.

In 1986 and 1987 Habré launched a series of stunning assaults on Goukouni's and Libya's heavily defended positions in B.E.T. In the process his forces captured immense quantities of war materiel (including hundreds of tanks and many jet airplanes and helicopters completely intact), raided deep into Libya itself, and at one time ousted the Libyans from Aouzou (q.v.) as well. The dramatic reverses convinced Muammar Qaddafi to sue for peace and seek resolution of the Aouzou Strip conflict by the International Court of Justice in The Hague. (Libya lost the case in 1994 and withdrew from the strip.) Habré's military successes also brought about a rallying to his regime most of the hitherto rebellious factions in the country. Indeed, by 1988 most of the key former rebel leaders were in his cabinet in N'Djamena. However, Habré's heavy-handed rule, paranoid quest for and rooting out of potential competitors for power, and his policy of having opposition leaders killed, drove a wedge between him and the Hadjeray (q.v.), who had helped him come to power in N'Djamena in 1982, and later, the Zaghawa (q.v.), who had also sided with him, among whom were found the real military geniuses—Djamouss (q.v.) and Déby—behind the victories against Libya.

When Déby fled N'Djamena he was pursued all the way into Sudan by Habré's elite troops. On several later occasions Habré's troops attacked Déby well inside Sudan in an attempt to disrupt his raising an army among Hadjeray-Zaghawa elements resident there. Well aware of Déby's military brilliance, Habré committed all of his elite forces in eastern Chad and personally led them in the deciding battles in November 1990 in Ouadai. In the ultimate tug-of-war Déby emerged victorious, decimating Habré's forces (with many of Habré's lieutenants dying in those battles), and then marching into N'Djamena unopposed on December 2, 1990. Habré, having been unable to secure the intervention on his side of French troops in the country, used a Zairean passport to escape into Cameroon with all of Chad's liquid assets. His last act before leaving was to order the killing of the remaining prisoners in the cellars of the presidency. With several lieutenants and remnants of his armies who escaped into Niger, he then mounted several counteroffensives in the Lake Chad region, but was unsuccessful in his comeback bid. Habré currently is based in Dakar. In his heyday he had a powerful lobby in Washington, employed U.S. ex-marines as personal bodyguards, and owned two houses in Denver.

HADDAD. A group of clans (also known as Aza) scattered throughout northern Chad, with some 30 percent of their 100,000 population living in the Kanem Préfecture, where they are subdivided into 40 subclans. Speaking the local vernacular wherever they are found (they have no language of their own) the Haddad are frequently considered an integral part of the ethnic group in the midst of which they live but of a specialized caste. They perform a variety of skills, such as weaving, dyeing, and salt-mining, and they are also excellent ironsmiths, tanners, and shoemakers. In many localities they are both despised and feared for the menial work they perform and for the magic they allegedly possess. They usually live in compounds at the fringes of villages and rarely intermarry with other ethnic groups. Many Haddad communities were in the past slaves or ex-slaves, of the Daza (q.v.) specifically, and most trace their origins to Ennedi, where some very ancient Haddad village sites have been discovered by archaeologists.

HADIDE see NIGERIA-CHAD BORDER SKIRMISHES, 1983

HADJ see HAJJ

HADJERAY. Collective name for a large number of ethnic groups found in the hilly areas between Mongo and Melfi in south-central Chad (in the Guéra Préfecture), whose most studied characteristic is their veneration of a series of oracles and spirits called *margai* (q.v.). Heavily converted to Islam during the colonial era, many *margai* priests are now *mallams* (q.v.); the French tried to prevent this mass conversion by encouraging Catholic schools in Hadjeray districts and by trying to preserve the *margai* traditions.

Hadjeray means literally "of the stones" (i.e., of the mountains) in Arabic and refers to the Hadjeray clans' domiciles. There are four major (agrarian) groups included, the most western ones being ethnically linked to the Daju (q.v.) and the eastern to the Kinga (q.v.). The Hadjeray have never been united in the past, nor have they any common origin, arriving in their present location around four centuries ago and settling in the rocky mountains in search of refuge from slave-raiding parties in the region. Essentially cultivators of the rocky ground, the only shared trait of the various groups is the belief in the *margai* spirits, which still exists in many villages off the beaten path. Other groups usually associated with the Hadjeray are the Dionkor, Dangaléat, Bidio, and Yalna. In the more-or-less reliable 1964 sample census it was estimated that there were 87,000 Hadjeray, and their number is currently assumed to be around 160,000.

Drawn into Chad's civil conflict in the 1960s, the Hadjeray rallied in particular behind Hissène Habré (q.v.) in his drive on N'Djamena in 1982. Indeed, together with the Daza Toubou (qq.v.) (called Gorane by the Arabs), the Hadjeray were the ones who brought Habré to power. They were, however, progressively driven into revolt by the purge and liquidation of some of their key members in government, beginning with Foreign Minister Idriss Miskine's (q.v.) 1983 "death from malaria" (actually poisoning), and culminating with the massive purge (and "disappearance") of many leaders of that group in 1987. By 1985 the Hadjeray east was again in a state of revolt, organized behind Maldoum Bada Abbas's (q.v.) MOSANAT (q.v.). Habré's ouster in December 1990 by Idriss Déby (q.v.), who entered N'Djamena together with Abbas, brought the Hadjeray back into the ruling coalition (Déby is a Zaghawa, and also from the east). But Déby's falling-out with Abbas (eventually rehabilitated) and Abbas Yacoub Kotti (q.v.) (killed) triggered a revolt that was only partly quelled in 1994.

HADJERO, ADOUM SENOUSSI see SENOUSSI, HADJERO ADOUM

HAGGAR, ABDERAHMAN (1916–). Sultan of the Zaghawa (q.v.), former president of the Conseil Supérieur de la Transition (CST) (q.v.), and the virtual overlord of Ennedi. Haggar served in Goukouni's (q.v.) GUNT (q.v.) government as secretary of state for agriculture and animal husbandry. Once the Zaghawa Déby (q.v.) regime rose to power Haggar set up his own personalist power formation and as a member of the CST was elected its secretary-general in 1993. He was forced to resign, however, together with the entire CST Bureau, in July 1995, when indicted for corruption.

HAGGAR, ADOUM ABOU (1931–1974). FROLINAT (q.v.) leader who replaced Abdel Hadj Issaka (q.v.) as commander of the First Liberation Army (q.v.) in the central-east district of Chad in 1971. A former student at Cairo's Al-Azhar University, Haggar was regarded as much more revolutionary and dedicated than Issaka, which is why he displaced his predecessor. The closure of the Sudan-Chad border on several occasions and Sudan's attempts to patrol the border greatly hampered Haggar's channels of communications with the outside world, though alternate ones were developed. The First Army launched its first attacks under his command in Guéra early in 1972. He was loyal to Dr. Abba Siddick (q.v.), though the long distances between Guéra and Libya made him practically autonomous in his operations. Haggar was executed in 1974 in Tripoli, Libya, following internal schisms in FROLINAT and was succeeded as field commander by Idriss Mahamat Amane (q.v.).

HAGGAR, AHMAT ABDERAHMAN. Foreign minister of Chad since May 1994. Haggar comes from the most powerful Zaghawa (q.v.) family in Chad.

HAIMARI, MAROUN (1933–). Diplomat and businessman. Born in Beirut, Lebanon, on September 27, 1933, and educated in political science, Haimari was a successful local merchant who was appointed honorary consul of Chad to Lebanon in 1964. In 1968 he applied for citizenship; he was naturalized as a Chadian and was then appointed ambassador of Chad to Lebanon. He was subsequently accredited to Jordan (1969) and to the Maghreb states (1973). His personal and diplomatic residence remained in Beirut.

HAITIANS. Significant attention was focused on the "Haitian connection" during the Tombalbaye (q.v.) era. Both Tombalbaye's son and nephew were dispatched to study in Port-au-Prince, Haiti, and a number of Haitians were brought over to staff senior posts in the Chadian civil service. These included the secretary-general of INTSH (q.v.) in 1974 and 1975, as well as Tombalbaye's personal advisor, Dr. André Vixamar (q.v.), who together with others gave support to the regime's authenticity drives, especially the renewed emphasis on the Yondo (q.v.) secret initiation rites. Haiti's original slave population traces its ancestry to Africa, of course, but to Benin specifically, and not to Chad; indeed, the sole Haitian embassy on the entire African continent was in Benin (then called Dahomey).

HAJJ (also HADJ). A duty required of all Muslims who have the means or possibility to make the pilgrimage to Mecca, the center of Islam. In 1970 official Saudi Arabian figures noted that 4,271 pilgrims had come from Chad in that year, the eighth highest number from Africa, after Nigeria (24,185), Egypt (13,547), Sudan (8,537), Morocco (6,935), Algeria (6,376), Tunisia (4,608), and Libya (4,570). The total from Africa was 90,109, though the actual number was undoubtedly higher. Many of the pilgrims originating in Chad make their way, in stages that sometimes last years, overland; Chad in fact, had been the traditional overland route for pilgrims from other parts of West Africa. In subsequent years the economic ravages of the Sahel drought and the highly unsettled conditions in eastern Chad (leading to Sudan, the final gateway to Mecca) kept numbers more or less at the same levels. Pilgrims who have concluded the Hajj are entitled to add the prefix al-Hajj to their name, though not everyone who uses the prefix has necessarily done the pilgrimage. (See also PILGRIMS.)

HALLATA, HAMED. Hissène Habré's (q.v.) last head of the DDS (q.v.) secret police, implicated in thousands of political killings.

HAMDALLAH, DJIBRINE ASSALI. Briefly one of the vice presidents of Hissène Habré's (q.v.) newly elected national assembly. Hamdallah served from July to December 1990, when Habré was ousted.

HAMIDI, MOUMINE TOGOI. Hamidi was appointed minister of information immediately after the fall of N'Djamena to Hissène Habré (q.v.)

in June 1982, but he was replaced by Mahamat Soumaila (q.v.) a few months later. He continued serving on the National Consultative Committee, and later served for another period as minister of information.

HANYAR RABIH. Hausa name for a southern pilgrim route to the Red Sea ports (see PILGRIMS) that passed through Dar Kouti (q.v.) and other territories conquered by Rabah (q.v.) in the 1890s. One of the few major centers of settlement on this route was N'Délé.

HARAZE-MANGUEIGNE. Souspréfecture with administrative headquarters in the village (population 1,700) of the same name, part of the Salamat Préfecture. Very sparsely populated, the souspréfecture encompasses 24,000 square kilometers (9,266 square miles) and has a population of 13,000.

HAROUN, ABOUBATKAYE. Since February 1991 representative and spokesman of Habré (q.v.) in Paris.

HAROUN, DANIEL (alias DANIEL DOUT). Chief in the central Guéra Préfecture and former leader of a group of rebels that rallied to the Tombalbaye (q.v.) government on November 15, 1970. Haroun had been the deputy of Hassane Karoubé, the commander of several guerrilla units until killed in August 1970. Defeated in his bid to succeed Karoubé as force commander, Haroun and his immediate followers rallied to the government. The event was given wide publicity by the government in an effort to portray the rebellion as ending.

HASSAN BAGUERI (1918–). Former key cabinet minister and vice president of the National Assembly. Born in 1918 in Oum-Hadjer, a retired sergeant of the French colonial forces, Hassan Bagueri entered politics in the mid-1950s. In March, 1957 he was first elected to the Territorial Assembly as PPT (q.v.) deputy and served as secretary of the assembly's Bureau in 1958 and 1959. In June 1959 he was appointed secretary of state for interior, serving successively after that as minister of civil service (April 1960–June 1960), minister of social affairs (June–August 1960), and minister of animal husbandry (August 1960–March 1962). In March 1962 he was dropped from the cabinet and regained his assembly seat, serving as fourth vice president of the assembly in 1966. In that year he was again briefly brought into the cabinet to replace the arrested Abderahim Djalal (q.v.), but he was himself arrested in June 1968 for plotting against the regime and for allegedly maintaining contact with FROLINAT. He was amnestied in 1971, and he entered private business.

HASSAN EL-GHARBI see HASSAUNA

HASSANE, ABDERAHMANE. Former FROLINAT (q.v.) leader based in the Central African Republic. Hassane, who controlled a small group of rebels operating along the border of Ouadai, rallied to the government early in 1971, a fact that was much exploited by the central government. He was disowned by Dr. Abba Siddick (q.v.) on the grounds that he was but a minor leader motivated by ethnic and personal considerations.

HASSANE GOGO, MAHAMAT (1933–). Former N'Djamena politician, born in Fort-Lamy in 1933. Hassane Gogo was AST (q.v.) deputy to the Territorial Assembly from June 1958 to March 1962 and represented Chari-Baguirmi. In June 1959 he was brought into Gabriel Lisette's (q.v.) cabinet as secretary of state in charge of economics, serving in the successive provisional governments as secretary of state for interior and (from September 1960 to March 1962) as secretary of state for information. Purged from the government in 1963, he then continued serving as a senior administrator in N'Djamena's court system.

HASSAUNA. Small group of seminomadic Arab clans claiming descent from Hassan el-Gharbi and coming into Chad from the north during the fourteenth to the nineteenth centuries. Among the Hassauna are the Ouled Mansur, Ouled Abu Isse, and Beni Wail clans that are found mostly in Kanem. In 1954 they were estimated at about 20,000 of the total 371,000 Arabs in Chad; the official 1964 ethnic breakdown put them at 26,000 of 460,000 Arabs; and in the latest estimate they numbered 46,000. (See also ARABS.)

HAUSA. A Muslim people numbering over 30 million and found mostly in northern Nigeria and southern Niger and in smaller concentrations throughout western and equatorial Africa. They speak the Hausa language that belongs to the Chad group of the Hamito-Semitic (Afro-Asiatic) language group, which is heavily infused with Arabic words consequent to heavy Arab influence and their conversion to Islam. Many terms also come from the Kanuri language as a result of their former close contact with, and domination by, the Bornu kingdom. In Chad the largest Hausa concentration is in N'Djamena, and there are also significant numbers in Abéché. (It has been estimated that fully one-third of Chad's Hausa are found in N'Djamena.) Usually traders in the major towns and villages of the area, many Hausa consider themselves temporary residents in their localities on their pilgrimage to Mecca. This was especially true during the colonial era (see PILGRIMS). Established in the past as large trading minorities in such localities as Massenya, Yao, and the Kotoko towns in the southwest, during the past 40 years they have gravitated strongly toward N'Djamena, where they have established several large ethnic quarters with their own chiefs. Their Abéché *zariba* (q.v.) is of particular historical importance.

HAUTE COUR DE JUSTICE. In the absence of a supreme court (abolished after the 1975 coup d'état), and replacing the 1976-inaugurated Cour de Securité de l'Etat that was itself abolished when N'Djamena fell to Goukouni (q.v.), the Haute Cour was set up by Hissène Habré (q.v.) in 1985. It was originally not a permanent court but one convened whenever the need arose, specifically to sit in cases involving major instances of corruption or of treason against the state. In 1990 its status was confirmed in Habré's new constitution, but shortly later it too was disbanded when N'Djamena fell to Idriss Déby's (q.v.) forces. The court was composed of members of the National Assembly.

HEL-BONGO, ADOUM (MAURICE) (1930–). Former cabinet minister and director of the International Labor Office (ILO) in Dakar, Senegal, and currently president of Chad's interim national assembly and presidential hopeful. Born on May 30, 1930, in Sarh, Hel-Bongo was educated locally and in France, where he studied at ENFOM and at the Political Science Institute in Paris, graduating with a law degree. At independence, as one of Chad's few highly educated individuals, Hel-Bongo served with the French government as counselor on administrative affairs, and upon his return home was immediately appointed (at the age of 30) to the key position of director of the civil service. Shortly thereafter he was promoted to the post of director of the cabinet of the minister of civil service; later he became director of economic affairs, and in January 1964 he became minister of agriculture. Elected in the meantime to the PPT (q.v.) Political Bureau, Hel-Bongo was transferred in November 1964 to head the Ministry of Public Health and Social Affairs, and in November 1966 he left Chad to become regional director of the ILO in Dakar, following which he was promoted to ILO's executive in Switzerland. He returned to Chad after more than 20 years abroad (something that may be used against his current presidential bid, a candidacy already announced) when he retired from ILO. With the liberalization of the political scene with the rise of the Idriss Déby (q.v.) regime, he set up his own political formation. When Chad's Conférence Nationale (q.v.) convened in 1993, Hel-Bongo was one of five candidates for the presidency of the conference, which he surprisingly won (with 409 of 780 votes) with heavy trade union support, against four other candidates, including a more radical candidate put forward by the Forum d'Opposition Démocratique (q.v.). Hel-Bongo continues to sit on the interim legislature, and he is considered one of the main contenders in the presidential elections—if they take place, and if Déby allows them to be held fairly. In July 1995 he formally announced that he would run for the presidency whenever the elections took place.

HISSA LULI ALI HUME. Successor to Wodei Kichidemi (q.v.), the derde (q.v.) of the Toubou (q.v.) in Tibesti. Wodei Kichidemi announced his choice in August 1975 shortly after his return from self-exile in Libya. In the process he disinherited his last surviving son, Goukouni (q.v.), who at the time was coleader (with Hissène Habré [q.v.]) of the Second Liberation Army (q.v.) in Tibesti.

HOHO see MUSSEY

HOUNO, MOUSSA BECHAR (General) (1953–1995). Idriss Déby's (q.v.) second chief of staff, replacing in September 1992 (with the rank of lieutenant colonel) the overly brutal Mahamat Ali Abdallah (q.v.) who had been implicated in several massacres of civilians, including the one in Doba in the south. Houno died in a car accident in Paris on July 4, 1995.

-I-

IBN OUMAR, ACHEIKH see ACHEIKH IBN OUMAR.

IBRAHIM, MOUSSA. Longtime imam of N'Djamena and spiritual leader of the capital's Muslim community during the 1960s and 1970s.

IBRAHIMI, MOUSTAFA ADOUM. Minister of women's and social affairs from December 1994 to July 1995.

ID EL-FITR. Muslim festival of breaking the fast at the end of Ramadan, celebrated throughout Chad in Muslim communities.

IDABAYE, IMBAI (JACQUES MORBAYE). Administrator and former key cabinet minister. Known previously under his pre-Tchaditude (q.v.) name of Jacques Morbayé, Idabaye was an administrator in the Ministry of Interior until promoted in August 1971 to director of the ministry and deputy director of the Sûreté Nationale. He served in these posts until October 1973, at which time he was transferred to head the Ministry of Defense. He was dismissed from that post with the coup of 1975 and returned to administrative duties, in the southern préfectures, until his retirement.

IDRIS ALOMA (c. 1574–1619). Possibly the best-known Sefuwa (q.v.) *mai* (q.v.) of the Kanem-Bornu Empire (q.v.), having utilized the services of an imam, Ahmed Ibn Furtua, as chronicler of his reign. Idris Aloma ascended to the throne when the kingdom was hard pressed from all directions. A dynastic factional struggle was going on, the economy was still suffering from a long drought, and the kingdom was being raided by Hausa, Bulala, and Tuareg (qq.v.) groups. Idris Aloma consolidated his rule by importing modern guns, hiring Turkish mercenaries, and building up his cavalry into a major force. One of the empire's greatest kings, Idris Aloma also installed religious courts and mosques. During his reign the empire's territorial boundaries expanded into Kouar, Aïr, and Kanem.

IMAM. The Muslim leader of a praying congregation; the title is usually conferred on a regular cleric serving as the prayer leader.

INDIGENAT. Civil status established in 1924 and in existence until the reforms of 1946, restricting the civil rights of the indigenous populations that had not attained the status of *évolué* or *assimilé* (q.v.). The restrictions included the obligation to perform *corvée* (q.v.) labor (including porterage) and legal jurisdiction under customary law and traditional authority with a French administrator presiding. The *indigénat* code was a major source of friction in francophone Africa during the colonial era. (See also ASSIMILATION POLICY.)

INFOTCHAD. Official daily news bulletin in Chad issued by the Agence Tchadienne de Presse (ATP). Mimeographed, with a circulation of between 700 and 2,000 copies in French, it was for long the only source of news in Chad apart from foreign newspapers and the radio. The ATP provides news bulletins to the radio as well. With the fall of N'Djamena to the north, a new newssheet in Arabic and French replaced *Infotchad,* but *Infotchad* was subsequently revived. In the late 1980s, and especially after Habré's (q.v.) ouster on December 2, 1990, a number of other private news publications appeared, the best known being the weekly *N'Djaména-Hebdo,* but most have fared poorly with the regime that has intermittently had them closed down, beating up reporters and editors and destroying presses and press-runs.

INSTITUT D'ENSEIGNEMENT ZOOTECHNIQUE ET VETERI-NAIRE D'AFRIQUE CENTRALE (IEZVAC). Veterinary school established in N'Djamena in 1964 by FESAC (q.v.) to train agents of animal husbandry and veterinarian engineers for the governments of the former colonies of the AEF (q.v.) federation. Students having completed secondary education undergo three years of studies, following which they are certified as superintendents of animal husbandry. They can then opt for two more years of study, leading to the title of engineer of animal husbandry. The numbers enrolled have remained more or less stable over the years, with some 35 percent of them from Chad.

INSTITUT NATIONAL DES SCIENCES DE L'EDUCATION (INSE). Organ created on August 18, 1975, to replace the former Institut Pédagogique National (IPN) and to prepare the personnel infrastructure necessary to promote social sciences and education in Chad.

INSTITUT NATIONAL DES SCIENCES HUMAINES (INSH). Important N'Djamena research institute founded in 1961 by Jean Lebeuf (q.v.) who remained its director until 1975. Until 1970 called the Institut National Tchadien pour les Sciences Humaines (INTSH), it had a staff of over 60, nearly all of whom were engaged in research in archaeology and ethnology. The institute had a library of some 3,000 volumes, was the depository of the Chadian archives, and housed a collection of artifacts from all over Chad, which in 1963 became part of the new Musée National (q.v.). INSH has published a number of valuable monographs, including a most complete and up-to-date bibliography of Chad. It has convened two major international conferences in N'Djamena and has immensely promoted the knowledge of Chadian and Central African prehistory in the wider community of scholars. INSH had to close down in 1979, and its staff—like most residents of the capital—fled into Cameroon during the internecine Battle for N'Djamena (q.v.). Like most of the capital, much of INSH's assets and buildings were either looted or destroyed in the fighting. In the mid-1980s INSH was revived and recommenced its activities, though on a more modest scale.

INSTITUT NATIONAL TCHADIEN POUR LES SCIENCES HUMAINES (INTSH). Pre-1970 name for INSH (q.v.).

IRAQ. Iraq has been among the various external powers to have been involved in intra-Chadian affairs. Being anti-Libyan, the regime in Baghdad gave Hissène Habré valuable financial and technical support, especially during his campaign to oust Libya from B.E.T. in 1986 and 1987. In particular, Iraqi funding and advice were tendered for the Chadian attack on the vast Libyan base of Maaten-es-Sarra (q.v.), which Iraq had actually built as an anti-Egyptian training base after the Camp David accords between Egypt and Israel.

IRIBA. Sparsely populated souspréfecture in Biltine covering 20,000 square kilometers (7,722 square miles) and with a population of 39,000, the souspréfecture's headquarters is in the village with the same name (population 3,600), which is the residence of the sultan of the Zaghawa (q.v.).

ISLAM. Though Muslim influences were prevalent in Central Africa from the tenth century and Islam was adopted as the state religion by all the former kingdoms in the region (Kanem-Bornu, Baguirmi, Ouadai), the faith did not sink truly deep roots among the wider population of the Sahel zone until the nineteenth century. The religion—though (until recently) relatively accommodating in Chad, except in Ouadai, and deeply permeated with pre-Islamic practices—made only slow and minor gains in the southern half of the country, largely because there it was associated with the slave-raiding activities of the kingdoms of the north. Moreover, the absence in the south of large and cohesive political units also impeded the growth of Islam. For all these reasons the southern half of the country is to this day a strong bastion of various animist beliefs or of Christianity.

During the colonial era several specific Islamic orders proselytized in Chad (see RELIGIOUS ORDERS), with the French colonial authorities in general supporting the local sects in opposition to those originating or based outside the country, usually in Libya or Sudan. The French in particular tried, with considerable success, to prevent the spread of the Sanusiya (q.v.) order, which had so strenuously resisted the French colonial expansion at the turn of the century. Islam became progressively politicized during the immediate pre-independence era (when Muslim parties emerged), the Tombalbaye (q.v.) presidency, and during the lengthy civil strife in the country. Though most of the academic attention to the rise of FROLINAT (q.v.) and its struggles against N'Djamena has been on its political and military manifestations in opposition to N'Djamena, the movement always had, at least among its eastern groups (the First Liberation Army [q.v.]), strong Muslim overtones. Indeed, the failure of the FLT (q.v.) and FROLINAT to merge in the mid-1960s was in part because of this.

The rise of fundamentalist Islam in other parts of the world eventually spilled over into Chad. This occurred especially in the late 1980s and after Sudan, specifically, joined the fundamentalist Muslim camp, as many of the armed groups seeking refuge in Darfur, and aid from Khartoum, fell under the sway of fundamentalist ideas to which they had already been susceptible. With their rallying (though not all have) in the 1990s to the regime of Idriss Déby (q.v.), who himself is from the "east" and came to power with armies recruited in Sudan, the call for the implementation of more Muslim (and fundamentalist) policies, and the elimination of the French language altogether (currently Arabic and French are official languages) has been heard for the first time in N'Djamena. Indeed, several of the political parties that sprang up in N'Djamena after the liberalization of party life have as central planks just that. Moreover, a religious-cum-liberation rebellion sprang up in the mid-1990s in Ouadai (historically the most xenophobic and fundamentalist regions of the country) calling for the creation of an Islamic state, and leaflets were openly circulated in Abéché warning all southerners (i.e., Sara teachers and civil servants) to leave for the south "or else." At the 1993 Conférence Nationale (q.v.) there were surprisingly strong pressures to hold and publish all proceedings in Arabic as well as to impose mandatory Islamic education in the entire country. These manifestations have created new sources of division between the north and the south.

Nevertheless, the Tidjaniya (q.v.) order, which is moderate, is by far the most popular and influential one in Chad. In the 1960s and 1970s it was estimated that between 40 and 50 percent of Chad's population was Muslim (with the northern two-thirds of the state solidly so), but more recent estimates suggest that the figure is likely to be more like 50–55 percent. (See also RELIGION; RELIGIOUS ORDERS.)

ISLAMIC LEGION. Largely mercenary and force-drafted Libyan force, recruited in order to avoid unpopular mobilizations at home, and used to supplement Libya's standing army in its more unpalatable tasks, mostly abroad. The Islamic Legion was first seen in a parade in Benghazi in September 1979 when it was a force of some 5,000–7,000 "strangers" caught in swoops on urban areas and given the choice of prison or paid military service. The Legion, which includes a considerable number of Sudanese as well as Druze from Lebanon, Palestinians, and Yemenites, has participated extensively in all of Libya's incursions into Chad, including in 1980 in N'Djamena, in the 1982–1983 conquest and retention of B.E.T., and again in 1988 to 1990 in Darfur, Sudan, where it assisted (and, according to some reports, actually provided ancillary military support to) Idriss Déby's (q.v.) insurgency against Hissène Habré (q.v.). At that time the Legion's strength in Darfur (wholly out of the control of Khartoum) was estimated at some 5,000, with 1,000 Libyan personnel, including officers.

Because the Legion is poorly trained, has very low morale, and is largely composed of criminals, illegal immigrants, and unemployed elements caught in Libya, it is hardly a viable fighting force, and though commanded by East German–trained Libyan career officers, it has fled more often than fought. Several thousand troops of the Legion, including senior professional Libyan officers, were captured by the Chadian army when Habré attacked and conquered most of B.E.T. from the Libyans in 1986 and 1987. They were kept in N'Djamena, and many were used by the CIA against Qaddafi's regime, despite strenuous and constant remonstrations by Tripoli, until Déby's rise to power. At that time, among Déby's first edicts, repaying Libya for its support while he was in the Darfur wilderness, were to release all Libyans to whatever destination they chose and to oust the CIA.

ISRAEL. Israel's contacts with Chad started very early, and indeed, Gabriel Lisette (q.v.) was on an official visit in Israel when he was ousted from power in 1960. During the subsequent Tombalbaye (q.v.) era Israel's role was small but important. The Technical Cooperation Pact of October 7, 1964, between the two states included assistance in national civic formation (via the creation and training of the Mouvement de la Jeunesse Tchadienne); the erection of model or pilot farms (specifically at Koundoul, near N'Djamena); health and educational aid; surveys and exploitation of natural resources; a loan (of US$400,000) for the Sarh refrigerated slaughterhouse; training of Chadian paratroopers at the Israeli-staffed Paratroopers' School in Zaire; training in N'Djamena of the Compagnies Tchadiennes de Sécurité (q.v.), and aid for Chad's government printer. In 1972 relations between Chad and Israel were ruptured by President Tombalbaye after he received Libya's assurance that in return for such an action Libya's assistance to FROLINAT (q.v.) would be terminated. (See LIBYA.) Israeli diplomatic and technical assistance missions in Chad were promptly evacuated. Subsequently Chad received some fiscal help from several Arab states, as promised, but hardly all that had been expected, and Libya's support for FROLINAT actually increased.

The fall of N'Djamena to northern elements (first Goukouni, then Habré [qq.v.]) increased the anti-Israel stance of the government, which became even more pronounced under Habré. Israeli contacts with southern opposition groups were discreetly maintained, however, during the entire GUNT (q.v.) era. By the mid-1980s, however, the Habré government shifted its stand vis-à-vis Israel, though this was not fully or formally acknowledged. (Indeed, in 1990 Chad angered Israel when Habré hosted Palestinian Yasser Arafat in N'Djamena and strongly courted Iraq, which had previously provided Habré with important aid against Libya.) Unlike the varied contacts of the 1960s and 1970s, however, Chad-Israel links in the 1980s were mostly military and, despite various rumors, not primarily of the state-to-state variety. Most of the officers of Habré's Presidential Security Unit were trained at the Israeli-staffed paratrooper college in Zaire, and a significant number of Israeli military trainers, advisers, and mercenary officers played a role in the actual fighting with Déby's armies along the Darfur boundary. Several Israeli officers (including one very senior one) were kiiled in Chadian attacks deep in Sudanese territory in 1989, and later, in the main battle between Habré's and Déby's forces, at least four more Israeli officers lost their lives. Notwithstanding this and the religious radicalization visible in N'Djamena in the 1990s, Chad-Israel relations have been diplomatically normalized.

ISSA, ABDALLAH MOHAMAD. Secretary-general of a segment of FROLINAT-Originel (q.v.) that refused to follow Dr. Abba Siddick's (q.v.) reconciliation with Hissène Habré (q.v.).

ISSA, AHMED. Former secretary of state for sports. Chad's former popular 800-meter runner in Mexico City's Olympic Games (1968), and a N'Djamena physical education instructor, Issa was imprisoned for several years by the Tombalbaye (q.v.) regime in 1972 for loose criticism of the N'Djamena elite. After the 1975 coup Issa was released and appointed secretary of state for education, culture, youth, and sports, serving for three years.

ISSA ALLATCHIMI, ALLATCHI YOUSSOUFMI (1922–). Former secretary of state, and son of Allatchi Aramimi, chief of the Gaida subgroup. Born in 1922 in Fada in the northern Ennedi souspréfecture, a former *chef de canton* of Gaida-Arami and mayor of Abéché, Issa Allatchimi first entered the Territorial Assembly in May 1957 as an independent (though allied to the UDIT [q.v.] party) and was reelected, as UDIT deputy, in March 1958. He remained deputy through December 1963. In 1957 he was the nominee of Jean Baptiste (q.v.) for one of the Chad seats on the Organisation Commune des Régions Sahariennes (OCRS) (q.v.), but his candidacy was blocked by Gabriel Lisette (q.v.). From September 1960 through March 1962 Issa Allatchimi was also President Tombalbaye's (q.v.) secretary of state for interior, following which he was attached to the presidency. In March 1963 he was arrested in the major purge of northern political figures opposing the imposition of a one-party system in Chad. Amnestied several years later, Issa Allatchimi has not occupied any important government position since. He was lucky to have escaped alive from Tombalbaye's prisons, since many of his compatriots died while in detention.

ISSAKA, ABDEL HADJ (1921–1972). FROLINAT (q.v.) Arab leader who took command of the rebel forces after the death of Ibrahim Abatcha (q.v.) in 1968. A trader from Batha (where he had been a chief and the *chef de canton* of Harazé-Djombo-Assinet), Issaka joined FROLINAT after being purged from the administration by the Tombalbaye (q.v.) regime. In exile in the C.A.R. and later in Sudan, Issaka organized a group of guerrillas from among the Chadian refugee community. Possessing no formal schooling, Issaka received guerrilla training in North Korea and until May 1970 led the field forces of FROLINAT in the Salamat region (the First Liberation Army [q.v.]). He was subsequently deserted by his followers because of his favoritism (in arms and allocations of funds) toward Arabs from Oum-Hadjer and due to allegations of fiscal improprieties. A supporter of "General" Mohamed Baghalani (q.v.) against Abba Siddick (q.v.), Issaka was murdered in January 1972 in Batha at the height of a bout of fratricidal strife in the First Liberation Army (q.v.).

ISSAKA, YOSKO. One of Hissène Habré's (q.v.) many chiefs of staff of the armed forces. A Daza (q.v.) Toubou (q.v.) like Habré, Issaka had previously been one of Goukouni's (q.v.) military commanders, until he switched sides. Issaka took command of the armies in 1987, after Hassan Djamouss (q.v.) retired.

ITNO, IBRAHIM MAHAMAT (1950–1989). Former Habré minister of interior, specifically charged with national reconciliation. Idriss Déby's (q.v.) half-brother, and of Zaghawa (q.v.) ethnicity, Itno had been Hissène Habré's (q.v.) military commander of Abéché in 1983, having recaptured the town from Goukouni's (q.v.) GUNT (q.v.) troops after temporarily conceding the town. In October 1983 Itno was rewarded for his military success by being integrated into Habré's cabinet as secretary of state for government inspection. In July 1984 he was promoted to minister of interior. As Habré began alienating and subsequently purging and liquidating members of those ethnic groups that had sided with him against Goukouni (namely the Hadjeray and later the Zaghawa), Itno and other key Zaghawa leaders in N'Djamena no longer felt secure. In April 1989 Itno was one of several key leaders (including Hassan Djamouss and Idriss Déby) who tried to flee N'Djamena. Itno was promptly captured, however, and summarily executed. Déby succeeded in reaching the sanctuary of Sudan, where he raised a largely Zaghawa army and then defeated Habré, marching into N'Djamena on December 2, 1990.

-J-

JELLABA. Sudanese Nilotic traders, many from the Dongola area, found in eastern Chad (since at least the middle of the eighteenth century) and engaged in trade between Darfur (q.v.) and Ouadai and Baguirmi. Their name, in Arabic, refers to their mercantile occupation.

JEREMIE, TOIRA. Leader of the Rassemblement du Peuple Tchadien (RPT) political party.

JEUNESSE DU PARTI PROGRESSISTE TCHADIEN (JEPPT). Youth branch of the Parti Progressiste Tchadien (PPT) (q.v.). The JEPPT was founded in a Constituent Congress on July 29, 1968, in Fort-Lamy, at which time some of the first tenets of the "Cultural Revolution" (q.v.)

were also announced. The creation of the JEPPT was declared part of the reorganization (along "revolutionary" lines) of the PPT. The JEPPT's executive secretary was Ouchar Tourgoudi (q.v.). One of the functions of the movement was to "fight foreign ideologies and influences."

JIMEMI, MAHAMAT (1910?–). Head of the Anakaza (q.v.) of Borkou, born around 1910. Jimemi's father had been executed by the French after deserting to the Sanusiya (q.v.) order at the time of the conquest of B.E.T. Jimemi is an intelligent, aggressive, and authoritarian leader.

JONKUR. Ethnic group found in the vicinity of Mongo and near Aboudeia, all in eastern Chad, between Melfi and Mongo. According to some they are a subgroup of the Banda, found in the C.A.R. The Jonkur (the name means "pagans"), claim to be the original inhabitants of the area before the arrival of the Kinga (q.v.). In 1980 they were estimated at around 40,000.

JOUR DE LA LIBERATION, D'UNITE, ET DES MARTYRS. State holiday commemorating the fall of N'Djamena to Hissène Habré (q.v.)—June 7, 1981. The holiday was totally ignored in the Sara south, and it was abrogated after the rise of Idriss Déby (q.v.) in 1990.

-K-

KABA. One of the larger of the many subgroups of the Sara. Not to be confused with the Sara-Kaba. Found on both sides of the international border between Chad and the C.A.R., in the immediate vicinity of Sarh, in the Moyen-Chari Préfecture. The terrain being totally without natural impediment, the Kaba were extensively raided by slave razzias from Baguirmi, Ouadai, Dar Rounga, and other kingdoms to the north and southeast. Never politically organized into large units and regarded as among the "backward" Sara subgroups, the Kaba are sedentary, growing cotton as their prime cash crop and engaging in fishing during the rainy season. They are best known abroad for the grotesquely elongated lips of Kaba women, a practice initiated in order to avoid capture and enslavement. Their numbers are estimated to be around 36,000. Only some 10,000 live in Chad, the rest in the C.A.R. In recent years the Kaba have been deeply influenced by the Ngambayé (q.v.).

KADALA. Title of the chiefs of the Daza (q.v.) clans of the Toubou (q.v.) people, whose hierarchy is less cohesive than that of the Teda (q.v.) to their northwest. The Borkou Kadala were nominally tributary to the sultan of Ouadai, while those farther to the southwest, to the Arab Awlad Sulayman (q.v.) tribes.

KADAM, MOUSSA (VICTOR) (1949–). Former cabinet minister under Hissène Habré (q.v.). Of Hadjeray (q.v.) ethnicity, Kadam was born in 1949 in Tabo (Mongo), and educated at Baro and Sarh and then at the Center of Higher Studies in Brazzaville, Congo, where he was in pedagogical studies from 1969 to 1973. He then spent a few years as deputy headmaster at Lycée Adoum Dallah in Moundou (1973–74) and as headmaster in N'Djamena, including at the prestigious Lycée Félix Eboué (1974–1978). In 1978 he went to the University of Paris for a further year's study, from which he joined Hissène Habré's FAN (q.v.). Following Habré's victory in the civil war Kadam was appointed in 1983 permanent secretary at the Ministry of Foreign Affairs. The following year Habré brought Kadam into his cabinet as minister of public works, mines, and petroleum, and in 1986 the portfolio was amended to public works, housing, and town planning. In 1987 Kadam was purged from the cabinet and arrested as part of Habré's elimination of most Hadjeray in high office.

KADAMA. Tunjur (q.v.) capital of Ouadai (q.v.) while the latter was under their rule in the sixteenth and early seventeenth centuries. The ruins of the palace of the Tunjur sultans are still visible southwest of Wara (q.v.).

KADE. Name of the distinctive papyrus canoes of the Boudouma on Lake Chad. (For the Kotoko equivalent, see ZEMI.) Ordinarily between five and nine meters (18 and 30 feet) in length, the boats are used for fishing, passenger transport on the lake, and the hauling of natron (q.v.) to Nigeria. Of interest is the fact that Boudouma craftsmen were recruited in 1965 to reconstruct the Thor Heyerdahl Kon-Tiki papyrus vessel.

KADJIDI. Small ethnic group, formerly slaves of the earliest Kanembu (q.v.), among whom they are currently found dispersed in Kanem and around Lake Chad. Due to similarities of lifestyle, custom, and language, the Kadjidi are frequently mistaken for Kanembu, but they occupy the same social status as the Kamadja (q.v.) among the Toubou. They take their name from an ancestor called Barko N'Jidi, rarely intermarry with the Kanembu and never with the Buduma, and are herders of zebu cattle. They are also found among the Kanuri of Bornu in Nigeria.

KADMUL. Symbol of authority among the various northern groups in Chad, especially the Toubou (q.v.). Among the Tomaghera (q.v.) clans, the *kadmul* is a green turban.

KADO. Fulani term designating pagans. Used to refer to a number of small ethnic groups in Mayo-Kebbi residing in the region of Pala. The Kado, including the Djimé and Pévé subgroups, number about 50,000.

KAGBE, NGUETBAYE (Captain). Little-known gendarmerie officer who was promoted to head the force on April 3, 1975, after the arrest of the gendarmerie's top senior officers in connection with an aborted anti-Tombalbaye (q.v.) plot. When the successful coup d'état 10 days later toppled the regime, Major Kottiga Guérinan (q.v.) assumed command of the force, and Kagbé was relegated to a subservient post.

KAIGAMA. Nonhereditary title of the commander in chief of the army of the Kanem-Bornu Empire (q.v.), who was usually a trusted and able slave in the *mai's* (q.v.) service. The title was not used following the rise of the al-Kanemi (q.v.) dynasty early in the nineteenth century.

KALGOA. Agricultural farm site some 70 kilometers (43 miles) from N'Djamena that in 1974 and 1975 became the focal point of President Tombalbaye's (q.v.) "Sacred Union" project—part of Opération Agriculture (q.v.)—that included the transportation (at great cost) of N'Djamena's population for labor-intensive agricultural work in Kalgoa in an effort to boost Chad's cotton production.

KALTHOUMA GUEMBANG (Mrs.). National Assembly deputy and former head of the PPT's (q.v.) women's section. Elected to the assembly on December 22, 1963 (and later vice president of that organ), Kalthouma Guembang served on the Political Bureau of the PPT between 1967 and 1968. In June 1968 she was arrested for allegedly providing funds to the FROLINAT (q.v.) movement. Amnestied and partly rehabilitated, and promoted to head the PPT's women's section, Kalthouma Guembang was arrested again in June 1973 in connection with the Black Sheep plot (q.v.), along with General Félix Malloum (q.v.). Placed on trial for "political sorcery and witchcraft" and for subversive opposition to the Tombalbaye regime, the low sentences meted out by the court (seven years' imprisonment) prompted President Tombalbaye to request—on the eve of the 1975 coup d'état that toppled him—that a new trial be held, citing the "errors" of the jurors. Following the coup, Kalthouma Guembang and other political prisoners were released from prison.

KAMADJA. Collective name for the approximately 4,000 descendants of slaves captured by the Toubou (q.v.) in their raids in the south or on passing caravans in the B.E.T. The Kamadja usually tend the Toubou palm groves in the oases, and they rarely intermarry with their masters. Though still in quasi peonage, they are progressively being paid (in kind) for their services.

KAMOUGOUE, WADAL ABDELKADER (General) (1939–). Former vice president of Chad and de facto ruler of southern Chad until August 1982, and later vice president of Goukouni's (q.v.) Gouvernement de Salut Nationale (q.v.), based in Bardai and in rebellion against Hissène Habré (q.v.) in N'Djamena. Born in Batam, Gabon, on May 20, 1939, Kamougoué was educated in Chad and later at the Ecole Général Leclerc in Brazzaville. Following his training he was posted in 1957 to Bouar, Ivory Coast, and at Pointe-Noire, Congo/Brazzaville, where he stayed until 1960. From 1960 to 1963 he was an instructor at the Ecole d'Enfants de Troupe, following which he trained in France, emerging from Saint Cyr as a second lieutenant in 1964. Upon his return to Chad the same year he was posted to the gendarmerie and later promoted to the rank of captain. One of the leading architects of the 1975 coup d'état that toppled the Tombalbaye (q.v.) regime, Kamougoué spearheaded the armed assault upon troops loyal to the president. Just prior to the coup, he had been on the high command of the army's general staff in charge of military operations against the FROLINAT (q.v.) in the north. One of the strongest personalities in the Conseil Supérieur Militaire (CSM) (q.v.), Kamougoué was minister of foreign affairs during the Félix Malloum (q.v.) presidency (1975–78). In mid-1976 he was also named to the newly created Commission de Défense Nationale (CDN) (q.v.) and as head of the tactical bureau of the high command of the armed forces general staff.

Promoted to lieutenant colonel in January 1977, following the collapse of N'Djamena to northern troops, Kamougoué retreated to Moundou, where he soon established a de facto state within a state, governed by the Comité Permanent du Sud (CPS) (q.v.), which was beholden to him. He was named a member of the provisional State Council following the Kano I peace talks, with responsibilities over agriculture and in command of the Forces Armée Tchadiennes (FAT) (q.v.) (1979–82). But his dominant role in the Sara south and his continued control over the gendarmerie (all of whose members had retreated to the south) gained him the GUNT (q.v.) vice presidency, thus displacing the more senior General Djogo (q.v.). Kamougoué served in that capacity under Goukouni from 1979 to 1982, at which time

Goukouni was ousted by Hissène Habré (q.v.). Even though when the Goukouni-Habré fighting was in progress (both in 1980 and in 1982) Kamougoué committed FAT (q.v.) troops on the side of Goukouni, he never lost sight of his prime goal—protection of the autonomy of the south. (Among some of his projects was one to set up a Chad-C.A.R. Sara Republic of Logone together with Ange-Félix Patassé of the C.A.R. His reticence in committing his full strength behind Goukouni (in part out of a hope that both northerners would exhaust themselves, allowing a southern comeback) played a major role in allowing Habré to emerge victorious in 1982, from Kamougoué's and the south's point of view, the worst possible outcome.

Shortly thereafter, dissident FAT officers, citing Kamougoué's autocratic methods—and ambitious to grasp political rewards offered by Habré in N'Djamena—mounted assaults in the south that rapidly delivered the Sara heartland to Habré and ousted Kamougoué from his stronghold. The assault came in two waves. In June 1982 Kamougoué was attacked by Lt. Colonel Samuel Rodai's (q.v.) troops and forced into a bunker with only 150 of his personal forces. Half of his men were killed before loyalist reinforcements arrived. In the process, however, some 800 FAT troops went over to the dissidents (under Rodai) and captured Bongor the following month. In August, because of Kamougoué's unwillingness to amnesty those officers who had earlier conspired against him, a second assault on Kamougoué was launched. Major Zamtato (q.v.) pushed out Kamougoué's forces from Doba and Sarh and with FAN (q.v.) assistance seized Moundou in a lightning strike. During this conflict, Ahmat Acyl's (q.v.) troops came to Kamougoué's aid, but to no avail. Kamougoué personally led the defense until the last moment, and then tried to make his escape in a light plane that crashed at takeoff. Suffering a leg injury, he was rescued and spirited into Cameroon by a Belgian priest. From there he made his way to Gabon and on to Bardai, to join Goukouni's Gouvernement de Salut National (GSN). His role was there reversed, as he was forced, militarily, to take second spot to General Djogo, but he assisted in the counteroffensive that brought Goukouni's forces back into Faya-Largeau and briefly into Abéché. It was in 1983 that he set up a political party, the Mouvement du Peuple Tchadien (MPT) (q.v.), as one of the formations in GUNT. (The party was taken over in the 1990s by Nadjita Beassomal [q.v.].) Regarded as a competent, professional, and pro-French officer, Kamougoué has also been viewed as autocratic (there have been allegations of financial improprieties during his governance of the south) and a prime opportunist. He was one of the last leaders to desert GUNT in 1986 to make his way to N'Djamena, having attempted to negotiate for a major position for a whole year. By that time he had become irrelevant, and in 1987 he was only named minister of agriculture. In 1988 he was reassigned as minister of justice, and in October 1990 minister of commerce and industry. With Idriss Déby's (q.v.) rise to power in December 1990, Kamougoué was kept out of the cabinet until the Conférence Nationale (q.v.) took place. Kamougoué participated in it as a leader of the URD (q.v.) party he helped to set up, and he was elected to the cabinet, as minister of the civil service. He was dropped from the cabinet in May 1994.

KANEM PREFECTURE. Immense sandy plain stretching from north of Lake Chad into the desert regions of Tibesti. Covering an area of 114,530 square kilometers (44,220 square miles), Kanem is transected by several large depressions separated by fixed dunes oriented in a northwest to southeast direction. Kanem's population of 250,000 belongs to the Kanembu, Daza Toubou (Gorane), and Tunjur ethnic groups, with sprinklings of other peoples. The préfecture has a low population density of 2.2 per square kilometer and is divided administratively into three souspréfectures (Mao, Moussoro, and Nord-Kanem) and three postes administratifs. The capital of the préfecture is in Mao (q.v.), which is some 325 kilometers (200 miles) from N'Djamena. The current political head of Kanem is Sultan Alifa Ai Zerzerti (q.v.), a large and imposing man with 11 wives and 45 children.

Mostly Muslim and semidesert, Kanem has had a long and tumultuous history as an area contested by all three kingdoms in the area, especially Bornu and Ouadai, falling briefly also under the control of both the Tunjur and the Awlad Sulayman. Until the devastating droughts of the late 1960s and early 1970s, the region had the largest herds of cattle in all of Chad. These have been greatly reduced since. The préfecture is little developed and has a low school attendance of 5.3 percent. However, oil was discovered in Kanem in the late 1970s though not in as large quantities as were discovered in the south near Doba. A small refinery is being built at Sédigui, with 43 percent of the funding from the World Bank (standing in for the totally bankrupt N'Djamena) and a Shell/Elf consortium, which is specifically aimed at meeting Chad's local needs. (See also KANEM-BORNU EMPIRE.)

KANEM-BORNU EMPIRE. The longest lasting and one of the most powerful and better known Sudanese states in Africa. Originally one of several small Zaghawa (q.v.) slave-trading principalities in the ninth century (at a time when the Zaghawa were more numerous as an ethnic group) in Kanem. First mentioned in A.D. 872 as the rulers of Kanem (q.v.), the Zaghawa kingdom began a serious expansion in the eleventh century and reached its height in the thirteenth century. Its first capital was Njimi (q.v.), 55 kilometers (34 miles) east of Mao (q.v.), founded in 1250. The Kanem kingdom was established with some Teda (q.v.) support as a loose association of clans under the leadership of the senior Sefuwa (q.v.) lineage of the Magumi (q.v.) clan, the head of which adopted the title of *mai* (q.v.). The twelfth *mai,* Hume (c. 1085–1097), was the first Muslim *mai,* though Islam did not make serious inroads into the kingdom until centuries later. Under the rule of Hume's son, Dunama (c. 1097–1150), the kingdom began to expand and came to control the north-south and east-west caravan routes (q.v.) connecting Hausaland, the Fezzan, and Darfur. (See maps on the extent of the Kanem-Bornu Empire over the centuries.) By 1242 pilgrimages to Mecca were a common occurrence for Kanemi devout Muslims, and a Cairo hostel existed to cater to their needs on their pilgrimage. Dunama himself made the hajj (q.v.) three times, and he drowned in the Red Sea on his last trip.

A major split among the federated clans in the middle of the thirteenth century (over unknown issues, possibly to do with sacrilegious acts by the *mais*) resulted in a sustained rebellion led by the Bulalas (q.v.). The revolt was ultimately successful, and the Sefuwa Magumi and their followers were driven out of Kanem to the west (around 1384–88) under *mai* Umar ibn Idris. There a long process of conquests of, and assimilation with, the numerous existing Sao (q.v.) clans resulted in the Kanuri ethnic mix and the consolidation of the powerful Bornu Empire, which was ruled by the Sefuwa dynasty until the beginning of the nineteenth century. The empire's capital (until 1811) was Birni Ngazargamo (q.v.), founded in 1484. Bornu reconquered Kanem from the Bulala early in the sixteenth century but allowed the region to remain in a quasi-tributary state. The frequent Bulala and other revolts in the region resulted in various Bornuan punitive expeditions. Bornu also exacted tribute from several Hausa states to the west, including Kano and Katsina, and conquered territory peopled by both Hausa and Fulani (qq.v.). Toward the end of the sixteenth century Islam began to strike deeper roots among the population, though it still tended to be the faith of the urban classes. Around this time firearms were introduced in greater quantities from Turkey, and camels were integrated into Bornuan military formations. During the seventeenth and eighteenth centuries Bornu's preeminence in the region slowly began to crumble, consequent to a series of major famines. Tuareg (q.v.) invasions and pressure from the Aïr (Niger) increased turbulence and unrest among the Fulani and led to the progressive loss of the Saharan caravan trails.

In the first half of the seventeenth century the Tunjur (q.v.)—recently expelled from Ouadai (q.v.)—arrived in Kanem, defeated the Bulala, and conquered the southern half of the province. A Bornuan military expedition was eventually sent to regain the region. Led by a

Hausa slave—Dala Afuno—the Tunjur were defeated and their sultan killed (1735). The Bornuan column established itself as a garrison force in Kanem; descendants of the force—called Dalatawa (q.v.), after the name of their leader—established in Mao (q.v.), continued to rule the province under a Khalif (later Alifa) who was the Bornuan viceroy in Kanem. Descendants of the dynasty are today the traditional rulers of the region.

At the beginning of the nineteenth century, growing Fulani strength began to tax Bornu's power. The kingdom's suzerainty over the Hausa states was challenged, and in the resurgence of Fulani power Bornu's capital, Birni Ngazargamo, was sacked around 1808. Under intense military pressure from all sides, the reigning *mai* appealed for help from Shaikh Muhammad al-Amin—better known as al-Kanemi (q.v.)—a scholar and warrior from Kanem. Recruiting a force of Shoa (Shuwa) (q.v.) Arabs, al-Kanemi succeeded in repulsing the Fulani threat to the autonomy of Bornu, though not without conceding the western provinces and being forced to relocate the capital to a less exposed position, Kukawa. In the process of helping the *mai* to ward off the Fulani threat, a de facto al-Kanemi dynasty was established in Bornu. The *mais* were kept on as puppet rulers, but al-Kanemi's son, Umar al-Kanemi (q.v.), removed the last *mai* from even nominal power and banned the centuries-old lineage. The much weakened and decayed kingdom collapsed in 1893 under Rabah's (q.v.) military assault—with the Shoa Arabs joining the Rabahist forces against Bornu—and just prior to Rabah's defeat at the hands of the invading French troops it appeared that a Rabahist dynasty (and empire) was in the process of being established on the ashes of that of al-Kanemi's Bornu. The Bornuan descendants from al-Kanemi still play an important traditional role today in northern Nigeria.

KANEM-BORNU, KINGS OF. As with most king lists, there is significant controversy as to names, dates, and even sequence of rulers.

Sefuwa Dynasty	Huwa
Sayif ibn Dhi Yazan	Selemma
Ibrahim	Humai (c. 1090)
Dugu	Dunama
Fune	Biri
Aritse	Bikur
Katuru	Selemma
Adyoma	Dunama Dibbalemi (c. 1250)
Bulu	Kadai
Arki	Kashim Biri

Dirko Kelem
Ibrahim Nikale (c. 1300)
Abdullah
Selemma
Kure Gana
Kure Kura
Muhammad
Idris (c. 1350)
Dawud
Uthman
Uthman
Bukar Liyatu
Idris Saradima Ladarem
Dunama
Umar Ibn Idris
Sa'id
Kadai Afuna
Biri
Uthman Kalinwama (c. 1425)
Dunama
Abdullah
Ibrahim
Kadai
Dunama (c. 1450)
Muhammad
Amar
Muhammad
Gaji
Uthman
Umar
Muhammad
Ali Gaji (c. 1500)
Idris Katagarmabe (d. c. 1526)
Muhammad

Ali
Dunama
Abdallah
Aisa Kili Ngirmaramma
Idris Aloma (d. c. 1619)
Muhammad
Ibrahim
Hajj Umar
Hajj Ali
Idris (c. 1700)
Dunama
Hajj Hamdun
Muhammad Irgama
Dunama Gana (c. 1750)
Ali
Ahmad Alimi (c. 1800)
Dunama
Muhammad Ngileruma
Dunama
Ibrahim (d. 1846)
Ali Minargoma (d. 1846)

Shehu Dynasty
al-Kanemi 1814–37
Umar 1837–53
Abdurrahman 1853–54
Umar 1854–81
Bukar 1881–84
Ibrahim 1884–85
Hashimi 1885–93
Kiyari 1893
Sanda Kura 1900–
Bukar Garbai 1901–22
Umar Sanda 1922–37
Sanda 1937–67

KANEMBU. From the Teda (q.v.) Anem-bu ("people of the south"), also known among the Hausa (especially in Niger) as Beriberi. Founders of the Kanem kingdom in the ninth century under the Sefuwa Magumi lineage, then still a Zaghawa (q.v.) admixture. The Kanembu are currently found in northeastern Nigeria, in Kaouar in Niger, and outside Kanem in Chad, in regions such as Massenya and N'Djamena. Most of the Kanembu in Kanem are found between Lake Chad and the 14th parallel, intermixed with the Haddad (q.v.), Tunjur (q.v.), and Awlad Sulayman (q.v.). Divided into a large number of subgroups, their most important clan is the Magumi (q.v.). Many of the latter migrated to what is now Nigeria after the fall of Kanem to the Bulala, and after intermarriage with the Sao (q.v.) they became the Kanuri. Other important subgroups include the Dalatawa (q.v.) and the Kogono, found around Mao (q.v.). (See also KANEM-BORNU EMPIRE; KANURI.) Related to the Toubou, Bulala, and Kotoko (qq.v.), the Kanembu, despite anthropological differences, are regarded by many scholars as the sedentary segment of the Toubou. There are no exact figures of their numbers, especially since certain of their branches have been Arabized and others thoroughly assimilated into related groups, as in N'Djamena and Massenya, where strong Kanembu-Kanuri assimilation is visible. Elsewhere the seminomadic Kanembu tend to be confused or lumped together with the Teda (q.v.) or the Daza (q.v.). One 1954 estimate placed their numbers in Kanem at 60,000 of the préfecture's total population (then) of 215,000. Current uncertain estimates would place their numbers some 50 percent higher. Their language is very close to Dazaga (see DAZA) and is written in a modified Arabic script. Most Kanembu belong to the Tidjaniya (q.v.) order, though some are affiliated with the Sanusiya (q.v.) and/or Quadriya (q.v.) orders. Few regard either N'Djamena or Mao (capital of the Kanem Préfecture) as their ethnic capital, looking rather toward Maiduguri in Nigeria.

KANO MEETINGS. Site in northern Nigeria where on March 16, 1979, the first meeting was held among protagonists in Chad's civil war following the fall of N'Djamena to Goukouni's (q.v.) armies. Held actually at a hotel in Baganda (10 kilometers from Kano), the meeting included only the key combatants and was aimed at determining, on neutral ground, the future shape of Chad. After five days of negotiation an agreement was reached for a cease-fire, release of prisoners, disbanding of private armies, demilitarization of the north, and formation of the interim government (GUNT, q.v.) as a prelude to national elections. Because the meeting included only Goukouni, Habré, Malloum, and Abderahmane (qq.v.) (Nigeria's protégé)—plus observers from several neighboring countries—the excluded rebel leaders (including Abba Siddick, Mahamat Abba Seid, Adoum Dana, and Ahmat Acyl [qq.v.]) began organizing a countergroup. To avoid factionalism and possible renewed strife, a second conference, called Kano II, was convened on April 3, 1979, at which Nigeria applied pressure on Goukouni and Habré (to the point of not allowing them to leave the conference) until all factions were given a role to play in the new interim government. Two further peace conferences (see LAGOS CONFERENCES) were needed before an acceptable GUNT array of power was reached.

KANURI. Descendants of the Magumi (q.v.) clan of the Kanembu (q.v.) and Zaghawa (q.v.) intermixed with Sao (q.v.) Kotoko (q.v.) elements. Found mostly between the Hausa areas and Lake Chad in northeastern Nigeria, the Kanuri were the dominant ethnic group of the Bornu (q.v.) Empire. In contemporary Chad, where they are called Bornuans, the Kanuri are sedentary agriculturalists or traders. Many of them supported the political campaigns of Ahmed Koulamallah (q.v.) in the 1950s. (See also KANEM-BORNU EMPIRE.)

KARAMANLI DYNASTY. A Tripoli (Libya) dynasty that maintained excellent relations with Bornu (q.v.) in the eighteenth and early nineteenth centuries, securing the safety of the north-south caravan routes (q.v.). The Karamanlis were toppled by a combination of internal schisms and the dispatch to Tripoli of an Ottoman governor and army (see TURKEY). The collapse of the dynasty (which coincided with the eclipse of the Bornu Empire) disrupted long-distance trade via the now unsafe Fezzan-Bornu trail (q.v.), shifting it eastward to the Ouadai route.

KASSIR, JEAN-NICHOLAS (1940–). Educator and former secretary of state. Born in Ati on January 15, 1940, and trained as an agricultural works engineer, Kassir worked as an instructor, and later director, of the Agricultural School of Ba-Illi (1962–71). From 1969 to 1971 he was also director of education and vocational (agricultural) training at the Ministry of Agriculture. He was appointed secretary of state for stockbreeding, waters, and forests in May 1971 and remained in that post until October 1973 when he returned to administrative-educational duties.

KASSIRE, NOURADINE KOUMAKOYE DELWA. Former prime minister under Idriss Déby (q.v.). Born in Tandjilé in the south, and with a power base in Mayo-Kebbi, Kassiré first entered politics when appointed to Hissène Habré's (q.v.) cabinet in August 1987 as minister of public works and housing. Later that year he was transferred to head the Ministry of Justice, and in September 1990 he was moved to the Ministry of Higher Education and Scientific Research. After Habré's ouster Kassiré set up on May 26, 1992, a political party, the Rassemblement National Démocratique Populaire (RNDP) (q.v.). The RNDP was actually an alliance of 16 small parties formed in opposition to the then pro-MPS (q.v.) government of Prime Minister Yodoyman (q.v.), calling for an early establishment of a wall-to-wall government. In January 1993 he was one of five candidates for the chairmanship of the Conférence Nationale (q.v.), but, being Idriss

Déby's choice, he was defeated in the vote that took place, with Adoum Hel-Bongo (q.v.) emerging in that post. Kassiré then served as prime minister in 1993 and 1994 but was defeated in favor of Djimasta (q.v.) when he proved incapable of rapidly scheduling national elections. In July 1995 Kassiré declared his presidential candidacy whenever they are ultimately held.

KATIALA (also KADIALA). Traditional title, among the Kanembu of Chad, of a dignitary in the court of the sultan of Mao, often the flag-bearer.

KEBZABO, SALEH (1947–). Publisher, journalist, and politician. Born in Léré on March 27, 1947, Kebzabo studied journalism in France and joined the Agence Tchadienne de Presse (ATP) in August 1971. He rapidly moved up to the post of chief editor and in 1975 became director of the ATP. With the fall of N'Djamena in 1980, Kebzabo moved to Bongor, where he continued his career. In 1990 he relocated to N'Djamena and set up the only independent newspaper, *N'Djaména-Hebdo*. On December 30, 1992, he also set up a new political party, the Union Nationale pour le Développement et le Renouveau (UNDR) (q.v.), and in 1993 he was a member of the Conférence Nationale (q.v.), and then briefly (1993–94) minister of trade. His newspaper has regularly been harassed by Chad's secret service, and his reporters and he himself have been sued for libel for alleging that Idriss Déby's (q.v.) Garde Républicaine (q.v.) was acting as a virtual occupation force in the south. Declaring himself a presidential candidate for whenever elections are held (they have been postponed by a year three times already), Kebzabo's newspaper office and home were again ransacked by Déby's forces in both August and September 1995. In the latter instance, he was also arrested on the grounds of illegal contacts with opposition elements abroad, a trumped-up charge. Though released on bail pending trial, his arrest triggered an already exasperated CPP (q.v.) alliance of parties in the interim legislature to threaten nonparticipation in any further political activities unless the head of the Agence National de Securité (q.v.), Déby's secret police, was dismissed.

KECHERDA. Small ethnic group found in the Moussoro region of Kanem. Of mixed origin, they have become integrated with the Daza (q.v.), whose language they speak.

KEDEI. The uniquely built Yedina (q.v.)-Buduma (q.v.) papyrus pirogues on Lake Chad. Called *tei-tei* in Arabic.

KEIRO, THOMAS (1933–). Former cabinet minister and diplomat. Born on May 12, 1933, in Bassao and for some time a technical agent with Chad's Health Service, Keiro was elected on the PPT (q.v.) party label to the National Assembly in March 1957, serving there through 1963. From June 1959 to August 1960 he was minister of production and rural cooperation and later, from August 1960 to March 1962, minister of public works and communications. From March to August 1961 he also served as foreign minister. Keiro was transferred again in March 1962, serving as minister of social affairs and of labor through January 1964. He was then dropped from the cabinet and appointed ambassador to the Central African Republic (and to Cameroon, Gabon, and Congo/Brazzaville, effective from different dates in 1965), serving in these capacities through 1972.

KEKE, ALI (1936–). Former minister of labor. Born in Bongor in August 1936, of Musey origins, and educated locally, Kéké was admitted to the Physical Education Center of Brazzaville and later studied in France. Upon his return to Chad he worked as a physical education instructor at the Collège Moderne de Bongor (1959–1962) while becoming an active PPT (q.v.) militant. In 1961 he was elected to Bongor's municipal council, and a year later he was elected to the National Assembly, becoming also a member of the PPT Political Bureau. In January 1964 he was brought into François Tombalbaye's (q.v.) cabinet as minister of labor, youth, and sports (and briefly served also as interim minister of health and social affairs). He was dropped from the cabinet in May 1971 in order to provide room for the recently amnestied top political prisoners. Since then he has performed administrative and technical duties in Bongor and in the Ministry of Youth.

KELO. Small but densely populated and important souspréfecture with administrative headquarters in the town of the same name, part of the Tandjilé Préfecture. Covering a territory of 4,500 square kilometers (1,740 square miles), with a population of 127,000, it has a relatively high population density. The town itself has 30,000 people and is Chad's fifth largest. Two decades ago it had only 4,000 people.

KEMTO, DOUNGOU (Colonel). Leader of a small opposition party, the Mouvement Patriotique National (MPN) (q.v.). A former director of the Sûreté Nationale (q.v.) and an FAT (q.v.) administrative officer, Kemto joined in the exodus to the south after the fall of N'Djamena to Goukouni (q.v.) in 1979. He set up the MPN in Moundou in June 1981. The party opposed current separatist sentiments in the south and was opposed to Colonel Kamougoué's (q.v.) leadership. It included a number of intellectuals and military officers, as well as southern FROLINAT (q.v.) sympathizers, uneasy over the increased Libyan role in Chad. Kemto personally supported the cleavage within FAT that led to the delivery of the southern préfectures to Hissène Habré (q.v.) in 1982.

KEMTO, FATIME (Mrs.). Minister of social and women's affairs since July 1984. A southerner, previously secretary of state for women's advancement, Mrs. Kemto was also appointed in June 1984 as second deputy commissioner for social and women's affairs in Hissène Habré's (q.v.) new party's (UNIR) (q.v.) executive bureau.

KERA. Ethnic group of some 25,000 people similar to the Toubouri (q.v.) in all respects except linguistically. They are found east and south of Lake Tikun.

KETTE, MOISE NODJI (Lt. Colonel). Minister of tourism since May 1994. Ketté was originally a DDS (q.v.) southerner with the rank of lieutenant, attached to Hissène Habré's (q.v.) embassy in France. After Idriss Déby's (q.v.) rise to power Ketté raised the banner of rebellion, together with troops who deserted with him, following the assassination in N'Djamena of Joseph Behidi (q.v.), the civil rights leader. He called his opposition movement the Comité de Sursaut National pour la Paix et la Démocratie (CSNPD). He operated out of bases in the Central African Republic, allegedly with as many as 5,000 troops. Some of his attacks against the regime triggered the atrocities of the Garde Républicaine (q.v.), including the slaughter of 150 civilians in Doba. In 1994 Ketté promoted himself to captain and began negotiations with Déby in Bangui, Central African Republic, which were ultimately fruitful in 1994. After the reconciliation Ketté was promoted to lieutenant colonel, 1,500 of his troops joined him in N'Djamena to be reintegrated into the Chadian army, and he himself joined Déby's cabinet. Part of the deal was that the Garde Républicaine was to be withdrawn from the south. The CNSPD was transformed into a legal political party.

KHALI, HISSENE ALI. Secretary of state for foreign affairs in the Habré-Malloum (qq.v.) government, and cause of the falling-out of the two leaders. Dispatched on a mission to Libya by Prime Minister Habré, Khali was not allowed to board his plane, at Malloum's orders. Malloum's action—a result of suspicion that Habré was in reality plotting with FROLINAT (q.v.) for a takeover of the capital—triggered the bout of fighting in N'Djamena that opened the door to Goukouni's (q.v.) advances.

KHATIR, HASSAN FADOUL. Cabinet minister in Idriss Déby's (q.v.) government. A Zaghawa (q.v.) who fought alongside Déby in 1989 and 1990, Khatir was first appointed secretary of state for youth and sports and later promoted to minister of planning in March 1991. In 1992 he was transferred to head the presidential office. While in a military hospital in Paris in March 1992 he was dropped from all government posts, having been accused of racketeering, but bounced back into the cabinet later that year as minister of youth. In April 1993 he was transferred to head the Ministry of Tourism, and in January 1994 he briefly served as minister of mines and energy.

KHATIR, MAHAMAT SENOUSSI. Idriss Déby's (q.v.) former head of the notorious ANS (q.v.) secret police, Khatir, a Zaghawa (q.v.), had been Acheikh Ibn Oumar's (q.v.) prime lieutenant in the CDR (q.v.), though when the organization split in 1984 he formed the anti-Libyan Comité d'Action et de Concertation du Comité d'Action Révolutionnaire (q.v.). In 1986 Khatir rallied to Hissène Habré's (q.v.) regime and was brought into the cabinet, first as minister of state and then as minister of public health. He was purged, together with other Zaghawa elements, in 1989, an event that was to spur the Zaghawa revolt and rise of the Déby regime. Khatir was reintegrated into the cabinet in September 1990 as minister of mines and energy. With Habré's ouster in 1990 and Déby (q.v.) replacing him, Khatir moved back into the limelight, though on January 1, 1995, he was arrested for the embezzlement of funds from a Cameroonian businessman visiting N'Djamena.

KHERALLAH, DJIBRINE ALI (1926–). Important former opposition member and cabinet minister. Born in Ati in 1926 and educated locally for a few years at a Koranic and elementary school, Kherallah was a clerk in the colonial administration before entering political life in 1946. In that year he was elected deputy from Batha to the Conseil Représentatif, running on the conservative UDT (q.v.) ticket. He was subsequently reelected in 1952 (UDT), in 1957 (AST, q.v.), in 1959 (GIRT, q.v.), and in 1962 as PPT (q.v.) deputy. During the 1940s and 1950s he continued working as a clerk in the administration of Ati and Doba. In the late 1950s Kherallah became one of the more influential leaders opposing the PPT alliance of Gabriel Lisette (q.v.) and François Tombalbaye (q.v.). In 1959 he became president of the GIRT formation, though his position in it was consistently challenged by other politicians. He first entered the cabinet in May 1957 when he was appointed Lisette's minister of finance; from December 1958 to February 1959 he served as minister of interior, and he continued in that capacity during the short tenure of the Sahoulba (q.v.) government. (See PROVISIONAL GOVERNMENTS.) Squeezed out of the cabinet during the equally brief Koulamallah government, Kherallah reemerged as minister of interior with the rise of Tombalbaye, serving in that capacity from March to June 1959 before being transferred to head the Ministry of Finance (June 1959 to January 1960). He later headed the Ministry of Justice (August to December 1960) and then returned briefly to the Ministry of Finance (December 1960 to April 1961). Between 1959 and 1961 he was also president of the assembly's Permanent Committee and president of the Chadian Union Douanière Equatoriale (UDE) (q.v.).

In February 1960 Kherallah helped to fuse all the anti-PPT parties into the PNA (q.v.), of which he was elected vice president. When the PNA—which had united all the conservative and Muslim parties in the country—was merged with the PPT (see POLITICAL PARTIES), Kherallah was brought into the cabinet as minister of foreign affairs (August 1961). He remained in that post until the massive Fort-Lamy riots of 1963 (q.v.), occasioned by a police raid on his home, where all the ex-PNA leadership had gathered. (The PNA had been formally dissolved by the Tombalbaye regime.) Arrested and imprisoned together with most of the country's Muslim and/or northern leadership, Kherallah was not amnestied until June 18, 1969. Largely out of public life for some two years, Kherallah was brought into the PPT in April 1971, integrated into the party's Political Bureau, and a month later appointed minister of finance. In December 1971 he was transferred to President Tombalbaye's office as minister of state; in October 1973 he was made minister of state in charge of the civil service, where he remained until the coup d'état of 1975. An intelligent, able, and modest politician, Kherallah has always had a very sizable Muslim following in N'Djamena.

KICHIDEMI, WODEI see WODEI KICHIDEMI

KIM. Confederation of four riverine city-states along the Logone River between Bongor and Laï. The confederation included Kim (the most important), peopled by the Kossopé; Djouman, inhabited by the Guerép on the right side of the river; Eré on the left side of the Logone, peopled by the Garap; and Kolobo, peopled by the Kolop on the right side of the river. There are also Kim found in N'Djamena, Bongor, and all along the river, comprising a total of 15,000 people. Originally from the east, they are linguistically linked to the Niellim. Admirably fortified, the Kim city-states have had alliances with the

Baguirmi kingdom (q.v.) to raid the Musey and Marba for slaves. Deeply influenced by Protestant missionaries arriving from Nigeria in the 1940s and 1950s, the Kim are currently advancing very rapidly socioeconomically.

KINDER, AHMAT. President of the Labor Court in N'Djamena.

KINGA. Collective name for a number of ethnic groups (only one of which is the Kinga proper) in the hilly country near Mongo and Melfi in Hadjeray (q.v.) country. In the north (Mongo), they are mingled with an important Daju (q.v.) colony, while in the south (Melfi), they are intermixed with several Arab clans. Most claim pre-fifteenth-century eastern (Darfurian) origins, and legends recount the role of the non-Muslim Kinga clans in the founding of Massenya (q.v.) and the Baguirmi kingdom (q.v.). It was estimated in the mid-1960s that there were some 26,000 Kinga, and an additional 87,000 members of related ethnic groups usually (casually) lumped together with the Kinga, the largest of which are the Junkun (or Diongor), the Dungal, and the Bidio. The various groups speak different dialects, most of which are linked to the Barma (q.v.) language. The people are essentially agriculturalists, and they tap the acacia trees for gum arabic (q.v.). Though converted to Islam during the colonial era, many of the villages still hold to the *margai* (q.v.) cults. The Kinga are considered by some scholars as part of the Hadjeray group of clans.

KINSARA see NIGERIA-CHAD BORDER SKIRMISHES, 1983

KIRDI. Pejorative term for the pagan groups of southern Chad, which was the hunting ground for slave raiders from Ouadai, Baguirmi, and Kanem-Bornu. Essentially, though not exclusively, applied in the past to the Sara and other ethnic groups in the south.

KODIO, LAUDERIM (formerly **NDOROUM, GASTON**) (1944–). Chad entrepreneur and former managing director of the Société Tchadienne d'Investissement (STI) from September 27, 1972 to 1979. Born in Sarh in 1944 and educated locally and in Paris, Kodio served briefly as director of the Agence Tchadienne de Presse (1969) before becoming principal secretary of the UEAC (q.v.) secretariat (1967–72). In 1972 Kodio became director of STI. With the fall of N'Djamena, Kodio relocated abroad.

KODOR FOURI. Common sixteenth-century ancestor of a number of Teda clans in Tibesti, including the Tomaghera (q.v.), the Gounda (q.v.), and the Tarsoa.

KODOY. A branch of the Maba (q.v.) clans found in the hilly regions (*kodok*=mountain people) north of Abéché in Ouadai. The Kodoy figured in the rebellions against the Tunjur kingdom in Ouadai (see OUADAI KINGDOM; TUNJUR) and, later, their assaults on Wara (q.v.) led to the relocation of Ouadai's capital to Abéché in 1850. Following the French occupation of Ouadai and the early heavy-handed administration of the region, unrest swept the Kodoy areas again. (See also MABA.)

KOKOI, ADOUM (Colonel). Key gendarmerie officer based in N'Djamena. Of mixed Kamadja-Daza origin.

KOLAK. Title of the kings of Ouadai. The *kolak* was an absolute monarch whose name could not be uttered by the population. Upon his acceding to the throne, all the *kolak*'s relatives were blinded so that they would not be able to participate in any power gambit against him. The *kolak* held a monopoly over all gold produced or imported into the kingdom, and he controlled long-distance trade. It was the *kolak* who granted charters for slave raids into the south, and he also sent razzias there for his own account. (See also OUADAI KINGDOM.)

KOLINGAR, ASSANE (1935–). Administrator. Born in Libreville, Gabon, on January 18, 1935, a graduate of France's Institut des Hautes Etudes d'Outre-Mer (IHEOM), Kolingar was appointed first secretary at Chad's embassy in France (1963) before returning home in 1965 to become administrative secretary-general of the government. He held that position until October 1973. Since then he has held several high-level administrative posts—some of which he had held previously also—including vice president of the Société Cotonnière Industrielle du Cameroun (CICAM), president of the Société Textile du Tchad (STT) and of SONACOT (q.v.), and most recently director general of Cotontchad (q.v.).

KONOMBAYE DJIMET, BERNARD (1935–). Educator and deputy. Born in Fort-Archambault in 1935 and educated locally and in Bongor, Konombaye Djimet entered the educational system as school director in Yao (Batha), staying in that post from 1956 to 1961 before moving to Mao. In 1962 he was appointed to the prestigious Collège Ahmed-Mangué in Fort-Archambault while also serving as deputy director of the Center of Pedagogical Documentation. Involved in youth activities throughout, he was one of the guiding spirits behind the creation of the PPT (q.v.) youth movement, the JEPPT (q.v.), of which he became first secretary of the Steering Committee. Later he became executive national commissioner of the movement. In 1969 Konombaye Djimet was elected deputy to the National Assembly and remained in that body until the 1975 coup d'état. He has since remained in instruction and in the administration of Chad's educational system.

KORANIC SCHOOLS. Islamic primary schools widely found throughout Chad's eastern and northern préfectures, including in the smaller villages. The highly informal schools offer a religious education, teach reading and writing of the Arabic script, and provide a rudimentary amount of secular education. Headed usually by a *faki,* the Koranic schools have, until fairly recently, competed effectively vis-à-vis the "Western" schools set up by both the colonial and the independent Chadian administrations.

KORO TORO. Village at the edge of the Bahr-el-Ghazal (q.v.), south of Djourab in the souspréfecture of Ennedi in B.E.T. In its vicinity are found remnants of a metallurgical civilization and traces of ancient Haddad (q.v.) villages.

KOSSEDA. One of the Teda (q.v.) clans in Tibesti, inhabiting the area near Zouar. The Kosseda are considered among the longest established clans in Tibesti, having come there from Zeila. They are also referred to as Yobat, meaning drawers of rainwater.

KOSSO, ALI (1922–). Former cabinet minister and senator to the French Community. Born in 1922 in N'Tiona, where he first worked as a farmer, Kosso rapidly became an important political figure and served as PPT (q.v.) deputy from Kanem to the National Assembly (1957–63). During these years he also served as Chad's delegate to the AEF (q.v.) Grand Council (October 1958 to April 1959), following which he went to Paris as senator to the French Community (through January 1961). An increasingly prominent figure in the PPT, Kosso was his party's deputy treasurer (1961–62) and entered the government as secretary of state for finance and the national plan (August 1960 to March 1962), following which he became full cabinet minister in charge of justice (March 1962 to March 1963). Shortly after this Kosso was purged in the major 1963 swoop against real and imagined opponents of President Tombalbaye (q.v.). Accused of opposing the creation of a one-party system in Chad, Kosso was imprisoned for a while and partly rehabilitated in the mid-1960s when he was appointed to the Conseil Economique et Social (q.v.), serving on it as vice president from 1967 to 1969. He was fully rehabilitated after the 1971 Fort-Archambault PPT Congress and was brought into the PPT Political Bureau and carried over into the Executive Committee of the MNRCS (q.v.), which replaced the PPT. He remained in this position and in secondary administrative positions until the 1975 coup d'état. He was one of the few members of the Tombalbaye regime to be briefly imprisoned after the fall of the regime.

KOTINGAR, GAYO (1939–). Educator, and director of INTSH (q.v.). Born in Doba on March 18, 1939, educated locally and abroad, Kotingar holds a doctorate in African history. After joining the University of Chad as a professor, he was appointed director of INTSH in October 1972. Early in 1973 he was integrated into the MNRCS (q.v.) party and in January 1974 was appointed secretary-general of the Ministry of Education. In 1975, after the coup, Kotingar was appointed rector of the University of N'Djamena.

KOTOKO. Ethnic group found along the lower course of the Logone River, the Chari River and delta, and on the other side of the international border in Cameroon. The Kotoko are also called Moria by the Kanuri, Mamka (or Mamaka) by the Massa, and Bala by the Barma. They are divided into a number of geographically localized clans, all of which trace their origins from the legendary Sao (q.v.) and are ethnically linked to the Yedina (q.v.) of the Lake Chad region. In the mid-1980s their numbers were estimated at around 60,000, most of whom are to be found in Cameroon near Goulfeil (q.v.) and Logone-Birni (q.v.). Converted to Islam by the influence of the Bornu (q.v.) Empire, the Kotoko suffered heavily from the wars among their various neighbors, during which they were continuously under military pressure. Ouadai in particular ravaged and destroyed most of their cities along the Chari River, and in the last years of the nineteenth century Rabah (q.v.) plundered their country for slaves. There is no common Kotoko language spoken by all the clans but rather a number of dialects, several of which are markedly different from the others. The people are mostly expert fishermen (some of their canoes are up to 10 meters [35 feet] in length), with agriculture constituting until recently only a very secondary form of economic activity. They catch huge quantities of fish by a variety of ingenious methods and sell most of the catch (in dried or smoked form) in neighboring markets. A few of the chiefly families possess cattle (tended by Arab nomads) and also exact a traditional tax on all cattle that cross "their" rivers from Chad into Cameroon (the Kotoko sultan of Logone-Birni, for example). The Kotoko were never organized into a single kingdom but rather in a series of walled city-principalities more or less independent of one another and owing nominal allegiance to Bornu. The most important of these were Goulfeil in the north, Logone-Birni in the south, and Kousseri in the center. Prior to the First World War, the Franco-German boundary in the region artificially split up some of these political entities, upset the traditional power hierarchy, and elevated Arab chiefs (previously their vassals) to positions of prominence. Most of the Kotoko are currently Muslim, though they still venerate a variety of water or riverine deities and practice pre-Islamic rites. Considering themselves the original owners of the land, they exact a variety of tributes for the right of cultivation, pasture, and crossing of their territories. (See also SAO.)

KOTOKO, AHMED (1918–1988). Former veteran Mayo-Kebbi politician, president of the National Assembly, and deputy to the French National Assembly. Kotoko was known to his friends as Hamai, and his real name was actually Ahmed Alifa, being of a lineage that came to Chad from Tombouctou (or Timbuktu, Mali) en route to Mecca in the nineteenth century. Born on October 18, 1918, in Goulfeil (in the extreme north of Cameroon) and a devout Muslim, Kotoko studied in France for a pharmaceutical career, though he only qualified as a male nurse. Between 1942 and 1946 he worked as a clerk and in transport, and once political liberalization reached Chad his leadership over the Kotoko (q.v.) ethnic group catapulted him into political prominence. In 1946 he was elected councillor of the French Union (q.v.)—as an independent—and in 1951 he was returned to Paris as delegate of the UDSR (q.v.) party to the French National Assembly. (An early cofounder of the PSIT [q.v.] party, Kotoko was involved in a harsh clash with Ahmed Koulamallah [q.v.], which resulted in his expulsion from the party and his establishing the UDSR.) In 1952 he aligned the UDSR with Gabriel Lisette's (q.v.) PPT (q.v.) to form the FACT (q.v.) alliance and was elected to Chad's Territorial Assembly. In 1957 he was reelected to the assembly as an Entente (q.v.) delegate, again part of the PPT coalition, and the same year he went to Brazzaville as Chad's councillor to the AEF (q.v.) Grand Council. From 1956 to 1961 he was also a member of N'Djamena's municipal council and the capital's deputy mayor. By 1959 a regular member of the PPT, Kotoko was again reelected to the Chadian National Assembly and served as PPT secretary of organization and as one of Lisette's principal lieutenants. The same year he was elected the assembly's president, a position he held until his purge in 1961. Kotoko joined the cabinet in March 1959, when he was appointed minister of education, and he became Tombalbaye's (q.v.) minister of finance in August 1960. In September 1961 he was crudely dropped from the cabinet as part of the major purge of Lisette's faction in the PPT. He was arrested and imprisoned in the northern Faya-Largeau, his citizenship was revoked (on the grounds that he was not actually a Chadian national), and he was deported to Cameroon. The same grounds were used to expel several other prominent politicians who were either of mixed parentage or had been born outside Chad.

After Kotoko was expelled from Chad, Cameroon put him to good use, first within its foreign ministry (1964–65) and then, from 1966 to 1972, as chargé d'affaires in Cameroon's first embassy in Saudi Arabia. He then served as Asian Affairs counselor in the foreign ministry (1973–77) and ambassador to Equatorial Guinea (1977–82). A major economic figure in Kousseri, his home, where he owned a hotel and several businesses, Kotoko died on October 7, 1988. His memoirs were published shortly thereafter.

KOTTI, ABBAS YACOUB (Colonel) (1950–1993). Idriss Déby's (q.v.) former chief of staff, and the regime's third most important personality. Kotti was a key Zaghawa (q.v.) military officer who greatly assisted Déby in recruiting Sudanese Zaghawa personnel for his army in Darfur (q.v.) during Déby's drive against Hissène Habré (q.v.). Kotti, previously Chad's military attaché in Khartoum, was a strong opponent of France and France's role in Chad, and he was a Muslim fundamentalist with links to Sudan's fundamentalists. He was also vice president of Déby's political party, the MPS (q.v.), and minister of defense before being demoted in March 1992 to head the Ministry of Public Works and Transport.

The cleavage between the two close allies began the moment Déby and Kotti marched into N'Djamena on December 2, 1990, as Kotti arrogated to himself, unilaterally, the second (old) presidential palace in the capital. Over the next few months he built up his private army in the capital to a force of over 1,000 (many nonnationals from Sudan), strutted around N'Djamena like a warlord, and grumbled about Déby's not giving him and his Zaghawa credit enough for defeating Habré. He thus not only became a destabilizing force in a context of reconciliation but also a personal threat to Déby. In the run-up to the 1993 Conférence Nationale (q.v.) Kotti tried to set up a political movement, the Comité National de Redressement (CNR), but Déby refused to recognize it, arguing that Kotti was the vice president of Déby's party, the MPS.

After progressively falling out with Déby, and continuing to recruit nonnationals (Sudanese) into the army at a time when global donor agents were calling for budgetary cuts, Kotti was dismissed in March 1992 as chief of staff and minister of defense and demoted to a lesser cabinet post. In June 1992 he fled the capital for the Lake Chad area with several hundred of his warriors, accused of plotting a coup d'état. He was arrested in Maroua, Cameroon, in December 1992, but succeeded in escaping from prison in March 1993. He was then lured back to N'Djamena in August 1993 with assurances of personal immunity (after his CNR was finally recognized as a party) but was assassinated on October 21, 1993, in N'Djamena's streets, allegedly when he resisted arrest by the security forces as he prepared a coup against Déby. With his assassination the alienation of the Zaghawa elements loyal to him was complete. Under the leadership of his brother, Hissein Kotti, a rebellion erupted in the east that spilled over into an attack on Abéché in January 1994. The rebellion smoldered until 1995.

KOTTI, HISSEIN. Brother of Abbas Yacoub Kotti (q.v.) and leader of the Zaghawa (q.v.) CNR (q.v.) rebellion in eastern Chad since 1993.

KOTTIGA, GUERINAN ANDRE ALPHONSE (Colonel). Former cabinet minister and head of the Chad commandos ("*codos*"). Little-known prior to the 1975 coup d'état, Kottiga—at the time deputy head of the gendarmerie under Colonel Djimé (q.v.)—was arrested on April 3, 1975, for a plot against the regime of President François Tombalbaye (q.v.). Severely tortured while under detention, he was flown to Paris after the coup for medical treatment and recovery. Upon his return to Chad he was given command of the gendarmerie (August 1975). A year later he passed the command back to Colonel Djimé and assumed the latter's cabinet position as minister of interior and security. In January 1977 Kottiga was promoted to the rank of lieutenant colonel, and the following year he became minister of foreign affairs. He served until 1979, when he left the government, and after Colonel Kamougoué's (q.v.) eclipse, Kottiga became head of all the *codos* in southern Chad, under their new title, Commandement des Groupements des Troupes Offensives (CGTO) (q.v.). The new "warlord of the south," like most major southern leaders he ultimately rallied to Habré in 1985, bringing over to the regime some 1,000 troops that were then integrated into the central Chadian armed forces. He was also appointed to Habré's cabinet as minister of public health and later of mines and energy, and in September 1990 as minister of posts. He and his units participated in the battles in eastern Chad in November 1990 against Idriss Déby, in which the latter emerged victorious. Kottiga was nevertheless integrated into Déby's first government (December 1990) as minister of tourism and the environment. His influence has been greatly eclipsed with the advent of political parties in 1992, but he was nevertheless used by Déby in the preparations for the Conférence Nationale of 1993 (q.v.).

KOUKA. A homogeneous ethnic group found mostly between Ati and Oum-Hadjer in the Batha Préfecture and numbering around 30,000. Some 10,000 more live on the eastern side of Lake Chad, among the Bulala. Mostly Muslim today, legends recount a Kouka role in the founding of the Baguirmi kingdom (q.v.).

KOULAMALLAH, ABDERAHMAN. One of Ahmed Koulamallah's (q.v.) sons, and founder of the resurrected Union Socialiste Tchadienne (UST) (q.v.) political party in Paris in 1986 (the original UST had been a coalition in the late 1950s).

KOULAMALLAH, AHMED (1912–1975). Chad's fiery and most prominent Muslim, pro-Arab opposition leader, founder of the Mouvement Socialiste Africain (MSA) (q.v.) and several other prior formations, and cofounder of the anti-PPT PNA (qq.v.) party. Also, very briefly, head of government during the period of the country's provisional governments (q.v.). Born in Massenya on February 11, 1912, and on his mother's side a member of the royal branch of the Baguirmi kingdom (q.v.), Koulamallah was by profession a merchant and a transporter of goods. Originally serving as Sultan Youssouf's personal aide and representative, Koulamallah's ambitions, radical views, and intrigues brought about his purge. With the advent of political life in Chad, he campaigned widely on an antichiefly plank. Popular and charismatic among the Chari-Baguirmi masses, part of Koulamallah's support there had always been because of his traditional credentials, his antichiefly vituperations notwithstanding. Yet his own impatience with his colleagues, his ambitions, and his proclivity for intrigues always prevented him from attaining his goals.

In the late 1940s Koulamallah served as the treasurer of the conservative chiefly UDT (q.v.) party with which he had thrown in his lot. He was forced out of the party in 1951 following accusations of embezzlement. Adopting a socialist credo, he cofounded the PSIT (q.v.) party together with Adoum Aganayé (q.v.) but failed in his bid that year to be elected to the French National Assembly. In 1952 he joined forces with the progressive FACT (q.v.), the PPT-led coalition, and was appointed president of the alliance. Shortly after that year's elections, in which he gained entry to the Chadian Territorial Assembly, he left FACT consequent to friction with both PSIT's Ahmed Kotoko (q.v.) and PPT's leader, Gabriel Lisette (q.v.). For some time he tried to organize grassroots support for his own personalist party among the masses of Chari-Baguirmi, and in the 1956 Fort-Lamy mayoralty elections he gained the second highest number of votes, becoming deputy mayor. Later that year a conflict between him and other PSIT leaders (including again Aganayé) led to his expulsion from the party, which then split into two bitter wings. Progressively isolated from all of Chad's political formations, and again defeated in his 1956 bid for a French National Assembly seat, Koulamallah formed the MSA party in 1957. The party was in essence a merger of elements from several formations he had led over the years, including the PSIT, PST, and PSK (q.v.), in different electoral contests. The strongly pro-Arab,

Nasserite, and pro-Sudan party won only one seat in the 1957 election and later was merged with other anti-PPT groups to form the Union Socialiste Tchadienne (UST) (q.v.). During the hectic months of Chad's provisional governments (q.v.), Koulamallah served as minister of state in Lisette's December 1958 government and as minister of tourism in the Gountchomé Sahoulba (q.v.) February 1959 government. In March 1959 Koulamallah engineered the fall of the Sahoulba government and headed—for 12 days—the next provisional formation. He himself was toppled by intrigues on the part of his old political (and religious) rival, Jean Baptiste (q.v.)—who had been the only major opposition figure Koulamallah had excluded from his own cabinet—and there Koulamallah's eclipse began. Never again included in any of the subsequent cabinets, Koulamallah and his MSA failed to gain any seats in the May 1959 elections. Though early in 1960 he was able to forge an anti-PPT alliance of all the remnants of the Muslim parties in Chad—the PNA (q.v.), in which paradoxically he shared power with Baptiste—he was to break with this formation as well, consequent to his unwillingness to accept the party's decision to try to cooperate with the PPT (then in power) or to serve in the PNA with Baptiste. In mid-1960 Koulamallah set up a new political movement, the UPT (q.v.), and tried to unite within it a variety of anti-PPT elements. When all opposition parties were banned in Chad in January 1962, Koulamallah defied the order and in September 1963 attended a high-level meeting of opposition leaders at the home of Djibrine Kherallah (q.v.) in Fort-Lamy. The meeting was broken up by the police, and most of those attending were arrested, provoking the bloody upheavals of Fort-Lamy that year. (See FORT-LAMY RIOTS.) Koulamallah, who had evaded the dragnet, was captured in Cameroon some time later and returned to Chad and imprisoned. He was not amnestied in 1969 (when most of Tombalbaye's [q.v.] enemies were rehabilitated), but only in mid-1971. A year later, after the guerrilla attack on N'Djamena's airport, Koulamallah was again arrested, allegedly for helping the raiders, and was kept under house arrest until his death in 1975.

KOUMAKOYE, DELWA KASSIRE see KASSIRE, NOURADINE KOUMAKOYE DELWA.

KOUMRA. Important Sara town, headquarters of the Koumra souspréfecture (125,000 people, 10,000 square kilometers [3,860 square miles]) in the Moyen-Chari. Near Koumra, which has a population of 13,000 and is Chad's ninth largest urban center, is the very important Yondo (q.v.) initiation center of Bédaya, which is also the hometown of former president François Tombalbaye (q.v.). During the colonial era the entire region was for some time attached to Oubangui-Chari, the contemporary Central African Republic.

KOURI. Small ethnic group whose members are devout Muslims, speak the Buduma-Kouri language, and are related to the Buduma (q.v.). They live along the banks of Lake Chad, but as in their locality there are no polders (q.v.) they are primarily farmers on small plots. Their oral legends refer to descent from immigrants from Yemen and co-lineage with the founders of the Kanem-Bornu Empire (q.v.).

KOUSSA, MARCEL (1920–). Merchant of Lebanese origins, educated in a Jesuit mission, Koussa joined his brother in a major trading enterprise in N'Djamena. In 1954 he branched off to supply the northern, and especially the Faya-Largeau, garrison, setting up a company—Société Commerciale de Borkou-Ennedi-Tibesti—which eventually became the major supplier of consumables in the north. During the rainy season, when B.E.T. is cut off from the south, his company used airplanes to supply the region. The civil strife in B.E.T. seriously impaired Koussa's operations, and in 1976 he terminated all activities in the north.

KOUSSERI. Known also as Fort-Foureau, Kousseri was the indigenous name of the site where Rabah's (q.v.) armies were finally defeated by a three-pronged French force on April 22, 1900. The French troops (one column coming from Algeria and led by Lamy, another from Niger, led by Voullet, and the third from the Congo under Gentil), converged on Lake Chad for the final battle that was to open up Chad to French influence, the Battle of Kousseri (q.v.), in which both Lamy and Rabah died. The Territoire Militaire des Pays et Protectorats du Tchad (q.v.) was founded during September 5–8, 1900, with its headquarters, opposite Kousseri on the right bank of the Chari River, named Fort-Lamy. Kousseri, currently in Cameroon, was the site of a very important Kotoko (q.v.) city in the precolonial era, with impressively high walls and fortifications. Its normal population of 11,000 swelled to 250,000 with the massive exodus from N'Djamena during the civil strife of 1978, and it still holds a significant, by now permanent, refugee population.

KREDA. Pejorative name the Arabs apply to the Toubou (q.v.) groups that nomadize the Chadian Bahr-el-Ghazal (q.v.).

KRIGA, MAHAMAT (1933–). Diplomat and former cabinet minister. Born in 1933 in Bongor and an educator and unionist in his earlier years, Kriga became deputy director of Chad's first diplomatic mission to France, and after the organization of the embassy in 1960, he remained as first secretary (1960–1962). Upon his return to Chad he was elected PPT (q.v.) deputy to the National Assembly (March 1962) and was immediately brought into the cabinet as minister of tourism and of information. His ministry was expanded to cover waters and forestry in 1963, and in 1964 he again assumed diplomatic duties when he was sent to Nigeria as Chad's ambassador. He remained in Lagos through 1968, when he was appointed ambassador to Sudan. In 1969 he returned to Chad to become secretary-general of the Foreign Ministry, and he remained in that position through 1976.

KUB KUB MASSACRE. Brutal November 1917 massacre by French troops of Abéché Senoussi (see SANUSIYA) leaders and marabouts (as well as two local chiefs and their entire households), who were (incorrectly) thought to be preparing a religious uprising against the French, following the imposition of direct French rule in Ouadai. The massacre (*kub*, from the French *coupe* as pronounced by the local population) of some 100 people was ordered by the nervous local commander, an alcoholic who had been transferred to the unattractive Ouadai posting for disciplinary reasons. The massacre came on the heels of severe French repression in the region and a series of severe droughts that reduced the Ouadai population by some 50 percent, bringing down the population of Abéché from 28,000 to less than 5,000. The Kub Kub massacre is still widely remembered in Abéché today.

KUFRA (also KOUFRA). Important desert oasis in Libya, some 1,000 kilometers (600 miles) from Faya-Largeau in B.E.T., and formerly an extremely important juncture and the main starting point on the caravan routes (q.v.) to the south. In 1895 Kufra became the political headquarters of the Sanusiya (q.v.) order. From there their influence radiated into Kanem, B.E.T., and even into Bornu. The Senoussi mounted fierce resistance to the expanding French effort in northern Chad. In 1927, after this resistance had died out, the oasis fell to Italian troops, and the Senoussi stranglehold over the Sahara regions abated.

KUKAWA (also KUKA). Post-1814 capital of the Bornu (q.v.) Empire. Founded by al-Kanemi (q.v.), who had been invited by the reigning *mai* (q.v.) to repel the Fulani (q.v.) invasions that had sacked the previous capital, Birni Ngazargamo (q.v.). Kukawa was located 130 kilometers (80 miles) northeast of contemporary Maiduguri (in Nigeria). The town was razed in turn by invading Ouadian troops in 1846 and destroyed by Rabah (q.v.) in 1893, when large segments of Bornu were annexed to Rabah's nascent and sprawling Central African dominions. With the onset of the colonial era, the traditional capital of the (al-Kanemi) Bornu emirate became Yerwa, where the current Shehu of Bornu resides.

KURI. Name of Lake Chad until roughly the sixteenth century, when, for the first time, the name "Chad," meaning "large body of water," is mentioned in the works of Ibn Fortu. Kuri was the name of the inhabitants of the western side of the lake, on the Karga archipelago. (See also YEDINA.)

KYABE. Souspréfecture in the Moyen-Chari Préfecture, Kyabé encompasses a population of 40,000 and a territory of 12,500 square kilometers (4,830 square miles). The administrative headquarters of the souspréfecture is in the village of the same name.

-L-

LAC PREFECTURE. Small (22,300 square kilometers [8,600 square miles]) préfecture carved out of Kanem after Chad's independence, covering the northern part of Lake Chad and its myriads of small islands and peninsulas. Lac has a population of 166,000 and a population density of 7.4 per square kilometer. The population is composed mostly of Buduma (q.v.), Kanembu (q.v.), and Kanuri (q.v.), only recently converted to Islam. The préfecture's capital is Bol (population 1,500); it contains two souspréfectures—Bol and Ngouri—and two *postes administratifs*. The region produces smoked fish, cattle, wheat, maize, and millet. (See also POLDERS.) The region was the refuge of Hissène Habré's forces when they fled N'Djamena in 1990 as well as that of the MDD (q.v.) of Moussa Medela (q.v.), whose operations against the government in N'Djamena have been mostly in the Lac region. For this reason the préfecture has been unsettled during much of the 1990s.

LAGOS CONFERENCES. Series of peace conferences, following the initial Kano meetings (q.v.).

Lagos I was attended by delegates from Chad's six neighboring states as well as from all movements excluded from Goukouni's GUNT (q.v.) government set up after the first Kano meeting. Taking place on May 27, 1979, the peace talks broadened the base of negotiations and forced the integration of Ahmat Acyl (q.v.), Abba Siddick (q.v.), and others into GUNT. Groups not participating at Lagos I included FAN (q.v.), MPLT (q.v.), and FAP (q.v.), all part of GUNT in N'Djamena.

Lagos II, the most all-inclusive peace conference, was held in two stages, on August 14 and August 19, 1979, and led to the creation of a new expanded GUNT government, with representatives from all 11 factions in the civil strife in Chad. The conference averted a threatened southern secession by promoting Colonel Kamougoué (q.v.), de facto strongman of the south, to the vice presidency of Chad. Goukouni assumed the presidency, shunting "Nigeria's" man in N'Djamena (Lol Mahamat Choua [q.v.], previously president), with Hissène Habré (q.v.) as minister of defense. Following a meeting at Dogouia that divided the lesser posts among all factions, the final GUNT cabinet emerged.

LAI. In the early days of the French occupation of Chad, also known as Fort Béhagle (when it was a major military outpost), Laï is the administrative headquarters of the Tandjilé Préfecture and of the Laï souspréfecture. The town of 8,000 is 405 kilometers (250 miles) south of N'Djamena and 125 kilometers (78 miles) northwest of Moundou north of the right bank of the juncture of two branches of the Logone River (q.v.). The souspréfecture of the same name covers 9,000 square kilometers (3,475 square miles) and has a population of 85,000 and a population density of 9.4 per square kilometer. Laï is on the main east-west Sarh-Pela and north-south N'Djamena-Bangui routes (see TANDJILE PREFECTURE) and in an area that produces cotton, fish, and rice. Largely isolated from the rest of the country during the August–November torrential rains, the region can also be reached (August to September) by barge up the Logone.

LAINA, LOUM HINASSOU (Colonel). Key Idriss Déby (q.v.) lieutenant. Laina joined the government in March 1991 as secretary of state for defense, while also chief of staff, though he was soon replaced by Abdallah Mahamat Ali (q.v.) on February 11, 1992. He kept his cabinet post right through the Conférence Nationale (q.v.) of 1993, until May 1994, when he was transferred to become minister of justice. He was finally dropped from the cabinet in March 1995, one of the longest-serving Déby ministers.

LAKA. Ngambayé subgroup. (See NGAMBAYE.)

LAKE CHAD. Large shallow freshwater lake on which converge the international boundaries of Chad, Niger, Nigeria, and Cameroon. The lake's major source of water is the Chari River (q.v.), which is augmented in N'Djamena by the Logone River (q.v.), both of which form a common delta on the lake. It has been estimated that some 90 percent of the water that flows into the lake evaporates promptly. The size of the lake varies tremendously, depending upon climatic conditions. In the past the lake encompassed from as much as 25,000 square kilometers (9,650 miles) to as little as 10,000 square kilometers (3,860 miles). (In 1955, and for several years previously, this has indeed been the size of the lake.) Major periods of expansion occurred from 1870 to 1892, 1934 to 1936, and especially from 1950 to 1964, during which times the Bahr-el-Ghazal (q.v.) flowed northward from the lake, a very rare occurrence. Contraction developed during the years 1936 to 1947, 1965 to 1973, and intermittently in the 1980s. In 1973 the lake was one-third of its normal size and at many points it was possible to cross on foot from Chad to either Niger or Nigeria; in the 1980s the lake port of N'Guigmi, in Niger, was in the middle of sand dunes 15 kilometers (10 miles) from any water.

As a consequence of the Sahel drought and poor rainfall throughout the region, some 90 percent of the lake's fish are believed to have perished during the contractions of the lake's surface and depth in the 1970s and 1980s. The salinity of the lake's waters did not increase appreciably until the 1980s, since the seepage of minerals to the northern and eastern desert areas of Kanem went unabated. In the 1980s, however, much salinization began to occur, sand barriers built up, and deforestation, overcultivation, and overpopulation along its shores by nomads-turned-sedentary-farmers changed the shoreline ecology, and amid alkalinization and wind erosion, Lake Chad was in 1986 declared a "disaster zone."

Along the lake's northern archipelago regions—during times of normal water levels—are numerous polders (q.v.), constructed mostly by Buduma (q.v.) villagers, aimed at trapping the very rich alluvial soil for the planting of wheat. During the major contraction of the lake's waters most of these polders have been high and dry, greatly undermining the livelihood of the amphibious populations of the islands and peninsulas of the lake. In prehistoric times Lake Chad was an immense inland sea, covering 300,000 to 400,000 square kilometers (116,000 to 155,000 square miles), probably connected with both the Nile and Benue River systems and with the Tibesti (q.v.) mountain ranges on its northern shores. Cave engravings and rock drawings in the B.E.T. support these hypotheses (see ARCHAEOLOGY).

LAKE FITRI. Small lake in the Batha Préfecture at the center of Bulala (q.v.) country. On its shores is found Yao (q.v.), the capital of the small Bulala sultanate. The lake (together with Lake Chad [q.v.]) is the remnant of the huge inland sea that covered the entire area in prehistoric times. The Batha River empties into Lake Fitri, though its course is often dry for long periods throughout the year. Vegetation is sparse in this region, though during the rainy season (June to September) huge marshes cover the area.

LAKOUE, ENOCH (1944–). Economist. Born in N'Djamena on November 5, 1944, and educated in Chad and in France in economics. In January 1968 Lakoué joined the Ministry of Economics and Transport as deputy director of commerce and industry, and in 1972 he was promoted to the directorship. Lakoué stayed in N'Djamena until 1978, when he left for France.

LALLIA, MARCEL (1920–1973). Prominent French expatriate businessman and political leader of various conservative parties prior to independence. Based originally in Abéché and later in N'Djamena, Lallia was an early deputy to the Chadian Conseil Représentatif on the URT (q.v.) label. First elected in 1946, he was reelected in 1952 (as RPT [q.v.] deputy), 1957 (on the AST [q.v.] label), and 1959 (UDIT [q.v.] party). A vocal critic of the progressive PPT (q.v.) party, Lallia was prominent in forging the PNA (q.v.) opposition alliance in 1960. Following the establishment of a one-party system in Chad he found himself deprived of a political base, though he remained a vocal critic of the regime. For some time the president of the local chamber of commerce, Lallia was on several occasions accused by President Tombalbaye (q.v.) of sympathizing with the FROLINAT (q.v.) rebellion. He was finally arrested on March 6, 1973, following which a number of Christian leaders appealed for clemency from Tombalbaye. In June of the same year it was announced that Lallia had died of a heart attack while in prison; it is assumed in N'Djamena that he had been killed.

LAMANA, ABDOULAYE (1933–). Former key cabinet minister and current political leader. Born in 1933 in Massenya, Chari-Baguirmi, though of Daye (Sara) origins, Lamana, a Muslim, was educated locally, at N'Djamena, and in Bongor. Entering the colonial administration, he worked as an administrative secretary (1955–57) before being attached to the governor's office in N'Djamena. In 1959 he went to Paris to continue his studies, obtaining a diploma in 1961 from the Institut des Hautes Etudes d'Outre-Mer (IHEOM), and upon his return to Chad was named inspector of public services and later deputy director of finance. A year later he joined the Tombalbaye (q.v.) cabinet as minister of finance, solidly entrenching himself as one of the president's inner circle of trusted ministers. In 1963 he was co-opted into the Political Bureau of the PPT (q.v.), and in 1964 he was named minister of economics and transport. Lamana built up the ministry into a major power base for himself and rapidly acquired secondary positions throughout the Chadian economy and administration. In 1968 his talents were further given their due when his ministry was expanded to include finance as well. An able administrator, by now one of the most influential figures in the cabinet, and widely regarded as Tombalbaye's heir apparent, Lamana was publicly criticized in March 1971 for "putting economic considerations above political ones"; the attack on his position occurred in conjunction with preparations by Tombalbaye to purge his technocrat followers in the cabinet and to offer their vacated posts to the recently amnestied Muslim leaders purged in the early 1960s. Dropped from the cabinet and removed from some of his other duties, Lamana remained in the PPT Political Bureau as treasurer general and vice president of the Committee on Economic and Financial Affairs. From 1971 to 1973 he also served as general manager of Cotontchad (q.v.). A general ministerial shuffle in October 1973 brought him back into prominence when he was appointed minister of state charged with the modern economy, planning, trade, and international cooperation, a position he held through the 1975 coup d'état. Lamana was put on trial in 1978 but absolved of charges of misuse of drought funds during the Tombalbaye era.

Lamana was largely on the political sidelines during the hectic 1980s. As a friend of Lol Mahamat Choua (q.v.), he rose to prominence again in the 1990s and participated in the 1993 Conférence Nationale (q.v.), where he was a candidate for its chairmanship. A leader of the Union Nationale (q.v.) political party, he is a presidential hopeful.

LAMI, PIERRE. First head of the French Mission de Réforme Administrative (MRA) (q.v.), replaced at Tombalbaye's (q.v.) strong insistence by Henri Paillard. Arriving in Chad in April 1969 and charged with the task of forcing the Chadian authorities to decentralize their power hierarchy and acknowledge former errors that had sparked the Muslim rebellion, Lami immediately clashed with Tombalbaye in connection with some of the specific policy suggestions prepared by his team, and especially the one that recommended the reinstatement with full powers of the traditional sultans of Chad. After Lami's replacement the very same proposals were made by Paillard and accepted by Tombalbaye. Lami had previously served under General Philippe Leclerc (q.v.) in the Fezzan and later in Indochina, and he had been governor of Côte d'Ivoire (1956) and of Senegal (1957).

LAMINE, AHMED (1937–). Administrator and former diplomat. A Hadjeray (q.v.) born in Mongo on December 28, 1937, Lamine was educated locally and at Brussels University in labor sociology. He served as director of social affairs from December 1970 to September 1971, at which time he was appointed prefect of the Lac Préfecture.

He remained in that posting until 1975, when he was transferred to the Ministry of Interior as head of a division. With the coming to power of Hissène Habré (q.v.) in 1982, Lamine rose to prominence, becoming mayor of N'Djamena. He was purged from all of his posts in 1987, however, after the falling-out between Habré and his former Hadjeray supporters, and he left for Mongo, where he was allegedly involved in the anti-Habré revolt. He bounced back into favor with Idriss Déby's (q.v.) capture of power and was briefly appointed director of Air Tchad, before being arrested by the CRCR (q.v.) in 1991 for sedition.

LAMINU NJITIYA (?–1871). Of Shoa (q.v.) Arab and Kanembu (q.v.) descent, Laminu Njitiya—originally an outlaw—became the prime lieutenant of Umar al-Kanemi, de facto ruler of Bornu (q.v.). Having assisted the latter to regain his throne in 1853 after a brief ouster, Laminu Njitiya was rewarded with a large fiefdom. A very popular and energetic figure, he greatly expanded Bornu's dominions in the *margai* country to the east.

LAO. Male initiation rites among the Ngambayé (q.v.). (See also YONDO.)

LAOKOLE, JEAN-BAPTISTE (1936–). Former postmaster, diplomat, and cabinet minister. Born in 1936 in Bendaidoura and educated in Chad in telecommunications and later in France in radio and electricity, Laokolé returned to N'Djamena in 1956 to assume the position of postmaster general. He stayed in that post until 1960, when he went to the Ecole Supérieure des PTT (1961–65). On his return he served as director of the post and finance section (1995), then head of personnel (1966–67), and then director of the post office and of the National Savings Bank of Chad (1967–73). In 1974 he was removed from postal duties, and after retraining in the Foreign Ministry he was appointed in 1976 ambassador to Zaire, Burundi, and Rwanda. He stayed in that post until 1982, when he was repatriated to head a division in the Ministry of Telecommunications in N'Djamena. When Idriss Déby (q.v.) came to power in December 1990 Laokolé was brought into the cabinet as secretary of state in charge of foreign affairs, serving from March 1991 to December 1992. He is currently in retirement.

LARGEAU see FAYA-LARGEAU.

LARGEAU, EMMANUEL (General) (1867–1916). French officer and conqueror of northern Chad. Born in Irún, Spain, in 1867 and raised in Niart, France, the son of Victor Largeau, the explorer of Central Africa, Emmanuel Largeau joined the army at a young age and rose up the ranks. In 1888 he entered St. Maixient Officers' School and eventually obtained a commission. Dispatched to Senegal, Côte d'Ivoire, and Gabon, Largeau participated in several important exploration and military missions. In 1902 he was attached to the French forces in Chad, and he helped expel the Senoussi (see SANUSIYA) from the northern B.E.T. regions, conquering and pacifying Ennedi (1910) and Borkou (1913). He died during the First World War on the Verdun front.

LEBEUF, JEAN PAUL. Founder and first French director of INTSH (q.v.), prolific author, and one of the foremost scholars of archaeology and history of the prehistoric civilizations of the Chad basin. A producer of publicity films prior to the Second World War, Lebeuf acquired overnight fame when in 1936 the Sao (q.v.) bronzework was discovered. Changing careers to study sociology and ethnology, Lebeuf realized the potential importance of the new Sao discoveries and their revelation of the former existence in the Chad basin of a civilization never before suspected to have developed there. He then led numerous excavation expeditions, over time writing hundreds of articles and 12 books. The creation of INTSH in 1961 in N'Djamena was very much his own work, and in 1962 and 1963 he was instrumental in the establishment of the Musée National, where a selection of Sao work is exhibited. His wife, whom he met while a student at the Musée de l'Homme in Paris, is also a noted scholar on Chad.

LE BOUCLIER. Moundou-based newspaper with a large readership in the south and among Sara refugees in Cameroon. Set up in Moundou after the 1978 disassociation of the Sara areas from N'Djamena.

LECLERC DE HAUTECLOCQUE, PHILIPPE (Marshal) (1902–1947). French officer, former colonial governor, and leader of the Free French force that invaded Libya from Chad during the Second World War. Born in northern France in 1902 and a graduate of St. Cyr (1924), Leclerc saw action in France and in Morocco and was captured twice during the war. A major at the time of the German invasion of France, he escaped to England, where he joined the Free French forces. Assigned as governor of Cameroon (1940) and later military commander of Chad (1941–42), Leclerc led a column of colonial and French troops that successfully attacked the Italian Fezzan from the totally unexpected southern direction after an epic 2,400-kilometer (1,500-mile), 39-day trek. His force of 3,200 troops (including 2,700 Africans, the majority Sara from southern Chad) crossed the B.E.T. wilderness into Libya, defeated the Italian garrisons there, and joined the British troops in Tripoli. Later Leclerc's division was to be the first to enter Paris, with the Marshal supervising the German surrender of the city. Before his death in 1947 he also served as commander of the French forces in Indochina.

LECOEUR, CHARLES (1903–1944). Educator and author. Born in Paris on May 14, 1903, and a graduate of the elite schools of France, LeCoeur became a teacher in Rabat, Morocco. He conducted field trips into the Chad-Niger area, publishing important works on the region. LeCoeur died in 1944 during the Second World War.

LELE. Ethnic group of some 40,000 people found mostly south of Kélo. Though slowly Christianized, they retain numerous animist practices, including ancestor worship. Their capital, Bargadjé, eventually became the contemporary Kélo, after the name of a Lélé chief. The Lélé are currently a minority in their own capital.

LERE. Small town of 3,500 people, headquarters of the souspréfecture of the same name (population 65,000; area 5,000 square kilometers [1,930 square miles]; population density 13.5 per square kilometer) in the Mayo-Kebbi Préfecture. The town of Léré is composed of four distinct ethnic quarters—Léré-Moundang, Léré-Foulbe (Fulani), Fouli-Léré, and Fouli-Hausa. The Fulani (q.v.) sector is the commercial center of the town. In front of a large square is found the palace of the *goléré* (q.v.), superior chief of the Moundang. The region had been the scene of intensive Fulani invasions from Cameroon in the nineteenth century, and Moundang-Fulani relations remain very tense to this day.

LIBERATION ARMIES see FIRST LIBERATION ARMY; SECOND LIBERATION ARMY; THIRD LIBERATION ARMY

LIBYA. Chad's northern neighbor and in precolonial times a major point of entry into the region of outside influences, prime trading partner, and terminus of the trans-Saharan caravan trails. One of the caravan trails' most important junctures was Kufra (q.v.) in the Fezzan, which connected the Bornu (q.v.) Empire with the outside world. In the nineteenth century Senoussi influence and power radiated southward from the Fezzan into Kanem, Ouadai, and the B.E.T. After the French occupation of Chad international trade was reoriented toward the southern routes (to the Atlantic Ocean) and the trans-Saharan trails diminished in importance. (See also CARAVAN ROUTES; SANUSIYA.) Though the Chad-Libya desert border artificially separated some ethnic groups in the region, relations between the two countries began to deteriorate only with the rise to power of the Muammar Qaddafi regime in Libya, and then not for ethnic reasons but for geopolitical, religious, and economic considerations. The new Libyan regime offered a base of operations to Dr. Abba Siddick's (q.v.) FROLINAT (q.v.)—this had been granted before but was of much less importance—and supplied the Toubou (q.v.) rebel movement with sophisticated materiel to wage a secession war against the southern-staffed armed forces of N'Djamena. Relations between the two countries fell to a low point in August 1971, when an anti-Tombalbaye (q.v.) Libya-sponsored attempted coup was discovered (see COUP [ATTEMPTED] OF AUGUST 27, 1971). Soon after, Chad broke relations with Libya and Tombalbaye publicly offered all anti-Qaddafi elements refuge in N'Djamena. Libya retaliated by granting de facto recognition to FROLINAT as the legitimate government of all of Chad. The break was mediated by Niger's President Hamani Diori, and relations were reestablished in April 1972. The reconciliation stipulated Libyan withdrawal of support from FROLINAT (including restraining their forays into B.E.T.) and financial credits to the Tombalbaye regime in exchange for Chad's breaking relations with Israel and tacit recognition of the Mussolini-Laval boundary agreement (q.v.) that runs deeply through northern B.E.T.

As part of the agreement (allegedly sealed by a large Libyan donation of never-traced U.S. dollars), Libyan troops moved into the Aouzou Strip (q.v.) and fortified it with ground-to-air missiles. Most of the pledged credits only slowly trickled into Chad, though in January 1974 the Banque Tchado-Arabe-Libyenne pour le Commerce Extérieur et le Developpement (BATAL) was set up with Libyan funds, and later a loan of 23,000 million CFA francs was delivered for a number of industrial projects in Chad. The 1975 coup d'état came as Chad-Libya relations had begun to sour again, though the new military regime was careful not to antagonize its powerful northern neighbor too much. Increasingly involved in the Chadian power struggle through its support for one or another (or several) of the rebel movements trying to unseat Félix Malloum (q.v.), Libya ultimately came to be viewed as sympathetic to a Goukouni (q.v.) victory—despite the fact that Libya's prime allies were Dr. Abba Siddick (q.v.) and Ahmat Acyl (q.v.). These two, however, were militarily weak; they could be used as pawns (which, indeed, Libya did) but could hardly be expected to wield real power and influence. Of the two major contenders for power, Hissène Habré (q.v.) was solidly opposed to a Libyan role in Chad, while Goukouni, militarily weak, was malleable. Thus during the fierce 1980 power struggle between Goukouni and Habré, the former's request for military aid from Libya was hastily acceded to, leading to the prompt ouster of Habré's forces from the capital. The Libyan troops that came to Chad were headquartered in Douzoma, near N'Djamena, and they also held positions in B.E.T. and Ouadai. Estimates, at the time, of 5,000 Libyans in Chad were later greatly revised upward. According to one scholar, one-third of Libya's entire army, or 15,000 troops, may have been in Chad in December 1980.

The Libyan role in 1981 triggered deep anxieties in both African and Western capitals, exacerbated by the later announcement of a treaty of union between Chad and Libya—another in Qaddafi's series of ill-fated unions. CIA funds, materiel, and assistance began reaching Habré, while internationally, U.S. and African pressure led to Goukouni's request that Libyan troops vacate Chad to be replaced by an OAU force. Goukouni's volte-face contributed directly to the swing of the military pendulum in favor of Habré, who then moved into N'Djamena unopposed on June 7, 1982. Goukouni's ouster brought a renewed Libyan role into Chad as he made his peace with Qaddafi. In mid-1983, assisted by Libyan air cover, materiel, and some troops, the GUNT (q.v.) counteroffensive began sweeping through B.E.T. and, temporarily, into Abéché. This in turn brought in additional U.S. financial and French military support for Habré, the announcement of the establishment of a "Red Zone" (q.v.) beyond which Goukouni's and Libya's advances would be repelled by French force of arms, leading to an armed stalemate along the 16th parallel. In mid-1984 a Mitterrand-Qaddafi agreement regarding a disengagement of external forces from Chad led France to withdraw part of its forces, though once it was clear that Libya had no intention of abiding by the agreement, the French returned.

By the mid-1980s, however, much of the GUNT fighting force had fallen apart, with most groups rallying to Habré, and even Goukouni had become disenchanted with Tripoli. In 1986 and 1987, moreover, bolstered by important U.S. military aid, Habré initiated a series of stunning attacks on Libya's officer-heavy and materiel-bogged forces in B.E.T., especially on the Ouadai-Doum base, whose East German and Czech officers fled a week before the assault. In the process a huge amount of war materiel was captured (to the value of over US$1.5 billion, and several thousand Libyan troops and senior Libyan generals were captured. The Libyan losses were so great that the entire regional balance of power was tilted, and Libyan military purchasing delegations were immediately dispatched to Brazil and other arms-exporting countries with shopping lists of war materiel. (The materiel destroyed or captured by Chad included 380 tanks and armored vehicles destroyed and 426 captured, 113 of which were T-55 tanks; the destruction of 28 aircraft and helicopters and the capture intact of 23, one of which was so new that the CIA flew in a team to examine its technology.)

Aouzou itself was also briefly liberated, falling into Chadian hands for the first time in 14 years, but French timidity and unwillingness to provide Habré with aircover brought a Chadian retreat from the town. In retaliation for the loss of Aouzou a daring September 1987 Chadian attack was launched against the sprawling Libyan base of Maaten-es-Sarra, 100 kilometers (60 miles) inside Libya proper. Using *wadi* (q.v.) beds for the deep penetration into the allegedly impregnable base, Chadian troops under the personal command of Chief of Staff Hassan Djamouss (q.v.) scored a complete surprise. Again more than 1,000 Libyan troops were killed (as well as two Soviet officers) and hundreds were captured (along with up to a dozen East European personnel), with massive destruction of Libyan materiel, before the Chadian troops withdrew. Although Libya—to salvage some pride—sent several jets to bomb Abéché (where the French Opération Epervier [q.v.] force was caught unprepared, and three civilians were killed) and N'Djamena (where no bombs were dropped after one Libyan aircraft was shot down), Libya had to acknowledge Chad's greater military might and resolve and its own defeat in the desert warfare, and Qaddafi agreed to pass on the resolution of ownership of the Aouzou Strip to the International Court of Justice (ICJ) in The Hague. A cease-fire between the two countries was negotiated in late 1987 and was followed by the resumption of diplomatic relations in October 1988.

However, Libya's military defeats at the hands of Habré grossly damaged Qaddafi's reputation. When Idriss Déby (q.v.) defected from N'Djamena in 1989, Qaddafi—smarting from his humiliation in Chad—extended to Déby both military and financial assistance, though Libya was to claim that it was not involved in Déby's raising an army in Darfur. Qaddafi was especially anxious to get back the thousands of Libyan troops still either POWs in Chad or being trained and used by the CIA as a destabilizing contra-force from Chadian bases. (Over 500 of them died in captivity.) Indeed, when in one of his forays against Habré's forces in Abéché Déby captured the Chadian chief of staff, Colonel Worimi (q.v.), Libya desperately tried to "buy" him from Déby in order to use him for bargaining for the 2,000 POWs in N'Djamena. (Déby refused, but he pledged—and later delivered on it—that as soon as he entered N'Djamena all Libyans would be freed.) Chad bitterly complained about the heavy support that Libya was offering Déby via its Islamic Legion (q.v.), which was contrary to the peace treaty signed between the two countries after the B.E.T. fighting. (Certainly there were daily Libyan flights between Kufra and Darfur).

Once Déby entered N'Djamena, Chad's relations with Libya immediately improved. Libyans under the control of the CIA were given the option of returning to Libya or going to some other country to continue their "liberation" activities. Indeed, Prime Minister Jean Alingué was even to argue in January 1992 in Tripoli that the 1989 bombing of the PanAm flight that crashed at Lockerbie was an American conspiracy. A grateful Libya gave Déby US$3 million in immediate aid, 20 Mercedes Benz cars, and three transport planes, including one for presidential use. However, a general cooperation agreement with Libya signed in 1992 was rejected by the interim legislature in June 1993. The Aouzou Strip dispute was resolved by the ICJ in favor of Chad (despite the introduction as evidence of a letter written by Tombalbaye), and Libya withdrew from the strip in 1994.

LIGUE TCHADIENNE DE DROITS DE L'HOMME (LTDH). One of several organs authorized by Idriss Déby (q.v.) in 1991, the LTDH published the following year a blistering report on abuses of human rights by his regime, including the slaughter of 150 civilians in Doba, and especially by his Garde Républicaine (q.v.). The LTDH lost its deputy president, Joseph Behidi, in an assassination in N'Djamena, and its head, Joseph M'Bayman, was fined one million CFA francs for defaming the Garde Républicaine by charging it with a variety of abuses.

LINGUISTIC GROUPS. Chad's population uses about 110 languages or dialects that are grouped into 12 distinct linguistic groups. Some of these contain a large number of languages/dialects and are used by a number of ethnic groups, while others are isolated, little studied, or seldom spoken within Chad. The 12 linguistic groups are as follows:

1. Central Saharan: including the Kanembou, Kanuri, Teda, Daza, and Baélé languages, spoken by the Kanembu, Bornuans, Teda, Daza, Zaghawa, and Bideyat, in Kanem, Chari-Baguirmi, B.E.T., and Biltine.

2. Chadic: including a large number of languages/dialects—formerly referred to as the Chado-Hamitic group—spread in a huge east-west arc that includes the Buduma, Kotoko, Massa, Marba, Miltou, Saorua, Djongor, Dangaléat, Moubi, and others, spoken by a variety of ethnic groups, in an arc including Chari-Baguirmi, Lac, Mayo-Kebbi, Tandjilé, Moyen-Chari, Guéra, Batha, Ouadai, Salamat, and Logone Occidentale.

3. Sara-Bongo-Baguirmi: including the mutually noncomprehensible Barma, Kouka, Bilala, Medogo, Kenga, and Sara languages, spoken by ethnic groups of the same name, numbering over 50 percent of Chad's population and found predominantly in the southern and western part of the country, but also in Batha and Guéra. Sometimes viewed as a subgroup of a larger Chari-Nile family.

4. Mabang: linguistic group encompassing Ouadai and Salamat

dialects, including Bora Mabang (of the Kodoy and Maba), Massalit, Marfa, and others.

5. Tama: including four minor dialects spoken in Biltine, Ouadai, and Salamat.

6. Daju (or Dadjo): encompassing one language—Daju—spoken in three localities in eastern Chad by the Daju ethnic group and by many more members across the border in Sudan.

7. Toubouri-Moundang-Mboum: encompassing these three languages plus the Kim and Mesmé, spoken by ethnic groups carrying the same names, mostly in Mayo-Kebbi, Logone Orientale, and Tandjilé.

8. Boua: includes Boua, Niellim Toun-no, and several other dialects spoken solely in Moyen-Chari and Guéra.

9. Mimi: single-language group. The language has not been analyzed by scholars, and it appears exclusively in Biltine, spoken by the Mimi ethnic group.

10. Banda-Nqbaka: including the Sango lingua franca of the Central African Republic (and Chad border areas, particularly around Sarh), and the Bolgo and Goula.

11. Fulani: spoken in several dialects by nonlocalized groups on transhumance treks.

12. Arabic: spoken in a number of dialects by up to one-third of Chad's population, in most of the northern two-thirds of the country.

LISETTE, GABRIEL (1919–). Founder of Chad's nationalist party, the Parti Progressiste Tchadien (PPT) (q.v.), architect of the party's rise to power, dominant early political leader, and first prime minister of Chad. Born on April 2, 1919, in Puerto Bello, Panama, to émigré parents, educated in Guadeloupe and at the Paris Ecole Nationale de la France d'Outre-Mer, Lisette served in the French army (1939–42), following which he began his career as a colonial administrator. In August 1944 he was posted to French Congo, and in 1946 he was transferred to Chad as deputy chief administrator of the Logone *département,* which he transformed into his political power base. After barely three months in his post he was elected Chad's deputy to the French National Assembly (defeating Jules Pierre Toura Gaba [q.v.], who was later to become his ally). As an early and ardent militant of the nascent RDA (q.v.) party (an interterritorial grouping of nationalist movements), Lisette became the party's secretary-general at the French National Assembly. Failing in his bid for reelection in 1951 (defeated by Bechir Mohamed Sow [q.v.], the UDT [q.v.] candidate), he was returned to Paris in 1956, serving there until 1959. In the meantime Lisette had set up an RDA branch in Chad, the PPT. Extremely hard-pressed at the outset, until 1956 and 1957 the PPT was not electorally very successful, losing consistently to the traditional chiefly parties that were supported both by the French colonial administration and by French expatriates in the country. Between 1952 and 1960 Lisette served as territorial deputy and as mayor of Fort-Lamy.

Following his party's smashing victory at the polls in 1957 he was called upon to head the country's first autonomous governments of 1957–59, and in 1959 he became vice president of Chad. Unpopular among the country's Muslim leaders, Lisette also came under constant attack for being a foreigner carving for himself an empire in Chad. In 1959 these pressures forced him to cede political leadership to his former lieutenant, François Tombalbaye (q.v.), though he remained deputy prime minister with responsibilities over economic coordination and foreign affairs. His highly unusual status and the creation of a veritable superministry under his control (a government within a government, according to many critics) continued to draw pressure for his total removal from power, especially by Ahmed Koulamallah (q.v.). He was finally purged on August 24, 1960; while attending an international conference in Israel he was deposed by Tombalbaye, and as an "alien" was prohibited from returning to Chad. (The same pretext was to be used later against ranking politicians that Tombalbaye wished to be rid of.) After Lisette's fall, Tombalbaye conducted a major purge of Lisette's many (and extremely devoted) supporters throughout the country, but especially in the Logone Préfecture. Indeed, for some time Tombalbaye was faced with a quasi revolt within the PPT itself over the political demise of Lisette; the Logone Préfecture was later carved up into three segments to prevent a "Lisettiste" comeback by his supporters, and a proconsul-type "permanent minister" to Logone was dispatched to control the region. Following his political demise, Lisette went to Paris and in 1963 became France's permanent representative to the Economic Commission for Latin America and later occupied similar high-level posts. In 1973 his name suddenly was resurrected in Chad when he was accused by Tombalbaye of plotting "against the security and happiness of the Chadian people" together with France's Jacques Foccart (q.v.).

LIVESTOCK. Chad has been traditionally a country with large numbers of livestock. The major drought in 1970s, however, greatly reduced local herds and also shifted their location to the wetter, more southern préfectures. Another drought/famine in 1984/85 likewise effectuated dramatic changes in livestock distribution in the country. (See also CAT-TLE.) In 1982, livestock distribution in Chad was estimated as follows:

B.E.T.: 110,000 camels; 35,000 cattle

Lac and Kanem: 1,500,000 cattle; 60,000 camels

Batha: 1,000,000 cattle; 115,000 camels

Biltine: 300,000 cattle; 40,000 camels

Chari-Baguirmi: 850,000 cattle; 3,000 camels

Guéra: 150,000 cattle

Ouadai: 600,000 cattle; 30,000 camels

Mayo-Kebbi and Tandjilé: 300,000 cattle

Moyen-Chari: 50,000 cattle

Salamat: 80,000 cattle

In the same year there were also an estimated 4,250,000 lambs/goats in the country, 150,000 horses, and 320,000 donkeys. While there are more recent figures, from 1992, these are very unreliable, in terms of both numbers and regional distribution; the real figures (when assembled) would underscore the serious, ongoing (and unsettling) encroachment of pastoralists on agricultural land in the south.

LOA AND SOU. Highest deities in Sara mythology, specifically among the Mbaï. Loa and Sou are twins symbolizing opposites in the physical and spiritual world.

LOGONE OCCIDENTALE PREFECTURE. Important southern préfecture created in the aftermath of the decision in 1962 to split the former united Logone Préfecture into three parts. With administrative headquarters in Moundou and three souspréfectures (Moundou, Beinamar, Bénoyé), and one *poste administratif,* Logone Occidentale encompasses a territory of 8,675 square kilometers (3,350 square miles) and a population of 365,000, giving it a population density of 42 per square kilometer, the highest by far in all of Chad, and up by 50 percent since the 1970s. Most of the population is Gambayé (q.v.) and other Sara clans. The region is a major producer of cotton, processed in four Cotontchad (q.v.) ginneries. Millet is traditionally smuggled for sale in the Central African Republic. If the Trans-Cameroonian railroad is extended to Chad it could link up at Moundou, making the latter a major transhipment point for Chadian imports and exports. The préfecture is one of the most developed in all of Chad and has the highest school attendance rate (61.4 percent) in the country.

LOGONE ORIENTALE PREFECTURE. Part of the pre-independence united Logone Préfecture that was split in 1962 into three segments. Logone Orientale covers a territory of 28,029 square kilometers (10,822 square miles) and has a population of 378,000, giving it a population density of 13.5 per square kilometer. The préfecture's capital is at Doba—whose major oil deposits may yet transform Chad's fate and are scheduled as of 1995 to be linked by a pipeline with an Atlantic port in Cameroon—and it is divided into four souspréfectures (Doba, Baïbokoum, Bébédjia, and Goré) and three *postes administratifs*. The population is a mixture of Sara and non-Sara groups, including Mbaï, Gor, N'gambayé, Kaba, Boum, and Laka. The préfecture is an important producer of cotton (two of its cantons have the highest cotton production in Chad) with several other crops being grown in sizable quantities, especially groundnuts and millet. Doba (population 13,300) is scheduled to be linked up with the Trans-Cameroonian railroad if it is extended into Chad. Such an eventuality would transform the town into a major transshipment center for the region. The préfecture is highly developed and has the second highest rate of school attendance (58.4 percent) in the country; it is also the center of Protestant influence in Chad.

LOGONE RIVER. One of Chad's major rivers. The 970-kilometer (600-mile) Logone is formed by two major branches: the M'Béré, which rises in Cameroon's Adamaoua Mountains, and the Pendé, which emerges from the Yadé massif. Downstream from the region of Mislippi and Ham (two small villages), the Logone constitutes the Chad-Cameroon border. It is joined at N'Djamena by the Chari River (q.v.), and the Chari-Logone forms a joint delta at Lake Chad. Between June and November the Logone overflows its banks, inundating vast stretches of land and making land communications impossible. The river links Moundou and Bongor with N'Djamena for several months of the year, though its winding course in several places makes navigation hazardous except for small barges.

LOGONE RIVER JOINT COMMISSION. A largely moribund Chad-Cameroon organization for the joint economic development of the Logone River (q.v.) regions. The commission (sometimes referred to as committee) met in N'Djamena in December 1967 for the first time in 15 years, having been set up prior to independence, and subsequently did not meet for another 10 years.

LOGONE-BIRNI. Historic ruined capital of the Sao (q.v.) sultanate, found on the left bank of the Logone River (q.v.) 65 kilometers (40 miles) south of Fort Foureau in Cameroon. The ruins are the site of the Kotoko (q.v.) ancestral tombs. The current sultan of the Kotoko exacts a personal tax on all cattle and produce crossing the river.

LOI-CADRE. The "enabling" act passed by the French National Assembly in June 1956. The act expanded the authority of the territorial assemblies in French colonies at the expense of the powers of the two federations (AEF and AOF) and gave colonies and mandates internal autonomy, made suffrage universal, and established a single electoral roll. The *loi-cadre* paved the way for the rise to power of nationalist parties—in Chad, Gabriel Lisette and his PPT (qq.v.).

LOL, MAHAMAT CHOUA see CHOUA, LOL MAHAMAT.

LOSSIMIAU, NAIMBAYE. Former cabinet minister and diplomat. A Ngambayé from Moundou, but with pro-Libyan sympathies, Lossimiau was minister of agriculture in the November 1979 GUNT (q.v.) government, and in July 1981 was named minister of rural development in Goukouni's (q.v.) cabinet. With Goukouni's ouster from power in N'Djamena in 1982 Lossimiau lost his post. He nevertheless assisted Hissène Habré in conquering the southern préfectures, in expectation of a cabinet post, and in November 1983 he was rewarded with an appointment as Chad's ambassador to the EC.

LYCEE FELIX EBOUE. Leading N'Djamena lycée named after the former governor-general of the AEF (q.v.) federation, who during the Second World War (when he was governor of Chad) rallied the AEF to the Free French cause, becoming a national hero (see EBOUE, FELIX). Located in the southeast part of the town near the hippodrome, the Lycée Félix Eboué was founded in 1947 as a primary school, becoming in 1955 one of the only three secondary schools in the entire country (see EDUCATION). Essentially exempted from President Tombalbaye's (q.v.) Africanization policies (see CULTURAL REVOLUTION) in 1970, the school maintained segregated classes. Student discontent over the privileged status of the expatriate children in the lycée resulted in a series of outbursts of strikes and violence in 1970 and 1971. Quelled by troops, the school erupted with anti-Tombalbaye demonstrations later in the year and in late 1972. It was briefly closed down by the government on three separate occasions.

LYCEE FRANCO-ARABE D'ABECHE. Primary and later secondary school set up by the French administration in Abéché in 1952.

Because of the ongoing suspicion and hostility in Ouadai to any form of outside Christian influence, the lycée offered a unique blend of secular, Koranic, and Arabic education. Despite these concessions to local demands, registration in the school was always low, with parents preferring to send their children to the more rudimentary facilities of the Koranic schools (q.v.) in order to be sure that no "contamination" occurred. The lycée was created by the French less from a desire to aid Ouadai (traditionally inimical to the French), than from a prudent desire to counter Islamic propaganda entering the region from outside its borders.

-M-

MAATEN-ES-SARRA. Major Libyan airbase 100 kilometers (60 miles) from the Chad border. It was attacked and overrun by Hissène Habré's (q.v.) armed forces in the Chad-Libya war of 1987. A large amount of sophisticated war materiel was destroyed and some captured and taken to Chad. Some tactical advice about the base was provided by Iraq which, after the Camp David peace accords, had helped to construct the base for the training of anti-Egypt terrorists, but which by now was hostile to Libya.

MABA. Collective name for a group of mountain ethnic groups in Ouadai and Biltine (q.v.) into which other ethnic groups, originating in Darfur (q.v.), have become assimilated. Under Abd-el-Kerim (q.v.), the Maba expelled the Tunjur (q.v.) dynasty in Ouadai and formed the backbone of the powerful and expanding Ouadai kingdom (q.v.). The principal Maba subgroups are the Kodoy (q.v.) and the Ouled Djema, formerly a Kodoy subgroup. All speak the same language—Bura-Mabang (q.v.). There are approximately 220,000 Maba in Ouadai, mostly in Abéché, in Am Dam, and in Biltine. Their main economic activity is stockbreeding (confined to Arab hands) and agriculture. Neither the harvesting of the acacia tree crops (gum arabic) nor ironwork is acceptable Maba work, and these are usually done by other ethnic groups. Within Maba society, and especially in Abéché's traditional hierarchy, chiefs and members of the royal clans still possess an inordinate amount of prestige and power.

MADANI, MAHAMAT OUMAR (1926–). Former attorney general of Chad. Born in 1926 in Massaguette and educated in Brazzaville and Paris, obtaining a degree from the Institut des Hautes Etudes d'Outre-Mer (IHEOM), Madani returned to Chad in 1963 to serve as magistrate in N'Djamena. From 1964 to 1969 he was president of the

N'Djamena Tribunal of First Instance; from 1969 to 1973 he served as prosecutor at the N'Djamena High Court; from 1973 to 1975 he was prosecutor at the Court of Appeals; and from 1975 to 1979 he was president of the Court of Appeals. Madani left the capital in 1979 to serve with the judicial system in Moundou.

MADJIMBANG, JOSEPH (1939–). Senior civil administrator and former diplomat. Born in Bébédjia on August 17, 1939, Madjimbang obtained a diploma from the IAP and was appointed, in succession, prefect of Moyen-Chari (1968), prefect of Chari-Baguirmi (1972), and prefect of Tandjilé (1976). In 1982 he moved to the civil administration of Moundou and was appointed prefect of Logone Occidentale, and in the mid-1980s, ambassador to Germany. Madjimbang is currently in retirement.

MADJINGAYE. Sara ethnic subgroup found in the Koumra and Sarh regions of Moyen-Chari préfecture. From a strictly purist point of view, it is the only group entitled to be called Sara. Numbering around 100,000, they are extremely homogeneous, arriving in their territory at the end of the seventeenth century. Raided extensively by the Baguirmi kingdom (q.v.), the Madjingayé twin centers of Koumra and Bédaya were conquered by Rabah (q.v.) in 1888–89. Bédaya remains to this day the seat of the Madjingayé *mbang* (q.v.) and a very important religious center. The Madjingayé were only minimally affected by Christian missionary efforts, with the first Protestant effort occurring in 1925 and the Catholic not until 1952. (See also SARA.)

MAGUMI. Major clan of the Zaghawa (q.v.) whose Sefuwa (q.v.) lineage founded—with Tomaghera (q.v.) assistance—the Kanem kingdom in the early years of the ninth century. The Sefuwa dynasty greatly expanded the nascent kingdom until the thirteenth century, when an internal cleavage forced it to relocate the center of power to Bornu. (See also KANEM-BORNU EMPIRE.)

MAHAMAT, ABDELKERIM (1933–). Former cabinet minister and diplomat. Born in 1933 in Goz-Beida in Ouadai, son of the sultan of Dar Sila, Mahamat was elected to the Territorial Assembly as UDIT (q.v.) deputy from Ouadai, serving from 1957 to 1963. From June 1959 to August 1960 Mahamat also served on Ahmed Mangué's (q.v.) ministerial cabinet, and from August 1960 to March 1962 he was Tombalbaye's (q.v.) secretary of state for defense. In June 1961 he was elected (with PPT [q.v.] support) mayor of Abéché, remaining in that post through 1963. He also served for a few weeks as secretary of state in charge of coordination (March–April 1962) and was elected president of the assembly in March 1962. On March 22, 1963, he was arrested in the major purge of Muslim and former opposition members. Together with other prominent northerners like Abo Nassour, Ali Kosso, and Al-latchi Issa Allatchimi (qq.v.), Mahamat had opposed the PPT creation of a one-party system. He was sentenced to life imprisonment but was amnestied in 1965 and appointed ambassador to Libya (June 1966 to April 1968). In 1967 he was further rehabilitated and was integrated into the Political Bureau of the PPT, though he soon fell from favor and was arrested again in May 1968. Amnestied again in 1970, Mahamat was appointed minister of stockbreeding, water, and forests in May 1971. He left the cabinet in October 1973 to occupy a succession of secondary administrative posts. With the fall of N'Djamena to the north, Mahamat was appointed ambassador to Sudan. Regarded as too much of a Habré ally, when the Goukouni-Habré (qq.v.) split developed in 1980 Mahamat was replaced as ambassador, but he refused to step down and vacate his offices. He bounced back to his ambassadorship later, with the emergence in N'Djamena of the victorious Habré. He is currently retired from public life.

MAHAMAT, CHAKROUN (1914–). Former sultan of N'Djamena and chief imam of the city. Mahamat Chakroun was elevated to the sultanship of N'Djamena at the recommendation of the French Mission de Réforme Administrative (MRA) (q.v.) despite the fact that a sultanate had not existed there since 1952 (when Sultan Kasser was deposed by the French) and that the institution had originally been a totally artificial French creation in the first place. The move was supposed to allow traditional elements in the area a measure of decentralized power. The sultanate was dissolved with the advent of military rule in 1976.

MAHAMAT, HASSAN DADJO (1935–). Former diplomat and cabinet minister. Born in Am-Timan (Salamat) on April 23, 1935, and educated locally and in N'Djamena, Mahamat was a schoolteacher from 1957 to 1962. He then passed a recruitment drive for police inspectors, took courses in public administration, and became a government functionary. He was appointed *chef de cabinet* of the minister of foreign affairs in 1966, and from that position gained appointment to Tripoli until 1968, and after his return to N'Djamena was appointed minister of waters, forests, and fisheries. He served in that post through 1971, before reassuming his diplomatic career. After the fall of the capital to northern troops, Mahamat briefly joined the Choua cabinet, as minister of stockbreeding, serving until 1980.

MAHAMAT, IBRAHIM MALLA. Deputy chairman of the anti-Déby MDD (qq.v.) operating in the Lake Chad region.

MAHAMAT, KASKANAYE (1907–1966). Important former Salamat PPT (q.v.) supporter. Born in 1907 in Am-Timan, and controlling much of the trade in the area, Mahamat was a key PPT leader in this region and was elected to the National Assembly in 1957 on the PPT ticket. He remained in the assembly until 1963 and was killed during the disturbances in Salamat in 1966.

MAHAMAT, MARTIN (1922–). Administrator, born in 1922 in Bédaya, and in his early years an instructor and educational inspector in Abéché, Sarh, Mongo, and Oum-Hadjer. Mahamat was an early supporter of the PPT (q.v.), tracing his membership to 1946. He actively began his political career in July 1959 when he served as *chef de cabinet* of both Thomas Keiro (q.v.) and Jules Pierre Toura Gaba (q.v.), the two ministers of public works. Since 1964 Mahamat has been with the Ministry of Interior, eventually rising to become director of Interior in the ministry. A member of the Political Bureau of the PPT, Mahamat was dropped from that organ in 1971 to make room for the recently amnestied Muslim opposition leaders. In 1977 he moved to Moundou, and soon after went into retirement.

MAHAMAT, OUMAR (1926–). Lawyer and former attorney general of Chad. Born in 1926 in Massaguette and educated at the Institut des Hautes Etudes d'Outre-Mer (IHEOM) in Paris, where he obtained his legal training, Mahamat joined the Ministry of Justice and served as president of the Court of Appeals from 1964 to 1969, when he was appointed attorney general.

MAHAMAT, OUTMAN. Former assembly deputy. Born in Fort-Lamy and by profession a trader, Mahamat helped in 1958 to found the militantly Muslim UNT (q.v.) party, which—allied with the UDIT (q.v.)—eliminated Ahmed Koulamallah's MSA (q.v.) from the latter's Chari-Baguirmi stronghold in 1959. Elected that year to the National Assembly, Mahamat served as secretary of the assembly's Bureau (1959–60). He was purged by Tombalbaye (q.v.) in 1962 for opposing the imposition of a one-party system in Chad, and he eventually retired from politics. In 1975 his name was resurrected in connection with the Outel Bono (q.v.) murder in Paris.

MAHAMAT DOUBA, ALIFA. Correct name of the Alifa of Bousso, better known abroad as Douba Alifa, Mahamat (q.v.).

MAHAMAT-EL-GONI (1923–). Former cabinet minister, opposition leader, and head of the conservative Action Sociale Tchadienne (AST) (q.v.) party. Born in Abéché on September 23, 1923 (the brother of Arabi-el-Goni [q.v.], also in politics), Mahamat-el-Goni was a prominent leader of the chiefly conservative coalition staunchly opposing the rise to power of the PPT (q.v.) of Gabriel Lisette (q.v.) and François Tombalbaye (q.v.). In March 1957 he was elected AST deputy to the Territorial Assembly, serving as president of the assembly's Social Affairs Committee. From March to June 1959 he was briefly secretary of state in charge of information before being elected AST senator to the French Community. He remained in Paris until 1961, when he returned to play an important role in the newly created anti-PPT party, the PNA (q.v.), of which he was elected secretary-general under Ahmed Koulamallah (q.v.). A pragmatist, Mahamat-el-Goni survived the major purges of 1963 by accepting the one-party system imposed by the PPT and was consequently appointed minister of stockbreeding (March 1963) and later minister of the civil service (January 1964). He was arrested in November 1965 for plotting against the regime and was amnestied in June 1970. Since then he has been involved in secondary administrative duties.

MAHAMAT SALEH, AHMET. Former minister of finance. A Kenga from Guéra, Mahamat Saleh was one of Hissène Habré's (q.v.) lieutenants, heading the short-lived Conseil National d'Union (q.v.) of the Malloum-Habré interregnum. Following the Kano I talks he was appointed secretary of state for finance and economics (April–November 1979) and also served briefly (November 1979–March 1980) as minister of territorial administration. After the Goukouni-Habré split, he followed Habré into self-exile and served as FAN (q.v.) field commander in Ouadai. Mahamat Saleh led the FAN counteroffensive on N'Djamena in 1982, following which he was installed as one of Habré's prime lieutenants and advisers.

MAHAMID. Djoheina (q.v.) Arab clans, part of the larger Rizegat (q.v.) subgroup. The Mahamid are found as nomads in northern Ouadai and Darfur (Sudan) and were estimated (in 1954) to number around 6,000. They have particularly good relations with the Zaghawa (q.v.). In the seventeenth century they played a role in toppling the Tunjur (q.v.) dynasty in Ouadai. (See also ARABS.)

MAHMOUD, ABDERAHMANE (Lt. Colonel) (1948–1980). Former minister of justice. Born in Iriba (Biltine) in 1948. Mahmoud was educated locally and at the Lycée Franco-Arabe d'Abéché (q.v.). He joined the Chadian armed forces in 1966 and was promoted to sergeant in December 1967. In 1970 he was again promoted, and after attending the Ecole Militaire d'Administration of Montpellier,

France, he was commissioned second lieutenant (October 1972). In October 1974 he was promoted to first lieutenant, and following the 1975 coup d'état he was named minister of information, tourism, parks, and reserves. At the same time he was appointed liaison officer between the Armed Forces of Chad and the Conseil Supérieur Militaire (CSM) (q.v.) and was made a member of the newly created Commission de Défense Nationale (CDN) (q.v.).

One of the very few Arab officers in the Chadian army (despite the high percentage of this group among the population at large), Mahmoud was rapidly promoted up the officer corps; in less than four years he had moved from lieutenant to lieutenant colonel, and in mid-1976 he was named to the key post of minister of justice in the Félix Malloum (q.v.) military regime. With the fall of N'Djamena to northern forces, Mahmoud had to choose sides between the two northern contenders. He opted for Goukouni (q.v.) and joined the military leadership of the latter's FAP (q.v.). He died in Abéché in 1980 in a skirmish between the FAP and Habré's (q.v.) troops.

MAI. Title adopted by the Sefuwa (q.v.) lineage of the Magumi (q.v.) clan that founded the kingdom of Kanem and later the Kanem-Bornu Empire (q.v.). Regarded as holy and omnipotent even after their conversion to Islam, the *mais* were shielded from their publics by an opaque screen. Their power declined dramatically with the onset of the Fulani (q.v.) invasions of the nineteenth century and Al-Kanemi's (q.v.) rise to de facto rulership over Bornu. In 1840 Umar al-Kanemi (q.v.) officially abolished the old dynasty and the Sefuwa claim to the throne. (See also BORNU.)

MAKKI, SALEH. Political leader and former cabinet minister. Makki, who is the leader of the Union des Forces Démocratiques (UFD) (q.v.), was briefly minister of animal husbandry in 1992.

MALBRANT, RENE (1903–1961). Veterinarian, colonial administrator, and early French politician in Chad. Born on March 8, 1903, and established in Chad since 1927 as a colonial veterinarian (through 1938), Malbrant moved to the AEF (q.v.) capital of Brazzaville to become head of Stockbreeding Services for the AEF federation. During the Second World War he rallied to the Free French cause and later benefited from this. He played an important role in the early political life of Chad, being elected to various posts from the first electoral college (see DOUBLE ELECTORAL COLLEGE). He served for 15 years as Chad's deputy to the French National Assembly, and by the time of his death in 1961 he had written some 50 specialized articles and books.

MALLAH, IBRAHIM. Vice president of the Forces Armées Occidentales (FAO) (q.v.) rebel force, part of which is still operating in the
western part of Chad.

MALLAM (MALLAMAI, plural). Islamic prayer leaders, teachers, and
counselors. As many as 10 percent of the Muslims in Chadian cities
consider themselves as *mallamai* and attach this prefix to their names.
They are experts on soothsaying, charm-making, numerology, theol-
ogy, Sharia law, and Muslim traditions and history. Frequently traveling from village to village, they preside over various ceremonies
and receive alms or payment in kind for their services. The term
comes from the Arabic for scholar or teacher but is often used very
loosely.

MALLOUM, ELOI BAIHON. Minister of mines, energy, and oil. A
leader of the southern CSNPD (q.v.) rebellion headed by Lt. Ketté
(q.v.), after the peace treaty negotiated with Idriss Déby (q.v.), Malloum
was one of two new CSNPD members integrated into the cabinet.

MALLOUM N'GAKOUTOU BEY'NDI, FELIX (General) (1932–).
Former president of Chad, minister of defense and veteran affairs, and
president of the Conseil Supérieur Militaire (CSM) (q.v.). Born in Sarh
on September 10, 1932, to a Sara father and a northern mother, Malloum (as he is usually called) was educated locally and at Bongor, following which he obtained military training at the Ecole Général
Leclerc in Brazzaville. In November 1952 he left the Congo with the
rank of sergeant and attended the Frejus military academy in France.
He then saw action in Indochina (1953–55), returned for more courses
at Frejus and St. Maixient, where he also received paratrooper training.
As lieutenant he saw further action in Algeria, and he returned to Chad
in August 1961. Malloum then rapidly rose up the ranks of Chad's new
national army, becoming captain in 1962, and then deputy chief of
staff. Suspended for three months in 1966 (on Tombalbaye's [q,v.] orders), he was later reinstated and in 1968 he was promoted directly to
the rank of colonel. He commanded the Chadian forces in their operations against the rebellion in Kanem, Guéra, and Chari-Baguirmi and
was for a time head of Tombalbaye's military cabinet, in charge of national defense and veterans' affairs. For several years the army's
strongman, despite his lower rank, Malloum replaced the purged General Doumro (q.v.) in December 1971 as chief of staff of the army and
on October 2, 1972, was named overall commander of Chad's armed
forces. He was promoted to general in January 1973 but soon fell afoul
of President Tombalbaye and was placed under house arrest on June
24, 1973, for "political sorcery." Tried for his role in the Black Sheep

plot (q.v.), Malloum's light sentence—and the defense's request for a retrial due to judicial errors—highly antagonized Tombalbaye. When the 1975 coup d'état erupted, Malloum was promptly released from prison, reassumed his rank in the armed forces, and became head of state and president of the Conseil Supérieur Militaire. One of his first acts once in power was an appeal to the northern rebel leadership to lay down their arms and work together with the new regime for the creation of a better Chad. The regime scored a major triumph when the derde (q.v.) of the Toubou (q.v.) agreed to return from self-imposed exile in Libya, while Moubi (q.v.) rebels in the eastern part of the country rallied to the new regime. Though suspected by Tombalbaye of having contacts with FROLINAT's (q.v.) Dr. Abba Siddick (q.v.) and being sympathetic to Siddick's goals, FROLINAT's response to the plea for an end to the civil war was negative; indeed, Malloum was the main target of a grenade attack on the first anniversary parade of the 1975 coup.

A dramatic last-ditch attempt to preserve a measure of Sara hegemony in Chad saw Malloum bring Hissène Habré (q.v.) into the premiership. Since Habré was not content with the shadow of power alone, the experiment was doomed from the outset, and as fighting between the two leaders erupted in the capital, Goukouni's (q.v.) troops marched in from the north unopposed. With the fall of the capital to the north, the process of hammering out a new balance of power between the north and the south commenced. As symbol of the defeated south, Malloum had to go; he went into exile, first to Nigeria, and then to France, where he maintains a residence.

MAMADOU, GABRIEL (1933–). Former prefect of Biltine. Born in 1933 in Sarh, Mamadou was trained as an educator and in 1959 served as principal of a school in N'Djamena. After advanced studies in Paris at the Institut des Hautes Etudes d'Outre-Mer (IHEOM), he joined the administration as prefect of Biltine (1963). After six years of loyal service to Tombalbaye (q.v.) in that sensitive post, Mamadou was transferred to the capital as director of the Sûreté Nationale (q.v.). The 1975 coup d'état cut short his career. Reassigned to technical duties in the Ministry of Interior, Mamadou relocated to Moundou with the fall of N'Djamena in 1978. Until 1982 he was active in the civil administration of Colonel Kamougoué (q.v.) in the southern préfectures. He continued serving in several administrative posts in the south, and he is currently in charge of the blood bank of the Red Cross.

MANANI, ADOUM RAKHIS. A former key lieutenant of Ahmat Acyl (q.v.) trained in southern Libya. The military strategist of the rebellious eastern group, Manani assumed leadership of the Conseil Démocratique de la Révolution (CDR) (q.v.) after Acyl's death in 1981, though he had to cede primacy to Acheikh Ibn Oumar (q.v.). When the movement split into three in 1986 and 1987 over Acheikh's proposal for rallying to N'Djamena, Manani became its secretary-general in Goukouni's GUNT (qq.v.) and replaced Acheikh as minister of defense in Goukouni's cabinet-in-exile in Bardai, becoming GUNT's (then largely irrelevant) second ranking leader. He retained with him 1,000 of the CDR armed complement. Some 500 troops followed Acheikh into reconciliation with Habré (q.v.), and some 500 remained loyal to the die-hard CDR, now under Dr. Moctar Moussa (q.v.). Manani rallied to Déby (q.v.) when the latter seized power in 1990.

MANDA see PARC NATIONAL DE MANDA

MANDJAFFA. Currently a small village, Mandjaffa is of significant historical interest as the Baguirmi kingdom's (q.v.) second most important city. The town was conquered by Rabah's (q.v.) forces in 1883 after a five-month siege.

MANDOUL VALLEY DEVELOPMENT PLAN. Agricultural modernization project under the French Bureau pour le Développement de la Production Agricole (BDPA), which had previously completed a plan (1962–69) in the central-eastern region of Chad. The Mandoul Valley project involves the southern area west of Sarh and east of Koumra (in the Moyen-Chari préfecture) and is bounded by the Bahr Sara and Pendé Rivers. The region of 11,400 square kilometers (4,400 square miles) has a cotton company (with low levels of productivity) and a high population density of 17.5 per square kilometer. After a number of preliminary studies, an integrated two-phased program of rural modernization was initiated for the area's 200,000 people. The first phase was completed in 1969; funded by the Fonds d'Aide et de Coopération (FAC) (q.v.), the project obtained satisfactory results in cotton harvests, stemming from earlier sowing of seed and better tending of the crop. Indeed, the yields achieved at the time were the highest in all of Chad. Diversification of crops (in favor of rice) also proceeded in the interim. The second phase, calling for the vaccination of cattle, cadre-formation, intensified rice cultivation, and a measure of mechanization, was a failure in many respects; rice production, for example, was barely 20 percent of what was anticipated in the BDPA plan.

MANGALME TAX RIOTS. Major antigovernment tax riots in 1965 in the village of Mangalmé (population 1,200) in the Batha Préfecture.

The riots erupted as a consequence of crass government mismanagement and marked the start of the general rebellion in Chad. According to President Tombalbaye (q.v.), the rioting in Mangalmé (500 kilometers [310 miles] east of N'Djamena) were due to "a misunderstanding about taxes"; in reality, the series of riots—which for several months the government did not even acknowledge had happened—were the result of Moubi (q.v.) frustrations with the administrative abuses of power on the part of the civil service in the area, the brutal collection of taxes up to three times the decreed rate by corrupt officials, and the haughty attitudes of petty functionaries posted to the "savage" east. The most serious upheaval occurred on November 1, 1965, and by the time government reinforcements arrived there were some 500 people dead, including the local National Assembly deputy, the director of the cabinet of the minister of interior, and eight other officials. After the riots spontaneous jacquerie erupted throughout the préfecture and in 1966 spread into neighboring regions, including Ouadai. Until mid-1971 the entire east was in constant turmoil and unsafe for travelers despite the 1969 establishment in nearby Mongo (in Guéra Préfecture) of the headquarters of the French Mission de Réforme Administrative (q.v.) and military aid mission. Only in January 1971 was a "peace treaty" negotiated with Moubi rebels, who then were integrated into the Chadian military forces. Intermittent unrest continued, however, and many of the revolts in eastern Chad have affected this region.

MANGUE, AHMED (1921–1961). Former deputy and cabinet minister. Though originally elected to the Conseil Représentatif (q.v.) in 1947 as a UDT (q.v.) deputy from Logone, Mangué joined forces with Gabriel Lisette's PPT (qq.v.) and was reelected in 1957 and 1959 on that ticket. In 1957 he served as PPT delegate to the AEF (q.v.) Grand Council in Brazzaville and was appointed—against Jean Baptiste's (q.v.) strong objections—to the OCRS (q.v.). Mangué joined the cabinet for the first time in June 1959 as minister of interior. In the subsequent hectic months of Chad's provisional governments (q.v.) he also served as minister of health and social affairs and as minister of education. Considered one of the rising stars of the PPT, Mangué died in an airplane accident in 1961. A secondary school is named after him in Sarh.

MANGUE, ISSA. Administrator and former diplomat. Mangué served as director of the Sûreté Nationale (q.v.) (September 1961 to March 1963), and as consul (March 1963 to April 1964) and permanent representative (April 1964 to February 1965) to Cameroon. Since then he has occupied a large number of administrative posts, including director of finance at the Ministry of Finance (1965–69) and technical counselor and comptroller at the Ministry of Interior (1969–75).

MANUFACTURE DE CIGARETTES DU TCHAD (MCT). Joint company founded in 1968 in Moundou to manufacture cigarettes. The government has a small (15 percent) share in the company, which is capitalized at 288 million CFA francs.

MAO. Historic town in Kanem, capital of the Alifa (q.v.) of Mao, of the Mao souspréfecture, and of the Kanem Préfecture. The souspréfecture encompasses 15,000 square kilometers (5,800 square miles), with a population of 40,000 people, giving it the low population density of 2.6 per square kilometer. The Alifas of Mao are of Dalatawa (q.v.) descent, tracing their origins from the Bornuan conqueror of Kanem in the seventeenth century, and are the traditional leaders in Kanem, commanding the loyalty of the Kanembu ethnic group. Oil deposits in the area and the construction of a small oil refinery are expected slowly to transform what has been until now a remote and undeveloped region.

MARABE. Important though small Sara religious center in the souspréfecture of Kyabé in the Moyen-Chari Préfecture.

MARAMBAYE, SILAS (1938–). Cabinet director of the minister of agriculture. Born in Bébalem in 1938, Marambayé was trained as a teacher, and he later became an educational inspector. Shortly after independence he was attached to the Ministry of Tourism, Water, and Forests (1960–62) in a technical capacity, and in 1963 he joined the Ministry of Agriculture as *chef de cabinet*. He served in that capacity until 1969, when he was nominated and elected PPT (q.v.) deputy to the National Assembly. After the 1975 coup Marambayé was attached to the Ministry of Interior as consultant.

MARBA. Southern ethnic group, part of a larger constellation of similar groups, including the Massa and Musey, and sometimes regarded as only a fraction of the latter. The Marba inhabit part of the Tandjilé Préfecture (specifically Kélo souspréfecture) and are separated from the rump of the Musey, consequent to chiefly and lineage disputes. (See also MUSEY.)

MARGAI. Deities (much studied by Westerners) of the Hadjeray (q.v.) in the Mongo region in Guéra Préfecture. The origin of the word is uncertain. The spirits are seen as living in various inanimate objects in specific locations, usually the heights of mountains and hills. Their powers are directed to controlling natural events such as rainfall, disease, and harvests and in providing individual and collective (village) protection from calamities. Miniature *margai* prayer areas are still found in many villages in Guéra even though the practice is allegedly dying out in the wake of the recent conversion of the population to Islam. In these prayer areas symbolic offerings are made to the *margai* for the protection of the village or, in the case of a "personal" *margai*, the individual compound. The chiefs of the villages are the *margai* priests, as is anyone who may be at that moment possessed by the spirits. (See also HADJERAY; KINGA.)

MARIA THERESA DOLLAR. Popular currency in Chad during the precolonial era and the first two decades of French rule in the country. Also, currency of the territories conquered by Rabah (q.v.) prior to his defeat by France. In was minted in Vienna and came into the area from Morocco. In certain regions (notably Ouadai) the French franc was virtually unknown until the 1930s; in Ouadai the Maria Theresa dollar and the Egyptian pound were, with great difficulty, replaced by the franc. Indeed, for the first 20 years of French rule in the country, France continued to import these dollars in order to be able to purchase local produce and pay for services. Also of note is that in Bornu and the other kingdoms of the region, cowrie shells and beads were not accepted as currency as they were along the African coast and immediate interior.

MARO. Small but very important trade center and traditional village, headquarters of the souspréfecture of the same name in the préfecture of Moyen-Chari.

MASALIT. Ethnic group found in Ouadai (especially along the Sudan border), originating in Darfur (q.v.), where they are found in much larger numbers. There are two branches of the group—the Masalit el Hauch, found along the border, and the Masalit el Batha, who reside along the Batha River. There are approximately 67,000 Masalit in Ouadai, mostly in the Ardé district. They speak a language that is related to though different from Bura-Mabang (q.v.). Their villages are very poor, and they do not own cattle. Though converted to Islam, the Masalit have retained many pre-Islamic practices. Many work in Sudan, some supporting the FLT (q.v.) rebel movement of Hassan Ahmed Moussa (q.v.), and later some of the other anti-N'Djamena movements that sprang up there.

MASIK see KORANIC SCHOOLS

MASSA (also BANANA). Southern ethnic group found in the Mayo-Kebbi Préfecture and especially in the Bongor souspréfecture. Possibly of Nilotic origin, the Massa came to Chad from the south up the Chari River some 200 years ago and installed themselves in small village groups. They are closely related to the Toubouri (q.v.) to the east and south. Extensively raided in the past by slave-hunting parties from Bornu and plundered in the nineteenth century by the Fulani (q.v.) sultanate of Adamaoua. Farther to the north the rise of the Baguirmi kingdom (q.v.) in the seventeenth century displaced a Massa clan that migrated to the south. There are currently an estimated 85,000 Massa in Chad.

The Massa do not live in towns or villages but in individual extended-family habitations. They are excellent stockbreeders and fishermen. Inhabiting regions that are inundated a good part of the year by the Logone River, and hence useless for cotton cultivation, they have been spared the abuses associated with the cultivation of that crop in Chad. Relatively untouched by modernization, the Massa are animists, have little contact with state organs, and have not pursued education very avidly. (See also MUSEY.)

MASSAKORY. Souspréfecture in the préfecture of Chari-Baguirmi with administrative headquarters in the village of the same name. The souspréfecture covers an area of 22,000 square kilometers (8,500 square miles), with 55,000 people; the village counts some 3,000 inhabitants.

MASSENYA (also MASSENIA). Former capital of the Baguirmi kingdom (q.v.). Currently the small town in the Chari-Baguirmi Préfecture bearing this name serves as the administrative headquarters of the 27,000–square kilometer (10,425–square mile) souspréfecture of the same name, with a population of 68,000 people and a population density of 2.5 per square kilometer.

Massenya is located 175 kilometers (110 miles) southeast of N'Djamena on the Ergig River, and the remains of the old Massenya are found some 20 kilometers (12 miles) to the northwest. The "current" Massenya is in reality the expanded village of Chekna (q.v.). Founded, according to legend, by a Kinga (q.v.) clan allied to Fulani (q.v.) merchants at the beginning of the sixteenth century, the town's name comes from "Mass"-"Ena," the latter part the name of a Fulani girl who sold milk on the site of the settlement. The town was attacked numerous times by various invading armies (see BAGUIRMI KINGDOM) and in 1871 was razed by Ouadai troops. It was again destroyed during the ravages of Rabah (q.v.) in 1898.

MAYE MOUSSA, ALIFA ZEZERTI (1937–). Educator and former cabinet minister. Born in Mao on September 17, 1937, of the reigning lineage, Mayé Moussa was educated locally and worked as an instructor in various localities from 1955 to 1963. In 1963 he joined the administration, and in April 1966 he was appointed minister of Saharan affairs, a new post. He served in this capacity through 1969, following which he returned to private life.

MAYO-KEBBI PREFECTURE. Important southern préfecture encompassing 30,100 square kilometers (11,600 square miles) and a population of 855,000 (Chad's largest), giving it also Chad's second highest population density of 28.4 per square kilometer. The region has its administrative headquarters at Bongor (q.v.) and is divided into the souspréfectures of Bongor, Fianga, Gounou-Gaya, Léré, Pala, and four *postes administratifs*. The bulk of the population is a variety of Sara and Sara-related subgroups, Massa (q.v.), Moundang (q.v.), and, near the Cameroon border, N'gambayé (q.v.) and Fulani (q.v.). For years the region was under direct French military control, with civilian rule being established only in 1921. On November 4, 1911, part of the area (bordering the Logone River) was ceded to Germany (and attached to the latter's then-colony of Cameroon) in exchange for a French protectorate over Morocco. During the First World War these regions were regained and reincorporated into the Chad colony.

Mayo-Kebbi is a major center of cotton production (Cotontchad [q.v.] has five factories in the area) and also produces groundnuts, rice, and millet. The préfecture is crisscrossed by a large number of roads, though most are impassable during the rainy season. The main arteries connect Bongor with N'Djamena (in use from mid-November to mid-July) and Bongor-Laï (December to July), while the Logone River (q.v.) is also navigable (between Bongor and N'Djamena) during the months of August and December. The préfecture has tourist potential and abundant wildlife, including elephants and panthers.

MBAI (also MBAYE). One of the Sara (q.v.) subgroups in southern Chad. The Mbaï are localized in the Doba and Moïssala regions, in the Logone Orientale Préfecture. Little is known definitively of their origins; though not Muslim, their traditions refer to a Nilotic origin. Linguists have also pointed out similarities between the Sara dialects and those spoken in Sudan's Bahr-el-Ghazal region.

The Mbaï were the target of numerous slave raids from Baguirmi (q.v.) and from the Fulani (q.v.) emirates (especially of Mben-Mben) in Cameroon. Formerly a large number of subgroups were linked together under the Mbaï category, swelling the size of the ethnic group to around 600,000. Currently most of these subgroups

(Gor, Ngambayé, Bedjond, etc.) are regarded as distinct from the Mbaï, whose number has thus "fallen" to barely 60,000. A large number of Chad's top civil and military leaders are Mbaï, including General Malloum, Colonel Kamougoué, and Toura Gaba (qq.v.).

MBAI-BEDIONDO See BEDJOND

MBAIBIKELE, NGARINA. Former political leader, head of the Mouvement Démocratique Tchadien (MDT) (q.v.), which was integrated into Hissène Habré's UNIR (q.v.).

MBAILEMDANA, N'DEINGAR (CHRISTOPHE N'DEINGAR) (1943–). Former president of the Banque des Etats de l'Afrique Centrale (BEAC) (q.v.) and cabinet minister. Born on February 14, 1943, in Beyama in the Logone Orientale préfecture. Mbailemdana studied in Doba and Sarh and finished his secondary education at the Lycée Félix Eboué in N'Djamena. He then continued his studies at the Ecole Nationale d'Administration (ENA) (1963–65) and at the Institut des Hautes Etudes d'Outre-Mer (IHEOM) in Paris (1967–68). With the Chadian civil service as of 1965, Mbailemdana was appointed deputy director of the Ministry of Health after his return from Paris in 1968. In 1970 he was named financial comptroller and later government commissioner to the Cour Spéciale de Justice and to the Commission d'Enquête Parlementaire. An extremely talented and upwardly mobile technocrat, Mbailemdana was brought into François Tombalbaye's (q.v.) cabinet in October 1973 as minister of finance, succeeding to the post of president of the BEAC in January 1974. Mbailemdana was temporarily involved in the southern quasi-secessionist movement of the "*codos*" (q.v.), and then was reintegrated into Hissène Habré's (q.v.) government in April 1988 as minister of finance, serving until Habré was ousted.

MBAITOUGARA, NADJALDO MADLONGAR (1949–). Civil administrator. Born in 1949 and educated in public administration and finance in Paris, Mbaitougara returned to N'Djamena in 1970 and was appointed head of the Budget Office. He was transferred in 1972 to head the department of economic control, personnel, and recruitment in the Ministry of the Civil Service, and in 1977 he was appointed head of the department of industry in the Ministry of the Civil Service. He served in a similar array of top administrative posts under Habré, and he published a number of books, including one on Chad's foreign policy.

MBAMI, YOUSSOUF MBOUDOU. Former diplomat and cabinet minister. Mbami served under Hissène Habré (q.v.) in a number of key posts, including ambassador to Nigeria until October 1989, and minister of higher education between that date and Habré's ouster. After the rise of Idriss Déby (q.v.) Mbami bounced back into the cabinet and in 1995 was minister of commerce.

MBANG. Title of the hereditary kings of the Baguirmi kingdom (q.v.). A quasi-sacred personage who was never directly seen except through a screen, the *mbang* was chosen from among the male members of the preceding king and enthroned after a 40-day retreat. The title *mbang* is also a fairly common one for chiefs of Barma (q.v.) and other ethnic groups in the region. In 1915 the *mbang*'s powers were greatly curtailed by the French administration, with the office-holder becoming essentially a simple *chef de canton*.

MBOUM. Ethnic group in southern Chad, part of larger settlements found in the Central African Republic and in Cameroon. The Mboum, numbering around 60,000 in Chad, are today greatly influenced by the neighboring Ngambayé (especially the chiefdom of Bessao), whose initiation ceremonies (Lao, q.v.), language, and names they have adopted. This cultural assimilation is linked with the strong spread of the Protestant faith in their region.

MEAR, ADOLPHE (1929–). High-level administrator. Born in Fada on April 29, 1929, and educated locally and in France at the Institut des Hautes Etudes d'Outre-Mer (IHEOM), Mear has occupied a series of top administrative posts, including deputy director and later director of economics and transportation (1965–71), and director of public works (1971–76), both in the Ministry of Economy. Briefly arrested after the guerrilla attack on N'Djamena in 1972, Mear has also been president of the Banque Tchadienne de Crédit et de Dépôts (q.v.) and has served on the board of the Société Textile du Tchad (q.v.). He has been in retirement since the mid-1980s.

MEDELA, MOUSSA (1955–). Leader of a faction in the Third Liberation Army (q.v.), which later adopted the name of Forces Armées Occidentales (FAO) (q.v.), and since 1991 fighting against the regime of Idriss Déby (q.v.)—intermittently with remnant forces of Hissène Habré—under the label of the MDD (q.v.). The FAO faction split from the control of Aboubaker Abderahmane (q.v.) over the latter's overly pro-Nigerian policies. Medela was appointed minister of public health in the November 1979 GUNT (q.v.) government and served in that capacity until 1981. Anti-Libyan and a supporter of the MPN (q.v.) of Doungou Kemto (q.v), he was in self-exile in Sudan for several years starting in April 1981, though he and his faction were affiliated with Goukouni's Gouvernement de Salut National (q.v.) in B.E.T.

MEDERSA. Muslim secondary schools for those completing the Koranic school (q.v.), or *masik,* curriculum. Popular in Chad since the 1950s, the Medersa offer a variety of secular and religious fields of study under local and (mostly) Sudanese teachers.

MEHARISTES. Camel corps. Extensively used by the French, in small units, to patrol Kanem and B.E.T., with headquarters in Moussoro. After independence the (largely Toubou) Garde Nomade (q.v.) continued the Méhariste tradition and function until it rebelled in the mid-1970s.

MELFI. Small but important town and market of 3,500 people in the souspréfecture of the same name in Guéra Préfecture.

MERRISE. Spirits distilled from dates, found in the Toubou (q.v.) areas in northern Chad, Niger, and parts of Algeria.

MIMI. Isolated, little-studied ethnic group, speaking a language that cannot be affiliated to any of the established family groups, found mostly in Ouadai. References to the Mimi in Ouadai come up in texts dating from the sixteenth century, suggesting a lengthy presence in that region.

MINISTER-RESIDENT IN BONGOR. Proconsul plenipotentiary post created in 1960 by President François Tombalbaye (q.v.) and originally filled by Minister of Economics and Transportation Aboudiguene Baba Hassane (q.v.). The post was created in order better to control the Logone region, at the time under the influence of lieutenants of the recently purged Gabriel Lisette (q.v.). The Logone Préfecture was later reorganized into three separate préfectures.

MIRGHANIYA. Small Islamic religious order that penetrated Chad from the Sudan. (See also ISLAM; RELIGIOUS ORDERS.)

MISIRIE. Nomadic Djoheina (q.v.) Arab group of clans found in the Ouadai Préfecture, divided traditionally into the "black" and "red" Misirié. Estimated in 1984 at over 110,000, the large majority of them are concentrated in the Oum-Hadjer district. Particularly aggressive and combative, they have engaged in bloody battles with neighboring groups periodically—right through the 1970s—leaving hundreds dead. The Misirié were heavily recruited by the various movements operating out of the east against Tombalbaye (q.v.) in N'Djamena, in part because they would fight for the booty, and later some of them joined other rebel movements that emerged in the east. (See also ARABS.)

MISKINE, ABDERAMANE IZZO. One of Idriss Déby's (q.v.) key cabinet members, and a powerful figure until 1995. Appointed in December 1991 as minister of the civil service and labor, Miskine was transferred in May 1992 to serve as government secretary-general, a post reconfirmed through several shuffles. In May 1994 he was appointed minister of interior, to be finally dropped from the government and appointed to a prefectural post in May 1995.

MISKINE, IDRISS (1948–1984). Former foreign minister of Chad. Born in N'Djamena of Hadjeray (q.v.) origins (from Guéra), Miskine first came to prominence when he joined the Malloum-Habré (qq.v.) government as Habré's minister of transport. With the falling apart of the subsequent Goukouni-Habré GUNT (q.v.) government, Miskine remained loyal to Habré and joined him in self-exile. A brilliant tactician, he was one of the chief architects of Habré's stunning comeback and one of the FAN (q.v.) commanders who led the troops into N'Djamena and later into the southern préfectures. Miskine was appointed minister of foreign affairs in 1982, but he died in January 1984, allegedly from complications from malaria. Rumors of his "unnatural" death were rife, however, especially after a purge of Hadjeray in government began, leading to the estrangement of the Hadjeray from Habré. After Habré was ousted it was confirmed that Miskine had been poisoned by the regime's specialized assassination squad, "The Vultures," in Habré's DDS (q.v.) secret police, headed by Ismail Bal (q.v.) (former prefect of Salamat), which had also been responsible for Ahmat Acyl's (q.v.) "accidental death" in 1982. Miskine was assassinated allegedly because he was the only person of stature who could replace Habré, and because he was allegedly negotiating with the CDR (q.v.) in Paris, which threatened Habré at the time.

MISSION DE REFORME ADMINISTRATIVE (MRA). French mission of administrative experts dispatched to Chad in April 1969 (in conjunction with French military assistance), with the aim of quelling the rebellion in the country and setting up a looser administrative hierarchy that would avoid the problems inherent to the old one. The MRA was empowered to enact major reforms—several of which were strenuously opposed by President François Tombalbaye (q.v.)—in order to soothe local complaints of governmental mismanagement. Operating essentially in the four central and eastern préfectures, in late

1970 the MRA fielded 31 experts in the countryside, with a team of 16 in N'Djamena. The group was originally headed by Pierre Lami (q.v.), who was replaced, at Tombalbaye's request, by Henri Paillard in June 1970. As part of the reforms, traditional authorities in the regions concerned were given back the powers they had had prior to 1967, and the sultans of Ouadai, Kanem, and Baguirmi were granted their former right to collect government taxes in exchange for their tithe. Also, Conseils de Préfecture (q.v.) were created, presided over by the local prefect and including 12 notables chosen for their competence and prestige, and the administration of justice was in part returned to local chiefs. Finally, the MRA recommended that the Toubou (q.v.) in the B.E.T. be allowed to forgo the payment of taxes, due to the ravages of the civil war and the effects of the Sahelian drought. The MRA also assisted in the setting up of new administrative structures, screening local government officials (and training or guiding existing ones) as well as recommending sites for the digging of wells to assist the drought-affected regions.

MOGOUMBAYE, LEON (1938–). Educator, unionist, and former assembly deputy. Born in 1938 in Dobara-Moundou, educated at a local Jesuit school and in France, Mogoumbayé entered the educational system in 1956 and taught in a number of local schools until 1967. In 1966 he was elected to the municipal council of Moundou and as second deputy major of the town. A year later he became second deputy secretary of the PPT (q.v.) in Logone Occidentale, and in 1969 he was elected to the National Assembly. There he served on the Political Bureau of the organ and as fourth vice president of the assembly.

MOISSALA. Souspréfecture with headquarters in the village of the same name, part of the préfecture of Moyen-Chari. The souspréfecture encompasses 10,000 square kilometers (3,860 square miles), with a population of 90,000 people. It is the center of the Mbaï ethnic group and capital of a chiefdom dominated for 32 years (until 1969) by the powerful Chief Tafala.

MONGO. Administrative headquarters of the souspréfecture of the same name and of the Guéra Préfecture, some 520 kilometers (322 miles) from N'Djamena. The town of 8,000 was also the headquarters of the French military assistance mission dispatched in 1969 to help quell the internal rebellion in Chad. Mongo is 153 kilometers (95 miles) from Ati (q.v.) and 372 kilometers (231 miles) from Abéché (q.v.).

MORBAYE, JACQUES see IDABAYE, IMBAI

MORTCHA. Rocky semidesert land between the 12th and 17th parallels, bounded in the east by the hills of Abéché and in the west by the Bahr-el-Ghazal (q.v.). The area is the prime nomadization terrain of the Mahamid (q.v.), who both in the precolonial and in the contemporary eras have had bloody clashes with the Toubou (q.v.) to the north. During the civil war in Chad the area was contested by various armies.

MOUBI. Ethnic group found mostly east of Abou Telfan in the Oum-Hadjer district, divided into two major subgroups—part of the general Hadjeray (q.v.) aggregation of tribes. Estimates of Chad's Moubi are subject to wide variations, with the 1964 census figure at 25,000. The Moubi speak a Daju (q.v.) dialect and, though converted to Islam, they retain many pre-Islamic beliefs and cults similar to those of the Kinga (q.v.) in the same region. In 1965 and 1966 the Moubi of Mangalmé, maladministered by the central government, revolted under indigenous leadership (see MANGALME TAX RIOTS). In 1970 and 1971 their leaders rallied again to the central government, but this allegiance was later shattered, and Moubi areas remained unsettled to this day.

MOUGNAN, ANDREW (1932–1973). Former deputy and founder of the Mouvement Révolutionnaire Tchadien (MRT). Born in Logone on August 18, 1932, of the Gambayé ethnic group (which disputed Tombalbaye's [q.v.] political leadership), Mougnan was trained as an agrarian technician. In April 1959 he was elected president of the Syndicat des Travailleurs Agricoles and vice president of the Cultural Center of Moundou. Very popular in his home region, he was elected PPT (q.v.) deputy to the National Assembly in November 1959, where he served on the Education and Arts Committee. In the assembly he strenuously opposed the purge of Gabriel Lisette (q.v.) and presented an unsuccessful motion of no confidence against the Tombalbaye regime. Increasingly disgruntled with Tombalbaye's conservative policies—and specifically with Tombalbaye himself, who had been his instructor in the past—Mougnan founded the MRT and was arrested soon after, to be interned in the far northern B.E.T. in 1962. Very popular in the south, and hence a major threat to Tombalbaye's paramountcy (indeed, a voice from the past, in many ways), Mougnan was formally amnestied in 1971 but died soon after, again in a Tombalbaye prison, allegedly tortured to death.

MOUKHTAR, MOUKHTAR BACHAR (1948–). One of Hissène Habré's (q.v.) political prisoners whose cause was particularly espoused by Amnesty International. A Maba (q.v.) from Abéché, and educated as a teacher, Moukhtar taught history before being appointed director general of education in 1985. He was later transferred to become secretary of state for agriculture before falling afoul of the regime, for reasons unclear, in July 1988. He was imprisoned at the notorious Camp du 13 Août (or as since referred to as Camp des Martyrs) and was only released after Habré's ouster in 1990.

MOULOUI. Small ethnic sliver found in the Mayo-Kebbi Préfecture (*cantons* Katoa and Mousgou). A large number of this group, which has been much studied by scholars, have migrated to N'Djamena. Their territory is normally totally inundated by water during the rainy season, making normal agricultural activity impossible.

MOUNDANG. One of the principal ethnic groups in southwest Chad. The Moundang are related to the Sara (q.v.) and are found in the Mayo-Kebbi Préfecture, especially in the Léré souspréfecture. They number about 100,000, a minority of which resides in neighboring Cameroon, from which they came to Chad in several waves. The town of Léré (q.v.) is their political and traditional capital and home of the *goléré* (q.v.), their chief or king. The Moundang are great farmers and grow cotton and millet while also raising cattle (tended by Fulani [q.v.]) for slaughter on ceremonial occasions. They are organized into totemic clans with no noble clans but with a king whose powers have by now been greatly eroded. They have been strongly influenced by the Fulani kingdom of Yola (center of the Adamaoua Mountains in Cameroon), whose advance into Chad they successfully checked. So strong was the Fulani influence upon Moundang development that colonial administrators at the outset referred to the *goléré* (mistakenly) as the *lamidu* (a Fulani chiefly title) of the Moundang. (Moundang traditional officers do, however, carry many Fulani titles.) One of the best-known Moundang on Chad's national scene was Gountchomé Sahoulba (q.v.), briefly prime minister of Chad in 1959.

MOUNDOU. Chad's third largest city, with a population of 39,600 (1972), which leaped to 65,000 after the fall of N'Djamena in 1979, and to an estimated 114,000 in 1994. The town is the administrative capital of both the Moundou souspréfecture and of the Logone Occidentale Préfecture. Founded in 1924, Moundou mushroomed tremendously during the Second World War, rapidly became Chad's second largest city in 1959, with 25,000 people to Fort-Archambault's 18,000, before falling behind the latter in the 1960s. Moundou is located near the Logone Occidentale branch of the Logone River (q.v.), which links it for several months during the year with Bongor and N'Djamena. After the de facto separation of Chad into two distinct halves, with the fall of N'Djamena to Goukouni's (q.v.) troops,

Moundou became the seat of Colonel Kamougoué's (q.v.) Comité Permanent du Sud (q.v.), the de facto government of the southern préfectures. Moundou finally fell under N'Djamena's control but only after the victory of Hissène Habré (q.v.) over Goukouni. The town was delivered to Habré by dissident FAT (q.v.) units, disgruntled with Kamougoué, on September 4, 1982.

MOUNGAR, FIDELE (DR.) (1948–). Former prime minister of Chad. Born in 1948, educated in France, and a surgeon by profession, Dr. Moungar served as head of the surgery department at Perrone Hospital before returning to N'Djamena in 1992. He was appointed to Idriss Déby's (q.v.) cabinet as minister of education in May 1992, serving on through the Conférence Nationale (q.v.) as head of the Action Tchadienne pour l'Unité et le Socialisme (ACTUS) (q.v.) political party. He was elected prime minister by the conference on April 6, 1993, but was unable to hold onto power in the divided interim national assembly since he could not in a timely fashion bring about the elections he was specifically charged with. He was ousted when President Déby manipulated the assembly to vote against him.

MOURDIA. Small nomadic and very heterogeneous population sliver, speaking Dazaga and assimilated with Daza (q.v.) culture, found in northern Ennedi in B.E.T.

MOUROUM. Sara subgroup found in the Doba (in Logone Orientale) and Läi (in Tandjilé) souspréfectures and encompassing some 70,000 people. In the precolonial era victims of slave raids by the Fulani (q.v.) and the Baguirmi kingdom (q.v.), the Mouroum evaded many such razzias by hiding in caves. Since they were good cultivators, though working on poor soil, the demand of the colonial administration for the planting of cotton on Mouroum lands triggered a spontaneous migration to Bousso. Since then large numbers have joined the Chadian army, the administration, and the Catholic Church.

MOUSGOUM. Ethnic people in the Bongor souspréfecture of the Mayo-Kebbi Préfecture, found squeezed between the Muslim Kotoko (q.v.) to the north and the animist Massa (q.v.) to the south. Their name comes from their chief village—Mousgoum. Though they share common origins with the Massa, they are differentiated by their language, Vouloum. Some 28,000 Mousgoum are found in Chad, with other concentrations across the border in Cameroon. Their traditional capital is Katoa. Though Islamized, they retain many pre-Islamic practices.

MOUSSA, ABDERAHMAN. Veteran diplomat and head of Idriss Déby's (q.v.) CRCR (q.v.) political police. Formerly a diplomat, Moussa was Tombalbaye's (q.v.) ambassador to Sudan and Ethiopia from 1970 to 1975, and he continued in that post after the 1975 coup. Temporarily repatriated to N'Djamena in 1977, he was appointed ambassador to France in March 1982. He was recalled from Paris after Hissène Habré's (q.v.) rise to power, but he refused to vacate his office, regarding GUNT (q.v.) as the legitimate government. No longer accredited to Paris, Moussa remained in the French capital as Goukouni's (q.v.) spokesman until 1988. In that year, with GUNT effectively defunct, Moussa resigned and joined Déby's rebellion, and after Habré was ousted from power in December 1990 he became head of Déby's intelligence service.

MOUSSA, HASSAN AHMED. Leader of the Front de Libération du Tchad (FLT) (q.v.). A local leader of the militantly Muslim Union Générale des Fils du Tchad (UGFT) (q.v.)—which in 1965 set up a political branch named the Mouvement National de Libération du Tchad (MNLT) (q.v.)—Moussa launched an antigovernment rebellion following the Mangalmé tax riots (q.v.). Most of the time based in Sudan, Moussa was temporarily imprisoned in 1966 in Khartoum, which led to the so-called Nyala congress and the creation, by FLT dissidents and some of Abatcha's (q.v.) forces, of FROLINAT (q.v.). The "joint" movement promptly collapsed when Moussa was freed and renounced it, with his group continuing to operate under the name of Front de Libération du Tchad. Supported by small contributions from Chadian workers in Sudan, Saudi Arabia, and Kuwait, and appealing mostly to Maba (q.v.) and Masalit (q.v.) elements, the hit-and-run guerrilla attacks scored some early successes against the poorly organized and underweaponed Chadian armed forces in the area between Abéché and Adré, Moussa's fiefdom. For the greater part of its existence, however, the FLT was mostly moribund, with Moussa rarely daring to cross into Chad. In 1974 and 1975 the movement rallied back to the government fold, marking the de facto end of the FLT rebellion in the east. In April 1977 Moussa announced the final dissolution of the FLT. He himself died in 1979 near Ati, killed by a FAN (q.v.) armed group.

MOUSSA, IBRAHIM. Long-term imam of N'Djamena, one of the few residents of the much-battered city to remain during the bitter fighting in 1980.

MOUSSA, MOCTAR (Dr.). Head of the Conseil Démocratique de la Révolution (CDR) (q.v.) faction after its three-way split, and not reconciled with Hissène Habré (q.v.) in 1988. Dr. Moussa remained in Tripoli, Libya, until 1990, when he rallied to the regime of Idriss Déby (q.v.).

MOUSSA, PAUL (1925–). Early key PPT (q.v.) deputy from Logone. Born in Laï in the Logone on December 18, 1925, and trained as a male nurse, Moussa was an early militant in the south who assured the party's rapid spread. In 1957 he was elected deputy to the legislative assembly and remained in the assembly until 1963, sitting on or chairing a variety of committees. After the events of 1963 Moussa was purged, but benefiting from an amnesty, he bounced back into the civil administration of Logone.

MOUSSA, PIERRE BOLTOUMI (1943–). Civil administrator. Born in 1943 in Mao, and educated at the Lycée Franco-Arabe d'Abéché (q.v.) and in Rennes, France, in agriculture (1961–63); in Paris, in law and economics (1963–66); at the International Institute of Public Administration in Paris (1965–68); and at the Academy of International Law in The Hague (1968–69). When Moussa returned to N'Djamena in 1970 he was appointed director of administrative and financial affairs in the Ministry of Foreign Affairs. In March 1972 he and his cousin, Georges Diguimbayé, were arrested on charges of embezzlement. In 1974 Moussa was reintegrated into the civil service and appointed director of transport in the Ministry of Transport and Communications, serving until 1977. For some time in eclipse, he emerged again in 1979 as director of the Second Division of the Secretariat in the Ministry of Foreign Affairs.

MOUSSAYE, AHMED. Leader of the Forces Armées du Peuple (FAP) (q.v.), not to be confused with Goukouni's Forces Armées Populaires (FAP) (q.v.) which had the same acronym. Moussaye's group was one that rallied to the regime of Hissène Habré (q.v.) in 1986, and he was integrated into Habré's cabinet as minister of housing. In 1988 he was transferred to head the post of secretary of state for public health.

MOUSSEY. Ethnic group, very closely related to the Massa (q.v.), found in the préfecture of Mayo-Kebbi, in the region of Bongor and the plains between the Logone River (q.v.) and the Toubouri depression. They are called the Hoho by some of their neighbors. Their number is estimated at around 180,000, and their language is quite similar to that of the Massa. They own numerous small horses, which they ride without saddles, and they have very picturesque initiation and other dances. Superb farmers, they raise over 10 percent of Chad's cotton harvest.

MOUSSORO. Souspréfecture with administrative headquarters in the village of the same name in the préfecture of Kanem, roughly 240 kilometers (150 miles) north of N'Djamena. The souspréfecture encompasses a population of 70,000, many of whom are seminomadic. The village was the headquarters of Chad's former Toubou (q.v.) Méhariste (q.v.) units and later was the radar headquarters for the French Opération Epervier (q.v.). The village has a large number of Kanembu (q.v.), most of whom relocated there from Mao (q.v.) at the outset of colonial rule in order to distance themselves from the aggressive rule of the Alifa (q.v.) of Mao.

MOUSTAPHA, IDRISS ADOUM (1939?–1979). Former leader of the Third Liberation Army (q.v.) and prime power rival of Aboubaker Abderahmane (q.v.), founder of the small force. In the power tug-of-war after Abderahmane's eclipse, Moustapha lost out to Lol Mahamat Choua (q.v.). He was killed trying to escape to Cameroon after the bitter fighting between his faction and the FAN (q.v.) in N'Djamena in June 1979. Moustapha served as minister of health in the short-lived GUNT (q.v.) government of March 23, 1978, as representative of the MPLT (q.v.).

MOUSTAPHA, MAHAMAT BABA (1952–1982). Administrator and major Chadian author. Born in Bogo, Cameroon, in 1952, of Fulani-Kanuri parents but a Chadian national, Moustapha obtained his education in N'Djamena and entered the Ecole Nationale d'Administration (q.v.) in 1973, receiving his diploma in administrative studies in 1975. Appointed deputy prefect of Chari-Baguirmi, he soon after went to France to obtain a law degree. Despite his youth, Moustapha was, at the time of his untimely death in 1982, a prolific author, with several stage plays to his credit, one of which won him the 1979 African Grand Prix. He died in an accident in Paris on November 1, 1982.

MOUSTAPHA, PHILIPPE (1919–1979). Veteran deputy to the National Assembly. Born in 1919 in Faya-Largeau, Mustapha was elected to the National Assembly in 1957 and remained in it for the next 17 years. He was in particular involved in the assembly's Transport and Economics Committee, which he headed for nearly a decade, building it into his personal fiefdom.

MOUVEMENT DE LA JEUNESSE TCHADIENNE (MJT). In its early phases, an Israeli-trained and staffed group of youth units. Created in the mid-1960s under a 1964 technical cooperation agreement, the MJT was involved in agrarian pilot projects and civic formation. All Israeli advisers left the units when Chad broke diplomatic relations with Israel in 1972. (See also ISRAEL.)

MOUVEMENT D'EMANCIPATION SOCIALE DE L'AFRIQUE NOIRE (MESAN). Small political party active for a few years in the late 1950s and early 1960s. The reigning party of neighboring Central African Republic (and of the latter's Boganda and David Dacko), MESAN campaigned in southern Chad in the May 1959 territorial elections, unallied with any other party in the region. Briefly campaigning also within the URT (q.v.), MESAN merged in 1961 with all the anti-PPT (q.v.) parties into the PNA (q.v.) coalition. Apart from scattered concentrations of support among ethnic groups divided by the Chad-C.A.R. border, MESAN had little impact upon Chadian politics.

MOUVEMENT DEMOCRATIQUE DE LA RENOVATION TCHADIENNE (MDRT). Stillborn opposition party created in Paris by Dr. Outel Bono (q.v.) that largely folded up after Bono's assassination, allegedly by Tombalbaye (q.v.) agents. The party's projected platform included demands for major administrative reforms, the creation of new internal regions of ethnic homogeneity, freedom of speech and of association, and an end to France's neocolonial relationship with Chad. Though opposed to FROLINAT's (q.v.) violent upheaval and armed struggle, the MDRT would have cooperated with that movement in achieving these goals.

MOUVEMENT DEMOCRATIQUE ET SOCIALISTE DU TCHAD (MDST). Southern political party, originally set up on November 15, 1988, in opposition to Hissène Habré (q.v.). Headed by Ahmat Mahamat Saleh (q.v.), it included an array of former cabinet ministers, including one of former president Tombalbaye's sons, Dr. Ngarbaye Tombalbaye (q.v.). In 1992 it was reconstituted as a political party in support of Sara causes, including the recognition of Sara as Chad's third language. At the time headed by Mbainaudo Djomia (q.v.), it was subsequently taken over by Tombalbaye.

MOUVEMENT DEMOCRATIQUE TCHADIEN (MDT). Largely moribund political movement formed on May 31, 1979, at a congress in Bédiondo, near Doba, following the fall of N'Djamena to the troops of Goukouni (q.v.) and Habré (q.v.). The main item in the MDT's platform was the reorganization of Chad along federal autonomous lines. It was headed by Ngarina Mbaibikelé, and later it merged with UNIR (q.v.) after the rise of the Habré regime.

MOUVEMENT DE SALUT NATIONAL DU TCHAD (MOSANAT). Rebel movement set up in 1986 by Lt. Maldoum Bada Abbas (q.v.) after Hissène Habré's (q.v.) liquidation of Foreign Minister Idriss

Miskine (q.v.) and the purge of the Hadjeray (q.v.) elements who had helped him come to power. Based in Guéra and coordinated by a five-man committee, MOSANAT opposed the centralized political system under Habré. Small and localized in their scope of action and unable to secure Libyan support for their cause (separated by Habré's control of Toubou [q.v.] regions to their north) MOSANAT nevertheless attracted to the rebellion a number of other small localized movements opposed to Habré's regime. It was progressively pushed eastward, out of Guéra, by Habré's forces, and linked up in Darfur with Libya's Islamic Legion (q.v.), which was dispatched to aid them in their rebellion against Habré. (See LIBYA.) Other splinter groups there, such as part of the FROLINAT-Originel (q.v.) and the Volcan Army (q.v.), and assistance from Ethiopia further allowed MOSANAT to build up its strength. However, MOSANAT's greatest ally was Idriss Déby (q.v.) after he fled N'Djamena, deserting Habré, who had alienated the Zaghawa (q.v.), another group that had helped Habré come to power in 1982; the Zaghawa-Hadjeray alliance would prove to be invincible. Together the two leaders built up their forces, merging their rebel movements, and in a number of sharp battles in November 1990 they defeated Habré and marched into N'Djamena on December 2, 1990.

MOUVEMENT DU PEUPLE TCHADIEN (MPT). Political party, originally set up by Colonel Kamougoué (q.v.) and then taken over by Major Nadjita Beassomal (q.v.), who rallied behind the regime of Hissène Habré (q.v.). (Not to be confused with the Mouvement Populaire Tchadien [q.v.] coalition with the same acronym.)

MOUVEMENT NATIONAL DE LIBERATION DU TCHAD (MNLT). Precursor of the Front de Libération du Tchad (FLT) (q.v.). Founded in 1966 by anti-Tombalbaye (q.v.) elements, headed by conservative Muslim leader Hassan Ahmed Moussa (q.v.), with the original purpose of "restoring" chiefly power and "the Muslim way of life," even at the cost of the secession of the eastern and northern provinces from Chad. In June 1966 the MNLT changed its name to the Front de Libération Nationale Tchadienne and later merged with the larger, more militant, and neo-Marxist Union Nationale Tchadienne (UNT) (q.v.) of Ibrahim Abatcha (q.v.) to form the Front de Libération Nationale (see FROLINAT). However, the merger had been arranged by renegade members of the MNLT during their leader's (Ahmed Moussa) imprisonment in Khartoum, and it was unacceptable to him on basic ideological and religious grounds. The MNLT therefore seceded soon after, opting for the name of FLT, while Abatcha's group retained the FROLINAT name.

MOUVEMENT NATIONAL DE REFORME TCHADIENNE (MNRT). Political party, set up in 1991 and headed by its secretary-general, Ali Muhammad Diallo (q.v.).

MOUVEMENT NATIONAL POUR LA REVOLUTION CUL-TURELLE ET SOCIALE (MNRCS). The "new" political movement that replaced the Parti Progressiste Tchadien (PPT) (q.v.) in September 1973, symbolizing the rebirth of Chad under the authenticity, Tchaditude, and "Cultural Revolution" (q.v.) drives of President Tombalbaye (q.v.). A number of new organs were also created, including a commission in charge of administrative and judicial reform (under Tougou Djimé [q.v.]) and a secretariat in charge of orientation and organization of the MNRCS (under Dikoa Garandi [q.v.]). The Executive Committee of the MNRCS (equivalent to the Political Bureau of the former PPT) included in September 1973: Ngartha (François) Tombalbaye, Abdoulaye Abo Nassour, Dono-Ngardoum Djidingar, Ahmadou Pallai, Mahamat Djerma, Tougou Djimé, Miangangbo N'Gangtar, Adoum Tchéré, Sohollot Bakouré, Ali Kosso, and Gayo Kotingar (all q.v.), some of whom had previously served on the PPT Political Bureau.

Through a variety of policies (see CULTURAL REVOLUTION; YONDO) the MNRCS attempted to revitalize the spirit of the southern populations, while through mass mobilization—which proved very costly—the party tried to uplift the Chadian economy, especially cotton cultivation. The movement was banned immediately after the 1975 coup d'état.

MOUVEMENT PATRIOTIQUE NATIONAL (MPN). Primarily anti-Libyan political movement set up by Doungou Kemto (q.v.) in June 1981 with the support of southern civilian and military officials concerned about the growing influence and presence of Libya in Chadian affairs. The party attracted a number of nonsouthern personalities—Mahamat Seid Abba (q.v.), Moussa Medela (q.v.), and Batram Adam Idriss, among others—but remained a minor caucusing group of intellectuals until Medela's faction gave it a more aggressive stance.

MOUVEMENT POPULAIRE DU SALUT (MPS). Idriss Déby's (q.v.) political party, an outgrowth of MOSANAT (q.v.). The party tried to include within it a wide array of elements, including southerners, but, especially with the advent of multipartyism in 1992, it is at its core a largely Zaghawa (q.v.) and to a lesser extent a Hadjeray (q.v.) party.

MOUVEMENT POPULAIRE TCHADIEN (MPT). The name of the anti-PPT (q.v.) coalition formed by the Union Socialiste Tchadienne

(UST) (q.v.) after the GIRT (q.v.) opted out of the Entente (q.v.), thus toppling the provisional government (q.v.) of Gabriel Lisette (q.v.) on January 30, 1959. The MPT coalition had 34 assembly seats to the Entente's 31, and former GIRT leader Gountchomé Sahoulba (q.v.) formed the next provisional government (q.v.). The government collapsed when Ahmed Koulamallah (q.v.) and his MSA (q.v.) deserted the MPT to join opportunistically in a temporary alliance with the PPT. Though at the time Lisette was in favor of forming a wall-to-wall coalition with the MPT, the opposition of Jean Baptiste (q.v.) prevented this course of action. In the May 1959 legislative elections the MPT's component factions competed under their old labels.

MOUVEMENT POUR LA DEMOCRATIE ET LE DEVELOPPEMENT (MDD). Currently the most important antigovernment guerrilla movement, operating in the Lake Chad region. Originally the MDD was an unholy coalition of the former FAO (q.v.), largely Kanembu army, and remnants of units loyal to Hissène Habré (q.v.) after his 1990 ouster from N'Djamena, loosely cooperating and led by Goukouni Guet (q.v.) until the latter was captured. The MDD (as then constituted) mounted attacks in December 1991, continuing through February 1992, in the Lac Préfecture (q.v.), capturing the regional capital Bol and reaching Boltram, in Massakory, 135 kilometers (85 miles) from N'Djamena, before it was stopped, with major losses, and repelled by Idriss Déby's (q.v.) ethnic forces. Though tactically united, the two former components of the MDD then fell apart and attacked each other, led (after Guet's capture, torture, and execution in N'Djamena) respectively by Moussa Medela (q.v.) and Ibrahim Malla Mahamat (q.v.). The remnants of Habré's Garde Présidentielle (q.v.) and other Daza (q.v.) followers then settled in a quasi-sedentary life in exile just across the border in Niger, while the former FAO, now the sole inheritor of the MDD label and allegedly left with only 600 troops, intermittently continued its armed thrusts at the Déby government. In April 1995 the two factions (Habré's and the former FAO) again reunited, but in an August 30, 1995, reorganization of the Political Bureau of the MDD Ibrahim Malla Mahamat was specifically excluded from any office (for disagreeing with the fusion of the two branches), though others from his branch were named to executive posts. This newly reunited MDD, however, does not include a large number of Habré's followers, some of whom have settled in Niger, while others have slowly made their way back to their original homes in B.E.T.

MOUVEMENT POUR LA LIBERATION DU TCHAD (MPLT). Name adopted by the rump of the small Third Liberation Army (q.v.) in

1979, following a split over its alleged preoccupation with Nigerian issues and Aboubaker Abderahmane's (q.v.) leadership. All factions were badly mauled between 1979 and 1980 in fighting with Hissène Habré's FAN (qq.v.) troops, and a segment broke off to follow Moussa Medela (q.v.), calling itself the Forces Armées Occidentales (FAO) (q.v.).

MOUVEMENT POUR L'UNITE ET LA DEMOCRATIE AU TCHAD (MUDT). Political movement founded in 1992 by Julien Marabayé, who has since died.

MOUVEMENT REVOLUTIONNAIRE DU PEUPLE TCHADIEN (MRPT). Southern opposition party, headed by Secretary-General Biré Titinan. Originally part of GUNT (q.v.) and headquartered in Brazzaville, Congo.

MOUVEMENT SOCIALISTE AFRICAIN (MSA). Interterritorial party in French Africa with which Ahmed Koulamallah (q.v.) aligned his political base, setting up a local Chadian branch with the same name, comprising former PSK, PST, and PSIT (all q.v.) elements after Koulamallah's break with Adoum Aganayé (q.v.) and PSIT. Though the new party was quite strong in Koulamallah's home base, Chari-Baguirmi, it only gained one seat in the 1957 Territorial Assembly elections. Later, his strength raised to four seats, Koulamallah merged the MSA with other anti-PPT (q.v.) elements to form the Union Socialiste Tchadienne (UST) (q.v.), and after the GIRT (q.v.) deserted the PPT coalition then in power (the Entente), the new anti-PPT alliance—which briefly came to power—was renamed Mouvement Populaire Tchadien (MPT) (q.v.). The MPT collapsed into its constituent parts very rapidly, and in the 1959 legislative elections the MSA failed to gain any seats, though Koulamallah was to participate in several other anti-PPT alliances.

MOYANGAR, NAIDEYAM (1930–). Historian. Born in 1930, earning an advanced degree in History, Moyangar has been head of the history department at the University of Chad since 1973.

MOYEN-CHARI PREFECTURE. Important, mostly Sara (q.v.) préfecture in southern Chad, with administrative headquarters in Sarh (formerly Fort-Archambault) and divided into the souspréfectures of Sarh, Koumra, Kyabé, Maro, Moïssala, and six *postes administratifs*. The préfecture is transected by numerous rivers and tributaries, including the Bahr Sara, the Chari (q.v.), the Bahr-Ko, and the Mandoul. Covering a territory of 45,174 square kilometers (17,442 square miles), its population of 646,000 (mostly Sara) gives the préfecture a density of 14.3 per square kilometer. Christian (both Catholic and Protestant) influences are much more prevalent in Moyen-Chari than farther to the north, though most of the population is animist, with considerable minorities of Muslims in the region. The préfecture's school attendance rate is quite high at 55 percent, the third highest in Chad. The préfecture, or parts of it, have in the past been intermittently attached to and detached from Chad, with Sarh in particular being always more strongly pulled by Bangui (q.v.) than by N'Djamena, since the former is its major riverine outlet to the outside world. Cotton production is the mainstay of the Moyen-Chari Préfecture; also produced are groundnuts, millet, and dried fish, with some cattle being brought into Sarh for processing in Sarh's meat plant before being shipped by air to neighboring countries. (The plant closed down in 1972.) Sarh is also an important tourist center and the starting point for safaris into the interior's abundant wildlife and national parks. Until 1982 under Sara administration from Moundou (q.v.), the préfecture was delivered to Hissène Habré (q.v.) by dissident FAT (q.v.) units in September of that year.

MUSEE NATIONAL. Chad's national museum, under the supervision of INTSH (q.v.). Founded in N'Djamena in 1963, with small branches in Wara (q.v.), Sarh (q.v.), and several other sites. The main branch specializes in prehistory, paleontology, and ethnography and includes the country's National Archives. Its collections include an important exhibit of Sao (q.v.) art and Sara masks.

MUSEY. Southern ethnic group found mostly in the souspréfecture of Gounou-Gaya (Mayo-Kebbi) in the Chari River valley. Estimated at around 130,000, the Musey are closely related to the Massa (q.v.) and share practically the same language. They are excellent farmers and produce one-tenth of all cotton in the region. Many of the Musey clans are quite recent arrivals in the Chari valley, having migrated there only in the past few decades from the east. Unlike the Massa, the Musey have been strongly pulled to modern life and education.

MUSSOLINI-LAVAL BOUNDARY AGREEMENT. A never ratified Franco-Italian boundary treaty that extended southern Libya (then an Italian possession) some 320 kilometers (200 miles) farther south into Chad's B.E.T. Préfecture and into northern Niger and a corner of Sudan. Since independence, Libya has regarded the treaty as binding, and as early as 1954 a motorized unit occupied Aouzou (q.v.), only to withdraw under French pressure. With the rise of the Muammar Qaddafi military regime in Libya the issue was revived and became a major source of contention between the two countries. According to widely publicized and only recently documented accounts, the (brief) 1972 Chad-Libya reconciliation (see LIBYA) included a secret proviso that conceded the 320-kilometer strip of B.E.T. to Libya, allegedly for several million U.S. dollars given to President François Tombalbaye (q.v.). Libya consequently sent garrisons into Aouzou and a few other outposts. The military junta that toppled Tombalbaye indicated its opposition to this agreement but was powerless to expel the stronger Libyan forces, and neither Goukouni nor Habré had any greater success until the mid-1980s. Though very heavily defended by sophisticated electronic weapons and with several airbases supported by Libya's Maaten-es-Sarra forward military base in Libya proper, starting in 1985 a series of humiliating military defeats (which brought Chad a great deal of war booty) finally forced Qaddafi to agree to have the boundary dispute litigated in the International Court of Justice in The Hague. In 1994 the court found against Libya, and with the withdrawal of Libyan forces the dispute was finally resolved.

MUSTAPHA, BATRAN (1922–). Former cabinet minister, and briefly ambassador to the Central African Republic. Born in Mao in 1922 and originally a trader, Mustapha was elected to the Territorial Assembly in May 1959 as AST (q.v.) deputy from Chari-Baguirmi. He served as the assembly's secretary in 1959 and 1960 and later became its questor. In March 1963 he was brought into François Tombalbaye's (q.v.) cabinet as minister of transport and served in that post until November 1964. After being dropped from the cabinet, he reassumed his assembly seat. In March 1970 he was briefly appointed ambassador to the Central African Republic, only to be brought back into Tombalbaye's cabinet in May 1971 as minister of the civil service. He served in that capacity until October 1973, when he resumed his private activities as a trader.

-N-

NACHTIGAL, GUSTAV (1834–1885). German explorer, author, and colonial administrator. A medical doctor in the Prussian army's medical corps, Nachtigal had to resign due to poor health. Moving to North Africa in 1862 and setting up his practice in Tunis—where he slowly regained his health—Nachtigal was selected in 1868 to bear Prussia's gifts to the Court of Bornu for assistance rendered in the past to German explorers, and especially to Heinrich Barth (q.v.). Nachtigal was delayed for over a year in his voyage in the Fezzan as he waited for a reliable caravan to the south, as the trade routes were no longer as safe as they had been in the past (see CARAVAN ROUTES). From 1869 to 1874 he visited parts of Libya, Chad, Niger, and the Sudan that had never been visited by Europeans (including Tibesti), his main mission taking him from Bornu across the breadth of Chad to Baguirmi, Ouadai, and on to Darfur, whence he progressed to Egypt. Everywhere he compiled meticulous notes, historical records, and king lists that are invaluable to historians today.

Nachtigal also played a key role in the German colonial effort in West Africa. After his Central Africa explorations he was appointed German consul in Tunis (1882) and was then dispatched to defend the German colonial aspirations in West Africa. He first sailed to Togo, annexing the region in the name of Germany, and later performed a similar function in Cameroon.

NADALI, NABIA. Coleader of the Alliance Nationale pour le Progrès et le Développement (ANPD), founded in 1993.

NAGUE ALSTHOM, KODEBRI (1919–). Former deputy, and president of the Cour Criminelle. Born in Banda near Sarh on February 3, 1919, a civil servant from his earliest days, Nagué Alsthom was elected deputy to the territorial legislature in 1946, serving on it until 1952. From 1952 to 1954 he worked with the French colonial administration in Abéché, and from 1954 to 1959 he was a postal inspector in Fort-Archambault (Sarh). At independence Nagué Alsthom was elected deputy mayor of Fort-Archambault (1960–63) and served as attorney general to the Supreme Court of Chad and president of the Cour Criminelle (1962–64). In 1969 he was elected to the National Assembly, and he remained a deputy until the 1975 coup d'état.

NAIMBAYE, LASSIMIAU (RAYMOND) (1940–). Former cabinet minister and ambassador to China. Born in Tilo in the Logone Occidentale Préfecture, Naimbayé was educated in Moundou, at the Ecole Félix Eboué (N'Djamena) and in Bamako, Mali, where he obtained a veterinarian's diploma (1959). Returning home in 1960, he was appointed deputy veterinarian of Abéché, and in 1961 head veterinarian of Oum-Hadjer. In 1962 he leaped into prominence when he was appointed *chef du cabinet* of the minister of stockbreeding and agriculture, and he was later moved to occupy the same post with the minister of foreign affairs. In 1965 he assumed diplomatic duties when he was sent to Khartoum as ambassador to Sudan, but he was repatriated shortly thereafter to join the government as minister of agriculture. A Catholic in a largely Muslim cabinet, Naimbayé served in this capacity for five years (April 1966 to May 1971) before being transferred to head the Ministry of Public Works; at the same time he was integrated into the PPT's (q.v.) Political Bureau. Early in 1974 he left the cabinet and was appointed ambassador to China. Pragmatic, opportunistic, and very ambitious, Naimbayé shifted his loyalties to Hissène Habré (q.v.) in the 1980s (after being ignored by Kamougoué [q.v.]) and with Habré's rise to power was appointed a political consultant.

NAINDOUBA, MAOUNOE (1948–). Author. Born on May 19, 1948, in Bénoyé and educated as a teacher in Brazzaville, Naindouba taught history and geography for several years in Pala before becoming the principal of his school. He is known for a number of plays and novels that were cited and received prizes for being among the best at various literary competitions in France.

NANGDA see BEDJOND

NAR. Small (60,000) ethnic sliver, part of the Sara constellation and closest to the core Madjingayé (q.v.) group. Found on both banks of the Mandoul River, mostly in the Koumra *canton*. The Nar have several distinctions among the Sara: they are excellent musicians (having invented the *balafon*), do not possess hierarchical chiefs, and are very much fetish-oriented. In their social structures the Nar are very democratically inclined and individualistic.

NASSOUR, ABDOULAYE SABRE ABO see ABO NASSOUR, ABDOULAYE SABRE

NATRON. Low-grade carbonate of soda (table salt) found in pans in several locations in Chad, especially northwest of Bol (q.v.) and in Tibesti. Used throughout the region, both for human and animal consumption, natron was one of the commodities traditionally carried by the various caravans crisscrossing the region prior to the colonial era. For quite some time local deposits have satisfied Chadian domestic needs, and surpluses have been exported to neighboring countries, especially Nigeria (3,000 tons annually) and the Central African Republic (500 tons). As of 1966 Chad's natron was under the monopoly of SONACOT (q.v.), though considerable quantities traditionally bypassed the company. During the height of the rebellion in Chad the transport of salt to the south and west was drastically disrupted, and this was mostly felt in external markets, especially Nigeria. Production of natron ground to a halt in 1970, for by then the state company had a three-year supply of natron in stock, and foreign demand had slackened, and the same year, SONACOT moved out of its natron commercialization monopoly. The highest production of natron occurred in 1966—6,514 tons. Natron extraction has traditionally been the occupation of the Haddad (q.v.); SONACOT's timid efforts to break the neopeonage of this group in the harsh natron mines of the north were not crowned with success.

NAYO-TOUMAR, JACOB (1942–). Civil administrator. Born in Bongor in 1942, a graduate of both the Institut International de l'Administration Publique (IIAP) and Ecole Nationale d'Administration (ENA), Nayo-Toumar was made deputy director of municipalities in the Ministry of Interior in August 1971. With the fall of N'Djamena, he relocated to Bongor, where he served on the mayor's staff.

N'DEINGAR, CHRISTOPHE see MBAILEMDANA, N'DEINGAR

NDILNODJI (Captain). Briefly minister of defense and veteran affairs under President Hissène Habré (q.v.). Little is known about Ndilnodji, who was one of the anti-Habré ex-FAT (q.v.) commando leaders in the southern préfecture who rallied to the regime in 1984. Being a southerner, he was promptly rewarded with high office, to signify Habré's magnanimity and desire for national reconciliation. He served for a few years and faded from public life.

N'DJAMENA. Capital of Chad and nerve center of the country, officially renamed N'Djamena on September 6, 1973. The name comes from the minute Arab fishing village, Am-Djamena (the original site of Fort-Lamy), which itself is the name of a shady tree found throughout the region. Located on the right side of the juncture of the Logone (q.v.) and Chari (q.v.) Rivers (which also constitute the border with Cameroon), 80 kilometers (50 miles) south of Lake Chad and some 3,000 kilometers (1,860 miles) north of Congo/Brazzaville's Pointe-Noire, one of the Atlantic seaports servicing the country via Bangui (Central African Republic) and Sarh, in the extreme south of Chad. Strategically located in the center of Africa, during the Second World War Fort-Lamy (as N'Djamena was then called) had the third busiest airport in the French Union, and it is still an important transit center as well as a major stop on the east-west pilgrim route to Mecca. The town's population was estimated in 1976 at 180,000, jumping to 360,000 in 1978 after the victory of the north in the civil war, declining dramatically at the time of the tug-of-war for the capital, and up again. Today it is estimated at over 650,000, with some projections that the city will attain a population of 1.5 million by the year 2010.

The city was founded on April 13, 1900, after the Battle of Kousseri (q.v.) and was named after Major Lamy, who died (along with his counterpart, the notorious slave raider Rabah) in the battle. Established opposite Kousseri for strategic reasons, the site at the time was a very minor Kotoko (q.v.) settlement. Its major period of growth came with independence. In 1958 Fort-Lamy's population stood at 53,000 — barely twice that of Moundou (q.v.) and only twice that of Abéché prior to the arrival of the French in Ouadai; by 1972 its population had more than doubled to 130,000 and grew another estimated 35 percent in the subsequent four years. The city is the center of all modern activity in Chad, with Sarh in the south taking a very secondary position. N'Djamena was also the base of the Sixth Régiment Inter-Armes d'Outre-Mer (RIAOM) (q.v.) and an important air junction on the north-south Saharan routes. Much of the town, and most of its installations, were destroyed or looted during the bitter intranorthern fighting that accompanied its fall to the north and the subsequent tug-of-war between the various northern factions. Virtually all of its population — 95 percent Muslim since Goukouni's (q.v.) entry into the city — fled to the opposite bank of the river to become refugees at Kousseri, Cameroon, returning only in 1981 and 1982. While facilities and services are by now largely operational, for several years, until 1984, electricity, water, and other essentials were either nonexistent or tightly rationed; schools and other educational facilities were closed, and civil servants were left without salaries for up to 18 months. (See also BATTLE FOR N'DJAMENA.)

N'DJAMENA-HEBDO. Independent journal operating in the capital since 1990. Its reporters and editors have been harassed, abused, and arrested several times for investigating and publishing stories on abuses of power by the Idriss Déby (q.v.) regime, and especially his Garde Républicaine (q.v.). Its managing director, Saleh Kebzabo (q.v.), founded a political party in December 1992 — the Union Nationale pour le Développement et le Renouveau (UNDR) — and is a presidential hopeful.

NDJEKERY, NOEL NETONON (1956–). Journalist and author. Born in 1956 in Moundou, not far from the Cameroon and C.A.R. borders, and educated abroad in mathematics and physics, Ndjekery started writing fiction and theatrical works at an early age. His first novel was published in Paris in 1977, before he was 21, and it was followed every few years by another book. In 1982 he won Radio France's first prize for literature.

NDO. The initiation rites among the Sara-Madjingayé (see MADJIN-GAYE), better known abroad as YONDO (q.v.).

NDOH MOUNGAR, RAYMOND (1927–). Important Sara official. Born in Nankessé on April 15, 1927, and educated for a teaching career, Ndoh Moungar eventually became an educational inspector attached to the Ministry of Education in N'Djamena. In April 1963 he also served for nine months as the personal secretary of the minister of education. In December 1963 he was elected deputy to the National Assembly and remained in the assembly until 1972. Simultaneously, between 1965 and 1968, Ndoh Moungar was municipal councillor and deputy mayor of Doba. After the 1979 fall of N'Djamena, Ndoh Moungar withdrew entirely to the southern préfectures, where he has been active in local municipal affairs.

NDOROUM, GASTON see KODIO, LAUDERIM

NGAKOUTOU, AHMED (VALENTIN) (1938–). Civil administrator. Born in Moïssala on December 28, 1938, Ngakoutou was educated locally and abroad, obtaining a diploma from the Institut International de l'Administration Publique (IIAP). For a few years in the early 1960s he worked as director of Tchad-Tourisme and with CIMEN-CAM—the Société des Cimenteries du Cameroun—and in January 1964 he was appointed director of development and of planning. In January 1965 he also joined the municipal council of N'Djamena. He held his first post until 1973 when he became director of Public Works. With the nationalization of SONASUT (q.v.), Ngakoutou was appointed director general of the state company, a post he still holds.

NGAMA. Sara ethnic sliver of 55,000, very close to the core Madjingayé group. The Ngama, found in the Maro, Modélé, and Nadili cantons, are among the most socioeconomically developed Sara clans. During the Tombalbaye (q.v.) era disproportionate numbers of Ngama were employed in the civil service, army, and police.

NGAMBAYE. Large Sara subgroup, previously considered part of the Mbaï group, and only in 1926 accepted by scholars as a separate ethnicity. Found in a vast arc west of the Pendé River in the Logone Orientale, Logone Occidentale, Mayo-Kebbi Préfectures, and, in general, in numerous fishing villages up the Logone and Chari Rivers, the Ngambayé are estimated at over 550,000. There are numerous Ngambayé also in Cameroon (Garoua area), Nigeria, and the Central African Republic.

　　Because of their large numbers, the Ngambayé are usually subdivided into the Makoula (of Bao, Krim-Krim, and Dadjilé); the Mang (of Bébalem and Bénoyé); the Mbaoua (along the Logone River); the Kilang (along the southern Chad border); the Dogo; and the Mbeur. The Ngambayé were extensively raided for slaves by Baguirmi (q.v.) razzias from the north as well as from the Fulani (q.v.) emirates in

Cameroon, with whom relations remain notoriously poor to this day. Both the French colonial presence and Christianity came late to Ngambayé areas—the first Europeans not until 1905, and the first missionary efforts only in 1911. Despite this late start, by 1945 Moundou had the greatest number of school graduates in all Chad. During the colonial era, opposition to the cultivation of cotton (q.v.) and the *cordes de chefs* (q.v.) scandals and riots were all localized in Ngambayé areas, including in Bébalem (q.v.), scene of the most violent explosion of resentment. Ngambayé territory also saw the birth of the PPT (q.v.)—originally opposing cotton cultivation—and Ngambayé supporters sustained the party during its lean days prior to 1959. Despite their electoral clout (they amount to 40 percent of all the Sara), the Ngambayé have had only a very few political offices, which has triggered resentments.

NGAMBAYE, ENOCH (1938–). Educator. Born in Nangda in 1938, and an instructor of mathematics by profession, Ngambayé joined the Ministry of Public Works in 1965 as director of the minister's cabinet. He served through February 1967, when he was appointed high commissioner of popular education and also joined the Conseil Economique et Social (q.v.), where he served as rapporteur of the Social Affairs Committee. He held both posts through 1979. With the fall of N'Djamena Ngambayé relocated to Sarh.

N'GANGBET, KOSNAYE (MICHEL) (1928–). Former critic of the Tombalbaye (q.v.) regime, and later cabinet minister. Born on March 22, 1938, in Doualet, N'Gangbet was educated locally and abroad and received a degree in political science and economics. A civil administrator by profession, N'Gangbet became deputy secretary-general of the Chadian Chamber of Commerce. In June 1969 he was arrested along with Dr. Outel Bono (q.v.), a vocal anti-Tombalbaye critic, for public criticism of the regime's corruption, mismanagement, and tribal favoritism. Placed on trial and sentenced to five years' imprisonment (for "inciting the population to revolt") N'Gangbet was amnestied on August 13, 1969, after a pledge to refrain from similar public criticisms of the regime. He reassumed his post in the Chamber of Commerce, later becoming its secretary-general. Following the 1975 coup d'état he was appointed minister of education, youth, and culture, but lost his post in a 1976 cabinet shuffle. After the fall of N'Djamena, N'Gangbet became minister of economics and finance in November 1979, and minister of finance in July 1981. He lost his post with the rise of the Hissène Habré (q.v.) regime, and in 1985 he joined the Front Démocratique du Tchad (q.v.) of General Djogo (q.v.), which rallied to Habré in 1986.

N'GANGTAR, MIANGANGBO MBAITENDJI (MAURICE) (1932–).
Former cabinet minister. Born in Bénoyé, of Ngambayé origins, in
1932, trained as a male nurse and health technician, N'Gangtar entered politics in the mid-1950s and was elected deputy to the Territorial Assembly on the PPT (q.v.) ticket in March 1957. He remained in
the assembly through December 1963. During these years he also
gained the mayoralty of Moundou (1961) and joined François
Tombalbaye's (q.v.) cabinet, first as minister of waters, forestry and
tourism (August 1960 to March 1962), then as minister of the civil service (March to May 1962), and later as minister of stockbreeding
(May 1962 to March 1963). In March 1963 he was promoted to the
key Ministry of Foreign Affairs, though in November 1964 he was
again transferred, this time to head the Ministry of Agriculture, a position he held until April 1966. A member of the PPT Political Bureau,
N'Gangtar was dropped from the cabinet in 1966 and has not rejoined
it since. Instead he became president of the Conseil Economique et
Social (q.v.) (in April 1967) and held that post until the 1975 coup d'é-
tat; in September 1973 he was also integrated into the Executive Committee of the new national political movement, the MNRCS (q.v.).

NGARBAROUM, DEMTITA (Major) (1935–1990). Former director of
national security from 1975 to 1978, and under Habré (q.v.) second
deputy chief of staff in 1990. With the fall of N'Djamena to northern
troops, Ngarbaroum joined the FAT (q.v.) withdrawal to the southern
préfectures, becoming military commander of one of the Sara districts. The grandson of the chief of Dounamanga, he was arrested after the fall of the south to Habré and was briefly imprisoned before being integrated into the regime's armed forces. Ngarbaroum was one of
the few senior officers not to fall in the battles in the east in 1990 defending Habré from Déby's (q.v.) onslaught, and he made his way to
N'Djamena. After the fall of N'Djamena to Déby on December 2,
1990, Ngarbaroum was captured, tortured, and killed in a settling of
scores.

N'GARDPBE, HOUD HADJ MOUSSA (1937–). Administrator. Born
in Sarh on January 15, 1937, and educated locally and in Paris at the
Institut des Hautes Etudes d'Outre-Mer (IHEOM), N'Gardpbé was
originally a teacher (1956–59) before becoming secretary-general of
the Sûreté Nationale in 1959. In 1963 he was transferred to Moyen-
Chari as prefect and in 1966 became municipal delegate from the city
of N'Djamena. Elected to the National Assembly, N'Gardpbé served
as its secretary-general from 1967 to 1971, as director of economic affairs in the Ministry of Economics from 1971 to 1972, and as prefect
of Logone Occidentale from 1972 to 1979. In 1979 N'Gardpbé joined

the regional administration of the south as one of Kamougoue's (q.v.) civilian lieutenants, and after the rise of the Habré (q.v.) regime in 1982 he became involved in local-level administration.

NGARE. Title of the kings of the Bulala, with their traditional capital in Yao on Lake Fitri. The title is a common one for nobility among other ethnic groups as well.

NGARIDOM, MARCEL (1943–). Diplomat and youth leader. Born in 1943 in Bémia-Laï, educated locally and abroad, Ngaridom joined the Chadian embassy to the United States in mid-1964 as first secretary. A year later he was transferred to N'Djamena to head the Protocol Section of the Ministry of Foreign Affairs, and in September 1969 he was appointed high commissioner of the JEPPT (q.v.), the party's youth wing. Following the 1975 coup détat and the banning of all symbols of the Tombalbaye (q.v.) past, he returned to administrative duties in the civil service.

N'AGARLEJY, KOJI-YARONGAR LE MOIBAN (1948–). Civil administrator. Born in Koro on June 21, 1948, and educated in Moundou and N'Djamena's Ecole Nationale d'Administration (ENA) (q.v.), Ngarlejy's career has been interspersed with study trips abroad to Ottawa (1971–73) and to Paris and Nanterre (1973–79), earning diplomas in public administration and in banking. He served as deputy subprefect of Moundou in 1970, subprefect of Beinamar, deputy prefect of Mongo (1973), and prefect of Guéra (1973) before becoming a consultant overseas. He returned to N'Djamena in 1979 to serve as minister of the civil service but left Chad again after the rise of the Habré (q.v.) regime.

NGARMANE. Head of the Eunuch Guard at the palace of the *mais* (q.v.) of the Baguirmi kingdom (q.v.). An important chief, the *ngarmane* was also in charge of razzias in the south mounted for the personal account of the king.

N'GARNIM, MOUSSA (1930–). Diplomat. Born on December 27, 1930, in Léré, trained in administration in both Brazzaville and in France (ENFOM), N'Garnim joined Gabriel Lisette's cabinet in May 1957 as minister of the civil service, staying in that position through Gabriel Lisette's (q.v.) December 1958 provisional government. After the fall of that government, he was shifted to administrative duties and joined François Tombalbaye's (q.v.) cabinet in October 1961 as administrative deputy secretary-general of the cabinet; in November 1962 he was promoted to secretary-general of the cabinet and served in that capacity until 1965, when he was appointed ambassador to France, remaining in Paris until April 1974. He was then repatriated to become councillor in the Ministry of Foreign Affairs. In 1976 he was appointed head of the Ecole Nationale d'Administration (ENA) (q.v.).

NGARYANA, NOUGALBAYE. Ngaryana, a former police commissioner, close to the Tombalbaye (q.v.) family, was appointed by Idriss Déby as minister of public health on June 23, 1994. In April 1995 he was transferred to head the Ministry of Public Security, recently created out of the Ministry of Interior.

NGOLBE, M'BAIDOUMINGA (1928–). Known also (prior to the authenticity [q.v.] campaigns) as Jules Golbert. Former cabinet director of President Tombalbaye (q.v.). Born in Boda (Logone) on October 21, 1928, Ngolbé was a former president of the Société Tchadienne de Crédit and instructor at the vocational school of Fort-Archambault (1953–56) and a training school in Pela (1956–57). From 1957 to 1960 he was head of the cabinet of Minister of Technical Education Maurice Coumatteau (q.v.), and from September 1960 to mid-1966 *chef du cabinet* of President Tombalbaye. In 1966 Ngolbé was appointed prefect of Mayo-Kebbi, returning to his previous post in August 1973. He remained with Tombalbaye's cabinet until 1974, when he was again assigned administrative duties within the Ministry of Interior. Ngolbé is Antoine Bangui's (q.v.) cousin.

N'GOTHE, GALI GATTA PIERRE. Cabinet minister under both Hissène Habré and Idriss Déby (qq.v.). N'Gothe was purged and imprisoned by Habré and was languishing in Habré's jails as a political prisoner at the time Déby seized power in December 1990. He was immediately released and appointed minister of higher education, and then in March 1991 he was given the finance and economy portfolio. He was dropped from the cabinet in July 1991 because he was acquiring a measure of popularity in N'Djamena, including unsubstantiated reports that he was one of France's preferences for head of state once democratization took place. He nevertheless rejoined the cabinet as leader of his party, the UFD-PR, after the Conférence Nationale (q.v.) of 1993, in which he participated. He was then appointed minister of education. Dropped in a cabinet shuffle in May 1994, he bounced back again in 1995 as minister of education.

N'GOURI. Souspréfecture with headquarters in the village of the same name, part of the Lac Préfecture. The village has 1,500 people and is an important stockbreeding center. A large proportion of the people are sedentary Haddad (q.v.), quite unusual, as well as Boudouma.

NGUELBAYE, MANASSE. Former minister of the economy. Nguelbayé was secretary of state to the minister of interior under Idriss Déby (q.v.) until July 1991, when he was promoted to assume the Ministry of the Economy. He resigned from the cabinet in February 1993.

NIELLIM. Sara clan found in southern Chad and, in much smaller numbers, in some locations farther to the north, on both sides of the Chari River until its confluence with the Salamat River. Organized in the middle of the nineteenth century as a small sultanate, the Niellim suffered from numerous assaults by the Barma (q.v.), becoming vassals of the Baguirmi kingdom (q.v.). Once the original inhabitants of the Melfi region, they have since become highly assimilated with the Barma.

NIERE. Ancient capital of the Tama (q.v.) whose ruins are still visible. Current sultans are enthroned at the site.

NIGERIA-CHAD BORDER SKIRMISHES, 1983. Series of border incidents in the Lake Chad area, centering on the islands of Hadidé and Kinsara, during the period of April 18–24, 1983. Officially stated casualties include 9 Nigerian and 75 Chadian soldiers dead, and 20 Nigerian and 32 Chadian soldiers captured. The clashes developed out of a combination of poorly demarcated borders, the "appearance" of "new" islands consequent to the low level of water in Lake Chad (triggering territorial disputes), and possible pillaging by destitute Chadian refugees and/or fishermen. The short-lived "war" was terminated in May 1983.

NIMRO. Village south of Wara (q.v.) that performed the commercial functions of the capital of the Ouadai kingdom (q.v.). With the transfer of the capital to Abéché, Nimro, no longer viable, disappeared.

NINGAYO, KARKYOM (1946–1982). Popular southern prefect in Moundou who was executed in front of his family by victorious FAN (q.v.) troops after their entry into Sarh and Moundou in September 1982. Though there were other examples of atrocities, the "Ningayo affair" electrified the south and eliminated any lingering feelings—especially in intellectual circles—about the possible advantages of a united Chad under northern control.

NIVELLE-MALLOUM, JEAN (1922–). Administrator and former diplomat. Born in N'Djamena on September 22, 1922, educated locally and abroad, Nivelle-Malloum began his career with the central (federal) French administration of the AEF (q.v.) federation in Brazzaville (1943–53). In June 1957 he joined the staff of the Chadian minister of the civil service as *chef du cabinet,* remaining in that post until October 1961. From 1961 to August 1965 he was director of the civil service, following which he became state comptroller attached to the presidential office. In June 1968 he left that post to become first counselor at Chad's embassy to Benelux and the EC. He was transferred in August 1970 to the embassy to France, with the same diplomatic rank. Repatriated in 1972, he was in charge of a department in the Foreign Ministry until 1979, when he relocated to Moundou.

NJIMI. Capital of the ancient kingdom of Kanem, which reached its height in the thirteenth century. The ruins of Njimi are currently to be found some 55 kilometers (34 miles) east of Mao, the contemporary administrative capital of the Kanem Préfecture. Njimi became the regular fixed capital of the hitherto seminomadic Kanem *mais* (q.v.) around 1250. In the middle of the fourteenth century the Bulala (q.v.) rebellions drove out the reigning Sefuwa (q.v.) Magumi (q.v.) dynasty, which resulted in the eventual shift of the capital of the Bulala to Yao (q.v.) on Lake Fitri. (See also KANEM-BORNU EMPIRE.)

NODJIMBANG, ALPHONSE (1931–). Former cabinet minister. Born on February 3, 1931, in Béboto (Logone) and trained as an educational inspector, Nodjimbang joined the PPT (q.v.) early in the 1950s and in March 1957 was elected to the Territorial Assembly as PPT deputy. He remained in the assembly until it was dissolved in December 1963, serving concurrently as the assembly's secretary (1957–59) and as its questor (1959). Becoming mayor of Doba in June 1961, Nodjimbang joined François Tombalbaye's (q.v.) cabinet in May 1962 as secretary of state for finance and the economy, and in March 1963 he was promoted to full cabinet status as minister of education. In November 1964 he was transferred to head the Ministry of Waters, Fisheries, and Forestry, serving until April 1966, after which he remained a member of the PPT Political Bureau (until 1969) and was appointed roving ambassador (i.e., without any particular country accreditation) and special emissary of President Tombalbaye. He remained in that capacity until the coup d'état of 1975. After the fall of N'Djamena, Nodjimbang served for six months in the April 1979 Choua (q.v.) government as minister of reconstruction.

NOI. A Sara caste with strict interdictions against (among other things) intermarriage. The Noï are found throughout Sara country in southern Chad and play a major religious and traditional role in Sara ceremonies by virtue of their function as fetish priests. Their number is difficult to estimate and may range from several hundred to a thousand. It is the Noï who install each new Sara *mbang* (q.v.).

NORD-KANEM. Officially designated "nomadic" souspréfecture within the préfecture of Kanem. It has as its administrative headquarters Nokou, a small village of 500, and encompasses a population of 40,000 and a territory of 70,000 square kilometers (27,000 square miles), giving it a low population density of 0.6 per square kilometer. One of the villages within Nord-Kanem, Rig-Rig, is a favorite transit point for contraband cattle on their way to Nigeria and Niger.

NOUR, MARIAM MAHAMAT. Minister of planning and cooperation. An economist by training, Mrs. Nour was integrated into Idriss Déby's (q.v.) government as secretary of state in charge of planning in March 1991 and retained through several cabinet shuffles, only to be dropped on May 20, 1992. In May 1994, however, she was brought into the government again, this time as a full minister, and serves in that capacity today.

NOURI, MAHAMAT. Key ex-FAN (q.v.) figure perpetually around the summit of power. Nouri was at Hissène Habré's (q.v.) side throughout his career. During Habré's short-lived alliance with General Félix Malloum (q.v.) in 1979, Nouri was first secretary-general to the government, and then Habré's minister of interior. In the interim GUNT (q.v.) government that followed, Nouri served as minister of transport, works, and communication. In the political wilderness with Habré between 1980 and 1982, Nouri came back to prominence after the capture of N'Djamena as head of Habré's Garde Présidentielle (q.v.), and in June 1984 he became commissioner for external affairs in the Executive Bureau of Habré's political party, UNIR (q.v.). In 1985 he joined the cabinet as minister of public health, and after Habré's ouster he was appointed in 1993 by the Conférence Nationale (q.v.) minister of public health again. In December 1994 he became minister of livestock, and in April 1995 Idriss Déby (q.v.) elevated him to minister of territorial administration, a post created out of the Ministry of Interior.

NOUVELLE SOCIETE COMMERCIALE DE KOUILOU-NIARI (NSCKN). One of the major expatriate (French) import-export houses in Chad, both prior to independence (minus "Nouvelle" in its name) and since. A N'Djamena-based Unilever subsidiary, the NSCKN for some time handled fully 50 percent of the country's registered imports. Though employing only 1,000 workers (including 22 Frenchmen) and with a turnover of only a few million dollars, the company was a powerful economic force in Chad against whose quasi monopoly the independent Chad government decided to compete by setting up its own import-export companies and state purchasing agencies, such as SONACOT (q.v.). Today the NSCKN—once powerful throughout the AEF (q.v.) federation—trades only in a few urban areas and handles only a specific number of commodities.

-O-

ODINGAR, MILAREW (NOEL) (General) (1932–). The most senior officer on the former Conseil Supérieur Militaire (CSM) (q.v.). Born to a chiefly family in Dowalé Béboto (Logone Orientale) in 1932, and of Sara origins, Odingar was prepared for a military career from youth. He attended the Ecole Général Leclerc in Brazzaville and in 1951 joined the French colonial armies, being attached to an artillery unit. In 1957 he attended the Frejus Training School for officers and in August 1961 was transferred to Chad's new national army with the rank of lieutenant. Rapidly rising up the ranks, he served as company commander, military prefect of B.E.T., and head of President Tombalbaye's (q.v.) military cabinet before becoming chief of staff of the army in 1973. According to the then-secret Galopin (q.v.) report, Odingar (as prefect of the B.E.T. until 1968) ordered the release of arrested women and children after the 1965 Bardai incidents (q.v.) (which eventually led to the Toubou [q.v.] uprising), and meted out disciplinary action to the rampaging Chadian troops, thus averting even more serious upheavals in the region. Just prior to the 1975 coup he was ordered arrested by Tombalbaye, which itself served as a catalyst for the coup. At the time of the coup, Odingar took command of operations against the Garde Présidentielle (q.v.) and announced the successful overthrow of Tombalbaye. Odingar was confirmed in his capacity as chief of staff after the coup but was retired after Hissène Habré (q.v.) joined the Félix Malloum (q.v.) government as prime minister, replaced by Lt. Colonel Gouemarou (q.v.). Though no longer in active service, Odingar remained loyal to the southern cause as manifested in the Kamougoué leadership out of Bongor.

OFFICE DE LA MISE EN VALEUR DU SATEGUI-DERESSIA (OMVSD). Autonomous state organ set up with the purpose of developing the Sategui-Deressia plains (some 360 kilometers [223 miles] south of N'Djamena) during the period of 1974 to 1979, and replacing altogether in 1976 the several SEMA (q.v.) organs then operating. Included in the project of regional development was the construction of a 6.2-kilometer (3.8-mile) canal off the Logone River as well as two polders (q.v.), 102 kilometers (63 miles) of desert roads, and the erection of rice plantations. The total cost of the project was estimated at 3,115 million CFA francs, all of which was to come from outside sources, such as 1,024 million CFA francs from the FED (q.v.) and US$7.5 million from AID. Most of the projects had to be postponed, then canceled, due to the unsettled conditions in Chad.

OFFICE DE LA RECHERCHE SCIENTIFIQUE ET TECHNIQUE OUTRE-MER (ORSTOM). Major French research organ. An important branch of ORSTOM in N'Djamena has conducted a large number of studies in geology, pedology, hydrology, hydrobiology, botany, archaeology, geophysics, and animal husbandry.

OFFICE NATIONAL DE DEVELOPPEMENT RURAL (ONDR). Principal governmental coordinating structure for the promotion of rural development. Established by decree on July 23, 1965, ONDR is operative in all the Secteurs Régionaux de Développement Rural (SRDR) (q.v.) through its activities to modernize their means of agricultural production, which include the allocation of new machinery and equipment (replacing the SMA [q.v.]), greater use of insecticides, encouragement of the formation of cooperatives, and in general tendering advice and suggesting reforms. The organ is prohibited by law from purchasing goods or crops and is especially charged with spurring the productivity of Chad's largest commercial crop, cotton. ONDR is not active in the Lac Préfecture, where SODELAC (q.v.) was in charge of agricultural modernization, nor in the rice areas of Tandjilé and Mayo-Kebbi, where SEMALK (q.v.) and SEMAB (q.v.), respectively, were involved, though ONDR is nominally the coordinating agency for the Mandoul Valley Development Plan (q.v.). Most of the activities of ONDR were terminated in the late 1970s.

OFFICE TCHADIEN D'ETUDES FERROVIAIRES (OTEF). State organ created in October 1962 under the supervision of the Ministry of Public Works and charged with examining the possibility of expanding the Trans-Cameroonian railroad to N'Djamena, via a number of intermediate Chadian towns. The agency has also—since the possibility has become more realistic in the 1970s—conducted surveys and mapping projects in anticipation of an actual link-up with the Transcamerounaise. A joint Chad-Cameroon commission was also established at the time, though its work has been, in general, minimal. (See also COMMUNICATIONS.) After the discovery of large oil deposits in the south, OTEF's work appeared more realistic, since the projected pipeline through Cameroon might involve also the construction of a rail spur to link up with the Transcamerounaise.

OIL. Until the mid-1970s all of Chad's oil reached the country through the expensive overland route, raising domestic prices in general. In December 1973 the Continental Oil Company (CONOCO) discovered oil deposits in the Mao region of Kanem and near Doba in the south. The American company had been granted drilling concessions over extensive areas (465,000 square kilometers [179,500 square miles] in the western and southwestern parts of Chad, having committed itself to investing a minimum of US$5.66 million in drilling explorations. By the mid-1970s Kanem Oilfield No. 1 (Mao) was producing 155 barrels a day. Conoco's discovery, however, was not pursued. In 1977 additional deposits were found at Sedigi in Kanem, on the northern edge of Lake Chad, with 70 million tons of crude reserves, allowing exploitation at the level of 1,500 barrels a day. Local processing in an oil refinery was envisaged that could meet all of Chad's domestic needs. The World Bank has recently committed 43 percent of the equity for the refinery since Chad has no resources of its own.

All work in Kanem had to cease in 1978, however, as the area became too dangerous. Serious oil exploration only really recommenced a decade later, in 1989, when additional, much larger oil finds were made, especially in the south (and in particular in 1994), but unsettled conditions made their exploitation problematic until recently. In 1988 an Esso-Chevron-Shell consortium was formed to exploit Chad's southern deposits (the second company involved in explorations is Hunt Petroleum), now estimated at 800 million barrels of oil. These will be evacuated from Doba to Douala, Cameroon, via a pipeline, with preliminary work beginning in 1995, and production is expected in the year 2000.

OLAFRIC see COMPAGNIE HUILIERE AFRICAINE

OPERATION AGRICULTURE. Also sometimes referred to as "Opération Coton" or "Project Agriculture." An unrealistic, overambitious program of agricultural development announced by President Tombalbaye (q.v.) on August 27, 1974. The program was supposed to mobilize over 1.5 million farmers and urban dwellers to raise Chad's cotton harvest to 750,000 tons on over 500,000 hectares (1.2 million acres) of land by 1974/75, without any significant fiscal outlays. If achieved, the 1974/75 crop would have represented a 600 percent increase over that of 1973/74. The operation was aborted immediately after the 1975 coup d'état (the harvest period had a few more months to run), and later the 1974/75 crop was revealed to have been a bumper crop but less than 25 percent higher than the previous year. Tombalbaye's handling of the massive mobilization effort was severely criticized on economic grounds, especially the labor dislocations it caused and the unscheduled (and prohibitive) costs it entailed. On the other hand, part of the increased higher cotton harvests since then must be attributed to the virgin islands opened up by Opération Agriculture.

OPERATION EPERVIER. Operation "Sparrowhawk" was France's defensive air shield against GUNT (q.v.) and Libya, after the latter's mid-1986 encroachments across the 16th parallel. The operation was in a sense the successor of Opération Manta (q.v.), terminated in 1984. At its height there were over 3,000 French troops and over a dozen jets in Chad with additional, roughly equivalent forces, in rear bases in Gabon, Senegal, and the Central African Republic. Though France refused to provide Habré with air cover against Libya after he had defeated the latter's forces in B.E.T. and had destroyed the Libyan airbase of Maaten-es-Sarra (and the lack of air cover forced Habré to evacuate the otherwise indefensible Aouzou), French antiaircraft batteries did repel Libyan retaliatory air attacks on N'Djamena. The French force was concentrated in the Abéché area, and they also operated a major radar station at Moussoro, 240 kilometers (150 miles) north of N'Djamena, which was closed down in January 1989. Indeed, French forces in Chad were scaled down after the peace accord with Libya, and reduced further after the Libyan withdrawal of troops from the Aouzou Strip (q.v.) in 1994 in light of the greatly reduced chance of conflict with Libya. By the mid-1990s there were fewer than 500 French troops in Chad, and these were mostly military retraining units.

OPERATION FIAT. Alleged mass embezzlement scheme tolerated by President Tombalbaye (q.v.) immediately prior to the 1975 coup d'état. The scheme was connected with the government's attempt to break out of the (French) Berliet truck monopoly through major authorizations to purchase Fiat equipment, during which thousands of millions of CFA francs were diverted into several ministers' pockets, including (it is alleged) Tombalbaye's. The "operation" was investigated by the military junta that came to power in 1975.

OPERATION MANDOUL see MANDOUL VALLEY DEVELOPMENT PLAN

OPERATION MANTA. Code name for the dispatch of a strong French military force to Chad in August 1983 to patrol and defend the so-called "Red Zone" (q.v.), or "Red Line" along the 16th parallel so as to prevent the further southward advance of Goukouni-led and Libya-supported troops of the GUNT (q.v.) armed forces. Opération Manta was mounted when it became clear that Libyan troops and tactical support were directly and actively involved in Goukouni's (q.v.) major assault, which led his troops into Faya-Largeau and Abéché. Some 3,500 French troops ultimately served in Chad, including jet squadrons based in Gabon. The operation was technically concluded after the September 17, 1984, agreement between France and Libya for mutual military noninvolvement in Chad's affairs, and a mutual pullout of forces. France then began evacuating its forces, but some time later discovered it had been tricked by Libya, and the 16th parallel was violated by Libyan-supported GUNT forces, which brought the return of French armed forces into the area in Opération Epervier (q.v.).

OPERATION REZZOU. Code name for Idriss Déby's (q.v.) 1990 assault into eastern Chad from his five bases in Darfur. Earlier he had either been confined within Sudan (raising and training his new armies) or only occasionally foraying into Chad. His insurgency had struck roots in the area, populated by Arab clans, Hadjeray (q.v.), and Zaghawa (q.v.), all of whom had been alienated by Hissène Habré (q.v.), a factor that ultimately led to Déby's victory and his entry into N'Djamena on December 2, 1990.

OPERATION SILURE. Code name for the French military withdrawal from Chad in accord with the Franco-Libyan agreement of September 17, 1984. Troops of both countries were supposed to withdraw from Chad between September 25 and November 15, 1984. The operation caused France's President François Mitterrand a major embarrassment, however, because after declaring the mutual withdrawal complete, he had to contradict himself and acknowledge that Libyan troops remained in Chad. A hurried meeting between Qaddafi and Mitterrand seemingly smoothed over the issue, though Libyan troops (between 600 and 1,200) remained in B.E.T. in contravention to the agreement. Some time later Opération Epervier (q.v.) was initiated, bringing French armed forces back into Chad. (See also OPERATION MANTA.)

ORGANISATION COMMUNE AFRICAINE, MALGACHE, ET MAURITIENNE (OCAMM). A grouping of most of francophone Africa (OCAM until later joined by Mauritius), for the purpose of economic, social, and cultural cooperation. Indirect successor to the Brazzaville Group, the Union Africaine et Malgache (UAM) and the Organisation Africaine et Malgache de Coopération Economique (OAMCE), OCAMM's most successful ventures to date have been the creation of Air Afrique—the multinational airline of French Africa—and a joint telecommunications system as well as cooperation on several joint technical colleges. Since 1970 OCAMM has suffered a measure of attrition as several states have resigned their membership and/or pulled out of some of the joint projects sponsored in the past by the organization.

ORGANISATION COMMUNE DES REGIONS SAHARIENNES (OCRS). Regional organization created on January 10, 1957, with the purpose of the socioeconomic development of the Saharan areas and the coordination of programs of research as well as interstate communications in the region. The organ had a High Commission and 32 members, 16 of whom represented the territorial assemblies involved, and 16 representatives of the various ethnic groups in the region. After independence Chad continued for a while to be represented by two state delegates; the OCRS's last program in Chad was in 1962; shortly after that, the organization collapsed as each independent territory opted for the separate and independent development and administration of its Saharan regions. The Chadian areas that fell at the time under the competence of the OCRS were B.E.T., Kanem, Biltine, and the Abéché and Adré sections of Ouadai.

ORGANISATION DE LIBERATION DU TCHAD DE FASCISME ET DE L'IMPERIALISME (OLTFI). Lagos-based movement set up in November 1983 that claimed credit for several attacks on a Zairean military camp in N'Djamena and a Kousseri-N'Djamena barge. OLTFI claimed allegiance to Goukouni's GSN (q.v.) in Bardai and later merged with the FAO (q.v.).

ORGANISATION DES FEMMES DE L'UNION NATIONALE POUR L'INDEPENDANCE ET LA REVOLUTION (OFUNIR). Former largely inactive women's branch of the Hissène Habré UNIR (qq.v.) political movement.

OTHMAN, DJALABO ABOUBAKAR (1930–1969). Early FROLINAT (q.v.) leader and opponent of Dr. Abba Siddick (q.v.). Of mixed Arab-Kreda (q.v.) origins, raised in Kanem and educated only in Koranic schools, Othman was the key leader of the radical Muslim Union Nationale Tchadienne (UNT) (q.v.), set up in 1958, and a member of its original steering committee. Following the ban of all opposition parties in 1962, Othman went into self-exile, including in Ghana. In 1968 he emerged as the first deputy secretary-general of FROLINAT in charge of foreign relations. Othman was killed soon after in internecine fighting in central Chad during a recruitment drive.

OUADAI KINGDOM. Powerful and expansionist Muslim slave kingdom centered on its capital of Abéché (q.v.)—or Abeshr—(until 1850, Wara) that encompassed much of eastern Chad, extending its suzerainty as far into the west as Kanem and Baguirmi. A quasi-independent state had existed in the Ouadai region since the fourteenth century but was conquered by the Tunjur (q.v.) early in the sixteenth century when they spread into the area from Darfur (q.v.) in the Sudan. The Tunjur dynasty was itself overthrown in a quasi-religious popular revolt led by Abd-el-Kerim (q.v.)—alternately placed in the year 1611 or 1635—who mobilized the local Maba (q.v.) clans and established a Muslim dynasty that was to remain in power until the colonial era. The history of the Ouadai kingdom is essentially a long succession of civil wars, conquests of adjoining areas, and slave raids deep into the south. The kingdom developed an elaborate hierarchical structure with a powerful absolute monarchy. Though at the outset Ouadai paid tribute to Darfur—and to Bornu (q.v.), which threatened to reinstate Tunjur rule—Ouadai broke these dependency links in the latter part of the eighteenth century, invading its former masters a couple of times. Darfur's power, as well as the mountainous geography of the region, prevented the expansion of Ouadai ambitions to the east, shifting them to the west and south; in the south Ouadai rapidly acquired preeminence over Dar Sila, Dar Kouti, Dar Rounga, and Salamat.

Much of Ouadai's prosperity and power rested on its ability to export large numbers of slaves to the north. Toward this end numerous slave-raiding expeditions were sent to the southern regions (as deep as parts of contemporary Central African Republic). Captured slaves were then sent north via the various caravans plying the routes to Egypt and Tripoli. Ouadai's trade received a major boost when around 1810 a new caravan route was opened to extensive trade, linking Abéché with the Mediterranean coast, via Kufra (q.v.) in the Fezzan (see CARAVAN ROUTES). This route rapidly became the most important one in the nineteenth century, due to the collapse of the Bornu-Tripoli route farther to the west. Better and easier communications with the coast also brought into Ouadai a more plentiful supply of firearms, crucial for their slave raids in the south.

Ouadai's rise to a position of cardinal importance in the nineteenth century was attested to when Ouadai was invited by Bornu's ruler, al-Kanemi, to assist in the imposition of Bornu's suzerainty over Baguirmi, geographically midway between the two. The reigning *kolak* (q.v.) of Ouadai, Abd-el-Kerim II, instead annexed the rebellious kingdom to Ouadai. In 1835 a Darfur attack on Ouadai succeeded due to the general anarchy that reigned in Wara (q.v.) as a result of intermittent succession crises. Darfur was able to install a puppet *kolak* in Ouadai, though later Ouadai was to break loose and retaliate against Darfur. The new *kolak,* Muhamad Sharif (1835–58), transferred the capital of Ouadai from Wara to Abéché in 1850 and attached himself to the nascent Sanusiya (q.v.) religious order.

The first Westerner to visit Ouadai—Vogel—did so the same year but was murdered prior to his departure from Abéché. Later other travelers reached the isolated and suspicious kingdom, including Gustav Nachtigal (q.v.). In 1889 Rabah (q.v.) ravaged much of southern Ouadai and placed the latter's dependencies of Dar Sila and Dar Kouti under Mohamed-es-Senoussi (q.v.), a trusted ally. When Rabah's conquests in Central Africa were cut short by the expanding French influence in the region, Ouadai provokingly demanded the return of its lost provinces that had been absorbed by France. Ouadai also rejected France's demand that the slave trade be ended and refused to allow free passage to French explorers and missions. Moreover, since French troops were soon in active combat with the Sanusiya lodges in Kanem and (later) in B.E.T. (the Sanusiya were the only force opposing France's influence in the area after the defeat of Rabah), Ouadai's close links with the Sanusiya order were viewed with suspicion by the French.

The first French advance against Abéché came when Yao (q.v.) and the Lake Fitri (q.v.) region were occupied in May 1909 with the assistance of Sultan Acyl (q.v.), of the reigning dynasty, who wished to topple the actual sultan, Doud Mourrah. Despite some Senoussi military help, Abéché was occupied on June 3, 1909, and Acyl was installed as France's puppet sultan. Doud Mourrah, who raised a new army in an attempted comeback, was again defeated on April 7, 1910, and escaped to Dar Massalit in what is today Sudan. Acyl himself fell afoul of the French when he reneged on pledges he had given them, and in 1911 there was a general revolt in Ouadai consequent to some of his excesses in court, and he was deposed by the French. These disturbances meshed with other unrest in the region, due to the harsh taxes imposed by the colonial authorities and the Kub Kub massacre (q.v.) of Abéché's marabouts by a demented French colonial officer. The inability of the peasantry to pay the heavy levies unleashed a heavy-handed French reprisal and rampage that prompted the massive exodus of much of Abéché's population to the countryside, and many Maba clans crossed the borders to Sudan. The exodus and devastation of the countryside brought about a collapse of the economy and, worsened by a severe drought, caused widespread starvation and epidemics (1913–14; 1916–18). As much as 60 percent of Ouadai's population may have perished during these years, which are still remembered in Abéché. (Between 1912 and 1914 the town's population plummeted from 28,000 to 5,000; the French authorities conservatively placed the number of those who died during the droughts and epidemics at 300,000.) The region never recovered from this blow, and its people maintained their inimical attitude toward French rule. The region was under direct French military rule until 1935, when the old sultanate was resurrected under Muhammad Ourada, with only nominal powers. Ourada, who tried to open his country to a modicum of outside and Western influences, was succeeded on the throne in 1945 by Ali Silek, the son of Sultan Doud Mourrah, who had so resisted the French entry into his country. The area remains distinctively apart from the rest of Chad, however, refusing integration with—and political domination by—the southern regions and tribes that until recently were regarded as merely hunting grounds for slaves. The region gravitates in all senses not toward the west, and N'Djamena, but toward the north and east, to Sudan and Egypt. For this reason the southern Sara parties, and especially the PPT (q.v.), never gained a significant stronghold in the area, and the rebellion in the mid-1960s found considerable support in the region. (See also OUADAI PREFECTURE.)

OUADAI KINGDOM, KINGS OF. As with other King lists, there is controversy regarding sequence and dates.

> Abd-el-Kerim (1635–55)
> Sharuf (1655–78)
> Sharif (1678–81)
> Yakob Arous (1681–1707)
> Kharut-es-Sarhir (1707–47)
> Muhamad Jawda (1747–95)
> Salih Deret (1795–1803)
> Abd-el-Kerim (also Sabun) (1803–13)
> Muhamad Busata (1813)
> Yusuf (1813–29)
> Ragib (1829)
> Abd-el-Aziz (1829–35)
> Muhamad Sharif (1835–58)
> Ali (1858–74)
> Yusuf (1874–98)
> Ibrahim (1898–1901)
> Mohamad Doud Mourrah (1902–09)
> Acyl (1909–12)
> Muhamad Urada (1935–45)
> Ali Silek (1945–)

OUADAI PREFECTURE. Eastern préfecture (formerly including also the Biltine) that covers the core of the precolonial Ouadai kingdom (q.v.). The préfecture encompasses 76,240 square kilometers (29,436 square miles) and 422,000 people—mostly Maba (q.v.) and related ethnic groups as well as nomadic Arab clans—giving it a population density of 5.5 per square kilometer. The préfecture is divided into the souspréfectures of Abéché-rural, Abéché-nomade, Adré, Am Dam, and Goz-Beida, and has its administrative headquarters in Abéché. The latter is also the seat of the current sultan and the former imperial capital of the Ouadai kingdom. Deeply troubled by the civil rebellion in Chad—in which many Maba (q.v.) clans participated—Ouadai has always been the second, and opposing, center of gravity in Chad. Its political leadership has traditionally and consistently been militantly Muslim, often Senoussi, conservative, and violently anti-PPT (q.v.), while its social ethos has been more conditioned by Arab influences and the proximity of neighboring Sudan. An important transit point for devout Muslim pilgrims (q.v.) on their way to Mecca, Ouadai's economic and political importance drastically declined with the advent of the colonial era. The arid region produces few goods for export other than gum arabic (q.v.)—harvests of which plunged with the Sahelian drought—and cattle (Chad's fourth largest cattle herds), which suffered even more in the last two decades. The préfecture has very low levels of school attendance (3.8 percent), a reflection of both the underdeveloped nature of the region and the antagonism of the populations to Western influences. Intermittent rebellion and unruliness, with banditry and brigandage in the peripheral areas, has also been an integral part of Ouadai history. (See also OUADAI KINGDOM; MABA.)

OUADI-DOUM. Small settlement 80 kilometers (50 miles) from Fada in B.E.T. that was the site of a major Libyan airbase during the period that GUNT (q.v.) and Libyan forces occupied the region. In 1986 the base had amassed a force of 300 tanks and 10,000 to 20,000 troops, and the runway was elongated to 4,200 meters to enable the landing of heavily loaded aircraft and jets. In February 1986 French jets strafed the base when GUNT-Libyan forces, in violation of a 1984 agreement, crossed the 16th parallel. When a Libyan column of 3,000 advanced to attack Fada (q.v.) only 80 kilometers (50 miles) away, the Chadian army destroyed it and in a major surprise assaulted Ouadi-Doum itself. There the Chadians routed the Libyans, killing 2,000 and capturing several hundred more plus a huge amount of war materiel. All the Czech and East German officers bolstering the Libyan force were evacuated a week before the assault. Part of the war booty was destroyed when Libyan bombers revisited the base for that purpose.

OUADI-RIME. Nomadic souspréfecture with administrative headquarters in the small (population 300) oasis of Djedaa, part of the préfecture of Batha.

OUANKOULOU. Title of the religio-political chief of the Toubouri (q.v.). (See also DORE.)

OUARA see WARA.

OUBANGUI-CHARI. Chad's southern colonial neighbor, now the Central African Republic. The name refers to the territory between the rivers

Oubangui and Chari. At various times in its history Chad was administratively subordinate to Oubangui-Chari (see OUBANGUI-CHARI-TCHAD), and at others portions of its territory were attached to its southern neighbor (see AFRIQUE EQUATORIALE FRANÇAISE). Most of the Sara areas in the south, for example, were for a considerable time directly governed from Bangui, capital of Oubangui-Chari, and much of Chad's imports and exports were, and still are, shipped via Bangui and the Congo/Brazzaville port of Pointe-Noire. (See also BANGUI.)

OUBANGUI-CHARI-TCHAD. Early name of the French colony established in Equatorial Africa on February 11, 1906, including what is currently Chad and the Central African Republic, and a constituent part of the French Congo (Congo Français). The capital of the area was first Fort de Possel and later (December 1906) Bangui (q.v.), and the colony was governed by a lieutenant governor, the first being Emile Merwart. In 1910 the Congo Français was replaced by the AEF (q.v.), and in April 1916 Oubangui-Chari was separated from Chad to become two separate colonies.

OULED ABU ISSE see HASSAUNA

OULED HEMAT. Djoheina (q.v.) Arab group of clans found throughout eastern Chad.

OULED MANSUR see HASSAUNA

OULED RACHID. Major group of Djoheina (q.v.) Arabs, composed of several clans found throughout the Batha valley and in southern Baguirmi. Their numbers were estimated in 1984 at around 140,000. (See also ARABS.)

OULED SLIMAN see AWLAD SULAYMAN

OUM CHALOUBA. Important and picturesque caravan stop, halfway between Abéché and Fada.

OUM-HADJER. Souspréfecture in the Batha Préfecture with administrative headquarters in the town with the same name (population 4,500). The souspréfecture encompasses 40,000 square kilometers (15,444 square miles) and 300,000 people (population density, 6 per square kilometer), most of whom are Misirié, allied subgroups, and Moubi (q.v.). Oum-Hadjer's second largest center is Mangalmé, scene of the major tax riots in 1965 (see MANGALME TAX RIOTS) that marked the beginning of the rebellion in the east. Major interethnic disorders also erupted in the souspréfecture in 1947 when over 180 people were killed in two days.

OUMAR, SAID ACHEIKH IBN see ACHEIKH, IBN OUMAR

OUNIANGA LAKES. Three small lakes some 220 kilometers (136 miles) north of Faya-Largeau in the Tibesti, one blue, one violet, and the third a light shade of red. The largest (called Ounianga Kebir or Great Ounianga) is roughly three kilometers by two kilometers; the second in size (Ounianga Kerir) covers barely four square kilometers and is a salt lake, the largest one in the Sahara desert. Apart from their stunning natural beauty, which has appealed to travelers throughout the years, the region was former President Tombalbaye's (q.v.) favored place of exile for many of his political opponents in the early 1960s.

OUSMAN, HISSENE. Early cabinet minister. A leader of the UDIT (q.v.) party, Ousman served as minister of transport in the December 1958 Gabriel Lisette (q.v.) cabinet, following which he was minister of stockbreeding in the governments of Gountchomé Sahoulba (q.v.) (February 1959), Ahmed Koulamallah (q.v.) (March 1959), and François Tombalbaye (q.v.) (March 1959). (See PROVISIONAL GOVERNMENTS.) He was dropped from the cabinet in 1962. In 1966 he was posted to Chad's embassy to Libya as first councillor, and in 1969 he was reassigned to Washington as first secretary at the Chadian Embassy to the United States. He remained in that post until 1975, when he was repatriated to head a division in the Ministry of Foreign Affairs. Since 1978 he has been in retirement.

OUTMAN, HANOUN. First president of Chad's Supreme Court (see COUR SUPREME). A lawyer and a magistrate, Outman served as the first president of the Supreme Court from 1963 to 1971, following which he went into retirement.

-P-

PALA. Souspréfecture with administrative headquarters in the town of the same name, part of the préfecture of Mayo-Kebbi. The souspréfecture encompasses a population of 126,000 and a territory of 8,000 square kilometers (3,088 square miles). The town of Pala includes 15,000 people, though at one time it had 30,000 people after the refugee influx from the north, following the fall of N'Djamena to northern troops in 1979.

PALLAI, AHMADOU (GASTON) (1936–1977). Banker and administrator. Born on October 26, 1936, in Guebanne-Léré, of Moundang origins, Pallai was educated locally and abroad and obtained a degree in political science. He has served in a variety of professional capacities, including as general director of the Banque Tchadienne de Crédit et de Dépôts (q.v.) and as president of the Professional Association of Banks of Chad. In April 1967 he became a member of the Conseil Economique et Social (q.v.), and in May 1968 he also became president of the Chadian Chamber of Commerce. He retained these posts after the 1975 coup d'état. From 1973 to 1975 Pallai also was a member of the Executive Committee of the MNRCS (q.v.) party.

PAPY, BAAL ZAHR HABI. Key military adviser to Idriss Déby (q.v.), and MPS (q.v.) security head. Originally, and for twelve years (1977–89), Papy had been Hissène Habré's (q.v.) top intelligence service officer; when Habré alienated the Zaghawa (q.v.) in 1989, Papy defected to Déby and joined him in exile. He served for a while as Déby's representative in Burkina Faso and then was a military aide during Déby's struggle against Habré's forces in 1990. After Déby's rise to power Papy was placed in charge of mobilizing the new MPS party and appointed its security head. There was an attempted assassination against him in his office in N'Djamena on January 25, 1991.

PARC NATIONAL DE MANDA. Game reserve of 108,000 hectares (266,760 acres) in the Moyen-Chari Préfecture, some 25 kilometers (16 miles) northwest of Sarh. The park has a large variety of wildlife, including lions, buffalo, giraffes, antelopes, and hippopotamuses. Formerly a wildlife reserve set up in 1953 to protect the rare Derby eland on the right bank of the Chari River, the park was opened to big game hunters in 1965.

PARC NATIONAL DE ZAKOUMA. Well-known wildlife reserve, 800 kilometers (500 miles) from N'Djamena, created in 1958 and officially renamed a national park in April 1963. Zakouma's 450,000 hectares (1.1 million acres) are a large plain drained from north to south by the Bahr Salamat (q.v.) and its tributaries. Open (and only accessible) between December 1 and May 31, it has a great abundance and variety of big game, including elephants (which roam in herds of hundreds), lions, giraffes, and antelopes (including the Grand Koudou and the rare Derby eland). One of the largest and finest game reserves in all of Africa—according to some, it rivals the greatest in East Africa—Zakouma is west of Am-Timan, east of Melfi, and northwest of Sarh, partly in the Guéra and partly in the Salamat Préfectures. In 1989, and again in 1990, the EC gave Chad 560 million CFA francs to improve the badly ravaged park. It remains empty of tourists, however, a victim of the image of constantly unsettled conditions in Chad.

Zakouma's animal density is much higher than that in other parks in East or South Africa. Communications are usually by air (DC-3) from N'Djamena to the large Campement du Bahr Tinga in the park, where accommodations are available for 130 people in huts containing four beds each. Nearby also is a fishing preserve. Zakouma is also surrounded by the Réserve du Bahr Salamat (300,000 hectares [741,000 acres]), created in 1965. Some 5,000 tourists visited the area each year in the 1970s, until the region became insecure due to guerrilla activities. Subsequently the park facilities and wildlife were greatly devastated by the fighting in the area from 1976 to 1983, with a near-total end to tourism. Though the facilities were on several occasions refurbished after guerrilla assaults, they remain mostly ruined, and very few tourists come to the park. The general peace that has descended on the region, however, has allowed a healthy replenishment of wildlife.

PARTI AFRICAIN POUR LA PAIX ET LA JUSTICE SOCIALE (PAPJS). Political movement set up by Neatobei Bidi (q.v.), with a federal platform.

PARTI COMMUNISTE TCHADIEN (PCT). Former small Marxist nucleus of (mostly) unionists and students during the Tombalbaye (q.v.) era. Its secretary-general and most noted member was Malla Djama Pleven, who was imprisoned by Tombalbaye until April 1971.

PARTI LIBERAL POUR L'UNITE ET LA SOLIDARITE (PLUS). Political party set up in 1992 by Abbas Mahamat Ambadi (q.v.).

PARTI NATIONAL AFRICAIN (PNA). Last legal political regroupment of all opposition elements (i.e., northern groups) in Chad prior to the imposition of a single-party system by the PPT (q.v.). Created on January 30, 1960, the PNA included elements of the UDIT, GIRT, AST, URT, MSA, and MESAN (qq.v.). Essentially a Muslim opposition party of conservative hues (despite the presence of the MSA bloc), the PNA was headed by its honorary president, MSA leader Ahmed Koulamallah (q.v.), with UDIT's Jean Baptiste (q.v.) as executive president, GIRT's Djibrine Kherallah (q.v.) as first vice president, URT's Seydou Tall as second vice president, AST's Mahamat-el-Goni (q.v.) as secretary-general, and MSA's Souleymane Naye as first secretary. The creation of the PNA reflected the sad reality of the sharp polarization of Chad, even so early in its political evolution, since the PNA encompassed most of the northern groups, while the southern ones were equally cohesively organized mostly behind the PPT. The PNA at the outset held 25 of the 85 assembly seats, though its strength plummeted to 17 and then to 10 as some members defected to the PPT. After the expulsion from Chad of former PPT leader Gabriel Lisette (q.v.), the PNA briefly agreed to form an alliance with the PPT, called the Union pour le Progrès du Tchad (UPT), essentially creating a virtual one-party system. The temporary reconciliation of all of Chad's parties was attested to by the UPT's first (and only) congress, which was held in April 1961 in Abéché, stronghold of the anti-PPT parties. The merger was temporary, however, and by May–June 1961 the various factions had left the UPT. In January 1962 all opposition parties were banned by the PPT and the National Assembly was dissolved.

PARTI POUR LES LIBERTES ET LE DEVELOPPEMENT (PLD). Political formation set up in 1992 by Ibn Oumar Mahamat Saleh (q.v.).

PARTI PROGRESSISTE TCHADIEN (PPT). A largely southern-based political party (with a solid core of ethnic support among the Sara) that after a long struggle against various administration-supported and chiefly conservative groupings, emerged as the dominant political force in Chad (1957) and banned all other political movements in 1962. In 1973 the party ceased to exist as it was succeeded by the MNRCS; after the 1975 coup d'état the MNRCS was banned. Founded in 1946 by Gabriel Lisette (q.v.), then a young colonial administrator from the West Indies (though born in Panama), and later joined by Jules Pierre Toura Gaba (q.v.), François Tombalbaye (q.v.), and Dr. Abba Siddick (q.v.), among others, the party became affiliated with the interterritorial RDA (q.v.) party in February 1947. Vehemently antichiefly and, in its early years, against cotton cultivation, the PPT slowly mellowed in the early 1950s, acquiring a centrist coloration. The party fought an uphill struggle against a variety of European and traditional Muslim parties, assisted by the French local administration, its principal opponent being the UDT (q.v.), and later the AST (q.v.). The party's political nadir was reached in 1951, though after the enactment of the *loi-cadre* (q.v.) it rapidly gained momentum and in 1957 finally emerged as the dominant party in the country. In its slow rise to power the PPT formed a variety of electoral alliances (see POLITICAL PARTIES) including the FACT (q.v.) and Entente (q.v.) coalitions. In 1957 the PPT formed the first African government in Chad, and in the territorial elections two years later the party strengthened its control by gaining 57 of the 85 assembly seats. Despite a period of government instability (1958–59) during which Chad had several provisional governments (q.v.), in two of which the PPT was excluded, the party emerged strengthened from the ordeal.

In 1960 Lisette was purged by his rival in the PPT, Tombalbaye, partly in order to conciliate the Muslim parties in the assembly. The following year the PPT merged with the PNA (q.v.)—itself a merger of all the remaining anti-PPT elements in the country—to form the UPT (q.v.) alliance that was to collapse shortly after its formation, and early in 1962 a one-party system was declared. From 1962 to 1973, when the PPT was succeeded by the MNRCS, the party was both moribund and in a violent state of flux—the former because party organization atrophied, with all decisions being made by Tombalbaye and his immediate cronies, and the latter because purge and counterpurge were a constant feature of Chadian political life, greatly complicating efforts to understand the dominant factions within the government hierarchy. During these years both real and imagined factions were arrested, only to be amnestied several years later and then again purged. Despite these purges, and possibly because of them, the regime in power was highly unstable, with constant cabinet shuffles, scandals, and turmoil, while the stagnation of the party—its lack of zeal, militancy, or cohesion—brought about calls for its replacement by a new organ. In 1973 the MNRCS (q.v.) replaced the PPT, though in the two years prior to the 1975 coup d'état it was obvious that the change was largely one in nomenclature, with the new movement including most of the politicians of the old party.

PARTI PROGRESSISTE TCHADIEN (PPT) FORT-ARCHAMBAULT CONGRESS, 1971. The seventh congress of the PPT (q.v.) party, held in Fort-Archambault (later named Sarh) in April 1971. The congress was the site of the government's admissions that in the past "injustices of all sorts . . . many errors and blunders . . ." had been committed, leading to the revolts in the north and the east of the country. (These were references to the Bardai incidents in 1965 [q.v.] that led to the Toubou rebellion, and to the conditions surrounding the Mangalmé tax riots [q.v.] that marked the beginning of the rebellion in the east.) Calling upon all Chadians to "reintegrate themselves into the Chad family," Tombalbaye had his earlier major amnesties ratified by the congress, fully one-half of the PPT Political Bureau was dropped to make room for some ex-prisoners, and important foreign policy changes were announced. Among the formerly purged politicians to join the PPT Political Bureau were Djibrine Kherallah (q.v.), Abdelkerim Mahamat (q.v.), Mahamat Seid Abba (q.v.), Ali Kosso (q.v.), and Mahamat Saleh Abouguene Baba Hassane (q.v.); those dropped from the Political Bureau on that occasion included Ali Kéké (q.v.), Georges Diguimbayé, Pierre Djimé (q.v.), Martin Mahamat (q.v.), and General Jacques Doumro (q.v.).

PARTI REPUBLICAIN POUR LE SALUT NATIONAL DU TCHAD (PRSNT). Separatist movement, successor to the ad hoc Front Uni du Sud (FUS) (q.v.), set up in Moundou by a number of civil and military leaders, headed by Kamougoué (q.v.), on April 28, 1979. The party had a strong pan-African platform and opposed the pro-Muslim and pro-northern bias of the GUNT (q.v.) government in power in N'Djamena.

PARTI SOCIALISTE DU TCHAD (PST). Short-lived personalist formation founded in 1950 by Ahmed Koulamallah (q.v.) after he was ousted from his post as UDT (q.v.) treasurer. He later linked up with Adoum Aganayé (q.v.) to form the PSIT (q.v.) party, and when he failed to get along with Aganayé formed the PSK (q.v.) party. (See also POLITICAL PARTIES.)

PARTI SOCIALISTE INDEPENDANT DU TCHAD (PSIT). Cleavage-ridden early political party. Set up in 1951 by Ahmed Koulamallah (q.v.)—recently forced out of the UDT (q.v.) under accusations of embezzlement as the party's treasurer—after his brief tenure as head of the Parti Socialiste du Tchad (q.v.), and by Adoum Aganayé (q.v.), aimed at competing in the 1951 French National Assembly elections. Essentially a Fort-Lamy party that, due to Koulamallah's chiefly descent, was also popular among the Barma-Arab masses in Chari-Baguirmi, PSIT joined the FACT (q.v.) coalition of the PPT (q.v.) party in 1952 (see POLITICAL PARTIES). Koulamallah's ambitions and his rivalry with Ahmed Kotoko (q.v.) within FACT broke up the coalition right after the 1952 territorial elections, when PSIT was resurrected as an autonomous party. During 1952–53 PSIT—affiliated with the French SFIO socialist party—tried to develop grassroots support and to project itself as a truly militant grouping. But its planks opposing chiefly powers antagonized traditionalist Chad more than its antitaxation positions could placate it. In 1956 a major schism developed between PSIT's main leaders, resulting in PSIT president Koulamallah's purging Aganayé, only to find himself thrown out of the party when Aganayé made a comeback. Koulamallah then set up his own party, the MSA (q.v.), and Aganayé—later joined by Ahmed Kotoko—retained control over PSIT. The party participated in the 1957 PPT coalition—the ERDIC (q.v.)—and eventually merged with the PPT.

PARTI SOCIALISTE KOULAMALLISTE (PSK). Temporary personalist formation of Ahmed Koulamallah (q.v.) set up to compete in the 1956 Fort-Lamy municipal elections and legislative elections. The PSK was set up after Koulamallah was forced out of his PSIT (q.v.)

alliance with Adoum Aganayé. (See also POLITICAL PARTIES.) In the municipal race the PSK obtained 22 percent of the vote, second to Lisette's ERDIC, which won 50 percent, and six of the 33 council seats, with ERDIC winning 18. In the territorial elections the PSK obtained 39 percent of the vote in Chari-Baguirmi (due to Koulamallah's traditionalist credentials in that region) and 38 percent of the vote in Kanem. After the 1956 elections the PSK gave way to the MSA (q.v.), set up for the 1957 elections.

PARTIES see POLITICAL PARTIES

PEUL see FULANI

PHARMAT. State pharmaceutical monopoly over imports into Chad, and manufacturer of a limited number of items.

PILGRIMS. Traditionally several of the most frequented pilgrim routes to Mecca (see HAJJ) cross Chadian territory. It is estimated that as many of 40,000 Muslims pass through N'Djamena alone, in both directions, many coming or returning to Nigeria and most (until the rebellion in Chad) using Abéché in Ouadai as their connection to Sudan and the Red Sea. The constant pilgrim movement through Chad—not abated by the onset of air travel—has resulted in thousands of transient traders who often live for years in one locality earning funds for the next stage in the hajj; for some the trek is a lifelong trip. The escalation of the fighting in Chad from 1978 to 1983 brought about serious dislocations to the pilgrimage routes through Chad.

PIRCOLOSSOU, BENOIT (1934–). Party militant and, briefly, secretary of state. Born on April 27, 1934, in Bajakala Kélo. Pircolossou was a postal agent who eventually, through party work, was elected to the Territorial Assembly in May 1959 and became one of the very few deputies to remain in the assembly through 1975. He was appointed secretary of state for finance and economics but held the post for only 11 months (1963–64). In 1966 he served as questor and vice president of the National Assembly, and in 1970 he was on the administrative committee of Cotontchad (q.v.) as well as president of the Société Hôtelière du Tchad. From 1972 to 1975 Pircolossou was also president of the Public Works Committee of the National Assembly and PPT secretary for Tandjilé Préfecture. Pircolossou is the nephew of Chief Azina of the Marba (q.v.) and himself *chef de canton* of Bagaye.

POLDERS. Series of dikes connecting a large number of the islands and peninsulas on the northern fjordlike shore of Lake Chad (q.v.), existing from the precolonial era but especially spurred since independence. The dikes tap the lake's waters during the flood season, and after they evaporate rich alluvial soil is deposited, which the populations (Buduma and Kotoko) cultivate to raise two and even three wheat crops a season. After about 10 years the dikes are opened up permanently for three years to refertilize the polders, following which the process is repeated. Because the dikes are quite primitive and fragile, they tend to be swept away during significant expansions of the lake's surface (see LAKE CHAD), and during periods of acute aridity (as during the 1970s and 1980s) the lake's waters do not extend to the inner polders. In 1950, 1954, and 1962, for example, nearly all the dikes were swept away by a major rise in Lake Chad's level. Planting of wheat is usually done from October to January, with the harvest four months later. Wheat is also planted along the *wadis* (q.v.) of Kanem and in the oases of B.E.T., but the yield is minimal. Available land for the erection of polders is estimated at around 60,000 hectares (150,000 acres), of which about half is under use—around 9,000 hectares (22,000 acres) actually under cultivation, the remainder either dry or being refertilized. The SEMA (q.v.) organ SEMABLE (q.v.) was in charge of developing wheat potential of the Lac Préfecture (in which most of the polders lie) until 1967, when SODELAC (q.v.) assumed that function. Neither was overly successful in marketing operations or in keeping the Grands Moulins du Tchad (q.v.) supplied with local wheat; indeed, wheat imports have been required from abroad for the mills, since the polder harvesters have preferred to sell their crops directly to buyers (many from Nigeria) at a higher price than that offered by Chad government agents. In 1972/73, for example, of 7,000 tons produced, only 448 tons were sold to SODELAC.

POLICE see ARMED FORCES; SURETE NATIONALE

POLICE MILITAIRE. Post-1983 successor to the Gendarmerie Nationale (q.v.). With much the same functions, though now subordinate to the FANT (q.v.) and its northern commanders in N'Djamena, the change in name was necessary in order to disassociate the new force from its former total allegiance to Colonel Kamougoué (q.v.) and southern separatist sentiments.

POLITICAL PARTIES: PRE-1975. The era of indigenous politics began in Chad in the aftermath of the Second World War when political parties were allowed to emerge. Even a cursory enumeration of the groupings and alliances that were set up between 1945 and the 1975 coup would total over 45, and this not taking into account a variety of local (regional) formations set up for specific electoral contests. The more important of the Chadian political parties, alliances, and movements of this era are discussed below, grouped into five broad categories: (1) the conservative, chiefly, and largely Muslim parties, including their European allies, that practically dominated the Chadian political scene until 1957; (2) the progressive non-Muslim parties and alliances, essentially the PPT and the various coalitions it formed throughout the years; (3) the major "socialist" or independent formations that in one way or another cooperated with the parties in the first two categories and most of which were the creation of Ahmed Koulamallah (q.v.); (4) minor or local groupings of lesser importance; and (5) the various pre-1975 opposition or rebel movements, including in particular FROLINAT. For detailed information on these parties, see the individual party entries. For post-1975 "parties," see the next entry, POLITICAL PARTIES: 1975–1996.

The conservative, chiefly, and Muslim parties and their European allies

European groupings. These were essentially narrow political vehicles for European (i.e., French) economic interests competing for local or foreign (French) representation from the first electoral roll (see DOUBLE ELECTORAL COLLEGE). In the early years, as many as half of the European delegates to the French National Assembly ran and were elected as independents, though many linked themselves with one or another of the French political parties. On the local (Chadian) level, European (first electoral college) parties were allied with African parties (of the second electoral college), invariably with those of deep conservative hues. All the parties were essentially right of center and became the Rassemblement du Peuple Français (RPF) (q.v.) in 1947.

Union Démocratique et Socialiste de la Résistance (UDSR). (See also party of the same name in category 2 below.) The UDSR was a European party created in 1946 to compete for the French Constituent Assembly's seats (electing René Malbrant [q.v.] from the first college and helping to elect de Boissoudy from the second), and to compete for the 1946 first electoral college French National Assembly seat (won by Malbrant). In 1947 the UDSR merged with the RPF (q.v.), and Chad's European delegates ran on the RPF ticket. The name of the Chadian branch of the RPF since 1950 was the Action Democratique et Sociale (ADS).

Union Républicaine du Tchad (URT). Not to be confused with "URT-1959." Early loosely knit European party created in 1946 under the leadership of, among others, Marcel Lallia (q.v.), to compete for the Conseil Représentatif and AEF Grand Council seats. Precursor to France's conservative RPF, of which the URT officially became the local Chadian branch in 1947. The URT-RPF was always closely allied on the domestic level with the African Union Démocratique du Tchad (UDT) (q.v.) and its offshoots. After the abolition of the double electoral college, several of the French URT-RPF-ADS leaders joined the UDT party, the AST (q.v.).

Rassemblement du Peuple Français (RPF). De Gaulle's party in France and also the name (1947–50) of its Chadian branch. Successor to the URT in Chad, competing for the first electoral college seats during 1947–50; the party was later renamed Action Démocratique et Sociale (ADS). For all practical purposes the same leadership strata participated in all three formations.

Action Démocratique et Sociale (ADS). Local RPF movement, successor to the URT and RPF parties in Chad. The ADS competed in the 1951 French National Assembly elections on the first electoral roll, allied to the RPF-affiliated second electoral roll party, the UDT. Following the abolition of the double electoral college (q.v.) the ADS (ex-URT, ex-RPF, ex-UDSR), European leaders joined the African conservative AST (q.v.) party with which they had been allied in the past.

Union Indépendante pour la Défense des Intérêts Communaux (UIDIC). AST-linked European party (with two Africans on its lists) that competed in the 1956 Fort-Lamy municipal elections in the European zones of the city. After the election the electoral list disbanded and merged with the AST.

(b) African parties.

Union Démocratique du Tchad (UDT). The first African party to organize, the UDT conservative loose chiefly alliance was allied, even directed, by the European first electoral college parties UDSR, URT, and RPF. The UDT in turn dominated indigenous political life in Chad from its founding in 1946 to 1954, and under a different name until 1956–57. Its most prominent leaders included Gountchomé Sahoulba (q.v.)—later to be briefly head of government—and Arabi-el-Goni (q.v.). All other successor chiefly or Muslim parties emerged first as factions within the UDT. By 1953, having suffered multiple cleavages and secessions, the party disappeared as a separate formation, its ideological successor being the AST (q.v.). The UDT was first deserted by the followers of Ahmed Koulamallah (q.v.) in 1950 (who set up his own PST, later PSIT, party), and in 1951 Ahmed Kotoko (q.v.)—briefly a member—also deserted the party to join the UDSR. In 1953 former governor Rogué—of the first electoral college—set up the UDIT party of rebel segments of the UDT, following which the badly truncated party was renamed the AST. The AST was also to suffer schisms and secessions, especially in 1956.

Action Sociale Tchadienne (AST). Post-1953–54 successor to the

UDT, formed as a highly independent faction within the UDT as early as 1952. Aligned with the first electoral college RPF, as was the UDT, the AST included the hard-core Muslim chiefly elements, with its strength in Ouadai, Batha, and parts of Mayo-Kebbi. The AST, like the UDT before it, suffered from severe schisms, including the 1956 desertion of Bechir Sow (q.v.), who left to form his Bloc Tchadien (BT) (q.v.) party, and the 1957 formation of the highly pragmatic GIRT (q.v.) party. In the 1957 elections the PPT coalition ERDIC (q.v.) offered to form an electoral compact with the AST under which the latter would be guaranteed 20 of the 65 seats. The offer was refused, and in the subsequent elections the AST was trounced, gaining only 14 seats. After a series of defections and secessions, in the 1959 elections the party retained only nine seats (in the larger 85-member assembly). Several European expatriates participated all along in AST politics, having joined the party once the double electoral college (q.v.) was abolished. Weakened over the years by its various splits and rivalries, the AST was compelled to join in several wider alliances, including the UST, MPT, PNA, and UNT (qq.v.). The AST disappeared as a separate party with the creation of the UST alliance, though all along in future formations an AST informal faction remained.

Union Démocratique Indépendante du Tchad (UDIT). Founded in 1953 by former governor Rogué and a segment of the UDT, controlled by Jean Baptiste (q.v.)—the UDIT's most dominant leader—the UDIT was strong in Ouadai and Batha. The party cooperated selectively with the PPT, despite its essentially conservative coloration, though in local contests in Ouadai it helped the AST. In 1957 Jean Baptiste was estranged from ERDIC (a PPT alliance) following the PPT's selection of its own stalwarts to represent Chad at the OCRS (q.v.), contrary to Baptiste's desire to head the delegation or to have one of his protégés (Issa Allatchimi) in that capacity. The UDIT, which had obtained seven of the 65 assembly seats in 1957 and 16 in 1959, then joined the AST and other anti-PPT parties to form the UST alliance (see below).

Groupement des Indépendants et Ruraux Tchadiens (GIRT). An AST faction that organized itself in 1956 and became a separate party in 1957. It selectively cooperated with the PPT in various electoral contests. Headed by Gountchomé Sahoulba (q.v.)—formerly a top AST leader—the party gained nine seats in the 1957 territorial elections and played a pivotal role in 1958–59, balancing the UST and the PPT alliances. In January 1959 the GIRT's desertion of the Entente (q.v.)-PPT coalition in favor of the UST brought down the Gabriel Lisette (q.v.) provisional government, and Sahoulba was called upon to form the next cabinet. Sahoulba's government soon collapsed as splits developed within the fragile coalition hammered out, and in subsequent developments and elections the GIRT lost its former pivotal position in Chadian politics. The party eventually merged into the PNA alliance of all anti-PPT parties.

Union Socialiste Tchadienne (UST). Short-lived AST-UDIT-MSA (qq.v.) 1958–59 alliance forged by Ahmed Koulamallah against the ERDIC coalition of Gabriel Lisette. In January 1959 the GIRT deserted ERDIC, toppling the Lisette provisional government and assisting in the creation of a Sahoulba-led cabinet. GIRT's move to the UST resulted in a change in the name of the wider anti-PPT group and the UST was renamed the Mouvement Populaire Tchadien (MPT).

Mouvement Populaire Tchadien (MPT). Successor to the UST following the GIRT's entry into the alliance after it left the PPT coalition ERDIC. The MPT formed the next provisional government under Gountchomé Sahoulba, holding 34 seats to ERDIC's 31. Ahmed Koulamallah's machinations and ambitions at this juncture, and his withdrawal of his MSA from the MPT, brought down the Sahoulba government within a month, ushered in a very brief provisional government under his aegis, and eventually paved the way for a PPT-dominated government under François Tombalbaye (q.v.). The remaining anti-PPT parties reunited in January 1960 to form the PNA.

Parti National Africain (PNA). The last legal anti-PPT coalition before the imposition of a one-party system. The PNA united remnants of the AST, GIRT, UDIT, MSA, and MESAN (qq.v.) that had not gone over to the PPT. Essentially a Muslim party with vocal leftist (MSA) Chari-Baguirmi and rightist (AST) Ouadai wings, the PNA was under the (honorary) presidency of Ahmed Koulamallah, the executive presidency of Jean Baptiste—these two being bitter enemies—and with Djibrine Kherallah (q.v.), Seydou Tall, and Mahamat-el-Goni (q.v.) in top executive positions as well. Starting out with 25 of the 85 seats of the National Assembly, the PNA suffered defections and declined in strength to 10 seats. In March 1961 the party agreed to merge with the dominant PPT—essentially creating a one-party state. The PPT-PNA alliance—the UPT—was short-lived despite a "unity congress" in Abéché, stronghold of the PNA, and vocal pledges of continued unity. The PNA broke out of the alliance when in the mayoralty races then scheduled, the PPT fielded its own candidates (without consultation with its PNA "partner") and disallowed the PNA lists when these were submitted somewhat later. The break occurred in mid-1961, and in January 1962 the government disbanded the PNA, declaring a single-party state. Hard-core opposition members who did not rally to the PPT at this stage were either driven underground (see category 4 below) or were eventually arrested by the Tombalbaye government.

The "progressive" non-Muslim parties and alliances

These were all—with the exception of Ahmed Koulamallah's various groupings—at one time or another linked with or cooperating with the RDA-affiliated PPT party of Gabriel Lisette and Francois Tombalbaye.

Parti Progressiste Tchadien (PPT). Southern Sara-based political party established in 1946 by Gabriel Lisette and affiliated from the outset with the African interterritorial movement, the RDA. The PPT faced a long struggle against the conservative and chiefly parties (especially the UDT and the AST) as well as expatriate-sponsored formations until 1957, when it clearly gained ascendance. In 1961 the PPT absorbed the last flexible remnants of its opposition (see PNA) and shortly later banned all other political parties in Chad. The PPT began with a strong militant anti-chiefly, anti-French, anti-cotton-cultivation program that both alarmed and antagonized the French administration (which supported the PPT's opposition) and traditional elements everywhere. Until 1957 the PPT sponsored very few chiefs (in 1952, only one) under its label in electoral contests, though later the need to acquire broader support—and the PPT's more centrist line—gained it a fair number of traditional leaders, especially in the south. (In like manner the PPT dropped most of its former more prominent platforms.) From 1952 the party very slowly gained electoral strength through the expansion of the electorate consequent to French reforms in their colonies (giving the heavily populated south greater political clout), the merger into the PPT of various former independent political formations or of more pragmatic politicians once associated with the PPT's opposition, and the forging of various alliances with other, like-minded parties. In 1957 the PPT coalition formed the first African government in Chad, and in the 1959 elections the alliance increased its electoral strength by garnering 57 of the territory's 85 seats. In the interim the country was ruled by a succession of provisional governments (q.v.), during which Gabriel Lisette was purged and exiled and Tombalbaye percolated to the top of the leadership hierarchy. Shortly thereafter, all other parties were banned, and purges, arrests, and disqualifications of citizenship (and hence expulsions) became the norm. From the time of independence these policies decimated the party as both former opposition members in it and loyal Tombalbaye supporters were purged for one reason or another. In 1973 the party was finally replaced by an allegedly more militant movement, the MNRCS (q.v.), which was supposed to carry out the "Cultural Revolution" (q.v.) in the country, revitalizing the spirit of the nation.

Front d'Action Civique du Tchad (FACT). First major PPT alliance, formed in 1951 and composed of the PPT, PSIT, UDSR, and other independents. FACT won six of the 30 seats of the Conseil Représentatif, the others going to the opposition UDT. The leaders of FACT were the leaders of the component groups in it, namely Lisette, Tombalbaye, Koulamallah, Kotoko, and Aganayé (qq.v.). Due to the PPT's then-acute weakness, FACT's president was Koulamallah. After the 1952 elections FACT fell apart consequent to Koulamallah's ambitions.

Entente Républicaine pour la Défense des Intérêts Communaux (ERDIC). Also referred to as "Entente," and practically identical in composition to the temporary alliance called Entente pour l'Application de la Loi-Cadre. Fluid coalitions were composed of the PPT of Lisette and the UDIT of Jean Baptiste, with the support of fragments of other, smaller groups. ERDIC won its first victory in the 1956 Fort-Lamy municipal elections, following which its majority increased as Ahmed Kotoko (q.v.) and his RPDT party as well as several independents joined the alliance. Despite internal tensions, ERDIC maintained its basic unity and scored a major victory in the 1957 elections, which led to the creation of Chad's first African government under Gabriel Lisette. (The Entente gained 47 seats, of which 32 were of the PPT.) In 1958 the PPT obtained the support of the pivotal ex-AST (q.v.) GIRT (q.v.) party (the PPT had been deserted by the UDIT over Lisette's rejection of Baptiste's nominees for the OCRS), though later the GIRT also deserted the PPT, leading to a period of instability (see PROVISIONAL GOVERNMENTS). Most of the "progressive" elements that had cooperated with the PPT in the formation of the various coalitions (such as ERDIC, Entente, etc.) fully merged with the PPT in 1960.

Union Tchadienne (UT). PPT-PSIT-UDSR electoral coalition headed by Gabriel Lisette in the 1956 elections for the French National Assembly. The UT garnered the largest number of votes.

Union Démocratique et Socialiste de la Résistance (UDSR). The former Gaullist precursor party label resurrected by Ahmed Kotoko for his campaign in the 1951 French National Assembly elections and in several subsequent contests. (See also category 1 European parties). The UDSR was always particularly close to the PPT. In 1952 it participated in the formation of the FACT alliance and later joined in ERDIC and in the Entente. In the 1957 elections the UDSR's share of the ERDIC seats in the National Assembly was seven of the 47 (of a total of 65 seats), and the PPT's share was 32. Some time later the UDSR fully merged with the PPT.

Regroupement des Partis Politiques du Tchad (RPPT). Local coalition based around Adoum Aganayé and Ahmed Kotoko and their respective parties, the PSIT and UDSR (qq.v.), in the 1956 Fort-Lamy municipal elections. After obtaining 20 percent of the vote, the RPPT disbanded and joined the PPT coalition, ERDIC.

Union pour le Progrès du Tchad (UPT). Brief merger of the PPT and opposition PNA (q.v.). Formed in March 1961 as a voluntary alliance that would have established a de facto one-party system in Chad, the union of all political factions—and the "historic reconciliation" of the animist/Christian progressive south with the Muslim-traditionalist east—was celebrated in a "unity congress" in Abéché in April 1961. The alliance soon collapsed over the PPT's unilateral designation of candidates for Chad's mayoralty elections (without consultation with its partner, the PNA) and the PNA's decision to run its own slates, which the PPT disallowed. Soon after, the PNA and all other political parties in Chad were declared illegal.

Mouvement National pour la Révolution Culturelle et Sociale (MNRCS). Successor to the PPT party, established in September 1973 after the PPT Sarh Congress of August 27–30, 1973. The new movement—with new structures, policies, and directives (including the promulgation of the "Cultural Revolution")—was supposed to revitalize the country, allegedly sunken into apathy, lethargy, and inertia by the PPT. The party was banned after the 1975 coup d'état.

The "Socialist" parties

These were mostly the political vehicles of Chad's mercurial and opportunistic Ahmed Koulamallah, who, as a devout Muslim (head of the Tidjaniya [q.v.] order), a militant socialist, and a traditional leader, gravitated from supporting the archconservative Ouadai parties to joining the PPT in opportunistic alliances, to setting up militant leftist groupings.

Parti Socialiste du Tchad (PST). Short-lived 1950 personalist formation headed by Koulamallah after he was expelled from his post as treasurer of the conservative-traditionalist UDT in 1950 and before he joined with Adoum Aganayé in setting up the PSIT party.

Parti Socialiste Indépendant du Tchad (PSIT). Cleavage-ridden political party founded late in 1951 by Ahmed Koulamallah and Adoum Aganayé. (See also PARTI SOCIALISTE DU TCHAD.) Essentially a Fort-Lamy party, though quite popular also among the masses of Chari-Baguirmi (due to Koulamallah's traditional credentials), the PSIT was internationally linked to the French Socialist Party, SFIO. PSIT joined the PPT-based FACT coalition but left it later due to Koulamallah-Kotoko friction as well as to Koulamallah's ambition to dominate the alliance. In 1956 PSIT was rent by a major falling-out of its two dominant personalities, with each one formally drumming the other out of the party. Eventually Koulamallah set up a new political party (at the outset called the Parti Socialiste Koulamalliste) while Aganayé retained control of the rump of the PSIT membership, later to be joined in it by Ahmed Kotoko. The party then joined the PPT-organized ERDIC alliance (1956)—adding only one seat to the Entente's 1957 total—and soon thereafter merged fully with the PPT.

Parti Socialiste Koulamalliste (PSK). Temporary 1956 name for Ahmed Koulamallah's political faction after he was expelled from PSIT consequent to a major personality clash between him and Adoum Aganayé. In the 1956 Fort-Lamy municipal elections, the PSK granted 22 percent of the votes (to the 50 percent of the PPT coalition, ERDIC) and six of the 33 seats (to ERDIC's 18), and in the same year's partial territorial elections the PSK won 39 percent of the vote in Chari-Baguirmi and 38 percent in Kanem. The party then worked out its formal name, becoming the Mouvement Socialiste Africain, under which name it competed in the 1957 Territorial Assembly elections.

Mouvement Socialiste Africain (MSA). Ahmed Koulamallah's 1957 successor party to the PSK, composed of elements who followed him out of PSIT after his personality clash with PSIT cofounder Adoum Aganayé. The party was internationally linked to the interterritorial party with the same name, which was unsuccessful, in Chad as elsewhere, in gaining political primacy. In both the 1957 and 1959 elections the MSA did not gain any seats in the Territorial Assembly, though Koulamallah retained his popularity in Kanem and Chari-Baguirmi. The party then joined in the anti-PPT Gountchomé Sahoulba government (the MPT alliance), though Koulamallah's desertion of the alliance brought it down and ushered in his own 12-day cabinet, following which power swung back to the PPT. Following this period of the unstable provisional governments (q.v.), the MSA joined in another additional anti-PPT coalition, the PNA, and in the aftermath of the collapse of the PNA-PPT alliance (UPT) the MSA was banned in Chad along with all other political parties. In 1963 Koulamallah and a large number of other opposition leaders were arrested.

Bloc des Travailleurs Démocrates Tchadiens (BTDT). Trade union list for the 1956 French National Assembly elections, headed by the radical Jean Charlot and Ahmet Mahamat Saleh (qq.v.). The list gained 4,843 votes to Gabriel Lisette's 130,843. In various guises and under various names the same group of leaders competed (futilely) in the elections up to 1959, hoping to draw support from "the proletariat"; in 1959 the party's major leaders joined the PPT.

Parti Communiste Tchadien (PCT). Minor nucleus headed by Malla Djama Pleven and composed mostly of unionists and students. Probably founded in 1957, and largely inactive, very little is known about the PCT.

Other minor or local groupings

Union de Guéra. A 1959 local electoral alliance between the UDIT and the MSA in Guéra Préfecture.

Union de Kanem. A 1959 local electoral compact between the UDIT and the MSA in Kanem against the PPT.

Union Logonaise. A local electoral alliance in 1959 between all the non-PPT parties (AST, GIRT, UDIT, MSA, and MESAN) to contest (unsuccessfully) the PPT's dominance in the Logone region.

Union Franco-Kanembu. Minor party contesting the Kanem seats in the 1952 elections.

Union Républicaine et Progressiste du Tchad (URPT). Early political list in the second electoral college 1946 elections. Headed by Jules Pierre Toura Gaba (q.v.), who later joined the PPT, and Ibrahim Babikir (q.v.). The party won four seats, three of which were from the Lac region. After Toura Gaba's defection in favor of the PPT, the URPT was absorbed by the UDT party.

Mouvement d'Emancipation Sociale de l'Afrique Noire (MESAN). Political movement of the Central African Republic (at the time Oubangui-Chari) that in 1959 ran a few candidates in Chad's southern border districts, appealing to ethnic groups divided by the C.A.R.-Chad border. The party was only moderately successful among these groups, and hardly at all at the national level. In 1959 MESAN/Chad forged the anti-PPT URT, and later (1961) joined the PNA, anti-PPT alliance.

Union Républicaine du Tchad (URT-1959). Not to be confused with the 1946 European party with the same name, the URT-1959 was the temporary label for MESAN's attempts to forge an anti-PPT coalition in the southern border districts. Headed by Seydou Tall in the 1959 elections, the party was only successful in a few areas and soon joined the PNA.

Union Progressiste Franco-Tchadienne (UPFT). Local Kanem list for the 1946 Conseil Représentatif elections in Kanem. Based in Mao and supported by chiefly elements, the UPFT was headed by Bechir Sow. It was later absorbed by the UDT party.

Bloc Tchadien (BT). A 1956 electoral list headed by Bechir Sow after his estrangement from the AST (q.v.). The party competed in the 1956 French National Assembly elections, gaining the lowest number of votes.

Rebel Movements

Union Nationale Tchadienne (UNT). Main precursor of FROLINAT. Established as an extremely radical and militantly Muslim party in November 1958, the UNT gained two seats in the 1959 elections (from Chari-Baguirmi). Mostly an Arab party, headed by Issa Danna, with other leaders like Abba Siddick (q.v.) and Mahamat Ousman, the party joined and then left the northern MPT alliance, trying to establish grassroots support among the peasants. After being banned in 1962 along with Chad's other political parties, the UNT was resurrected by Mahamat Seid Abba and Ibrahim Abatcha (qq.v.), and established itself in Sudan, beginning guerrilla operations in Chad around 1965. Its political headquarters later shifted to North Africa, and after merging with the MNLT and UGFT (qq.v.), formed the FROLINAT rebel movement.

Union Générale des Fils du Tchad (UGFT). Conservative Muslim sociocultural movement, with Muslim Brotherhood links and support, led by Hassan Ahmed Moussa (q.v.), who, with UGFT support, members, and funds, founded the MNLT, which later merged with the UNT to form the FROLINAT. The merger soon collapsed, and Moussa's group continued antigovernment operations under the name of Front de Libération du Tchad (FLT).

Mouvement National de Libération du Tchad (MNLT). Precursor of the Front de Libération du Tchad (FLT). Founded by Hassan Ahmed Moussa as a traditionalist Muslim party aiming at the secession of eastern and northern Chad and supported by funds and members from the UGFT. In June 1966 the MNLT briefly merged with Ibrahim Abatcha's UNT to form FROLINAT; personality and ideological cleavages caused the dissolution of the union, following which the MNLT began armed rebellion in eastern Chad under the name Front de Libération du Tchad (FLT).

Front de Libération du Tchad (FLT). Not to be confused with the Front de Libération Nationale (FROLINAT), which was in many respects a more bitter enemy to the FLT than the Chad government. Successor to the MNLT after the latter's 1966 withdrawal from its brief union with the UNT in the form of FROLINAT. Largely moribund, more involved in occasional brigandage than in revolutionary struggle, and "led" by Moussa from Khartoum in Sudan, the FLT has operated mostly in Ouadai and other areas in eastern Chad. The FLT rallied back to the government in the early 1970s.

Front de Libération Nationale (FROLINAT). Successor to the UNT and dominant political and military Muslim guerrilla organization, still fighting the regime in N'Djamena. Based in Algiers and in Tripoli, and led by Dr. Abba Siddick—whose leadership was repudiated, however, by the Toubou (q.v.) Second Liberation Army (q.v.) in the B.E.T.—FROLINAT was a radical neo-Marxist movement aiming, alternatively, at overthrowing the N'Djamena government and/or at withdrawing Chad's Muslim regions (the east and north) from the control of the Sara southern leadership.

Mouvement Révolutionnaire Tchadien (MRT). Led by former Tombalbaye aide André Mougnan (q.v.), the MRT was founded in

1966 in southern Chad to dispute the political dominance of Tombalbaye and to promote the ethnic interests of the Gambayé (q.v.) people. Of little practical import except in a few Gambayé districts, the MRT collapsed with the arrest and imprisonment of Mougnan; the latter rallied to the government after his release in 1971.

Front National al-Khoumi. Little-known Khartoum-based anti-Tombalbaye political movement set up in 1969.

Mouvement Démocratique de la Rénovation Tchadienne (MDRT). Stillborn Paris-based opposition party set up in 1973 by Dr. Outel Bono (q.v.), who was promptly murdered by Chadian secret agents. The party would have entered into a dialogue with FROLINAT—though it opposed a political compromise—and would have adopted more nationalist domestic and foreign postures.

POLITICAL PARTIES: 1975–1996. Most of the post-1975 political formations have been "parties" largely in name only. Essentially elitist formations, some of the more pretentious groupings had/have fewer than 100 adherents, temporary or intermittent. Others were splinters of FROLINAT (q.v.) after it became divorced from Dr. Abba Siddick (q.v.) and taken over, in different name, by Goukouni (q.v.). Finally, none of the post-1975 parties faced an electoral battle, seriously organized grassroots support (though Hissène Habré's UNIR [qq.v.] did make an effort to mobilize the vote), developed programs or platforms (as distinct from simple catch-all slogans), or indeed performed any of the tasks that parties normally perform at one time or another.

The most important groups that have formed since 1975 may be organized into five categories: (1) The offshoots of FROLINAT; (2) Goukouni's or his GUNT alliance partners; (3) Habré's governmental party; (4) Various elitist groupings that arose in opposition to Habré's rule; and (5) the large number of parties that sprang up, or were legalized, in the period since the liberalization of the 1990s. For further details, see the individual entries of all parties. For readers seeking only contemporary political formations, the parties listed in category 5 will also include parties that may have been formed (under the same or different leadership) prior to 1990 and survived to the contemporary era.

Offshoots of FROLINAT

After Dr. Abba Siddick's (q.v.) ouster from FROLINAT and the emergence of Goukouni and Habré as the main military power-wielders of the rebel movement, FROLINAT rapidly disappeared. For some time Goukouni referred to his military force as CCFAN-FROLINAT, and later as FAP-FROLINAT, but by 1977 the old acronym was no longer used. Several of the original FROLINAT leaders, however, continued to use the name.

FROLINAT-Originel: grouping of core Arab pro-Siddick loyalists, headed by Abba Siddick. A minute grouping, FROLINAT-Originel suffered from attrition, and in 1984 split into two as one segment, unhappy with Siddick's alliance with Habré (as the latter's minister of education), joined in the anti-Habré and anti-Goukouni Rassemblement des Forces Patriotiques (see category 4 below) under Abdelkadir Yacine (q.v.).

FROLINAT-Fondamental: pro-Sudanese, pro-Islamic grouping, always separatist within the original FROLINAT, and beholden to Mahamat Seid Abba (q.v.), Adoum Hadjero Senoussi (q.v.) and Mamadio Balassane (q.v.), it possessed some guerrilla strength.

FROLINAT-Orthodoxe: personalist following of Mohammed Hajero Senoussi. This party was pro-Sudanese, and religiously more fundamentalist. It had, however, only a limited number of guerrilla fighters. In 1995 a "FROLINAT" of minuscule proportions still exists, however, headed in exile by Mahmoud Ali Mahmoud.

GUNT political formations

Rassemblement National pour la Démocratie et le Progrès (RNDP). Political party set up in January 1982 in N'Djamena, by Minister of Justice Delwa Kassiré Koumakoyé, with political power pretensions within the GUNT government. It later rallied to Habré and merged with his UNIR (q.v.). It was resurrected as an alliance, with the same name, during the Idriss Déby (q.v.) era (see category 5 below).

Rassemblement pour l'Unité et la Démocratie au Tchad (RUDT). Political movement founded with some fanfare by Dono-Ngardoum Djidingar (q.v.), a southerner, after his appointment as prime minister in the GUNT government in 1982. Another cofounder, later to become prime minister of Chad, was Jean Bawoyeu Alingué (q.v.). Aimed at a reconciliation between the north and the south—under Djidingar's ambitious aegis—RUDT grouped together several ex-Tombalbaye officials seeking new legitimacy and credentials. There was little organizational effort, and Habré's military assault from the east foredoomed the party, which then rallied to Habré in 1984 and merged with his UNIR.

Organisation de Libération du Tchad de Fascisme et de l'Imperialisme (OLTFI). Lagos-based, politico-military grouping claiming to have launched attacks on Habré bases in Chari-Baguirmi and in the south. Formed in November 1983, the party is a vehicle for the Goukouni's GSN in B.E.T.

Mouvement Populaire et Révolutionnaire du Tchad (MPRT). Colonel Kamougoué's GUNT-affiliated movement.

Conseil Démocratique de la Révolution (CDR). Successor to the Second FROLINAT Army, which after Acyl's (q.v.) death came under the leadership of Acheikh Ibn Oumar (q.v.) and became the major fighting force of GUNT. In the mid-1980s, however, it was rent by a bitter crisis over its orientation vis-à-vis Libya and Sudan, complicated by secular-Muslim issues, and it split into three. Acheikh some time later rallied to Habré; Adoum Rakhis Manani (q.v.), its number two leader, retained the CDR rump behind the increasingly irrelevant GUNT; and Dr. Moctar Moussa (q.v.) remained in Tripoli with a small segment of the original movement.

Comité d'Action et de Coordination (CAC). One of the factions of the CDR set up in 1984 by Mahamat Senoussi Khatir (q.v.). It seceded completely from the CDR in August 1984 over the latter's overly pro-Libyan postures and rallied to Habré in 1985.

The Habré governmental party

Union Nationale pour l'Indépendance et la Révolution (UNIR). Founded in June 1984 (indicative of Habré's low priority on political mobilization) as the governmental party. It was not very active, though it did set up women's and youth branches, and it had a minor presence in much of the south. UNIR's main branches were in N'Djamena, where office-holders and office-seekers from all the préfectures tended to congregate. UNIR presented a slate for the 1990 single party/multicandidate elections that ushered in a national assembly, but shortly later Idriss Déby came to power and UNIR was banned. The "successor" of UNIR was one branch of the MDD (see category 5 below), which is still intermittently launching military assaults in the Lake Chad region.

Antinorthern and anti-Habré groupings

A number of these sprang up, starting with the 1975 coup, and especially after the disengagement of the Sara south from the northern préfectures. Only the most well-known or longest-lasting formations are listed here, chronologically.

Union Nationale Démocratique (UND). Formed by Dr. Facho Balaam (q.v.) as an underground movement in the last year of Tombalbaye's regime (1974) and becoming more prominent in 1975, the UND originally had its headquarters in the C.A.R., with a small ethnic base in southwestern Chad. Seen by Tombalbaye as a FROLINAT front group, the UND actually was in opposition to both Tombalbaye and FROLINAT. After the coup of 1975, the UND played an independent and equivocal role favoring a north-south reconciliation but rejecting the credentials of both Habré and Goukouni. After the latter's ouster in 1982, the UND joined in the Goukouni-led GSN opposition in B.E.T. However, in 1984, alarmed at the Libyan role in the Goukouni military advances, the UND joined with several other groups, including former FROLINAT splinter factions, to form the Rassemblement des Forces Patriotiques (RFP).

Rassemblement des Forces Patriotiques (RFP). Political alliance between the UND, headed by Dr. Facho Balaam (q.v.), and several splinter groups, including elements of FROLINAT-Originel, FROLINAT-Fondamental, and others. Formed at a congress in Ouagadougou, Burkina Faso, on August 12, 1984, the movement, headed by Balaam, was both anti-Goukouni and anti-Habré.

Front Uni du Sud (FUS). The classic and first antinorthern (or south-firster) movement, set up in Moundou by a group of civil and military leaders after the fall of N'Djamena in 1978 and the Sara disengagement from the capital. Aimed at unifying the south in light of the dangers attending the civil war defeat, the FUS led to the setting up of the Comité Permanente du Sud (CPS) along more structured lines as the administration of the southern préfectures, and the following year (1979) to the founding of the PRSNT.

Parti Républicain pour le Salut National du Tchad (PRSNT). Successor to the Front Uni du Sud (FUS), formed in Moundou by Colonel Kamougoué on April 28, 1979. The PRSNT had a strong pan-Africanist platform, grouped together many civil and military leaders of the south, and had as its prime goal the conservation of the autonomy of the Sara south. The PRSNT cooperated on the national level with Goukouni, who respected the quasi autonomy of the south while giving its leaders a significant share in the government of Chad.

Mouvement Démocratique Tchadien (MDT). Moribund party set up on May 31, 1979, at a congress in Bédiondo (near Doba) with much the same goals as the FUS. It merged with Habré's UNIR in 1984.

Mouvement Patriotique National (MPN). Political movement set up by Doungou Kemto (q.v.) in June 1981, grouping southern and eastern civil and military leaders concerned about the increasing role and presence of Libya in Chad. The movement had the distinction of allying to the south a number of former FROLINAT pro-Sudan leaders such as Moussa Medela (q.v.) and Batram Adam Idriss.

Action Tchadienne pour l'Unité et le Socialisme (ACTUS). Originally one of several small political groups to spring up in 1984 in the south in opposition to the Habré administration. ACTUS was a southern quasi-socialist party that joined in Facho Balaam's 1984 Rassemblement des Forces Patriotiques (RFP) and merged with the Mouvement Révolutionnaire du Peuple Tchadien (MRPT) in 1990. It was resurrected in 1992 by Fidèle Moungar (q.v.), who was to become prime minister.

Mouvement pour le Socialisme et la Démocratie au Tchad (MSDT). A Sara opposition group set up in 1988 by Ahmet Mahamat Saleh (q.v.), which was to become influential after 1992. (For more details, see category 5.)

Front Démocratique du Tchad (FDT). Political movement set up in September 1984 by General Djogo (q.v.) after he gave up his post as commander in chief of the ANL (q.v.) forces of GUNT. He attracted the support of Colonel Djimé (q.v.), Jean Bawoyeu Alingué (q.v.), and several former southern cabinet ministers, and in early 1986 rallied to the Habré regime.

Mouvement de Salut Nationale du Tchad (MOSANAT). This was a new kind of movement, in that it was formed by former Hadjeray (q.v.) allies of Habré, led by Lt. Maldoum Bada Abbas (q.v.), disenchanted with Habré after he started systematically to purge and liquidate their leaders. Formed in October 1986, it began guerrilla activity in Guéra and later merged with Déby's Zaghawa (q.v.) revolt to triumph against Habré.

Union Socialiste Tchadienne (UST). Political formation of Abderahman Koulamallah (q.v.), son of former Chadian master politician Ahmed Koulamallah (q.v.), set up in 1986 in Paris, but it did not attract much attention.

Groupe des Démocrates et Patriotes (GDP). Another of Jean Alingué's several political formations. Set up in 1984, the GDP stood for an independent posture vis-à-vis Goukouni and Habré.

Union Populaire Tchadienne. Party set up in Paris in opposition to Habré under Secretary-General Yacoub Mahamat Ourada, who rallied to Habré in July 1988.

Post-1990 political parties and rebel movements.

A large number of such formations were formed after the political liberalization ushered in by Idriss Déby once he came to power. (In mid-1995 there were an estimated 55 parties, not counting former parties, merged groupings, and rebel movements.) Elections were promised for as early as 1992 but have been postponed several times, and are now not anticipated before mid-1996. Conceivably they could be postponed again, since Déby is unlikely to relish losing parliamentary control, his ethnic base being minor and his enemies many. Some other "parties," having secured representation in the 1993 Conférence Nationale (q.v.) and in the subsequent interim national assembly, are also none too anxious to put to the test the strength of their electoral support. Since no competitive elections have taken place since 1962, and much has changed in Chad, it is extremely difficult to estimate the real strength and the likely staying power of many of these formations or the various intraparty alliances among them. All observers note that most parties are totally devoid of platform or ideology and are primarily personalist, ethnic, and regional political vehicles. Most of those parties currently playing a role in Chad are listed here; as noted in the entry's introduction, some were founded in earlier periods.

Mouvement Patriotique du Salut (MPS). Idriss Déby's political party, grouping in particular his own Zaghawa (q.v.) ethnic followers, but also strong among some Hadjeray (q.v.) despite the fact that he alienated some of their leaders. The MPS has also absorbed a variety of other political fragments such as the FROLINAT-Fondamental under Mamadio Balassane.

Mouvement pour la Démocratie et le Développement (MDD). There are actually two wings of the MDD. One is remnants of the FAO, expressing Kanuri grievances, that never put down their arms and have been fighting N'Djamena from holdout camps in Nigeria and around Lake Chad, led by Moussa Medela (q.v.). A second group is composed of remnants of Habré's forces, after he was ousted from power, headed by Goukouni Guet (q.v.) until captured, and then by Ibrahim Malla Mahamat (q.v.). They jointly tried to advance on N'Djamena, especially from 1991 to 1993. The two distinctly different groups were briefly united under the MDD banner in 1991 but later fell apart to fight each other. In April 1995 it was announced that they had reunited again.

Forces Armées de la République Fédérale (FARF). Dissident armed groups in southern Chad, increasingly active since 1994, when another group (CSNPD) was enticed to rally to Habré. Operating out of bases in the Central African Republic under the overall command of Laokein Bardé Frisson (q.v.), FARF stands for a loose federal system that would separate the south from the control of N'Djamena.

Front National Tchadien (FNT). Together with the MDD and FARF, the FNT was until late 1994 the sole serious armed opposition to N'Djamena. (Some small southern rebel movements do exist, however.) It started a rebellion in eastern Chad in 1992 and called for the establishment of an Islamic state in Ouadai. The FNT signed a peace agreement with N'Djamena on October 12, 1994.

Conseil National de Redressement (CNR). Zaghawa (q.v.) political vehicle of Colonel Abbas Kotti (q.v.) until he was liquidated by Déby in October 1993. The party had a strong religious fundamentalist orientation, and Déby refused to grant it representation in the national conference of 1993. After Kotti's death the movement was taken over by his brother, Hissein Kotti, who began an armed struggle (at times allied with the FNT) along the border with Sudan. It was involved in the January 1994 attack (with the FNT) on Abéché.

Mouvement Révolutionnaire du Peuple Tchadien (MRPT). South-ern political party headed by Biré Titinian strongly standing for fed-eralism, originally allied with GUNT, and based in Brazzaville.

Action Tchadienne pour l'Unité et le Socialisme (ACTUS). South-ern party, in 1990 merged with the MRPT, and headed by Fidèle Moungar (q.v.).

Mouvement pour le Démocratie et la Socialisme au Tchad (MDST). Political party originally set up in opposition to Habré in Lagos on November 15, 1988, and headed by Secretary-General Ah-met Mahamat Saleh (q.v.), grouping a large number of former cabi-net ministers and Sara influentials, among which was Tombalbaye's son, Dr. Ngarbaye Tombalbaye (q.v.). After the liberalizations in N'Djamena, the latter assumed a much larger role in the party, be-coming its president.

Mouvement National de Réforme Tchadienne (MNRT). Political party set up in 1991 and headed by its secretary-general, Ali Muham-mad Diallo (q.v.).

Mouvement du Peuple Tchadien (MPT). Southern political party, originally set up by Colonel Kamougoué and taken over in the 1990s by Nadjita Beassomal (q.v.).

Union des Forces Démocratiques (UFD). Headed by the former Déby minister of animal husbandry Saleh Makki (q.v.) and Ngawara Nahor. Not to be confused with the UFD-PR.

Comité de Sursaut National pour la Paix et la Démocratie (CSNPD). Originally a southern "*codo*" (q.v.) rebellion headed by Lt. Ketté (q.v.). The CSNPD began fighting the Déby regime in 1992, and despite several bouts of negotiations was not reconciled with the regime until 1994. After reconciliation the movement was legalized, Ketté was promoted to colonel, and one of its members, Eloi Baihon Malloum (q.v.), was integrated into the cabinet.

Union pour le Renouveau Démocratique (URD). General Kamougoué's most recent political vehicle, formed in 1992 and allied within the RNDP (q.v.) alliance to oppose the government of Prime Minister Joseph Yodoyman (q.v.).

Rassemblement pour la Démocratie et le Progrès (RDP). Political vehicle of Lol Mahamat Choua (q.v.) and his Arab and Kanembu sup-porters, formed in 1991. The party was very close in orientation to Ab-doulaye Lamana's (q.v.) Union Nationale (UN).

Alliance Nationale pour la Démocratie et le Renouveau (ANDR). Political party created in December 1992 by Joseph Yodoyman (q.v.), prime minister of Chad.

Alliance Démocratique Tchadienne (ADT). Political party under the leadership of former GUNT foreign minister Tidjani Thiam (q.v.).

Front d'Action pour l'Instauration de la Démocratie au Tchad

(FAIDT). Guerrilla group that started operating in eastern Chad in November 1994.

Rassemblement Révolutionnaire Tchadien (RRT). Radical movement formed in February 1990 after a charter conference in Libya, and headed by Secretary-General Adoum Togoi (q.v.).

Rassemblement Nationaliste Tchadien (RNT). Political movement set up by Chadians overseas, headquartered in Brussels and headed by Issaka Ramat Alhamdou (q.v.), former GUNT representative to the EC.

Rassemblement du Peuple Tchadien (RPT). Party formed by the rector of the faculty of letters of the University of Chad, Laoubelé Damaye Dangbé (q.v.), and including Toira Jeremie (q.v.).

Convention pour le Progrès et le Développement (CPD). Political party set up February 4, 1992, with the aim of stopping the fighting in the Lake Chad region. The party included a number of opposition leaders back from exile abroad, was headed by Adoum Hadjero Senoussi (q.v.), and included Seydou Sahoulba (q.v.).

Alliance Nationale pour le Progrès et le Développement (ANT). Political party set up by Nabia Nadali (q.v.).

Union pour la Démocratie et la République (UDR). Political party set up by Djimasta Koibla (q.v.).

Union Nationale. Political party set up by Abdoulaye Lamana (q.v.), on many stands very close to the RDP of Choua.

Front des Forces d'Action pour la République (FAR). Political party set up in 1992 by N'Garledji Yarongar (q.v.).

Mouvement pour l'Unité et la Démocratie du Tchad (MUDT). Political party founded by Julien Maraby, who died in 1994.

Parti Libéral pour l'Unité et la Solidarité (PLUS). Party formed by Abbas Mahamat Ambadi (q.v.).

Alliance Nationale pour le Changement (ANC). Political party formed in 1992 by Yacoub Goukouni. It has a radical plank calling for the abolition of the use of French in Chad.

Parti Africain pour la Paix et la Justice Sociale (PAPJS). Southern political party set up by Neatobei Bidi (q.v.), standing for federalism.

Union Démocratique pour le Progrès au Tchad (UDPT). Party headed by Elie Romba (q.v.).

Mouvement Social pour la Démocratie au Tchad (MSDT). Sara political party with a strong cultural platform, including the recognition of Sara as Chad's third official language. It is headed by Mbainaudo Djomia (q.v.).

Union des Forces Démocratiques—Parti Républicaine (UFD-PR). Party formed in 1992 by Gali Gatta N'Gothe (q.v.).

Convention Nationale Démocratique et Sociale (CNDS). Party set up by veteran opposition politician Adoum Moussa Seif (q.v.), with a strong antifederal platform.

Convention Sociale-Démocrate Tchadienne (CSDT). Party formed in 1992 by Younous Ibeidou and grouping some former Habré elements, including Bilal Soubiane (q.v.). One of its leaders, Abbas Ali (q.v.), emerged as president of the CST in July 1995 when the entire Bureau was indicted for corruption.

Union Nationale pour la Démocratie et le Progrès (UNDP). Party headed by Abdelkadir Yacine (q.v.), formerly leader of the FROLINAT-Originel.

Union Nationale pour le Développement et le Renouveau (UNDR). Party set up by the editor of N'Djamena's only independent newspaper, Saleh Kebzabo.

Parti pour les Libertés et le Développement (PLD). Party set up by Ibn Oumar Mahamat Saleh (q.v.).

Rassemblement des Forces Démocratiques du Tchad (RFDT). Political party headed by a former cabinet minister under Habré, Djemberé Le Soromian.

Parti Social-Démocrate Tchadien (PSDT). Social-democratic political party headed by Miambé Romain (q.v.).

Convention Nationale des Socio-Démocrates (CNSD). A second social-democratic party, headed by Younous Ibeidou.

Tchad-Avenir (TA). Progressive pro-rural party founded in 1993 and headed by Joel Oulator, advocating the creation of a senate to represent Chad's rural populations.

Parti Démocratique Tchadien (PDT). Party formed in 1993 by Dr. A. Djigdjag.

Mouvement pour la Paix et le Développement (MPD). A largely northern political movement set up in 1992 by Mahamat Abdoulaye (q.v.).

Several of the intraparty alliances/coalitions created since 1992 are notable: The *Front d'Opposition Démocratique* (FOD) was set up in September 1992 by 15 political parties in their effort to pressure Déby into convening a national conference. The grouping renamed itself on November 15 as the Forum pour le Changement Démocratique (FCD). The 16-party alliance *Rassemblement National pour la Démocratie et le Progrès* (RNDP), headed by Nouradine Koumakoyé Delwa Kassiré, was formed on May 26, 1992, to oppose the government of Prime Minister Yodoyman. The *Concertation des Partis Politiques* (CPP) was the largest of these alliances. Formed in 1994 and grouping 40 of the 45 parties in Chad at that time under spokesman (and former premier) Jean Alingué (q.v.). The *Alliance des Partis Politiques pour la Démocratie* (APPD) was a June 1994 intraparty alliance in opposition to the largely southern CPP. The *Entente pour une Alternative Démocratique* (Entente) was a July 1994 alliance of eight small parties not included in the

CCP and APPD. The *Collectif des Partis pour le Changement* (COPAC) was a small but influential eight-party alliance formed in November 1994 and including the parties headed by former premier Fidèle Moungar, Adoum Moussa Seif (q.v.) and Saleh Kebzabo, editor of N'Djamena's only independent daily newspaper, *N'Djaména-Hebdo.*

POLITICAL PARTIES: INITIAL NATIONAL ASSEMBLY STRENGTH, 1947–1959. The following figures indicate party strengths immediately after the various elections in Chad between 1947 and 1959. In subsequent years, until the 1990s, only the PPT (q.v.) was allowed to campaign. Sharp swings in party strength occurred from time to time between elections consequent to defections from one formation to another. For the full party names, see the list of acronyms and abbreviations. (See also POLITICAL PARTIES.)

1947 Conseil Représentatif (30 seats)
(a) first electoral college: 5 URT, 5 independents
(b) second electoral college: 11 UDT, 2 UPFT, 4 URPT, 1 PPT, 2 independents

1952 Territorial Assembly (45 seats)
(a) first electoral college: 15 RPF and independents
(b) second electoral college: 24 UDT, 6 FACT

1957 Territorial Assembly (65 seats)
32 PPT, 9 GIRT, 8 AST, 7 UDSR, 7 UDIT, 1 PSIT, 1 independent

1959 National Assembly (85 seats)
59 PPT, 16 UDIT, 9 AST, 2 GIRT, 1 UNT

POLITICAL PRISONERS. A large number of Chad's leadership strata have, at one time or another, been imprisoned by the Tombalbaye (q.v.) regime on real or trumped-up charges, and they may be grouped into four general categories: (1) political leaders shunted aside by Tombalbaye in his drive to achieve preeminence in Chadian political life, following the purge of Gabriel Lisette (q.v.), founder of the PPT (q.v.); (2) opposition elements refusing to accept Sara or southern political hegemony as manifested by the abolition of party politics and the establishment of a one-party system; (3) FROLINAT (q.v.) and other rebel groups and their sympathizers in N'Djamena; or (4) members of Tombalbaye's immediate entourage regarded as becoming threats or challenges to the president's hegemony in the country, whether true or not. After the 1975 coup d'état, inquiries began on "disappearances" from prison rolls during the Tombalbaye era of numerous political prisoners. At least 33 are known to have been liquidated.

Sara political preeminence ended in 1978, and the concept of "political prisoners" acquired both a newer, broader meaning and a much more sinister significance. While the first northern regime, that of Goukouni (q.v.), was remarkably conciliatory and benevolent, the Habré (q.v.) dictatorship and the current Déby (q.v.) authoritarian regime have been gross violators of human rights. During the nine years Habré was in power thousands of political prisoners were arrested. Some were arrested with cause, others on suspicion, and many more merely by virtue of being their relatives. Detained without trial, sometimes for years in appalling conditions, most have been tortured, and many were executed in secret prisons and even in the presidential complex. Many more were simply killed by Habré's secret service and other forces of repression that included a unit specializing in liquidating VIPs and making their deaths appear natural or accidental. (It is now assumed, for example, that former foreign minister Idriss Miskine [q.v.] did not die of malaria but was poisoned, and that opposition leader Ahmat Acyl [q.v.] was likewise murdered rather than killed in an aviation accident.) Before fleeing the capital (with all of Chad's liquid reserves) Habré ordered the liquidation of an additional 300 political prisoners at the time being held in the presidential compound.

While Déby has been less vicious in his personal vendettas (in the sense that some of those who dared to cross swords with him actually left prison alive), he has used the same forces of repression (including some of the same commanding officers and executioners that Habré used, and the torture and killing of enemies and suspected enemies continue to this day.

POPULATION. Chad has never had a comprehensive population census, and the last reliable population survey took place in 1964. At that time the country was believed to have 3.3 million people. Projections from that survey lead to the current estimate of a population of some 6.5 million.

POSTE DE CONTROLE ADMINISTRATIF (PCA). Basic administrative unit for regions where existing traditional units with administrative structures could be integrated in toto into the central administration. Elsewhere the most basic unit is the *arrondissement*. (See also ADMINISTRATIVE ORGANIZATION.)

PREFECTURES. Successors to the colonial era's *départements* (q.v.), divided into a number of *souspréfectures* and in some regions also include one or more *postes de contrôle administratif* (q.v.). The number of départements/préfectures has risen slowly over the years. Until 1956 there were nine: in that year Gúera was formed as a separate district to accommodate the administrative needs of central Chad, and in 1959 the eleventh préfecture, Biltine, was carved out of Ouadai. After independence the Tombalbaye (q.v.) regime divided the highly populated Logone département into three préfectures (1962), in part to isolate residual loyalties to the purged Gabriel Lisette (q.v.), who was very popular in parts of the Logone. In 1969 a fourteenth préfecture, Lac, was created. Each préfecture is headed by a prefect who is nominated by the central government and who serves as the representative of the minister of interior; the prefect controls the subprefect and other subordinate officials in the souspréfectures. There are currently 52 souspréfectures and 20 administrative posts in Chad (see also ADMINISTRATIVE ORGANIZATION). The 14 préfectures and their headquarters are as follows:

1. Chari-Baguirmi	(N'Djamena)
2. Batha	(Ati)
3. B.E.T.	(Faya)
4. Biltine	(Biltine)
5. Guéra	(Mongo)
6. Kanem	(Mao)
7. Lac	(Bol)
8. Logone Occidentale	(Moundou)
9. Logone Orientale	(Doba)
10. Mayo-Kebbi	(Bongor)
11. Moyen-Chari	(Sarh)
12. Ouadai	(Abéché)
13. Salamat	(Am-Timan)
14. Tandjilé	(Laï)

PREMIERE ARMEE VOLCAN. Adoum Abdoulahi Dana's (q.v.) faction of the Volcan Army (q.v.), most of whom followed Ahmat Acyl (q.v.), whose group became known as the Volcan Nouveau, and later the Conseil Démocratique de la Révolution (q.v.). The Première Armée Volcan, and Dana, were separated from Acyl's group on the issue of Libya. Dana was staunchly anti-Libyan (and pro-Sudanese), while Acyl was usually regarded by Libya's puppet.

PRODEL see SOCIETE FRIGORIFIQUE DES PRODUITS DES ELEVEURS TCHADIENS

PROTESTANTS see CHRISTIAN MISSIONS

PROVISIONAL GOVERNMENTS (1958–1959). Series of four successive, unstable, provisional governments of short duration, from December 1958 to June 1959 when the PPT (Entente)–UST struggle for power was at its height, with the GIRT (q.v.) party playing a pivotal role. The governments were those of:

1. Gabriel Lisette (q.v.) December 16, 1958–January 30, 1959). Including 8 PPT, 2 AST, 2 UDIT, 2 MSA members, or 8 Muslims, 6 Sara, and 2 Europeans. The government collapsed when the GIRT deserted the Entente (q.v.) for the UST (q.v.) opposition to form the MPT (q.v.) alliance that formed the next cabinet.

2. Gountchomé Sahoulba (q.v.) (February 11, 1959–March 12, 1959). Fluid government of the opposition UST/MPT alliance in which the PPT refused to serve, it raised the call of the possible withdrawal of southern Sara areas from Chad and finally weaned away the MSA (q.v.) component, toppling Sahoulba and ushering in Ahmed Koulamallah's attempt at a cabinet.

3. Ahmed Koulamallah (q.v.) (March 12–24, 1959). Including 4 PPT, 2 MSA, 2 GIRT, 2 AST, and 2 UDIT members. The brief government was toppled due to the intrigues of Jean Baptiste (q.v.), the only prominent anti-PPT leader excluded from it, and the continued opposition of the Entente to recognizing the ascendance of the Muslim/traditionalist elements.

4. François Tombalbaye (q.v.) (March 24–June 16, 1959). Including 7 PPT, 3 GIRT, 3 UDIT members during which a stabilization of power developed, leading to the next regular government by Tombalbaye on June 16, 1959.

-Q-

QUADRIYA. Minority Muslim religious order that spread into Chad from the west. (See also RELIGIOUS ORDERS.)

-R-

RABAH ZUBEIR (also RABIH FADL ALLAH) (1845?–1900). Infamous Sudanese slave raider and builder of a vast personal empire in Central Africa just prior to the entry of European forces in the area. Born around 1840–45 in Halfaya, near Khartoum in the Sudan, of Funj or Jellabi parents, and probably a slave in his youth, Rabah rose to prominence in the personal armies of Zubeir Rahma Mansur al-Abbasi (see ZUBEIR

PASHA) in the Sudan, becoming one of his principal standard-bearers and lieutenants. He was a prominent commander in Zubeir's invasion and conquest of Darfur (q.v.) in 1873, and after Zubeir's imprisonment in Cairo and the death of his son, Sulayman, Rabah took command of the remaining forces. With these armies he raided vast areas to the south and west of Darfur (in contemporary Chad and the Central African Republic), depopulating them for the slave trade. Between 1884 and 1890, Rabah conquered Dar Kouti (q.v.), later expanding his control over other Ouadai tributary states, including Salamat. Requested to join forces with the Mahdi of Sudan, Rabah ordered his troops to wear the Mahdist patched *jubba* and intermittently declared that his conquests were in the name of the Mahdi, but he did not swerve from his goal of expanding into Central Africa. In 1889 Rabah conquered Dar Rounga (q.v.), another Ouadai tributary, and in 1890 he consolidated some of his possessions under Mohamed-es-Senoussi (q.v.), who became sultan of these areas. Regrouping his armies, and prospering from the slave trade, Rabah then turned to the north, against Baguirmi, bypassing completely the Ouadai kingdom (q.v.). In 1892 he defeated and razed Baguirmi (q.v.), advanced and conquered by surprise the Chari and Logone River regions, and then, heavily outnumbered (allegedly with only 3,000 troops), his forces assaulted the Bornu (q.v.) Empire, defeating the Shehu's armies and ruthlessly pillaging Kukawa, the capital, in 1893. Rabah then established his own capital (in 1894) in Dikwa, south of Lake Chad. At the height of his power Great Britain toyed with the idea of accepting—and recognizing—his hegemony over Bornu and the interior, while France all along regarded him as its main obstacle in Central Africa.

Preparing for an expansion into yet-unconquered Bornu tributary states and into Kano itself (he had married off his daughter to the son of the emir of Sokoto), Rabah's plans were disrupted by the French arrival in Baguirmi and by Sultan Guarang's (see GUARANG II) request for French protection against him. Rabah then returned to pillage Baguirmi and the Logone regions again, in the process razing Massenya for the second time, in 1898. His forces clashed a few times in small and inconclusive battles with the French until in 1900 the major armies of the two foes met in the Battle of Kousseri (q.v.). There, three French columns (led by Foureau and Lamy, Gentil, and Joalland and Meynier) that had advanced overland from the south, north, and west, converged to demolish Rabah's forces in the April 22, 1900, battle that saw both Rabah's and Lamy's death.

Rabah's successful conquests were a direct function of his well-disciplined and well-armed troops. Though he initially began his raids from Darfur with probably no more than 2,000 men, his forces swelled to possibly 20,000 men (grouped into battalions), of whom some 5,000 had repeating firearms and adequate ammunition. (Resupplying his forces was a constant problem for Rabah, who was forced to import all his needs over the lengthy Fezzan route.) Though not religious, Rabah carried his campaigns in the name of the Mahdi, and his forces chanted the Mahdist song. He tried to ally himself with the powerful Sanusiya (q.v.) in the north (also expanding in the interior into Kanem and B.E.T.), but Mohammad al-Mahdi es-Senoussi would have nothing to do with him. Though in the 1970s some of Rabah's descendants, as well as other sympathizers, have attempted to have his exploits rehabilitated and seen as part of an early "anticolonialist" struggle, other scholars (e.g., Hugot) regard Rabah's massacres in the regions he raided and/or occupied as more than matching those of Genghis Khan in Eurasia. The remaining Rabahist forces continued to resist the French until 1901, when Rabah's son, Rabih-ibn-Fadl-Allah was killed, and in 1911 the last Rabahist lieutenant, Mohamed-es-Senoussi, was also killed. Remnants of Rabah's Dikwa "court" were brought by the French forces to newly established Fort-Lamy, where they formed the original Shoa (q.v.) Arab nucleus of the city. (See also HANYAR RABIH; ZUBEIR PASHA.)

RADIO NATIONALE TCHADIENNE (RNT). Renamed in 1972 "The Voice of Unity and Progress" (Voix de l'Unité et du Progrès), and in 1974 "The Voice of the Chadian Cultural Revolution," RNT transmitted in nine languages: French, Arabic, Sara, Toubouri, Massa, Gorane, Moundang, Fulani, and Kanembu. In 1972 the station obtained a new 100-kilowatt transmitter that allowed it to cover the entire country. The number of radios in Chad jumped dramatically from 6,000 in 1960 to 70,000 in 1972 after the installation of a radio assembly plant in N'Djamena, but by 1983 there were still only 83,000 radios in Chad. The radio station itself was heavily damaged during the "first" fall of N'Djamena. Repaired by France, it was controlled by Hissène Habré (q.v.) until 1981 and again damaged in the Goukouni-Habré fighting.

RAHAMA SALEH, MAHAMAT see SALEH, MAHAMAT RAHAMA

RAILROADS see COMMUNICATIONS

RAKHIS, MANANI see MANANI, ADOUM RAKHIS

RARIKINGAR TAMADJI, PAUL (1912–). Born on February 15, 1912, in Balemba, near Sarh; educated locally and served as a school teacher and educational inspector (1932–56) in Sarh, Léré, and Fort-Lamy. A founding member of the PPT (q.v.) party, he was *chef de canton* of Balemba in 1957, and joined the National Assembly in 1959 as Moyen-Chari deputy. Mayor of Sarh from 1964 to 1974, he was one of the few deputies to survive until the 1975 coup, serving the National Assembly as third vice president (1966–70) and president of the Foreign Affairs Committee.

RASSEMBLEMENT DEMOCRATIQUE AFRICAIN (RDA). Francophone Africa's first and most influential political movement, with branches in all of France's African territories. Founded in 1946 by Félix Houphouët-Boigny, future president of Côte d'Ivoire, the party was initially very militant, allied with the Communist Party in the French National Assembly. Its territorial affiliate in Chad was the Parti Progressiste Tchadien (q.v.), whose founder, Gabriel Lisette (q.v.), also played a prominent role in the RDA. Essentially defunct since the independence of francophone Africa.

RASSEMBLEMENT DES FORCES PATRIOTIQUES (RFP). Opposition movement set up in Ouagadougou, Burkina Faso, on August 12, 1984. Hostile to both Goukouni's (q.v.) GUNT (q.v.) and Libya's role in Chad, the RFP combined several factions previously associated with GUNT. The leader of the RFP was Dr. Facho Balaam (q.v.), secretary-general of the UND (q.v.), one of the GUNT former factions. The other factions in the RFP included Abdelkadir Yacine's (q.v.) dissident wing of FROLINAT-Originel, Adoum Hadjero Senoussi's (q.v.) FROLINAT-Fondamental, Adoum Dana's (q.v.) Volcan Army (q.v.), and remnants of the FAO (q.v.) under Moussa Medela (q.v.). A fifth group, little known before its association with the RFP, was the Action Tchadienne pour l'Unité et le Socialisme (ACTUS) (q.v.). All of these groups were fragments of original fighting forces.

RASSEMBLEMENT DU PEUPLE FRANÇAIS (RPF). Party begun in France in 1947 by Charles de Gaulle, after which various second electoral roll parties declared affiliation (see DOUBLE ELECTORAL COLLEGE). In Chad, of second electoral college parties, UDT (q.v.) and later AST (q.v.) affiliated with RPF (see also POLITICAL PARTIES). Of first electoral college groupings, URT (q.v.) changed its name to RPF in 1947, becoming the local branch of the French parent party. Most European politicians in URT-RPF were traders or functionaries, e.g., René Malbrant and Marcel Lallia (qq.v.). After the double electoral college ended, most such expatriates joined conservative parties of the second electoral college aligned with the RPF in the past.

RASSEMBLEMENT DU PEUPLE TCHADIEN (RPT). Political party set up in mid-1992 by Laoubelé Damaye Dangbé, former rector of the faculty of letters of the University of N'Djamena, and Toira Jeremie.

RASSEMBLEMENT NATIONAL DEMOCRATIQUE POPULAIRE (RNDP). Political movement set up in January 1982 by Minister of Justice Nouradine Koumakoyé Delwa Kassiré. It was later merged with Hissène Habré's (q.v.) UNIR (q.v.). With the political liberalizations of the Idriss Déby (q.v.) era, the party was refounded on May 26, 1992, as an alliance of 16 mostly southern anti-Déby parties to oppose the government of Prime Minister Joseph Yodoyman (q.v.).

RASSEMBLEMENT NATIONALISTE TCHADIEN (RNT). Anti-Habré opposition group established in February 1990 in Brussels by Issaka Ramat Alhamdou (q.v.), a former ambassador to the EC.

RASSEMBLEMENT POUR LA DEMOCRATIE ET LE PROGRES (RDP). A largely Kanembu political party set up in 1992 by former mayor of N'Djamena Lol Mahamat Choua (q.v.), originally illegally, and then within the RNDP (q.v.) alliance, to oppose the government of Prime Minister Joseph Yodoyman (q.v.). In its platform the party was virtually identical to that of the Union Nationale (q.v.) of Abdoulaye Lamana (q.v.).

RASSEMBLEMENT POUR L'UNITE ET LA DEMOCRATIE AU TCHAD (RUDT). Movement founded in 1982 by Dono-Ngardoum Djidingar (q.v.), shortly before his appointment as prime minister by Goukouni (q.v.). The party tried to bridge the chasm between north and south and included former Tombalbaye (q.v.) supporters as well as Toubou (q.v.) personalities. The former GUNT (q.v.) minister Naimbayé Lossimiau (q.v.) was a prominent member of RUDT. The party dissolved itself and merged with UNIR (q.v.) after the rise of Hissène Habré (q.v.).

RASSEMBLEMENT REVOLUTIONNAIRE TCHADIEN (RRT). Anti-Habré movement founded in February 1990 in Libya by secretary-general Adoum Togoi, a former key GUNT (q.v.) leader.

REBELLIONS. Widespread rebellions in northern and eastern Chad occurred in the 1960s and were a direct result of (1) long-standing center-periphery tensions; (2) regionalism (q.v.); (3) unsettled conditions in semidesert northern regions, until 1965 governed by a French military prefect and military administration; (4) crude and corrupt administration by the central government, civilian and military; and (5) the natural sociocultural and religious diversity of the country, upon which a one-party system was artificially and forcefully imposed. Also leading to a massive societal deflation of authority and legitimacy were: the withdrawal of many powers, including traditional taxing rights, from Chad's major customary chiefs and sultans; emphasis upon compulsory cotton cultivation in the south and prohibitions on big-game hunting in Ouadai; and new compulsory contributions for the National Development Loan, corruptly collected by state agents.

In essence, the rebellions arose directly from the government's attempt to impose control (frequently insensitive to local feelings) over regions never truly controlled, even by France.

One of the first incidents erupted during the night of September 2, 1965, in Bardai (q.v.) in Tibesti (q.v.) during a rowdy dance in which a squabble resulted in the death of a Chadian soldier. The local subprefect immediately ordered harsh sanctions leading to the rounding-up of the inhabitants of the entire village (including women and children), who were then paraded nude, roughed up, and humiliated. Nine of the villagers—including the derde (q.v.) of the Toubou (q.v.) and his son Goukouni (q.v.)—were arrested and charged with various offenses. Following this, a variety of "fines" were imposed arbitrarily for the wearing of turbans (5,000 CFA francs), assembly of more than two people (5,000 CFA francs), growing of beards, and so on. Because of these gross humiliations and a history of grudges since the Chadians took over in the B.E.T. (q.v.) from the French, an immediate revolt began; the derde and his entourage escaped to Libya, while three of his sons took up arms against the central government.

The brutality and insensitivity of the local administration in the north was brought sharply into focus by the then-confidential report (of May 1968) of Captain Pierre Galopin (q.v.), which was released only much later and which formed the backbone of the reforms of the Mission de Réforme Administrative (MRA) (q.v.) dispatched by France. In September 1965 there also erupted tax riots in Batha Préfecture over the increased governmental levies, and in October came the famous Mangalmé tax riots (q.v.) that marked the start of the rebellion in the east. These riots were also a direct result of the corruption of local officials (who tried to collect up to five times the decreed taxes, pocketing the difference). The uprising then spread into Ouadai, and in February 1967 there was a rebellion in Salamat, where 56 people were killed, including the local prefect and his deputy. The revolt continued to spread—assisted now by the formation of both the FLT (q.v.) and FROLINAT (q.v.) rebel movements that mounted assaults from abroad—and several regional capitals were threatened, including Mongo (capital of Guéra), Mangalamé and villages in Chari-Baguirmi, including Bokoro, barely 100 kilometers (60 miles) from N'Djamena.

The gradual loss of control of the provinces by the central government (land communications were totally cut off between Chad's east and west with guerrillas controlling the countryside) led to Tombalbaye's (q.v.) appeal for French assistance (in accord with the 1960 Franco-Chadian defense treaty) in mid-1968. At that time a contingent of gendarmes was encircled by former Toubou members of the Garde Nomade (q.v.) that had rebelled and killed most of the non-Toubou garrison of Aouzou keeping at bay rescue columns sent from the regional headquarters. A small contingent of French paratroopers was promptly dispatched to break the siege, and these were withdrawn in September 1968; only later, in April 1969, were larger French forces sent to Chad both to quell the rebellion in the country and to undertake a massive retraining of the Chadian army and administration. The Moubi (q.v.) rebellion in the east was slowly calmed by 1970–71, with the more prominent tribal chiefs being brought back to the governmental fold and other opposition elements rallied to the new military regime after the 1975 coup d'état. In the north, after a series of prolonged search-and-destroy missions by Franco-Chadian forces, and after several major battles with Toubou forces, the rebellion was contained to several small and distant pockets in the B.E.T. By June 1971 most of France's combat troops were withdrawn, though sizable contingents remained in the country to retrain the Chadian armed forces and to staff the MRA. (The issue of French troops in Chad had deeply polarized public opinion in France, contributing to the speed with which French forces were withdrawn.)

Through the activity of the MRA some 800 incompetent civil servants were dismissed, including one prefect; traditional authority was returned to the sultans; the various supplementary taxes previously imposed were canceled (and regular head and cattle taxes temporarily lifted); and large segments of the civil service involved with the peripheral areas of Chad were retrained. Though the derde of the Toubou was invited to return to Tibesti with his former powers restored (Abdoulaye Abo Nassour [q.v.] was specially dispatched to Libya to extend an offer in 1971), the final reconciliation did not occur until 1975, after the coup in which Tombalbaye was killed. Goukouni, however, the derde's last surviving son, continued the armed revolt against N'Djamena, in conjunction with Hissène Habré (q.v.), and later—after Habré succumbed to Félix Malloum's (q.v.) offer to accept the premiership—alone, as head of a small band of warriors. The falling apart of the Malloum-Habré bicephalous leadership, an unnatural and unlikely partnership in the first place, coupled with Goukouni's military advances against a totally demoralized Chadian army, brought about the fall of N'Djamena and the "end" of the northern rebellion, since power was assumed by one or another of the two northern leaders, usually at the head of a coalition of the former guerrilla heads. In essence, however, the Sara south—not conquered—was transformed under General Kamougoué (q.v.) into a state of "passive resistance," a state within a state. The falling-out in N'Djamena of the northern victors and Habré's ouster following Goukouni's appeal for Libyan troops created a "new" rebellion, Habré's, now emanating from his Biltine bastion. His comeback, with CIA funds and assistance, transformed the GUNT (q.v.) coalition into rebels as Goukouni, driven to

B.E.T., launched his counteroffensive on N'Djamena. Finally, the delivery to Habré of the Sara south by dissident FAT (q.v.) troops rebelling against Kamougoué triggered "liberation" movements in the south, either linked to or autonomous from that waged in B.E.T. by Goukouni in alliance with Kamougoué and other officers who fled the south.

The Goukouni rebellion was terminated, however, by France's denying him any advances below the 16th parallel (see RED ZONE) and by Habré's sharp attacks on Libya's forces in B.E.T. and within Libya itself, leading Muammar Qaddafi to sue for peace. Habré's victory brought him much acclaim, helped to shatter Goukouni's shaky GUNT alliance as many factions rallied to N'Djamena, and also led to the withdrawal of Libyan support for Habré's foes.

Another wave of rebellions developed, however, in the east, as Habré simultaneously began to alienate some of the very groups that had brought him to power. First the Hadjeray (q.v.), many of whose leaders were either purged or liquidated, were driven into rebellion, with Maldoum Bada Abbas (q.v.) becoming their leader under the banner of MOSANAT (q.v.); later, the Zaghawa (q.v.) were persecuted, with Idriss Déby (q.v.) becoming their leader. The two groups united in Darfur, and after smashing Habré's armies entered victoriously into N'Djamena on December 2, 1990.

Though a couple of separatist rebellions subsequently broke out in the east (e.g., the FNT [q.v.]), with a fundamentalist Muslim rebellion possibly in the offing in Ouadai as well, in the mid-1990s the greatest danger is in the south. For more than a decade there has been armed resistance to both Habré's and Déby's regimes and their excesses. But in essence the real grievance is over the spread of pastoralists, and Muslims, from the north and east into the south. Though Lt. Ketté (q.v.), one of the military leaders, was weaned back to the fold in 1994, there is a growing separatist and/or federal demand that will probably have to be met.

RED ZONE (also RED LINE). Zone established by France at the 15th parallel to separate Habré-controlled Chad from the GUNT-held northern segment of the country. France made it clear that any rebel advances south of this line would be repulsed by French forces in the area. In January 1984 the Red Zone was penetrated by GUNT forces that reached the village of Ziguey before retreating with prisoners, including two Belgian doctors. In subsequent fighting one French Jaguar plane was downed and some 12 rebel vehicles destroyed. The Red Zone was subsequently moved farther north (16th parallel), to the Koro Toro–Oum Chalouba axis, and aerial reinforcements were brought into N'Djamena from French bases in Gabon. French forces were briefly withdrawn but then reinstated after a mutual withdrawal of forces agreement with Libya collapsed, and during the Habré assaults on Libya there was some exchange of fire between Libya and France. French forces began to withdraw after the Libya-Chad peace accord, and especially after Libya withdrew from the Aouzou Strip (q.v.).

REFERENDUM OF DECEMBER 10, 1989. A spurious constitutional referendum that also automatically returned Hissène Habré (q.v.) to a seven-year term of office. The 15-page, 200-article constitution, which provided Chad with an executive with extremely strong executive powers, was allegedly ratified by more than 94 percent of the country's voters, and by 100 percent in some (mostly northern) préfectures. Slightly less than a year later, Habré was ousted from power by Idriss Déby (q.v.).

REFUGEES. Chad has been an area of major population migrations from time immemorial. This did not change in the twentieth century, during which population dislocations in both directions have been frequent. The eastern frontier has been especially porous, along which a virtual no-man's-land has prevailed when populations—at times entire clans—have crossed the border with little concern for or even knowledge of territorial sovereignty. In like manner, in the desert north, Toubou (q.v.) and other groups have historically, and to this day, freely crossed from Chad to Libya and back again. The onset of the civil rebellions in Chad aggravated these dislocations, triggering an outmigration of politicoeconomic refugees in all directions. Their total number was estimated in 1970 at over 1,136,000, found mostly in Sudan, Libya, Niger, C.A.R., Nigeria, Cameroon, Congo, and Saudi Arabia. Such figures, huge though they are, are only official estimates, with the real figures being probably higher. In 1982, for example, the officially registered refugees in Maiduguri in northern Nigeria numbered 13,000, yet international refugee officials estimated that there were 110,000 in this area alone. Similarly, at the height of the "first" Battle for N'Djamena (q.v.) (between Habré and Goukouni [qq.v.] in 1980) roughly half of the population of N'Djamena (over 100,000 people) fled across the river to Kousseri, Cameroon. Officially, most returned after hostilities died off; unofficially, fully 17,000 remained in scattered camps around Kousseri. And when in 1983 Nigeria expelled its illegal aliens, some 700,000 Chadians were repatriated. Around 50 percent of these were seen as refugees from the civil strife in Chad, yet the total number of official refugees in Nigeria in that year stood only at 35,000. There are no current reliable figures on the dimensions and locations of Chad's refugee populations. While the

Chadian community in Sudan may have declined, it is assumed that the number of Sara Chadians in Cameroon and C.A.R., as well as Kanembu in Nigeria, has increased significantly, as southerners have relocated to escape the brutality of Idriss Déby's (q.v.) Garde Républicaine (q.v.) and the steady encroachments into the south of pastoralists and Muslims.

REGIMENT DE DEFENSE OPERATIONNELLE DU TERRITOIRE (RDOT). Elite force founded in 1986 by the Hadjeray Minister of Interior Mahamat Itno (q.v.), of mostly Daza (q.v.) Toubou (q.v.) and Hadjeray (q.v.) desert fighters that brought Hissène Habré (q.v.) to power in 1982, southern gendarmes who threw their lot behind him, and a number of European mercenaries recruited by a former crony of Bob Denard, and receiving U.S. and French military assistance. The unit was headquartered in the Dabut camp in N'Djamena's outskirts and was one of Habré's main military props.

REGIMENT INTER-ARMES D'OUTRE-MER (RIAOM). French military units intended for overseas intervention. In the case of Chad, until 1975, when all French troops were ordered out of the country in the aftermath of the Claustre (q.v.) fiasco, the French forces in the country were stationed in the N'Djamena infantry and airbase (No. 142) and elsewhere in the countryside. Their number varied (see FRANCE, FORCES IN CHAD) over the years but usually included some 900 troops of the Sixth RIAOM and some 600 air force personnel. In 1975 their total number amounted to 2,500; they were withdrawn in October 1975 but twice returned to assist Hissène Habré (q.v.) against the rebellion of Goukouni (q.v.) and his Libyan support.

REGIONALISM. Chad's regionalism is a function of both the country's size—encompassing a large number of regions and ethnic groups that have been unable to reconcile historic animosities—and the country's geographic location, straddling the black-white, east-west, north-south, Muslim-animist, Sahel-tropical dividing lines that run through the center of Africa. The territory has thus been the backdrop for powerful historic competitions between Ouadai, Baguirmi, and Kanem-Bornu (qq.v.), the scene of continuous Arab-Muslim slave raids into the southern areas, and the arena of competing outside influences and forces, including those of the Sanusiya (q.v.), Rahab (q.v.), and the Awlad Sulayman (q.v.). The differing manner in which the French were originally received in the area—in Baguirmi as allies against Rabah and Ouadai predatory attacks; in Sara regions as saviors against the slave raiders from the north; in Ouadai and B.E.T. as infidel invaders—illustrates to some extent some of the basic cleavages in the country that remain intense to this day. In Ouadai, for example, there has always been reluctance on the part of the largely Muslim population to participate in Chadian social, economic, political, or educational structures or to accept the de facto supremacy in the country of the populations formerly regarded as mere slave-material. On most socioeconomic indicators the various Chadian regions score statistics resembling data from completely different countries, and this has not changed much over the years. During the 1980s this sense of regionalism was greatly compounded by Sara resentments in the south over the spread of pastoralists and Muslims from the north and east, and a call for federalism or secession has emerged. In the east, in the meantime, fundamentalist Islam has taken root, so that the country is more polarized today than at independence.

REGIONS. Colonial administrative units into which Chad was divided, and precursors of the post-independence *préfectures* (q.v.). Each *région* was divided into a number of *districts,* which in turn were subdivided further into *cantons* grouping several villages. The districts were precursors to the souspréfectures. The number of régions differed over the years; in 1950, for example, there were nine: Chari-Baguirmi, Ouadai, Kanem, B.E.T., Batha, Salamat, Moyen-Chari, Logone, Mayo-Kebbi. A tenth région—Guéra—was established in 1956, and in 1959 Biltine was carved out of northern Ouadai. After independence the number of divisions in Chad went up to 14. Each région possessed administrative Conseils de Région (q.v.) presided over by the central government's prefect. (See also ADMINISTRATIVE ORGANIZATION.)

REGNY, MAHAMADOU MAHAMAT. Minister of women's and social affairs, serving until December 1994.

REGROUPEMENT DES PARTIS POLITIQUES DU TCHAD (RPPT). Temporary political coalition of the PSIT (q.v.), UDSR (q.v.), and other local groups, led by Ahmed Kotoko (q.v.) and Adoum Aganayé (q.v.) to compete the 1956 Fort-Lamy municipal elections. Obtaining only 20 percent of the vote, the RPPT was disbanded after the elections, its leaders merging with the winning ERDIC (q.v.) coalition.

RELIGION. Estimates of Chad's religious composition are unreliable and widely divergent, largely due to persistent gross overestimates of the number of Christians and underestimates of the number of animists in the southern parts of the country. Many who profess to be Christian are more often than not only nominally so, and in essence animist. Similarly, while the northern two-thirds of the country is acknowledged to be solidly Muslim, there is controversy as to the precise number of people residing there, since Chad has never had a census. One recent religious breakdown of the country has it that 41 percent of the population is Muslim, 29 percent Christian, and 30 percent animist. Another, however, maintains that 51 percent of the population is Muslim, 19 percent Christian, and 30 percent animist. Of the southern Christians, many are Protestants. (See also CHRISTIAN MISSIONS; ISLAM; RELIGIOUS ORDERS.)

RELIGIOUS ORDERS. The most important Muslim religious orders in Chad are the Tidjaniya, Quadriya, Sanusiya, Mirghaniya, and Tarbiya. In the mid-1990s the predominant order, the Tidjaniya, has been under direct attack and is losing ground, especially in the east and in particular in Ouadai (q.v.), to powerful fundamentalist influences seeping in from Sudan. Not only was a rebellion, the FNT (q.v.), operating in the east on essentially a religious platform, but also, beginning in November 1994, leaflets were distributed in Abéché calling on all expatriates and Christian/animist southerners (primarily Sara) to vacate their posts as teachers and administrators and leave the region or face death, as had occurred in Algeria.

Tidjaniya. Still Chad's most important order, established at the turn of the century and encouraged by the local French administration throughout the colonial era because of its emphasis on submission to temporal authority. The order was founded by Umar al-Tidjani (1737–1815) in Fez, Morocco. Though the order was well established, a national organization was not set up in Chad until 1951. The orthodox order made serious inroads into the Quadriya order, and it was long led by Koulamallah (q.v.), until he was ousted from Chad. Most of the country's Arab population (except for the Awlad Sulayman, who are Senoussi) used to belong to the Tidjaniya order, as were most of the Kanembu in the country; some of the Arab groups have recently been influenced by fundamentalism coming from the East.

Quadriya. The oldest order, and still very important in northern Nigeria, though it was not originally overly successful in Chad. The Quadriya has strength in Ouadai and in scattered pockets in Kanem and Chari-Baguirmi. Much of its strength was weaned away by the Tidjaniya, but this may be changing.

Sanusiya. Founded in Libya by the Grand Sanusi, and during the precolonial era strongly contesting French colonial ambitions in Central Africa (see SANUSIYA), the order—once expanding vigorously into Kanem and B.E.T. from Libya—has scattered pockets of adherents in these areas and in Ouadai, but especially in Tibesti.

Mirghaniya. A small order whose members are found mostly in Ouadai, and which has been gaining converts.

Tarbiya. An offshoot of the Tidjaniya, headed by Cheikh Ibrahim Nyass of Kaolock, Senegal, the Tarbiya order was gaining considerable support in Chad (mostly in intellectual circles) before being banned by President Tombalbaye (q.v.) in 1962. (See also ISLAM.)

REPUBLIQUE DU LOGONE. Oft-discussed and seriously deliberated secessionist alternative in the south to rule by northerners from N'Djamena. At times during the years between 1979 and 1982 Kamougoué's (q.v.) administration in Bongor was referred to as such as well, partly because he had initiated discussions with Ange-Félix Patassé, the Sara political leader in the Central African Republic. Only the certain knowledge that formal secession would not be tolerated by Paris dissuaded leaders in the five southern Sara préfectures from opting for this course of action. In the 1990s the option has been revived by several of the Sara parties in reaction to the reign of repression imposed on these préfectures by both the Habré and the Déby (qq.v.) regimes. More ominously, partly due to the prolonged droughts in the Sahel, and partly under the aegis (and protection) of a decade and a half of northern leadership in N'Djamena, there has been a large spread of pastoralist Muslim peoples southward, with both ethnic and religious clashes occurring. Many of these have been little reported outside the country but are indicative of worsening interethnic relations. The secessionist option is thus currently very much a possibility, especially since few truly expect Idriss Déby to vacate power.

RESERVE DE ABOU-TELFAN. Wildlife reserve created in 1955 to protect the rare Grand Koudou. Located between Mongo and Baro and stretching in a north-south direction, the reserve covers 110,000 hectares (271,700 acres).

RESERVE DE FAUNE DE MANDELIA. Small (138,000 hectares [340,860 acres]) wildlife refuge for elephants, some 20 kilometers (12 miles) from N'Djamena, between Mandelia and Moundoul. In recent years its elephant herds have been greatly reduced.

RESERVE DE SINIAKA-MINIA. Large (450,000 hectares [1.1 million acres]), little-developed national park in the southwestern part of Guéra Préfecture, with limited access via Djember in its opposite extremity in southeastern Chari-Baguirmi. Situated southeast of Melfi and created in 1961, Siniaka-Minia's animal density and variety place it well ahead of Zakouma (q.v.) National Park, though the latter is well known abroad while Siniaka-Minia is not. The park is difficult to reach and even harder to penetrate, due to thick brush and other vegetation, and so it draws few visitors. Small parts of the park are open to big-game hunters searching for buffalo, lions, and elephants.

RESERVE DU BAHR SALAMAT. Large wildlife reserve covering over 300,000 hectares (741,000 acres), surrounding the Parc National de Zakouma (q.v.), linked at Alaway with the Réserve de Siniaka-Minia (q.v.). The reserve was created to protect Zakouma's wildlife.

REVOLUTION CULTURELLE see CULTURAL REVOLUTION; MOUVEMENT NATIONAL POUR LA REVOLUTION CULTURELLE ET SOCIALE; YONDO.

RIZEGAT. Large Djoheina (q.v.) subgroup of Arab clans, named after its ancestor Rizeg. Rizeg's three sons gave their names to component subgroupings, including the Mahamid (q.v.). Found largely in Ouadai and in neighboring Darfur, Sudan.

ROASNGAR, M'BAINDOLOUMAL (Major) (1940–). Former minister of agriculture and natural disasters. A relatively little-known professional officer trained in Paris, Roasngar was brought into the cabinet as minister of territorial development and the environment after the 1975 coup d'état. His post was later changed, and he became minister of agriculture and natural disasters, serving in that capacity until 1978. He was Hissène Habré's (q.v.) choice to replace Major Camille Gourvenac (q.v.) as head of the Chadian Secret Service, and Habré's views on this important appointment were heeded by General Félix Malloum (q.v.). After the fall of the capital to Goukouni (q.v.), and the de facto partition of the country, Roasngar became Lt. Colonel Kamougoué's (q.v.) deputy in Sarh, ruler of the district in the name of the Comité Permanent du Sud (q.v.). Kamougoué's ouster by dissident FAT (q.v.) officers spelled the end of Roasngar's political career.

ROB-MBA, DJOTOIBET (1936–). Agricultural engineer. Born in 1936 and educated in France in tropical agriculture, Rob-Mba was appointed secretary-general of the Ministry of Agriculture and Animal Husbandry on his return from France. In the 1980s he worked in Burkina Faso as an expert from the Food and Agriculture Organization, and more recently has been residing in Le Havre, France.

ROCK PAINTINGS see ARCHAEOLOGY

RODAI, SAMUEL (Lt. Colonel). As an inexperienced young southern (Ngambayé) second lieutenant and subprefect of Tibesti, Rodai was the cause of the civil rebellion in B.E.T. His harsh punitive policies (see BARDAI INCIDENTS) in 1965 sparked the Toubou (q.v.) uprising. After the deaths of several Toubou prisoners in their cells, Rodai was recalled from Tibesti and reassigned to other duties. (His successor, Lt. Allafi (q.v.), continued Rodai's inept policies and aggravated the rebellion.) Promoted to first lieutenant and later to captain, Rodai commanded FAT (q.v.) forces in Ouadai after the pacification of the region by the French army in 1972. Further promoted to major and then to lieutenant colonel, Rodai was briefly chief of staff during the Malloum-Habré (qq.v.) interregnum (September 1978). With the disengagement of the south after the fall of N'Djamena, Rodai withdrew to Mayo-Kebbi. There he constantly clashed with his nominal superior, Colonel Kamougoué (q.v.), and tried to have the latter removed from his leadership role on the Comité Permanent du Sud (q.v.), the governing body of the Sara préfectures. Unsuccessful in these efforts, Rodai joined in the FAT upheaval that delivered the south to Habré shortly after the latter's triumphal entry into N'Djamena in 1982. Though Rodai expected a major political reward, he was merely retained in the new FANT (q.v.) army, being both disliked in the Sara south and unacceptable in the north due to his role in the Bardai incidents.

ROMAIN, MIAMBE. Head of the post-1992 Parti Social-Démocrate Tchadien.

ROMBA, ELIE ADOLPHE (1942–). Former cabinet minister under both Hissène Habré (q.v.) and Idriss Déby (q.v.). A southerner born in Fort-Lamy on December 28, 1942, Romba was trained in Paris as a customs inspector, returning to Chad to occupy a post in the Department of Customs. In June 1967 he became director of Civil Registrations, and in May 1971 he was brought into the cabinet as secretary of state in charge of finance. In December 1971 he was promoted to full ministerial rank but was dismissed in March 1973 for alleged mismanagement of resources. After the 1975 coup, Romba was appointed director of the Caisse Autonome des Amortissements, but was brought back into the cabinet in 1982 as Habré's minister of finance. He has also been head of Cotontchad (q.v.). In 1992 Romba set up a vehicle for his political ambitions, the Union Démocratique pour le Progrès du Tchad (UDPT), and he was viewed favorably by Paris as a potential prime minister. He participated in the Conférence Nationale (q.v.) in 1993 and was appointed by it as minister of justice, serving until May 1994.

ROUELENGAR, AMOS. Formerly Hissène Habré's (q.v.) minister of industry and commerce, leaving the cabinet in February 1990. In 1992 Rouelengar, a southerner, escaped an attempted kidnapping by Major Ahmat Taher Sodigui, a DDS (q.v.) veteran, who wanted to settle scores with him dating from the Habré era. After the rise to power of Idriss Déby, Rouelengar served for a few months (Sept. 1993–Jan. 1994) as Minister of Finance.

ROUSTAN, RENE (1918–). Colonial administrator and former Tombalbaye (q.v.) consultant. Born in Marseille on November 14, 1918, Roustan joined the colonial civil service after obtaining a law degree and a diploma in oriental languages. After serving briefly in Indochina (1943–45), he was appointed subprefect of Kyabé (Moyen-Chari) and in 1950 became director of budgets, pensions, and accounts and later deputy director general of finances for the AEF (q.v.) federal administration. He served in these capacities until 1959. On January 1, 1960, he became secretary-general of the government of Chad (the top administrative post in the executive), and in January 1962 he was renamed technical counselor, attached to the presidency. He remained in this top advisory role until 1968.

RUNGA. Small ethnic group and a Mbang language (see MABA) that is spoken over wide areas of the Salamat Préfecture (q.v.) and in part of the Central African Republic. The Runga, who were in particular decimated by the ravages of Rabah (q.v.) in their precolonial sultanate of Dar al-Kuti, are also found as herders in Ouadai. In 1992 the Runga population was estimated at only 24,000.

-S-

SABIT, AZIZ (1937–). Senior civil administrator. Born in Ati on July 4, 1937, and educated in civil aviation, Sabit has been director of civil aviation since October 1967. He has also served on a variety of boards, including that of the Chad Electric Company.

SABUN, ABD-EL-KARIM, KING (1805–1815) OF OUADAI. One of Ouadai's greatest kings, he impelled the kingdom to the heights of its power. Personally violent and cruel, Sabun rose to power in 1805. He promoted Islam, expanded Ouadai to the west into Baguirmi and Kanem and, utilizing a court schism in the former, razed its capital and set up a puppet *mai* (q.v.) in Massenya.

SAFI, ABDELKADER. Former cabinet minister. Safi entered Idriss Déby's (q.v.) regime as minister of livestock on May 20, 1992, and in

October of that year was promoted to head the Ministry of Finance, serving until the Conférence Nationale (q.v.) government of April 1993.

SAHARAN ROCK DRAWINGS see ARCHAEOLOGY

SAHEL. Climatologically arid, transitional zone between the desert north and the subtropical south. Running across much of Central Africa, the zone encompasses in Chad most of the Kanem, Chari-Baguirmi, and Biltine Préfectures. Though the Sahelian regions have a regular rainfall, any disruption of the climate (as in a prolonged drought) can transform the affected areas into desert. (See also DROUGHT.)

SAHOULBA, GOUNTCHOME (1909–1963). Early political leader and, briefly in 1959, head of government. As the *gong* (chief) of the Moundang (q.v.) in Mayo-Kebbi, and sultan of Léré, Sahoulba also played an important political role in the pre-independence period. An early member of the conservative traditionalist and pro-chiefly party, the UDT (q.v.), Sahoulba was elected to the Conseil Représentatif (q.v.) from Logone in 1947 and remained a deputy until 1961. In 1951 he was elected by the assembly to serve as senator to the French Union (q.v.). In 1957 Sahoulba split with the AST (q.v.) leadership (the party was the successor of the UDT), to form the GIRT (q.v.) party that selectively cooperated with Gabriel Lisette's (q.v.) PPT (q.v.) in a number of electoral races under the ERDIC and Entente (qq.v.) labels. In 1957 he was elected president of the National Assembly after reelection on the Entente list. Sahoulba's chiefly credentials prevented him from playing a more prominent role in Chad, then rapidly approaching independence. But on January 30, 1959— his party for some time in a pivotal power-balance role in the assembly—Sahoulba switched support from the Entente to the opposition and engineered the fall of the Lisette provisional government. Joining with the opposition groups to form the MPT (q.v.) coalition (see POLITICAL PARTIES), Sahoulba then briefly headed the successor provisional government (q.v.) before being toppled by his erstwhile ally Ahmed Koulamallah's (q.v.) switch of support for the Entente. In the next provisional government, which lasted 12 days, under Koulamallah, Sahoulba was retained as minister of transport, a post he continued to occupy after Koulamallah's fall and the formation of Tombalbaye's (q.v.) provisional government. In subsequent elections, however, the GIRT's political strength was greatly eroded, and neither the party nor Sahoulba were to play the kind of pivotal role they had played in 1959. Indeed, in 1960 Sahoulba was gently eased out of the spotlight and appointed ambassador to Cameroon (where a segment of the Moundang also reside).

SAHOULBA, SEYDOU. Son of Gountchomé Sahoulba (q.v.), and prominent founder in January 1992 of the Convention pour le Progrès et le Développment (CPD), which tried to play a role in ending the fighting in the Lake Chad area.

SALAH, MOHIDDINE. Former Idriss Déby (q.v.) cabinet minister. Salah joined the cabinet as secretary of state for the economy in March 1991 and was shifted to public works (December 1991), and then to finance as full minister (May 1992) before being dropped from the government.

SALAMAT ARABS. Group of clans belonging to the Djoheina (q.v.) branch of Arab tribes in Chad (see ARABS) that arrived in waves from the Sudan from the fourteenth to the nineteenth centuries and trace their descent to Abdallah el-Djoheini. Found throughout the region between the Chari River and Ouadai, subdivided into a large number of subgroups, including the Hilal (in Baguirmi), the Essala (who live among the Kotoko and the Barma), the Ouled Moussa (found in Ouadai), and the Sherafa (in northwestern Ouadai, assimilated into the Daza). In 1992 their number was estimated to be over 160,000.

SALAMAT PREFECTURE. Southern préfecture bordering the Central African Republic, with administrative headquarters in Am-Timan (q.v.). The préfecture covers 63,000 square kilometers (24,325 square miles) and contains three souspréfectures—Am-Timan, Adoudeia, and Harazé-Mangueigné. Its small nomadic population, depleted recently, numbers around 131,000, giving the préfecture a population density of 2.1 per square kilometer. The main ethnic groups in the préfecture are the Salamat Arabs (q.v.), the Ouled Rachid (q.v.), the Runga, and several other Arab subgroups. Part of the important Zakouma (q.v.) national park is within the Salamat Préfecture. Much of the region is a vast marshy plain drained by the Bahr Salamat (q.v.) and its tributaries. The préfecture's main products are cattle (on the hoof, exported to neighboring C.A.R. or to other centers), cotton, millet, groundnuts, sorghum, and dried and smoked fish. There is abundant big game throughout the area. The school attendance rate is 14.6 percent. The préfecture was the scene of significant antigovernment action in the late 1960s, and rebel groups are still operating today in the sparsely populated region in opposition to the current regime.

SALEH, ADOUM MAHAMAT. Idriss Déby's (q.v.) former minister of interior, and MPS (q.v.) secretary for communications. Saleh was appointed to Déby's cabinet immediately after Hissène Habré (q.v.) was ousted in December 1990. After fundamental policy disagreements with Déby, Saleh was dropped from both party and cabinet and appointed ambassador to Libya.

SALEH, AHMAT MAHAMAT (1946–). Opposition leader and cabinet minister under several presidents. Ahmat first came to prominence in 1978 when he was appointed minister of finance in the government of General Félix Malloum (q.v.). He was then driven into self-exile in Nigeria, and on November 14, 1988, he set up the MSDT (q.v.) opposition political movement in Lagos. After the rise to power of Idriss Déby (q.v.), Ahmat returned to N'Djamena and in March 1991 joined the government as minister of information. In December 1991 he was promoted to foreign minister, serving in that capacity until May 1992. He was then out of the government until April 1993, when he was appointed, and confirmed by the Conférence Nationale (q.v.), as minister of agriculture, staying on until May 1994.

SALEH, IBN OUMAR MAHAMAT. Frequent cabinet minister under both Habré and Déby (qq.v.). A northerner, and originally a professor at the University of N'Djamena. Saleh first joined Habré's cabinet in 1988 as minister of livestock and rural water supplies. He was later appointed minister of higher education, and from October 1989 to December 1990 he served as minister of planning. After Habré's ouster in December 1990 Saleh was again integrated into the cabinet, appointed minister of planning and cooperation in March 1991, surviving all the cabinet shuffles, being reconfirmed in that post by the Conférence Nationale (q.v.) in 1993, and only leaving the government in May 1994.

SALEH, MAHAMAT RAHAMA (1933–). Former cabinet minister and prefect of Batha. Born in Abéché in 1933, and briefly a student at Cairo's Al-Azhar University, Saleh worked as a municipal clerk in his hometown between 1948 and 1960 before joining the central administration, first as subprefect of Am Dam, then of Abéché and Am-Timan (1960–62). During the 1950s Saleh was a member of the militant Bloc des Travailleurs Démocrates Tchadiens (q.v.) of Jean Charlot (q.v.), running on that political ticket in the 1956 French National Assembly elections. In 1962 he was appointed *chef du cabinet* of the minister of the civil service, and the same year he was admitted for higher studies at France's prestigious Institut des Hautes Etudes d'Outre-Mer (IHEOM), completing his work in 1964. Upon his return to Chad he was reappointed to his old post as subprefect of Am-Timan, where he had served for a few weeks in 1961, and in 1966 he was brought into the cabinet as minister of the civil service. He served in that post through 1971, though he was for some time under house arrest under suspicion of maintaining contact with FROLINAT (q.v.). In 1971 he was dropped from the cabinet and appointed prefect of Batha, a position he held until the 1975 coup d'état. Saleh occupied a variety of other posts until the rise of the Hissène Habré (q.v.) regime, when he was appointed secretary of state in charge of agriculture (1988) and later of commerce and industry, serving until March 1990.

SALEM. FAC-funded, briefly published bimonthly. The name means "peace," and the publication emphasized reconciliation under FAC. The journal collapsed in 1982 after the entry of Habré (q.v.) troops into N'Djamena and the ouster of GUNT (q.v.).

SALIM, ALI DOUKORE. Administrator. For several years administrative director of the urban district of N'Djamena. Salim, better known as Ali Salim Doukoré, was brought into President Tombalbaye's (q.v.) cabinet in October 1968 as secretary of state for economics and finance. He served in that post until May 1971, at which time he was reassigned to his former administrative duties.

SANGHO (also SANGO). Lingua franca in neighboring Central African Republic, spoken mostly by the Oubangui riverine trading populations. The language is also understood along Chad's southern border, and especially in Sarh, by both Sara and Sangho ethnic elements. For a variety of reasons—one of which was that it was the prime language of Protestant proselytizing in the south—the use of Sangho was formally forbidden by the government of Chad in 1964.

SANUSIYA. A Sunni (orthodox) Sufi (mystic) order, emphasizing the return to the basic precepts and sources of Islam, avoidance of foreign contamination (though not in favor of asceticism), and direct interpretation of Islam, that struck roots in northern Libya in the nineteenth century. From there it radiated southward, including into areas currently part of Chad. The founder of the order was the Algerian scholar al-Sayyid Muhammad bin Ali al-Khattabi al-Sanusi (called in Libya the Grand Sanusi or al-Sanusi al-Kabir). Born of a distinguished family of Sharifs around 1787 and educated locally and at Fez (Morocco) and Mecca, al-Sanusi set up his order in Mecca in 1837, gathering a large number of Bedouin adherents. Forced out in 1841 by the local Muslim establishment and prevented by the French colonial expansion from returning to Algeria, al-Sanusi settled in Libya, in Tripoli and later in Benghazi, and in 1843 he founded the mother-lodge of the new order in Cyrenaica. After another pilgrimage to Mecca, he moved his headquarters to the interior Jaghbub (250 kilometers [160 miles] from the coast), where he founded an Islamic university, the second in the world after Al-Azhar in Cairo. Winning over tribes involved in the long-distance trans-Saharan caravan trade (and thus directly bringing peace and security to the Benghazi-

Ouadai caravan trail and a spurt of commerce on it), the order aggressively expanded southward, especially in Ouadai, where it was greatly aided by al-Sanusi's ties with the reigning Muhammad Sharif from their Mecca pilgrimage days. Al-Sanusi died in Jaghbub on September 7, 1859, and his two surviving sons continued his work, al-Sayyid Muhammad al-Mahdi taking over the general administration of the order and al-Sayyid Muhammad al-Sharif taking over religious leadership. The former greatly expanded the influence of the order in the Sahara by moving the center of the order to Kufra (q.v.) in 1895—wishing to avoid contact with the coastal "infidels" and Turks—consequently coming into very intimate contact with the B.E.T. (q.v.) regions of Chad and the various groups in the region. Much of the proselytizing in these southern areas was conducted by al-Mahdi's two principal lieutenants, Sidi Muhammad al-Barrani (q.v.)—in Kanem and B.E.T.—and Muhammad al-Sunni in Bornu and Baguirmi. The serious inroads the order scored in Kanem and other neighboring regions and the threat to the mushrooming de facto Sanusi empire by the French entry in the area prompted the relocation of the Sanusiya headquarters farther to the south, to Quru in Chad, between Borkou and Tibesti, as well as to the organization of anti-French movements in the entire area utilizing the Toubou (q.v.) and other solidly sympathetic ethnic groups. Resistance to the French was bitter, and one by one the 10 Sanusi *zawiyas* (q.v.) fell, though not without major French assaults (see BIR ALALI). By 1914 the Sanusi stranglehold over the north had been broken (though scattered fighting continued at least until 1919). Already in 1902 the fall and destruction of the Bir Alali lodge in Kanem resulted in a withdrawal of the Sanusiya capital from Quru to the safer Kufra. With the Italian declaration of war on Turkey and invasion of Libya, the order was further drawn to the threat of the infidels in the north (neglecting the south) and cooperated with the (hitherto despised) Turks in an effort to check the Italians. This effort was not successful, and in 1929 Kufra fell to Italian forces, finally destroying Sanusi power in the entire area. In 1952 the head of the Sanusiya order—Sidi Muhammad Idriss—was made king of newly independent Libya (he was toppled 17 years later by the military coup d'état of Muammar Qaddafi). The order still has many adherents in Chad, especially in the north and in Ouadai, though it is very much a minority sect. (See also RELIGIOUS ORDERS.)

SAO. Common name given to all the ethnic groups founded by the Sefuwa (q.v.) Magumi (q.v.) dynasty in Bornu after their expulsion from Kanem in the fourteenth century (see BORNU-KANEM EMPIRE). The Sao are an ethnic group long since extinct, though their descendants are the contemporary Kotoko (q.v.) and, through Magumi-

Kanembu and Sao intermarriage, the Kanuri (q.v.) of Bornu. According to legend the Sao were established from the tenth century onward in a wide arc stretching from Kouar in Niger to Lake Fitri in Chad. Their origins are not clear, but Kanembu legends recount their arrival from the east via the north, their gigantic stature—allowing them to lift elephants single-handedly—and their crafts. Contemporary archaeological research (in both Chad and Cameroon) has revealed that the Sao lived in compact settlements and, later, in walled cities. There is no evidence of a written language, but numerous relics remain of their artwork, including impressively large burial urns, highly developed lost-wax cast-iron work, and artistically highly regarded bronze figurine work. Kano's mudwalls, among others, were reputedly built by the Sao. With the establishment of the Kanem kingdom the Sao were pushed southward, and after the rise of the Bornu Empire they began to be systematically raided until their population greatly diminished, and the Sao disappeared as a separate people at the beginning of the seventeenth century. Traces of their former residence in western Chad are widely evident.

SARA. A large group of mostly non-Muslim agricultural and fishing clans living along the Chari and Logone River valleys and assimilated into an ethnic aggregate over the generations. They are estimated to number over 1.5 million people, or roughly one-third of the population of Chad. Some of the more important Sara clans are the Gambayé (q.v.)—the largest—Mbaï, Goulaye, Madjingayé, and Kaba (qq.v.). Other Sara groups include the Mboum, Laka, Moundang, Toubouri, Niellim, Massa (qq.v.), Kabalayé, Gabri, Soumrayé, Boa, N'Dam, Miltou, Saroua, and others. Extensively and semiannually raided for slaves by razzias from the Bornu, Baguirmi, and Ouadai kingdoms, some Sara groups artificially elongated the lips of the women to make them unattractive as slaves. In the west the Sara were also raided by the Fulani from the Adamaoua Mountains sultanate (in Cameroon). These perennial raids resulted in a great deal of depopulation in the south, exacerbated by the onset of Rabah's (q.v.) invasions, and they explain the sincere welcome accorded to the French when they arrived in the area pledging an end to the slave trade. Organized into relatively autonomous extended-family units (*golbai*, [q.v.], *tafourounda*, etc.), with a few exceptions the Sara were not (as were the Moundang [q.v.]) organized into any large viable territorial units. Chiefly authority in the independent Sara villages was not powerful, the chiefs usually being assisted by a council of elders. Though the slave trade was ended with the onset of French rule, the French recruited forced labor from the Sara villages (see CORVEE) for the construction of the Congo-

Océan railroad in Congo/Brazzaville and other infrastructure projects, causing population dislocations in the south and local disturbances. Moreover, from the 1930s on, the large-scale introduction of cotton cultivation—virtually forced upon the native population so that they could pay the taxes exacted on every village—also caused a great deal of discontent. The French reliance on local chiefs for the enforcement of the cultivation of cotton and collection of the tax in kind—and abuses connected with it (see CORDES DE CHEFS)—resulted in the artificial bolstering of traditional authority, a phenomenon that was at times violently resisted by the villagers. Notwithstanding this, the rapid spread of cotton in the south resulted in the area's designation as "Chad-utile," as the other regions contributed little to the overall economic development of the country. Though many have recently become converted to Islam, Sara country is still largely animist, with significant inroads having been achieved by both Catholic and Protestant missionaries (see CHRISTIAN MISSIONS; PROTESTANTS; RELIGION). With the extension of the franchise to all individuals of voting age, the numerical strength of the Sara was immediately manifest at the political level, leading to the rise to power of the PPT (q.v.) party of Gabriel Lisette (q.v.) and François Tombalbaye (q.v.). The coming of age of the south exacerbated ethnic animosities and regionalism (q.v.), since the east and north had become accustomed to thinking of the Sara as either subject peoples or merely slaves, while the Sara regions (still) harbor grievances against the Arabs and other groups that had until so recently raided them for the slave trade. Also, largely because the Sara grasped earlier the various meager educational possibilities offered them, much of the armed forces and civil administration of Chad is staffed with their members. In contrast, much of the Muslim areas of Ouadai and the north were deeply suspicious of the "contamination" aspects of Western education and fought off its inroads in their areas. Properly speaking, the term Sara refers to only one ethnic group—the Sara-Madjingayé, also a misnomer. Their closest ethnic cousins are the Nar, Goulaye, and Ngama (qq.v.). A second group of clans, assimilated into Sara culture, include the Daye, Noï, and Mboum (qq.v), while all the other groups—Sara-Kaba, Mbaï, Bedjond, Gor, Ngambayé, Kaba, Mouroum, and Doba—are "merely" Sara speakers, but ethnically further distant.

No accurate statistical breakdown of the various Sara groups exists. Population estimates in 1977, based on projections made from 1968 surveys, the most recent relatively reliable ones, suggest the figures that follow. However, these figures should only be seen as indicative, since if to these one adds the—again estimated—1.5 percent annual demographic growth of the Sara, the total figure for the Sara falls short of most estimates of their percentage of the population.

Sara	92,000
Nar	32,000
Goulaye	112,000
Ngama	37,000
Kaba	72,000
Mbaï	45,000
Bedjond	34,000
Gor	58,000
Doba	40,000
Mouroum	49,000
Gambayé	425,000
Gore	5,000
Total	1,006,000

SARA-KABA. Group of ethnically assimilated peoples residing on the right bank of the Chari River up to Lake Iro, between Salamat and Bahr Keita and farther south. Their supreme religious and ritual leader resides at Bedaya (q.v.). Scattered groups are also to be found in the big cities, such as Sarh and (prior to 1979) N'Djamena, making up a grand total of around 120,000. Frequently raided for slaves by both the Ouadai kingdom (q.v.) and Sultan Senusi at Ndeli, some Sara-Kaba served in Rabah's (q.v.) armies. During the colonial era the Sara-Kaba were recruited in large numbers as forced labor for the construction of the Congo-Océan railroad (in Congo), leaving them very hostile to the French and their collaborationist village chiefs. During much of the colonial era, Jean Charlot Bakouré (q.v.), of mixed parentage and from Djoko, was the Sara-Kaba prime political leader, and he remained so until the coup that toppled Tombalbaye (q.v.). Indeed, in 1974 he was named the Sara-Kaba Superior Chief. Other prominent members of this upwardly mobile group have been General Djogo and General Djimé (q.v.).

SARH. Prior to President Tombalbaye's (q.v.) Tchaditude policies of the "Cultural Revolution" (q.v) Sarh was known as Fort-Archambault and for several years prior to the Second World War was attached to Oubangui-Chari and governed by Bangui. In 1994 it was Chad's second largest city, with more than 120,000 people (nearly tripling in the past two decades from 43,000 people in 1972), and administrative headquarters of both the important Moyen-Chari Préfecture and the Sarh souspréfecture, which encompasses some 130,000 people. The city is the main point of entry and exit for goods coming/going to Congo/Brazzaville's Atlantic port of Pointe-Noire via the Oubangui and Congo Rivers and Bangui (see COMMUNICATIONS). Sarh is connected by unpaved but relatively well-maintained roads with N'Djamena (600 kilometers [370 miles] away) and with all other major centers in the country, and it can also be reached from the capital by river during three months of the year.

Founded as a fort on the Chari River on August 15, 1899, by French forces entering the regions via the Congo and Bangui, the town was originally named after one of Gentil's young officers who died there; the post-1973 name means in the Sara language "encampment" and refers to the forced labor camps into which Sara and other southerners were brutally interned during the construction of the Congo-Océan railroad in the Congo. Sarh is a very dull agricultural town with broad tree-shaded streets that belie its commercial importance and former strategic significance. It is the starting-out point for safaris into the interior and is greatly aided in its tourist attractions by the accessibility of abundant big game (elephants, giraffes, panthers, etc.). Sarh is also the cotton center of Chad (the systematic cultivation of the crop was launched first in Sarh in 1931), the second largest industrial center (after the capital) in the country, and the most important transportation juncture in the country by virtue of the very heavy volume of imports and exports that use the Sarh–Bangui–Pointe Noire route. For all these reasons Sarh also has a sizable resident European community.

The population of both town and préfecture increased dramatically after the 1978 fall of N'Djamena to the northern forces, but no up-to-date estimates exist. Sarh then became the military headquarters of General Djogo (q.v.), though Moundou, under Colonel Kamougoué (q.v.) and his gendarmerie, was the political center of the southern préfectures. After Goukouni's (q.v.) ouster from N'Djamena, Sarh fell to dissident FAT (q.v.) troops that ousted Djogo and delivered the region to Hissène Habré (q.v.). There is considerable anti-N'Djamena feeling in the town, and some elements advocate an all-Sara "République du Logone" (q.v.) or a federal option. In any such eventuality, however, Moundou would likely be the capital rather than Sahr.

SEBHA-BARDAI ROAD. One of the tangible, but rapidly deteriorating, remnants of former Chad-Libya cooperation. The Sebha-Bardai road, a wide paved road linking Sebha to the Kourizo pass inside Chad, was built by Libya as part of its technical assistance to Chad.

SECOND LIBERATION ARMY. Original and alternate name for the Forces Armées du Nord (FAN) (q.v.), the force led by Goukouni and Habré (qq.v.) in their fight against Tombalbaye (q.v.) and the successor regime of Malloum (q.v.). The name was adopted in July 1969 following a congress of B.E.T. guerrilla leaders under the chairmanship of Mahamat Ali Taher (q.v.). After the Goukouni-Habré split of 1976 the army fell under the exclusive leadership of Goukouni, and in 1978 it merged with the Volcan Army (q.v.), then led by Ahmat Acyl (q.v.), successor to "General" Baghalani (q.v.). It then renamed itself the Forces Armées Populaires (FAP) (q.v.).

SECTEUR EXPERIMENTAL DE MODERNISATION AGRICOLE DE BONGOR (SEMAB). One of the SEMA (q.v.) organs set up in 1958 and charged with the development and marketing of rice in the Bongor region.

SECTEUR EXPERIMENTAL DE MODERNISATION AGRICOLE DE LAI ET KELO (SEMALK). One of the SEMA (q.v.) organs set up in 1960 to operate in the souspréfectures of Laï and Kélo and charged with the expansion and modernization of rice production in these areas. The organ was involved in 1968 in the modernization of rice production on 20,000 hectares (49,400 acres) in these two souspréfectures, though later, in 1970, some of its operations in Laï were removed from its jurisdiction and attached to the FDAR (q.v.).

SECTEUR EXPERIMENTAL DE MODERNISATION AGRICOLE DU BLE (SEMABLE). One of the SEMA (q.v.) organs set up in 1961 and charged with the development and marketing of wheat grown on the polders (q.v.) of Lake Chad's Lac Préfecture and with helping farmers to construct and maintain the fragile polders on the lake. The company was not successful in its prime areas of responsibility and grossly failed to satisfy the raw-materials needs of N'Djamena's flour mills. It was replaced in 1967 by SODELAC (q.v.). In its first year of operations SEMABLE purchased only 900 tons of the 1,600 tons of wheat produced in the region, and in 1965–66 it purchased only 1,100 of the 2,422 tons produced. In 1967 only 500 of the 9,000 tons produced in Lac were sold to the state. Farmers in general (including under SODELAC's tenure) regarded the state organs as the purchaser of last resort, largely because market prices were much higher than the prices offered by the state organs. Much of the wheat produced was therefore sold directly to other farmers or purchasers or smuggled across into Nigeria where even better prices were obtained.

SECTEURS DE MODERNISATION AGRICOLE (SMA). Not to be confused with the SEMA (q.v.) organs (i.e., SEMAB, SEMALK, SEMABLE). Created in 1963 — and in 1965 replaced by ONDR (q.v.) — the Secteurs de Modernisation Agricole were charged with the furthering of agricultural modernization through the centralization of tools, machinery, work cattle, and technical assistants. For more details, see the entry for the SMA successor, Office National de Développement Rural.

SECTEURS EXPERIMENTAUX DE MODERNISATION AGRICOLE (SEMA). Not to be confused with the SMA (q.v.), the SEMA were a number of state organs set up between 1958 and 1967 and charged with the development of specific agricultural crops and the modernization of specific geographical régions or préfectures, empowered to guarantee an outlet for the crop via state purchases and sales of the commodity at fixed official prices. The various organs had a great deal of latitude as well as fiscal autonomy. Among the structures created were: (1)Secteur Expérimental de Modernisation Agricole de Bongor (SEMAB), created in 1958 and charged with encouraging rice cultivation in the Bongor souspréfecture; (2) Secteur Expérimental de Modernisation Agricole de Laï et Kélo (SEMALK), set up in 1960, in charge of spurring rice cultivation in the souspréfectures of Läi and Kélo; and (3) Secteur Expérimental de Modernisation Agricole du Blé (SEMABLE), created in 1961 to assist in the development of Lake Chad's polders (q.v.) in the Lac Préfecture and to encourage the production of wheat and its sale to the Grands Moulins du Tchad (q.v.). In December 1967 SEMABLE was replaced by SODELAC (q.v.). The SEMA organs recorded very mixed results, and in 1976 they were replaced by the Office de la Mise en Valeur du Sategui-Deressia (q.v.).

SECTEURS REGIONAUX DE DEVELOPPEMENT RURAL (SRDR). Territorial development sectors into which Chad is divided. There were 12 such regions in 1972 and 57 subsectors in which the Office National de Développement Rural (ONDR) (q.v.) is active, coordinating modernization projects and allocating developmental aid.

SEF. The hot dry season in the Sahel (q.v.) belt, lasting from around mid-March to mid-May.

SEFUWA. Lineage of the Magumi (q.v.) clan that founded the Kanem kingdom (see KANEM-BORNU EMPIRE) in the ninth century. The latter rapidly expanded in the eleventh century, reaching its height in the thirteenth. In the fourteenth century the Sefuwa were challenged in a religious dispute by another clan, the Bulala (q.v.), and after a series of defeats were ousted from power. They retreated to the western reaches of the kingdom where a new kingdom was founded, eventually to become Bornu (q.v.). The latter became extremely powerful and eventually reconquered the Kanem region. The Sefuwa traced their descent from Saif ibn Dhi Yazan (and were also known as Yazani) from Yemen (as do many other ethnic groups, though the geographical point of origin is usually mythical). Their dynasty was one of the longest in Africa, coming to an end in 1846 when their last *mai* (q.v.) was toppled by Umar al-Kanemi (q.v.).

SEID, BRAHIM. Déby's first minister of alimentary needs, appointed in December 1990 and dropped a year later.

SEID, JOSEPH BRAHIM (1927–1980). Lawyer, longtime cabinet minister, diplomat, and one of Chad's towering intellectuals. Born in Fort-Lamy on November 27, 1927, of Gor-Bulala parentage, Seid was educated locally, at Brazzaville, and at the College of the Holy Family in Cairo, becoming Chad's first university graduate in 1949. He continued his education in law at the University of Paris (having originally trained for a pharmaceutical career) and at Lyons, and he also attended ENFOM. In 1955 he returned to Africa to become deputy state prosecutor in Brazzaville, and in 1957 he was appointed justice of the peace in Djambala, also in Congo. In 1959 he finally returned to Chad to serve as public prosecutor in Moundou (1959–60), following which (in December) he was appointed Chad's first ambassador to France, the highest diplomatic office in the foreign service. Seid served in Paris until April 1966, when he was repatriated to Chad to join Tombalbaye's (q.v.) government as minister of justice, a position he held for nine years, until the 1975 coup d'état. His noninvolvement in factional politics in the cabinet, his unswerving loyalty to the head of government—as well as his high reputation in foreign circles—explain his longevity in office during one of the most turbulent eras of Chadian politics. Yet, though widely respected abroad (where he was considered a brilliant lawyer and a towering intellectual, by virtue of some of his writings), at no time did Seid have any serious power or influence in the cabinet. Even though some cabinet policies were known to be personally repugnant to him, he did not resign his post. Seid was the author of two novels (published in 1962 and 1967) and various brief articles. Following the 1975 coup d'état he served for a few years as attorney general (1975–78) and then retired into private law practice until his death.

SEID, MAHAMAT ABBA see ABBA, MAHAMAT SEID

SEIF, ADOUM MOUSSA. Former cabinet minister under both Habré and Déby (qq.v.). Appointed Habré's minister of the economy and trade in July 1984, Seif was transferred to head the Ministry of Mines and Energy in 1986, and then to head the Ministry of Information in 1988. He lost his post with the rise of the Déby regime and was arrested on January 8, 1992, for involvement in Habré's attempted comeback via the MDD (q.v.) invasion in the Lake Chad region. He bounced back into the government in the aftermath of the Conférence Nationale, when he was elected minister of administrative reform in April 1993, a post he occupied for one year.

SEKIMBAYE, ANDRE (1939–). Educator. Born on November 24, 1939, in Belama Gore, Sekimbayé was educated locally and in France; he was instructor of psychology of education and director of the National Pedagogic Institute in N'Djamena from 1969 to 1973. He then became director of primary education at the Ministry of Education, relocating to Moundou in 1979 after the fall of N'Djamena to Goukouni's (q.v.) troops.

SELINGAR, SILAS BENOIT (1928–1970?). Former cabinet minister and close Tombalbaye (q.v.) associate. A Sara from the south, Selingar served as Tombalbaye's *chef du cabinet* from March 1962 to March 1963. In January 1964 he joined the cabinet as minister of public works and was for some time also responsible for the Ministry of Interior. In his latter capacity he was the one who ordered the government troops to quell the Mangalmé tax riots (q.v.)—which resulted in 500 deaths. Regarded once as Tombalbaye's right-hand man, Selingar was purged from the cabinet in October 1966 on charges of corruption, embezzlement, and maladministration. Placed under house arrest, he was then imprisoned on charges of maintaining contact with FROLINAT's (q.v.) Ibrahim Abatcha (q.v.). In December 1967 he was further accused of plotting—from his prison cell—the dissolution of the National Assembly and the overthrow of the Tombalbaye regime. The charges were never proven, though most probably Selingar's major crime was engaging in factional politics in Tombalbaye's entourage. He was killed while in prison.

SEM MIANTOLOUM, BEASNAEL (1948–). Educator. Born in 1948 and trained in African literature, Sem Miantoloum taught for a few years at the University of N'Djamena before assuming the post of head of personnel at a local parastatal. In 1982 he left the country for Ghana, becoming the scholarships program officer of the Association of African Universities.

SENOUSSI see SANUSIYA

SENOUSSI, ADOUM HADJERO. Former FROLINAT (q.v.) leader. A Chadian born in Sudan and formerly an officer in the Sudanese Army (and hence widely regarded as "Sudan's Man"), Senoussi was one of FROLINAT's earliest leaders. Recruited by Ibrahim Abatcha (q.v), Senoussi's role was to liaise with the Sudanese government and to recruit and train Chadian refugees in Sudan. Senoussi was also, from 1966 to 1969, FROLINAT's secretary of the armed forces. Because of this lengthy and early association with both

Abatcha and FROLINAT, Senoussi only grudgingly accepted the post-Abatcha emergence of Abba Siddick (q.v.) as head of the movement. He kept himself and his Sudanese following as a distinct armed clique, not beholden to Siddick, in the Maghreb. Later, in 1978, his faction was to adopt the name FROLINAT-Fondamental (q.v.). Following the fall of N'Djamena to Goukouni (q.v.), Senoussi was invited to the KANO II peace talks but was not given a post in the subsequent GUNT (q.v.) government. This was partly because he never had many troops, and he had allegedly never been engaged in combat within Chad. Joining in the Libyan-sponsored FACP (q.v.)—which grouped all the Kano "losers"—Senoussi was eventually integrated in GUNT in November 1979 and served as minister of reconstruction. He was expelled from GUNT soon after because he sided with Hissène Habré (q.v.) in the Goukouni-Habré falling-out in 1980, fleeing to exile in Khartoum. Not given a role in the new Habré administration of 1982—following Habré's comeback—Senoussi joined Goukouni's GUNT government-in-exile, based in Bardai. He was one of the last to rally to Habré, in December 1987, after GUNT had for all practical purposes ceased to exist and after Habré's attacks on the Libyan positions in B.E.T. After the rise of the Idriss Déby (q.v.) regime, Senoussi set up several political parties, one of which was the Front de Libération Démocratique Tchadien (FLDT) (q.v.).

SENOUSSI, MAHAMAT (1918–1965). Former vice president of the National Assembly. Born in Mangalmé (Batha) on February 16, 1918, and a merchant by profession, Senoussi was elected to the Territorial Assembly in March 1957 as PPT (q.v.) deputy from Guéra Préfecture and was reelected in 1959. Already a municipal councillor of Fort-Lamy (November 1956), he served as vice president of the National Assembly (1957–58) and as its questor (1958–60). Shortly after Chad's independence, Senoussi was purged for opposition activities, and he later retired from public life. Amnestied by Tombalbaye, Senoussi died during the 1965 Mangalmé tax riots (q.v.).

SENOUSSI, MAHAMAT (1944–). Former minister of defense and of veteran affairs. Born in 1944 in Oum-Hadjer (Batha) and educated in Ati and Abéché, Senoussi joined the Foreign Ministry in 1962 and was transferred to the Sûreté Nationale (q.v.) in 1963. He obtained specialized training in France during the next 18 months, after which he returned to Chad, becoming commissioner of police at Sarh and later at Abéché (1965–68). On October 16, 1968, he moved into the cabinet as minister of defense and of veteran affairs. Three years later, in

May 1971, he left the cabinet and resumed administrative duties with the Ministry of Interior.

SENOUSSI, MOHAMED-ES- (1850?–1911). Sultan of Dar Kouti and of Dar Rounga (qq.v.) at the time of the French entry into Chad, and major ally of Rabah (q.v.). Born around 1850 in Ouadai and surnamed Senoussi by his father, an early follower of the Sanusiya (q.v.), Mohammed-es-Senoussi moved to Dar Kouti in Chad at an early age and was raised by his uncle. Briefly captured as a slave by a raiding party belonging to Zubeir Pasha (q.v.), Senoussi escaped and in 1890 assisted in toppling the local reigning dynasty. Nephew of the deposed ruler (Kobur), Senoussi was named sultan of these former Ouadai provinces by Rabah. Shortly later a French advance mission (led by Crampel) that reached Dar Kouti was murdered at Senoussi's orders, and the captured arms were added to the Rabahist arsenal. The furor aroused in France by this action bolstered demands for a major French advance in the region. In the meantime a strong Ouadai force reached Dar Kouti to punish the rebellious province; thousands were killed or taken into slavery, with Senoussi himself forced into hiding for over a year. When he finally returned to his throne, the political picture for him looked bright in light of major new Rabahist successes in the area. Within five years, however, Rabah was killed and his armies dispersed (see BATTLE OF KOUSSERI). For some time preoccupied with the conquest of Ouadai and other areas in the north, the French allowed Senoussi to retain his throne, and he continued his slave raids in the countryside. Finally in 1911 a French force was dispatched against him and he was killed the same year.

SHARI RIVER see CHARI RIVER

SHEHU. Regal title—from sheikh or sultan in Arabic—adopted by the al-Kanemi (q.v.) dynasty following its rise to power in the Kanem-Bornu Empire (q.v.). The title was adopted to distinguish between the (nominal) sovereign of the Sefuwa (q.v.) lineage—the *mai* (q.v.)—and the new de facto rulers of the al-Kanemi lineage. The Sefuwa dynasty was finally abolished in 1848. After Rabah's (q.v.) defeat at the hands of the French and Bornu's incorporation into the British colony of Nigeria, the Shehu was recognized as titular ruler over Bornu. The current Shehu is Umar Abubakar Garbai el-Kanemi, Nigeria's second most important Muslim leader after the Fulani sultan of Sokoto, who resides in his new capital of Yerwa.

SHEHU LAMINU. One of several Bornuan names for Mohammad al-Kanemi (q.v.).

SHOA (or SHUWA) ARABS. Collective name—used by most ethnic groups in western Chad—for the various Arab clans in the country, with the exception of the Awlad Sulayman and the Tunjur (qq.v.). (See also ARABS.)

SHOFFAI BOGARMI (Derde) (1860?–1939). Last fully independent leader of Tibesti's Teda (q.v.) branch of the Toubou (q.v.) ethnic group. Shoffai Bogarmi (also Chai Bogar-mi) was twelfth derde (q.v.) of the Teda between 1894 and 1939. When French troops entered into B.E.T. he resisted their intrusion with all his might, seeking military allies from all quarters, but he was finally defeated and pushed into the Fezzan in 1914. He returned to Tibesti in 1920 and was accepted by the French as derde, subject to his ensuring law and order in his domains. After Shoffai Bogarmi's death, Wodei Kichidemi (q.v.) was elected derde. (See also DERDE.)

SIDDICK, ABBA (Dr.) (1924–). Former minister of higher education and former secretary-general of FROLINAT (q.v.). Born in Mobayé in the Central African Republic on December 25, 1924, of a Chadian father and a C.A.R. mother, Siddick is the grandson of a Rabahist (see RABAH) general. An early militant in the PPT (q.v.) in Abéché, he rapidly moved up the party hierarchy, becoming Gabriel Lisette's (q.v.) secretary-general of the PPT, and in 1957 he joined the cabinet as minister of education. He remained in that post through the provisional governments (q.v.) of Chad—except under Sahoulba—but was dropped from François Tombalbaye's (q.v.) provisional government of 1959, at which time he was also stripped of his party leadership. Siddick left the country for France, where he studied for the next eight years and qualified as a surgeon. Secretly a FROLINAT supporter, Siddick assumed active leadership of FROLINAT after his graduation, becoming its secretary-general after Ibrahim Abatcha's (q.v.) death the same year. Originally not very doctrinaire, Siddick rapidly developed a neo-Marxist stance, though he was increasingly attacked (especially after 1971) for not being sufficiently revolutionary, and his leadership was rejected by both Hissène Habré (q.v.) and his Second Liberation Army (q.v.) as well as by Chadian students abroad (in France and at El Beida University). Indeed, the cleavage between Siddick and the Chadian students in Benghazi was so embarrassing that Siddick had to appeal to Muammar Qaddafi to have their Libyan scholarships revoked after they set up an autonomous Comité Populaire in 1972 that disowned him. Siddick's control over the fighting forces in Chad has also been more on paper than in reality. The eastern armed guerrillas have always been highly autonomous and often more interested in brigandage than in revolutionary action, while the highly independent Toubou (q.v.) (and later Habré) complained that he paid little attention to them and did not help to evacuate their wounded into Libya. Indeed, a circular was sent out to Arab capitals specifically disowning Siddick's leadership, though Qaddafi's largesse continued to prop him up in FROLINAT headquarters in Tripoli. By the mid-1970s, however, Siddick's personal reputation as well as FROLINAT's (badly truncated as it was by its trouncing at the hands of the French and by massive desertions) was at its lowest since the rebellions began in Chad. Continuously under pressure for being a backseat tactician who had never led troops in battle, nor for that matter had ever slipped into "liberated" territory, Siddick was also regarded as an agnostic nonbeliever by FROLINAT factions for whom the religious struggle was paramount. Seen as a usurper of Abatcha's mantle of leadership—and one who refused to call a congress to ratify his leadership—Siddick was widely ignored by many of the actual fighting factions. He was finally ousted in 1976–77 by a coalition of Goukouni (q.v.) and some of his allies. All of Siddick's Algiers and Tripoli subordinates were also removed from office. Siddick, refusing disassociation from FROLINAT, continued to call his small following FROLINAT-Originel (q.v.), which later also split, while the Goukouni rump preferred to use the FAN (q.v.), and later FAP (q.v.) label. Totally locked out of power following the first Kano peace talks (see KANO MEETINGS), Siddick was brought into the GUNT cabinet of November 1979 as minister of education only because of pressure from Nigeria (aimed at granting cabinet representation to every conceivable faction). Straddling the fence during the Goukouni-Habré tug-of-war, with Habré returning to power in 1982, Siddick was reconfirmed in the same ministry in which he had served for four years before being dismissed in 1986 and retiring from public life.

SIDDICK FADOUL (?–1989). Brother-in-law of Hassan Djamouss (q.v.), whose murder in a Habré (q.v.) jail drove the final wedge between Habré and the Zaghawa (q.v.), caused their defection, and ultimately led to Habré's ouster by Déby (q.v.) in 1990.

SILEK, ABDERAMAN ALI (1942–). Ouadaian nobleman and deputy in the National Assembly. Born in 1942 in Abéché, the son of Sultan Ali Silek of Ouadai, Silek was educated locally in a traditional school. He served as subprefect of Adré and from 1969 to the 1975 coup d'état was a deputy in the National Assembly.

SILEK, MAHAMAT GAMAR (1937–). Former secretary of state in Tombalbaye's (q.v.) government. Born on August 4, 1937, in Am-Timan in the Salamat Préfecture, and an administration agent by occupation, Silek was defeated in 1960 when he ran for a seat in the National Assembly. Two years later he was attached to Tombalbaye's presidential office as an administrative assistant (June 1962–April 1963) and was later appointed deputy prefect of Léré (May–December 1963). In January 1964 he returned to N'Djamena, this time as secretary of state in charge of information attached to the presidential office. He was arrested in 1967 on the charge of plotting against the government and was amnestied in April 1970. He then served for four years in an administrative capacity with the Ministry of Interior.

SLAVES. Prior to the French occupation of the territory that was to become Chad—though in some respects right through the early 1920s—large numbers of slaves were captured in the southern areas and exported to the north and east to the Maghreb, Turkey, and Arabia. All the major kingdoms in the area—Bornu, Baguirmi, and Ouadai—mounted frequent expeditions into Sara areas for slaves, who were then promptly sent north and east along the various caravan routes (q.v.). As late as the 1920s two Senegalese marabouts making the hajj (q.v.) through Chad found themselves abducted and sold as slaves in Chad. Rabah's (q.v.) extensive raids in the area in the late 1800s also resulted in a massive depopulation of Central Africa. Various European travelers in the region observed some of these slave raids and have left written testimonials to the cruelty of the practice. According to the French authorities, the slave trade did not formally end in Chad until 1926.

SMUGGLING. With lengthy, porous, and uncontrollable borders, smuggling has always been rife in Chad. It has long been estimated that the vast majority (as much as 90 percent) of all trade enters and leaves the country via traditional channels. There are many routes, and the one skirting Lake Chad via Rig Rig (to Nigeria/Niger) was a favorite until it became highly insecure in the late 1980s and was replaced by a more southerly route to Cameroon and then through Cameroon to and from Nigeria. Much oil, for example, reaches Chad along the latter route, as well as fabrics, vehicles, and cigarettes. There is also considerable smuggling of cattle (on the hoof) from Chad, primarily to Nigeria, as well as illicit trade to and from the Central African Republic.

SOCIETE AGRICOLE LOGONE-TCHAD see COTONFRAN

SOCIETE BAGUIRMIENNE DE TRANSPORTS FLUVIAUX. Commercial company set up in 1954 by Ahmed Koulamallah (q.v.) to break the monopoly and customary transit rights of chiefs along the

Chari River who controlled the cross-river traffic. Set up in Bousso to transport riverine traffic between there and N'Djamena, the company linked up with several discredited chiefs against the traditional establishment. The company went to court and won its case against the vested interests along the river but eventually found itself paying off a variety of chiefs to facilitate its activities.

SOCIETE COMMERCIALE DU BORKOU-ENNEDI-TIBESTI (SCBET). Former major supply company in B.E.T., and longtime prime supplier of the Faya-Largeau garrison. The company ceased to operate when Faya-Largeau fell to rebel hands in the late 1970s, rupturing communication between it and N'Djamena. (See also MARCEL KOUSSA.)

SOCIETE COMMERCIALE DE KOUILOU-NIARI (SCKN) see NOUVELLE SOCIETE DE KOUILOU-NIARI

SOCIETE COTONNIERE DU TCHAD (COTONTCHAD). Successor to Cotonfran (q.v.). Cotontchad was established as a mixed-economy company on April 21, 1971, with a capitalization of 600 million CFA francs, of which the Cotonfran combine held 30 percent of the shares, the Chadian government 45 percent, private French interests 17 percent, and various banks 8 percent. At its height in the 1970s the company had 24 gin mills in the country and some 3,200 purchasing agents/centers in the countryside, and it held a total monopoly over the purchase, processing, export, and marketing of all of Chad's cotton crop—the mainstay of the economy. At the time that the company replaced Cotonfran, its director was the former finance minister Abdoulaye Lamana (q.v.). Between 1966 and 1971 Cotonfran subcontracted the transport of purchased cotton equally between Unitchadienne (q.v.) and the CTT (q.v.) cooperative, while Cotonfran slowly augmented its own trucking fleet. Between 1972 and 1975 Cotontchad accelerated this process of controlling all aspects of its activities by allowing the CTT only 20 percent of the traffic, with Cotontchad's own fleet transporting 80 percent of the crop. In 1975 the company established a total monopoly over the transportation of all cotton. For a listing of Cotontchad's affiliates, see COTONFRAN. (For details on the cotton crop and exports of cotton, see COTTON and the appropriate tables.) The company's capitalization has progressively gone up to 2.5 billion CFA francs, with the state's share at 75 percent. The CFDT holds 17 percent, Chad banking consortia 6 percent, and the CCCE (q.v.) 2 percent.

Cotontchad entered a period of major decline in the late 1970s, which worsened in the mid-1980s, partly because of the unsettled conditions in many parts of the country, but primarily because the company was unable to market cotton effectively. The prices paid to producers neither covered production costs nor Cotontchad's marketing costs, with the result that the company was losing money and kept afloat largely via foreign subsidies. In 1988 the company nearly collapsed completely but was rescued by major infusions of French, EC, and AID funds, totaling US$47 million at which time it was also forced to embark on a painful program of restructuring and downsizing that saw the closure of half of the country's 26 cotton gins, the dismissal of half of its workers, the closure of its branch in Bangui, and the sale of its two aircraft and 150 trucks. Cotton production was likewise to be limited to 100,000 tons, explaining the major plummeting of production from Chad's bumper crop of 160,000 tons in 1984 to the 90,000 tons of 1987. However, production had again rebounded to 174,000 tons in 1991, since cultivators have few other options, despite low producer prices—though it declined again to 122,000 tons in 1992. The company made a profit of 2.7 billion CFA francs in 1990 but piled up deficits again in 1991 and 1992, when it had a 3 billion CFA franc loss. The fall of global market prices in 1992 again depressed Cotontchad's activities, and the company had to close down two of its eight factories and dismiss 500 workers initially, and later 1,000 more. Apart from those directly working for Cotontchad, more than 2 million Chadians make a living growing cotton in the country.

SOCIETE COTONNIERE FRANCO-TCHADIENNE (COTONFRAN). Cotton monopoly established in Chad in 1925 to purchase the entire country's produce and to transport, gin, export, and market it abroad. Producer prices were fixed in 1964 by the Caisse de Stabilisation des Prix du Coton (CSPC) (q.v.), which ensured stability of prices paid to farmers, irrespective of world market fluctuations; prior to 1964 the same function was performed by a joint C.A.R.-Chad stabilization fund. At Chad's independence, Cotonfran's contract was renewed for another 10 years, and in 1971 the company took a new name—Société Cotonière du Tchad (Cotontchad)—and the Chadian government now had a larger financial stake in it. Cotonfran had some 3,200 purchasing agents/stations in the country and 22 ginning mills. Between 1966 and 1971 it subcontracted the collection of raw cotton to two local firms (Unitchadienne and CTT) but after 1972—under Cotontchad—this arrangement was changed. Cotonfran itself has several affiliates, including: Société des Oléagineux du Logone-Tchad (SOLT), the oil mills of Moundou, set up in 1956; Société Agricole Logone-Tchad (SALT), set up in 1956 with Congolese and C.A.R. participation to encourage the growth and production of certain specific crops; and Constructions Métalliques du Tchad (COMAL), established in 1959 with a link to and investment in the C.A.R. textile factory in Boali, the Industrie Cotonnière de l'Oubangui et du Tchad. (See also COTTON; SOCIETE COTONNIERE DU TCHAD.)

SOCIETE DES OLEAGINEUX DU LOGONE-TCHAD (SOLT) see SOCIETE COTONNIERE FRANCO-TCHADIENNE.

SOCIETE D'ETUDES SUCRIERES DU TCHAD (SESUCHARI). State company established in 1965 to conduct research and experiments with local cane sugar planting and production, following successful first efforts in 1963. SESUCHARI has already invested over 5.8 billion CFA francs in the experimental planting of sugar in the southern préfectures (especially in irrigated plots near Sarh) with the goal of reaching the production initially of 20,000 tons of sugar annually, and an ultimate goal of 40,000 tons from 3,000 hectares (7,410 acres) of land.

SOCIETE DU MATERIEL AGRICOLE DU TCHAD (SOMAT). State organ officially set up in May 1976 with a capitalization of 290 million CFA francs and based in N'Djamena. The company became fully operational in 1978, producing a wide array of agricultural materials. The plant was destroyed during the 1979 fighting in the capital and has been only partly rebuilt since.

SOCIETE FRIGORIFIQUE DES PRODUITS DES ELEVEURS TCHADIENS (PRODEL). French company controlling the Farcha slaughterhouse outside N'Djamena and frozen meat exports out of Chad. The only slaughterhouse to be profitable (the ones in Abéché and Sarh had to close down), PRODEL nevertheless never developed into a major source of supply for the tsetse-infested regions in the south—a prime expansion possibility envisaged since the 1960s.

SOCIETE HOTELIERE DU TCHAD (SHT). Largely moribund parastatal company set up to direct the state-owned Chadian hotels and camps. Since many of these were in unsettled areas or were destroyed in Chad's civil wars, SHT's responsibilities were greatly curtailed. Moreover, with the fall of N'Djamena to northern troops in 1980 and the fighting in the capital in 1982, tourism never recovered.

SOCIETE INDUSTRIELLE DE MATERIEL AGRICOLE DU TCHAD (SIMAT). State company set up to produce a variety of agricultural implements, but in particular plowing equipment for cotton cultivators. As the company's fate is directly linked with that of the cotton industry, it suffered declining sales in the 1980s, and again in the 1990s, as cotton cultivation plummeted.

SOCIETE INDUSTRIELLE DE VIANDE DU TCHAD (SIVIT). Ambitious but ill-conceived industrial project in Sarh involving a meat cannery, a can factory, tanneries, a shoe factory, and several allied workshops. Set up in 1967 with Israeli, French, and German capital, the project had persistent problems in obtaining its raw material—cattle on the hoof—due to the severity of the Sahelian drought farther to the north (which decimated vast herds), the paucity of cattle in the immediate vicinity (due to tsetse infestation), and the inclination of cattle herders to sell their cattle across the border, to much nearer, traditional markets at a higher price than that offered by SIVIT. The plant's conceptualization was also much too ambitious for the Chadian reality; if working at full capacity, for example, which it never did, SIVIT would have exhausted all cattle resources in the south in barely two years. Moreover, the location of the abattoir was a result of a political decision—this being Tombalbaye's (q.v.) region—and necessitated a long, exhausting cattle trek south from the Sahelian pasturelands, thinning cattle to the detriment of producer prices. For all of these reasons, SIVIT was never an economical proposition, and it closed down completely in 1971.

SOCIETE NATIONALE DE COMMERCIALISATION DU TCHAD (SONACOT). Mixed-economy company created in November 1965 and given a monopoly over the local purchase of a number of commodities (and their marketing abroad) and the sale of certain specific consumer goods within Chad. Unlike the specialized or geographically restricted SEMA (q.v.) organs, SONACOT operated statewide and handled a variety of commodities, though the more important ones were confined to the specialized companies. Among its responsibilities were gum arabic (q.v.)—previously under SMR and FDAR (qq.v.) monopoly—natron (q.v.), demonopolized in the 1980s due to the glut in the market and the large stockpiles available to Chad, and groundnuts, even though the bulk (96 percent) of the latter are consumed in Chad. With the collapse of central authority in Chad in 1979 SONACOT disappeared.

SOCIETE NATIONALE SUCRERIE DU TCHAD (SONASUT). Sugar processing company founded at Banda in 1965 with an original capitalization of 420 million CFA francs. SONASUT has a capacity of over 40,000 tons (augmented several times, most recently in 1993, from its original 8,000-ton capacity), and it refines crude sugar imported from Congo-Brazzaville. Virtually from the outset the company operated at full capacity, producing both refined sugar and confectionary. Originally known as SOSUTCHAD, the company was nationalized in 1976 and capitalized at 4,711 million CFA francs. The company then immediately entered into a decline, and in 1975 needed a loan from the CCCE (q.v.) to bail it out of financial difficulties. In 1987 SONASUT received 40 million French francs from the CCCE to allow it to finance a technical and financial restructuring. In 1990 the company, which produces the lowest priced sugar in Africa, produced 30,000 tons of raw sugar and 290,000 tons of cane sugar. It then owned 3,500 hectares (8,650 acres) of canefields and employed some 3,000 workers. High energy costs and smuggling from Nigeria, Gabon, Central African Republic, and Cameroon hamper its efforts to become solvent.

SOCIETE POUR LE DEVELOPPEMENT DE LA REGION DU LAC (SODELAC). State organ in charge of helping to develop the potentials of the Lac Préfecture and especially the polders (q.v.) of Lake Chad. Among its more important responsibilities, SODELAC is empowered to purchase from local producers wheat crops from the polders and to market them, especially to the flour mills of N'Djamena. The official price was originally fixed at 20 CFA francs, and there were great expectations that the Grands Moulins du Tchad (q.v.) would reach their full capacity of 12,000 tons through the local raw material. These hopes were dashed when it became apparent that SODELAC was unable to purchase more than a fraction of the produce of the préfecture. In 1968, for example, SODELAC purchased 500 tons of the total production from the polders of 9,000 tons. The major cause of the disinclination of farmers to sell to SODELAC was that the free-market prices were much higher than those offered by the government. An inquiry revealed, for example, that SODELAC could have offered as much as 40 or even 50 CFA francs, thus cornering much of the crop and still remaining within the bounds of fiscal responsibility.

SOCIETE SUCRIERE DU TCHAD (SOSUTCHAD) see SOCIETE NATIONALE SUCRERIE DU TCHAD (SONASUT)

SOCIETE TCHADIENNE DE CREDIT see BANQUE DE DEVELOPPEMENT DU TCHAD (BDT)

SOCIETE TCHADIENNE D'ENERGIE ELECTRIQUE (STEE). Mixed-economy electricity/water utilities company in which the government holds 60 percent of equity. STEE was formed in 1968 after the reorganization of the previously private company, with capitalization of 238 million CFA francs, since augmented to 5 billion CFA francs. Most of STEE's installations in N'Djamena were either destroyed or severely damaged in the battles for the capital. Electricity and water supplies were virtually nonexistent between 1979 and 1982 and sporadic until the 1990s. The company, which employs 500 workers, is in constant fiscal trouble, losing money every year (2 billion

CFA francs in 1991), as few customers pay their bills. In 1988 it received a French loan of 33 million CFA francs to rehabilitate power stations in N'Djamena, Sarh, and Moundou. Electricity costs are the highest in Africa, and six times Nigeria's.

SOCIETE TCHADIENNE D'EXPLOITATION DE RESSOURCES ANIMALES (SOTERA). A mixed-economy organ set up in 1978 with a monopoly over the export of meat to neighboring countries. The company was closed down in 1988 because the bulk of cattle exports (on the hoof) bypassed the modern economy altogether, making the deficitory company unnecessary.

SOCIETE TCHADIENNE D'INVESTISSEMENT (STI). State company established in 1973 after a September 27, 1972, decision to set up an autonomous organ to spur investments in the lagging sectors of the Chadian economy. The company was set up with a capitalization of 350 million CFA francs.

SOCIETE TEXTILE DU TCHAD (STT). Mixed-economy company founded in Sarh in November 1966 with capitalization of 300 million CFA francs (later 680 million), shared by the Chadian government (22 percent), the Cameroon Investment Society (8 percent), and French (35 percent) and German (35 percent) investment combines. STT started operations in 1967 with some 650 African workers and 23 expatriates, and in the mid-1980s had the capacity to process 2,400 tons of cotton and to produce 15.5 million meters of textiles, nearly doubling its original capacity of 8 million meters. STT alone accounted for 50 percent of "industry" in Chad. The company at first was extremely successful, and it reached peak capacity in 1971. Since then, output declined, and STT piled up deficits. Starting in the late 1980s it was forced to downsize and dismiss segments of its workforce as a result of a massive flow of illicit imports flooding Chad from Nigeria. The company closed down in 1992.

SOM YABA. Short-lived experiment in February 1980 by the Agence Tchadienne de Presse (ATP) to issue a French-Arabic newspaper in N'Djamena. The Goukouni-Habré (qq.v.) falling-out ended the effort, as indiscriminate shelling damaged ATP facilities. The name "Som Yaba" means, in Arabic, "Seven Days."

SOUBIANE, AHMAT ASSABALLAH. Former minister of interior and President Idriss Déby's (q.v.) second in command after the purge of Maldoum Bada Abbas (q.v.). Soubiane, a close Déby ally during the wars against Hissène Habré (q.v.), first joined Déby's cabinet in

March 1991 as secretary of state in charge of transport and in December 1991 was promoted to minister of interior. He was transferred to prefectural duties in May 1992.

SOUBIANE, BILAL. Former Goukouni (q.v.) ally, who rallied to Hissène Habré (q.v.) in 1986. He was subsequently integrated into the cabinet as minister of commerce, later trade and industry. In September 1990 he was appointed minister of urban planning and housing. He lost his post with the rise of the Idriss Déby (q.v.) regime.

SOUDURE. The annual period of grain storage during the heavy rain season in the south. Lack of adequate storage facilities, hoarding by merchants, poor communications—or total absence of contact—during several months of the rainy seasons, and recently the Sahelian drought, make this period one of major hardship to farmers who face a shortage of grain. In 1968 a catastrophic famine was only narrowly averted during the *soudure* when emergency relief supplies (including some from the U.S.) were widely distributed.

SOUGOUMI, CHAIMI (1924–). Son of the derde (q.v.) of the Toubou (q.v.) preceding Wodei Kichidemi (q.v.). At the time of the succession, both father and son tried to falsify Teda (q.v.) tradition in order to persuade the French colonial administration to elevate Sougoumi to the derdeship. This was the origin of the mortal enmity between Kichidemi, who was ultimately confirmed as derde, and Sougoumi. It had wider repercussions in that Tombalbaye (q.v.), aware of the derde's enmity, favored Sougoumi and his clan; and when the Toubou rebellion broke out after the 1965 Bardai incidents (q.v.), Sougoumi rallied to the government rather than joining the call to arms. Sougoumi was subsequently rewarded by Tombalbaye with a seat at the National Assembly as the "representative" of B.E.T. When the rebellion began to sap Tombalbaye's power and secret negotiations began with rebel leaders, the derde demanded, as a sine qua non, Sougoumi's removal from office and humiliation. This ultimately did occur, though under the succeeding military administration of General Félix Malloum (q.v.), which formally and explicitly repudiated Sougoumi's "leadership" over the Toubou and feted the derde in N'Djamena when he finally arrived from his self-exile in Tripoli.

SOUGOUMI, YOUSSOUF SIDI. Under Hissène Habré (q.v.) secretary-general of the government, appointed to give the Teda (q.v.), from whose noble lines he descends (see SOUGOUMI, CHAIMI), a highly visible political post, thus undermining Goukouni's (q.v.) sway over that ethnic group.

SOUMAILA, MAHAMAT (1956–1989). Former Habré (q.v.) minister. Born in Bol, capital of the Lac Préfecture, on June 25, 1956, and educated at the Lycée Franco-Arabe d'Abéché, at the University of Chad (1975–77), and in public administration in Paris, Soumaila joined the civil service in 1982 as adviser to President Habré. He was appointed secretary of state in charge of information soon after, and in 1986 he was appointed secretary of state for planning. He died in the September 20, 1989, explosion over the Sahara desert of a UTA Paris-bound plane.

SOUNGOI, AHMED. Former diplomat and former Idriss Déby (q.v.) foreign minister. Soungoi served as ambassador to Algeria under Hissène Habré (q.v.) and then defected to Déby. When the latter came to power in December 1990 Soungoi was immediately appointed foreign minister. He was transferred to head the Ministry of Information in December 1991, and dropped from the cabinet in May 1992.

SOUSPREFECTURES. Successors to the pre-independence administrative *districts* (q.v.) of which the former *régions* were composed. The number of souspréfectures has increased since independence with the creation of several new préfectures. Chad currently is divided into 14 préfectures, 54 souspréfectures, and 20 *postes administratifs*. (See ADMINISTRATIVE ORGANIZATION.)

SOW, ADAM MALICK (1922–). Diplomat. Born in Massakory on December 22, 1922. In his early days one of the deputy mayors of Fort-Lamy and *chef du cabinet* of the minister of interior, Sow was appointed ambassador to the United States and representative to the United Nations in June 1961. In April 1964 and in February 1965, respectively, he vacated these twin posts, and in 1966 he became prefect of the Tandjilé Préfecture with headquarters in Laï. In August 1971 he was made director of the civil service, serving in that post until January 1974.

SOW, BECHIR MOHAMED. Important early political leader and former deputy to the French National Assembly and ambassador to Libya. A high-level Fort-Lamy administrator and secretary to French Governor Rogué, Sow was an early dominant political figure in the post–Second World War era. A conservative traditionalist, he was elected in 1946 to the AEF (q.v.) Grand Council in Brazzaville on the UDT (q.v.) ticket, to the local Conseil Représentatif, and to the French Union (q.v.) as senator. In 1951 he continued to represent Chad when he was elected—again on the conservative UDT list—deputy to the French National Assembly (where he joined the I.O.M. faction), and in 1952 he was reelected to Chad's Territorial Assembly as UDT deputy from Kanem. By 1956, however, the more liberal forces in the country were on the upswing, and Sow was defeated in his effort to be reelected to the French National Assembly; his schism with the traditionalist groupings brought his second defeat when his Bloc Tchadien (BT) (q.v.) list lost out in Kanem, his stronghold, to the AST (q.v.) and UT (q.v.) parties. Returning to administration, Sow was appointed prefect of Kanem in 1960, and in 1968 he was made ambassador to Libya, a post he held until 1974. He has been in retirement since.

STUDENT UPHEAVAL OF NOVEMBER 1971. Chad's student population, abroad (mostly in France) and at home, progressively became radicalized in the 1960s and alienated from the Tombalbaye (q.v.) regime. Abroad a segment of the militant association of Chadian students in France (ATF) has been sympathetic to FROLINAT's (q.v.) goals, while others flocked in droves to the nascent opposition movement announced in 1973 by Dr. Outel Bono (q.v.). And the announced creation of the University of Tchad (q.v.) in N'Djamena and the imminent repatriation of many students from France greatly antagonized those who preferred to continue their education abroad.

Domestically, an indication of the hostility of Chad's student population to the Tombalbaye regime was the November 29–30, 1971, student upheaval that first erupted in the elitist Lycée Félix Eboué (q.v.) in N'Djamena and then spread to other urban centers and to the primary schools. The immediate causes of the demonstrations were largely academic and nonpolitical in the strict sense of the term—gripes over the racial segregation in the lycée of the school's French pupils (organized into more advanced classes with special and allegedly better instructors). The strike was the first major one in the city and required the active intervention of military units to contain it, with at least one student killed and over a score injured. Most disturbing to Tombalbaye was the fact that as the strikes spread the students started to chant "Vive l'Armée, Vive le Général Doumro [q.v.] [the chief of staff], A bas la police, A bas Tombalbaye." Some time later Doumro—only nominally chief of staff of the armed forces—was purged and Colonel Félix Malloum (q.v.) was elevated to his post. The riots resulted in the smashing of the windows of the U.S. embassy, minor damage elsewhere, and the politicization of the primary school system; all educational establishments were then closed for a week until tempers cooled off. Several French instructors were then expelled from the country for joining with the demonstrators, and Tombalbaye announced the wholesale repatriation of Chad's students in Benelux who had occupied the Chadian embassy in Brussels as an act of solidarity. A similar takeover had occurred in Paris, but there were too many students in France to be brought back; in the end most of the Benelux students were allowed to continue their studies. Other student complaints were later acknowledged (by Tombalbaye) as valid, though their call for a coup was regarded as treasonable. Africanization of the educational establishment was given higher priority, and some of the student grievances were addressed in the soon-to-emerge authenticity drives (see CULTURAL REVOLUTION), though paradoxically the Lycée Félix Eboué—where the whole upheaval had started—was exempted from many of the reforms. After the 1975 coup d'état that elevated General Malloum to power, Chad's students presented the new regime with detailed lists of their demands, and on March 15, 1976, Chadian students stormed and briefly occupied Chad's embassy in Paris in retaliation for Malloum's abrogation of unionists' and students' right to strike.

SUDAN. Chad's eastern neighbor, with which relations have frequently been strained and at times ruptured. Since in the precolonial era there had been intense competitions between Ouadai and Darfur (q.v.), facing each other across what was to become the Chad-Sudan border, each disputing the other's claims over tributary states (most in Chad). The Anglo-French delineation of the border was only the beginning of friction between the two territories. Indeed, on that occasion thousands of Africans caught on the "Chadian" side fled to Sudan—a flight that was repeated in more recent times with the onset of the civil rebellions in Chad in the 1960s. Between 250,000 and 500,000 former Chadians—many Masalit (q.v.)—fled to Sudan during the height of the rebellion in Chad, and only some have returned since the 1975 "reconciliation." In Sudan they usually contributed funds to and joined in the ranks of the FLT (q.v.) in opposition to the central government in N'Djamena. There was also a great deal of sympathy for the plight of the Ouadai and Biltine ethnic groups under Tombalbaye (q.v.), among their ethnic kin-groups in Sudan, many artificially separated by the international border; this manifested itself in sympathy in Khartoum itself for the rebellion in Chad, though in this case religious and geopolitical considerations may have been much more important. In mid-1965, following the beginning of unrest in Ouadai, the Chadian government accused Sudan of harboring a government-in-exile in Khartoum and of offering rebel groups refuge across the border. Though the difficulties were smoothed over and a frontier delimitation committee was appointed to deal with certain perennial problems, in August 1966 the outbreak of the rebellion in Chad's eastern provinces (see MANGALME TAX RIOTS; REBELLIONS) brought Chad-Sudan relations to the breaking point. All border crossing points were officially closed by Chad, an ultimatum was issued to Khartoum to stop harboring rebel groups, and Tombalbaye even hinted at the possibility of war between the two countries. Again the friction was eased—by Niger President Hamani Diori—and the border was reopened (essentially to the hajj [q.v.] pilgrims) on September 30, 1967. Since then, despite the continuation of Sudanese sympathy for their coreligionists in Chad, relations between the two nations remained proper. In May 1972 Sudanese army units went into action against Chadian rebels trying to cut off interstate traffic by terrorizing villages on the Sudanese side of the border. Numerous rebels were killed in this operation, and from then on, the Sudanese were less sympathetic to the Chadian rebel cause. After the falling-out of the victorious northern factions, Sudan again became a place of refuge for opposition elements, and it was from Sudan that Hissène Habré (q.v.) marched back to power in N'Djamena.

In the late 1980s Sudan again figured prominently in Chadian affairs. Earlier Chad's Hadjeray (q.v.) had been antagonized by Habré, and many were in exile in Darfur; and then came the alienation of the Zaghawa (q.v.), which brought Idriss Déby (q.v.) to Darfur. There the two ethnic groups joined hands and raised and trained an army, with many non-Chadians in their ranks. On a number of instances Habré sent his armies deep into Darfur to hit at Déby's bases and growing strength, but to no avail. Libya's Muammar Qaddafi also sent to Darfur airplanes loaded with arms for Déby and over 1,000 members of his Islamic Legion. (Khartoum had an interest in blocking Libyan help to its own rebellion in southern Sudan, and hence acquiesced to this Libyan presence.) Déby's ultimate assault on N'Djamena in 1989 was launched from Darfur. Sudan was again a base for the raising of an anti-N'Djamena army in 1992, when former chief of staff Abbas Yacoub Kotti (q.v.), alienated from Déby, raised a force in Darfur.

SURETE NATIONALE. Originally a combined civil police force for all of the AEF (q.v.) federation, and then in 1961 Chad set up its own Sûreté Nationale units. By 1971 the force had been increased to 1,000 men, serving as the police in the major urban areas, in charge of immigration, criminal records and archives, crime prevention, border patrols, and antismuggling activities. The Sûreté also guarded the president of the republic and other high officials. In 1967 the special Compagnies Tchadiennes de Sécurité (CTS) (q.v.) were created as quasi-military units. The Sûreté is under the command of the minister of interior; despite its light police work, the Sûreté had (separately from the CTS) light infantry units equipped with mortars and semiautomatic weapons. In the 1970s it was secretly retrained by Moroccan officers. With the fall of N'Djamena to northern troops in 1979, the Sûreté—composed of mostly Sara personnel—virtually closed down. Those who relocated south were integrated into Colonel Kamougoué's (q.v.) gendarmerie, while both Habré and (later) Déby were to set up completely different forces packed with their own ethnic kinsmen.

SYNDICAT AUTONOME DU TCHAD (SAT). Powerful autonomous nonaffiliated trade union in the pre-independence era of which Tombalbaye (q.v.) was at one time (1946) president.

SYNDICAT DE TRAVAILLEURS DU TCHAD (STT). Early Communist-leaning CGT-affiliated trade union in the pre-independence era, with Jean Charlot (q.v.) as president. Tombalbaye's SAT (q.v.) union was set up in opposition to the STT.

-T-

TAGO. Important archaeological site on the N'Djamena-Moussoro road, 21 kilometers (13 miles) northeast of the capital, near the small village of Mogo. A very large number of archaeological objects of great significance have been recovered from this site.

TAHA, ABDEL MOUTI ABDERAHMAN (1940–). Former cabinet minister. Born in 1940 in Abéché and educated locally and abroad (where he obtained a *license* degree in economics), Taha joined the Ministry of Economics in 1968, becoming deputy director of planning and development (1968–69). He then served with the United Nations Social and Economic Council as Chad's delegate (1969–70) and as first councillor at Chad's embassy to the United States (1970–71). In May 1971 he returned to Chad to join the cabinet as minister of commerce, serving in that capacity until the end of 1973.

TAHER, ALLAHOU LIMANE (1934–). Early Gabriel Lisette (q.v.) associate and former cabinet minister. A Muslim from Kanem, born in Mao in 1934, Taher was educated in law in the Brussels Free University between 1959 and 1968. He returned to Chad to join the government as secretary of state for public works, having been elected to the assembly on the PPT (q.v.) label in 1957 and again in 1959. In 1959 he also served as president of the National Assembly. Taher then served briefly in François Tombalbaye's (q.v.) provisional government, but after the purge of Lisette he lost his assembly seat and was purged from the government for leading the attempted censure of Tombalbaye in the assembly (together with Jules Pierre Toura Gaba [q.v.]) for Lisette's purge. Imprisoned in the remote B.E.T., he was quietly released several years later and appointed to a top post in the civil service. Some time later he was briefly arrested after the 1972 guerrilla attack on N'Djamena airport. Appointed secretary of state for agriculture in the CSM (q.v.) military regime, Taher was arrested again in 1978 for membership in FROLINAT (q.v.). After the fall of N'Djamena to northern troops, Taher reemerged as a senior administrative coordinator in the Ministry of Interior.

TAHER, MAHAMAT ALI (1929–1969). Early UNT (q.v.) and FROL-INAT (q.v.) organizer and leader. Born in Kanem in 1929, and for some time a member of the Egyptian police, Taher was a leading figure on the Steering Committee of the Union Nationale Tchadienne (UNT) (q.v.), set up in 1958. A master tactician, Taher was one of Ibrahim Abatcha's (q.v.) FROLINAT lieutenants, and he was responsible for the unification and organization of the rebellion of the Toubou (q.v.) in B.E.T. in 1969, while field commander of the troops in Borkou specifically. As such he was in essence the founding father of FROLINAT's Second Army. He was also personally behind the Garde Nomade (q.v.) (Toubou) uprising in Aouzou, which directly brought about French military assistance for Tombalbaye, and it was he who personally recruited Goukouni (q.v.) into the rebellion. Taher was killed in action against the French in September 1969 and was succeeded as commander in chief by Goukouni.

TALBA, MOHAMMED. Former secretary of state for agriculture. Talba began his career with trade union activities and moved to head a department in the Ministry of Finance. Purged and then amnestied for alleged opposition to the regime in August 1965, he was soon appointed secretary of state for agriculture and animal production. He remained in that post until November 1968, when he was dispatched to Libya as first counselor at Chad's embassy, a position he held until 1975.

TAMA. Ethnic group residing in Ouadai and Biltine Préfectures and estimated at some 40,000. They speak an eastern Sudanic dialect similar to that of the Asangori. Their ancient capital was located at Niéré, whose ruins may still be seen and where new sultans are still enthroned to this day. Nominally Muslim, they have a variety of pre-Islamic customs. The Tama nobility was linked to the Daju (q.v.) rulers of Ouadai prior to the arrival of the Tunjur (q.v.).

TANDJILE PREFECTURE. Southern préfecture formed in 1962 as a result of the breaking into three parts of the former Logone Préfecture. Tandjilé covers an area of 18,050 square kilometers (6,970 square miles), with a population of 372,000 people and a population density of 20.6 per square kilometer. It is composed of the souspréfectures of Laï and Kélo and one *poste administratif* and has its headquarters in the town of Laï on the Logone Orientale branch of the Logone River. The préfecture's main product is cotton, which is refined in the Cotontchad (q.v.) factories in Guidari and Kélo and then shipped to Sarh for export to Europe via Bangui. The region also produces fish and rice, the latter marketed by SEMALK (q.v.). The préfecture is crossed by two major communication arteries, the north-south route that links Bangui in the Central African Republic with N'Djamena via the Logone valley (Laï-N'Djamena, 405 kilometers [251 miles]), and the east-west route linking Sarh with Pela. All roads in the préfecture are impassable during the heavy rainy season (August to November) when some three-quarters of the préfecture is inundated by water. During August and September Laï is accessible, however, by barges up the Logone River. The region has a relatively high school attendance rate of 40.5 percent and has been the scene of several projects aimed at agricultural diversification and modernization.

TARBIYA. Religious sect, offshoot of the Tidjaniya (q.v.). Headed by Sheikh Ibrahim Nyass of Kaolack, Senegal, the Tarbiya was gaining major inroads among the Chadian urban intelligentsia in the 1950s when it was formally banned by Tombalbaye (q.v.) in 1962.

TARSO AHON. Second highest peak in the rugged Tibesti, reaching 3,325 meters (10,908 feet), slightly less than Emi Koussi (q.v.), the highest peak in the Sahara, also in Chad.

TATALA, REMY (1942–). Journalist. Born on October 1, 1942, in Moïssala to a traditional chiefly family, Tatala was educated locally and continued his studies in a journalism school in West Germany. He entered politics in December 1969 when he was elected to the National Assembly, where he presided over the Legislation Committee. Since 1975 Tatala has been with the Ministry of Information.

TAUER, AHMET (1913–1976). Key entrepreneur in B.E.T. Born in Faya-Largeau in 1913, the son of a Libyan father who served in the Sanusiya (q.v.) armies in Chad. Tauer established himself as the key commercial agent of Faya-Largeau and specialized in particular in supplying the military garrison in that center. The only entrepreneur in the north with his own truck fleet, Tauer's importance was recognized by his election to the National Assembly on the UDIT (q.v.) ticket (later PPT [q.v.]) from 1959 through 1962. Originally respected and left unmolested by both protagonists in the civil war in B.E.T., Tauer had to discontinue his operations there in 1973, shortly before his death.

TAXE CIVIQUE. Former principal personal tax in Chad, payable annually by all men (and since 1968, with a great deal of resistance, by all women as well) between the ages of 18 and 60 with an income of less than 60,000 CFA francs per year. (Direct taxes constituted in 1974 fully 25 percent of government receipts, and indirect taxes 57.2 percent.) The tax varied in the past from 300 CFA francs in the north to 1,400 CFA francs in the more prosperous south and urban centers, but in 1968—when also extended to women—a uniform 900 CFA franc tax was imposed plus 100 francs for the Rural Development Fund, for an effective total of 1,000. A variety of other nuisance taxes were also levied, including an even more unpopular one on livestock (e.g., 170 francs per head of cattle), which various highly independent ethnic groups went to great lengths to avoid. Taxes were assessed and levied by village and regional chiefs who normally kept a certain amount for themselves, usually 10 percent. In 1965 the tax brought the central government in N'Djamena a total of 1,116 million CFA francs, estimated at the time as barely half of what should have been the revenue on the basis of estimations of the country's human and livestock demography. With the increased fiscal stresses on the Chadian budget in the mid-1960s major efforts were made to collect more efficiently and completely the various taxes, causing serious unrest, which was exacerbated by corrupt tax collectors who doubled or tripled the taxes assessed and pocketed the difference. A direct result of these practices were the various rebellions that erupted in the country (see also MANGALME TAX RIOTS; REBELLIONS). One of the first actions of the Mission de Réforme Administrative (MRA) (q.v.) dispatched from France to help quell the civil disturbances in the country was to recommend that all taxes be annulled for a number of years in light of the ravages of the civil war and the Sahelian drought. Effective in 1971, this was indeed decreed for the B.E.T. and other parts of Chad's northern and eastern préfectures.

"LA TCHADIENNE." Pre-1979 national anthem of Chad. Also, name of N'Djamena's major hotel.

TCHADITUDE see CULTURAL REVOLUTION; MOUVEMENT NATIONAL POUR LA REVOLUTION CULTURELLE ET SOCIALE; YONDO

TCHAD-NON-VIOLENCE. An association for the defense of human rights, founded in N'Djamena in 1991. Part of the interim legislation (CST, q.v.), it suspended its participation in April 1993 in protest against the continued massacres of villagers and abuses of human rights by Idriss Déby's (q.v.) forces of repression.

TCHAD-UTILE. Frequently used term in the press to refer to the "useful" southern (mostly Sara) parts of Chad that product cotton, the basis and the mainstay of the Chadian economy, as opposed to the "nonproductive" north and east.

TCHEKNA see CHEKNA

TCHERE, ADOUM (1925–). Veteran Hadjeray (q.v.) politician, former cabinet minister, deputy secretary-general of the PPT (q.v.), and one of the dominant political leaders of Chad up to 1975. Born in 1925 in Mongo (Guéra), a veteran of the Free French forces during the Second World War (in which he won the Croix de Guerre, Légion d'Honneur, and other decorations), Tchéré joined the Chad health department after the war (being trained as a dental assistant) and began political activities in 1951. He was brought into Gabriel Lisette's (q.v.) cabinet in December 1958, serving for a few months (until February 1959) as minister of labor and social affairs; in the succeeding Sahoulba (q.v.) provisional government he was shifted to head the Ministry of Agriculture, and in June 1959 he again moved, this time to head the Ministry of Animal Husbandry and Water Supplies. In August 1960 he was reassigned to another post as minister of agriculture, serving there until May 1962. He was elected deputy from Guéra to the National Assembly in 1959 on the AST (q.v.) ticket (soon becoming a PPT [q.v.] member) and retained his assembly seat throughout the turbulent years until the 1975 coup d'état, serving as president of the assembly from 1966 and December 1968. In 1969 Tchéré proposed a costly campaign of "psychological warfare" in Guéra to counter the spread of the civil rebellion in that préfecture. Most of the funds allocated for that purpose found their way into his own building projects in N'Djamena instead. In May 1962 Tchéré's Ministry of Agriculture was expanded to include Water Resources and Forestry, though these were dropped in March 1963. He remained minister of agriculture until January 1964, when he was dropped from the cabinet. For some time eclipsed from the power hierarchy, Tchéré became deputy secretary-general of the PPT in July 1970, and in May 1971 he took over the sensitive position of minister of defense and of veterans affairs. Later, in December, the latter post was removed from him (after the student upheavals that called for a coup d'état, though he was named minister of state in charge of party organization. When the MNRCS (q.v.) was set up on the ashes of the PPT, Tchéré was named to the Executive Committee and remained there until the 1975 coup d'état. He was one of the few politicians arrested (briefly) after the coup.

TEDA. A branch of the Toubou (q.v.) in northern Chad who call them-selves Tedagada (those who speak Tedaga). The other branch, the Daza (q.v.) (or Dazagada) speak a similar dialect, both being related to Kanuri (q.v.). Notwithstanding many similarities, the two Toubou branches have more often than not been fiercely antago-nistic to each other. (The Goukouni-Habré [qq.v.] tug-of-war is partly traceable to these tensions.) Teda groups in neighboring Niger (especially in the Djado area and between Agadem and Soutellan) are called collectively Braouia. The Teda are in general found in the northwestern regions of Chad and are divided into some 20 clans that nomadize specific areas. Even rough estimates of the total Teda population vary widely, but they probably number at least 50,000, with two-thirds of them (around 30,000) to be found in Chad in Tibesti (14,000), Borkou (13,000), and Kanem (2,500). The Tomaghera (q.v.) clan, residing in Tibesti, is the most noble and pure, and from its leading three families the derde (q.v.) has tra-ditionally been chosen. The derde is both the superior chief of the Tomaghera and the nominal head of the Teda, though his powers are more symbolic than real. The derde has often been referred to (erroneously) as the sultan of Zouar, after the chief headquarters of the Tomaghera. The Teda are Muslim, with most clans in the north-ern areas belonging to the Sanusiya (q.v.) order, while those to the south are Tidjaniya (q.v.). They spearheaded the 1968 rebellion in the B.E.T. when the derde was humiliated (see REBELLIONS) and went into self-exile in Libya. Only in 1975 did the new military regime succeed in getting him to return, with the pledge that there would be no more central government interference with the tradi-tional rights of the Toubou people. The Teda clans include the: Tomaghera, Tarsoa, Tameurtioua, Tozoba, Gouboda, Factoa, Kosseda, Dirsina, Bardoa, Odobaya, Terintere, Keressa, Tchioda, Mogode, Aozouya, Taizera, Gounda, Fortena, Mada, Tegua, Ka-madja.

TERRITOIRE MILITAIRE DES PAYS ET PROTECTORATS DU TCHAD. Original (1900–15) name, fixed by decree on September 5, 1990, for the general region of delineated French territory in Equato-rial Africa, at the time little explored. There existed military outposts in Fort-Archambault and Fort-Lamy; protectorate agreements had been signed with Lal, Baguirmi, and Alifa Djerab between 1892 and 1899. On February 11, 1906, the area was designated as the colony of Oubangui-Chari-Tchad (q.v.), part of the French Congo (Congo Français); the latter became the AEF (q.v.) federation in 1910, and in 1916 Chad was separated from Oubangui-Chari (i.e., the Central African Republic) and became a separate colony within the federation.

THIAM, TIDJANI. A Chadian of Mali-Mauritanian origin, Thiam is a rich petroleum trader and was an adviser to Mali's former president Moussa Traoré. He also served as a key CDR (q.v.) representative and spokesman in Paris from 1982 to 1988. He returned to N'Djamena after the CDR was reconciled with Habré (q.v.), and in 1992 he formed an independent party, the Alliance pour la Démocratie au Tchad (ADT).

THIRD LIBERATION ARMY. Small, intermittently active group of guerrillas, supported and backed by Nigeria, immediately prior to the collapse of the Malloum-Habré (qq.v.) administration. Set up by Aboubaker Abderahmane (q.v.), following his desertion from FROLINAT (q.v.) in May 1977, the minuscule force attracted world headlines after the attack on an American oil exploration camp in Kanem and a grenade attack on a N'Djamena cinema. Calling itself also the Mouvement Populaire pour la Libération du Tchad, most of the force shifted allegiance to Lol Mahamat Choua (q.v.) and later to Moussa Medela (q.v.) and his Forces Armées Occidentales (q.v.). Holdouts were decimated in internecine fighting in N'Djamena in 1979 with Habré's FAN (q.v.) units. A segment still survives in the Lac Préfecture in opposition to the Idriss Déby (q.v.) regime in N'Djamena and was involved in fighting with Déby's forces during 1991–33.

TIBBU see TOUBOU; also DAZA; TEDA

TIBESTI. Large western souspréfecture in B.E.T. (q.v.), with administrative headquarters in Bardai (q.v.). A desert mountain massif encompassing 150,000 square kilometers (57,900 square miles), Tibesti was in prehistoric times much wetter and probably constituted the northern shore of an extended Lake Chad (q.v.). (See also BODELE DEPRESSION.) Estimates of Tibesti's population, which is seminomadic, vary greatly, with the median figure around 16,000, giving the souspréfecture the lowest population density (0.1 per square kilometer) in all of Chad. The most productive areas are a few villages near Bardai, Zouar, and Zoumri, where herding and tending of date and palm groves (on the northern slopes of Tibesti and in the oases) are the prime economic activities. The region was little explored by Europeans, with no one crossing the area, for example, between Gustav Nachtigal's (q.v.) explorations and the Tilho mission in 1911. The area was contested by several powers, including the Senoussi (see SANUSIYA)—who mounted several expeditions into the area and established one major garrison—and the French, who finally incorporated the area into their sphere of occupation. Fully pacified only in the early 1920s, Tibesti was originally part of Afrique Occidentale

Française (AOF) and only in 1930 was it attached to Chad and transferred to the Afrique Equatoriale Française (AEF) federation. East Tibesti offers easy and direct access to Kufra in Libya and was used extensively in the past by caravans from Bornu on their way to the coast (see CARAVAN ROUTES). The entire region is graced with natural beauty in its volcanic massifs, gorges, craters, spectacular scenery, and small desert lakes.

Administered until 1965 by French military forces (despite the fact that Chad acquired independence in 1960), Tibesti was the site of major rebellions once administrative control was passed over to indigenous personnel. The rebellions (q.v.)—spearheaded by the major ethnic group in the region, the Teda (q.v.)—ultimately led to the fall of N'Djamena and the rise of Goukouni (q.v.), son of the Teda derde (q.v.), as president of Chad. Goukouni himself was ousted in 1982 by the rival Toubou clan, the Daza (q.v.), rallied behind Hissène Habré (q.v.) (himself ousted in 1990 by Déby). The entire Tibesti experiences great variations of temperatures, with the highlands often recording temperatures below 15°F.

TIBESTIENNE DE TRANSPORTS. Former trans-Saharan trucking company operating in Chad's Tibesti region. The company was a sub-branch of the Transafricaine (q.v.) combine.

TIDEI, BRAHIM MAHAMAT. Former cabinet minister. Tidei was brought into Idriss Déby's (q.v.) government in May 1992 as secretary of state for interior, and in an October 1992 shuffle he was appointed minister of public works. He left the cabinet for an administrative appointment in April 1993.

TIDJANI, MAHAMAT (1938–). Youth leader and National Assembly deputy. Born in 1938 in Faya-Largeau in the far north, and a teacher (later educational inspector) by profession, Tidjani was appointed to the Executive Council of the youth branch of the PPT (q.v.) (the JEPPT, q.v.) in 1968 and was promoted to secretary of state in charge of the JEPPT in 1969. He then briefly served as deputy prefect of the B.E.T. Préfecture (also in 1969), and in December of that year he was elected deputy to the National Assembly, remaining in office until the coup of 1975.

TIDJANIYA (also TIJANIYA). Important Muslim religious order, the dominant one in Chad. (See also ISLAM; RELIGIOUS ORDERS.)

TOGOI, ADOUM (Major). Key Goukouni (q.v.) lieutenant and former commander in chief of the FAN (q.v.) (Goukouni-Habré) forces.

Completely unschooled, an accountant only consequent to night classes in N'Djamena, Togoi joined the Chadian army in 1969 to serve as a cashier. In 1971 he absconded with army funds and deserted to FROLINAT (q.v.). He rapidly attained prominence, and his military command was confirmed at the CCFAN (q.v.) congress of 1972. The same year he spearheaded the guerrilla assault on N'Djamena and several other daring raids. Badly wounded in 1978 during fighting against Libyan troops—and in captivity for some time—during the Goukouni-Habré split in 1980, he remained loyal to the former and was named deputy chief of staff of the national integrated army in 1980, and in July 1981 secretary of state for defense. He suffered loss of status and was virtually demoted when his command of troops in 1982 could not prevent a Habré (q.v.) victory, leading to Goukouni's exile. He then briefly commanded one of the GUNT (q.v.) units in B.E.T. in support of Goukouni's attempted comeback but soon set himself up as an independent leader of a Zaghawa (q.v.) armed band against Habré based in Tripoli, Libya. He was the last of the GUNT leaders to remain in opposition to Habré. After Idriss Déby's (q.v.) rise to power Togoi shifted allegiance to him, and in December 1991 he briefly served as minister of tourism.

TOGOI, KERIM. Former secretary general of Hissène Habré's (q.v.) presidential office. A technocrat appointed minister of the economy, planning, and transport following the 1975 coup d'état, Togoi was retained in the subsequent Malloum-Habré (qq.v.) government as personal consultant to Habré. He was integrated into the GUNT (q.v.) government of 1979, and after Habré's rise to power in 1982, he was appointed (in January 1983) head of the presidential office staff. He was transferred to prefectural duties in 1986.

TOGOIMI, YOUSSOUF. Former cabinet minister. Togoimi, a close Déby (q.v.) ally, joined the government in March 1991 as minister of justice, staying in that post until the government formed by the Conférence Nationale (q.v.) in April 1993.

TOIRA, JEREMIE BEADE. Minister of commerce and industry from December 1990 to October 1992, when he resigned from Déby's (q.v.) cabinet. Toira is a member of the RPT (q.v.) political party.

TOKINON, PIERRE (Captain). A former southern "*codo*" (q.v.) sergeant, Tokinon rallied to Hissène Habré (q.v.) and was promoted to captain and appointed secretary of state for public health in 1988. He was then sent for military training at the elite Israeli academy in Zaire and returned to N'Djamena to be appointed to the Presidential

Security unit. Tokinon rallied to Idriss Déby (q.v.) after Habré's ouster and was appointed in January 1991 director of the presidential military cabinet. In July 1991 he was appointed secretary of state in the cabinet, and in December that year he was promoted to minister of public health. In May 1992 he was transferred to head the Ministry of Tourism, serving in that capacity until the Conférence Nationale (q.v.) government of April 1993.

TOMAGHERA (or TOMAGRA). The most noble and prestigious Teda (q.v.) clan of the Toubou (q.v.) people in northern Chad, from whose three leading families the derde (q.v.) of the Teda of Tibesti is customarily chosen. Tomaghera oral history refers to their origins from the Sudan (see TOUBOU), though existing evidence suggests descent into Chad from the Fezzan (Libya). The Tomaghera are found only in western Tibesti (between Zouar and Sherda) and in Kanem. The name of the clan is cited in the Bornu chronicles as associated with the Kanem kingdom (see KANEM-BORNU EMPIRE) and its reigning dynasty. In 1966 the Tomaghera clan led the Teda-Toubou rebellion in Chad after the derde was humiliated in the Bardai incidents (q.v.). The revolt was only contained with French military assistance and simmered on until the coup of 1975 and President Tombalbaye's (q.v.) death. At that time the derde consented to return from self-imposed exile in Libya to his capital in Zouar, in return for a pledge of non-interference in his people's affairs by the central government. (See also TEDA; TOUBOU.) Though the derde called on the Teda to end their rebellion, his last surviving son, Goukouni (q.v.), continued the struggle, for which the derde disinherited him.

TOMBALBAYE, NGARBAYE (Dr.) One of François Tombalbaye's (q.v.) sons, and as the latter has now been fully rehabilitated, one of the key political leaders of the Sara. Tombalbaye was educated in medicine in France, and in the late 1980s set up there a political party the MSDT (q.v.) in opposition to Hissène Habré (q.v.). After the rise of Idriss Déby (q.v.), Tombalbaye relocated to N'Djamena, participated in the 1993 Conférence Nationale (q.v.), and had his party recognized. Tombalbaye was appointed minister of health in the May 1994 government, but he refused the appointment three days later, after belatedly realizing that he was compromising his future political viability by associating with Déby.

TOMBALBAYE, NGARTHA (FRANÇOIS) (1918–1975). Former president of Chad, killed in the coup d'état of 1975. Born in Bessada (near Koumra) in the heart of Sara country on June 15, 1918, the Protestant Tombalbaye—son of a trader—obtained primary and secondary education in Sarh and in Brazzaville, following which he began work as an instructor in various locations, including Sarh, N'Djamena, Koumra, and Kyabé (1946–49). In 1946 Tombalbaye helped to set up the PPT (q.v.) and headed its Sarh branch, swinging to it the support of his own clan, the Madjingayé; later he was placed in charge of organizing the masses behind the PPT in the Logone and Moyen-Chari regions. Actively discriminated against by the local French administration (for his political activities), Tombalbaye was reduced to the manual manufacture of bricks in 1951 in order to sustain himself. Other PPT leaders, including Gabriel Lisette (q.v.), were also in dire financial circumstances. In the 1952 territorial elections the PPT began making its first strides toward breaking the political stranglehold of the Muslim and European parties in the country, and Tombalbaye secured his election as a deputy and was reelected again in 1957, 1959, and 1962. From 1957 to 1959 he also served as councillor and vice president of the AEF (q.v.) Grand Council in Brazzaville as well as ideological secretary of the PPT under Lisette. As Lisette began to find himself attacked by the northern leadership in the country for his expatriate credentials—and following a period of instability during which Chad had three provisional governments (q.v.)—Lisette relinquished power to Tombalbaye in March 1959. Immediately Tombalbaye began to eliminate Lisette's power base, and in mid-1960, while Lisette was on a mission to Israel he was purged from his positions and forbidden to return to Chad. Lisette's dauphin and Tombalbaye's main rival during the period of 1956 to 1960, Jules Pierre Toura Gaba (q.v.), was purged in 1962 as well (as were many other Lisettist supporters) and exiled to the remote B.E.T. Tombalbaye survived a minirevolt within his own party (incensed over his cavalier treatment of Lisette), and after an effort at absorbing the greatly truncated Muslim parties into a PPT-UNT coalition (see POLITICAL PARTIES), competitive politics were banned and a single-party system was established. Somewhat later a wide array of former top opposition politicians were arrested on a variety of charges and incarcerated in the B.E.T. The National Assembly was then dismissed, to be later reinstated, after a thorough purge of troublesome or opposition elements (1963). In the mid-1960s Tombalbaye was confronted with the rebellions in southern and eastern Chad, a result of mismanagement on the part of the central administration and a long record of grievances against Tombalbaye in the peripheral regions. Practically cut off from all other urban centers in the country, Tombalbaye finally appealed for French military assistance (see REBELLIONS) but had to pay the price of revamping his administration and tolerating a decentralization of power to the provinces and to the country's traditional rulers—conditions imposed by the French Mission de Réforme

Administrative (MRA) (q.v.). In 1972 Tombalbaye secretly reached an accord with Libya (q.v.), the principal backer of the rebel FROLINAT (q.v.), in which he accepted the Mussolini-Laval boundary (q.v.) between the two countries, thus renouncing the Aouzou Strip (q.v.) in exchange for a large sum of money. He also broke diplomatic relations with Israel in exchange for Libya's promised fiscal largesse and restraints on FROLINAT. In the meantime Tombalbaye had survived coup attempts (see COUP [ATTEMPTED] OF 1971; COUP [ATTEMPTED] OF 1972), had continued his cycle of continuous purges of real or imagined enemies, finally reaching into the armed forces, had pulled Chad out of the UDEAC (q.v.) and into the newly created UEAC (q.v.), and had charted Chad's course of "Cultural Revolution" (q.v.) and authenticity. The latter policies, especially the forced Yondo (q.v.) initiation rites, persecution of Christian missionaries, and wildly overambitious projects (see, for example, OPERATION AGRICULTURE), rapidly gained him international notoriety and the desertion of many of his former domestic allies. Just prior to the coup d'état, and sparked by revelations of conspiracies within the armed forces, a major purge of the officer corps appeared in the offing. When the coup d'état erupted, Tombalbaye allegedly died in a cross fire between the assaulting force and his palace guard, though more recently reports have surfaced that he was actually summarily executed. His body was secretly buried in Faya, which lends further validity to that interpretation. After Tombalbaye's reputation was fully rehabilitated during the 1993 Conférence Nationale (q.v.), his body was exhumed on April 3, 1994, and reburied in his home village, and his property, confiscated after the coup, was returned to his legitimate heirs. His son, Ngarbaye Tombalbaye (q.v.), has inherited a certain amount of political clout in the Sara south for his new political party, the MSDT (q.v.).

TOUADE, PIERRE OUSMAN (1931–1982). Journalist and lawyer. Born in Nyouh on August 15, 1931, Touadé joined the PPT (q.v.) in his twenties and became an administrative secretary in the PPT Political Bureau and simultaneously the personal secretary of the minister of the civil service (November 1957–April 1959). After specialized training abroad, he returned to Chad in 1963 to become director of Radio Chad, and later (1968–71) director general of tourism and information. Late in 1971 he left Chad to become an instructor in the Yaoundé, Cameroon, School of Journalism, but he returned to N'Djamena after the 1975 coup to be appointed minister of state in charge of information and civil orientation in the CSM (q.v.) government. A supporter of Goukouni (q.v.), Touadé was arrested in N'Djamena in August 1982 after the fall of the city to Hissène Habré (q.v.) troops. He has not been heard of since and is presumed to have been liquidated.

TOUBOU. Collective name for the various seminomadic pastoral clans inhabiting northern Chad and especially the B.E.T. region. Their name comes from the Kanuri (q.v.) for "inhabitants of Tu," the latter being the local name for the Tibesti mountains. (However, only some 25,000 Toubou currently live in Chad's Tibesti souspréfecture.) The two major Toubou clans are the Teda and Daza (qq.v.), who call themselves Tedagada and Dazagada ("those who speak Teda" and "those who speak Daza," closely related dialects that are linked to the Kanuri language). The two groups inhabit an area stretching from the Fezzan in Libya to the Kouar oasis and Djado in Niger, to Ennedi in northeastern Chad, with smaller groups to be found farther south, in Kanem (right up to Lake Chad) and in an arc stretching to northern Ouadai. In general the Daza clans populate the southeastern areas, the Teda the western. Relations between the two have more often than not been antagonistic, in part explaining the tug-of-war between Habré (Daza) and Goukouni (qq.v.), their two main leaders.

Estimates of the entire Toubou population vary widely. In 1975 they were estimated to number 250,000, with the majority found in Chad; because of their relatively low demographic growth and heavy casualties during the several civil wars in Chad, their numbers were estimated in 1992 at barely 300,000. The two main groups are divided into a large number of small clans that nomadize specific territorial areas, and the Tomaghera (q.v.) (or Tomagra) Teda clan, considered the most pure and noble, is the one from whose three leading families are chosen the derdes (q.v.) of the Toubou. The ethnic origin of the Toubou is still clouded in mystery, especially since in their dark coloration and their language they are quite different from the Berbers from whom they are thought to have originated and with whom they share strikingly similar ABO blood group patterns. According to one reconstruction of the past, the Toubou are descended from white nomads from the Nile valley that established themselves in Borkou, then Tibesti, in the seventh to the ninth centuries, helping the creation of the Kanem kingdom (see KANEM-BORNU EMPIRE) and dynasty. In the early thirteenth century they were expelled to the north, into the Fezzan, and in the following centuries—by now intermixed with other ethnic groups—they returned southward searching for new pastures. Early in the nineteenth century this migration escalated under Turkish pressure (see TURKEY), though later the Toubou (and the Sanusiya [q.v.] brotherhood in their areas) fiercely resisted French penetration into B.E.T. under the Turkish flag. Finally defeated only around 1920, the Toubou were in general left alone and in turn kept away from the French. The French ruled the northern préfecture with a light hand, interfering little with the fiercely individualistic Toubou and demanding only law and order and the safety of the north-south communication routes. In 1965—five years after Chad's independence—the French garrison and military prefect were pulled out of the B.E.T., and within months incidents multiplied (see REBELLIONS), until the derde went into self-exile in Libya and the Toubou took up arms against N'Djamena. Only in the mid-1970s was the revolt quelled by both French military forces (dispatched at Tombalbaye's [q.v.] request) and major N'Djamena concessions—forced upon Chad by the French and enacted by the Mission de Réforme Administrative (q.v.)—as well as by President Tombalbaye's death in the 1975 coup d'état that brought about the return of the Toubou's derde to his Zouar capital in western Tibesti. However, the Toubou rebellion continued, despite the derde's call for a cessation of hostilities, under the separate banners (briefly united) of Goukouni (q.v.) leading the Teda branch, and Hissène Habré (q.v.) leading the Daza. Both leaders were at one time or another to be heads of state of Chad, though Habré's reign (1982–90) was by far the longer one.

Muslim nomadic warriors (especially the Teda) who value their freedom highly, the Toubou were in the past great raiders, exacting a 10 percent tribute from trans-Saharan caravans. They have rarely been united and have frequently been ravaged by blood feuds and interclan squabbles, taking offense at the slightest provocation. Their religion is deeply imbued with pre-Islamic influences and practices (e.g., most genealogies trace origins to a female progenitor, and the status of women in the clans is markedly higher than in other Islamized groups) and, despite oral legends of Islam reaching them in the seventeenth century, it is believed that many converted only around 1820. They are mostly vegetarians who tend—or have tended for them by ex-slaves— date and palm trees in desert oases; they keep goats, sheep, and camels and in the past also kept some cattle. (Their livestock suffered greatly from the near-decade of the Sahelian drought coupled with the effects of the civil war in the region.) Most of the Toubou in Tibesti and Borkou are Senoussi (see SANUSIYA), while those in the south are of the Tidjaniya order.

TOUBOURI (also TOUPOURI; TUPURI). Ethnic group in the Fianga souspréfecture, numbering around 80,000 and closely linked to the Massa (q.v.). Not to be confused with the Toubou. Great farmers, many Toubouri also served in the pre-1979 Chadian armed forces. Much larger concentrations of Toubouri are to be found across the border in Cameroon. The border, fixed in 1908 by an Anglo-German treaty, effectively cuts the ethnic group into two.

TOUKA, ALI. Hissène Habré's (q.v.) former police chief. Touka was arrested in N'Djamena on January 8, 1992, after the failure of Habré's attempted comeback via the Lake Chad insurrection.

TOUKA, MAINA. Déby's ambassador to France, appointed in December 1990.

TOUPOURI see TOUBOURI

TOURA GABA, JULES PIERRE (1920–). Cofounder of the PPT (q.v.), prominent early political leader, and purged heir apparent to Gabriel Lisette (q.v.). Born on December 18, 1920, in Mabiyan (Moïssala), a Sara schoolteacher educated in a Protestant mission, Toura Gaba rapidly became one of the nascent PPT's most important leaders. Together with Lisette—whom he had opposed at the outset—Toura Gaba helped to organize the Sara behind the PPT. In 1946 he was elected deputy to the local territorial council (as URPT [q.v.] delegate, soon to switch to the PPT) and remained a (PPT) deputy through 1962, serving as the assembly's president for several years and as vice president of the PPT from 1959 until his purge in mid-1962. Unsuccessful in his early bid to be elected in 1952 as Chad's representative to the French Union, Toura Gaba helped to build up the strength and organization of the PPT and saw it emerge victorious in 1957. He then joined Lisette's cabinet, first as minister of agriculture, stockbreeding, waters, fisheries, and forestry (May 1957–December 1958), then as minister of agriculture (December 1958–February 1959), minister of public works (March–June 1959), minister of public works and telecommunications (June 1959–August 1960), moving under Tombalbaye (q.v.) to become minister of foreign affairs (August 1960–March 1961), minister of education (August 1961–March 1962), and prior to his purge, minister of public works and telecommunications (March–June 1962). In mid-1962 Tombalbaye's drive to consolidate his power base in the PPT—never truly secure after his purge of former leader Lisette, due to the latter's many staunch supporters in the party—resulted in an escalating campaign of vilifying Toura Gaba, ending with his arrest. Exiled to Ounianga Kebir in the B.E.T., Toura Gaba's personal reputation brought several impassioned efforts to have him freed; in two of these, military officers were involved, for which they were severely disciplined. Eventually amnestied from the harsh conditions in the B.E.T., Toura Gaba was "exiled" abroad when he was posted as ambassador to West Germany and Italy in September 1966, serving there for eight years until 1974. At that time, incensed with the excesses of the "Cultural Revolution" (q.v.) back home, and especially the torture and murder of Christian missionaries and the forced initiation to the Yondo (q.v.) rites, Toura Gaba formally resigned his post and declared his intention not to return to Chad. In retaliation the Tombalbaye regime barred his uncle, Ousman Ndakran—an important Protestant church official—from all religious activities. After the coup d'état of 1975 Toura Gaba was called back from his self-exile in Europe and appointed diplomatic counselor to the Conseil Supérieur Militaire (CSM) (q.v.), serving through 1978.

TOURE, MOUSSA (1928–). Former press attaché in the office of the presidency. Born in N'Djamena on June 28, 1928, Touré was educated locally and in Bongor, becoming an administrative official. A youth leader in the Parti National Africain (q.v.), he was elected its president in 1959, and the same year he became president of the Football (Soccer) League. In 1957 he was also elected municipal councillor from N'Djamena and MSA (q.v.) territorial deputy from Chari-Baguirmi (to May 1959). Brought into the Ministry of Justice as press attaché of Djibrine Ali Kherallah in 1960, he became Tombalbaye's (q.v.) principal press attaché. After obtaining a diploma from the IAP, Touré was appointed as magistrate and presided over the Labor Court from 1971 to 1978. Following the reconstitution of the collapsed civil administration in N'Djamena, Touré was integrated back into the court system as a judge, serving until his retirement.

TOURGOUDI, OUCHAR (1936–). Educator and former cabinet minister. Born in Abéché in 1936 and a schoolteacher and youth leader by profession, Tourgoudi taught in a variety of schools in Ouadai, Batha, and Kanem. He was integrated into the PPT (q.v.) Political Bureau in August 1964 and two years later was brought into Tombalbaye's (q.v.) cabinet as minister of tourism and information. In 1968 he was transferred to become executive secretary of the JEPPT (q.v.) youth structures and secretary of state attached to the presidency, in charge of Youth, posts he held until 1978.

TOURKOU. The Chadian dialect of Arabic.

TOUSSIDE. Volcanic peak in the Tibesti (q.v.) massif, reaching to 3,315 meters (10,876 feet), or slightly less than the Emi Koussi (q.v.), highest mountain in the Sahara, also in Tibesti. Tousside is located southwest of Bardai (q.v.).

TRADE UNIONS. Since Chad's salaried workers were originally relatively few and most were not members of unions, the country's trade union movement started off relatively weak (even by African standards) and splintered until the 1964 creation of the Union Nationale des Travailleurs Tchadiens (UNTT) (q.v.). In 1968 the UNTT was transformed into the Union Nationale de Travailleurs du Tchad (UNATRAT) (q.v.), with the full consolidation of the single trade union confederation, following the forced merger into it of the few minor Christian unions. In 1972 UNATRAT had around 12,000 members, an increase of 4,000 from 1964. Unionists under the former UNTT and UNATRAT resisted increased taxes, salary freezes (as in 1968), voluntary labor contributions (as during the "Cultural Revolution" [q.v.] phase), and other austerity measures introduced by the Tombalbaye (q.v.) regime. Some members were secret sympathizers of the FROLINAT (q.v.) or (more usually) of more radical ideologies than the official positions of their trade movement. In general, however, unionists played a very minor role in Chadian politics.

This was to change after the fall of N'Djamena, first to Goukouni (q.v.) (1979), then to Hissène Habré (q.v.) (1982), and then to Idriss Déby (q.v.) (1990), all northern leaders, and acting (with the notable exception of Goukouni) as brutal, conquering warlords. The ravages of Habré's takeover of southern Chad (which Goukouni very astutely left alone during his brief reign), the brutalization of southern populations with no recourse to law in a system dominated by northerners, and the acute uncertainty of life in N'Djamena—where Habré's and later Déby's kinsmen strutted about bullying all and sundry—triggered an oppositional mentality on the part of unionists, most of whom are southern, even in N'Djamena. This was greatly compounded by the fact that many civil servants were not paid (and indeed, did not work) during the armed tug-of-war for N'Djamena (during which more than half the population fled the city), or for months after, and again in 1990 after Déby inherited empty state coffers, subsequent to Habré's escaping with all the country's liquid reserves.

For much of Déby's tenure the trade unions—now largely grouped under the renamed Union des Syndicats du Tchad (a second federation, Confédération Libre des Travailleurs du Tchad, now exists)—have been pressing for higher wages, back-pay, and also for a faster pace toward representative elections. Notwithstanding several prolonged strikes, little concrete has come out of their efforts.

TRANSAFRICAINE. Long-distance trucking concern in northern and eastern Chad, as well as in certain other parts of Africa. Controlled by the Société Mory et Compagnie, the Transafricaine is the result of the merger of the CCCI (Compagnie Coloniale Commerciale et Industrielle) of Guinea, the Compagnie Générale Transaharienne, and the Société Africaine de Transports Tropicaux (plus two other minor concerns) to produce one of the greatest trucking combines in Africa. The Transafricaine services Guinea, Côte d'Ivoire, Burkina Faso, Mali, Benin, Niger, and Chad. The Transafricaine's subsidiaries included the Compagnie Tchadienne de Transports (1957) and La Tibestienne de Transports as well as the Transnigerian Co. (Kano, Nigeria) and others. The Société Mory et Compagnie also controlled the Union Routière Centre-Africaine (Uniroute) (q.v.), which long held the monopoly over the evacuation of Chad's cotton harvest.

TRANS-CAMEROONIAN RAILROAD. First conceived by the German administration in Cameroon, the first section of the railroad (Douala-Yaoundé) was begun during the German era (prior to 1914) and completed by the subsequent French administration in 1927. During 1930 and 1931, the groundwork was laid to extend the line northward to N'Gaoundéré with the possibility of linking N'Djamena (via M'Béré) into the network. The line was not extended, however, due to the economic conditions in the 1930s and the onset of the Second World War. After the war the idea was revived, new feasibility plans were made, and preliminary work began in 1950, though no serious concrete construction occurred until 1964 under an independent Cameroonian government. N'Gaoundéré was reached nine years later, opening up the interior of the country but also providing Chad an alternate route to the coast via the railroad and the paved roads leading from N'Gaoundéré and Garoua (also in Cameroon) to the Chad border. A definitive decision regarding the extension of the Trans-camerounaise even farther to the north (which would benefit Chad more than Cameroon at this stage) was never reached, though all parties accept the desirability of such a course of action. On the other hand, the discovery in the late 1970s, and exploitation in the early 1990s, of large amounts of oil in southern Chad has opened the way to an oil pipeline from Doba to the Cameroonian coast. This project was initiated in 1994 and reconfirmed in 1995, and as a result the whole issue of extending the Transcamerounaise to a now potentially more prosperous Chad has been reopened.

TRANS-SAHARAN ROUTES see CARAVAN ROUTES

TRAORE, ABAKAR SANGA (1932–). Former minister of finance. Born in Mao in Kanem on October 12, 1932, and a civil administrator by profession, Traoré studied in France, obtaining a diploma from the Institut des Haute Etudes d'Outre-Mer (IHEOM). Since then he has served as director of foreign affairs (1961–62), deputy secretary-general of the government (1964–65), director general of fiscal controls (i.e., auditor-general), director of information, and director of the

Agence Tchadienne de Presse (ATP) (all between September 1965 and March 1966), finally entering the Tombalbaye (q.v.) cabinet on April 20, 1966, as minister of finance. A longtime member of the PPT (q.v.) Political Bureau, Traoré was dropped from the cabinet in November 1968 and reassigned to his previous high-level administrative duties. In April 1970 he was appointed inspector general of administration with the rank of cabinet minister; in August 1971 he was transferred to become prefect of Logone Occidentale, serving in that capacity until 1975, when he was transferred to Tandjilé. He is currently in retirement.

TREATY OF UNION OF CHAD AND LIBYA. Treaty signed on January 6, 1981, following the earlier (June 15, 1980) Treaty of Friendship and Alliance between the two countries. The alleged Union of Chad and Libya followed several earlier federation experiments by Libya's Muammar Qaddafi to bring about Libya-dominated federations elsewhere in Africa. It caused immense trepidation both in the West and in African capitals, and it swung public opinion overwhelmingly against Goukouni (q.v.) and triggered secret CIA funding for his adversary, Hissène Habré (q.v.), who, despite his role in the Claustre (q.v.) affair, suddenly appeared far more acceptable as a head of state. The treaty, which aimed at stabilizing Goukouni's rule in N'Djamena (aware that he was in command of a minimal armed force and unwilling to use brute force to crush opposition), was ultimately repudiated under world pressure. Though the alternative promised to Goukouni, OAU troops, to protect his regime from Habré's insurgency, was dispatched to N'Djamena, they did not fight, and they did not prevent the CIA-financed and heavily armed Habré from marching, virtually unopposed, into N'Djamena.

TROU AU NATRON. Large crater in Tibesti, of major scenic and tourist interest.

TRUCKING MONOPOLIES see COOPERATIVE DES TRANSPORTEURS TCHADIENS; TRANSAFRICAINE; UNIROUTE; UNITCHADIENNE.

TUAREG. Nomadic Saharan ethnic group normally resident farther to the northwest, in Niger and Algeria, but who from time to time entered the regions to their south. In 1855, for example, the Tuareg defeated the southward-moving pillaging columns of the Awlad Sulayman (q.v.), and later, in alliance with the Teda (q.v.) of Tibesti, exerted effective control over much of northern Kanem and its caravan routes (q.v.). In 1871 the Tuareg broke their alliance with the Teda and attacked them, but some 30 years later they formed another alliance to resist the French invasion in the B.E.T.

TUNJUR. Ethnic group that played a major role in Chadian history and that is currently found in very small numbers in Kanem (in the vicinity of Mondo, northeast of Mao) and Ouadai. The Tunjur are assumed to descend originally from a non-Arab, pre-Islamic (and possibly Christianized) Nilotic tribe in the Sudan; their own traditions recount their origin as a Beni Hilal (see ARABS) clan originally from Tunisia. The Tunjur ousted the Daju (q.v.) dynasty in Darfur (q.v.), displacing the Daju into Ouadai. The Tunjur were themselves replaced in Darfur in the sixteenth century by the Keira dynasty, and, moving to Ouadai, they established there a kingdom stretching into some areas of Batha and Dar Sila that lasted roughly a century. Following a Maba quasi-religious upheaval led by Abd-el-Kerim (q.v.) in 1611, the Tunjur were ousted from power in Ouadai, and they migrated farther west, eventually reaching Kanem. There they defeated the Bulala (q.v.) kingdom based in Mao—which had earlier ousted the Sefuwa (q.v.) Magumi (q.v.) into Nigeria, where the Bornu kingdom was to emerge—and established their hegemony over the various tribes in the region. The Tunjur established a tacit alliance with Ouadai, but this did not help much since they were soon subdued by a Bornuan military expedition (see DALATAWA) that reconquered normally tributary Kanem. In the middle of the nineteenth century, what remained of Tunjur power in Kanem was demolished by the rampaging waves of Awlad Sulayman (q.v.) that surged into Kanem from the north, where they had been expelled by the Turkish occupation of Tripolitania. The purest Tunjur are currently found in Dar Zioud, northeast of Oum-Hadjer, with other elements in Mondo in Kanem. Small groups of Tunjur are also found farther west in Nigeria.

TUPURI see TOUBOURI

TURKEY. At least from the sixteenth century, and possibly much earlier, sporadic contacts existed between the various kingdoms in Chad (but primarily Bornu) and the Ottoman Empire in Constantinople. Certainly slaves and other gifts (ostrich feathers, ivory) for the caliphs were from time to time dispatched northward from Bornu, and later from Ouadai and Baguirmi; and in the nineteenth century eunuchs became the specialty export of Baguirmi. The reverse trade brought a variety of commodities unavailable locally, including guns and ammunition, European steel products, and other goods, as well as instructors. The fact that the Ottomans captured Tripoli from Spain in 1551 greatly facilitated this mutual contact. Later, in the eighteenth and nineteenth centuries, the local Karamanli dynasty (q.v.) in Tripoli (1711–1833) performed an important middleman role between Bornu and Constantinople. The control of the trans-Saharan caravan trail terminals at either extremity by the powerful Bornu and Karamanli dynasties assured the safety of commerce during the heyday of the Bornu-Fezzan-Tripoli trade (see CARAVAN ROUTES; KARAMANLI DYNASTY). When the Ottoman conquest of Libya occurred in 1833 (with a weak local governor being appointed) a host of factors were set loose that led to the decline in trade on the caravan trail and the eruption of interethnic conflict in the northern regions of Bornu during much of the period of the Turkish control of the coast (1833–1911). The Awlad Sulayman (q.v.), pushed to the south by Turkish conquests in the Fezzan, ravaged much of Kanem before swinging into Nigeria. Turkish expeditions reached into Tibesti where, inter alia, a Turko-Senoussi outpost was created in Ain Galakka (q.v.). Later the Turks appeared poised for a possible penetration into Bornu itself, though the weakness of Turkish strength in the area made this a highly questionable enterprise. Still, in 1911 the French in Borkou clashed with a Turkish *kaimakan* in the area, and earlier, in 1907, the Turks gave military help—and a *kaimakan* commission and Turkish flag—to the derde (q.v.) of the Toubou (q.v.), who, having repelled the advancing Turkish forays into his area (in 1900), now appealed for Turkish help against the "greater" French infidels. Despite these ambitions in B.E.T., the Italian-Turkish war of 1912 led to the conquest of Libya by Italy and the elimination of Turkish power in the area. In 1913, in turn, the French finally captured Ain Galakka—which had changed hands a couple of times—forestalling any possible claims that might be advanced against this former Turkish outpost deep in the Sahara desert.

TURKU. Chadic Arabic, the lingua franca in Chad. (See ARABS.)

-U-

UMAR IBN IDRISS (?–c. 1388). King of Kanem-Bornu, who moved the empire's capital west of Lake Chad. Five of his immediate predecessors had been killed in repulsing Bulala (q.v.) attacks after Dunama Dibbalemi's (q.v.) sacrilegious actions had precipitated the Bulala revolt the previous century.

UNION DEMOCRATIQUE DU TCHAD (UDT). Early conservative and chiefly political party that dominated Chadian politics between 1946 and 1954 (and under a different name until 1957) with the support of its ally (with the same name), which contested the first electoral roll seats in the era of the double electoral college (q.v.). Founded in 1946 as a coalition of chiefs and traditional elements, including *chef de canton* Gountchomé Sahoulba (q.v.) and Arabi-el-Goni (q.v.), the UDT was affiliated with the French RPF (q.v.). In the 1946 elections the UDT won all of four seats of Ouadai and all four of Logone (which was at the time a single region) and also sent two delegates to the AEF (q.v.) Grand Council in Brazzaville. Assisted by the French administration and by the URT (q.v.) first electoral college party, the UDT absorbed a variety of small splinter groups after the 1946 elections, including the UPFT and URPT (qq.v.). In 1950 the party was rent by internal division as Ahmed Koulamallah (q.v.) was ousted to form his own political party (eventually the MSA [q.v.]), and in 1951 Ahmed Kotoko (q.v.)—briefly a member—also opted out to set up the UDSR (q.v.). In 1951 the UDT was nevertheless able to elect Bechir Sow (q.v.) and another delegate, Sou IV, to the French National Assembly as deputies from Chad. (The unwillingness to field a Kotoko candidacy for the assembly caused the rift leading to the creation of the UDSR.) The following year, however, the internal divisions in the UDT became acute. The UDT still managed in the 1952 territorial elections to sweep all of the seats in eight of the ten Chadian *circonscriptions* (electing candidates such as Bechir Sow, the Alifa of Kanem, the sultan of Fitri, Babikir Ibrahim, and Sahoulba) for a total of 24 of the 30 seats contested; but later the UDT suffered a split as Rogué, in opposition to Malbrant's (q.v) domination of the UDT's first electoral roll ally, joined hands with Jean Baptiste (q.v.) to lead a UDT faction to form a separate party, the UDIT (q.v.), in 1953, following which the UDT changed its name to the AST (q.v.). (See also POLITICAL PARTIES.)

UNION DEMOCRATIQUE ET SOCIALISTE DE LA RESISTANCE (UDSR). French National Assembly faction to which Chad's first European deputies (Malbrant and Boissoudy) affiliated themselves in 1946. After the formation of the RPF (q.v.) the UDSR merged with it, and Chad's deputies also made the transition and campaigned on the RPF label. Later, the RPF's first electoral roll party in Chad was the ADS (q.v.), while Ahmed Kotoko (q.v.), councillor to the French Union, took command of the party's second electoral roll campaigns for the 1951 French National Assembly elections and other contests. A centrist party based on Kotoko's ethnic clientele in the Fort-Lamy area, the UDSR in 1952 joined the PPT (q.v.) alliance to form FACT (q.v.). After that the UDSR remained closely aligned with the PPT—in contrast to its previous stance—though in 1956 in the Fort-Lamy mayoralty elections, Kotoko joined Adoum Aganayé (q.v.) to form a temporary local list, the RPPT (q.v.). In the 1957 territorial elections the UDSR won seven seats in the assembly, and by 1959 it had fully merged with the PPT. (See also POLITICAL PARTIES.)

UNION DEMOCRATIQUE INDEPENDANTE DU TCHAD (UDIT). Early Chadian political party. Founded in 1953 by Rogué, former governor (1944–49) of Chad, after his defection from the European RPF (q.v.) party. Among the UDIT's other prominent personalities were Jean Baptiste (q.v.), who later dominated the party. Running on the UDIT party label (the party had been formed of a faction of the UDT [q.v.]), Rogué was elected in 1954 to the Territorial Assembly and to the Council of the French Union. Especially powerful in Ouadai and Batha, the UDIT drained the strength of its former parent party, the UDT, leading to the latter's eventual collapse and renaming to AST (q.v.). In the 1956 Fort-Lamy municipal elections the UDIT joined its former rival, the PPT (q.v.), in forming the ERDIC (q.v.) coalition, which scored an impressive victory by pulling in 50 percent of the votes. Baptiste continued the UDIT's selective cooperation with the PPT (with which it was fundamentally mismatched in terms of ideology) while cooperating in local races with the conservative Muslim parties, especially the AST. In the 1957 territorial elections, the UDIT gained seven seats, and in 1959 fourteen. Shortly after the 1957 race the PPT leadership rejected the UDIT's strongly requested demand to send two of its own members to be Chad's delegates to the OCRS (q.v.). (The delegates suggested were Baptiste and Allatchi Issa Allatchimi [q.v.].) When the PPT showed no sign of compromise, Baptiste pulled his party out of the Entente (q.v.) coalition and shifted to cooperation with the AST. Some time later the GIRT (q.v.) party also deserted the Entente, and the PPT government of Gabriel Lisette (q.v.) collapsed. The UDIT participated briefly—directly as a separate party or more usually as a faction in an anti-PPT, wall-to-wall coalition—in the several successor governments during the period of provisional governments (q.v.) (see also POLITICAL PARTIES) and was finally banned, along with all other parties, when a one-party system was imposed in January 1962.

UNION DES ETATS DE L'AFRIQUE CENTRALE (UEAC). Rival regional organization to the UDEAC (q.v.), set up on April 2, 1968, by Zaire, Chad, and the Central African Republic after the latter complained that it had been neglected by the UDEAC, in which both of the latter states had been members. The UEAC had in essence the same purposes as the UDEAC; the organization was largely moribund, however, especially after the December 1968 change of heart on the part of President Jean-Bédel Bokassa of the C.A.R.—consequent to a dispute with Zaire—and in the subsequent rearray of members the UEAC remained with only two (Zaire and Chad) members with noncontiguous borders. Despite the fact that the economic rationale of the UEAC had disappeared, Chad maintained its membership until the coup of 1975. Following the coup, in 1976, it was announced that Chad would rejoin the UDEAC. The UEAC's Executive Secretariat was opened in N'Djamena in July 1970.

UNION DES FORCES DEMOCRATIQUES (UFD). Political party set up in 1992 by Saleh Maki, who was briefly Idriss Déby's (q.v.) minister of animal husbandry. Restructured and renamed Union des Forces Démocratiques–Parti Républicain, it reemerged in 1993 under the leadership of Gali Gatta N'Gothe (q.v.).

UNION DES REPUBLIQUES DE L'AFRIQUE CENTRALE (URAC). Regional association created on May 18, 1960, in Fort-Lamy by Chad, Congo-Brazzaville, and the Central African Republic. Aimed at coordinating defense, foreign policy, and economic policy and at continuing the cooperation between the territories that existed in the colonial era within the AEF (q.v.) federation, URAC did not have Gabon (the richest of the territories) as a member; Gabon participated in the conference to create URAC but did not ratify the resolution. The whole issue soon became irrelevant since the various states of the region requested, and obtained, separate independence, and a new organ was needed to take into account the changed circumstances. (For the economic common structures created in the region, see UNION DES ETATS DE L'AFRIQUE CENTRALE; UNION DOUANIERE EQUATORIALE; UNION DOUANIERE ET ECONOMIQUE D'AFRIQUE CENTRALE.)

UNION DES SYNDICATS DU TCHAD (UST). Chad's largest trade-union confederation. The UST was the successor, after the fall of the Habré (q.v.) regime, of the Union Nationale des Travailleurs Tchadiens (UNTT) (q.v.), though at the time a second, much smaller confederation, the Confédération Libre des Travailleurs du Tchad (CLTT) (q.v.), was also legalized. The UST has been constantly engaged, especially since 1992, in a tug-of-war with Idriss Déby (q.v.) over issues such as back-pay, salary increases, layoffs, the new income tax, privatization, the assassination of League of Human Rights vice president Behidi, the Doba massacres in the south by Déby's Garde Républicaine (q.v.), and the degree and pace of democratization in general. The unionists have at times declared strikes lasting for months but have usually succeeded in their economic rather than their political demands. UST leaders have on several occasions been arrested by the Déby regime. Its president is Djimbagué Dombal, and Loukoura Sa-Ndoudjinang is his deputy.

UNION DOUANIERE EQUATORIALE (UDE). Predecessor to the UDEAC (q.v.), established as a customs union in 1959 by the four AEF (q.v.) territories, with Cameroon becoming an associate member in 1961 and Equatorial Guinea in 1987. In January 1966 the UDE transformed itself into a broader customs and economic union, the UDEAC. (The actual treaty creating the UDEAC had been signed as early as late 1964.) The goals of the UDE were: free movement of capital and goods between member states; common import taxes; the creation of a solidarity fund from part of the customs collected (the proceeds to be allocated along the following ratios: Gabon, 0.15 percent; Congo/Brazzaville, 3 percent; C.A.R., 35 percent; and Chad, 61.85 percent); and the introduction of a single tax system.

UNION DOUANIERE ET ECONOMIQUE D'AFRIQUE CENTRALE (UDEAC). Successor to the Union Douanière Equatoriale (q.v.). A broader customs and economic union than the former, the UDEAC was set up on January 1, 1966, aimed at harmonizing customs, fiscal, and investment policies through uniform investment codes, a single tax on locally manufactured goods, common customs, and a modification of the UDE's solidarity fund aimed at greater compensations to inland insular states for the advantages accruing to the coastal states from the transit traffic through their territories. Originally signed late in 1964, the UDEAC's treaty was later expanded to include Cameroon. The organization's secretariat is in Bangui. In April 1968, complaining that they had been neglected and had benefited very little from association with the UDEAC, Chad and the Central African Republic left the organization and set up, together with Zaire, the rival UEAC (q.v.). The C.A.R. rapidly became disenchanted with the UEAC and returned to the UDEAC in December of the same year, while Chad announced its intention to do so only after the 1975 coup d'état that toppled President Tombalbaye (q.v.). Chad remains a member and in December 1987 hosted the organization's 23rd summit meeting.

UNION DU GUERA. Temporary local UDIT-MSA (qq.v.) electoral alliance for the May 1959 Territorial Assembly elections against the PPT (q.v.) in the Guéra région.

UNION DU KANEM. Temporary local UDIT-MSA (qq.v.) electoral compact in Kanem against the PPT (q.v.) in the 1959 Territorial Assembly elections.

UNION FRANCO-KANEMBU (UFK). Local Kanem list for the 1952 territorial elections led by a Cameroonian and a Dahomean. The party did not survive beyond the 1952 contest.

UNION GENERALE DES FILS DU TCHAD (UGFT). Originally a nonpolitical students' organization, set up in Cairo by Chadic-Arab youth early in 1959. Following the anti-Muslim incidents in N'Djamena in 1963 (see FORT-LAMY RIOTS), the UGFT split into two: one supportive of the PPT (q.v.) in power and the other calling for the overthrow of Tombalbaye (q.v.). In 1965 Tombalbaye set up a small secret committee that liaised with Ibrahim Abatcha (q.v.), cofounder of what was to become FROLINAT (q.v.), and in 1966, with Muslim Brotherhood support and led by Ahmed Moussa (q.v.), formed the Mouvement National de Libération du Tchad (MNLT) (q.v.), which soon after briefly joined with Abatcha's UNT (q.v.) to form the militant FROLINAT (q.v.). The union between the radical UNT and conservative MNLT promptly collapsed (as it had actually been forged by cliques in each), with the Moussa faction opting for the name of Front de Libération du Tchad (q.v.) and the Abatcha group retaining the name FROLINAT.

UNION INDEPENDANTE POUR LA DEFENSE DES INTERETS COMMUNAUX (UIDIC). An AST (q.v.) electoral list that ran in the 1956 Fort-Lamy municipal elections in the European zones of the city. Its list included six Europeans (headed by William Tardrew) and two Africans. Together with the AST—its African ally, campaigning in the native areas of the city—the UIDIC obtained barely 15 percent of the total vote, compared to the 50 percent of the PPT (q.v.) alliance of ERDIC (q.v.) and the 22 percent of Koulamallah's (q.v.) PSK (q.v.). After the elections three of the AST elected members rallied to ERDIC; the European UIDIC members later joined the AST party.

UNION LOGONAISE (UL). Regional (Logone) electoral list for the May 1959 Territorial Assembly elections. The UL grouped together a number of parties against the PPT, including the AST, GIRT, UDIT, MSA, and MESAN (qq.v.). Since the PPT was strongest in Logone, the efforts of the Union Logonaise were unsuccessful.

UNION NATIONALE (UN). Political party set up in 1992 by Abdoulaye Lamana (q.v.), the former Chadian ambassador to the EC. Its vice president is Mahamat Djerma (q.v.), one of Goukouni's (q.v.) former deputies and a prominent former member of both FROLINAT and GUNT (qq.v.).

UNION NATIONALE DEMOCRATIQUE (UND). Small underground movement set up by the southern veterinarian Dr. Facho Balaam in 1974 in an effort to bring about a north-south reconciliation. Despite its southern leadership, the UND was in essence a front for FROLINAT (q.v.). With an ethnic base in the extreme southwest of Chad and headquarters across the border in the Central African Republic, the UND adopted a very independent stance vis-à-vis Kamougoué, Goukouni, and Habré (qq.v.). After the fall of N'Djamena to Habré in 1982, and especially after the conquest of the southern préfectures by the FAN (q.v.) with dissident FAT (q.v.) support, the UND swung into open support for Goukouni and joined his GUNT-in-exile administration in Bardai. This was to change in 1984, however. In August the UND became part of a new formation—the Rassemblement des Forces Patriotiques (q.v.)—with Balaam at its head and the RFD rejecting both Habré and Goukouni as legitimate leaders for Chad.

UNION NATIONALE DES TRAVAILLEURS DU TCHAD (UNATRAT). Formerly Chad's unified trade union movement, formed in January 1968 under government direction after the absorption into the UNTT (q.v.) of several small Christian trade union splinter groups. UNATRAT had some 8,000 members and has been under the leadership of Robert Gorallah (q.v.). After the rise of the Idriss Déby (q.v.) regime in 1990 the name of the trade union confederation was changed to UST (q.v.), and a second, smaller, organ of independent unionists was also legalized.

UNION NATIONALE DES TRAVAILLEURS TCHADIENS (UNTT). Chad's former trade union formed by the 1964 fusion of all but a few recalcitrant Christian splinter groups, shortly after the imposition of a one-party system in Chad. In 1968 the confederation changed its acronym to UNATRAT (q.v.) to mark the total consolidation under its umbrella of the Christian unionists. As a union, the UNTT, and its successor the UNATRAT, was weak and ineffective; as a control mechanism for the PPT (q.v.) government, the structure was also ineffective since a certain proportion of the membership was sympathetic to more radical causes, including that of FROLINAT (q.v.). The UNTT disappeared after Idriss Déby's (q.v.) rise to power in 1990, when the trade union confederation was renamed the UST.

UNION NATIONALE POUR LA DEMOCRATIE ET LE PROGRES (UNDP). Political party set up and legalized in October 1992 by Yassin Bakhit.

UNION NATIONALE POUR LE DEVELOPPEMENT ET LE RE-
NOUVEAU (UNDR). Political party set up on December 30, 1992,
by Saleh Kebzabo (q.v.), the editor of N'Djamena's only independent
newspaper, *N'Djaména-Hebdo,* who in 1995 also declared his candidacy for the presidency if and when elections are held.

UNION NATIONALE POUR L'INDEPENDANCE ET LA REVOLU-
TION (UNIR). President Hissène Habré's (q.v.) political party, set up
as the political successor to his FAN (q.v.) military organization.
UNIR was formed in June 1984 with a central committee of regional
representatives that elected (on June 28) an Executive Bureau of 14
members and (originally) a Central Committee of 80. Under Habré's
chairmanship the bureau's composition was as follows: executive secretary: Gouarra Lassou; deputy secretary: Youssouf Sidi; commissioner for guidance, information, and education: Djimé Tougou; first
deputy commissioner: Robert Kadjangaba; second deputy commissioner (social and women's affairs): Fatimé Kemto; commissioner for
external relations: Mahamat Nouri; deputy commissioner: Adoum
Moussa Seif; commissioner for the armed forces: Idriss Déby; deputy
commissioner: Yorongar Moibian; commissioner for security: Issaka
Hassan; deputy commissioner: Ahmat Dadji; commissioner for finance, economy, and rural development: Nouradine Koumakoyé
Delwa Kassiré; deputy commissioner: Mahamat Gig Yi.
    UNIR was not popular in the south, being viewed as little more than
a Gorane (q.v.)-dominated successor to FAN (q.v.) and FROLINAT
(q.v.), and was joined only by southerners who wished to move up the
governmental ladder. Strong efforts were made late in 1987 to increase
the party's minuscule membership: a youth branch (RAJEUNIR),
a women's branch (OFIUNIR), and a trade union branch (UNACOT)
were also formed, though membership remained stagnant. At its second congress in November 1988 the Central Committee integrated
with great fanfare several new members who had formerly led six opposition groups but who had rallied to the regime, including the southerners Generals Djogo and Kamougoué (qq.v.). The Central Committee was at the time expanded to 110 members. Under UNIR
single-party parliamentary elections were held in 1990, and a new National Assembly was elected. The party was banned after Hissène
Habré was ousted, and his movement (in exile) became the MDD
(q.v.).

UNION NATIONALE TCHADIENNE (UNT). Precursor of FROLI-
NAT (q.v.). The UNT was set up in November 1958 to contest the
May 1959 territorial elections, in which it won one seat in Chari-
Baguirmi, forcing the MSA (q.v.) out of the préfecture. Indeed,

extremely radical in its appeal, the UNT totally outflanked the MSA and became Chad's most militant faction. The UNT's president at the time was Issa Danna, and its central bureau was composed only of Arabs. Among its other prominent leaders were Outman Mahamat, Othman Aboubakar Djalabo, Mahamat Ali Taher, Ibrahim Abatcha, Mahamat Abba, and Abba Siddick (qq.v.)—the latter just out of his cabinet post in the PPT (q.v.) government. In July 1959 the UNT deserted the MPT (q.v.) coalition in which it had temporarily participated and tried to develop grassroots support among the peasantry, youth, and "proletariat." Later it announced its international affiliation with the extremist interterritorial PFA. After its dissolution along with all Chadian parties when a one-party system was imposed in January 1962, remnants of the UNT, led by Ibrahim Abatcha (q.v.)—a Marxist and militant Muslim unionist—established themselves in Khartoum, Sudan, and began an anti-Tombalbaye (q.v.) campaign while preparing for armed struggle. Early in 1966 the UNT began quick hit-and-run forays into Ouadai. In June 1966 the UNT formally merged with conservative elements in the UGFT and MNLT (qq.v.) to form FROLINAT (q.v.). The opportunistic union of extreme opposites soon collapsed, however, largely because it had been formed by splinter groups from both, with UNT opting to continue under the name of FROLINAT while Ahmed Moussa's (q.v.) group of MNLT-UGFT opted for the name of FLT (q.v.).

UNION POPULAIRE TCHADIENNE (UPT). Former overseas political opposition movement, headed by Secretary-General Yacoub Mahamat Ourada, that rallied to the Hissène Habré (q.v.) regime on July 15, 1988.

UNION POUR LA DEMOCRATIE ET LA REPUBLIQUE (UDR). Political party, one of several set up by Jean Alingué (q.v.), who joined the Conférence Nationale (q.v.) under its ticket.

UNION POUR LE PROGRES DU TCHAD (UPT). Temporary merger of the PPT (q.v.) and PNA (qq.v.) in March 1961 that essentially created a voluntary one-party system in Chad. The "reconciliation" of the PNA (which included just about every possible conservative, Muslim, and formerly anti-PPT leader in the country) and the dominant PPT, was witnessed by the fact that the founding (and only) congress of the new "unity" party was held in Abéché, stronghold of anti-PPT sentiment in the past. The alliance collapsed a few months later, however, when the PPT unilaterally designated all candidates for the municipal elections in Chad without consulting its new ally. This sparked an angry denunciation on the part of the UPT leaders, who presented an alternate list for the races. This list was declared void, and some time later all parties in Chad were banned. (See also POLITICAL PARTIES.)

UNION POUR LE RENOUVEAU ET LA DEMOCRATIE (URD). Political party, one of several set up by General Kamougoué (q.v.) in 1992 in preparation for his entry into the country's Conférence Nationale (q.v.).

UNION PROGRESSISTE FRANCO-TCHADIENNE (UPFT). Early local Kanem electoral list for the 1946 Conseil Représentatif elections. Based in Mao, the list included Sultan Ali Alifa and Bechir Sow (q.v.) and won the two Kanem seats. After the election the party was absorbed by the UDT (q.v.).

UNION REPUBLICAINE DU TCHAD (URT), 1946. Early (and first fully local) European party created in 1946 to contest the first electoral roll seats. A conservative extension of the French Right, the URT won five of the ten seats of the first electoral college, the rest going to independents. One of its 1946 leaders was Marcel Lallia (q.v.). Late in 1947 the URT became formally affiliated with the RPF (q.v.) and in the next elections campaigned under that name.

UNION REPUBLICAINE DU TCHAD (URT), 1959. Temporary minor 1959 political party led by Seydou Tall, its only important personality. Formed by MESAN (q.v.) as its local branch in Chad (see POLITICAL PARTIES), the URT joined the PNA (q.v.) coalition against the PPT (q.v.), with Tall becoming vice president of the new party. The URT had little if any impact on Chadian politics and appealed mostly to ethnic elements in border areas transected by the C.A.R.-Chad boundary. Not to be confused with the European party of 1946 in the previous entry.

UNION REPUBLICAINE ET PROGRESSISTE DU TCHAD (URPT). Early political party that presented itself in the 1946 elections for the local assembly, campaigning for the second electoral roll seats. Its most prominent members were Jules Pierre Toura Gaba (q.v.), who later joined the PPT (q.v.), and Ibrahim Babikir (q.v.), at the time a postal agent. The URPT won the three seats of the Lac région and one in Moyen-Chari. The rump of the party was later absorbed by the conservative UDT (q.v.) while the more liberal elements went over to the PPT.

UNION ROUTIERE CENTRE-AFRICAINE (UNIROUTE). Giant expatriate transportation company that in the colonial era had a quasi monopoly over cotton transport in Chad and Central African Republic, and to a lesser extent was also active in Cameroon. Controlled by the Société Mory et Compagnie, the holding company of Rothschild interests, Uniroute totally dominated trucking on the crucial Fort-Lamy–Fort-Archambault–Bangui route. In 1957–58 Uniroute ceded part of its monopoly to the CTT (q.v.) and later changed its name to UNITCHADIENNE (q.v.). (See also COTTON.)

UNION SOCIALISTE TCHADIENNE (UST). Short-lived (1957–59) coalition of anti-PPT (q.v.) Muslim parties. Forged by Ahmed Koulamallah (q.v.) out of his former MSA (q.v.), together with the AST and a segment of the UDIT. The coalition was successful in the partial elections in Chari-Baguirmi and held 26 seats to the PPT coalition's 39 seats. The UST's internal power distribution was AST 14, UDIT 5, MSA 4, independents 3. In January 1959 the GIRT (q.v.) (formerly a faction within the AST that moved to selective cooperation with the PPT) deserted the PPT alliance, which resulted in the collapse of the Gabriel Lisette (q.v.) government. The GIRT joined the UST coalition, which was then renamed the MPT (q.v.). The new alliance formed the next (brief) provisional government under the leadership of GIRT leader Sahoulba (q.v.). The party was resurrected in Paris in 1986 by Koulamallah's son, Abderahman Koulamallah (q.v.), and in 1992 it was transferred to Chad. (See also POLITICAL PARTIES.)

UNION TCHADIENNE (UT). PPT-PSIT-UDSR (qq.v.) electoral coalition headed by Gabriel Lisette (q.v.) for the 1956 French National Assembly elections. The UT won the largest number of votes (130,843 to the AST's 105,258), and Lisette was elected as Chad's deputy.

UNIROUTE see UNION ROUTIERE CENTRE-AFRICAINE

UNITCHADIENNE. Giant transport company, successor to the Union Routière Centre-Africaine (q.v.) of the colonial era, sharing with the CTT (q.v.) a monopoly over all trucking into and out of Chad, and with activities in the C.A.R. and Cameroon as well. In 1970 Unitchadienne controlled, with the CTT, fully 80 percent of all public and private transport in Chad. Until 1957–58, as Uniroute, the company had a total monopoly over the evacuation of all of Chad's cotton crop, a monopoly progressively shared with the CTT; during the 1958–65 period the proportion was 80–20, and in the 1966–73 period it was 50–50. In 1972–73 Unitchadienne left the cotton sector completely (leaving it to be shared by the CTT and Cotontchad and progressively monopolized by the latter), though it still had a dominant role in other trucking sectors. In 1970 Unitchadienne had 232 trucks with a capacity of 2,129 tons and was the only company with regular transport schedules between N'Djamena and Bongor, Moundou, Sarh, and Abéché, and prior to the civil wars maintained a regular trucking link with Tripoli, Libya. (See also UNION ROUTIERE CENTRE-AFRICAINE.)

UNITED STATES. The U.S. political stake and involvement in Chadian affairs began in earnest with Goukouni's (q.v.) rise to power in N'Djamena. Until then Washington was largely content to work through France, whose paramountcy it recognized. However, the fact that Goukouni was closely supported by Libya, and that France was unwilling to risk antagonizing Muammar Qaddafi, brought about direct, though originally covert, U.S. support for Hissène Habré (q.v.) after—and, some suggest, before—his falling-out with Goukouni in N'Djamena. Libya's move to reinforce Goukouni's control of N'Djamena in 1981 with thousands of troops was in particular regarded as ominous, and soon planeloads of sophisticated weapons were being supplied by the CIA to Habré's forces. There is no doubt that it was this war materiel, as well as Goukouni's leaning over backwards to accommodate Washington in asking that the Libyan forces be withdrawn, that led to his ouster and the installation of Habré in his stead. Subsequently Habré became one of the most pliable and useful U.S. allies in the region, continuing to benefit from relatively large amounts of economic and military aid (including presidential aid) as well as military training, including via CIA and other "advisers" who were installed in several bases near N'Djamena.

During Habré's stunning military victories over Libya in 1987, U.S. military experts were the first (much to the chagrin of the French) to inspect sophisticated Soviet war booty that was captured intact. (Habré then received 24 Stinger antiaircraft missiles, seven launchers, and antitank missiles.) The CIA moved in in greater strength to train and use 700 of the more than 2,000 Libyan POWs captured in these battles as a contra-force, though its exploits, if any, are not known. (They were part of an anti-Qaddafi organization, the National Front for the Salvation of Libya.) The murderous aspects of the Habré regime were glossed over, and indeed, U.S. support for Habré was steadfast to the very end. In his last battles in eastern Chad against Déby's forces (financed and assisted by Libya), Habré moved his best and most loyal ethnic troops aboard American Hercules C-130 planes allegedly flown by Zairean pilots with American copilots.

The result of this close U.S. support for Habré was that when Habré was finally militarily defeated and ousted in December 1990, the very first action of the new leader in power, Idriss Déby (q.v.), was to close down the CIA camps, expel remaining American military officials (most had left once Habré's defeat was known), and order Libyan

POWs repatriated or released, while moving into a much more cordial relationship with Libya, which had supported his comeback.

UNIVERSITY OF CHAD. National university of Chad, officially founded with substantial French fiscal assistance in 1970/71 and fully operative in 1972. In that year the university, under rector Jean Cabot, formerly of Vincennes University, had a library of 3,000 volumes, 25 instructors, and 200 students. The Université du Tchad, whose operating language is French, has three institutes: Applied Linguistics, Literature, and Humanities; Law, Economics, and Management; and Applied and Pure Science. With the creation of the university the activities of the Foundation for Higher Education were wound up. By 1974, when the university turned out its first graduates (45 students), some 500 students were registered in classes. The next year (1974/75) was seriously disrupted due to the imposition of compulsory *Yondo* (q.v.) rites. With the fall of N'Djamena to the north and the partition of the city between FAN and FAP (qq.v.), the university was closed down in 1979. Heavily damaged in subsequent fighting between the opposing armies in the capital, it remained closed for three years. By 1987 the university was fully restored, and during that academic year it enrolled 1,500 students. Five hundred additional Chadians were studying in universities outside the country. These numbers have only slightly increased in recent years, partly because the number of government scholarships has remained stagnant, and because the Habré-Déby (qq.v.) tug-of-war consumed a large proportion of the government's fiscal resources.

URADA, MUHAMMAD (Sultan). Sultan of Ouadai, who was restored to his throne in Abéché in 1934. The previous sultan, recognized by the French, had been deposed by them in 1912 (see ACYL). Urada's son, Abdalhedi Urada, assumed a minor political role in the 1960s, as PPT (q.v.) deputy to the National Assembly.

URBANIZATION. Starting off in the 1960s with one of the lowest percentages of urban populations in Africa, urbanization has been very rapid in Chad. It reached 11 percent in 1970, 30 percent in 1990, and is currently estimated to stand at around 33 percent of the country's population. The prime motive behind this demographic shift has been the greater physical security in urban conglomerations, but the devastating series of droughts in the Sahel in the 1970s and 1980s also contributed to a rural-urban shift. Also the fact that northern groups have in turn "captured" N'Djamena (Teda, Daza, the Hadjeray-Zaghawa alliance, etc.) has brought members of these groups into the capital and into regional centers. The highest increases in percentage growth have been in the small southern towns, some of which quintupled in size in two decades. Some of this growth took place during the major influx of southerners fleeing the first Battle for N'Djamena (q.v.), since many did not return to the capital after conditions there stabilized. Estimates of the size of Chad's main towns vary widely; the following is one ranking as of mid-1994.

1. N'Djamena	650,000	6. Bongor	20,000
2. Sarh	120,000	7. Doba	18,000
3. Moundou	114,000	8. Pala	14,000
4. Abéché	85,000	9. Koumra	13,000
5. Kélo	30,000		

-V-

VANDOME, CHARLES (1928–). Former archbishop of N'Djamena. Born in Colombes, France, in 1928, Vandome was ordained in 1960 and immediately took up duties in Chad in the Catholic missions at Bousso, Sara-Kenga, and Baro. In 1969 he became father superior of the Chad Jesuit Order and later spent several years in Douala, Cameroon. In 1981 he returned to Chad as archbishop of N'Djamena, replacing Dalmais. He is the author of several books, mostly on Ngambayé-Moundou linguistics.

VIXAMAR, ANDRE (Dr.). Haitian intellectual and physician, for a time in the employ of President Tombalbaye's (q.v.) presidential staff as personal adviser. He was the principal adviser and assistant in the project to revive and revitalize the Yondo (q.v.) rites in Chad. (See also CULTURAL REVOLUTION.)

VOIX DE LA LEGALITE. N'Djamena transmitting station that for some nine months in 1980 competed with Radio Tchad, then under Habré's control. Operated by GUNT (q.v.), it was less powerful but broadcast the government's version of events in the capital. Part of its equipment was transferred in 1982 to Bardai, where it transmitted the GUNT-in-exile message as Radio Bardai.

VOIX DE LA REVOLUTION CULTURELLE TCHADIENNE see RADIO NATIONALE TCHADIENNE

VOIX DE L'UNITE ET DE PROGRES see RADIO NATIONALE TCHADIENNE

VOLAIT, ANDRE EMILE (1923–). Senior colonial administrator and administrative functionary. Born in Lausanne, Switzerland, on October 1, 1923, Volait joined the French colonial civil service after obtaining a law degree and studying political science at the University of Paris. Head of the Paris office of the governor-general of the AEF federation from 1948 to 1950, Volait next served for six years (1952–57) with the Ministry of Colonies in Paris, in charge of economic affairs and planning. In 1957 he joined the emerging national administration in N'Djamena as deputy director of economic affairs and in 1959 became cabinet director of the secretary of state for economic coordination. He served in similar capacities in the cabinets of other ministers charged with economic and financial issues until he returned to France in 1972.

VOLCAN ARMY. Segment of the original First Liberation Army (q.v.), organized and headed by Mohamed Baghalani (q.v.) in 1975. Intermittently engaged in border assaults from the Sudan frontier, the Volcan Army (also called Volcan Force) was about to merge with Goukouni's (q.v.) Second Liberation Army (q.v.) when Baghalani died in an accident and the plans were shelved. Ahmat Acyl (q.v.) emerged as the new leader, and the Volcan Army acquired a strong pro-Libya orientation. A small faction opted to follow Adoum Dana (q.v.) instead, who remained true to the original pro-Sudan line of the organization. Acyl brought the group, variably estimated as fielding between 500 and 2,000 fighting men, into the GUNT (q.v.) coalition in 1980 and changed its name to the Conseil Démocratique de la Révolution (CDR) (q.v.). As usual with such forces, a splinter group refused to follow the CDR into GUNT and retained the original name. Later it was joined by another splinter group after the CDR itself broke up into three factions. The Volcan Army, then headed by Secretary-General Abdoulkassim Gamar, officially disbanded on August 4, 1989, and rallied to Hissène Habré (q.v.). However, a small faction within it remained in Sudan, having linked up with the Hadjeray (q.v.) MOSANAT (q.v.) rebellion, and later with Idriss Déby (q.v.).

VOLCAN NOUVEAU. Brief appellation of the Ahmat Acyl (q.v.) rump of Volcan Army (q.v.) after the Acyl-Dana split and before the Acyl faction adopted its new name, the CDR (q.v.).

-W-

WADAI see OUADAI

WADI. Seasonally dry streambeds.

WAJUNGA. Small Toubou (q.v.) group of allegedly different origin than either the dominant Teda or Daza (qq.v.) groups. More sedentary, and residing east of Tibesti near the small Ounianga lakes (north of Faya-Largeau), the Wajunga have tended to support political candidates in opposition to the Teda. For this reason, during the civil upheavals in the region in the 1970s there were pitched battles between the Teda and the Wajunga that had nothing to do with the anti-N'Djamena rebellion.

WARA. Former capital of the Ouadai kingdom (q.v.), some 35 kilometers (22 miles) from Abéché. The ritual and political center of the kingdom, Wara (also spelled Ouara) was closed to commercial activity with Nimro, a few kilometers south, fulfilling this function. Founded in the second half of the seventeenth century, Wara's isolated strategic location led to its abandonment in 1850, when the capital was shifted to Abéché (q.v.). The impetus for the relocation was continuous tribal attacks on the city from the hilly areas around it. Remnants of the imperial city (including its large ruined walls, the sultan's quarters, and a large mosque reputedly built by Abd-el-Kerim [q.v.]) can be reached at the end of a very difficult trek from Abéché. Nearby are also located the burial tombs of the former kings of Ouadai. Wara's name translates to "difficult crossing-place."

WASILI. Kanembu (q.v.) name for the Awlad Sulayman (q.v.).

WHEAT see POLDERS; SEMABLE; SODELAC

WODEI KICHEDEMI (Derde) (1903–1977). Former derde (q.v.) of the Teda (q.v.) in Chad. Originating from Seguédem, the nonhereditary chief of the Tomaghera (q.v.) clan was selected along traditional criteria to serve as successor derde in 1939, after the death of Shoffai Bogarmi (q.v.), becoming spiritual leader of all the Teda in Tibesti. During his selection, attempts by a competing clan and candidate to mislead the French administration into accepting their qualifications resulted in a lifelong animosity that had political repercussions in the 1960s. After the transfer of B.E.T. to Chadian hands, maladministration, especially the demeaning 1965 Bardai incidents (q.v.) and Tombalbaye's (q.v.) appointing as minister of Saharan affairs the derde's lifelong enemy (and his refusal to appoint one of his sons to the administration) resulted in the call to arms by his four sons and the derde's trek into exile. He was to return to Chad only after Tombalbaye's death in the 1975 Malloum (q.v.) coup. After being accorded state honors, he withdrew to Zouar, his capital. There he disinherited his only remaining son—Wodei Goukouni (q.v.)—for not obeying him and laying down his arms, and he died in 1977. Goukouni was to emerge a year later as president of Chad. (See also DERDE; TEDA; TOUBOU.)

WORIMI, ALLAFOZA KONI (Colonel). Former Habré chief of staff. Worimi was named chief of staff in 1989 after the Zaghawa (q.v.) defections that included that of Chief of Staff Djamouss (q.v.) and Idriss Déby (q.v.). He had been one of Hissène Habré's (q.v.) key lieutenants during the latter's drive on N'Djamena against Goukouni in the 1980–82 period. In the conflict with Déby, Worimi personally led his forces on assaults against Déby's troops. In an August 1989 raid by Déby on Abéché, Worimi was captured and taken to the Bamissi oasis and Déby's base at Kutum, 200 kilometers (125 miles) inside Darfur. There then followed a daring Chadian rescue mission headed by Worimi's deputy. Badly wounded in the process, Worimi was airlifted by an Iraqi plane and flown to Paris for treatment and recovery.

-X–Y-

YACINE, ABDELKADIR. A member of Dr. Abba Siddick's (q.v.) FROLINAT (q.v.), Yacine was appointed secretary of state in charge of refugees in the Goukouni GUNT (qq.v.) government of July 1981. With the fall of N'Djamena to Habré (q.v.) forces a year later, he lost his post and joined the anti-Habré GUNT with his small faction of FROLINAT-Originel (q.v.).

YACOUB, ADOUM. Key Habré aide. Longtime secretary of state for external relations in the GUNT (q.v.) government-in-exile in B.E.T., Yacoub served primarily as GUNT spokesman abroad, often based in Tripoli, Libya. He remained in this capacity until GUNT fell apart in 1987, at which point he rallied to Hissène Habré (q.v.) and was appointed deputy chief of staff of the Garde Présidentielle (q.v.). He led the Chadian assault 200 kilometers (125 miles) into Sudan to rescue the captive Colonel Worimi (q.v.). Later he was sent to attend a Sandhurst, England, officers' school, where he was when Habré's regime collapsed, and on graduating he joined Habré's rebellion in the Lake Chad region. After Goukouni Guet (q.v.) was captured by Idriss Déby's (q.v.) forces, Yacoub assumed command of the Habré rebellion, and it was under his aegis (and that of Habré's notorious nephew Korei Guini [q.v.]) that a second front was briefly opened in the south, at the Central African Republic border, with some 1,000 troops recruited in Ouadai and Batha and trained in Nyala, Sudan. That front collapsed since his troops, northerners, were not granted asylum among the southerners in Chad, and he then returned to lead the northern rebellion. After the rebellion was repulsed, Yacoub settled with the remnants of Habré's followers in the Nguigmi region of Niger but was expelled by the Niger government in January 1994 for his forays into Chad.

YAERE see CHARI RIVER

YAKOUMA, MAHAMAT. Former mayor of N'Djamena. A high-level civil administrator by profession, Yakouma was deputy director of finance in the Ministry of Finance until November 1965, when he was elected mayor of Chad's capital. He served in that position until the end of 1971. He was then appointed prefect of Guéra and in October 1973 was brought back to the capital to join Tombalbaye's (q.v.) cabinet as secretary of state in charge of interior. Following the 1975 coup d'état he was reappointed to the same position. With the rise of Goukouni's GUNT (qq.v) government, Yakouma was appointed prefect of Salamat but lost the post when Hissène Habré (q.v.) seized power in N'Djamena in 1982. He is currently in retirement.

YAMOKO BEZO, NICOLAS (1941–). Bank administrator. Born in Sarh on December 6, 1941, by profession a civil administrator, Yamoko Bezo was educated locally and in France, graduating from the prestigious Institut des Hautes Etudes d'Outre-Mer (IHEOM) and Institut International de l'Administration Publique (IIAP). He has been deputy director (1970–1973) and director (1973) of the African Development Bank, and previously was a member of Chad's Social and Economic Council.

YAO. Small village on the northern shore of Lake Fitri (q.v.), which is the major center of the Bulala (q.v.) ethnic group in Chad, and core of the small Bulala sultanate set up after their defeat at the hands of the Tunjur (q.v.), following the latter's invasions into Kanem. The founding date of the sultanate is disputed and is alternately placed either at the beginning of the fifteenth century or at the beginning of the seventeenth century. Currently Yao is inhabited by only a few hundred people. In the *cirana* walled-quarter resides the Bulala sovereign, who has the title of *Ngaré*. (See also BULALA.)

YARMARKE, KA MAKAILA (1943–). Journalist and former director of programs at Radio Chad from 1973 to 1977. Born on June 7, 1943, and educated in N'Djamena and in Belgium in telecommunications,

Yarmarké returned to N'Djamena to assume the post of deputy coordinator of programs (1971–72) and was promoted to director of programs in 1973. Yarmarké left Chad with the collapse of Sara power in the capital.

YARMARKE, KA NADJI. Former mayor of Kélo (Tandjilé) during the brief Goukouni (q.v.) presidency, Yarmarké switched loyalties to Hissène Habré (q.v.) in 1982 and was brought into his cabinet as secretary of state in charge of natural disasters. He lost his post after Habré's ouster.

YARONGAR, N'GARLEDJI. Political head of the Front des Forces d'Action pour la République (q.v.), a party set up in 1992.

YAZANI see SEFUWA

YEDINA. Better known as the Buduma (q.v.) and frequently (though incorrectly) lumped together with the Kanembu (q.v.) or Kotoko (q.v.), the Yedina are a distinct ethnic group of some 33,000 found in the Bol district of the Lac Préfecture (where 25,000 of them live on the islands and peninsulas) and in the Massakory district. Linked to the Kotoko via alleged descent from a union of Kanembu and Sao (q.v.) progenitors, the Yedina are divided into two large groups (the Buduma and the Kuri) and many small subgroups, among which the Guria are the most numerous. Their name comes either from that of the village of Yedi (southwest of the lake), where Sao used to live, or from the Kanuri "*yedi*" which means "east." Their language is similar to that of the Kotoko and is usually placed in the Kotoko-Hausa group of the Chado-Hamitic language family. Their main occupation is fishing in distinctively styled pirogues, as well as stockbreeding and tending the polders (q.v.) of the lake. The Yedina are essentially animist, having only recently been exposed to Islam.

YOBAT see KOSSEDA

YODOYMAN, JOSEPH. Former prime minister of Chad. A southerner, Yodoyman first gained political office in November 1979 when he was appointed deputy secretary-general of the GUNT (q.v.) government. He was promoted in July 1981 to secretary of state for interior, and he made an easy transition into Hissène Habré's (q.v.) cabinet in 1982, appointed minister of planning. A leader of one of the parties that sprang up after the Idriss Déby (q.v.) liberalizations, Yodoyman replaced Jean Alingué (q.v.) on May 20, 1992, as Déby's prime minister, serving for 18 months.

YOMA, ROTOUANG (Captain). Former minister of justice. A former aide-de-camp to Colonel Kamougoué (q.v.), during the latter's tenure as head of the Sara administration based in Moundou (1978–82). In 1982 Captain Yoma sided with the dissident FAT (q.v.) officers who ousted Kamougoué and delivered the southern préfectures to Habré's control. Yoma was rewarded with the Ministry of Defense in October 1982, and in July 1984 he was transferred to the Ministry of Justice.

YOMADJI, OSCAR. Early Déby (q.v.) cabinet member. Yomadji was appointed in December 1991 deputy secretary-general of the government, and in May 1992 he was promoted to secretary of state in charge of planning. In October 1992 he was promoted to full ministerial rank and appointed in charge of livestock. He remained in the cabinet until the Conférence Nationale (q.v.) in 1993 selected its own cabinet.

YONDO. Name of the male youth initiation ceremonies among the Goulaye, Miltou, Niellim, and many Sara clans in Chad. Among the Gambayé, the equivalent rite is called *lao*. As part of the program of Tchaditude, authenticity, and "Cultural Revolution" (q.v.), President Tombalbaye (q.v.) first decreed the Yondo rites as a basic prerequisite for public office for all Sara non-Muslims; later Sara Muslims were included in the decree (though it was anathema to them), and finally all civil servants were required to undergo Yondo initiation or its ethnic functional equivalent. Still later, possibly without overt and direct central government encouragement, just about any Western-educated or Muslim citizen could find himself being forcibly required to undergo the rites at the pain of torture or even death. Apart from disrupting many institutions (such as the schools and the local university) the rites were condemned by many as pagan, heretic, and barbaric, as well as personally traumatic to some of those forced to undergo them, especially those who had been long divorced from Sara traditional life. Numerous accounts of the torture and killing of Christian missionaries and priests percolated to the outside world at the height of the drive to force all noninitiates to undergo the rites. The rites are conducted by the *Nge-kor-bang-ndo* ("opener of the camp doors") in a number of specific sites, to which young people from surrounding villages are dispatched. One very important site is Bedaya, Tombalbaye's hometown, where up to 1,000 youths were initiated at one time in the 1970s. The purpose of the rites, previously held only every five to ten years, is to transform uninitiated youth—who cannot marry—to the status of full-fledged Sara adults through the learning of ancient Sara traditions and secret symbols and, after suffering humiliating and painful ordeals, being given absolution for their sins. The rites are essentially a socialization process by which ancient values are transmitted to the new generation, and Christian missionaries had long opposed them, even petitioning to have them completely abolished in 1960. In mid-1965 a compromise was reached by which uninitiated Christian youths (who hitherto had been barred from participating in adult Sara life, since without the rites they were not "traditionally" of age even if chronologically so) were allowed to attend the rites, some of which were not required of them, addressing their prayers to God rather than to the Sara spirit world. The compromise broke down in the early 1970s—coinciding with the start of Tombalbaye's "Cultural Revolution"—when traditional chiefs complained that now that the stigma of noninitiation had been removed from Christian (and Muslim) youth, there had developed a major surge of requests for abbreviated Yondo rites, followed by conversion to Christianity. As a consequence of the coincidence of Tombalbaye's "Cultural Revolution" and the pressures from traditional chiefs for unfettered freedom to demand of all youth initiation in Yondo, the rites—in their entirety—came to be imposed upon all.

YOSKO see ANGATA YOSKOIMI

YOSSENGAR, ENOCH (1933–). Civil administrator. Born in 1933 in Deboto (near Doba, Logone Orientale) and educated abroad, including at the Institut des Hautes Etudes d'Outre-Mer (IHEOM), Yossengar occupied a variety of administrative posts, including court clerk in the Fort-Lamy Court of Appeals (1958–59) and deputy secretary-general of the Chadian government (1959–61). He was also an administrator with the Banque Tchadienne de Crédit et de Dépôts, director general of the Office d'Exploitation des Carrières (OECA), president of the Ati branch of the PPT (q.v.) (1967), and member (1967) of the Social and Economic Council. With the collapse of Sara power in N'Djamena in 1979, Yossengar moved to the south.

YOUSSOUF, MAHAMAT (Sultan). Twenty-fourth sultan of Baguirmi. Formerly the *chef de canton* of Massenya—the core of the Barma people and of the Baguirmi kingdom (q.v.)—and father of Ahmed Koulamallah (q.v.), Youssouf was officially enthroned on June 14, 1970, in Massenya in the presence of President Tombalbaye as part of the recommendations of the French Mission de Réforme Administrative (q.v.). There has always been bad blood between Youssouf and Koulamallah.

YOYANA, BANIARA. Habré's minister of agriculture and rural development from 1984 to 1988.

-Z-

ZAGHAWA. Group of seminomadic Arab (q.v.) clans found in a broad arc across northern Chad and in parts of Darfur (q.v.) in Sudan. Formerly much more widespread and found in greater numbers, especially in Kanem and in eastern Niger, the Zaghawa were estimated in 1964 to number 25,000, mostly in the Biltine Préfecture. Their language is closely related to that of the Teda (q.v.) and hence indirectly to Kanuri, though a segment speaks only Arabic (which is for all a primary language) and strongly identifies with the Mahamid Arabs (q.v.). The Zaghawa are also related to the Bideyat (q.v.) to their north and jointly refer to themselves as Beri. In the Middle Ages the Zaghawa—thought to be of nomadic Berber origins—who were then more numerous and controlled much of the trans-Saharan trade, helped to found the original Kanem kingdom and dynasty (see KANEM-BORNU EMPIRE), as well as Gobir, a Hausa state, and several other principalities. The Zaghawa were one of the ethnic groups that threw their support behind Hissène Habré (q.v.) in his tug-of-war with N'Djamena, and they gained politically with Habré's victory and rise to power in 1982. Indeed, some of their leaders were among the key military commanders who secured victory for Habré. Progressively disenchanted with Habré's reign, they rebelled when his spate of purges started affecting them, and Djamouss (q.v.), Déby (q.v.), and Itno (q.v.) defected in 1989. Forging an alliance with the equally disaffected Hadjeray of the east and with ethnic kinsmen in Darfur (where Déby raised his armies), the Zaghawa emerged triumphant in December 1990 when Déby marched into N'Djamena. Today most of the key posts in the government, the entire Garde Républicaine (q.v.), and many positions in Déby's other forces of repression are staffed by Zaghawa.

ZAKA. From the Arabic *zakat,* the *zaka* is the traditional 10 percent "Koranic tax" payable in kind to local chiefs especially in northern and eastern Chad. In some areas, including Kanem, despotic chiefs—including Kanem's Alifa (q.v.)—have extracted much more than this tithe, right into the contemporary era.

ZAKARIA, WAWA DAHAB (Major). Former minister of public works, mines, geology, and transport. Born in Ati, Zakaria joined the armed forces in 1964 and was trained locally and at Saint-Cyr at the Ecole Militaire Inter-Armes and attended supplemental courses at St. Maixient (for infantry officers) and Pau (paratroop officers). In 1969 he completed courses at the Ecole de Pilotage Avion at Dax, Cognac, and Toulouse. He was appointed to the Conseil Supérieur Militaire (q.v.) and became minister of public works after the coup of 1975. In mid-

1976 Zakaria was appointed aviation counselor to the chief of staff of the armed forces and was also named to the Commission de Défense Nationale (CDN) (q.v.) formed that year. Early in January 1977 he was promoted to major, and with Habré's entry into the Malloum (q.v.) government in 1978 Zakaria became commander of the air force, leaving the cabinet. He made his peace with Goukouni (q.v.) when the latter seized N'Djamena, and he was given charge of training the new unified national army. Zakaria was later retired from the army.

ZAKOUMA see PARC NATIONAL DE ZAKOUMA

ZAMTATO, GANAMBANG (Major). Little-known Sara officer who linked forces with Lt. Colonel Rodai (q.v.) and Habré's FAN (qq.v.) army to bring about the ouster of Kamougoué (q.v.) from his southern bastion and that region's delivery to central control under Habré. Heading a dissident FAT (q.v.) force, Zamtato personally took Doba from loyalist forces and later headed the assault that ousted Kamougoué from Sarh in August 1982. Zamtato, a former interim minister of justice, received military support for his troops from Habré's FAN. Zamtato was widely despised in the Sara south, being regarded as a traitor, especially when the FAN troops that moved into the south began a series of atrocities and pillaging. Though he expected political reward from Habré, Zamtato's aspirations were gratified instead in the military sphere with his appointment as deputy commander of the FANT (q.v.) forces in the southern préfectures. He was retired in 1989.

ZARIBA. "Encampment." A term that replaced "*zongo*" in Chad to refer to strangers' quarters, especially those of the Hausa. From the Arabic, referring to a stockage of thorn-bushes within which travelers congregate. In N'Djamena the size of the hajj (q.v.) or pilgrim inflow (see PILGRIMS) that utilizes the city as a major staring-out point—as well as colonial urban regulations—assured that the Hausa communities are scattered throughout the city. (See, for example, DJEMB EL-BAHR.)

The first *zariba* officially set up in the city was the Djemb el-Gato, near the river, where caravans from Cameroon used to cross. In Abéché the Hausa quarter (originally called Zariba Hausa, later Zariba Babalay [q.v.]) is much more compact, as is the Hausa community in that town. The bulk of Abéché's Hausa live within the *zariba*, and its economic importance has practically made it the focal point of town—"downtown," in essence, though it was originally an encampment on the outskirts of the town. The *zariba* has a distinctive Hausa atmosphere more reminiscent of northern Nigerian towns than of eastern

Chad. The main entrance faces the Jellaba mosque of Am Segu and has the decaying remains of the gatehouse of Hassan Babalay (q.v.), the Hausa founder (though not the first arrival) of the *zariba* that is now named after him. Some 2,500 Hausa now live in the Abéché *zariba,* though some estimates put the numbers lower. Its location is on the same plot of land originally granted to Hausa pilgrims in the early 1870s by Ouadai's Sultan Yusuf.

ZARIBA BABALAY. Hausa quarter in Abéché, originally called Zariba Hausa (see ZARIBA). The vast bulk of Abéché's Hausa reside in the *zariba* that was founded to cater to the needs of pilgrims (q.v.) on the way to Mecca. The quarter, which is the commercial center of the town, has a distinctive northern Nigerian flavor. Its main entrance faces the Jellaba mosque of Am Segu and has the decaying remains of the gatehouse of Hassan Babalay, founder of the *zariba,* who controlled the quarter and much of the trade in the town until his death in 1936.

ZAWAYA. Religious centers or chapter-houses established by the Sanusiya (q.v.) brotherhood at which religious and basic education was provided. In Chad these were set up in Borkou, Tibesti, and Kanem and were the strongholds of anti-French resistance, which was eventually brutally crushed. Capitalizing on the caravan routes (q.v.) to the south (to Kanem and Ouadai), the *zawayas* prospered from long-distance trade.

ZEBU. Breed of most of the cattle herded in Chad, adaptable to the harsh sub-Saharan climate.

ZEMI. Name of the large canoes of the Kotoko, master fishermen on the Chari-Logone and Lake Chad. Originally used also for raids, the canoes are up to 11 meters (36 feet) in length and can accommodate 20 to 25 people.

ZENE ALI FADEL, MAHAMAT (1929–). Former secretary of state, longtime deputy to the National Assembly and, more recently, Déby cabinet member. Born in 1929 in Djouna and by profession a transporter, Mahamat Zene Ali (as he is usually referred to) was PPT (q.v.) secretary for Salamat and in 1959 joined the National Assembly for the first time as deputy from Salamat. For several years secretary of the assembly's Bureau (1959–63), Zene Ali Fadel remained a deputy until 1969, though he was briefly purged in one of the periodic swoops on real or imagined anti-Tombalbaye (q.v.) opposition elements. In May 1971 he was appointed secretary of state attached to the presidency and served in that capacity until shortly before the 1975 coup d'état. Zene came back to prominence with Idriss Déby's (q.v.) rise to power in 1990, when he served as minister of livestock from March 1991 to May 1992, and again as minister of public health from October 1992 to April 1993, when the Conférence Nationale (q.v.) selected its own cabinet.

ZERZERTI, ALIFA AI. Current sultan of Kanem. A key traditional leader, in 1993 Zerzerti, a very imposing individual, had 11 wives and 45 children.

ZONGO see ZARIBA

ZOUAR. Tibesti (q.v.) capital of the derde (q.v.) of the Teda (q.v.). Also, during the Tombalbaye (q.v.) era, the important northern garrison town of the Chadian armed forces. The region is one of volcanic peaks of spectacular beauty, grottos of prehistoric cave drawings (q.v.), and small oases where the sparse populations of the region congregate. Zouar is 520 kilometers (322 miles) from Faya-Largeau (q.v.), the capital of Tibesti and of B.E.T. Zouar, in the Aouzou Strip (q.v.), was under Libyan and Goukouni (q.v.) control until 1986 and 1987, when it changed hands several times when the Teda and Goukouni became disenchanted with Libyan overlordship. It finally and definitively reverted to Chad in 1994 after the International Court of Justice ruled that the Aouzou Strip falls under Chadian sovereignty.

ZOUIA. One of the longest established Teda clans in Tibesti, inhabiting an area north of Bardai.

ZUBEIR PASHA, RAHMA MANSUR (1831–1913). Sudanese slave trader and conqueror of Darfur (q.v.), in whose forces Rabah (q.v.) fought prior to the latter's invasion of territories west of Darfur, in Chad. A Jalali (of the Nilotic Djimeab tribe), Zubeir first worked as an agent for an Egyptian trader before entering the slave and ivory trade on his own account. Very ambitious, Zubeir began penetrating regions previously untapped in the southwest of Sudan, developing a personal army of some 1,000 men with which he established absolute control over the Bahr-el-Ghazal. Developing trade outposts throughout the area, by 1865 he had a virtual monopoly over the slave trade, exporting up to 1,800 slaves annually. Though appointed by the Khedive in Cairo as official governor of the territory he had conquered (in exchange for a tribute paid in ivory), Zubeir rapidly came to be viewed as a threat to the Khedive's territorial ambitions in the area, especially when in 1874 Zubeir—at the head of a well-disciplined and trained army—defeated and conquered Darfur and made forays into Ouadai. (Despite this, the remnants of the local Keira dynasty in Darfur were only fully subjugated in 1916.) When Egypt proclaimed the region as its own, Zubeir was tricked into returning to Cairo to protest and was there prevented from returning to his empire in the south. He remained under virtual house arrest for some time, his conquering exploits being continued by his son, and later by Rabah. Between 1885 and 1887 Zubeir Pasha was interned by the British at Gibraltar (he had helped raise a force for the Mahdi), but he returned to Sudan in 1899 and settled as a wealthy landowner until his death in 1913.

Bibliography

As is true for much of francophone Africa, the student of Chad must rely to a large extent upon written material in French. With a few notable exceptions, the first books in English only began appearing in the 1970s. The bibliography that follows (which omits much of the more ephemeral material included in the second edition), though substantial, is not all-inclusive, and it emphasizes the social sciences in particular. It lists many of the English-language sources on Chad and a comprehensive selection of the more important literature in French and other European languages, arranged under a number of broad topical headings. Unlike in several other African states, few books or pamphlets of any substance are published in N'Djamena, and those that are, tend to be extremely difficult to trace or obtain abroad. (The exception is, of course, government material and publications of INTSH.) For this reason, only the most valuable and/or easily accessible locally published material is listed here. As a further guide to prospective researchers, the following very brief bibliographic comments might be of some use.

For general information on this region of Africa (the former Afrique Equatoriale Française) and/or Chad's role within its historical evolution, Balandier's book *The Sociology of Black Africa* is invaluable (see General Works), as are the works of Bovill, Cornevin, Gide, Hallett, and Thompson and Adloff. The substantial bibliography on archaeology and prehistory is merely a very selective sampling of the voluminous amount of material published on Chad's distant past. That so much has been written in this field is both a tribute to the many archaeological puzzles and gems in Chad (see ARCHAEOLOGY) and to the large number of world-renowned scholars who have devoted their energies to their discovery and deciphering. Even the archaeological neophyte can point out the significance of the various writings of Arkell, Coppens, Fuchs, Courtin, Griaule, Huard, Jean Paul Lebeuf, Lhote, and Mauny.

Published accounts of early missions of exploration tend sometimes to confuse the contemporary reader with data that are either contradictory, since disproved, or crowded with minutiae of lesser importance today. This has never been the case with the works by the two foremost explorers of the Chad region, Heinrich Barth and especially Gustav Nachtigal. The latter's multivolume *Sahara und Sudan* is now available

453

in English, with the expert translation and annotations by Allan and Humphrey Fisher; the volumes dealing with Nachtigal's trek from Fezzan to Bornu and, after side-trips, on to Ouadai and Egypt remain to this day invaluable, highly readable and vivid testimonials to an era barely past in Chad. One could also read with great profit the twin books by the French author André Gide, though these refer to his travels in the region in the early part of the 1920s.

The historical section of the bibliography encompasses a large number of works. Among those especially valuable are those by Boahen (whose work is seminal), Cohen (especially important for the study of Bornu, which is not thoroughly covered in this dictionary), Ferrandi (interesting for his summary, at times biased, of the French conquest of the region), Berre and Bret (who have helped open up the history of Dar Sila and the Daju), the Fishers, the two Gentils, Malval (whose work, flawed by the inclusion of trivia, gossip, and inaccuracies, still provides a useful chronological summary), P. Gentil (on the French campaigns in Chad), the Lebeufs, B. G. Martin, Palmer (*The Bornu, Sahara, and Sudan* is a classic), Pacques, Tubiana, Urvoy, and Zeltner. Also noteworthy are the works that attempt (Adeleye, Babikir) to rehabilitate the slave-raiding reputation of Rabah (descendants exist in the area) by casting him as an early anticolonialist hero, and the slow addition to the works (listed here, and under Religion) on the Franco-Sanussiya campaigns in the Sahara.

The range of anthropological-sociological works is especially comprehensive, though not every ethnic group or subject matter has received equal treatment by scholars (and some groups still remain relatively ignored). There is also a paucity of comparative studies and a nearly complete absence of comprehensive studies encompassing all the ethnic groups within the territorial limits of Chad. Among the best studies are those of the prolific Adler (see in particular his joint work with Zempleni, *Le Baton de l'Aveugle,* on the Moundang), d'Arbaumont, Bouquet, Briggs (whose work *Tribes of the Sahara,* along with Capot-Rey's *Le Sahara Français,* is seminal), Cabot, Jean Chapelle, Cline, Dumas-Champion on the Masa, Fuchs (whose important research is in German, which unfortunately limits his academic audience), Hagenbrucher's study of the Bulala, and Jaulin (especially his *La Mort Sara*).

The Lebeuf husband-wife team dominates many fields of research on Chad. Though somewhat dated, Annie Lebeuf's *Les Populations du Tchad* is still an excellent summary of the Sahelian ethnic groups, while her *Les Principautés Kotoko* is the seminal study of this ethnic group. She has also published widely in collaboration with other scholars and with her husband, Jean Paul Lebeuf. The latter's voluminous work is, of course, widely cited, and especially his *Etudes Kotoko.* Of prime importance also is Le Rouvreur's seminal *Saheliens et Sahariens du Tchad,* probably the best and most comprehensive compendium on Chad's northern and central ethnic groups, including their history. Though for long out of print, this monumental study and Le Cornec's equally widely cited study of Chadian politics in the colonial era (see the section on Politics) are the best introductory combinations for the novice on Chad. Le Rouvreur's focus on the Sahelian/Saharan ethnic groups (also the focus of the forementioned Annie Lebeuf book) can be supplemented, for the Sara south, by the excellent Lanne summary article. Pairault's rather specialized research also deserves to be noted as well as Pouillon's (especially his article on power among the Hadjeray, published in *L'Homme*) and the Tubianas' extremely voluminous research on the Zaghawa. Finally, one should note Harmattan's 1994 publication of the important recent INTSH colloquium on problems of Chadian identities, and Reyna's several studies of marriage, divorce, and family planning.

For those interested in politics and contemporary affairs, coverage in English is at last adequate, though for more detailed or in-depth insights French sources still remain vital. Of note are the various annuals that carry solid chapters on Chad, and the various periodicals and/or weeklies that provide intermittent coverage (*West Africa, Afrique Contemporaine, Politique Africaine.*) For sometimes remarkably detailed information, not easily available even in French sources, the fortnightly *Africa Confidential* is indispensable, though its coverage of Chad is intermittent. Unfortunately some former staple sources of information, such as the venerable *Revue Française d'Etudes Politiques Africaines* (also known as *Le Mois en Afrique*) and the annual *African Contemporary Record,* stopped publishing in the late 1980s. One should also note Ballard's brief, and by now dated, treatment of Chad in the joint chapter on the AEF states in Carter's *National Unity and Regionalism in Eight African States,* the important articles by Biarnes, Casteran, Decraene, Gueriviere, and Lemarchand (the latter in English).

Gonidec's slim, and dated, volume in the "Political and Constitutional" series on Africa, which he edited for Berger-Levrault, is useful for Chad's former constitutions and structures, as are many of the articles appearing in the French journals *Penant* and *Revue Juridique et Politique* (and in particular those by Seid). As previously noted, Le Cornec's *Histoire Politique du Tchad de 1900 à 1962* is seminal and without any competition. The study pays particular attention to Chad's traditional framework and provides a survey, in great detail, of the critical 1945 to 1960 years—replete with lists of assembly delegates and the like not available in any other secondary source.

As one approaches the more contemporary era, articles in English become plentiful. The Adloffs' *Conflict in Chad* is a good summary of the causes and evolution of the rebellion, as are Kelly's and Nolutshungu's books, also in English. However, the two extremely meticulously researched books by the modest Buijenhuijs are without peer, just as his third work, on Chad's 1993 national conference, is at present the only one available on this recent event. Finally, one must mention the well-prepared second edition of the *Area Handbook for Chad* (published by the U.S. Government Printing Office), which covers practically the entire range of subjects connected with Chad. Not only is it an invaluable work for all who must rely exclusively upon English sources for an understanding of Chad, but also it could well serve as the first work to be read.

In economics, a variety of annuals, periodicals, and official documents provide ongoing coverage of Chad. Among those one could note *Marchés Tropicaux et Méditerranéens,* the publications of the French government and the Bureau pour le Développement de la Promotion Agricole, and the "Etudes et Statistiques" series of the Banque des Etats de l'Afrique Centrale (formerly the BCEAEC). Bouquet's articles are also invaluable, as well as those by Cabot, the ORSTOM reports of Couty, and Diguimbayé's contributions. The latter, as minister of planning and coordination, edited the key—though now dated—*L'Essor du Tchad,* which contains valuable data and maps widely cited and used by other scholars and publications. Equally excellent summaries and surveys of Chad's economy are to be found in English as well, as in the International Monetary Fund's volume 1 of *Surveys of African Economies* (1968) and in the World Bank's booklet *Chad: Development Potential and Constraints* (1974) and more recent publications. (It should be noted that some of the statistics in the latter publications are difficult to reconcile with those provided in equally authoritative French studies or with data published in N'Djamena.)

In the area of scientific studies one should note in particular the numerous projects undertaken under the auspices of ORSTOM. (Most of the more technical works are not listed in the bibliography, but a comprehensive catalogue is available directly from N'Djamena or Paris.) Also of importance is the early work of Arnaud, Cabot's research on the Logone, Capot-Rey's *Borkou et Ounianga,* Beadle's *Inland Waters of Tropical Africa* (where, in jargon-free language, conditions in Lake Chad and Ounianga are presented), Le Coeur's research, the *Missions Berliet Ténéré-Tchad* report, the early but still very important three-volume *Documents Scientifiques de la Mission Tilho, 1906–1909,* and the publications of Pias, Servant, and Urvoy.

The literature on education in Chad has all along been sparse, but it is slowly being augmented. Of note is the interpretive analysis of Khayar, Clauss's book (in German), and Mbaisso's monographic survey of the educational field in general. Published work on religious themes has encompassed both traditional religion (see in particular the important work of Dalmais; that by Fuchs in German; and by Vincent in French) and Islam in Chad. Research on Islam was of particular interest to the local

French administration in light of ever-present fears of the resurgence of militant anti-French Islam. For some of the best work of this genre, see the various Mémoires of CHEAM, which are, unfortunately, quite difficult to refer to unless studied in Paris or duplicated from the original. Significantly more work on Islam has appeared in the last decade or so, and that of the Tubianas on the Zaghawa and Magnant's more general one are particularly useful.

André Clair has written/assembled various books and compendia of popular literature (he is, of course, especially known for his work on Niger), as have also Bebnoné and Fortier. In the field of linguistics, scholars still refer to the seminal work of Heinrich Barth. Of extreme importance is the meticulous and voluminous work by the two prolific Germans, Lukas and especially Jungraithmayr, by Le Coeur (on the Toubou), Roth-Laly (Chadic Arabic), Tubiana (Zaghawa and Mbaï), Caprile and Fortier (Mbaï), and Fedry (Dangléat), among others. There is also by now much specialized linguistic work in English, only part of which could be included here. In the field of Chadian art and music the work of Monique Brandily is solidly established. Also noteworthy is the handsome *L'Art Sao* published in 1972 by Editions Delroisse, a tribute to the artistic genius of the long-gone Sao.

Readers who wish to locate data and sources beyond what is provided in this dictionary will no doubt refer to the section on sources. For bibliographic data, especially recommended are the thorough and comprehensive publications of the Institut National Tchadien des Sciences Humaines (N'Djamena). These include the 1968 *Bibliographie du Tchad* (Sciences Humaines) by J. P. Lebeuf et al. and its 1974 supplement (M. M. Berief, *Complément à la Bibliographie du Tchad* (Sciences Humaines), and Jean Chapelle's 1968 *Documents du Dépôt Officiel d'Archives de Fort-Lamy*—all of which are among the best of their kind published by any public or private organ in Africa. For comprehensive bibliographic searches, these should be supplemented by reference to the standard sources of ongoing Africana bibliography available in most large academic libraries. For biographical or economic references, the former EDIAFRIC directories (the press is now defunct) were unequalled, though they did not always provide more than the minimum detail required by scholars.

Finally, for general sources on Chad's political and economic evolution, a number of staple publications can be recommended, most of which have been mentioned previously. These are, in particular, *Africa Research Bulletin* (both series), *West Africa, Politique Africaine, Africa Confidential,* and BEAC's "Etudes et Statistiques" series.

The books and articles in this bibliography have been organized under the following subject headings:

General Works

Balandier, Georges. *The Sociology of Black Africa.* New York: Praeger, 1970.

Bangui, Antoine. *Les ombres de Koh.* Paris: Hatier, 1984.

Bary, Erika de. *Die Flammenbäüme. Erlebtes vom Fezzan bis Kamerun.* Herranalb, Schwarzwald: Erdmann, 1966.

Berrier, J. C., and R. Denizet. *Hauts lieux d'Afrique: L'expédition française Tibesti-Congo-Ethiopie.* Paris: Amiot-Dumont, 1953.

Blanc, Paul. "A Propos des migrations dans l'ancienne Afrique Française." *Afrique et Asie,* no. 54, 1961, pp. 16–36.

Boulanger, Daniel. *Tchadiennes.* Paris: Gallimard, 1965.

Bourges, Hervé, and Claude Wauthier. *Les 50 Afriques.* Paris: Le Seuil, 1979.

Bovill, E. W. *The Golden Trade of the Moors.* London: Oxford University Press, 1958.

Bruel, Georges. *La France Equatoriale Africaine.* Paris: Larose, 1935.

Burthe d'Annelet, Col. de. *A travers l'Afrique Française.* 2 vols. Paris: Larose, 1932.

Cervenka, Z. *Land-locked Countries of Africa.* Uppsala: Scandinavian Institute of African Studies, 1973.

Chasseloup Laubat, F. de. "Le lac Tchad, route impériale?" *Revue des Deux Mondes,* 56, no. 7, 1940, pp. 503–32.

Cornevin, Robert. *Histoire de l'Afrique.* Paris: Payot, 1966.

Delafosse, M. *Les Sociétés primitives de l'Afrique Equatoriale.* Paris: Société Française d'Imprimerie et de Librairie, 1911.

Deschamps, Hubert. *L'Europe découvert l'Afrique.* Paris: Editions Berger-Levrault, 1967.

Dorato, M. "Il Lago Ciad e le terre ai confini meridionali della Libia." *Rivista delle colonie,* vol. 11, no. 2, 1973, pp. 161–74.

"Enquête pour un film contre l'impérialisme français." *Cinéthique,* vol. 15, no. 3, 1972, pp. 1–30.

France. Ministère des Affaires Etrangères. *Niger et Tchad.* Paris: Cussac, 1918.

Gide, André. *Kongo und Tschad.* Stüttgart: Deutsche Verlags Anstalt, 1930.

———. *Le retour du Tchad.* Paris: Gallimard, 1928.

Guernier, Eugène (ed.). *Afrique Equatoriale Française: Encyclopédie Coloniale et Maritime.* Paris: Encyclopédie Coloniale et Maritime, 1950.

Haardt, G. M., and L. Audouin-Dubreuil. *Across the Sahara by Motor Car.* New York: D. Appleton and Company, 1924.

Hallett, Robin. *Africa to 1875: A Modern History.* Ann Arbor: University of Michigan Press, 1970.

Hance, William A. *Geography of Modern Africa.* New York: Columbia University Press, 1967.

Hanotaux, G., and A. Martineau. *Histoire des colonies françaises.* 6 vols. Paris: Plon, 1932.

Helfritz, Hans. *Schwarze Ritter zwischen Niger und Tschad: ein Reisebericht von Westafrika.* Berlin: Safari-Verlag, 1958.

Heseltine, Nigel. *From Libyan Sands to Chad.* London: Museum Press, 1960.

Histoire et épopée des troupes coloniales. Paris: Presses Modernes, 1956.

Kimble, George H. T. *Tropical Africa.* New York: Twentieth Century Fund, 1960.

Lapie, Pierre Olivier. *My Travels through Chad.* London: J. Murray, 1943.

Maquet, E., I. B. Kake, and J. Suret-Canale. *Histoire de l'Afrique centrale des origines au milieu du 20ᵉ siècle.* Paris: Présence Africaine, 1971.

Maran, René. *Le Tchad de sable et d'or.* Paris: Alexis Rédier, 1931.

Martel, André. "Pour une histoire du Sahara français." *Revue Française d'Histoire d'Outre-Mer,* vol. 55, no. 200, 1968, pp. 335–51.

Paluel-Marmont, Albert. *Rendez-vous au Tchad.* Paris: Larousse, 1952.

Salacuse, J. W. *An Introduction to Law in French-Speaking Africa.* Vol. 1, *Africa South of the Sahara.* Charlottesville, VA: The Michie Company, 1969.

Sophie, Ulrich. *Le gouverneur-général Félix Eboué.* Paris: Larose, 1950.

Soret, M. *La carte ethnique de l'A.E.F.* Paris, ORSTOM. 1957.

Stride, G. T., and Caroline Ifeka. *Peoples and Empires of West Africa.* New York: Africana, 1971.

Suret-Canale, Jean. *Afrique noire occidentale et centrale: De la colonisation aux indépendances.* 2 vols. Paris: Editions Sociales, 1972.

——. *French Colonialism in Tropical Africa, 1900–1945.* London: C. Hurst and Company, 1964.

Susset, Raymond. *La vérité sur le Cameroun et l'A.E.F.* Paris: Editions de la Nouvelle Revue Critique, 1934.

Swann, Alfred J. *Fighting the Slave-Hunters in Central Africa.* London: Frank Cass and Company, 1969.

Tchad. Service de l'Information. *L'Essentiel sur le Tchad.* Paris: 1960.

"Le Tchad." Special issue of *Vivant Univers,* May–June, 1978.

Temple, O.S.M. *Chiefs and Cities of Central Africa: Across Lake Chad by Way of Britain, French, and German Territories.* Freeport, NY: Books for Libraries Press, 1971.

Tenaille, Franck. *Les 56 Afriques.* 2 vols. Paris: Maspero, 1979.

"Terre d'Afrique: Le Tchad." *Nations Nouvelles,* No. 4, May 1965, pp. 19–27.

Tersen, Emile. *Histoire de la colonisation française.* Paris: Presses Universitaires de France, 1950.

Thompson, Virginia M., and Richard Adloff. *The Emerging States of French Equatorial Africa.* Stanford: Stanford University Press, 1960.

Trézenem, Edouard. *L'Afrique Equatoriale Française.* Paris: Editions Maritimes et Coloniales, 1955.

Tschad. Stuttgart: W. Kolhammer, 1964.

Vezinet, General. *Le Général Leclerc de Hautecloque, Maréchal de France.* Paris: Presses de la Cité, 1974.

Zieglé, Henri. *L'Afrique Equatoriale Française.* Paris: Berger-Levrault, 1952.

Archaeology and Prehistory

Adams, L. J., and G. Tetzlaff. "Did Lake Chad Exist around 18,000 B.C.?" *Archives for Meteorology, Geophysics, and Bioclimatology* (Vienna), vol. 34, no. 3, 1984, pp. 299–308.

Alionen, H. *Préhistoire de l'Afrique.* Paris: N. Boubée, 1955.

Alverny, F. d'. "Vestiges d'art rupestre au Tibesti oriental." *Journal de la Société des Africanistes,* vol. 20, no. 2, 1950, pp. 239–72.

Arkell, A. J. "The Aterian of Great Wanyanga." *Actes du 4ᵉ Congrès Panafricain de Préhistoire,* 1962, pp. 233–342.

——. "Preliminary Report on the Archaeological Result of the British Ennedi Expedition 1957." *Kush* (Khartoum), vol. 7, 1959, pp. 15–26.

——. *Wanyanga and an Archaelogical Reconnaissance of the South West Libyan Desert: The British Ennedi Expedition 1957.* London: Oxford University Press, 1964.

Ba, Amadou Hampaté, and G. Diéterlen. "Les fresques d'époque bovidienne du Tassili, N'Ajjer et les traditions des Peul: Hypothèses d'interprétation," *Journal de la Société des Africanistes,* 36, i, 1966, pp. 141–57.

Bailloud, G. "L'évolution des styles céramiques en Ennedi (République du Tchad)." *Actes du Premier Colloque International d'Archéologie Africaine, Fort-Lamy, 1966.* Fort-Lamy: Institut National Tchadien pur les Sciences Humaines, 1969.

———. "Les peintures rupestres archaiques de l'Ennedi (Tchad)" *L'Anthropologie,* vol. 64, no. 3/4, 1960, pp. 211–34.

Beck, P., and P. Huard. *Tibesti, carrefour de la préhistoire saharienne.* Paris: Arthaud, 1969.

Beltrami, Vanni. "Arte parietale dello Djado e delle regioni prossime al margine occidentale del Tibesti." *Africa* (Rome), vol. 44, no. 3, 1989, pp. 445–72.

Bodin, V. "Examen de fragments de terre cuite provenant de la région du Tchad" *Etudes Camerounaises,* vol. 2, no. 49, March–June 1978, pp. 25–26.

Bonnet, A. "Les gravures rupestres de Niola Doha en Ennedi et les peintures corporelles actuelles de certaines tribus du Soudan nilotique." *Actes du 6e Congrès International des Sciences Anthropologiques et Ethnologiques,* vol. 1, II, 1963.

Bottcher, U., P. J. Ergenzinger, S. H. Jaeckel, and K. Kaiser. "Quartare Seebildungen und ihre Mollusken-Inhalte im Tibesti-Gebirge und seinen Rahmenbereichen der Zentralen Ostsahara." *Zeitschrift für Geomorphologie,* N.F., 16, 2, 1972, pp. 182–234.

Bouesnard, L., and R. Mauny. "Gravures rupestres et sites néolithiques des abords est de l'Aïr," *Bulletin de l'IFAN,* 24(B), 1/2, January–April 1962, pp. i–ii.

Camps-Fabrer, Henriette. *Matière et art mobilier dans la préhistoire nord-africaine et saharienne.* Paris: Arts et Métiers Graphiques, 1966.

Capot-Rey, R. "Découvertes archéologiques au Borkou." *Travaux de l'Institut de Recherches Sahariennes* (Algiers), vol. 17, 1958, pp. 203–5.

———. "Premiers effets des forages artésiens au Borkou." *Travaux de l'Institut de Recherches Sahariennes,* no. 24, 1965, pp. 171–76.

———. "Le Vent et le modèle éolien au Borkou." *Travaux de l'Institut de Recherches Sahariennes,* vol. 15, no. 1, 1957, pp. 149–57.

Carpenter, Rhys. "A Trans-Saharan Caravan Route in Herodotus." *Journal of American Archeology,* vol. 60, 1956, pp. 231–42.

Carrique, A. "Notice sur la ville inconnue découverte à N'Galaka." *Journal de la Société des Africanistes,* vol. 5, no. 1, 1935, pp. 85–92.

Cartier, J.A. "Fresques du Tchad." *France-Eurafrique,* no. 159, February 1965, pp. 43–44.

Connah, G. *Three Thousand Years in Africa: Man and His Environment in the Lake Chad Region of Nigeria.* London: Cambridge University Press, 1981.

Coppens, Yves. "L'Afrique Equatoriale: Une étape de l'histoire de l'humanité." *Cahiers d'Explorateurs,* no. 19, December 1967, pp. 18–19.

―――. "Les cultures protohistoriques et histoires du Djourab." *Actes du Premier Colloque Internationale d'Archéologie Africaine.* Fort-Lamy: Institut National Tchadien pour les Sciences Humaines, 1969.

―――. "Découverte d'un Australopithécine dans le villafranchien du Tchad." *Comptes Rendu de l'Académie de Sciences,* vol. 251, 1960, pp. 2385–86.

―――. "Deux Gisements de vertébrés villafranchiennes au Tchad: Note paléontologique." In G. Mortelmans and J. Nenquin (eds.), *Actes du 4e Congrès Panafricain de Préhistoire et de l'Etude du Quaternaire.* Tervuren: Musée Royal de l'Afrique Centrale, 1962, pp. 299–315.

―――. "An Early Hominid from Chad." *Current Anthropology,* vol. 7, December 1966, pp. 584–85.

―――. "L'époque Haddadienne." *Revista de Faculdade de Letras,* vol. 9, no. 9, 1965, pp. 3–8.

―――. "La paléontologie au Tchad, *Sao,* no. 5, January 1972, pp. 5–8.

―――. "Les Proboscidiens du Tchad: Leur contribution à la chronologie du quaternaire africain." In *Actas del V Congreso Panafricano de Prehistoria y de Estudio del Cuaternario.* Santa Cruz de Tenerife: Publicaciones del Museo Arqueologico, 1965, pp. 331–87.

―――. "Le Tchadanthropus." *L'Anthropologie,* vol. 70, 1966, pp. 5–16.

Courtin, J. "Cabrets préhistoriques en quartz au Borkou." *Bulletin de la Société Préhistorique Française,* vol. 62, no. 4, April 1965, pp. 543–601.

―――. "Découverte de harpons en os au Borkou." *Bulletin de la Société Préhistorique Française,* vol. 62, no. 2, February 1965, pp. 120–25.

―――. "Découverte d'un sanctuaire Sao à Fort-Lamy, Tchad." *West African Archaeological Newsletter* (Ibadan), vol. 6, 1967, pp. 20–22.

―――. "Engins de pêche du Nord Tchad." *Travaux de l'Institut de Recherches Sahariennes* (Algiers), no. 26, 1967, pp. 103–111.

―――. "Le néolithique du Borkou, Nord-Tchad." *L'Anthropologie,* vol. 70, no. 3/4, 1966, pp. 263–81.

―――. "Pierres de pluie du pays Sara." *Bulletin de la Société Préhistorique Française,* vol. 62, no. 4, April 1965, pp. 535–38.

―――. "Récentes découvertes préhistoriques et protohistoriques au Tchad." *West African Archaeological Newsletter* (Ibadan), vol. 6, 1967, pp. 17–19.

―――. "La sanctuaire 'Sao' de Bait-al-Kabir." *Bulletin de la Société Préhistorique Française,* vol. 62, no. 2, March 1965, pp. 5–503.

―――. "Sites préhistoriques du Borkou." *Bulletin de la Société Préhistorique Françoise,* vol. 61, no. 6, June 1964, pp. 528–31.

―――. "La Ténéréen du Borkou, Nord Tchad." *La Préhistoire, Problèmes et Tendances.* Paris: CNRS, 1968, pp. 133–38.

Delibrias, G., et al. "Trois datations de sediments sahariens récents par le radiocarbone." *Libyca,* vol. 6, 1959, pp. 267–70.

De Neufville, Richard L., and Arthur A. Houghton. "A Description of Ain Farah and of Wara." *Kush* (Khartoum), no. 13, 1965, pp. 195–204.

Denis, P. "Pendeloques en pierre polie chez les pasteurs tchadiens." *Notes Africains,* no. 114, 1967, pp. 69–70.

Essomba, J. M. "L'archéologie et le problème de chronologie du fer aux abords sud du Lac Tchad." *Afrika Zamani* (Yaoundé), no. 6/7, December 1977, pp. 1–11.

Fagan, B. M. "Radiocarbon dates for sub-Saharan Africa." *Journal of African History,* vol. 8, 1967.

Fantin, Mario. "Graffiti del Tibesti." *Universo,* vol. 44, no. 6, November/December 1964, pp. 1005–30.

Forkl, Hermann. *Die Beziehungen der zentralsudanischen Reiche Bornu, Mandara und Bagirmi sowie der Kotoko-Staaten zu ihren sudlichen Nachbarn unter besonderer Berucksichtigung des Sao-Problems.* Munich: Minerva, 1983.

Fuchs, Peter. "Felsmalereien und Felsgravuren in Tibesti, Borku und Ennedi." *Archiv für Volkerkunde,* vol. 12, 1957, pp. 110–35.

Gabriel, B. "Bauelemente praislamischer Grabertypen im Tibesti-Gebirge." *Acta Prehistorica et Archaeologica,* vol. 1, 1970, pp. 1–28.

Gaden, H., and R. Verneau. "Stations et sépultures néolithiques des territoires du Tchad." *L'Anthropologie,* vol. 30, 1920, pp. 513–43.

Griaule, Marcel. "Les Sao légendaires." *La Revue de Paris,* September 15, 1937, pp. 321–56.

———. *Les Sao légendaires.* Paris: Gallimard, 1943.

Griaule, Marcel, and Jean Paul Lebeuf. "Fouilles dans la région du Tchad." *Journal de la Société des Africanistes,* vol. 18, 1948, pp. 1–116; vol. 20, 1950, pp. 1–151; vol. 21, 1951, pp. 1–95.

Hamelin, Pierre. "Les bronzes du Tchad." *Tribus,* no. 11, 1952/53, pp. 379–99.

Hartweg, R., and F. Trienen. "Ossements anciens de Mdaga." *Etudes et Documents Tchadiens,* vol. 2, 1967, pp. 35–39.

Hermann, B., and B. Gabriel. "Untersuchungen an vorgeschichtlischen skeletten-material aus dem Tibesti-Gebirge." *Berliner Geographischen Abhandlungen,* vol. 16, 1972, pp. 143–52.

Huard, Paul. "L'age pastoral au Tibesti" *Notre Sahara,* no. 10, January 1959; no. 12, July 1960.

———. "A propos de deux objets modernes du Tchad en cuivre coulé à la cire perdue." *Odu,* vol. 1, no. 1, 1964, pp. 59–61.

———. "A propos des bucranes à corne deformée de Faras." *Kush,* vol. 12, 1964, pp. 63–81.

———. "Archéologie et zoologie: Contributions à l'étude du Sahara oriental et central." *Bulletin de l'IFAN,* vol. 24, no. 1/2, 1962, pp. 86–104.

———. "Art rupestre au Tchad." *Encyclopédie Mensuelle d'Outre-Mer,* no. 39, 1953, pp. 313–17.

———. "Contribution à l'étude des prémiers travaux agraires au Sahara Tchadien." *Bulletin de la Société Préhistorique Française,* vol. 67, no. 2, 1970, pp. 539–58.

———. "Contribution à l'étude du cheval, du fer, et du chameau au Sahara oriental." *Bulletin de l'IFAN,* 22 (B), 1/2, January–April 1960, pp. 134–78.

———. "La datation de squelettes néolithiques, post-néolithiques, et pré-Islamiques du Nord Tibesti." *Bulletin de la Société Préhistorique Française,* vol. 70, 1973, pp. 100–102.

———. "Etat des recherches rupestres au Tchad." *Tropiques,* no. 345, August/September 1952, pp. 41–45.

———. "Etat des recherches sur les rapports entre cultures anciennes du Sahara Tchadien, du Nubie, et du Soudan." *Bibliotheca Orientalis,* vol. 21, no. 5/6, September–November 1964, p. 289.

———. "La faune disparue du Tibesti." *Vétérinaires,* July–October, 1953.

———. "Les figurations d'animaux à disques frontaux et attributs rituels au Sahara oriental." *Bulletin de l'IFAN,* 23 (B), 3/4, July–October 1961, pp. 476–517.

———. "Gravures et peintures rupestres du Borkou." *Bulletin de la Société des Etudes Centrafricaines,* no. 6, 1953, pp. 149–60.

———. "Les gravures rupestres de Gonoa (Tibesti)." *Tropiques,* no. 346, October 1952, pp. 38–46.

———. "Gravures rupestres de l'Ennedi et des Erdis." *Bulletin de l'Institut de Recherches Scientifiques au Congo* (Brazzaville), vol. 2, 1963, pp. 25–39.

———. "Gravures rupestres des confins nigéro-tchadiens." *Bulletin de l'IFAN,* vol. 15, no. 4, 1953, pp. 1569–81.

———. "Les gravures rupestres d'Oudingueur." *Tropiques,* no. 360, March 1954, pp. 35–45.

———. "Gravures rupestres du Tibesti." *Magazine de l'Afrique du Nord* (Algiers), June 1953.

———. "Influences culturelles transmises au Sahara tchadien par le Groupe C. de Nubie." *Kush* (Khartoum), 15, 1970.

———. Introduction et diffusion du fer au Tchad." *Journal of African History,* vol. 7, no. 3, 1966, pp. 377–404.

———. "Les mains à doigt manquant du incomplet sur les peintures rupestres du Tibesti." *Bulletin de la Société Préhistorique Française,* vol. 65, no. 1, January 1968, pp. 19–20.

———. "Nouvelle contribution à l'étude du fer au Sahara et au Tchad." *Bulletin de l'IFAN,* 26 (B), 3/4, July–October 1964, pp. 297–396.

———. "Nouvelles figurations sahariennes et nilo-soudanaises de boeufs porteurs, montés et attéles." *Bulletin de la Sociéte Préhistorique Française,* vol. 65, no. 4, April 1968, pp. 14–20.

———. "Nouvelles gravures rupestres du Djado, de l'Afafi, et du Tibesti." *Bulletin de l'IFAN,* vol. 19, no. 1/2, 1957, pp. 184–223.

———. "Nouvelles peintures rupestres du Tibesti oriental." *Actes du 6ᵉ Congrès Panafricain de Préhistoire, Dakar 1967.* Chambery: Imprimeries Réunies de Chambery, 1972, pp. 199–206.

———. "Les peintures rupestres du Tchad." *Encyclopédie Mensuelle d'Outre-Mer,* no. 71/72, July–August 1956, pp. 317–20.

———. "Préhistoire et archéologie au Tchad." *Bulletin de l'Institut des Etudes Centrafricaines,* no. 17/18, 1959, pp. 5–20.

———. *Recherches rupestres au Tchad.* Paris: Tropiques, 1953.

———. "Répertoire des stations rupestres du Sahara oriental français (Confins Nigéro-Tchadiens-Tibesti-Borkou-Ennedi)." *Journal de la Société des Africanistes,* vol. 23, no. 1/2, 1953, pp. 43–76.

———. "Le Tibesti des chasseurs." *Notre Sahara,* no. 7, January 1959.

Huard, Paul, G. Breaud, and J. M. Massip. "Répertoire des sites paléolithiques du Sahara central, tchadien, et oriental." *Bulletin de l'IFAN,* vol. 31(B), no. 3, 1969, pp. 853–74.

Huard, Paul, and Jean-Claude Feval. "Figurations rupestres des confins algéro-nigéro-tchadiens." *Travaux de l'Institut de Recherches Sahariennes,* 23, 1/2, 1964, pp. 61–94.

Huard, Paul, and Christian Le Masson. "Peintures rupestres du Tibesti oriental et méridional." *Objets et Mondes,* vol. 4, no. 4, Winter 1964, pp. 237–62.

Huard, Paul, and Jean Marie Massip. "Gravures rupestres du Tibesti méridional et du Borku." *Bulletin de la Société Préhistorique Française,* vol. 60, no. 7/8, 1963, pp. 468–81.

———. "Gravures rupestres de Ye Lulu Loga." *Bulletin de la Société Préhistorique Française,* vol. 61, no. 8, 1964, pp. 192–97.

———. "Harpons en os et céramiques à decor au Sahara tchadien." *Bulletin de la Société Préhistorique Française,* vol. 61, no. 1, 1964, pp. 105–23.

———. "Monuments du Sahara nigéro-tchadien: 1. Grands cercles et pièrres levées." *Bulletin de l'IFAN,* vol. 29(B), no. 1/2, January–April 1967, pp. 1–27.

———. "Nouveaux centres de peintures rupestres au Sahara nigéro-tchadien." *Bulletin de l'IFAN,* vol. 28(B), no. 1/2, January–April 1966, pp. 44–81.

———. "Nouveaux groupes de grands personnages du style gravé de Guirchi Nialadoia (Ennedi)." *Actes du prèmier Colloque International d'Archéologie Africaine, Fort-Lamy, 1966.* Fort-Lamy: Institut National Tchadien pour les Sciences Humaines, 1969, pp. 210–23.

Huard, Paul, et al. "Grands outils de pierre polie du Sahara nigéro-tchadien." *Bulletin de la Société Préhistorique Française,* vol. 65, no. 2, February 1968, pp. 629–41.

———. "Matériaux pour l'étude de l'age du fer au Djourab (Tchad)." *Bulletin de l'IFAN,* vol. 25(B), no. 3/4, July–October 1963, pp. 435–51.

Hugot, Henri (ed.). *Missions Berliet Ténéré-Tchad. Documents Scientifiques.* Paris: Arts et Métiers Graphiques, 1962.

Humbert, Jean-Charles. *Sahara: Les traces de l'homme.* Paris: R. Chaband, 1989.

Institut de Sociologie Solvay. "Recherches d'ethno-archéologie dans la République du Tchad (10e Mission Lebeuf)." *Revue de l'Institut de Sociologie Solvay,* no. 1, 1960, pp. 174–75.

Lapparent, A. F., and H. Breuil. "Le massif montagneux de l'Ennedi et les danseuses préhistoriques de Niola Doa." *Cahiers d'Art,* 1956, p. 16.

Lebeuf, A., and J. P. Lebeuf. "Monuments symboliques du palais royal de Logone-Birni." *Journal de la Société des Africanistes,* vol. 25, 1955, p. 25–34.

Lebeuf, A.M.D. "Enceintes de briques de la région tchadienne." *Actes du 4e Congrès Panafricain de Préhistoire,* Tervuren, 1962, pp. 437–43.

Lebeuf, Jean Paul. "Afrique et histoire." *Le Sao* (Fort-Lamy), no. 1, 1967, pp. 3–12.

———. *Archéologie tchadienne: les Sao du Cameroun et du Tchad.* Paris: Hermann, 1962.

———. "Beyond the Lake Chad." *Geographical Magazine,* January 1953, pp. 434–43.

———. "Une boîte à antimoine." *Notes Africaines,* no. 18, April 1943, p. 8.

———. "Boules de pierres de la région tchadienne." *Notes Africaines,* no. 59, July 1953, pp. 67–68.

———. "Bracelets anthropomorphes de Gawi." *Homme,* vol. 5, no. 2, June 1965, pp. 125–26.

———. *Carte archéologique des abords du Lac Tchad (Cameroun, Niger, Tchad).* Paris: Centre National de la Recherche Scientifique, 1969.

———. "Une civilisation disparue." *Afrique Equatoriale,* no. 4–5, December 1956, pp. 36–39.

———. "Les collections archéologiques du Tchad au Musée de l'Homme," *Bulletin, Musée National d'Histoire Naturelle,* vol. 14, no. 2, 1942, pp. 100–105.

———. "Essai de chronologie Sao." *Actes du Premier Colloque International d'Archéologie Africaine, Fort-Lamy, 1966.* Fort-Lamy: Institut National Tchadien pour les Sciences Humaines, 1969, pp. 231–41.

———. "Fouilles archéologiques dans la région du Tchad." *Zaïre* no. 5, May 1947, pp. 543–53.

———. "Mission Logone–Lac Fitri." *Anthropologie,* vol. 53, 1949, pp. 156–58.

———. "Nouvelle découvertes archéologiques à Fort-Lamy (République du Tchad)." *West African Archaeological Newsletter,* no. 4, March 1966, pp. 29–30.

———. "Petits objets de terre cuite du Tchad." *Notes Africaines,* no. 55, July 1955, p. 69.

———. "Prehistory, Proto-History, and History in Chad." *Journal of the Historical Society of Nigeria,* vol. 2, no. 4, December 1963, pp. 593–601. (Also in Boun and Crowder [eds.], *Proceedings of the First International Congress of Africanists.* London: Longmans, 1964, pp. 72–81.)

———. "Recherches d'ethno-archéologie dans la République du Tchad," *Africa,* vol. 30, no. 2, April 1960.

———. "Signification de la céramique Sao (Tchad)." *Comptes Rendus des Séances Académie des Inscriptions et Belles-Lettres,* Paris, 1960, pp. 394–405.

———. "The Site of Warra." *Journal of the Historical Society of Nigeria,* vol. 2/3, December 1962, pp. 396–99.

———. "Terres cuites du Tchad." *Tropiques,* no. 322, June 1950, pp. 35–37.

———. "Les travaux de la mission Lebeuf, 1949–50 en AEF." *Bulletin d'Information de la Ministère de la France d'Outre-Mer,* November 1950, pp. 6–7.

Lebeuf, Jean Paul, and Johannes Hermann Immo Kirsch. *Oura, ville perdue.* Paris: Editions Recherches sur les Civilisations, 1989.

Lebeuf, Jean Paul, and A. Masson Detourbet. *La civilisation du Chad, suivi d'une étude sur les bronzes Sao.* Paris: Payot, 1950.

———. "A Newly Discovered Bronze Culture from the Shores of Lake Chad." *Illustrated London News,* June 23, 1951.

———. "Nouvelles découvertes au Tchad." *France Illustration,* May 21, 1949.

———. "Sao et Kotoko livrent leurs secrets." *La Documentation Française,* 1952, pp. 84–95.

———. "Le site de Tago (Tchad)." *Préhistoire,* vol. 11, 1950, pp. 143–92.

———. "Strange Sculpture of Lake Chad." *Illustrated London News,* December 17, 1949.

Lebeuf, Jean Paul, et al. *Le gisement Sao de Mdaga.* Paris: Klinchsieck, 1981.

Lelubre, M. "Contribution à la préhistoire du Sahara: Les peintures rupestres du Dohone (Tibesti nord-oriental)." *Bulletin de la Société Préhistorique Française,* vol. 45, no. 5, 1948, pp. 163–71.

Lhote, Henri. "Au sujet du port du voile chez les Tuareg et les Teda." *Notes Africaines,* no. 52, October 1951, pp. 108–111.

————. "La Mission Berliét-Ténéré." *Europe-Outremer,* no. 263, February 1960, pp. 20–23.

————. "Les peintures parietales de l'Ennedi." *Bulletin de la Société Préhistorique Française,* vol. 58, no. 1, January 1966, pp. 34–40.

————. "Le peuplement du Sahara néolithique d'après l'interprétation des gravures et des peintures rupestres." *Journal de la Société des Africanistes,* 40, no. 2, 1970, pp. 91–102.

————. "Route antique de Sahara central." *Encyclopédie Mensuelle d'Outre-Mer,* no. 15, 1951, pp. 300–315.

————. "Saharan Rock Art." *Natural History,* vol. 69, no. 6, June–July 1960, pp. 28–43.

Lhote, Henri, and Yves Lorelle. "Tchad: La Vie depuis 6 millions d'années sans discontinuité." *France Eurafrique,* no. 216, April–May 1970, pp. 39–43.

Masson Detourbet, A. *Le Kotoko, citadins, et pêcheurs de la région tchadienne.* Lagos: Nigerian Museum, 1956.

————. "Le passé de la plaine du Tchad." *Tropiques,* no. 328, January 1951, pp. 58–61.

————. "Recherches archéologiques dans la région du Tchad 1949–1950." *Encyclopédie Mensuelle d'Outre-Mer,* no. 4, 1950, pp. 96–98.

Mauny, Raymond. "Une belle performance française: La mission Berliét-Ténéré." *Tropiques,* no. 426, March 1960, pp. 10–17.

————. "Un harpon en os du Tchad." *Bulletin de la Société Préhistorique Française,* vol. 49, no. 10, 1952, pp. 469–71.

————. "Objets subactuels en fer trouvés en pays Teda et à l'est de l'Aïr." *Notes Africaines IFAN,* no. 97, January 1963, pp. 24–25.

————. "Poteries engobées et peintures de tradition nilotique de la région de Koro Toro (Tchad)." *Bulletin de l' IFAN,* vol. 25(B), no. 1/2, January–April 1963, pp. 39–46.

Moreau, J., and D. Stordeur. "Un lissoir de potière arabe du Tchad." *Notes Africaines,* no. 126, April 1970, pp. 51–52.

Muzzolini, Alfred. *L'art rupestre préhistorique des massifs centraux sahariens.* Oxford: BAR, 1986.

Ngouanken, Tchoumba. *Autour du Lac Tchad.* Paris: Harmattan, 1980.

Pales, Léon. "Découverte d'un important gisement préhistorique à Fort-Lamy." *Journal de la Société des Africanistes,* vol. 7, 1937, pp. 125–72.

Passemard, E., and H. De Saint-Floris. "Les peintures rupestres de l'Ennedi." *Journal de la Société des Africanistes,* vol. 5, 1935, pp. 97–112.

Petit, J. "Une mission ethnographique et archéologique au Tibesti." *Travaux de l'Institut de Recherches Sahariennes,* vol. 17, 1958, pp. 219–20.

Posnansky, Merrick, and Roderick McIntosh. "New Radiocarbon Dates for Northern and Western Africa." *Journal of African History,* vol. 17, no. 2, 1976, pp. 161–65.

Quechon, G. "Vers une préhistoire de la mort." In *Sciences et Avenir,* 1971, pp. 84–95.

"Recherches d'ethno-archéologie dans la République du Tchad." *Revue de l'Institut Sociologique* (Brussels), vol. 1, 1960, pp. 174–75.

Regelsperger, G. "Du Niger au Tchad: La Mission Tilho." *Mois Coloniale et Maritime,* vol. 1, 1909, pp. 97–109.

Rivallain, J., and W. Van Neer. "Inventaire du matériel archéologique et faunique de Koyam, Sud du Tchad." *L'Anthropologie,* vol. 88, no. 2, 1984, pp. 441–48.

Robert-Chaleix, Denise. *Tegdaoust: Recherches sur Aoudaghost.* Paris: Recherches sur les Civilisations, 1989.

Roset, J. P. "Contribution à la connaissance du peuplement néolithique et protohistorique du Tibesti. *Cahiers ORSTOM,* vol. 11, no. 1, 1974, pp. 47–84.

———. *Quatre Sépultures pré-islamiques dans la région de Zouar (Tibesti).* Fort-Lamy: Office de la Recherche Scientifique et Technique Outre-Mer, 1968.

Saxon, Douglas Esche. "The History of the Shari River Basin ca. 500 B.C.–1000 A.D." Ph.D. diss., University of California, Los Angeles, 1980.

Schneider, J. L. "Evolution du dernier lacustre et peuplements préhistoriques aux pays-bas du Tchad." In *Actes du Premier Colloque International d'Archéologie Africaine, Fort-Lamy, 1966.* Fort-Lamy: Institut National Tchadien pour les Sciences Humaines, 1969.

Servant, Michel. *Séquences continentales et variations climatiques: Evolution du bassin du Tchad au Cénozolque supérieur.* Paris: ORSTOM, 1983.

Staewen, Christophe, and Karl Heinz. *Gonoa: Felsbilder aus Nord-Tibesti.* Stuttgart: F. Steiner, 1987.

Tillet, Thierry. *La paléolithique du bassin tchadien septentrional.* Paris: CNRS, 1983.

———. "Recherches préhistoriques dans le sud-ouest tchadien." *Bulletin de l'IFAN,* vol. 40, no. 3, July 1978, pp. 447–57.

Trienen, Françoise. "Découvertes pré-historiques dans la région de Fort-Lamy (Tchad)." *Notes Africaines,* no. 130, April 1971, pp. 30–41.

———. "Fresques du Tchad." *Homme,* vol. 5, no. 2, April–June 1965, pp. 123–126.

———. "Un nouveau site Sao au Tchad: Korno." *Notes Africaines,* no. 127, July 1970, pp. 65–74.

————. *Sahara et Sahel à l'age du fer: Borkou, Tchad.* Paris: Société des Africanistes, 1982.

Trienen-Claustre, Françoise. "Le nécropole de Nemra. *West African Journal of Archaeology,* vol. 5, 1976.

————. "Nouveaux éléments de datation absolue pour l'age du fer de la région de Koro Toro." *Anthropologie,* vol. 82, no. 1, 1978, pp. 103–9.

————. "Les tombes de Namanamassou (Tibesti) et leur contexte céramique et lithique." *Archéologie,* 1981.

Tubiana, J. "Découverte récente d'une pièce archéologique à l'ouest du Tibesti." *Notes Africaines,* no. 86, April 1960, pp. 41–42.

————. "La mission du Centre National de la Recherche Scientifique." *Cahiers d'Etudes Africaines,* no. 1, January 1960, pp. 115–20.

Verron, Guy. "Céramique de la région tchadienne II, culture Sao." *Fiches Typologiques Africaines.* Fort-Lamy: Institut National Tchadien pour les Sciences Humaines, vols. 8 and 9, pp. 226–59, 260–93.

Vire, M. M. "Stèles funéraires musulmanes soudano-sahariennes." *Bulletin de l'IFAN,* vol. 21, 1959, pp. 459–500.

Wulsin, Frederick R. "An Archaeological Reconnaissance in the Chari Basin." *Harvard African Studies,* vol. 10, 1932, pp. 1–88.

Early Explorations

"A propos de l'exploration du Ouadai," *Afrique Française,* no. 12, 1910, pp. 390–91.

Alexander, Boyd. "From the Niger, by Lake Tchad, to the Nile." *Annual Report of the Smithsonian Institution,* 1909, pp. 335–400.

————. "Lake Chad." *African Society Journal* (London), vol. 7, 1908, pp. 225–38.

Al-Tunisi, Muhammad b. Umar. *Voyage au Darfur.* Paris, 1845.

————. *Voyage au Ouadday.* Paris: Gide et Baudry, 1951.

Arjanse, J. d'. *Vers le Tchad mystérieux.* Paris: Jules Tallandier, 1933.

Avon, C. "Du Congo au Tchad." *Bulletin de la Société de Géographie Commerciale de Paris,* vol. 25, 1903, pp. 120–40.

Ayasse, L. "Première Reconnaissance N'guimi, Agadem, Bilma." *Revue des Troupes Coloniales,* vol. 1, 1907, pp. 552–82.

Ballif, L. "Le Tibesti." *Renseignements Coloniaux,* 1921, pp. 41–74.

Baquet, L. *La pénétration saharienne: Resumé historique (1899–1905).* Paris: Charles-Lavauzelle, 1908.

Barth, Heinrich. *Travels and Discoveries in North and Central Africa. From the Journal of an Expedition Undertaken . . . in the Years 1849–1856.* 5 vols. London: Longman Co., 1857–58.

Baudon, A. "Les voies d'accès vers le Tchad: Reconnaissance d'une nouvelle route." *Bulletin de la Société de Géographie et d'Etudes Coloniales de Marseille,* vol. 37, 1914, pp. 301–23.

Bauer, F. *Die Deutsche Niger-Benue-Tschadsee Expedition 1902–1903.* Berlin: D. Reimer, 1904.

Béhagle, F. de. "Le Bassin du Tchad." *Bulletin de la Société de Géographie* (Lille), vol. 20, 1893, pp. 344–58.

Belinay, F. de. "En Kadei sur le Tchad." *Renseignements Coloniaux,* no. 11, November 1938, pp. 293–97.

Bernard, A., and N. Lacroix. *La pénétration saharienne, 1830–1906.* Algiers: Imprimerie Algérienne, 1906.

Berthelot, A. *L'Afrique saharienne et soudanaise: Ce qu'en ont connu les Anciens.* Paris: Les Arts et les Livres, 1927.

Beurmann, K. M. von. *Voyages et explorations, 1860–63: Nubie, Libye, Soudan, Fezzan, Lac Tchad, Bournou.* St. Illide: Gibanel, 1973.

Blaizot, R. "Le Tibesti d'hier et de demain." *Renseignements Coloniaux,* 1921, pp. 6–14.

Bordeaux Züge östlich und nordöstlich vom Tschadsee." *Globus,* no. 95, 1909, pp. 46–50.

Bourbon-Parme, Sixte de. "Great Routes of the Sahara, Past and Future." *The Geographical Journal,* vol. 81, no. 2, February 1933, pp. 97–107.

———. "La première exploration automobile du Tibesti, Borkou et Mordja." *Renseignements Coloniaux,* 1932, pp. 369–78.

Bourbon-Parme, Sixte de, and H. de Bearn. *Au coeur du grand desert: Explorations sahariennes: Journal de la mission Alger-Tchad.* Paris: La Portique, 1931.

Bourdarie, P. "The Ouaddai." *Revue Indigène,* no. 56, December 1910, pp. 737–43.

Bruel, Georges. "La région civile du Haute-Chari." *Géographie,* no. 5, 1902, pp. 165–74.

Brunache, Paul. *Au centre de l'Afrique: Autour du Lac Tchad.* Paris: Alcan, 1893.

Bruneau de Laborie, Emile Louis Bruno. *Du Cameroun au Caire par le désert de Libye.* Paris: Flammarion, 1924.

Burckhardt, John Lewis. *Travels in Nubia.* London: J. Murray, 1819.

Canal, J. "De Tunis au lac Tchad et à Kotokou: Exploration faite par le Colonel Courtot, janvier–mai 1925." *Bulletin de la Société de Géographie d'Alger et d'Afrique du Nord* (Algiers), vol. 40, no. 142, April–June 1935, pp. 185–212.

Chapiseau, Felix. *Au pays de l'esclavage (moeurs et coutumes de l'Afrique centrale).* Paris: J. Maisonneuve, 1900.

Chaudron, C. "Tchad-Ouadai." *Revue de Troupes Coloniales,* vol. 2, 1910, pp. 246–67.

Chavanne J. *Die Sahara.* Vienna: Hartleben, 1879.

Chevalier, A. "Exploration scientifique dans les états de Snoussi, Sultan du Dar el Kouti." *Géographie,* vol. 8, 1903, pp. 89–95.

———. "Mission A. Chevalier dans les territoires du Tchad." *Géographie,* vol. 9, 1904, pp. 35–37.

———. "Mission scientifique au Chari et au Tchad." *Géographie* vol. 7, 1903, pp. 354–60.

Chudeau, R. "De Zinder au Tchad." *Comptes Rendus de l'Academie des Sciences,* vol. 143, 1906, pp. 193–95.

———. "L'Ouaddai." *Géographie,* vol. 30, 1914/15, pp. 292–94.

Cornet, Charles J. A. *Au Tchad: Trois ans chez les Senoussistes, les Ouaddaiens, et les Kirdis.* Paris: Plon Nourrit et Cie, 1910.

Cortier, M. *D'une rive à l'autre du Sahara.* Paris: Larose, 1908.

Crowther, S. *Journal of an Expedition up the Niger and Tchadda Rivers Undertaken by MacLaird.* London: Church Missionary Society, 1855.

Dalla Vedova G. "Pellegrino Matteuci ed il suo diario inedito." *Bolletino di la Società Geografica Italiana,* 1855, pp. 641–73.

D'Annelet, Col. Burthe. *A travers l'Afrique Française.* 2 vols. Paris: Didot, 1939.

———. "La deuxième mission du Lt. Col. Burthe d'Annelet en Afrique Centrale." *Afrique Française,* no. 8, August 1933, pp. 456–61.

———. "La Mission du Lt. Colonel Burthe d'Annelet en Afrique Centrale." *Afrique Française,* April 1930, pp. 163–67.

Deburaux, E. *Le Sahara et le Soudan en Ballon.* Paris: Hachette, 1902.

Decorse, J. *Du Congo au Lac Tchad.* Paris: Asselin et Houzeau, 1906.

———. "Rapport économique et zoologique sur la région du Tchad." *Renseignements Coloniaux de l'Afrique Française,* May, June, July 1905, pp. 189–97, 221–27, 268–75.

Deloncle, F. "Le Bénoué et le Chari: Voyage d'un moine franciscan." *Bulletin de la Société Géographique du Lyons,* vol. 2, 1876, pp. 473–76.

Denham, Dixon, and H. Clapperton. *Narrative of Travels and Discoveries in Northern and Central Africa in the Years 1822, 1823, and 1824.* London: Murray, 1826.

Descorps, C. "Victor Largeau." *Bulletin de la Société Géographique d'Alger,* 1897, pp. 372–73.

Destenave, Georges Mathieu. "Deux années de commandement dans la région du Tchad." *Revue de Géographie,* July 1903.

———. "Le Lac Tchad." *Revue Générale des Sciences,* vol. 14, 1903, pp. 649–62, 717–27.

———. "Exploration des Iles du Tchad." *Géographie,* vol. 7, 1903, pp. 421–26.

———. "Rapport sur les îles du Tchad." *Revue Coloniale,* 1902/1903, pp. 331–38.

Devedeix, A. "Au centre tropical Ouaddien: Contre-rezzou en pays Ouaddien." *Armée et Marine,* no. 142, February 1911, pp. 231–33.

Dominik, H. "Bericht des Oberleutnants Dominik uber Gebiete zwischen dem oberen Benue und dem Tschadsee." *Deutsches Kolonialblatt,* vol. 14, 1903, pp. 105–7, 130–32, 148–52.

————. *Vom Atlantik zum Tschadsee.* Berlin: E. S. Mittler et Sohn, 1908.

Dubois, R. "Bas Chari, rive sud du Tchad, Bahr-el-Gazal." *Annales de Géographie,* vol. 12, 1903, pp. 339–56.

Duchêne, A. "La France au Lac Tchad." *Questions Diplomatiques et Coloniales,* vol. 9, 1900, pp. 449–58.

Dujour, G. "Notes sur le Moyen-Chari." *Revue Coloniale,* vol. 6, 1906, pp. 1–20.

Dybowski, Jean. "La Mission Jean Dybowski vers le Tchad." *Tour du Monde,* 1893, pp. 113–76.

————. *La Route du Chad.* Paris, 1893.

Forster, B. "Die Arbeiten der englisch-franzosischen Grenzkommission zwischon Niger und Tschadsee." *Globus,* vol. 87, 1905.

————. "Geografische und ethnographische Ergebruisse der Expedition F. Foureau." *Globus,* vol. 81, 1902, pp. 247–53.

Foureau, E. "De l'Algérie au Congo-Français par l'Aïr et le Tchad." *Bulletin de la Société Normande de Géographie,* vol. 23, 1901, pp. 170–99.

————. "La Traversée du Sahara." *Bulletin de la Société Géographique de Lyons,* vol. 17, 1901, pp. 138–45.

Fourneau, Alfred. "Deux années dans la région du Tchad." *L'Afrique Française, Renseignements Coloniaux,* vol. 14, 1904, pp. 121–25, 145–52.

François, G. "La Mission Tilho: La frontière entre le Niger et le Tchad." *Afrique Française,* no. 2, 1909, pp. 56–62.

Froidevaux, H. "D'Alger au Congo par le Tchad." *Questions Diplomatiques et Coloniales,* vol. 13, January–June 1902, pp. 493–97.

Gadel, A. "Liaison avec Bilma." *Bulletin de la Société Géographique d'Alger,* vol. 19, 1914, pp. 21–37.

————. "Notes sur Bilma et les oasis environnantes." *Revue Coloniale,* no. 51, June 1907, pp. 361–86.

Garnier, R. "Conférence sur la Mission Gentil." *Bulletin de la Société Géographique d'Alger,* 1901, pp. 112–128.

Gide, André. *Le retour du Tchad.* Paris: Gallimard, 1928.

————. *Voyage au Congo.* Paris: Gallimard, 1927.

Godard, A. "Etude sur le Bar-el-Ghazal (région du Tchad)." *Bulletin de la Société de Géographie d'Alger et de l'Afrique du Nord,* vol. 18, 1913, pp. 283–315.

Goumbe, Afa Ti. "Notes sur le Senoussi." *Le Courrier Européen,* 1911, pp. 313–16.

Guilleux, A. *Journal de route d'un caporal de tirailleurs de la mission saharienne, 1896–1900.* Paris: Schachter, 1900.

Hanolet, A. "Exploration au nord du Bornou et au bassin du Tchad-Chari." *Bulletin de la Société Royale de Géographie d'Anvers,* vol. 30, 1906, pp. 93–100.

Hilaire, J. *Du Congo au Nile: Ouadai, cinq ans d'arrêt.* Marseille: Editions de l'ASCG, 1930.

Huart, Marie J. E. "Le Tchad et ses habitants: Notes de géographie physique et humaine. *Géographie,* vol. 9, 1904, pp. 161–76.

Hulot, A. "De l'Océan Atlantique au Lac Tchad: Mission du Capitaine Lenfant." *Revue des Deux Mondes,* vol. 21, 1904, pp. 694–707.

———. "La découverte des grandes sources du centre de l'Afrique." *Géographie,* vol. 19, 1909, pp. 169–70.

———. "Mission Chari-Sangha." *Géographie,* vol. 3, 1901, pp. 197–202.

———. "La mission télégraphique du Tchad." *Géographie,* vol. 23, 1911, pp. 236–38.

———. "Mission Tilho: Notes du Lieutenant Mercadier." *Géographie,* vol. 17, 1908, pp. 173–74.

———. "Retour de la Mission Lenfant." *Géographie,* vol. 17, 1908, pp. 171–73.

———. "Mission Chari-Sangha." *Revue Coloniale,* 1901, pp. 61–75.

———. "Les peuplades de l'Oubangui et du Bahr-el-Ghazal." *Revue de Science,* vol. 17, no. 10, 1902, pp. 301–6; vol. 17, no. 13, 1902, pp. 394–400.

Hutchinson, T. J. *Narrative of the Niger, Tshadda, and Binue Exploration.* London: Frank Cass and Co., 1966.

Hutter, D., and A. Hauptmann. "Die Wissenschaftlichen Ergebusse der Expedition Foureau-Lamy 1898–1900." *Globus,* vol. 90, 1906, pp. 362–67, 380–83.

Julien, A. "Du Haut-Oubangui vers le Chari per le bassin de la Kota." *Bulletin de la Société de Géographie de Paris,* vol. 18, 1897, pp. 129–78, 496–518.

———. "La situation économique du Dar el Kouti." *Afrique Française,* no. 1, 1904, pp. 38–40.

Kannengiesser, Georg A. "Der Tsäde oder Tsädsee." *Zeitschrift für Kolonialpolitik,* vol. 6, 1904, pp. 522–38.

Kleist, von. "Die Oese Bilma." *Globus,* vol. 91, 1907, pp. 65–66.

Lacoin, L. "Région de l'Oubangui, du Chari, et du Tchad." *Bulletin de la Société Géologique de la France,* vol. 3, 1904, pp. 484–96.

Lancrenon, P. "Exploration entre la Sangha et le Logone." *Géographie,* vol. 16, 1907, pp. 423–26.

———. "Les travaux de la mission télégraphique du Tchad, 1910–13." *Renseignements Coloniaux,* 1914, pp. 34–40, 55–68.

Lauture, P.H.S. *Mémoires sur le Soudan.* Paris: A. Bertrand, 1855.

Le Herissé, H. "Au Tchad." *Armée et Marine,* no. 138, December 15, 1910, pp. 161–65.

Lemoine, F. "Exploration du Borkou." *Géographie,* vol. 7, 1903, pp. 372–76.

———. "Exploration entre la Sangha et le Logone." *Géographie*, vol. 6, 1907, pp. 423–26.

Lenfant, Eugene A. "Conférence du 26 Fevrier 1908." *Quinzaine Coloniale*, 1908, pp. 255–62.

———. "La Grande Route du Tchad." *Tour du Monde*, vol. 10, 1904, pp. 493–588.

———. *La Grande Route du Chad: Mission de la Société de Géographie*. Paris: Hachette, 1905.

———. "La Mission du Haut-Logone." *Renseignements Coloniaux*, no. 6, 1908, pp. 152–56.

———. "La Mission du Haut-Logone." *Géographie*, no. 17, 1908, pp. 337–41.

———. "Opérations de la Mission Lenfant dans les bassins du Bahr-Lara et du Logone." *Géographie*, vol. 16, 1907, pp. 281–86.

Leotard, J. "Bahr-el-Ghazal." *Bulletin de la Société Géographique de Marseille*, vol. 23, 1899, pp. 323–25.

———. "Chronologie géographique de l'AEF." *Bulletin de la Société Géographique de Marseille*, vol. 35, 1911, pp. 115–25.

———. "La France au Bahr-el-Ghazal et au Tchad." *Bulletin de la Société Géographique de Marseille*, vol. 23, no. 1, 1899, pp. 103–5.

———. "La Mission Gentil-Bretonnet." *Bulletin de la Société Géographique de Marseille*, vol. 23, no. 3, 1899, pp. 321–23; vol. 23, no. 4, 1899, pp. 397–400.

———. "La Retour de Marchand." *Bulletin de la Société Géographique de Marseille*, vol. 23, no. 2, 1899, pp. 198–205.

Lhote, Henri. "La Mission Berliét-Ténéré ouvre la route directe Alger-Tchad." *Europe-France-Outremer*, no. 363, February 1960, pp. 20–23.

Loefler. "De la Sangha au Chari et à la Bénoué." *Renseignements Coloniaux*, 1902, 121–28.

———. "Les régions comprises entre la Haute-Sangha, le Chari, et le Cameroun." *Renseignements Coloniaux*, no. 9, 1907, pp. 224–40.

Lorin, H. "Autours du Tchad." *Bulletin de la Société Géographique de Lille*, vol. 49, 1908, pp. 41–45.

Lucien, A. "Ouadai Aouali." *Renseignements Coloniaux*, 1911, pp. 12–15.

MacLeod, C. *Chiefs and Cities of Central Africa: Across Lake Chad by Way of British, French, and German territories*. Edinburgh: Blackwood, 1912.

Maistre, C. "Du Congo au Niger par l'Oubangui et la Bénué." *Bulletin de la Société Géographique de Paris*, 1893, pp. 368–86.

———. "La Mission Maistre." *Afrique Française*, no. 6, 1893, pp. 2–8.

———. "La Mission Maistre dans l'Afrique Centrale 1892–3." *Comptes Rendu de Séances de la Société Géographique*, 1893, pp. 270–88.

————. "Retour de la Mission Maistre." *Afrique Française,* no. 6, 1893, pp. 8–11.

Mangin, G. "Région du Tchad: Le Borkou." *Revue Française de l'Etranger et des Colonies,* vol. 32, 1907, pp. 273–83.

Marquardseu, H. "Die Geographischer Erforschung des Tschad-seege-bietes bis zum Jahre 1905." *Mittelingen Deutschen Schutzgebieten,* vol. 18, 1905, pp. 318–51.

Maunoir, C. "Voyage du Dr. Nachtigal dans le Wadai, le Darfour, et le Kordofan." *Rapports Annuels sur le Progrès de la Géographie,* 1867–92, vol. 1, pp. 637–45.

Mecklenburg, A. F., Duke of. *From the Congo to the Niger and the Nile.* 2 vols. London: Duckworth and Company, 1913.

Mercier, P. "La mission de revitaillement du Tchad par Kano." *Renseignements Coloniaux,* no. 7, 1914, pp. 261–82.

Mercuri, T. "Au Chari: La Mission de Behagle." *Bulletin de la Société Géographique d'Alger et de l'Afrique du Nord,* 1900, pp. 386–99.

Meynier, O. "La France dans l'Afrique Centrale." *Bulletein de la Société de Géographie de Lille,* vol. 39, 1903, pp. 414–43.

————. "Un raid au Chari." *Revue Française,* vol. 26, 1901, pp. 352–57.

"La Mission du Haut-Logone." *Revue des Troupes Coloniales,* vol. 1, 1908, pp. 498–512.

"Les Missions du Chari et de l'Afrique Centrale: La Mission Joalland-Meynier." *L'Afrique Française,* no. 6, 1901, pp. 184–97.

Mizon, L. "L'itinéraire de Yola à Dingui sur le Mayo-Kebbi." *Bulletin de la Société Géographique de Paris,* vol. 17, 1896, pp. 65–98.

Modat, A. *Une Tournée en pays Fertyt.* Paris: Comité de l'Afrique Française, 1912.

Moll, C. "La boucle du Logone Occidental: Les Lakas, les Moundous, les Toubouri." *Mois Coloniale et Maritime,* 1909, pp. 205–17.

————. "Rapport du Capitaine Moll, commandant de Poste de Zinder-Tchad." *Revue Coloniale,* 1901/1902, pp. 44–58.

Montbel, M. "Nos marches sahariennes." *Questions Diplomatiques et Coloniales,* vol. 37, June 1 and 16, 1914, pp. 647–58; 725–37.

Monteil, C. *De Saint Louis à Tripoli par le Lac Tchad.* Paris: Alcan, 1894.

Monterin, Umberto. "Attraverso il deserto Libico fino al Tibesti." *L'Universo* (Florence), October 1935, pp. 803–43.

————. *L'esplorazione del Tibesti settentrionale e delle zone confinarie del Sud Libico.* Rome: Società Italiana per il Progresso della Scienza, 1937.

Mourey, C., and L. Brunet. "La marche vers le Tchad." *Année Coloniale,* 1899, pp. 82–91.

————. "Région Chari-Tchad." *Année Coloniale,* 1902/1903, pp. 130–40.

Nachtigal, Gustav. "Doktor G. Nachtigal's Reise zu den Tibbu Reschade." *Petermanns Geographische Mitteilungen,* vol. 16, 1870, pp. 25–29, 47–51, 273–87.

———. "Doktor G. Nachtigal's Reise nach Baghirmi." *Globus,* vol. 39, 1881, pp. 209–15, 225–31, 241–47, 257–63, 273–79, 289–93, 305–10.

———. *Sahara and Sudan.* 4 vols., translated by A.G.B. and H. J. Fisher. London: C. Hurst, 1971+.

Prins, P. "Bassin du Tchad." *Comptes Rendus des Séances de la Société Géographique,* 1898, pp. 236–41.

———. "Vers le Tchad: Une année de résidence auprès de Mohamed Abd-er-Rhaman Gaourang sultan de Baguirmi—avril 1898–mai 1899." *Géographie,* vol. 1, no. 3, 1900, pp. 177–92.

———. "Voyage au Dar Rounga." *Géographie,* vol. 1, no. 3, 1900, pp. 193–96.

Rebillet, A. "Etat politique du Bornou et du Baghirmi." *Comptes Rendus des Séances de la Société Géographique,* June 1, 1894, pp. 265–67.

Segni, P. F. da. "Viaggio da Tripoli di Barbaria al Bornu nel 1850." *Bolletino della Società Geographica Italiana,* vol. 4, no. 1, 1870.

Terrier, A., and C. Mourey. *L'Expansion française et la formation territoriale.* Paris: Larose, 1910.

Thesiger, W. "A Camel Journey to Tibesti." *Geographical Journal,* vol. 94, December 1939, pp. 433–46.

Tilho, J. "A propos du Lac Tchad." *Afrique Française,* no. 5, 1937, pp. 265–71.

———. "Avenir du Tchad." *Afrique Française,* no. 4, 1935, pp. 236–39.

———. "Exploration du Capitaine Tilho dans le bassin du Tchad." *Géographie,* vol. 2, 1905, pp. 226–30.

———. "Exploration du Lac Tchad." *Géographie,* vol. 13, 1906, pp. 195–214.

———. "Reconnaissance dans le pays-Bas du Tchad." *Géographie,* vol. 28, 1913, pp. 372–74.

Tilho, J., and E. P. O'Shee. "Du Tchad au Niger: Notice historique." *Documents Scientifiques de la Mission Tilho.* vol. 2. Paris: Imprimerie Nationale, 1910–14, pp. 309–552.

Toutée, A. *Dahomey, Niger, Touareg: Récit du Voyage.* Paris: Hachette, 1908.

Truffert. "Région du Tchad." *Revue de Géographie,* vol. 52, 1903, pp. 481–502; vol. 53, 1903, pp. 14–35.

Van Vollenhoven, J. "Conférences sur le voyage de Nachtigal au Ouaddai." *Bulletin de la Société Géographique d'Alger et de l'Afrique du Nord,* 1902, no. 4, pp. 544–57.

———. *Le Voyage de Nachtigal au Ouaddai.* Paris: Afrique Française, n.d.

Varigault, A. "La vraie route du Tchad." *Géographie,* vol. 28, 1913, pp. 67–69.

———. "Une tribu nomade: Les Bororo." *Renseignements Coloniaux,* vol. 13, 1913, pp. 110–112.

Vischer, H. "A Journey from Tripoli across the Sahara to Lake Chad." *Geographical Journal,* vol. 33, 1909, pp. 241–66.

———. "De Tripoli au Lac Tchad." *Géographie,* vol. 20, 1909, pp. 349–56.

History

Abadie, Jean-Claude, and François Abadie. *Sahara-Tchad 1890–1900: Carnet de route de Propser Haller, medicin de la mission Foureau-Lamy.* Paris: Harmattan, 1989.

Adefuye, Ade I. "The Kanuri Factor in Nigeria-Chad Relations." *Journal of the Historical Society of Nigeria,* vol. 12, no. 3/4, 1984/85, pp. 121–37.

Adeleye, R. A. "Rabih b. Fadlallah and the Diplomacy of European Imperial Invasion in the Central Sudan, 1893–1902." *Journal of the Historical Society of Nigeria,* vol. 3, December 1970, pp. 399–411.

———. "Rabih b. Fadlallah, 1879–1893: Exploits and Impact on Political Relations in the Central Sudan." *Journal of the Historical Society of Nigeria,* vol. 2, June 1970, pp. 223–42.

Adler, A. "Le royaume moundang de Léré." In C. Tardits (ed.), *Princes et serviteurs: Cinq études de monarchies africaines,* Paris: Société d'Ethnographie, 1987.

Adoum, H. "L'Empereur Rabah et son temps." *Mémoires E.N.F.O.M.,* Paris, 1959.

Aerts, P. "Les Tchadiens et le service militaire." *Tropiques,* vol. 52, no. 362, May 1954.

Alamdou, Ramat Issaka. *Les relations franco-tchadiennes de la Conférence de Berlin à nos jours.* Paris: Institut d'Etudes des Relations Internationales Contemporaines et de Recherches Diplomatiques, 1972.

Alfassa, P. "Le Rattachement du Tibesti à l'Afrique Equatoriale Française." *L'Afrique Française,* no. 5, May 1930, pp. 281–82.

Alis, Harry. *A la Conquête du Tchad.* Paris: Hachette, 1891.

Alkali, M. Nur. "The Political System and Administrative Structure of Kanem Bornu under the Saifawa." In J. F. Ade Ajayi and Bashir Ikara (eds.), *Evolution of Political Culture in Nigeria,* Ibadan: Ibadan University Press, 1985, pp. 33–49.

Amegboh, Joseph. *Rabah, conquérant des pays tchadiens.* Paris: Editions ABC, 1976.

Arbaumont, J. d'. "Le Tibesti et le domaine Téda-Daza." *Bulletin de l'IFAN,* July–October 1954.

————. "Refléxions sur les Toubou." *Tropiques,* August/September 1954.

Arkell, A. J. "The History of Darfur, 1200–1700: The Influence of Bornu." *Sudan Notes and Records* (Khartoum), no. 33, 1952, pp. 129–55.

————. "The Influence of Christian Nubia in the Chad Area between A.D. 800–1200." *Kush* (Khartoum), 11, 1963, pp. 315–19.

Auphan, P. *Histoire de la décolonisation.* Paris: France-Empire, 1967.

Azevedo, Mario J. (ed.). *Cameroon and Chad in Historical Perspectives.* Lewiston: Edwin Mellen Press, 1988.

————. "The Human Price of Development: The Brazzaville Railroad and the Sara of Chad." *African Studies Review,* vol. 24, no. 1, March 1981, pp. 1–19.

————. "Power and Slavery in Central Africa: Chad 1890–1892." *Journal of Negro History,* Fall 1982, pp. 198–211.

————. "Sara Demographic Instability as a Consequence of French Colonial Policy in Chad, 1890–1940." Ph.D. diss., Duke University, 1977.

Babikir, Arbab Djama. *L'Empire de Rabeh.* Paris: Dervy, 1950.

Bachar, M. *Mangalmé, préfecture du Guéra et ses habitants, les Moubi.* Fort-Lamy: Ecole Nationale d'Administration, 1970.

Balfour-Paul, H. G. "Sultans' Palaces in Darfur and Waddai." *Kush* (Khartoum), no. 2, 1954, pp. 5–18.

Ballif, L. "Le Tibesti." *Renseignements Coloniaux de l'Afrique Française,* no. 3, 1921, pp. 41–47.

Bedes, Yusuf. "Tales of the Wadai Slave Trade in the Nineties." *Sudan Notes and Records* (Khartoum), vol. 23, no. 1, 1940, pp. 169–83.

Benoit, J. "La guerre au desert: La Sénoussisme et l'attaque du Sahara et du Soudan, décembre 1914–octobre 1919." *Revue des Sciences Politiques,* vol. 49, April–June 1926, pp. 224–45.

Berre, Henri. "El Hadj Mustapha Oule Bekhit Sultan du Dar Sila." *Mémoires du CHEAM,* no. 1804, 1951.

————. "Entre Ouaddai et Dar For: Annales des sultans dadjo (1664–1912)." *Le Mois en Afrique,* no. 201/202, October–December 1982, pp. 144–148.

————. "Grossard le mai-aimé." *Le Mois en Afrique,* no. 188/189, August/September 1981, pp. 96–116.

————. "Origines dadjo." *Le Mois en Afrique,* April/May 1983, pp. 141–160.

————. *Sultans dadjo du Sila, Tchad.* Paris: CNRS, 1985.

————. "Les Sultanats du Tchad." *Mémoires du CHEAM,* no. 2005, 1951.

Biobaku, Saburi, and Muhammad al-Hajj. "The Sudanese Mahdiyya and the Niger-Chad Region." In I. M. Lewis (ed.), *Islam in Tropical Africa,* London: Hutchinson, 1966, pp. 226–239.

Bivar, A.D.H., and P. L. Shinnie. "Old Kanuri Capitals." *Journal of African History,* vol. 3, no. 1, 1962, pp. 1–10.

Bjorkelo, A. "State and Society in the Central Sudanic Kingdoms: Kanem-Bornu, Bagirmi, and Wadai." Ph.D. diss., University of Bergen, 1976.

Blondiaux, P. "Cinquante années d'administration française à Melfi (1903–1952)." *Mémoires du CHEAM,* no. 2149, 1953.

Boahen, A. Adu. *Britain, the Sahara and the Western Sudan, 1788–1861.* Oxford: Clarendon Press, 1964.

———. "The Caravan Trade in the Nineteenth Century." *Journal of African History,* vol. 3, no. 2, 1962, pp. 349–59.

———. "The Caravan Trade in the Nineteenth Century." In P.J.M. McEwan (ed.), *Nineteenth-Century Africa,* London: Oxford University Press, 1968, pp. 90–98.

Boisson, Jacques. *L'histoire du Tchad et de Fort-Archambault.* Paris: Editions du Scorpion, 1966.

Bordeaux. "Deux Contre-rezzou dans le Ouaddai, l'Ennedi, et le Borkou." *Géographie,* vol. 18, 1908, pp. 209–26.

Botting, A. *The Knights of Bornu.* London: Hodder Stoughton, 1960.

Boudon, C. "Le Batha." *Revue Militaire A.E.F.,* no. 12, 1938, p. 39–44.

Boujol, R. "Le Baguirmi, royaume musulman de l'Afrique centrale." *Mémoires du CHEAM,* no. 281, 1939.

Boulnois, J. "Le migration des Sao au Tchad." *Bulletin d' l'IFAN,* vol. 5, nos. 1–4, 1943, pp. 80–120.

Bourda, L. "L'Ounianga." *Revue des Troupes Coloniales,* no. 223, March/April 1935, pp. 130–86.

Bret, René-Joseph. *La Vie du Sultan Mohamed Bakhit, 1856–1916: La pénétration française au Dar Sila.* Paris: CNRS, 1987.

Britsch, Gabriel. *La Mission Foureau-Lamy et l'arrivée des Français au Tchad, 1898–1900: Carnets de route du Lieutenant Gabriel Britsch.* Paris: Harmattan, 1989.

Britsch, J. "Le Sahara et ses pionniers." *Eurafrique,* no. 26, April 1961, pp. 15–20.

Brochot, C. "Marche, stationnement, et combat au territoire du Tchad." *Revue des Troupes Coloniales,* vol. 2, 1912, pp. 621–53.

Bru, L. "Le Tchad d'hier et d'aujourd'hui: La conquête, les realisations, les tendances actuelles." *Revue Militaire A.E.F.,* no. 1, 1935, pp. 19–32.

Bruel, Georges. "Mohammed-es-Senoussi et ses états." *Bulletin de la Société de Recherches Congolaises,* no. 11, 1930, pp. 93–101.

———. "L'occupation du bassin de Tchad. Moulins: Crepin-Leblond, 1902.

Buijtenhuijs, R. "La dialectique nord-sud dans l'histoire tchadienne." *Africa Perspectives* (Leiden), no. 2, 1977, pp. 43–61.

Buret, Joseph. *Le territoire français Niger-Tchad.* Brussels: Société d'Etudes Coloniales de Belgique, 1905.

Cabot, Jean, and Christian Bouquet. *Le Tchad.* Paris: Presses Universitaires de France, 1973.

Caillat. "Contribution à l'étude du Ouaddai." *Mémoires du CHEAM,* no. 1545, 1950.

Caix, Robert de. "Au pays du Tchad." *Afrique Française,* no. 4, 1910, pp. 119–26.

———. "La délimitation de l'extrême sud: Les possibilités de notre politique saharienne." *Renseignements Coloniaux,* no. 9, 1901, pp. 181–97.

———. "La politique saharienne." *Afrique Française,* no. 3, 1910, pp. 77–80.

———. "La question du Tibesti." *Afrique Française,* vol. 21, 1911, pp. 88–92.

Caprile, J. P. *A travers le pays toumak avec Gustav Nachtigal, 1874–1974.* Bremen: Übersee-Museum, 1977.

Casenave, M. A. "Les chefs au Ouaddai." *Mémoires du CHEAM,* no. 2099, 1952.

———. "Les minorités musulmanes du nord-est tchadien: Sultanats des Dar Zaghoua et Sar Tama." *Mémoires du CHEAM,* no. 1987, 1952.

Cerf, J. de. *Bahr el Ghazal: Terre du Tchad.* Monte Carlo: Regain, 1957.

Chambrun, General de. "Souvenirs de la mission Foureau-Lamy." *Revue des Vivants,* 1930, pp. 52–61.

Chapelle, Jean. *Souvenirs du Sahel: Zinder, Lac Tchad, Komadougou.* Paris: Harmattan, 1987.

———. "Tchad." *Mémoires du CHEAM,* no. 2799, 1957.

Charbonneau, J. R. *Marchés et marchands d'Afrique Noire.* Paris: La Colombe, 1961.

Chauvet, Jacques. "Les Quartiers de Sarh, ex Fort-Archambault (République du Tchad)." Ph.D. diss., University of Bordeaux, 1974.

Ciammaichella, Glanco. *Libyens et Français au Tchad (1887–1914): La confrérie sénoussie et le commerce transsaharien.* Paris: CNRS, 1987.

"Cinquantenaire du Tchad, 1900–1950." *Tropiques,* no. 328, 1951.

Clanet, J. "Une ville précoloniale en declin: Abéché." University of Vincennes Mémoire, 1972.

Cohen, Ronald. "The Bornu King List." In *Boston University Papers on Africa,* vol. 2, 1966, pp. 39–83.

———. "From Empire to Colony: Bornu in the Nineteenth and Twentieth Centuries." In V. Turner (ed.), *Colonialism in Africa, 1870–1960,* vol. 3, Cambridge: Cambridge University Press, 1971.

———. *The Kanuri of Bornu.* New York: Holt, Rinehart and Winston, 1967.

Cohen, Ronald, and Louis Brenner. "Bornu in the Nineteenth Century." In J. F. A. Ajayi and Michael Crowder (eds.), *A History of West Africa,* vol. 2, London: Longman Group, 1974, pp. 93–128.

Conte, Edouard. *Marriage Patterns, Political Change, and the Perpetuation of Social Inequality in South Kanem.* Paris: ORSTOM, 1983.

Coquery-Vidrovitch, C. "Le pillage de l'Afrique Equatoriale." *Histoire* (Paris), no. 3, 1978, pp. 43–52.

Cordell, Dennis Dale. "Dar Al-Kuti: A History of the Slave Trade and State-formation in the Islamic Frontier in Northern Equatorial Africa." Ph.D. diss., University of Wisconsin, 1977.

———. *Dar al-Kuti and the Last Years of the Trans-Saharan Slave Trade.* Madison: University of Wisconsin Press, 1985.

———. "The Labor of Violence: Dar al-Kouti in the Nineteenth Century." In Catherine Coquery-Vidrovitch and Paul E. Lovejoy (eds.), *The Workers of African Trade,* Beverly Hills, CA: Sage Publications, 1988, pp. 169–192.

Cornevin, Robert. "Les bien faits de l'esclavage arabe en Afrique centrale et orientale par le Capitaine Jerome Becker en 1887." *France-Eurafrique,* vol. 19, no. 184, May 1967, pp. 36–41.

———. "Tschad." *Internationale Afrikaforum,* vol. 5, no. 7/8, July/August 1969, pp. 496–99.

Cortier, M. "Les Turcs en Afrique Centrale: La frontière franco-tripolitaine." *L'Afrique Française,* no. 9, September 1911, pp. 320–28.

Costa, P. "Abéché 1957." Paris: Mémoire E.N.F.O.M., 1958.

Courville H. de. "Chefferie traditionnelle, administration française, et partis politiques au Ouaddai." *Mémoires du CHEAM,* no. 3095, 1959.

Cruciani, Marc. "La Senoussaya et la conquête des confins libyques du Tchad." *Eurafrique,* no. 12, 1954.

Curtin, Philip. "Epidemiology and the Slave Trade." *Political Science Quarterly,* vol. 83, no. 2, 1968, pp. 190–212.

Daigre, R. P. *Oubangi-Chari, témoignage sur son évolution (1900–1940).* Issoudun, Indre: Dillen et Cie, 1947.

Dalmais, Paul. *L'histoire de Fort-Archambault.* Fort-Lamy: Institut National Tchadien pour les Sciences Humaines, 1950.

Darcy, Robert. "L'enjeu." *Revue Militaire Générale,* vol. 5, 1971, pp. 641–53.

Davidson, Basil. "From Kanem to Bornu." *West African Review,* vol. 33, no. 417, September 1962, pp. 20–24.

———. "The Sao and Kanem" and "Darfur." In *The Lost Cities of Africa.* Boston: Little, Brown and Company, 1959, pp. 104–16.

Decobert, C. "Le Conseil des anciens: Islamisation et arabisation dans le bassin tchadien." *Annales,* July/August 1982, pp. 764–82.

Decorse, J., and M. Gaudefroy-Demombynes. *Rabah et les Arabes du Chari.* Paris: Guilmoto, 1906.

Deese, Patrick Herbert. "From Empire to Independence: An Analysis of the Legal Status of French Equatorial Africa, 1939–61." Ph.D. diss. University of Tennessee, 1970.

Delacommune L. "Au Ouaddai: Un gouvernement de l'Afrique Centrale." *Revue Indigène,* no. 46, February 1910, pp. 78–84.

De Neufville, R. L., et al. "A Description of Ain Farah and Wara." *Kush,* vol. 13, 1965, pp. 195–204.

Denis, Jacques. "Fort-Lamy: Croissance et destin d'une ville africaine." *Bulletin de la Société d'Etudes Géographiques,* vol. 27, no. 1, 1958, pp. 35–54.

Devallée, A. "Le Baghirmi." *Bulletin de la Société de Recherches Congolaises,* no. 7, 1925, pp. 3–76.

Diolé, Philippe. *Dans le Fezzan inconnu.* Paris: 1957.

Djonfené, R. E. "Le Canton de Léré." Fort-Lamy, Ecole Nationale d'Administration, Mémoire, 1968.

Doornbos, P. "Enkele opmerkingen over Tsjaad en noord-ost Afrika." In W. Van Bingsbergen and G. Hessling (eds.), *Aspekten van Staat en Maatschappi j: Recent Dutch and Belgian Research on the African State.* Leiden: African Studies center, 1984.

Dorobantz, J. "Les Evénements du Ouaddai et l'ingérence turque dans notre empire africain." *Questions Diplomatiques et Coloniales,* vol. 31, 1911, pp. 65–75.

———. "Les Turcs au Bourkou." *Questions Diplomatiques et Coloniales,* vol. 32, 1912, pp. 284–85.

———. "Les Turcs au Tibesti." *Questions Diplomatiques et Coloniales,* vol. 31, 1911, pp. 364–66.

Dujarric, Gaston. *La vie du sultan Rabah: Les Français au Tchad.* Paris: J. André, 1902.

Dumont, H. P. "La Colonie du Chari-Tchad." *Bulletin de la Société de Géographie de Marseille,* vol. 54, 1933, pp. 56–79.

Duriez. "Le sultanat de Fort-Lamy." *Mémoires du CHEAM,* 1950.

Eboué, Felix. *Politique indigène de l'A.E.F.* Brazzaville: Imprimerie Officielle, 1941.

Elliot, G. S. McD. "The Anglo-French Niger-Tchad Boundary Commission." *The Geographical Journal,* vol. 24, 1904, pp. 505–24.

El-Nager, O. A. "A Note on the Material for the Study of Rabah's Career." *Bulletin of the African Studies Association of the United Kingdom,* no. 6, November 1965, pp. 20–23.

Emerit, M. "Les liaisons terrestres entre Le Soudan et l'Afrique du Nord au XVIIIe et au début du XIXe siècle." *Transactions de l'Institut des Recherches Sahariennes,* vol. 11, 1954.

Estienne, G. "Les voies de communicataions entre l'Afrique du Nord et l'Afrique Centrale." *Renseignements Coloniaux,* October 1929, pp. 550–60.

Etienne, E. "Discours de 24 decembre 1910 au sujet des événements de Massalit." *Afrique Française,* no. 1, January 1911, pp. 15–19.

———. "Interpellation sur la politique saharienne." *Renseignements Coloniaux,* no. 3, 1910, pp. 67–71.

———. *Evolution du Tchad depuis 1950.* Fort-Lamy: Archives Nationales, 1958.

Fabre, P. *Les heures d'Abéché.* Marseille: Cahiers du Sud, 1935.

Favardi, L. *Sahara et Soudan: Essai sur la mise en valeur du Sahara et sur les communications du centre Africain avec l'Europe.* Paris: Imprimerie F. Levé, 1905.

"Félix Sylvester Eboué, Governor of Chad Territory." *Journal of Negro History,* 29, no. 4, October 1944, pp. 501–3.

Ferrandi, Jean. *Abéché, capitale du Ouaddai.* Paris: Editions de l'Afrique Française, 1913.

———. *Le Centre-africain français: Tchad, Bourkou, Ennedi: Leur conquête.* Paris: Charles Lavauzelle, 1928.

———. "Des procédés de combat des nomades des oasis du Sahara Oriental." *Revue de Troupes Coloniales,* vol. 1, 1910, pp. 362–74.

———. "Le Kanem," *Dépêche Coloniale Illustrée,* 1910, pp. 39–54.

———. "L'occupation du Borkou et de l'Ennedi," *Renseignements Coloniaux de l'Afrique Française,* nos. 8–12, 1914, pp. 289–317.

———. "La vérité sur l'occupation turque au borkou idans le Tibesti et l'Ennedi avant 1914." *Le Saharien,* no. 107, 1988, pp. 8–20.

Ferrandi, Jean, and Lame. "Fort-Lamy, chef lieu du territoire du Tchad." *Renseignements Coloniaux de l'Afrique Française,* no. 3, 1912, pp. 101–11.

"Les Fils de Senoussi." *L'Afrique Française,* no. 5, 1912, pp. 201–2.

Fisher, Allan G. B., and H. J. Fisher. "Nachtigal's Experience in Tibesti, 1869: African Immigration Restrictions in the Mid-Nineteenth Century." *Adab,* vol. 1, 1972, pp. 24–45.

———. *Slavery and Muslim Society in Africa: The Institution in Saharan and Sudanic Africa and the Trans-Saharan Trade.* London: Hurst, 1970.

Fisher, Humphrey J., and V. Rowland. "Firearms in the Central Sudan." *Journal of African History,* vol. 12, no. 2, 1971, pp. 215–40.

Fleischhacker, H. "Rassen und Bevölkerungs-geschichte Nordafrikas unter besonderer Berücksichtigung der Athiopiden, der Libyer und der Garamanten." *Paideuma,* no. 15, 1969, pp. 12–53.

Forkl, Hemann. *Die Beziehungen der zentralsudanischen Reiche Bornu, Mandara und Bagirmi sowie der Kotoko-Staaten zu ihren sudlichen Nachbarn unter besondered Berucksichtigung des Sao-Problems.* Munich: Minerva, 1983.

———. *Der Einfus Bornus, Manadaras, Bayirmis, der Kotoko staaten und der Jukum-Konfederation auf die Kultur-entwicklung ihrer Nachbarn sudlich des Tschadsees.* Munich: Minerva, 1985.

————. "Untersuchungen zur Geschichte des Ostlichen Zentralsudan." In R. Vossen and U. Claudi (eds.), *Sprache, Geschichte und Kultur in Afrika,* Hamburg: Buske, 1983, pp. 433–459.

Fortier, Joseph. "Bédaya et ses rois." Ph.D. diss., University of Paris, 1976.

————. *Le couteau de jet sacré: Histoire des Sar et leurs rois au sud du Tchad.* Paris: Harmattan, 1982.

Foulkes. "The New Anglo-French Frontier between the Niger and Lake Chad." *The Scottish Geographical Magazine.* vol. 22, 1906, pp. 505–75.

France. Ministère des Colonies. "La delimitation Ouadai-Darfur." *Renseignements Coloniaux,* no. 5, 1924, pp. 211–14.

Fresnel, M. "Mémoires sur le Ouadai." *Bulletin de la Société de Géographie,* vol. 11, no. 3, January/February 1949, pp. 5–74.

Fuchs, Peter. "Die Migrationen der Tunjer (Tschad)." *Gedenkschrift Gustav Nachtigal 1874–1974.* Bremen: Übersee-Museum, 1977, pp. 33–53.

Furneaux, Rupert. *Abdel Krim.* London: Secker and Warburg, 1967.

Gabriel, Baldur. *Von der Routenaufnahme zum Weltraumphoto Die Erforschung des Tibesti-Gebirges in der Zentralen Sahara.* Berlin: Verlag-Kiepert KG, 1973.

Gaden, H. "Les états musulmans de l'Afrique Centrale et leurs rapports avec la Mecque et Constantinople." *Questions Diplomatiques et Coloniales,* vol. 24, no. 225, October 1907, pp. 436–47.

Gaffarel, P. "L'Afrique equatoriale." *Histoire d'Expansion Coloniale de la France.* Mascella: Barlafier, 1905, pp. 216–77.

————. *Notre expansion coloniale en Afrique de 1870 à nos jours.* Paris: Alcan, 1918.

Ganslmayr, Herbert. *Gustav Nachtigal, 1869–1969.* Bad Godesberg: Inter Nationes, 1969.

————. "Gustav Nachtigal und Wara." *Africana Marburgensia,* 2, 1, 1969, pp. 14–21.

Gardinier, David E. "Mihammad Awuda Oulech at Abéché: A Reformist Islamic Challenge to French and Traditionalist Interests in Ouaddai, Chad, 1947–1956." *Islam et Sociétés au Sud du Sahara,* vol. 3, 1989, pp. 159–185.

Gentil, Emile. *La chute de l'empire de Rabah.* Paris: Hachette, 1902.

————. "La chute de l'empire de Rabah." *Tour du Monde,* 1901, pp. 529–624.

————. "La conquête du Tchad." *Revue Française de l'Etranger et des Colonies et Exploration,* vol. 26, 1901, pp. 321–35.

————. "Occupation et organisation des territoires du Tchad." *Géographie,* vol. 3, 1901, pp. 353–68.

Gentil, Pierre. *Confins Libyens, Lac Tchad, Fleuve Niger.* Paris: Lavauzelle, 1946.

―――. *La Conquête du Tchad (1894–1916).* 2 vols. Château de Vincennes: Service Historique de l'Armée, 1970.

―――. "Explorateurs français vers le Tchad de 1890 à 1894." Ph.D. diss., University of Paris, 1966.

―――. "Tchad, décolonisation, indépendance." *Mémoires du CHEAM,* no. 4004, 1965.

Gervais, Raymond. "La plus riche des colonies pauvres: La politique monétaire et fiscale de la France au Tchad, 1900–1920. *Canadian Journal of African Studies,* vol. 16, no. 1, 1982, pp. 93–112.

Giri, Jacques. *Le Sahel au XIXᵉ siècle: Un essai de réflexion prospective sur les sociétés saheliennes.* Paris: Karthala, 1989.

Goetz, François. *Méharistes et Touaregs: Récit saharien.* Paris: La Pensée Universelle, 1991.

Gouraud, Henri J. *Zinder-Tchad: Souvenirs d'un Africain.* Paris: Plon, 1944.

Grech, A. "Essai sur le Dar Kouti au temps de Senoussi." *Bulletin de la Société des Recherches Congolaises,* vol. 4, 1924, pp. 19–54.

Gros, R. "Histoire des Toundjours de Mondo." *Mémoires du CHEAM,* no. 1774, 1951.

Grossard, A. *Mission de délimitation de l'AOF et du Soudan Anglo-Egyptien.* Paris: Larose, 1925.

Hallam, W.K.R. "An Introduction to the History of Bornu." *Nigerian Field,* 35, no. 4, 1970, pp. 147–69.

―――. "The Itinerary of Rabih Fadl Allah, 1879–1893." *Bulletin de l'IFAN,* vol. 30, no. 1, 1968, pp. 165–81.

―――. *Life and Times of Rabih Fadl Allah.* Ilfracombe: Stockwell, 1977.

―――. "Rabeh: The Tyrant of Bornu." *Nigeria Magazine,* no. 86, September 1965, pp. 164–75.

Hanoteaux, G. "La négociation franco-allemande, Congo et Maroc." *Revue Hebdomadaire,* 1911, pp. 577–98.

Hayer, Jeffrey E. "A Political History of the Maba Sultanate of Wadai, 1635–1912." Ph.D. diss. University of Wisconsin, 1975.

Heseltine, Nigel. "Toubbou and Gorane, Nomads of the Chad Territory." *South African Archeological Bulletin,* vol. 14, no. 53, 1959, pp. 21–27.

Hilaire, A. *Du Congo au Nil, Ouadai ... cinq ans d'arrêt:* Marseille: Editions de l'A.S.C.G., 1930.

―――. "L'occupation du Dar Sila." *Renseignements Coloniaux,* no. 5/6, 1917, pp. 105–18.

Hirshffeld, Claire. "British Policy on the Middle Niger, 1890–1898." In

N. N. Barker and M. L. Brown (eds.), *Diplomacy in an Age of Nationalism,* New York: Columbia University Press, 1968, pp. 192–208.

Horowitz, Michael M. "Ba Karim: An Account of Rabah's Wars." *African Historical Studies,* vol. 3, no. 2, 1970, pp. 391–402.

———. "A Reconsideration of the 'Eastern Sudan'." *Cahiers d'Etudes Africaines,* vol. 7, no. 27, 1967, pp. 381–98.

Huard, Joel. *Au Tchad sous les manquiers.* Paris: La Pensée Universelle, 1979.

Huard, Paul. "Aires ou origines de quelques traits culturels des populations pré-islamiques du Bas-Chari-Logone dites Sao." *Actes du Premier Colloque International d'Archéologie Africaine, Fort-Lamy, 1966.* Fort-Lamy: Institut National Tchadien pour les Sciences Humaines, 1969.

Hugo, Pierre. *Le Tchad.* Paris: Nouvelles Editions Latines, 1965.

———. "Tchad et Soudan." *Afrique et Asie,* no. 37, 1957, pp. 3–10.

Ibn Fartua, Ahmed. *History of the First Twelve Years of the Reign of Mai Alooma of Bornu.* London: Frank Cass, 1970.

———. "The Kanem Wars." In H. R. Palmer (ed.), *Sudanese Memoirs,* vol. i. Lagos: Government Printer, 1928, pp. 15–72.

Ifemesia, C. C. "Bornu under the Shehus." In J.F.A. Ajayi and Ian Espie (eds.), *A Thousand Years of West African History,* Ibadan: Ibadan University Press, 1965.

———. "The States of the Central Sudan." In J.F.A. Ajayi and Ian Espie (eds.), *A Thousand Years of West African History,* London: Nelson, 1965, pp. 72–112.

Ingold, F.J.J. *L'épopée LeClerc au Sahara, 1940–1943.* Paris: Berger-Levrault, 1945.

———. *Les troupes noires au combat.* Paris: Berger-Levrault, 1940.

Jackson, H. C. *Black Ivory and White, or the Story of El Zubeir Pasha, Slaver and Sultan, as Told by Himself.* London: Oxford University Press, 1912.

Jennings Bramey, W. E. "Tales of the Wadai Slave Trade in the Nineties Told by the Yunes Bedis of the Majabra." *Sudan Notes and Records,* vol. 23, no. 1, 1940, pp. 169–83.

Joos, L.C.D. "Le Ouaddai, le Dar Kouti et la Senoussia en 1904." *Etudes Camerounaises,* no. 53/54, October–December 1956, pp. 3–17.

Joubert, G. "Le faki Naim." *Bulletin de la Société de Recherches Congolaises,* no. 24, November 1937, pp. 5–63.

Jourdier, F. "Oubangui-Char-Tchad." *Depêche Coloniale,* no. 15, August 15, 1910, pp. 183–92.

Julien, C. "Le Dar Ouadai." *Renseignements Coloniaux,* no. 2, February 1904, pp. 51–62; no. 3, March 1904, pp. 108–110; no. 5, May 1904, pp. 138–43.

———. "Mohammed es Senoussi et ses états." *Bulletin de la Société de*

Recherches Congolaises (Brazzaville), nos. 7, 8, 9, 10; 1925, 1927, 1928, 1929; pp. 104–77, 55–122, 49–96, 45–88.

Kake, I. B. "Genèse des états africains: Le Tchad." *Bingo,* March 1971, pp. 14–16.

Kapteijns, Lidwien. "Dar Sila, the Sultanate in Pre-colonial times." *Cahiers d'Etudes Africaines,* no. 92, 1983, pp. 447–70.

———. "The Organization of Exchange in Precolonial Western Sudan." In Leif Ole Manger (ed.), *Trade and Traders in the Sudan,* Bergen (Norway): University of Bergen Department of Social Anthropology, 1984, pp. 49–80.

Kapteijns, Lidwien, and J. Spaulding. *After the Millennium: Diplomatic Correspondence from Wadai and Darfur on the Eve of Colonial Conquest, 1885–1916.* East Lansing: Michigan State University, African Studies Center, 1988.

Kelinguen, Y. "Renaissance d'un sultanat dans l'Afrique Centrale Française: Le Ouadai." *Afrique et Asie,* no. 13, 1951, pp. 34–40.

Khayar, Issa Hassan. *Tchad, regards sur les élites ouaddaiennes.* Paris: CNRS, 1984.

Kieffer, J. "La France au Tchad." *Bulletin de la Société Normande de Géographie,* vol. 32, 1910, pp. 181–95.

———. "Le Kouti: Le massacre de la Mission Crampel." *Bulletin de la Société Géographique d'Alger et de l'Afrique du Nord,* 1905, pp. 290–303.

Kirk-Greene, A.H.M. "The British Consulate at Lake Chad: A Forgotten Treaty with the Sheikh of Bornu." *African Affairs,* vol. 58, no. 233, October 1959, pp. 334–39.

Kogongar, Jean Gayo. "Introduction à la vie et à l'histoire précoloniale des populations Sara du Tchad." Ph.D. diss., University of Paris, 1976.

Kollmannsperger, A. *Auf der Strasse der Zugvöget. Bericht einer Afrika-Expedition.* Pfaffenhofen: Ilmgan Verlag, 1961.

Kryszanowski, L. "La pénétration du Sahara par l'Algérie et la mission Foureau-Lamy." *Questions Diplomatiques et Coloniales,* vol. 7, 1899, pp. 129–45.

Kund. "Bericht über enine Bereisung der deutschfranzosischen Grenze zwischen Schari-Logone-Tuburi." *Mitteilungen Deutschen Schutzgebieten,* vol. 19, 1906, pp. 1–30.

Labatut. "Le territoire militaire du Tchad (Kanem, le Lac Tchad, Ouaddai)." *Bulletin de la Société de Géographie d'Alger et de l'Afrique du Nord,* vol. 16, 1911, pp. 119–53.

Lacorre. "Le Tibesti et la colonne Loefler, 1913–1914." *Revue des Troupes Coloniales,* 1920, pp. 172–202.

Laigret-Pascault, Denyse E. *Fort-Lamy, capitale de la République du Tchad.* Monaco: Paul Bory, 1961.

Lampden, G. D. "History of Darfur." *Sudan Notes and Records,* no. 31, December 1950, pp. 177–209.

Landeroin, M. "Du Tchad au Niger: Notes historiques." In Auguste Jean Marie Tilho, *Documents Scientifiques de la Mission Tilho, 1906–1909,* 3 vols., Paris: Larose, 1911.

Lange, Dierk. *Chronologie et histoire d'un royaume africain.* Wiesbaden: Franz Steiner Verlag, 1977.

———. "L'eviction des Séfuwa du Kanem et l'origine des Bulala." *Journal of African History,* vol. 33, no. 3, 1982, pp. 315–31.

———. "The Kingdoms and Peoples of Chad." In *General History of Africa,* vol. 4, London: Heinemann, 1984.

———. "Préliminaires pour une histoire des Sao." *Journal of African History,* vol. 30, no. 2, 1989, pp. 189–210.

———. "Trois hauts dignitaires Bornouans du XVIe siècle: Le Digmo, le Grand Jamma, et le Cikama." *Journal of African History,* vol. 29, 1988, pp. 177–189.

Lange, Dierk, and B. W. Barkindo. "The Chad Region as a Crossroads." In M. El Fasi (ed.), *Africa from the Seventh to the Eleventh Century,* London: Heinemann, 1988, pp. 436–460.

Lange, Fried. *Mossa, Wann Kommst du Wieder: Zwischen Tschad-see und Gütterberg.* Dusseldorf: Volkischer Verlag, 1942.

Lanier, H. "L'ancien royaume de Baghirmi: Histoire et coutumes." *Renseignements Coloniaux de l'Afrique Française,* no. 10, 1925, pp. 457–74.

Lanne, Bernard. "Histoire d'une frontière, ou la 'Bande d'Aouzou.' " *Afrique et l'Asie Modernes,* no. 154, 1987, pp. 3–15.

———. *Liste des chefs, des unités administratives du Tchad.* Paris: Ecole des Hautes Etudes en Sciences Sociales, 1983.

———. "Le Tchad pendant la guerre, 1939–1945." In C. R. Ageron (ed.), *Les chemins de la décolonisation de l'empire colonial français,* Paris: CNRS, 1986, pp. 439–54.

Lapie, Pierre Olivier. *Le Tchad fait la guerre.* Paris: Hachette, 1945.

Lapierre, L. "Deux épisodes de la guerre au Sahara." *Renseignements* no. 4, 1920, pp. 69–82.

———. "Situation des pays et protectorats du Tchad au point de vue économique." *Revue Coloniale,* vol. 3, 1903, pp. 642–60; vol. 4, 1904, pp. 79–97.

———. "La situation du territoire militaire du Tchad au début de 1912." *Renseignements Coloniaux,* no. 1, 1913, pp. 3–20; no. 2, 1913, pp. 73–91.

Lavers, John E. "An Introduction to the History of Bagirmi, c. 1500–1800." *Annals of Borno,* vol. 1, 1983, pp. 29–44.

———. "Kanem and Borno under Three Dynasties." In J. F. Ade Ajayl and Bashir Ikara (eds.), *Evolution of Political Culture in Nigeria,* Ibadan: Ibadan University Press, 1985, pp. 18–32.

Lavit, F. "La colonie du Tchad en 1923." *Renseignements Coloniaux de l'Afrique Française,* vol. 34, 1924, pp. 117–29, 232–42, 255–56.

Law, R.C.C. "The Garamantes and Trans-Saharan Enterprise in Classical Times." *Journal of African History,* vol. 8, no. 2, 1967, pp. 181–200.

Lebeuf, Annie M. D. "Boum Massenia, capitale de l'ancien royaume du Baguirmi." *Journal de la Société des Africanistes,* vol. 37, no. 2, 1967, pp. 215–44.

———. "Les dignitaires de la cour de Massenya." *Paideuma,* no. 23, 1977, pp. 41–93.

———. "Le royaume du Baguirmi." In Claude Tardits (ed.), *Princes et serviteurs du royaume: Cinq études de monarchies africaines,* Paris: Société d'Ethnographie, 1987, pp. 171–225.

Lebeuf, Jean Paul. "Contribution à l'étude de l'histoire de la région Tchadienne et considerations sur la méthode." In J. Vansina (ed.), *The Historian in Tropical Africa.* London: Oxford University Press, 1964, pp. 239–56.

———. *Quand l'or était vivant: Aventures au Tchad.* Paris: J. Susse, 1945.

———. "Les Sao du Tchad: La renaissance d'une civilisation disparue." *Comptes Rendus de l'Académie des Sciences Coloniales,* vol. 5/6, 1944, pp. 257–67.

———. "The Site of Wara (Republic of Chad)." *Journal of the Historical Society of Nigeria,* no. 2/3, 1962, pp. 396–99.

Lebeuf, Jean Paul, and M. Rodinson. "Les mosquées de Fort-Lamy." *Bulletin de l'IFAN,* vol. 14, no. 3, July 1952, pp. 970–74.

Lebrun, A. "Préface à la pénétration française au Tchad de Ferrandi." *Afrique Française,* no. 3, March 1930, pp. 103–4.

Le Coeur, Marguerite. *Les oasis du Kawar, une route, un pays.* Niamey (Niger): IRSH, 1985.

Le Cornec, Jacques. "Baguirmi and Kanem." In P.J.M. McEwan (ed.), *Africa from Early Times to 1800,* London: Oxford University Press, 1968, pp. 122–33.

Lemarchand, René. "Les émeutes de Fort-Lamy (1946) et Fort-Archambault." *Le Mois en Afrique,* no. 231/2, April/May, 1985, pp. 3–15.

Lenier, H. "L'ancien royaume du Baguirmi." *Renseignements Coloniaux et Documents,* vol. 35, 1925, pp. 457–74.

Leroy-Beaulieu, P. "La pénétration de la France au Sahara." *Economiste Française,* no. 49, December 8, 1906, pp. 828–30.

Le Rumeur, Guy. *Méhariste et chef de poste du Tchad.* Paris: Harmattan, 1991.

"Une lettre inédité de Marchand à Gentil." *Revue d'Histoire des Colonies,* vol. 40, no. 140/141, 1953, pp. 431–442.

Leviel, A. *Deux grand coloniaux: Victor Largeau, explorateur du Sa-*

hara; *Le Général Largeau, organisateur et pacificateur de la colonie du Tchad*. Niort: G. Lavadoux, 1928.

Lewicki, Tadeusz. "A propos du nom de l'oasis de Koufra chez les géographes arabes du XIe et du XIIe siècle." *Journal of African History,* vol. 6, no. 3, 1965, pp. 295–306.

———. "L'état nord-africain de Tahert et ses relations avec le Soudan occidental à la fin du 18e et 19e siècle." *Cahiers d'Etudes Africaines,* vol. 28, 1962, pp. 513–35.

———. "Traits d'histoire du commerce transsaharien: Marchands et missionnaires ibadites au Soudan occidental et central au cours des VIIIe–XXe siècles." *Ethnografia Polska,* vol. 8, 1964, pp. 291–311.

Lippert, Julius. *Rabah*. Berlin, 1899.

Loefler. "La pacification du Tibesti (1913–1914)." *Renseignements Coloniaux de l'Afrique Française,* no. 7, July 1916, pp. 173–99.

MacMichael, A.A.A. *History of the Arabs in the Sudan and Darfur*. 2 vols. Reprint of 1935 edition. London: Cass. 1965.

Magendie, A. "Les ruines de Ouara." *Bulletin de la Société des Recherches Congolaises* (Brazzaville), no. 22, 1936, pp. 148–54.

Magnant, Jean-Pierre. "Terre de lignage et état chez les populations Sara du Sud du Tchad." *Revue Française d'Histoire d'Outre-Mer,* vol. 68, no. 250/253, 1981, 394–426.

———. *La troisième mort de l'Empire du Borno*. Bordeaux: CEAN, 1989.

Maillard, Jean. "Au Ouaddai de 1909 à 1912." *Encyclopédie Mensuelle d'Outre-Mer*. November 1953.

Maillard, M. "Histoire du Kanem." *Mémoires du CHEAM,* no. 1903, 1951.

Malowist, M. "The Social and Economic Stability of the Western Sudan in the Middle Ages." *Past and Present,* vol. 33, April 1966, pp. 3–15.

Malval, Jean. *Essai de chronologie tchadienne (1707–1940)*. Paris: Editions du Centre National de la Recherche Scientifique, 1974.

———. "Les premiers médecins du Tchad." *Concours Medical,* no. 4, January 26, 1963, pp. 601–6; no. 5, February 2, 1963, pp. 767, 775.

Martin, B. G. "Kanem, Bornu, and the Fazzan: Notes on the Political History of a Trade Route." *Journal of African History,* vol. 10, no. 1, 1969, pp. 15–27.

———. "Mai Idris of Bornu and the Ottoman Turcs." *International Journal of Middle East Studies*. no. 3, 1972.

Martin, Gaston. *Histoire de l'esclavage dans les colonies françaises*. Paris: Presses Universitaires de France, 1948.

Martine, F. "Essai sur l'histoire du pays Salamat." *Bulletin de la Société de Recherches Congolaises,* vol. 5, 1924, pp. 19–95.

———. "Essai sur l'histoire du pays Salamat et les moeurs et coutumes et ses habitants." *Géographie,* vol. 43, March 1925, pp. 296–316,

April/May 1925, pp. 423–41; vol. 44, June 1925, pp. 36–44, July/August 1925, pp. 155–64.

Masson, A. "L'organisation politique de la région du Tchad." *Mémoires du CHEAM,* no. 241, 1938.

Mauny, R. "La Savane nilo-tchadienne, voie de pénétration des influences egyptiennes et orientales?" In *Conferencia International des Africanistes Occidentales,* vol. 2, Santa Isabel de Fernando Poo, 1951, pp. 83–115.

Meillassoux, Claude. *L'esclavage en Afrique précoloniale.* Paris: Maspero, 1975.

Menier, M. A. "La Marche au Tchad de 1887 à 1891." *Bulletin Institut d'Etudes Centre-Africaines,* vol. 5, 1953, pp. 5–18.

Meunier, D. "Le commerce de sel de Taoudeni." *Journal des Africanistes,* vol. 50, no. 2, 1980, pp. 133–144.

Meyerowitz, E.L.R. "The Origins of the 'Sudanic' Civilizations." *Anthropos,* vol. 67, no. 1/2, 1972, pp. 161–75.

Meynier, Octave F. *Les conquérants du Tchad.* Paris: Flammarion, 1923.

———. *La Mission Joalland-Meynier.* Paris: Editions de l'Empire Français, 1947.

Migeod, Frederick William H. "The Ancient So People of Bornu." *Journal of the African Society.* vol. 23, no. 89, 1923/24, pp. 19–29.

Millam, J. J. "Découverte et pacification du Sahara." *Revue Historique de l'Armée,* vol. 15, no. 4, 1959, pp. 55–66.

Modat, C. "Une tournée en pays Fertyt." *Renseignements Coloniaux,* May 1912, pp. 177–98; June 1912, pp. 218–37; July 1912, pp. 270–98.

Mohammadou, Eldridge. *Idriss Aloma ou l'épopée du Kanem-Bornu.* Dakar: Nouvelles Editions Africaines, 1983.

Monteil, V. "Les manuscrits historiques arabo-africains." *Bulletin de l'IFAN,* vol. 28, no. 3/4, July–October, 1966, pp. 668–75.

Monterin, Umberto. "Missione della Reale Società Geografica nel Deserto Libico e nel Tibesti." *Bolletino Geografico* (Tripoli), no. 7, July–December 1934, pp. 9–33.

Moran, Denise. *Tchad.* Paris: Gallimard, 1934.

Morin, M. "Fort-Lamy, capitale et métropole incomplète." Ph.D. diss., University of Lyons, 1972.

Moullet, A. "Le Ténéré, Kaouar: Du Tibesti au Hoggar." *Revue des Troupes Coloniales,* vol. 28, 1934, pp. 105–25, 269–90.

Nachtigal, Gustav. *Sahara und Sudan.* 3 vols. Berlin: Weidmannsche Buchhandlung, 1879–89.

———. "Übersicht über die Geschichte Wadai's." *Zeitschrift der Gesellschaft für Erdkunde zu Berlin,* vol. 6, 1871, pp. 345–66.

———. "Zur Geschichte Baghirmi's." *Zeitschrift der Gessellschaft für Erdkunde zu Berlin,* vol. 9, 1874, pp. 39–59, 99–133.

Nojigoto, Adda. *La Naissance d'une Colonie: Le Tchad de 1900 à 1909.* Abidjan: Institut d'Histoire, 1981.

O'Fahey, Rex S. *A Catalog of Dar Fur Documents.* Bergen (Norway), University of Bergen, 1981.

———. *Enigmatic Saint: Ahmad Ibn Idris and the Idrisi Tradition.* London: Hurst, 1990.

———. *Land in Dar Fur.* Cambridge: Cambridge University Press, 1983.

———. "Slavery and the Slave Trade in Darfur." *Journal of African History,* vol. 14, no. 1, 1973, pp. 29–43.

———. *State and Society in Dar Fur.* New York: St. Martin's Press, 1980.

———. *States and State-formation in the Eastern Sudan.* Khartoum: University of Khartoum Research Unit, 1970.

———. "The Tunjur: A Central Sudanese Mystery." *Sudan Notes and Records,* no. 61, 1980, pp. 47–60.

O'Fahey, Rex S., and J. L. Spaulding. *Kingdoms of the Sudan.* London: Methuen, 1974.

Oppenheim, Max von. *Rabeh und das Tschadseegebiet.* Berlin: D. Reimer, 1902.

Pacques, V. "Origine et caractère du pouvoir royal au Buguirmi." *Journal de la Société des Africanistes,* vol. 37, no. 2, 1967, pp. 183–214.

Palmer, H. R. "The Bornu Girgam." *Journal of the African Society,* vol. 12, 1912, pp. 71–83.

———. *The Bornu, Sahara and Sudan.* London: J. Murray, 1936.

———. "History of Katsina." *Journal of the African Society,* vol. 26, 1926, pp. 216–36.

———. *A History of the First Twelve Years of the Reign of Mai Idris Alooma of Bornu.* Lagos: 1926.

———. "The Kano Chronicles." *Journal of the Royal Anthropological Institute,* vol. 38, 1908, pp. 58–98.

———. "Origin of the Name Bornu." *Journal of the African Society,* vol. 28, October 1928, pp. 36–42.

———. "The Pre-Tunjur Rulers of Wadai." *Sudan Notes and Records,* vol. 5, 1922, pp. 197–99.

Perez Mazarredo, Marie-Claire. "Enfoques." Special issue no. 2, 1984.

Pimlott, J. "The French Army: From Indochina to Chad, 1946–1984." In I. F. W. and J. Pimlott (eds.), *Armed Forces and Modern Counterinsurgency,* London: Croom Helm, 1985.

Poux-Crsnsac, Germaine. "Tage Rabebe, chanson de Rabah." *Journal de la Société des Africanistes,* vol. 7, no. 2, 1937, pp. 173–87.

"Rabah." *L'Afrique Française,* no. 7, 1899, p. 222; no. 8, 1899, p. 267.

Relations interethniques et culture matérielle dans le bassin du Lac Tchad. Paris: ORSTOM, 1990.

Reyna, S. P. *Wars without End: The Political Economy of a Precolonial State*. Hanover, NH: University Press of New England, 1990.

Rivallain, Josette. "Palémonnaies africaines: Moyens d'approche et fonctionnement: Une exemple en pays Sara, sud du Tchad." *Economies et Sociétés,* vol. 20, no. 2, 1986, pp. 31–48.

Roberts, Allen F. "A Note on the Precolonial Iron Currency of the Lake of Southwestern Chad." *Journal des Africanistes,* vol. 58, no. 1, 1988, pp. 99–105.

Roche, Jean de la. *Le Gouverneur Général Eboué.* Paris: Hachette, 1957.

Rodd, F. "A Fezzani Military Expedition to Kanem and Bagirmi in 1821: Major Denham's Manuscript." *Journal of the Royal African Society,* vol. 35, April 1936, pp. 153–65.

Rodinson, M. "Généalogie royale de Logone-Birni." *Etudes Camer-ounaises,* vol. 3, no. 29/30, March–June 1950, pp. 75–82.

Rolland, G. "Rabah." *Afrique Française,* no. 3, 1895, pp. 73–74.

Roncière, C. de la. "Une histoire du Bornou au XVIIe siècle par un chirurgien français captif à Tripoli." *Revue Historique des Colonies Françaises,* vol. 27, no. 3, 1919, pp. 73–88.

Rosenkrantz, Esther. "Survivances coloniale: Les problèmes politiques du Kanem." *Politique Africaine,* March 1989, pp. 124–29.

Rottier, C. "Une mission au Tibesti." *Renseignement Coloniaux,* 1928, pp. 425–43.

———. "Le Sahara oriental: Kaouar, Djado, Tibesti." *Renseignement Coloniaux,* no. 1, 1924, pp. 1–24; no. 2, 1924, pp. 78–88; no. 3, 1924, pp. 101–8.

Rouard, Decard E. *La France et la Turquie dans le Sahara Oriental.* Paris: Pedone, 1910.

Roucaud, C. "Une reconnaissance vers l'Equii et le Toro." *Renseigne-ments Coloniaux,* no. 10, 1911, pp. 229–33.

Roure, G. "Le Tibesti, bastion de notre Afrique Noire." *Illustration,* April 1, 1939, pp. 411–16.

Saidu Bi Hayatu, Sultan. *Sultan Saydu Bi Hayatu Tells the Story of His and His Father's Life.* Edited by Hermann Jungraithmayr and Wil-fried Gunther. Munich: W. Fink, 1978.

Schneider, J. "Le Département du Borkou-Ennedi-Tibesti." *Revue des Troupes Coloniales,* vol. 30, January/February 1936, pp. 10–51.

———. "Le Tibesti." *Bulletin de la Société de Recherches Congolaises* (Brazzaville), no. 27, June 1939, pp. 5–93.

Schultze, A. *The Sultanate of Bornu.* London: Cass, 1968, reprint of 1913 edition.

Seid, Joseph Brahim. "Ouaddai dans le passé." *Liaison,* no. 42, 1954, pp. 69–76.

———. "Saboun, roi du Ouaddai." *Liaison,* no. 44, 1954, pp. 81–86; no. 45, 1955, pp. 48–54.

————. "Les Senoussistes pendant la guerre, 1914–1918." In *Les troupes coloniales pendant la guerre, 1914–1918.* Paris: Imprimerie Nationale, 1931, pp. 483–98.

————. *Le Tchad.* Casablanca: Editions Fontane, 1958.

Smith, M. G. "The Beginnings of Hausa Society, A.D. 1000–1500." in J. Vansina, R. Maunyand, and L. V. Jones (eds.), *The Historian in Tropical Africa,* London: Oxford University Press, 1964, pp. 339–357.

Spaulding, Jay, and Kidwien Kapteijns. *An Islamic Alliance: 'Ali Dinar and the Sanusiyya, 1906–1916.* Evanston, IL: Northwestern University Press, 1994.

Spittler, Gerd. "Karawanenhandel und kamelrazzia bei den kel ewer: Die kontrolle des salz-und hirsenhandels zwischen Air, Bilma und Kano, 1850–1900." *Paiedeuma,* vol. 30, 1984, pp. 139–160.

Sturzinger, U. "The Introduction of Cotton Cultivation in Chad: The Role of the Administration, 1920–1936." *African Economic History,* vol. 12, 1983, pp. 213–225.

Terrier, A. "Après le départ des Turcs." *Afrique Française,* no. 11, 1912, pp. 429–30.

————. "La campagne du Tchad." *Journal des Voyages,* vol. 9, 1900/1901, pp. 313–16; 331–33; 346–47; 365–67; 378–79.

————. "La défaite et la mort de Fadel Allah." *Afrique Française,* no. 1, 1902, pp. 2–6.

————. "Le drame de Bir Taouil." *Afrique Française,* no. 5, 1910, pp. 181–84.

————. "Les Français au Lac Tchad." *Journal des Voyages,* vol. 8, 1900, pp. 241–44.

————. "La France autour du Lac Tchad." *Afrique Française,* no. 6, 1902, pp. 222–25; no. 7, 1902, pp. 251–54; no. 9, 1902, pp. 314–26; no. 12, 1902, pp. 414–17.

————. "Le massacre de la Mission Bretonnet." *Afrique Française,* no. 11, 1899, pp. 362–68.

————. "La Mission Joallnd-Meynier." *Journal des Voyages,* vol. 100, 1901, pp. 95–96; 101–3; 121–23; 133–35.

————. "La pacification du territoire militaire du Tchad: La soumission des sultans Doudmourrah et Bakjit." *Afrique Française,* no. 111, 1912, pp. 77–83.

————. "La prise d'Abéché." *Afrique Française,* no. 10, 1909, pp. 334–36.

————. "La Région du Chari." *Afrique Française,* no. 4, 1901, pp. 100–4.

————. "La Route Soudanaise du Lac Tchad." *Questions Diplomatiques et Coloniales,* vol. 17, 1904, pp. 873–83.

————. "Sénoussi d'El Kouti." *Afrique Française,* no. 12, 1903, pp. 393–98.

————. "La soumission de Senoussi." *Afrique Française,* no. 9, 1901, pp. 290–92.

————. "La situation au Ouaddai." *Afrique Française,* no. 11, 1903, pp. 362–64.

————. "Traversée de l'Afrique: La Mission Foureau-Lamy." *Journal des Voyages,* vol. 9, 1900/1901, pp. 25–27; 43–45; 57–59; 75–77; 93–95; 110–14; 127–30; 137–40; 163–65; 174–75; 190–91.

Theobald, A. B. *Ali Dinar, Last Sultan of Darfur.* London: Longmans, 1965.

Toura Gaba, M. J. "Gakol et Gaguel: Deux héros de la légende Pen." *Liaison,* no. 49/50, 1955, pp. 55–57; no. 51, 1956, 51–53; no. 53, 1956, 71–75.

Triaud, Jean Louis. *Tchad 1900–1902: Une guerre franco-libyenne oubliée? Une confrérie musulmane, la Sanusiyya, face à la France.* Paris: Harmattan, 1989.

Tubiana, Marie-José. "Un document inédit sur les sultans du Wadday [Ousman ibn Fodé. Etude sur l'histoire du Ouaddai]." *Cahiers d'Etudes Africaines,* no. 2, May 1960, pp. 49–112.

Tubiana, Marie-José, and Joseph Tubiana. "Mission au Darfur." *L'Homme,* vol. 7, no. 1, 1967, pp. 89–96.

Tubiana, Marie-José, et al. *Adb-el Karim, propagateur de l'Islam et fondateur du royaume du Ouaddai.* Paris: CNRS, 1978.

"Les Turcs et l'Afrique Centrale." *Afrique Française,* no. 5, 1906, pp. 133–34.

Urvoy, Yves F. "Bornu Conquest and Empire." In P.J.M. McEwan (ed.), *Africa from Early Times to 1800,* London: Oxford University Press, 1968, pp. 47–59.

————. "Chronologie du Bornou." *Journal de la Société des Africanistes,* vol. 11, 1941, pp. 21–32.

————. *L'histoire de l'Empire du Bornou.* Paris: Larose, 1949.

Usman, Bala, and Nur Alkali (eds.), *Studies in the History of Precolonial Borno.* Zaria (Nigeria): Northern Nigeria Publishing Company, 1983.

Van Kretschmer, J. A. "Tibesti: Ben bargwoestigien in de Sahara." *Mededelingen van het Afrika-instituut* (Leiden), 1950, pp. 282–287.

Van Vollenhoven. *Le Voyage de Nachtigal au Ouadai.* Paris: Larose, n.d.

Vossart, J. "Histoire du sultanat du Mandara." *Etudes Camerounaises,* vol. 4, no. 35/36, pp. 19–52.

Wright, John. "Chad and Libya: Some Historical Connections." *Maghreb Review,* vol. 8, no. 3/4, 1983, pp. 91–95.

————. *Libya, Chad, and the Central Sahara.* London: Hurst and Co., 1989.

————. "The Wadai-Benghazi slave route." *Slavery and Abolition* (London), vol. 13, no. 1, 1992, pp. 174–184.

Yagoussou, A. "Un nouveau prophète au Baghirmi: Mohamed Ali." *Revue Indigène,* no. 34, February 1909, pp. 72–74.

Zachariah, K. C., and J. Condo. *Migration in West Africa,* Washington: B.I.R.D., 1981.

Zeltner, Jean-Claude. *Les arabes dans la région du Lac Tchad.* Sarh (Chad): C.E.L., 1977.

————. "Histoire de Rabeh." *Tchad et Culture,* no. 95, June 1976, pp. 17–21.

————. "Histoire des arabes sur les rives du Lac 'Tchad.' " *Annales de l'Université d'Abidjan.* (Abidjan), Ser. F, 2, no. 2, 1970, pp. 109–237.

————. "Histoire du Kanem." *Tchad et Culture,* no. 96–100, November 1976–May 1977.

————. "L'Imam Ibn Fortu . . . sur le Kanem." *Tchad et Culture,* no. 112, November 1978.

————. "L'installation des arabes au sud du Lac Tchad." *Abbia* (Yaoundé), 16, March 1967, pp. 129–53.

————. "Le May Idris Alaoma et les Kotoko." *Revue Camerounaise d'Histoire,* vol. 1, 1971, pp. 36–40.

————. *Pages d'histoire du Kanem.* Paris: Harmattan, 1980.

————. *Les pays du Tchad dans la tourmente (1880–1903).* Paris: Harmattan, 1988.

————. *Tripoli, carrefour de l'Europe et des pays du Tchad, 1500–1795.* Paris: Harmattan, 1992.

————. "Tripolitaine et pays toubou et des pays du Tchad, XIXe siècle." *Islam et Sociétés au Sud du Sahara,* vol. 3, 1989, pp. 90–105.

Anthropology and Sociology

Abras, A. "Le Canton Diongor-Aboutelfan." N'Djamena: Ecole Nationale d'Administration, 1967.

Adler, Alfred. "Essai sur la signification des relations de dépendance personnelle dans l'ancien systeme politique des Moundan du Tchad." *Cahiers d'Etudes Africaines,* vol. 9, no. 35, 1969, pp. 441–60.

————. "L'ethnologie et les fétiches." *Nouvelle Revue de Psychoanalyse,* no. 2, 1970, pp. 149–58.

————. "Faiseurs de pluie, faiseurs d'ordre." *Libre,* no. 2, 1977, pp. 45–68.

————. "La fillette amoureuse des masques: Le statut de la femme chez les Moundang." *Journal des Africanistes,* vol. 52, no. 1/2, 1989, pp. 63–97.

————. "Les jumeaux sont rois chez les Moundang [Tchad]." *L'Homme,* vol. 13, no. 1/2, January–April 1973, pp. 167–92.

————. *La mort et le masque du roi: La royauté sacrée des Moundang du Tchad.* Paris: Payot, 1982.

————. *Les pays de Boura: Notes sur la vie sociale et religieuse d'une population du Moyen-Chari.* Fort-Lamy: Institut National Tchadien pour les Sciences Humaines, 1966.

————. "Le pouvoir et l'interdit: Aspects de la royauté sacrée chez les Moundang." In *Systèmes de signes: Textes réunis en hommage à Germaine Dieterlen.* Paris: Hermann, 1978, pp. 25–40.

————. "Rapport sur une mission en pays Mbay (sud du Tchad), juillet 1963–février 1964." *Cahiers d'Etudes Africaines,* vol. 5, no. 2 (18), February 1965, pp. 341–47.

————. "Royauté et sacrifice chez les Moundang du Tchad." In M. Cartry (ed.), *Sous la masque de l'animal: Essais sur le sacrifice en Afrique Noire.* Paris: Presses Universitaires de France, 1987, pp. 89–130.

————. "La transgression et sa dérision." *L'Homme,* vol. 2, no. 3, 1972, pp. 5–63.

Adler, Alfred, and John Leavitt. "The Ritual Doubling of the Person of the King." In Michel Izard et al. (eds.), *Between Belief and Transgression: Structuralist Essays in Religion, History, and Myth.* Chicago: University of Chicago Press, 1982, pp. 180–192.

Adler, Alfred, and A. Zempieni. *Le baton de l'aveugle: Divination, maladie, et pouvoir chez les Moundang du Tchad.* Paris: Hermann, 1972.

————. "La divination chez les Moundang du Tchad." *Sciences,* no. 73, 1971, pp. 4–11.

Agblemagnon, Ferdinand N'sougan. "Approccio critico alla problematica attuale dello sviluppo nazionale." *Quaderni di Sociologia* (Milan), vol. 20, no. 3/4, 1971, pp. 287–94.

Agostini, J. de. "Promotion sociale au pays Hadjerai." *Latitudes,* no. 1, 1957, pp. 23–30.

Akester, R. "Tibesti: Land of the Tebou." *Geographical Magazine,* vol. 31, 1958, pp. 12–26.

Ala, R. "Notes sur les relations entre les hommes et la terre dans les zones à berbéré du Bas-Chari Tchadien." Paris: Mémoires E.N.F.O.M., 1959.

Amady, G. "Aperçu sur le régime successoral chez les Moundangs du Tchad." *Revue Juridique et Politique,* vol. 26, no. 4, 1972, pp. 819–26.

Antonini, Ange-Raymond. "Les fondements métaphysiques de la morale chez les Kirdis du Tchad et du Cameroun." *Bulletins et Mémoires de le Société d'Anthropologie de Paris,* vol. 9, no. 4, October–December 1966, pp. 367–76.

Arbaumont, J. d'. "Notes sur un voyage au Tibesti (Avril 1950): Tableau des clans." *Mémoire du CHEAM,* no. 2355, 1953.

————. "Organisation politique au Tibesti." *Bulletin de l'IFAN,* vol. 18, 1956, pp. 148–55.

————. "Réflexions sur les Toubous." *Tropiques,* no. 365, August/September 1954, pp. 35–38.

———. "Santons du Tibesti oriental: Désignation des chefs coutumiers au Tibesti et au Borkou." *Mémoires du CHEAM,* no. 2354, 1963.

———. "Le Tibesti et le domaine Teda-Daza." *Bulletin de l'IFAN,* vol. 16, no. 3/4, 1954, pp. 255–306.

———. "Traditions du Tibesti oriental." *Encyclopédie Mensuelle d'Outre-Mer,* no. 45, May 1954, pp. 163–65.

Arditi, Claude. "La mise sur la natte: Rites de possession et condition féminine en milieu islamisé à N'Djamena." *Objets et Mondes* vol. 20, no. 2, Summer 1980, pp. 49–60.

———. "Les populations de la moyenne vallée du Chari (Tchad): Vie économique et sociale." *Cahiers d'Etudes Africaines,* vol. 11, no. 44, 1971, pp. 614–43.

———. "Troubles mentaux et rites de possession au Tchad." *Coopération et Développement,* no. 38, 1971, pp. 34–38.

Authier, D. "L'ethnographie et l'anthropologie des Toubous du Tibesti méridional et du Borkou-Ennedi." *Anthropologie,* vol. 30, 1920, pp. 577–78.

Azevedo, Mario Joaquim. "Power and Slavery in Central Africa: Chad (1890–1925)." *Journal of Negro History,* vol. 67, no. 3, Fall 1982, pp. 198–211.

———. "Sara Demographic Instability as a Consequence of French Colonial Policy in Chad." Ph.D. diss., Duke University, 1976.

Bachar, M. *Mangalmé, préfecture du Guéra et ses habitants, les Moubi.* Fort-Lamy: Ecole Nationale d'Administration, 1970.

Baguerri, Hassane. "Chez les Nomades du Batha." *Communauté France-Eurafrique,* no. 138, January 1962, pp. 17–18.

Balfour-Paul, H.G. "A Prehistoric Cult Still Practiced in Muslim Darfur," *Journal of the Royal Anthropological Institute,* vol. 86, 1956, pp. 77–86.

Bardinet, C. "La population des vendeurs du grand marché de N'Djamena en 1976." *Cahiers d'Outre-Mer,* vol. 31, no. 121, July–September 1978, pp. 225–50.

Baroin, Catherine. "Anarchie et cohésion chez les Toubous." Ph.D. diss., University of Paris, 1982.

———. "Effets de la colonisation sur la société traditionnelle Daza." *Journal des Africanistes,* vol. 47, no. 2, 1977, pp. 123–39.

——— (ed.). *Gens du roc et du sables: Les Toubou.* Paris: CNRS, 1988.

———. "Une histoire honteuse: Le chef et la viande." In C. Baroin (ed.), *Gens du roc et du sables: Les Toubou.* Paris: CNRS, 1988, pp. 111–137.

———. "Les masques de bétail chez les Azza et Daza du Niger." *Etudes Nigeriennes,* no. 29, 1972.

———. "Organisation territoriale, organisation sociale: La logique du système toubou." *Journal des Africanistes,* vol. 56, no. 2, 1986, pp. 7–27.

Bary, Erica de. "Erlebtes Leben im Tschadsee Distrikt." *Neues Afrika,* vol. 2, no. 9, September 1965, pp. 280–83.

Bataillon, C. "Modernisation du nomadisme pastorale." *Nomades et Nomadisme au Sahara,* Paris: UNESCO, pp. 165–77.

Behm, E. "Das Land und Volk der Tebu: Versuch einer geographischen und ethnographischen Skiz ze der Ostlichen Sahara," *Petermanns Geographische Mitteilungen,* part 2, supplement no. 8, 1862, pp. 31–67.

Beling-Nkroumba. "L'Afrique et les peuples du bassin méditerranéen: Les Sao." *Echos Pédagogigues,* vol. 3, no. 10, December 1966, pp. 5–9.

Bemmoiras, J-P. *La situation démographique du Tchad: Résultats provisoires de l'enquête démographique 1964.* Paris: SEDES, 1964.

Benton, P. A. *The Languages and Peoples of Bornu.* 2 vols. London: F. Call Co., 1968.

Bernus, Edmond, and Suzanne Bernus. *Photos de Tuaregs.* Paris: Harmattan, 1983.

Berre, H. "Daju." In R. V. Weekes (ed.), *Muslim Peoples: A World Ethnographic Survey,* London: Aldwych, 1984, pp. 219–223.

Bertaud, M. "Coutume urbaine de Fort-Lamy." *Mémoires du CHEAM,* no. 2224, 1953.

———. "La répartition des dommages corporels ou Dia devant les tribunaux indigènes de Fort-Lamy." *Mémoires du CHEAM,* no. 2175, 1953.

Beyassoum, Samuel. "La formation du lien matrimonial au Tchad." *Revue Juridique et Politique,* vol. 20, no. 1, January–March 1966, pp. 16–29.

Biasutti, R. "I Tebbu secondo recenti indagini italiane." *Archivio per Antropologia e la Ethnografia* (Florence), vol. 43, 1933, pp. 168–201.

Blaizot, R. "L'agriculture au Tibesti." *Renseignements Coloniaux de l'Afrique Française,* no. 12, 1918, pp. 243–47.

———. "Du Tibesti d'hier et de demain." *Renseignements Coloniaux de l'Afrique Française,* November 1921, pp. 6–14.

Bonfiglioli, Angelo Maliki. *Agro-pastoralism in Chad as a Strategy for Survival: An Essay on the Relationship between Anthropology and Statistics.* Washington, DC: World Bank, 1993.

Boucher, A. "Aspects du nomadisme au Tibesti-Borkou." In *Questions Sahariennes,* CHEAM no. 1009, 1945, pp. 147–63.

Bouillez, M. "De l'usage du phallus au Tchad. *Anthropologie,* 1911, pp. 41–42.

———. "Deux légendes du Tchad: Réflexions sur les So." *Institut Français d'Anthropologie: Comptes Rendus des Séances,* March 1912, pp. 80–84.

————. "Notes sur les 'Goranes' (Toubou au sens large)." *L'Anthropologie,* vol. 24, 1913, pp. 399–418.

Bouillié, R. *Les Coutumes Familiales au Kanem.* Paris: Domat-Montchrestien, 1937.

Boujol, M. "Les Arabes du Tchad." *Mémoires du CHEAM,* no. 603, 1939.

Boujol, M., and R. Clupot. "La subdivision de Melfi." *Bulletin de la Société de Recherches Congolaises* (Brazzaville), vol. 28, December 1941, pp. 13–82.

Bouquet, Christian. "Aperçu démographique et sociologique-économique du groupe Babalia (Tchad)." *Cahiers d'Etudes Africaines,* vol. 16, no. 3/4, 1976, pp. 615–26.

————. "Buduma." In R. V. Weekes (ed.), *Muslim Peoples: A World Ethnographic Survey,* London: Aldwych, 1984, pp. 180–183.

————. "Genèse et évolution de l'habitat rural dans le Bas-Chari tchadien." *Etudes Rurales,* vol. 70, April–June 1978, pp. 51–64.

————. "Les incertitudes de la démographie africaine: L'exemple du Tchad." *Les Cahiers d'Outre-Mer,* 24, no. 96, 1971, pp. 410–32.

————. *Insulaires et riverains du Lac Tchad.* 2 vol. Paris: Harmattan, 1990.

————. "Kanembu." In R. V. Weekes (ed.), *Muslim Peoples: A World Ethnographic Survey,* London: Aldwych, 1984, pp. 372–75.

————. "Kuri." In R. V. Weekes (ed.), *Muslim Peoples: A World Ethnographic Survey,* London: Aldwych, 1984, pp. 427–29.

————. "Les limites d'une étude de régionalisation au Sud Kanem." *Les Cahiers d'Outre-Mer,* no. 103, July–September 1973, pp. 262–78.

————. "Un peuple insulaire qui vit au rythme de l'eau: Les Buduma." In A. Singaravelou (ed.), *Pauvreté et développement dans les pays tropicaux.* Bordeaux: Centre de Recherches sur les Espaces Tropicaux, 1989.

Boussarie, L. "L'habitat européen au Tchad." *Mémoires du CHEAM,* no. 1524, 1950.

Bout, R. "Le Margaye et les relations de pouvoir chez les Hadjerayes du Tchad." Aix: Mémoire I.E.P., 1962.

Boyeldieu, Pascal, and Christian Seignobos. "Contribution à l'étude du pays Niellim." *Annales de l'Université du Tchad,* no. 3, May 1975, pp. 67–98.

Branche, A. "Superstitions et pratiques de médecine indigènes au Kanem (Tchad)." *Annales de Médecine et Pharmacie Coloniales,* vol. 2, April–June 1936, pp. 387–405.

Brandily, Monique. "Les inégalités dans la société du Tibesti." In C. Baroin (ed.), *Gens du roc et du sables: Les Toubou,* Paris: CNRS, 1988, pp. 37–71.

———. "Piègeage des oiseux au Tibesti." *Objets et Mondes,* vol. 20, no. 4, 1980, pp. 141–48.

———. "Au Tibesti, l'investiture du dernier Derde." *Balafon,* no. 51, 1981.

———. "Un exorcisme musical chez les Kotoko." *La Musique dans la Vie* (Paris), vol. 1, 1967, pp. 33–75.

Braukamper, Ulrich. "Wanderungen und Transhumanzzyklen von Rindernomaden in Darfur." *Paideuma,* vol. 35, 1989, pp. 17–38.

Bremaud, O. "Nomadisme et transhumance en Afrique subsaharienne." *Revue d'Elevage et Médicine Tropicale,* vol. 8, no. 4, 1955, pp. 327–55.

Bremaud, O., and J. Pagot. "Grazing Lands, Nomadism, and Transhumance in the Sahel." *Problems of the Arid Zone,* Paris, UNESCO, 1962.

Briey, D. "Industrialization and Social Problems in Central Africa." *International Labour Review,* vol. 43, no. 5, May 1951, pp. 475–506.

Briggs, Lloyd Cabot. "Aperçu sur l'anthropologie des Teda." *Bulletin de l'IFAN,* vol. 18, 1956, pp. 280–85.

———. *Tribes of the Sahara.* Cambridge: Harvard University Press, 1960.

Brown, Ellen P. *Nourrir les gens, nourrir les haines.* Paris: Société d'Ethnographie, 1983.

Bruel, Georges. "Le cercle du Moyen-Logone." *Renseignements Coloniaux,* no. 10, October 1905, pp. 357–76; no. 11, November 1905, pp. 434–47.

Brusseaux. "Notes sur les Moundans, Mission Moll, 1905–1907." *Bulletin de la Société de Recherches Congolaises,* vol. 1, 1922, pp. 23–49.

Buisson, E. M. "Monographie de la subdivision de Pala." *Notions théoriques et pratiques de géologie et minéralogie coloniales,* Paris, Bureau d'Etudes Géologiques, 1945, pp. 328–42.

———. "Note sur les droits fonciers, en particulier les droits du cueillette, en pays Sara-Madjingayé." *Bulletin de la Société de Recherches Congolaises,* no. 23, August 1937, pp. 17–20.

———. "Notes éthniques sur le pays dit 'N'Gama-Suto' (Subdivision de Fort-Archambault)." *Bulletin de la Société de Recherches Congolaises,* no. 27, June 1939, pp. 107–13.

Cabot, Jean. *Le bassin du Moyen Logone.* Paris: ORSTOM, 1965.

———. *Carte ethnodémographique du bassin du Moyen-Logone.* Paris: ORSTOM, 1965.

———. "Kim, village du Moyen-Logone." *Bulletin de l'Institut d'Etudes Centrafricaines* (Brazzaville), no. 5, 1953, pp. 41–67.

———. *Population du Moyen Logone.* Paris: ORSTOM, 1953.

Cabot, Jean, and Christian Bouquet. *Atlas pratique du Tchad.* N'Djamena: Institut National Tchadien pour les Sciences Humaines, 1972.

Cabot, Jean, and Roland Diziain. *Population du Moyen-Logone.* Paris: Office de la Recherche Scientifique et Technique Outre-Mer, 1955.

Cames, A."Les Teddas Djagadas Moussouas." *Revue Militaire A.E.F.,* no. 12, 1938, pp. 45–67.

Candille, A. "Aperçu sur la médecine indigène au Ouaddai." *Revue Militaire A.E.F.,* no. 14, 1938, pp. 31–44.

Capot-Rey, R. *L'Afrique blanche française.* Vol. 2, *Le Sahara français.* Paris: Presses Universitaires de France, 1953.

———. "La bordure méridionale de l'Ennedi." *Travaux de l'Institut de Recherches Sahariennes* (Algiers), 24, 1965, pp. 47–64.

———. "Le Bourkou et Ounianga." *Travaux de l'Institut de Recherches Sahariennes,* no. 5, 1961.

———. "Introduction à une géographie humaine du Borkou." *Travaux de l'Institut de Recherches Sahariennes,* vol. 16, no. 2, 1957, pp. 41–72.

———. "Le nomadisme des Toubous." *Nomades et Nomadisme au Sahara,* Paris, UNESCO, 1963.

———. "Le nomadisme pastoral dans le Sahara français." *Travaux de l'Institut de Recherches Sahariennes,* vol. 1, 1942, pp. 63–86.

———. "La sédentarisation des nomades." *Journées d'Information Socio-médicales Sahariennes,* 1959, pp. 235–39.

———. "Le sel et le commerce du Bet." *Travaux de l'Institut de Recherches Sahariennes,* no. 18, 1959.

Carbou, Henri. *La région du Tchad et du Ouaddai.* 2 vols. Paris: E. Leroux, 1912.

Carl, L., and Petit. *Le ville du sel: Du Hoggar au Tibesti.* Paris: Julliard, 1954.

———. "Une technique archaïque de la fabrication du fer dans le Mourdi." *Ethnographie,* no. 51, 1956, pp. 60–81.

Carniaux, N. "Le mariage chez les nomades du Bahr el Ghazal." *Encyclopédie Mensuelle d'Outre-Mer,* no. 42, February 1954, pp. 68–69.

Caron, J. "Le Borkou Ennedi Tibesti." *Mémoires du CHEAM,* no. 3966, 1964.

———. "La justice coutumière dans le District de l'Ennedi." *Mémoires du CHEAM,* no. 3924, 1964.

———. "Le nomadisme des Toubous du B.E.T." *Mémoires du CHEAM,* no. 3967, 1964.

Catala, R. "L'évolution des chefferies africaines du District de Mao de 1899 à 1953." *Mémoire du CHEAM,* no. 2328, 1954.

Catherinet, M. "Quelques rites agricoles chez les Banana-Kolon et les Maïba de la région du Logone (Tchad)." *Notes Africaines,* no. 62, April 1954, pp. 40–42.

Chabrelie, L. "Note sur la langue Sara." *Journal de la Société des Africanistes,* vol. 5, 1935, pp. 125–51.

———. "Notes sur quelques croyances des Sara." *Journal de la Société des Africanistes,* no. 3, 1933, 315–18.

Chaker, Salem. *Etudes Touareges: Bilan des recherches en sciences sociales: Institutions, chercherus, bibliographie.* Aix-en-Province: Edisud, 1988.

Chalmel. "Notice sur les Bideyat." *Bulletin de la Société de Recherches Congolaises* (Brazzaville), vol. 15, October 1931, pp. 33–91.

Chapelle, Jean. "Etude sur les Toubous nègres sahariens." *Mémoires du CHEAM,* no. 804, 1946.

———. *Kreda et Kecherda du Soro.* Maison-Alfort: IEMVPT, 1965.

———. "Les nomades du Sahara méridional: Les Toubous." *Tropiques,* no. 318, February 1950, pp. 29–38; no. 319, March 1950, pp. 16–24.

———. "Les Toubous." *Mémoires du CHEAM,* no. 1039, 1947.

———. *Nomades noirs du Sahara.* Paris: Plon, 1935; Paris: Harmattan, 1982.

———. *Le peuple tchadien.* Paris: Harmattan, 1980.

———. "Tchad." *Mémoires du CHEAM,* no. 2799, 1957.

Charbonneau, R. *Essais sahariens: Au Tibesti.* Paris: L. Fournier et Cie, 1938.

Charpin, H. "Contribution à l'étude des groupes sanguins des Téda du Tibesti." *Médicine Tropicale,* vol. 20, no. 1, January/February 1960, pp. 73–75.

———. "Recherches d'anthropologie physique sur les Téda du Tibesti." *Bulletins et Mémoires de la Société d'Anthropologie de Paris,* vol. 2, 1961, pp. 439–51.

Chauvet, J. "Traditions et modernisme dans les quartiers de Sahr." *Cahiers d'Outre-Mer,* vol. 30, no. 117, January–March 1977, pp. 57–82.

Chauvet, Jacques. "Croissance urbaine et incidents de 1979 de Sarh." *Cahiers d'Outre-Mer,* no. 158, April–June, 1987, pp. 205–11.

———. "Evolution de la famille et croissance des villes moyennes: Sarh (Tchad) et Toumoudi (Côte d'Ivoire)." *Cahiers d'Outre-Mer,* no. 158, April–June 1987, pp. 173–203.

"Chez les Tchadiens." *Peuples du Monde* (Paris), no. 51, May 1972, pp. 19–34.

Clanet, J. "Les éleveurs de l'ouest tchadien." Ph.D. diss., University of Paris, 1975.

Cline, Walter. *The Teda of Tibesti, Borku, and Kawar in the Eastern Sahara.* Menasha, WI: George Banta, 1950.

Coblentz, Alex. "Goranes et Toubous des confins nord du Tchad: Etude anthropologique et biologique." Ph.D. diss., University of Paris, 1961.

"Cohabitation de nomades et de sédentaires en Afrique Noire: Les problèmes actuels du Tchad." *L'Afrique et l'Asie,* no. 63, July–September 1963, pp. 33–38.

Cohen, Ronald. "The Just-so So: A Spurious Tribal Grouping in Western Sudanic Culture." *Man,* vol. 62, October 1962.

———. "The Kingship in Bornu. In Michael Crowder and Obaro Ikime (eds.), *West African Chiefs: Their Changing Status under Colonial Rule and Independence,* New York: Africana Publishing Corporation, 1970, pp. 187–210.

———. "The Structure of Kanuri Society." Ph.D. diss., University of Wisconsin, 1960.

Conte, Edouard. "Castes, classes, et alliance au sud-Kanem." *Journal des Africanistes,* vol. 53, no. 1/2, 1983, pp. 147–69.

———. "La dynamique de l'alliance parmi les chasseurs sédentarisés Duu Rea du Sud-Kanem." *Paideuma,* vol. 32, 1986, pp. 129–61.

———. *Marriage Patterns, Political Change, and the Perpetuation of Social Inequality in South Kanem, Chad.* Paris: ORSTOM, 1983.

Courtecuisse, Louis. "Territoire du Tchad, Région du Ouadai: Les Arabes Mahamid du District de Biltine." *Mémoires du CHEAM,* n.d.

Courtecuisse, Louis, et al. *Quelques populations de la République du Tchad: Les Arabes du Tchad.* Paris: Centre des Hautes Etudes Administratives d'Afrique et d'Asie Modernes, 1971.

Courtex C. "Les Mahamid du Tchad." *Tropiques,* no. 328, January 1951, pp. 38–46.

Courtier and Gosselin, G. *Etude sur l'urbanisation et l'amélioration de l'habitat dans les quartiers africains de Fort-Lamy.* Paris: S.M.U.H., 1961.

Couvy, Dr. "Notes anthropométriques sur quelques races du territoire militaire du Tchad." *L'Anthropologie,* vol. 18, 1907, pp. 549–82.

Cransac, G. "Une fable de la Fontaine sur les bords du Chari." *Bulletin de la Société de Recherches Congolaises,* no. 20, 1935, pp. 109–15.

Crognier, E. "Adaptation morphologique d'une population africaine au biotope tropical: Les Sara du Tchad." *Bulletins et Mémoires de la Société d'Anthropologie de Paris,* vol. 10, Ser. 12, 1973.

Croqueville, J. "Le District de Kélo, Région du Logone." *Afrique Française,* April 1954, pp. 180–82.

———. "Essai d'étude démographique des Kaba du District de Kyabé, Région du Moyen-Chari." *Mémoires du CHEAM,* 1955.

Cuvillier-Fleury, R. "Monographie de la circonscription du Mayo-Kebbi." *Bulletin de la Société de Recherches Congolaises* (Brazzaville), no. 12, 1930, pp. 11–36.

Dagnac, C. "Les traditions historiques des clans habitant actuellement le Tibesti." *Bulletin de l'Institut d'Etudes Centrafricaines* (Brazzaville), vol. 1, 1945, pp. 7–31.

Dainville, Jacques de. "Habitations et types de peuplement sur la rive occidentale du lac Tchad." *Revue de Géographie Humaine et Ethnologie,* no. 2, April–June 1948, pp. 59–69.

Dalloni, M. *Mission au Tibesti (1930–1931).* 2 vols. Paris: Gauthier-Villar, 1935.

Decorse, J. "La chasse et l'agriculture chez les populations du Soudan." *L'Anthropologie,* 1905, pp. 457–73.

————. "L'habitation et le village du Congo au Tchad." *L'Anthropologie,* vol. 16, 1905, pp. 639–56.

————. "Le tatouage, les mutilations éthniques, et la parure chez les populations du Soudan." *L'Anthropologie,* 1905, pp. 129–47.

Decoux. "Au pays Sara." *Tropiques,* no. 328, January 1951, pp. 48–54.

Dehuz, L. "La toute puissante Margai." *Connaissance du Monde,* no. 23, October 1960, pp. 31–38.

Delafosse, M. *Essai sur le peuple et la langue Sara.* Paris: André et Cie, 1897.

Delange, Jacqueline. "Les arts anciens de la plaine du Tchad." *Objets et Mondes,* vol. 2, no. 3, Fall 1962, pp. 135–48.

Dennis, Pierre. "Les calebasses au Tchad." *Notes Africaines de l'IFAN,* no. 118, April 1968, pp. 53–57.

Derendinger, Général. *Autour de Melfi, un peuple d'affranchis, les Yal-Nas.* Paris: L. Fournier, 1912.

————. "Contribution à l'étude des langues nègres du centre africain." *Journal de la Société des Africanistes,* vol. 19, 1949, pp. 143–94.

————. "Les curieuses usines de fer de Télé-Nugar." *Journal de la Société des Africanistes,* vol. 6, 1936, pp. 197–204.

————. "Un peuple d'affranchis, les Yal-Nas." *Revue Indigène,* no. 71, March 1912, pp. 191–202.

Desio, A. "Una Recognizione nel Tibesti settentrionale." *Bolletino della Reale Società Geografica Italiana,* vol. 6, August/September 1941, pp. 401–8.

————. *Il Tibesti Nord-Orientale.* Rome: Società Italiana Arti Grafiche, 1942.

Devallée, J. "Le Baguirmi." *Bulletin de la Société de Recherches Congolaises* (Brazzaville), vol. 7, nos. 2–4, 1925, pp. 3–76.

Deysson, A. "Etude de la race Doza." *Bulletin de la Société de Recherches Congolaises,* no. 24, 1937, pp. 137–89.

Dizain and Cabot. *Population du Moyen Logone.* Paris: ORSTOM, 1955.

Djasgarel, L. "Grosses différences dans les droits accordés aux hommes et aux femmes." *OAMCE,* no. 5, March 1964, pp. 56–59.

————. "La polygamie est une handicap." *OAMCE,* no. 5, March 1964, pp. 59–60.

Djian, A. "Notes sur les populations musulmanes du Territoire du

Tchad." *Bulletin de la Société de Recherches Congolaises* (Brazzaville), vol. 4, no. 1, 1924, pp. 9–17.

Duisberg, A. von. "Untersuchung über die Bedeutung einiger Bornu-Namen." *Anthropos,* vol. 26, 1931, pp. 563–68.

Dumas-Champion, Françoise. *Le Masa du Tchad: Bétail et société.* New York: Cambridge University Press, 1983.

———. "Recherches sur l'organisation sociale des Masa." Ph.D. diss., University of Paris, 1977.

———. "Le role social et rituel du bétail chez les Massa du Tchad." *Africa,* vol. 50, no. 2, 1980, pp. 161–81.

———. "Le sacrifice comme procès rituel chez les Massa." *Systèmes de Pensée en Afrique Noire,* no. 4, 1979, pp. 95–116.

———. "Sacrifice et homicide en pays Massa." *Systèmes de Pensée en Afrique Noire,* no. 5, 1981, pp. 175–94.

———. "Le sacrifice ou la question du meurtre." *Anthropos,* vol. 82, no. 1/3, 1987, pp. 135–149.

Dupont, K. "Les goitres et Koumra." *Journal de la Société des Africanistes,* vol. 11, no. 1/2, 1941, pp. 225–26.

Durand, C. "Les noms de personnes au Tchad." *Penant,* no. 746, October–December 1974, pp. 429–47.

Echard, Nicole (ed.). *Les relations hommes-femmes dans le bassin du Lac Tchad.* Paris: ORSTOM, 1991.

Edwige, Charles. "Notes sur la subdivision de Melfi." *Bulletin de la Société Recherches Congolaises* (Brazzaville), no. 8, 1927, pp. 3–43.

Elgard, L. "Largeau (Faya): Confins Tchadiens." *Mémoires du CHEAM,* no. 1517, 1949.

Erceville, A. "La rive occidentale du Tchad: Le pays et les gens." *Mémoires du CHEAM,* no. 1690, 1950.

Essing, D. "Menschliches und Sprachliches vom Tchad-See." *Neues Afrika,* vol. 6, no. 9, September 1964, pp. 313–14.

"Etats et sociétés nomades." *Politique Africaine,* special issue no. 34, June 1989.

"L'évolution démographique dans les Républiques Gabonaise, du Congo, Centrafricaine, et du Tchad." *Chroniques de la Communauté,* 2, October 1959, pp. 53–55.

Feckoua, Laurent. "Les hommes et leurs activités en pays Toupouri." Ph.D. diss., University of Paris, 1977.

Ferrandi, J. "Les oasis et les nomades du Sahara oriental." *Renseignements Coloniaux,* 1910, pp. 3–8, 38–46.

Foedermayer, F. "Lieder der Bale-Bilia." *Mitteilungen der anthropologischen Gessellschaft im Wien,* 1969, pp. 64–76.

Foly, Ayélé Antoinette, and Alain Lafitte. "Animation féminine dans les communautés villageoises du Moyen Chari." *Institut Pan-Africain pour le Développement,* no. 2, January–March 1981.

Fortier, Joseph. *Le couteau de jet sacré: Histoire des Sar et de leurs rois au sud du Tchad*. Paris: Harmattan, 1982.

———. "Rites et coutumes d'une tribu Sara: Les Mbaye de Moïssala." *Bulletin de l'IFAN,* 20, no. 1/2, 1958, pp. 142–69.

Fotius, G. *Etude phytosociologique du triangle Fort-Lamy–Bousso–Laï.* Fort-Lamy: ORSTOM, 1973.

Fuchs, Peter. *Afrikanische Dekamerone: Erzahlungen aus Zentralafrika.* Stuttgart: Deutsche Verlags Anstalt, 1961.

———. "Die Bale von Ennedi." *Umschau,* vol. 62, no. 2, January 1962, pp. 40–44.

———. "Chad and the Sahara." *Visual Anthropology,* vol. 1, no. 3, 1988, pp. 251–61.

———. "Eisengewinnung und Schmiedetum in Nordlichen Tschad." *Baessler Arch. Beitrage Zur Nolkerkunde* (Berlin), 18, no. 2, 1970, pp. 295–334.

———. "Entwicklungen und Verfinderungen der Institution des Priester-Hauptlings in Sud-Wadai, Sudan." *Sociologus,* vol. 11, no. 2, 1961, pp. 174–86.

———. "Forschungen in Wadai." *Wiener Volkerkundliche Mitteilungen,* vol. 7, no. 2, 1959, pp. 85–86.

———. "Der Margai-Kult der Hadjerai." *Mitteilungen der Anthropologischen Gesellschaft in Wien,* 1960.

———. "Téda et Kanouri: Les relations interethniques à Fachi." In C. Baroin (ed.), *Gens du roc et du sable: Les Toubou,* Paris: CNRS, 1988, pp. 251–261.

———. "Traditionelle und nicht-traditionelle Hauptlinge in der Sudost Sahara und im zentralen Sudan [Tubu, Hadjerai]." *Zeitschrift für Ethnologie,* vol. 87, no. 2, 1962, pp. 234–43.

———. *Tschad.* Bonn: Kurt Schroeder, 1966.

———. "Über die Tubbu von Tibesti." *Archive für Volkerkunde,* vol. 11, 1956, pp. 43–66.

———. "Der Ursprung der Tubu." *VIe Congrès International de Sciences Anthropologiques,* Paris: Musée de l'Homme, 1964.

———. *Die Volker der Südost-Sahara: Tibesti, Borku, Ennedi.* Vienna: Braumüller, 1961.

———. *Weisser Fleck im schwarzen Erdteil. Meine Expedition nach Ennedi.* Stuttgart: Engelhornverlag, 1958.

———. "Zwei dringeude Aufgaben in Afrika [Kara (Birao) und Haddad (Kanem)]." *Bulletin of the International Committee on Urgent Anthropological and Ethnological Research,* vol. 5, 1962, pp. 52–53.

Gabe, M. "Les Boas de la région de Korbol." *Mémoires du CHEAM,* 1950.

Gaillard, R., and L. Poutrin. "Etude anthropologique des populations des régions du Tchad et du Kanem." *Documents Scientifiques de la Mission Tilho.* Paris: Larose, 1914.

Galaty, John G., and Philip C. Salzman. *Change and Development in Nomadic and Pastoral Societies.* Leiden: E. J. Brill, 1981.

Gallais, Jean. "Les péul en question." *Revue de Psychologie des Peuples* (Le Havre), no. 3, 1969, pp. 231–51.

Gamory-Dubourdeau, P. M. "Notes sur les coutumes des Toubous du Nord." *Bulletin du Comité d'Etudes Historiques et Scientifiques de l'Afrique Occidentale Française* (Dakar), 1926, pp. 131–52.

Ganay, Solange de. "Le génie des eaux chez les Dogons, les Kouroumba et les Sara." *Comptes Rendus de la Séance de l'Institut Française d'Anthropologie,* November 1940–December 1943, pp. 4–5.

Ganay, Solange de, and Marcel Griaule. "Notes sur les pirogues de la pêche dans la région du Bahr Salamat." *Journal de la Société des Africanistes,* vol. 13, 1943, pp. 187–204.

Garcia. "Moeurs et coutumes des Téda du Tou." *Bulletin de l'Institut d'Etudes Centrafricaines,* no. 10, 1955, pp. 167–209.

Gardi, R. *Kirdi parmi les peuplades païennes des monts et des marais du nord Cameroun.* Paris: Albin Michel, 1957.

Garine, Igor de. "Approaches to the Study of Food and Prestige in Savannah Tribes: Massa and Mussey of Northern Cameroon and Chad." *Social Science Information,* 1980/1, pp. 39–78.

———. "Au Tchad chez les Moussey." *Atlas,* no. 26, September 1968, pp. 60–67.

———. *Les Massa du Cameroun.* Paris: Presses Universitaires de France, 1964.

———. "Traditions orales et cultures au Mayo-Kebbi, Tchad: L'homme, hier et aujourd'hui." *Recueil d'Etude en Hommage à A. Leroi Gourhan.* Paris: Cujas, 1973.

Gast, M. "Notes d'éthnographie touarègue." *Libyca,* 12, 1964, pp. 325–34.

Gedenkschrift Gustav Nachtigal 1874–1974. Bremen: Im Selbstverlag des Museums, 1977.

Geo-Fourrier, G. "Les Bororos, pasteurs nomades du Tchad." *Le Nature,* no. 2922, February 1, 1934, pp. 106–10.

———. "Les Burma du Bahr-Sara." *Art et Décoration,* vol. 61, May 1932, pp. 157–60.

———. "Les civilisations agonisantes du Tchad." *La Nature,* December 1933, pp. 436–89; December 1934, pp. 500–503.

Gide, André. "Les villages des tribus Massas." *Illustrations,* March 5, 1927, pp. 236–37.

Gilg, Jean Paul. "Dobadene: Etude d'un village de la zone cotonnière du Tchad méridional." Ph.D. diss., University of Paris, 1962.

Gillet, Hubert. *Le peuplement végétal du massif de l'Ennedi.* Paris: Imprimerie Nationale, 1968.

Godrie, J. "Les populations riveraines du Tchad." *Mémoires du CHEAM,* no. 3316, 1960.

Goepp, Jean-Claude. "Rites, mythes, et cohésion dans une société du sud-ouest du Tchad." *Journal des Africanistes,* vol. 50, no. 2, 1980, pp. 59–71.

Gourou, P. "Une géographie du sous-peuplement." *L'Homme,* vol. 7, no. 2, April–June 1967, pp. 85–93.

Grall, A. "Le Secteur Nord du Cercle du Gouré," *Bulletin de l'IFAN,* vol. 7, 1945, pp. 1–46.

Griaule, M. "Cinq missions éthnographiques en Afrique tropicale." *Comptes Rendus Mensuelles des Séances de l'Académie des Sciences Coloniaux,* vol. 9, 1943, pp. 680–88.

———. "Les Goula du Lac Iro." *Comptes Rendus Sommaire du Séance de l'Institut Français d'Anthropologie,* vol. 20, 1940–43.

———. "Notes sur l'Agriculture des Goula et des Koulfa." *Bulletin de l'IFAN,* vol. 8, 1946, pp. 88–99.

Gros, R. "Histoire des Toundjours de Mondo." *Mémoires du CHEAM,* no. 1774, 1951.

Hagedorn, H. "Beobachtungen zur Siedlungs und Wirtschaftsweise der Toubous im Tibesti-Gebrige," *Erde,* no. 97, 1966, pp. 268–88.

Hagen, G. von. *Einige Notizen über die Musqu.* Berlin: Teubrier, 1911.

Hagenbrucher, F. *Les arabes dits 'Suwa' du nord Cameroun.* N'Djamena: ORSTOM, 1973.

———. *Magie et sorcellerie chez les arabes 'Suwa.'* N'Djamena: ORSTOM, 1974.

———. "Notes sur les Bilala du Fitri." *Cahiers ORSTOM,* vol. 5, no. 4, 1968, pp. 39–76.

Hallaire, Jacques. *Au confluent des traditions de la savane et de la forêt.* N'Djamena: CEFOD, 1987.

———. *Des noms qui parlent, hommes et femmes dans la société Sar d'après les noms d'initiation.* Sarh: Centres d'Etudes Linguistiques, 1977.

———. "Fiancailles chez les Sara de Bedaya." *Revue de l'Action* (Paris), 180, July/August 1964, pp. 833–40.

Herse, P. L. "Note relative au Didjiellé." *Bulletin de la Société de Recherches Congolaises,* no. 20, 1935, pp. 126–29.

———. "Rites funéraires des Toubouris." *Bulletin de la Société de Recherches Congolaises* (Brazzaville), no. 23, August 1937, pp. 21–30.

Heseltine, Nigel. "Toubou and Gorane, Nomads of the Chad Territory: Notes on Their Origins." *South African Archaeological Bulletin,* 14, no. 53, 1959, pp. 21–27.

Heusch, Luc de. "Myth as Reality." *Journal of Religion in Africa,* vol. 18, no. 3, 1988, pp. 200–215.

Hiernaux, J. "Les populations du Moyen-Chari." *Etudes et Documents Tchadiens,* no. 2, 1967, pp. 1–33.

———. "La réflectance de la peau dans une communauté de Sara Madjingay (République du Tchad)." *Anthropologie,* 76, no. 3/4, 1972, pp. 279–99.

Hocquet, Yves. "Le Nomadisme au Tchad." *Mémoires du CHEAM,* no. 4036, 1966.

Hofman, I. "Eine meroitische Stadt in Wadai?" *Meroitic Newsletter,* June 1972, pp. 14–18.

Holt, P. M. "Funj Origins: A Critique and New Evidence." *Journal of African History,* 4, 1, 1963, pp. 39–55.

Houlet, G. "Tchad ensorcelant." *Connaissance du Monde,* vol. 32, 1961, pp. 53–60.

Hovermann, J. "Vorlaufiger Bericht uber eine Forschungsreise ins Tibesti-Massiv." *Erde,* vol. 92, no. 2, 1963, pp. 126–35.

Huard, Paul. "Les groupes sanguine des Téda du Tibesti." *Bulletin de l'IFAN,* 23(B), 1/2, January–April 1961, pp. 328–29.

———. "Nouvelles données séro-anthropologiques sur les Téda du Tibesti." *Bulletin* de l'IFAN, 25(B), 3/4, July–October 1963, pp. 451–53.

———. "Populations anciennes du Tibesti." *Encyclopédie Mensuelle d'Outre-Mer,* vol. 5, no. 60/61, August/September 1955, pp. 366–70.

Huard, Paul, and Max Charpin. "Aspect sociologique d'une enquête anthropologique sur les Téda du Tibesti." *Bulletin de l'IFAN,* vol. 24, (B), no. 3/4, July–October 1962, pp. 575–83.

———. "Contribution à l'étude anthropologique des Téda du Tibesti." *Bulletin de l'IFAN,* vol. 22(B), no. 1/2, January–April 1960, pp. 179–201.

Huber, H. "Tod und Trauer im Westsudan." *Anthropos,* vol. 46, 1951, pp. 453–86.

Hugot, H. J. "Les missions Berliet au Sahara." *Libyca,* vol. 8, 1960, pp. 323–35.

———. "La poterie néolithique saharienne." *Congrés Préhistorique de France,* Paris, 1965, pp. 645–52.

Hugot, Pierre. "La transhumance des Arabes Myssirié et les origines des batailles inter-tribales d'Oum-Hadjer-Tchad de 1947." *Mémoires du CHEAM,* no. 1580, 1950.

Identités tchadiennes: L'héritage des peuples et les apports extérieurs. Paris: Harmattan, 1994.

Israel. Ministry of Foreign Affairs. *Les centres urbains et régionaux de la République du Tchad.* Jerusalem, 1963 [by Zarhy].

Issaka, Alamdou-Ramat. "Origine et descendance des Sawa." *La Voix de l'E.N.A.* (N'Djamena), no. 2, May 1966.

Jacob, M. and J. P. Lelagarde. *Enquête démographique par sondage: Zone des cuvettes lacustres et ouaddis du Lac Tchad. Rapport Définitif.* Paris: Bureau pour le Développement de la Production Agricole, 1964.

Jacolin, Pierre. "What Do Young People in the Countryside Mean by 'Success'?" *African Environment* (Dakar), vols. 14–16, 1980, pp. 341–80.

Jaulin, Robert. "Le Coté Sara." In *Gens du soir, gens de l'autre,* Paris: Union Générale d'Edition, 1973, pp. 43–132.

———. "La distribution des femmes et des biens chez les Sara." *Cahiers d'Etudes Africaines,* vol. 6, no. 23, July–September 1966, pp. 419–62.

———. *La mort Sara: L'ordre de la vie ou la pensée de la mort au Tchad.* Paris: Plon, 1967; 1992.

———. "Note sur Marabe, le village Mara." *Cahiers d'Etudes Africaines,* no. 4, December 1960, pp. 85–98.

———. "Notes sur l'analyse d'un système divinatoire." *Psyche,* no. 104, June 1955, pp. 353–61.

Jungraithmayr, Hermann, and Henry Tourneux (eds.), *Etudes Tchadiques.* Paris: CNRS, 1988.

Kinder, Ahmat. "Les mouvements de population en République du Tchad." *Revue Juridique et Politique,* vol. 34, no. 1, January–March 1980, pp. 218–36.

Kogongar, Gayo Jean. "Introduction à la vie et à l'histoire pré-coloniales des populations Sara du Tchad." Ph.D. diss., University of Paris, 1971.

Konrad, Walter. "Aufbau und Funktion eines Trittwebstuhls der Kanembu. Tschadsee-Gebiet." *Encyclopedia Cinematographica.* Gottingen: Institut fur den Wissenschaftlichen film, 1973.

———. "Beschneidung und Beschneidungsgerat der Salamat-Araber von Djimtilo." *Baessler-Archiv,* vol. 6, no. 1, 1958, pp. 61–65.

———. "Die Fruchtbarkeitskulte bei den Buduma." *Ethnographische Archaeologische Forschungen,* vol. 4, no. 1/2, 1958.

———. "Neue Beitraege zur Kenntnis der Buduma." *Zeitschrift fur Ethnologie,* 88, no. 2, 1963, pp. 332–36.

———. "Sara-M'bai (Zentralafrika, Mittlerer Schari). Herstellen einer Maske fur die Knaben Initiaiton." *Encyclopaedia Cinematographica, Tographica.* Gottingen: Institut fur den Wissenschaftlichen Film, 1973.

———. "Über Fruchtbarkeitskulte bei den Buduma." *Ethnographische Archaologische Forschungen,* vol. 6, no. 1/2, 1960, pp. 46–57.

———. "Über Tracht und Schmuck der Buduma." *Baessler Archiv,* vol. 7, no. 2, 1964, pp. 373–98.

——. "Die Wasserfahrzeuge der Tschadsee-Region." *Buessler Archiv,* vol. 5, no. 1, 1957, pp. 121–43.

Kraton, Sadinaly. *La chefferie chez les Ngama.* Paris: Harmattan, 1993.

Kronenberg, Andreas. "The Fountain of the Sun: A Tale of Herodotus, Plony, and the Modern Teda." *Man,* vol. 55, no. 88, May 1966.

——. "Die Sonnenquelle und Alexander der Grose." *Paideuma,* vol. 35, 1989, pp. 169–75.

——. "Das Hfiupthngswesen in Tibesti." *Mitteilungen der Anthropologie Gesellshaft zu Wien,* no. 84–85, 1955, pp. 46–55.

——. *Die Teda von Tibesti.* Horn-wieh: Verlag F. Berger, 1958.

Laboubée, J. "Les Tédas au Tibesti et au Borkou." *Mémoires du CHEAM,* no. 1931, 1951.

Lafarge, Francine, and Christian Seignobos. "Rapport préliminaire sur le pays Kim." *Annales de l'Université du Tchad,* no. 3, May 1975, pp. 99–157.

Lagopolous, Alexandros P. "Sociological Urbanism: An Analysis of the Traditional Western Sudanese Settlement." In M. Gottdiener and A. P. Lagopoulos (eds.), *The City and the Sign,* New York: Columbia University Press, 1986, pp. 259–87.

Lami, Pierre. "Les Houes de Dieu." *Bulletin de la Société de Recherches Congolaises,* no. 24, November 1937, pp. 102–11.

Landra, G. "Sulla morfologia del capello presso alcune populazioni africane." *Atti del Società Italiane por Progresso Scienze,* no. 3, 1937.

Lange, Dierk. *Chronologie et histoire d'un royaume africain.* Wiesbaden: Steiner Verlag, 1977.

——. *Le Diwan des sultans du Bornu.* Wiesbaden: Steiner Verlag, 1977.

——. "L'éviction des Sefuwa du Kanem et l'origine des Bulala." *Journal of African History,* vol. 23, no. 3, 1982, pp. 315–331.

Lanne, Bernard. "Les populations du Sud du Tchad." *Revue Française d'Etudes Politiques Africaines,* July/August 1979, pp. 41–81.

Latruffe, J. "Un problème politique au Tchad: Les arabes Myssyrié." *Mémoires du CHEAM,* no. 1388, 1949.

Latruffe, J., G. Serre, and J. Vossart. *Quelques populations de la République du Tchad.* Paris: CHEAM, 1971.

Lavelle, A. "Mutations villageoises et développement urbain au Tchad: L'absorption de Milezi Farcha (2) par Fort-Lamy." Ph.D. diss., University of Bordeaux, 1971.

Lebeuf, Annie M. D. *Les dignitaires de la cour de Massenya.* Paris: Paideuma, 1977.

——. *Les populations du Tchad.* Paris: Presses Universitaires de France, 1959.

——. *Les principautés Kotoko: Essai sur le caractère sacré de l'autorité.* Paris: Centre National de la Recherche Scientifique, 1969.

————. "Le rôle de le femme dans l'organisation politique des sociétés africaines." In Denise Paulme (ed.), *Femmes d'Afrique Noire,* Paris: Mouton, 1960, pp. 93–119.

————. "The Role of Women in the Political Organization of African Societies." In D. Paulme (eds.), *Women of Tropical Africa,* London: 1963, pp. 93–119.

Lebeuf, Annie M. D., and Jean Paul Lebeuf. "Monuments symboliques du palais royale de Logone-Birni." *Journal de la Société des Africanistes,* vol. 25, 1955, pp. 27–34.

Lebeuf, Jean Paul. *L'application de l'ethnologie à l'assistance sanitaire.* Brussels: Université Libre, 1957.

————. "Broderie et symbolisme chez les Kanouri et les Kotoko." *Objets et Mondes* (Paris), 10, no. 4, 1970, pp. 263–82.

————. "Centres urbains d'AEF." *Africa,* vol. 23, no. 4, 1955, pp. 285–97.

————. "Chez les Kotoko, pêcheurs dans le Logone et le Chari." *Au Bord de l'Eau,* January 1955.

————. "La circoncision chez les Kotoko, dans l'ancien pays Sao." *Journal de la Société des Africanistes,* vol. 8, 1938, pp. 1–9.

————. "La civilisation du Tchad." *Proceedings of the Third International West African Conference,* 1949, pp. 293–96.

————. *Les collections du Tchad.* Paris: Musée de l'Homme, 1941.

————. *Du Cameroun au Tchad.* Paris: Nathan, 1954.

————. "L'Empire des Sao." *Marianne,* January 19 and 26, 1938.

————. *Etudes Kotoko.* Paris: Mouton, 1976.

————. *Fort-Lamy, Tchad A.E.F.; Rapport d'une enquête préliminaire dans les milieux urbains de la Fédération.* Paris: Editions de l'Union Française, 1954.

————. "Les fouilles dans la région du Chari et du Tchad." *Anthropologie,* vol. 48, 1938, pp. 215–16.

————. "Foyers Kotoko." *Journal de la Société des Africanistes,* vol. 12, 1942, pp. 260–63.

————. "La mission Sahara-Cameroun." *Géographie,* vol. 49, no. 4, April 1938, pp. 225–30.

————. "La pêche chez les Kotoko." *Sciences et Voyages,* no. 89, June 1943, p. 113.

————. "Personne et système du monde chez les Kotoko." *Colloque Internationaux du C.N.R.S. no. 544: La notion de personne en Afrique noire, Paris, October 1971.* Paris: CNRS, 1973.

————. "Les peuples des Républiques de l'Afrique Centrale (Congo-Kinshasa excépté)." *Ethnologie Régionale I.* Paris: Gallimard, 1972, pp. 508–65.

————. "Pipes et plantes à fumer chez les Kotoko." *Notes Africaines,* no. 93, January 1962, pp. 16–17.

———. "Les populations de l'entre Chari-Nil." *Handbuch des Ange-wandten Volkerkunde,* 1947, pp. 427–69.

———. "Probing the Mystery of Lake Chad's Earliest Dwellers." *Sphere,* vol. 157, no. 2048, November 22, 1938.

———. "Quelques bijoux provenant de l'ancient pays Sao." *La Terre et la Vie,* no. 6, November/December 1938.

———. "Quelques pierres sacrées du pays Kotoko." *La Terre et la Vie,* vol. 9, no. 1, January/February 1939, pp. 10–18.

———. "Les Sao du Tchad." *France-Illustration,* April 27, 1946, pp. 445–48.

———. "Les Sao et les Kotoko du Tchad." *Zäire,* no. 3, March 1947, pp. 297–311.

———. "Sociologie en Oubangui-Chad et au Tchad." *Encyclopédie Coloniale et Maritime,* vol. 6, February 1951, pp. 42–43.

———. "Les souverains de Logone-Birni." *Etudes Camerounaises,* no. 47/48, March–June 1955, pp. 3–8.

Lebeuf, Jean Paul, and A.M.D. Lebeuf. *Le gisement Sao de Mdaga.* Paris: Société d'Ethnographie, 1980.

Lebeuf, Jean Paul, and M. Rodinson. "Génealogies royales de villes Kotoko (Goulfeil, Kousseri, Makari)." *Etudes Camerounaises,* vol. 1, no. 23/24, September–December 1948, pp. 31–46.

———. "L'origine et les souverains du Mandara." *Bulletin de l'IFAN,* no. 1/2, 1956, pp. 227–55.

Leblanc, E. "Anthropologie et ethnographie." *Mission Scientifique du Fezzan 1944–45,* Algiers, Imbert, 1948.

Le Coeur, Charles. *Dictionnaire ethnographique Téda.* Paris: Larose, 1950.

———. "L'honneur et le bon sens chez les Toubous du Sahara central." *Etudes Nigériennes,* no. 1, 1953.

———. "Les 'Mapalia' numides et leurs survivance au Sahara." *Hes-peris,* vol. 24, 1937, pp. 29–45.

———. "Methodes et conclusions d'une enquête humaine au Sahara nigéro-tchadien." *Conférence Internationale des Africanistes de l'Ouest,* Dakar, 1951, pp. 374–81.

———. *Mission au Tibesti: Carnets de route, 1933–4.* Paris: CNRS, 1969.

———. *Le rite et l'outil.* Paris: Presses Universitaires de France, 1939.

———. "Le système des clans au Tibesti." *Etudes Nigériennes,* vol. 1, 1953, pp. 11–16.

———. "Technique, art et point d'honneur, d'après l'inventaire d'une collection Toubou." *Etudes Nigériennes,* no. 1, 1953.

———. "Le Tibesti et la Téda." *Journal de la Société des Africanistes,* vol. 5, no. 1, 1935, pp. 41–60.

————. "Le Tibesti et ses habitants." *Bulletin de la Société des Amis du Musée d'Histoire Naturelle de Paris,* vol. 14, 1935, pp. 15–16.

————. "Un Toubou conciliateur de l'Islam et du Christianisme." *Travaux de l'Institut de Recherches Sahariennes,* vol. 3, 1945, pp. 155–59.

Le Coeur, Charles, and M. Le Coeur. "Borkou." *Encyclopédie de l'Islam.* Leyden: Brill, 1960, pp. 1295–96.

Le Coeur, H. "Mission au Niger, juillet–decembre 1969." *Journal de la Société des Africanistes,* vol. 40, no. 2, 1970, pp. 160–68.

Lembezat, B. *Les populations païennes du nord Cameroun.* Paris: Presses Universitaires de France, 1961.

Le Rouvreur, Albert. "Agadem et Djado: Deux aspects du Téda." *Mémoires du CHEAM,* 1948.

————. *Saheliens et Sahariens du Tchad.* Paris: Berger Levrault, 1962.

————. "Une saison sèche en Ennedi (1949–50)." *Etudes Rurales,* no. 42, 1971, pp. 172–77.

Lespinois de Mangolini, et al. *Etude de la vallée du Mandoul.* Fort-Lamy: Bureau pour le Développement de la Production Agricole, 1968.

Lieurade, L. "Le Cameroun Tchadien." *La Terre et la Vie,* vol. 5, no. 5, May 1935, pp. 214–35.

————. "Kotoko." *Togo-Cameroun,* January 1934, pp. 11–36.

Lopatinsky, O. "Armes tedda." *Objets et Mondes,* vol. 8, no. 3, Autumn 1968, pp. 205–26.

————. *Les Tedda du Tibesti et le problème de survie.* Paris: Institut d'Ethnologie, 1973.

————. *Vêtement, parure, parfums et coiffure chez les Tedda du Tibesti.* Paris: Institut d'Ethnologie, 1973.

Lopinot, B. "Aspects particuliers du problème des chefferies chez une population anarchique: Les Gambayes du Logone." CHEAM document, 1954.

Luhi, Charles. "Les Bororos et leur legendes: L'homme, le zebu, et la femme." *France-Eurafrique,* no. 218, July 1970, pp. 28–31.

Lukas, J. "Aus der Literatur der Badawi-Kanuri in Bornu." *Zeitschrift fur Eingeborenen Sprachen,* vol. 26, no. 1, 1935, pp. 35–56.

————. "Tschadische Studien I. Beitrage zur Kenntnis des Mukulu." *Afrika und Ubersee* (Hamburg), vol. 60, no. 1/2, 1977, pp. 1–58.

Lukas, R. *Nicht-Islamische Ethnien im sudlichen Tschadraum.* Frankfurt: Frankfurt University, 1973.

Luxeil, E. "Les Boudoumas: Population lacustre." *Mémoires du CHEAM,* no. 3004, 1959.

MacMichael, H. A. "Notes on the Zaghawa and the People of Gehel Midob, Anglo-Egyptian Sudan." *Journal of the Royal Anthropological Institute,* vol. 42, 1912, pp. 288–344.

Magnant, Jean-Pierre. "Les arabes et la terre au sud du Lac Tchad." In

R. Verdier and A. Rochegude (eds.), *Systèmes fonciers à la ville et au village*. Paris: Harmattan, 1986, pp. 257–80.

———. "Peuples, ethnices, et nation: Le cas du Tchad." *Droits et Cultures,* no. 8, 1984.

———. *La terre Sara, terre Tchadienne.* Paris: Harmattan, 1986.

Maillard, P. "Les redevances coutumières au Tchad." *Mémoires du CHEAM,* no. 1906, 1951.

Mainet, Guy, and Nicolas Guy. *La vallée du Gulbi de Maradi: Enquête socio-économique.* Paris: IFAN-CNRS, 1964.

Margarido, Alfredo, and Pierrette Ceccaldi. "Presentation du fichier ethnique du centre d'analyse et de recherche documentaires pour l'Afrique noire (CARDAN) et du projet de publication de l'inventaire provisoire des populations du Tchad." *Africa,* 38, 2, April 1968, pp. 204–8.

Marnay, Pierre, and Pierre Thenevin. *Etude socio-économique de la ville d'Abéché.* Paris: S.E.D.E.S., 1964.

Martin, Charles. *Au coeur de l'Afrique Equatoriale.* Lille: Lefebvre Ducrocq, 1912.

———. "Notes sur les Toubous." *Revue du Monde Musulman,* no. 34, 1917/1918, pp. 151–69.

Martin, Françoise. "De l'identité des personnes au Nord Tchad et de quelques problèmes juridiques annexes." *Mémoires du CHEAM,* no. 3324, 1960.

Martin, R. "Notes sur les Mundang de la région de Léré." *Bulletin de l'Institut d'Etudes Centre-Africaines,* vol. 2, no. 1, 1947.

Massip, J. M. *Contribution à l'inventaire des ressources du Tibesti.* Paris, Institut d'Ethnologie, 1967.

———. *Nomades et nomadisme en Ennedi.* Paris: Insitut d'Ethnologie, 1966.

Masson Detourbet, A., and M. P. Vincent. "Essai d'étude démographique des Kotoko." *Population,* July–September 1951, pp. 445–58.

Mathias, A. "La population de l'Afrique Equatoriale Française, Cercle de Batha." *Renseignements Coloniaux,* July 1928, pp. 451–52.

———. "La Route du Chari au Ouadai." *Afrique Française,* no. 12, December 1928, 530–31.

Matthey, Piero. "Brief Notes on the Noey, a Former Tribe of Hunters and Fishers in Southern Chad." *Bulletin of the International Committee on Urgent Anthropological and Ethnological Research,* vol. 8, 1966, pp. 37–38.

———. "I Miti non precedono la storia." *L'Uomo* (Milano), vol. 4, no. 1, 1980.

May, Roy. "Internal Dimensions of Warfare in Chad." *Cambridge Anthropology,* vol. 13, no. 2, 1988/89, pp. 17–27.

Mazoudier, A. "Le rythme de vie indigène et les migrations saisonnières dans la colonie du Tchad." *Annales de Géographie,* October–December 1945, pp. 296–99.

Meillassoux, Claude. "Recherche d'un niveau de détermination dans la société cynégétique Mbuti." *L'Homme et la Société,* 6, October–December 1967, pp. 95–106.

Michaut, F. "Pratique médicale au lac Tchad en 1966 et 1967." MD thesis, University of Paris, 1969.

Le milieu et les hommes: Recherches comparatives et historiques dans le bassin du Lac Tchad. Paris: ORSTOM, 1988.

Monino, Yves. *Forge et forgerons.* Paris: ORSTOM, 1991.

Monod, T. "Un problème à étudier: La question Sao." *La Terre et la Vie,* vol. 2, no. 4, April 1939, pp. 239–41.

Morel, J. "Discours au sujet des événements du Massalit." *Afrique Française,* no. i, January 1911, pp. 9–15.

Mouchet, J. "Contribution à l'étude des Gula." *Bulletin de l'IFAN,* no. 3/4, July–October 1958, pp. 593–611.

Moulinard, A. "Essai sur l'habitat indigène dans la colonie du Tchad." *Journal de la Société des Africanistes,* vol. 17, 1947, pp. 7–18.

Moussy, Bernadette. "Des jardins d'enfants au Togo et au Tchad." *Les Carnets de l'Enfance,* no. 21, January–March 1973, pp. 63–75.

Moylinard, C. "Essai sur l'habitat indigène dans la colonie du Tchad." *Journal de la Société des Africanistes,* vol. 17, 1947, pp. 7–18.

Muraz, A. "Les superstitions dans la race Sara." *BSRC,* no. 9, 1928.

Nachtigal, Gustav. "Die Tibbu, Ethnographische Skizze." *Zeitschrift der Gesellschaft für Erdkunde Zu Berlin,* vol. 5, 1870, pp. 216–42, 289–316.

Nassal, R. "Le Tchad est un pays pilote dans le domaine des recherches en sciences humaines." *France-Eurafrique,* vol. 19, no. 181, February 1967, pp. 43–45.

Nguembélé, S. V. "Coutumes du mariage entre famille chez les Kanembou des environs de Fort-Lamy." *Liaison,* no. 31, Janaury 1953, pp. 28–30.

Nicolaisen, Johannes. "The Haddad, a Hunting People in Tchad: Preliminary Report of an Ethnographical Reconnaissance." *Folk* (Copenhagen), no. 10, 1968, pp. 91–109

———. "The Pastoral Kreda and the African Cattle Complex. *Folk* (Copenhagen), no. 19/20, 1977/78, pp. 251–307.

Nodinot, J. F. "Une vieille société dirigeante baguirmienne au contact d'une poussée démographique de non-baguirmiens." ENFOM Mémoire, 1957.

Nöel, P. "Etude ethnographique et anthropologique sur les Tédas du Tibesti." *L'Anthropologie,* vol. 30, 1920, pp. 115–35.

Nomades et nomadisme au Sahara. Paris: UNESCO, 1963.

"Notes sur les Moundans." *Recherches Congolaises,* vol. 22, no. 1, 1922, pp. 23–49.

Nzekwu Onuora. "From Maiduguri to Lake Chad." *Nigeria Magazine,* no. 79, December 1963, pp. 237–47.

Pacques, V. "Mouvements cosmiques et mouvements des eaux en pays Baguirmi (Tchad)." *Proceedings of the Eighth Congress of Anthropological and Ethnological Sciences 1968, Tokyo and Kyoto,* vol. 3. Tokyo: Science Council of Japan, 1970, pp. 72–75.

———. "Origine et caractères du pouvoir royal au Baguirmi." *Journal de la Société des Africanistes,* vol. 37, no. 2, 1967, pp. 183–214.

———. *Le roi pêcheur et le roi chasseur.* Strasbourg: Institut d'Anthropologie, 1977.

Pairault, Claude. "Boum (Tchad) après trente ans." *Afrique Contemporaine,* October–December 1992, pp. 88–98.

———. "Boum-Kabir en présence de la mort." *Journal de la Société des Africanistes,* vol. 34, no. 1, 1964.

———. *Boum-le-Grand, Village d'Iro.* Paris: Institut d'Ethnologie de Paris, 1966.

———. "Le Kuro des Goula Iro." *Actes du VIe Congrès des Sciences Anthropologiques, Paris, Musée de l'Homme,* 1964, pp. 435–40.

———. "Parenté d'origine et parenté initiatique chez les Goula Iro." *L'Homme,* vol. 6, no. 1, January–March 1966, pp. 95–99.

———. "Structure de la parenté chez les Goula Iro." *Africa* (Belgium), 24, no. 4, October 1964, pp. 360–69.

Parkin, David, and David Nyamwaya (eds.), *The Transformation of African Marriage:* Manchester: Manchester University Press, 1987.

Patterson Brown, Ellen. "The Ultimate Withdrawal: Suicide among the Sara Nar." *Archives Européens de Sociologie,* vol. 22, no. 2, 1981, pp. 199–227.

"Les Paysannats du Tchad." Paris: S.E.D.E.S., 1965.

Pedrals, Denis Pierre de. *Antilopes et calebasses.* Paris: Durel, 1948.

Podlewski, André Michel. *La dynamique des principales populations du Nord-Cameroun (entre Bénoué et Lac Tchad).* Paris: ORSTOM, 1966.

Pouillon, J. "A quelque chose malheur est bon: Croyances des Hadjerai, Tchad." *L'Homme,* 13, 3, July–September 1973, pp. 93–100.

———. "Rapport d'enquête au Tchad." *Cahiers d'Etudes Africaines,* 3, 1960, pp. 153–55.

———. "Rite, histoire, structure chez les Kenga." *L'Homme,* vol. 15, no. 1, January–March 1975, pp. 29–41.

———. "La structure du pouvoir chez les Hadjerai." *L'Homme,* 4, no. 3, September/October 1964, pp. 18–70.

Poutrin, L. *Esquisse ethnologique des principales populations de L'Afrique Française.* Paris: Masson, 1914.

"Printemps à Fort-Lamy." *Europe France Outremer,* no. 503, December 1971, pp. 40–42.

Pujo, A. "Le Borkou et ses habitants, vie et moeurs." *Revue Militaire de l'AEF,* vol. 12, 1938, pp. 19–30.

———. "La vie et les moeurs au Borkou." *Revue Militaire de l'AEF,* vol. 16, 1939, pp. 35–54.

Quelques populations de la République du Tchad: Les Arabes du Tchad. Paris: Centre des Hautes Etudes Administratives sur l'Afrique et l'Asie Modernes, 1971.

Requin (Lt.). "Les clans Tedda du Tibesti." *Renseignements Coloniaux,* vol. 45, January 1935, pp. 55–59; April 1965, pp. 259–64.

Revault d'Allones, J. G. "La chasse au buffle dans le Logone oriental." *Notes Africaines,* no. 117, January 1968, pp. 10–11.

Reyna, S. P. "The Costs of Marriage: A Study of Some Factors Affecting Northwest Barma Fertility." Ph.D. diss., Columbia University, 1972.

———. "Family Planning, Residence Rules and Preferences, and the Extended Family among the Northwest Barma of Chad." Paper presented at the African Studies Association Meeting, 1972.

———. "Marriage Payments, Household Structure, and Domestic Labour-Supply among the Barma of Chad." *Africa,* vol. 47, no. 1, 1977, pp. 81–88.

———. "The Rationality of Divorce: Marital Instability among the Barma of Chad." *Journal of Comparative Family Studies,* vol. 8, no. 2, 1977, pp. 269–88. Reprinted in G. Kurian (ed.), *Cross-Cultural Perspectives of Mate Selection and Marriage,* Westport, CT: Greenwood Press, 1979, pp. 322–41.

Reyna, S. P., and C. Bouquet. "Le Tchad." In John Caldwell (ed.), *Croissance démographique et évolution socio-économique en Afrique de l'Ouest,* Paris: 1973, pp. 767–802.

Ricci, E. "Richerche sui gruppi Sanguini nei Tebu." *Revista de Antropologia,* vol. 30, 1933/34, pp. 353–71.

Rivallain, Josette. "Contribution à l'étude des groupes Sara, sud du Tchad: Implantation des populations, importance des échanges à valeur monétaire." *Annales de l'Université d'Abidjan,* vol. 9, 1981, pp. 23–51.

Roberts, Allen F. "The Myths of Sou, the Sara Trickster: Structure and Anti-structure in the Contents and Context of Prose Narratives." M.A. thesis, University of Chicago, 1972.

———. "A Note on the Pre-colonial Iron Currency of the Laka of Southwestern Chad." *Journal des Africanistes,* vol. 58, no. 1, 1988, pp. 96–101.

Robin, A. "Pêche chez les Kotoko." *Togo-Cameroun,* January 1934, pp. 27–29.

Rottier, A. "Etude sur le Tibesti." *Bulletin du Comité d'Etudes Historiques et Scientifiques de l'AOF,* 1922, pp. 26–56.
———. "Le Sahara oriental." *Renseignements Coloniaux,* 1924, pp. 1–14, 78–88.
Sabatini, Arturo. "Anthropologie der Tebu von Kufra." *Zeitschrift für Rassenkunde,* vol. 3, no. 3, 1936, pp. 253–69.
Santandrea, Stefano. *A Tribal History of the Western Bahr el Ghazal.* Verona: Editions Nigrizia, 1964.
Schiffers, Heinrich. "Le Borkou et ses habitants." *Travaux de l'Institut de Recherches Sahariennes,* vol. 15, no. 1, 1957, pp. 65–88.
———. "Neue Forschungen zum Problem der saharischen Tubu (Tibbu)." *Erdkunde,* vol. 16, no. 2, 1962, pp. 143–46.
Sechaud. "Le Pays Hadjerai, Morgo, Melfi, Abou Déia." *Mémoires du CHEAM,* 1949.
Seid, Joseph Brahim. "Le bonnet, la bourse, et la canne magique." *Presence Africaine,* no. 32/33, 1960, pp. 156–59.
———. "Coutumes successorales traditionnalles au Tchad islamisé." *Revue Juridique et Politique,* vol. 26, no. 4, 1972, pp. 81–118.
Seignobos, Christian. "Des gens du poney: Les Marba-Mousseye." *Revue de Géographie du Cameroun,* vol. 4, no. 1, 1983, pp. 9–38.
———. "Instruments aratoires du Tchad mériodinal et du Nord-Cameroun." In J. Peltres-Wurtz (ed.), *Les instruments aratoires en Afrique tropicale,* Paris: Cahiers ORSTOM, vol. 20, no. 3/4, 1984.
———. "Les transformations de l'habitation traditionelle au Tchad." *Cahiers d'Outre-Mer,* no. 95, July–September 1971, pp. 294–324.
Seligman, C. G. *Pagan Tribes of Nilotic Sudan.* London: Routledge and Sons, 1932.
Serre, Gérard. "Nomadisation d'hivernage des arabes de l'Oued Rime (Tchad)." *Mémoires du CHEAM,* no. 2737, 1957.
"La situation démographique au Tchad." Paris: S.E.D.E.S., 1964.
"Situation et problèmes de l'emploi au Tchad." *Revue Internationale du Travail,* vol. 85, no. 5, 1962, pp. 548–56.
Tailleur, J. "Les droits régaliens au Tchad." *ENFOM Mémoire,* 1955.
Talbot, P.A. "The Buduma of Lake Chad." *Africa,* vol. 41, 1911, pp. 245–59.
"Tchad: Nouvelle urbanisme à Fort-Lamy." *Afrique,* November 1962, pp. 50–57.
Tchad. Service de la Statistique Générale. *Enquête démographique au Tchad, 1964.* Paris, 1966.
Teisserene, Pierre. *Le Dieu des autres.* Paris: Union Générale d'Editions, 1975.
Tesmann, G. "Die Mbaka-Limba-Mbum und Lakka." *Zeitschrift für Ethnologie,* vol. 60, no. 2, 1928, pp. 305–52.

Thomas, F. C., Jr. "The Juhaina Arabs of Chad." *Middle East Journal,* vol. 13, 1959, pp. 143–55.

Tidanbay Madjingar, Gaby. *La pêche en pays Sar.* Sarh: Collège Charles Lwanga, 1982.

Toqué, G. *Essai sur le peuple et la langue Banda (région du Tchad).* Paris: J. André, 1904.

Tourneux, Henry. "Bibliographie linguistique Teda-Dazza." In C. Baroin (ed.), *Gens du roc et du sable,* Paris: CNRS, 1988.

———. "Première note sur le Mbara." *Africana Marburgensia,* vol. 11, no. 2, 1978, pp. 37–42.

Tourneux, Henry, Christian Seignobos, and Francine Lafarge. *Les Mbara et leur langue (Tchad).* Paris: SELAF, 1986.

Triaud, Jean-Louis. *Chad 1900–1902.* Paris: Harmattan, 1987.

Tubiana, Joseph. "Mission au Darfur." *Homme,* vol. 7, no. 1, 1967, pp. 89–96.

———. "La mission du Centre National de la Recherche Scientifique aux confins du Tchad." *Cahiers d'Etudes Africaines,* vol. 1, 1959, pp. 115–20.

Tubiana, Joseph, Claude Arditi, and Claude Pairault (eds). *L'identité Tchadienne: L'héritage des peuples et les apports extérieures.* Paris: Harmattan, 1994.

Tubiana, Marie José. "Une coiffure d'apparat des femmes zaghawa (Kobé et Kapka) et bidéyat (bilia)." *Objets et Mondes,* vol. 8, no. 2, 1968, pp. 129–44.

———. "Introduction du numéraire dans les circuits matrimoniaux za-ghawa." *Le Mois en Afrique,* no. 211/212, August/September, 1983, pp. 166–73.

———. "Le marché de Hila-ba [Ouaddai]: Moutons, mil, sel, et con-trebande." *Cahiers d'Etudes Africaines,* vol. 2, no. 6, 1961, pp. 196–243.

———. "Mariages zaghawa: Les changements liés à l'économie et l'idéologie." In David J. Parkin and David Nyamwaya (eds.), *The Transformations of African Marriage,* Manchester: Manchester University Press, 1987.

———. "Nature et fonction du sacrifice chez les Beri du Tchad." *Systèmes de Pensée en Afrique Noire,* no. 4, 1979, pp. 139–66.

———. "Pouvoir et confiance: La relation oncle maternel–neveu utérin et le système politique des Zaghawa." *Cahiers d'Etudes Africaines,* vol. 19, no. 1–4, 1979, pp. 55–68.

———. "A propos du lévirat chez les Zaghawa: Un problème de méthodologie." In B. Koechlin et al. (eds.), *De la route céleste au terroir du jardin du foyer: Mosaïque sociographique,* Paris: Editions de l'Ecole des Hautes Etudes en Sciences Sociales, 1987.

———. "Une rite de vie: La sacrifice d'une bête pleine chez les

Zaghawa Kobe du Ouaddai." *Journal de Psychologie Normale et Pathologique,* vol. 3, July–September 1960, pp. 291–310.

———. *Survivances pre-islamiques en pays Zaghawa.* Paris: Institut ethnologique, 1964.

———. "Systéme pastoral et obligation de transhumer chez les Zaghawa (Soudan-Tchad)," *Etudes rurales,* no. 42, 1971, pp. 120–71.

———. *Des Troupeaux et des femmes: mariage et transfers de biens chez les Beri (Zaghawa et Bideyat du Tchad et du Sudan).* Paris: Harmattan, 1985.

Tubiana, Marie José, and Joseph Tubiana. *Contes Zaghawa: Trente-sept contes et deux legendes recueillis au Tchad.* Paris: Les Quatre Jeudis, 1962.

———. "Un peuple noire aux confins du Tchad du Soudan: Les Béri aujourd'hui." *Cahiers d'Outre-Mer,* no. 103, 1973, pp. 250–61.

———. "La pratique actuelle dela cueillette chez les Zaghawa du Tchad." *Journal de l'Agriculture Tropicale et Botanique Appliquée,* vol. 41, no. 2–5, 1969, pp. 55–84.

———. *Système pastoral et obligation de transhumance chez les Zaghawa.* Paris: Mouton, 1971.

———. "Tradition et développement au Soudan oriental: L'exemple zaghawa." In Théodore Monod (ed.), *Pastoralism in Tropical Africa,* London: Oxford University Press, 1975, pp. 468–86.

———. *The Zaghawa from an Ecological Perspective: Food-gathering, the Pastoral System, Tradition and Development of the Zaghawa of Sudan and Chad.* Rotterdam: A. A. Balkema, 1977.

Urvoy, Y. *Petit Atlas ethnodémographique du Soudan entre Sénégal et Tchad.* Dakar: IFAN, 1942.

Vallois, H. V. "Ossements anciens de la région de Fort-Lamy." *Revue Anthropologique,* no. 10–12, October–December 1938, pp. 251–70.

Vandome, Charles. *Manuel d'initiation au Ngambay.* Fort-Lamy: Mission Catholique, 1961.

———. "Les Ngambayé-Moundou." *Mémoires de l'IFAN,* no. 69. Dakar, 1962.

———. *Terminologie de la parenté en pays Ngambayé.* Fort-Lamy: SNO, 1963.

Verheyt, L. "Pour une approche synthétique, psychanalytique, et fonctionnelle des contes: Application à un conte zaghawa." Ph.D. diss., University of Paris, 1971.

Verlet, Martin. "Le gouvernement des hommes chez les Yidéna du Lac Tchad dans le courant du XIXe siècle." *Cahiers d'Etudes Africaines,* vol. 7, no. 1, 1967, pp. 190–93.

Verlet, Martin, et al. *Aspects humains de la pêche au Lac Tchad: Etude socio-économique.* 6 vols. Paris: BDPA, 1964–65.

Vieillard, G. "Note sur deux institutions propres aux populations péules d'entre Niger et Tchad." *Journal de la Société des Africanistes,* vol. 2, no. 1, 1931, pp. 85–93.

Viguier, J. "Dromadaires de la région de Batha." Paris, *Mémoires de CHEAM,* no. 2165, 1953.

Vincent, Jean-François. *Cultes agraires et relations d'autorité chez les Gaba.* Yaoundé, 1967.

———. *Le pouvoir et le sacré chez les Hadjeray du Tchad.* Paris: Anthropos, 1975.

Vivien, A. "Essai de concordance de cinq tables génealogiques du Baguirmi (Tchad)." *Journal de la Société des Africanistes,* vol. 37, no. 1, 1967, pp. 25–39.

Vossart, J. "Notes sur les populations du district de Bongor, Mayo Kebbi, Tchad." *Mémoires du CHEAM,* no. 2304, 1954.

Works, John A. "Pilgrims in a Strange Land: The Hausa Community in Chad, 1890–1970." Ph.D. diss., University of Wisconsin, 1972; also Columbia University Press, 1974.

Wyss-Dunant, E. "Recherches anthropologiques dans le Tibesti occidental." *Archives Suisses d'Anthropologie Générale,* no. 13, 1948, pp. 125–55.

———. "Les Toubous du Tibesti, peuplade d'origine berbère." *Bulletin de la Société des Sciences Naturelles du Maroc,* vol. 28, 1948 (1950), pp. 83–84.

Zeltner, J. C. *Les arabes dans la région du Lac Tchad: Problèmes d'-origine et de chronologie.* Sarh: Collége Charles Lwanga, 1977.

Politics

Abakar, Mahammat Hassan. "La codification du droit au Tchad." *Revue Juridique et Politique,* vol. 40, no. 3/4, 1986, pp. 447–50.

———. *Un Tchadien à l'aventure.* Paris: Harmattan, 1992.

"Accords de Lagos." *Afrique Contemporaine,* September/October 1979, pp. 31–32.

Adloff, V. T., and R. Adloff. *Conflict in Chad.* Institute of International Studies. University of California, 1981.

Agoro, I. O. "The Establishment of the Chad Basin Commission." *The International and Comparative Law Quarterly,* vol. 15, no. 2, April 1966, pp. 542–50.

Alhamdou, I. R. *Ma vérité sur le Tchad.* Brussels: Editions Africa, 1984.

Amady, Nathé. "La condition des étrangers au Tchad." *Revue Juridique et Politique,* vol. 34, no. 1, January–March 1980, pp. 237–48.

Amos, John W. "Libya in Chad: Soviet Surrogate or Nomadic Imperialist?" *Conflict,* vol. 5, no. 1, 1983, pp. 1–18.

"Anarchie et confusion." *Afrique Contemporaine,* April/May 1979, pp. 14–16.

Aquarone, Marie-Christine. *Les frontières du refus: Six séparatismes africaines.* Paris: CNRS, 1987.

Arbaumont, J. d'. "Organisation politique au Tibesti." *Bulletin de l'IFAN,* vol. 18, no. 1-2, January–April 1956.

Arditi, Claude. "Tchad: Chronique d'une démocratie importée." *Journal des Anthropologues,* no. 53–55, Autumn 1993–Spring 1994.

"Au Tchad avec Général Cortadellas." *France-Eurafrique,* March 1970.

"Au Tchad: Naissance difficile d'un état moderne." *Marchés Tropicaux,* no. 1370, February 11, 1972, pp. 369–72.

Aurillac, M. "France-Tchad: L'Afrique au coeur." *Politique Internationale,* no. 39, 1988, pp. 157–63.

Azevedao, Mario. *Cameroun and Chad in Historical and Contemporary Perspective.* Lewiston, NY: Edwin Mellen Press, 1980.

Azevedao, Mario, and G. Prater. "Foreign Assistance and Dependence: Post-colonial Chad, 1960–1985." *Journal of African Studies,* vol. 13, no. 3, 1986, pp. 102–10.

Bach, D. "Le Nigeria et le Tchad: Echec d'une politique de stabilisation du conflit." *Politique Africaine,* no. 16, December 1984, pp. 125–28.

Bachard, M. "Mangalmé, préfecture du Guéra et ses habitants." Fort-Lamy, Mémoire E.N.A., 1969.

Ballard, John A. "Four Equatorial States: Central African Republic, Chad, Congo/Brazzaville, Gabon." In G. M. Carter (ed.), *National Unity and Regionalism in Eight African States,* Ithaca, NY: Cornell University Press, 1966, pp. 231–335.

Bangui, Antoine. *Les ombres de Koh.* Paris: Hatier, 1984.

———. *Prisonnier de Tombalbaye.* Paris: Hatier, 1980.

Baroine, C. "Organisation territoriale, organisation sociale: La logique du système toubou." *Journal des Africanistes,* vol. 56, no. 2, 1986, pp. 7–28.

Bearman, Jonathan. "The conflict in Chad." In *Qadhafi's Libya,* London: Zed Press, 1986, pp. 203–26.

Belgium. Office de la Coopération au Développement. Service Etudes. Statistiques et Documentation. *La République du Chad.* Brussels, July 1968.

Beringaye, Marc. "Le retrait du Tchad de l'UDEAC." Ph.D. diss. University of Poitiers, 1988.

Bertin, Jean, and Jean Chaussade. "La République du Tchad." *Europe-France-Outremer,* no. 366, May 1960, pp. 42–51.

Beyassoum, Samuel. "Le formation du lien matrimonial du Tchad." *Revue Juridique et Politique,* January–March 1966, pp. 16–29.

Biarnes, Pierre. "Tchad." In *L'Année politique africaine 1970.* Dakar: Société Africaine d'Edition, 1971.

———. "Tchad: Entre Paris et Tripoli." *Le Mois en Afrique,* no. 113, May 1975, pp. 12–16.

————. "Tchad: Intervention militaire française." *Revue Française d'E-tudes Politiques Africaines,* no. 33, September 1968, pp. 5–8.

Biarnes, Pierre, and Léon Dutrieux. *L'Economie africaine en 1974.* Dakar: Société Africaine d'Edition, April 1974.

Bloch, Jean. *Tchad: Une néo-colonie.* Paris: Git-le-Coeur, 1972.

Bloch, Jean, and Monique Vernhes. *Guerre coloniale au Tchad.* Montreux, Switzerland: La Cité, 1972.

Bontemps, Louis. "Nord et sud dans l'évolution politique du Tchad." *Afrique Contemporaine,* September/October 1978, pp. 1–7.

Bouquet, Christian. "Les limites d'une étude de régionalisation au Sud-Kanem." *Cahiers d'Outre-Mer,* no. 103, 1973, pp. 262–78.

————. *Tchad, genèse d'un conflit.* Paris: L'Harmattan, 1982.

————. "Tchad: Huit questions pour mieux comprendre." *Françias du Monde,* no. 27, October 1983.

————. "Tchad: Une saison des pluies chaudes." In *Année Africaine 1983,* Paris: Pedone, 1985, pp. 212–36.

Boyd, H. "Chad: A Civil War without End." *Journal of African Studies,* vol. 10, no. 4, 1983/84, pp. 119–26.

Brandily, Monique. "Le Tchad face nord 1978–79." *Politique Africaine,* no. 16, 1984, pp. 45–65.

————. "Au Tibesti l'investiture du dernier derde." *Balafon,* no. 51, 1982, pp. 12–21.

Breton, J. M. "Le contrôle supérieur de l'administration et des finances publiques au Tchad." *Bulletin de l'Institut International d'Administration Publique,* July–September 1974, pp. 125–74.

Buijtenhuijs, Robert. "L'art de ménager la chèvre et le chou: La politique tchadienne de François Mitterrand." *Politique Africaine,* no. 16, 1984.

————. "La conférence nationale du Tchad comme vous y étiez." *Politique Africaine,* no. 50, June 1993.

————. *La conférence nationale souveraine du Tchad.* Paris: Karthala, 1993.

————. "La dialectique nord-sud dans l'histoire tchadienne." *African Perspectives,* no. 2, 1977, pp. 43–61.

————. "Le Frolinat à l'épreuve du pouvoir." *Politique Africaine,* no. 16, 1984.

————. *Le Frolinat et les guerres civiles du Tchad (1977–1984).* Paris: Karthala, 1987.

————. *Le Frolinat et les révoltes populaires du Tchad, 1965–76.* The Hague: Mouton, 1978.

————. "Guerre de guérilla et révolution en Afrique Noire: Les leçons du Tchad." *Politique Africaine,* vol. 1, no. 1, January 1980, pp. 23–33.

————. "La mort du commandant Galopin: Une mise au point." *Politique Africaine,* no. 20, December 1985, pp. 91–95.

————. "Les partis politiques africains ont-ils des projets de société?" *Politique Africaine,* no. 56, December 1994, pp. 119–36.

————. "La situation dans le sud du Tchad." *Afrique Contemporaine,* July–September, 1995, pp. 20–30.

————. "Is Tsjaad nog een staat?" In W. van Bingsbergen and G. Hesseling (eds.), *Aspecten van staat en maatschappij in Afrika: Recent Dutch and Belgian Research on the State.* Leiden: African Studies Center, 1984, pp. 303–7.

————. "Notes sur l'évolution du FROLINAT." *Revue Française d'Etudes Politiques Africaines,* no. 138/39, June/July 1977, pp. 118–25.

————. "Les potentialités révolutionnaires de l'Afrique Noire: Les élites dissidentes." *Cahiers d'Etudes Africaines,* no. 69/70, 1978, pp. 79–92.

————. "Révolutionnaire informanten en 'révolutionnaire antropologie.'" *Sociologische Gids,* vol. 27, no. 5, September/October 1980, pp. 426–32.

————. "Tchad 1985–1986." *Année Africaine 1985–86.* Bordeaux: Presses Universitaires de Bordeaux, 1988, pp. 73–86.

————. "Tchad: une conférence nationale et des massacres." In *L'Afrique Politique 1994.* Paris: Karthala, 1994.

————. "Thierry Desjardins, Mme. Claustre, et le Tchad." *Politique Aujourd'hui,* March/April 1976.

————. "Tsjaad: Twee of drie opstanden en een halve revolutie." *Kroniek van Afrika,* vol. 13, no. 2, 1973.

Cabot, Jean. "Le Tchad écartelé." *Hérodote,* no. 18, April–June 1980, pp. 133–53.

Calchinovati, G. "Ciad: L'ultima battaglia dei para." *Astrolabio,* vol. 7, 1969, pp. 25–26.

Camara, A. "Tchad: Tombalbaye sacrifié." *Zone des Tempêtes,* July/August, 1973.

Caron, Louis-Jean. "La justice coutumière dans le district de L'Ennedi." Paris: *CHEAM-Mémoire,* no. 3924, 1964.

Casteran, Christian. "La rébellion au Tchad." *Revue Française d'Etudes Politiques Africaines,* no. 73, January 1972, pp. 35–53.

————. "Tchad: Difficultés pour M. Tombalbaye." *Revue Française d'Etudes Politiques Africaines,* no. 69, September 1971, pp. 9–11.

————. "Tchad: Histoire d'un grève." *Revue Française d'Etudes Politiques Africaines,* no. 73, January 1972, pp. 8–10.

————. "Tchad: L'assassinat d'un opposant au régime." *Revue Française d'Etudes Politiques Africaines,* no. 93, September 1973, pp. 18–20.

"Chad." In *Africa,* special annual issue of *Jeune Afrique.*

"Chad." In *Africa.* New York: Africana Publishing Corporation, annual.

"Chad." In *Africa South of the Sahara.* London: Europa Publications Limited, annual.

"Chad." In Colin Legum (ed.), *Africa Contemporary Record*. London: Africa Research Limited, later Rex Collings and New York, African Publishing Corporation, annual.

"Chad: Are the French Leaving?" *Africa Confidential,* vol. 21, no. 10, March 7, 1980, pp. 5–6.

"Chad: Before the Storm?" *Africa Confidential,* vol. 20, no. 3, January 31, 1979.

"Chad: Can FROLINAT Unite?" *Africa Confidential,* vol. 18, no. 21, October 21, 1977, pp. 1–2.

"Chad: Carrot and Stick." *Africa Confidential,* August 19, 1987, pp. 3–5.

"Chad: A Conciliatory Government." *Africa Confidential,* vol. 23, no. 22, October 20, 1982, pp. 6–7.

"Chad: The Consequences of Victory." *Africa Confidential,* April 15, 1987, pp. 2–4.

"Chad: Deby and Democracy." *Africa Confidential,* March 17, 1995, pp. 4–6.

"Chad: Diplomatic Zigzags." *Africa Confidential,* vol. 20, no. 11, May 23, 1979, pp. 4–5.

"Chad: Exit Tombalbaye." *Africa Confidential,* vol. 16, no. 8, April 25, 1975, pp. 1–3.

"Chad: The Factions Return." *Africa Confidential,* July 22, 1987, pp. 5–6.

"Chad: Final Disintegration." *Africa Confidential,* vol. 21, no . 17, August 13, 1980, pp. 3–5.

"Chad: Finding Oil in Troubled Waters." *Africa Confidential,* February 19, 1993, pp. 5–7.

"Chad: France Hedges Its Bet." *Africa Confidential,* April 20, 1990, pp. 4–5.

"Chad: France's New Colonial War." *African Communist,* vol. 40, 1970, pp. 79–81.

"Chad: France's Search for a Compromise." *Africa Confidential,* vol. 19, no. 15, July 21, 1978.

"Chad: From Rebel to Ruler." *Africa Confidential,* vol. 19, no. 19, September 22, 1978.

"Chad: Great Power Rivalry." *Africa Confidential,* vol. 19, no. 2, January 20, 1978, pp. 4–6.

"Chad: Habré at a Turning Point." *Africa Confidential,* April 28, 1989, pp. 1–3.

"Chad: Habré out, Déby in." *Africa Confidential,* December 7, 1990, pp. 1–3.

"Chad: Habré's Prospects." *Africa Confidential,* June 23, 1982, pp. 6–8.

"Chad: Habré's Strong Hand." *Africa Confidential,* September 22, 1982, pp. 5–7.

"Chad/Libya: Qadaffi Turns Diplomat." *Africa Confidential,* July 1, 1988, pp. 3–5.

"Chad: The Long Arm of the Elysée." *Africa Confidential,* May 22, 1992, pp. 4–6.

"Chad: One Palace Too Many." *Africa Confidential,* June 28, 1991, pp. 4–6.

"Chad: Perilous Peace." *Africa Confidential,* vol. 19, no. 8, April 14, 1978, pp. 4–5.

"Chad: Quelling the Unrest." *Africa Confidential,* vol. 11, no. 7, April 3, 1970, pp. 2–5.

"Chad: The Return of Goukouni." *Africa Confidential,* May 31, 1992, pp. 6–7.

"Chad: The Shaping of the New Alignments." *Africa Confidential,* vol. 22, no. 15, July 15, 1981, pp. 1–3.

"Chad: A State of Anarchy." *Africa,* March 1979, pp. 18–19.

"Chad: The Threat from Darfur." *Africa Confidential,* December 15, 1989, pp. 6–7.

"Chad: Victim of a Race War." *Bulletin of the African Institute of South Africa* (Pretoria), vol. 9, 1972, pp. 27–35.

"Chad? Who Is Winning?" *Africa Confidential,* vol. 20, no. 6, March 14, 1979, pp. 5–8.

"Chad: Who Will Help Whom?" *Africa Confidential,* November 21, 1975, pp. 5–7.

"Chadian Newspaper." *Africa Confidential,* August 24, 1973.

"Changement de noms de lieux en Afrique." *Europe-Outre-Mer,* no. 591, April 1979, pp. 44–46.

Charlot, Michel. "French Imperialism and the Developing Countries." *Freedomways,* 13, 1973, pp. 55–62.

Charlton, Roger, and Roy May. "Warlords and Militarism in Chad." *Review of African Political Economy,* no. 45/46, 1988, pp. 12–25.

"Charte Fondamentale du Tchad." *Afrique Contemporaine,* September/October 1978, pp. 16–20.

Chauler, Pierre. "Au Tchad: Naissance difficile d'un état moderne." *Marchés Tropicaux et Mediterranéens,* no. 1370, February 11, 1972, pp. 369–72.

Chauvet, Jacques F. "Croissance urbaine et incidents de 1979 à Sarh: Analyse géographique et problèmes du développement." *Cahiers d'Outre-Mer,* vol. 40, no. 158, 1987, pp. 205–11.

———. "Les quartiers de Sarh, ex-Fort-Archambault." Ph.D. diss. University of Bordeaux, 1974.

Chéramy, Pierre. "Au Tchad." *France-Eurafrique,* no. 215, March 1970, pp. 6–9.

Chipman, J. "France, Libya, and Chad." *The World Today,* October 1983, pp. 361–64.

"Chute du President Goukouni." *Afrique Contemporaine,* no. 122, July/August 1982, pp. 26–27.

Claustre, Pierre. *L'affaire Claustre: Autopsie d'une prise d'otages.* Paris: Karthala, 1990.

Codo, Léon. "Les Etats-Unis, la France, et le conflit tchadien." *Géopolitique,* no. 9, 1988, pp. 81–121.

————. "Tchad: Militaire ou negociée, une solution toujours introuvable." *Année Africaine 1984.* Paris: Pedone, 1986, pp. 196–204.

Combe, Marc. *Otage au Tibesti.* Paris: Flammarion, 1976.

Comte, Gilbert. "Tchad: Le temps à travailler pour M. François Tombalbaye." *Revue Française d'Etudes Politiques Africaines,* no. 51, March 1970, pp. 12–14.

————. "Tchad: Mystère autour de l'intervention militaire française." *Revue Française d'Etudes Politiques Africaines,* no. 36, December 1968, pp. 16–19.

Conac, Gérard (ed.). *Les institutions administratives des états francophones d'Afrique Noire.* Paris: Economica, 1979.

"Constitution of the Republic of Chad." In Amos J. Peaslee (ed.), *Constitution of Nations.* vol. 1, *Africa.* The Hague: Martinus Nijhoff, 1965, pp. 65–81.

Cornevin, Robert. "Tchad." *Afrika-Forum,* July/August 1969, pp. 496–99.

Costadoni, Giancarlo. "Ciad: Un precario equilibro." *Politica Internazionale.* no. 8/9, August/September 1979, pp. 11–22.

————. "Il conflitto nel Ciad." *Aggiornamento Sociale,* vol. 32, no. 3, March 1981, pp. 185–98.

Coulon, Christian. "Tchad." In *Année Africaine 1972.* Paris: Editions A. Pedone, 1973, pp. 593–603.

"Council Informed Agreement Reached in Chad-Libya Issue." *UN Chronicle.* March 1978, pp. 5–8.

Courville, B. de. "Chefferie traditionnelle, administration française, et partis politiques au Ouaddai." *Mémoires du CHEAM,* no. 3095, 1959.

————. "Le Ouaddaï." *Mémoires du CHEAM,* no. 3971, 1964.

Cox, J.J.G. "France in Africa." *Army Quarterly and Defense Journal,* vol. 118, no. 2, 1988, pp. 161–67.

Dadi, Abderahman. *Tchad: L'état retrouvé.* Paris: Harmattan, 1987.

Dadi, Abderahman, and Alain Moyrand. "La juridiction administrative au Tchad: Du conseil du contentieux administratif à la Chambre administrative et financière de la Cour d'appel de N'Djamena." In *Les Cours Suprêmes en Afrique,* Paris: Economica, 1988, pp. 263–311.

Dagui, N'Gabo. "Le fondement du code pénal tchadienne." *Revue Juridique et Politique,* vol. 40, no. 1/2, January–June 1986, pp. 153–59.

Déby, Idriss. *Discours du colonel Idriss Déby.* N'Djamena, 1992.

Decalo, Samuel. "Chad: The Roots of Center-Periphery Strife." *African Affairs,* October 1980, pp. 490–509.

————. "Regionalism, Political Decay, and Civil Strife in Chad." *Journal of Modern African Studies,* vol. 18, no. 1, 1980, pp. 23–56.

Decker, Marie-Laure, and Ornella Tondini. *Pour le Tchad.* Paris: 1979.

"Declaration de N'Djamena." *Afrique Contemporaine,* May/June 1982, pp. 36–38.

Decraene, Phillipe. "Chad at World's End." *Africa Report,* January 1968, pp. 54–58.

————. "Tchad: Intervention française." *Revue Française d'Etudes Politiques Africaines,* no. 48, December 1969.

————. "Le voyage de M. Pompidou au Niger et au Tchad." *Revue Française d'Etudes Politiques Africaines,* no. 74, February 1972.

Delwa Kassiré, Koumakoyé. "Problématique de l'administration territoriale au Tchad." Ph.D. diss., University of Paris, 1988.

Desjardins, Thierry. *Avec les otages du Tchad.* Paris: Presses de la Cité, 1975.

————. *Les rébelles d'aujourd'hui.* Paris: 1977.

————. "La deuxième guerre civile." *Afrique Contemporaine,* no. 109, May/June 1980, pp. 31–33.

Devoluy, Pierre. "Stratégie et tactique des forces armées nationales." *Géopolitique,* vol. 5, 1987, pp. 33–44.

Dimanche, Georges Nestor. "Tchad und Deutschland." *Afrika-Forum,* November 1966, pp. 489–501.

Diop, Assane. "Plus ça change." *Africa Report,* March/April 1992, pp. 25–27.

Djarangar, Djita Issa. "Description phonologique du Bédjond." Ph.D. diss., University of Grenoble, 1989.

Doh, Dominique. "Tchad: Ce n'est pas une guerre de religion." *Africasia,* no. 3, 1969, pp. 8–10.

Doornbos, P. "La révolution dérapée: La violence dans l'est du Tchad, 1978–1981." *Politique Africaine,* vol. 2, no. 7, September 1982, pp. 5–13.

Douence, Jean-Claude. "Tchad." In *Année Africaine 1964,* Paris: Editions Pedone, 1965, pp. 421–28.

"Les douze états de la zone franc en 1979–80." *Bulletin de l'IFAN,* no. 1081, February 1981, pp. 20719–32.

Dreux-Brézé, Joachim de. *Le problème du regroupement en Afrique Equatoriale,* Paris: Librairie Générale de Droit et de Jurisprudence, 1968.

Dronne, Raymone. *Le serment de Koufra.* Paris: Les Documents du Temps, 1965.

Ducat, Marc. "La réforme foncière et domaniale au Tchad." *Penant,* vol. 78, no. 721, July–September 1968, pp. 393–415.

Duic, Walter Z. *Africa Administration.* 3 vols. Munich: Verlag Dokumentation, 1978.

Dunn, Michael Collins. "Chad: The OAU Tries Peacekeeping." *Washington Quarterly,* Spring 1982, pp. 182–88.

Durand, C. "L'ancien droit coutumier répressif au Tchad." *Penant,* vol. 86, no. 756, April–June 1977, pp. 170–91.

————. "Le droit pénal de la famille dans la République du Tchad." *Penant,* vol. 80, no. 729, 1970, pp. 273–80.

————. "La nouvelle organisation judiciaire du Tchad et renforcement des pouvoirs des magistrats au pénal." *Penant,* vol. 80, no. 728, 1970, pp. 181–90.

————. "Observations sur les statistiques judiciaires de 1968 de la République du Tchad." *Penant,* vol. 81, no. 731, 1971, pp. 127–39.

————. "Les tendances du droit pénal au Tchad depuis l'indépendance." *Penant,* vol. 83, no. 741, July–September 1973, pp. 350–87.

Ediafric. *La Politique Africaine en 1969.* 2nd edition. Paris, 1969.

El-Kikhia, Mansour O. "Chad: The Same Old Story." *Journal of African Studies,* vol. 10, no. 4, Winter 1983, pp. 119–26.

"Les événements du Tchad." *L'Afrique et l'Asie,* no. 86, 1969, pp. 39–50.

Foltz, William J. "Chad's Third Republic: Strengths, Problems, Prospects." *CSIS Africa Notes,* no. 77, 1987.

Fortier, Joseph. *Le couteau de jet sacré: Histoire des Sar et de leur rôle au sud du Tchad.* Paris: Harmattan, 1982.

France. La Documentation Française. "La législation du travail dans les états africains et malgache d'expression française." *Notes et Etudes Documentaires,* no. 3018, September 13, 1963.

————. "La République du Tchad." *Notes et Etudes Documentaires,* no. 2696, August 1960.

————. "La République du Tchad." *Notes et Etudes Documentaires,* no. 3411, 1967.

————. "Tchad Constitution du 16 Avril 1962." In "Les constitutions des républiques africaines et malgache d'expression française." *Notes et Etudes Documentaires,* no. 2995, 1963.

"France: Chad and the Francophones." *Africa Confidential,* October 10, 1975, pp. 5–7.

"France et Tchad." *Revue Générale de Droit International Publique,* vol. 75, 1971, pp. 199–205.

Franziska, James. "Chad: Habre's Push North." *Africa Report,* March/April 1987, pp. 41–43.

————. "Habre's Hour of Glory." *Africa Report,* September/October 1987, pp. 20–23.

Frémaux, P. "La rébellion tchadienne." Ph.D. diss., University of Paris, 1973.

Froelich, J. C. "Tensions in the Chad." *Adelphi Papers,* 93 December 1972, pp. 42–52.

Fuchs, P. *Tschad.* Bonn: K. Schroeder, 1966.

———. "Vergessene Krieg. Tschad. Unabhängigkeit in der Sackgasse." *Westermanns Monatshefte,* 1973.

Gabas, Jean-Jacques. *Aides extérieures dans les pays membres du CILSS.* Paris: OCDE, 1987.

Gabriel, I. "Chad: The Inside Story." *New African Developments,* vol. 11, no. 11, November 1977, pp. 1057–59.

Gali Ngothe, Gatta. *Tchad: Guerre civile et désagrégation de l'état.* Paris: Présence Africaine, 1985.

Galmaye Youssou Bomi. "La responsabilité des agents publics au Tchad." *Revue Juridique et Politique,* vol. 24, no. 4, October–December 1973, pp. 909–24.

Galtier, Gérard. "Pour en finir avec la guerre du Tchad." *Le Mois en Afrique,* no. 223/224, 1984, pp. 4–17.

Gardot, P. "L'enjeu de la guerre au Tchad." *Africasia,* no. 33, February 1, 1971.

Gautron, Jean-Claude. "La force de maintien de la paix au Tchad." In *Année Africaine, 1981,* Paris: Pedone, 1983, pp. 167–89.

Gentil, Pierre. "Le Tchad: Décolonisation et indépendance." *Comptes Rendus Trimestriels des Séances de l'Académie des Sciences d'Outre-Mer,* vol. 29, January 1969, pp. 1–24.

———. "Tchad, décolonisation, indépendance." *Mémoire du CHEAM,* no. 4004, 1965.

Gérard, Claude. "Qui êtes-vous Monsieur le Président Tombalbaye." *France-Eurafrique,* no. 181, February 1967, pp. 9–12.

Gilbert, François. "Tchad: Une réconiliation intéressée." *Revue Française d'Etudes Politique Africaines,* no. 108, December 1974, pp. 17–19.

Golhor, Kando. "L'intégration politique d'un état africain nouveau, problèmes et perspectives: Le cas du Tchad (1960–1979)." Ph.D. diss., University of Laval, 1991.

Gomez, Tello. "La confusa guerra de Chad." *Africa* (Madrid), 348, 1970, pp. 489–92.

Gonidec, P. F. "La Constitution du Tchad." *Penant,* no. 671, 1959.

———. *La République du Tchad.* Paris: Berger Levrault, 1971.

Grandin-Blanc, Nicole, and Robert Buijtenhuijs. *Tensions politiques et ethnies au sahel.* Leiden: Afrika-Studiecentrum, 1977.

Guerivière, Jean de la. "Tchad: La guerre du B.E.T. aura lieu." *Revue Française d'Etudes Politiques Africaines,* no. 59, November 1970, pp. 14–17.

———. "Tchad: La minute de vérité." *Revue Française d'Etudes Politiques Africaines,* no. 66, June 1971, pp. 16–18.

———. "Tchad: Président Diori Hamani réconcile les frères ennemis."

Revue Française d'Etudes Politiques Africaines, no. 77, May 1972, pp. 14–18.

Guernier, H. "Une institution nouvelle en République du Tchad: Les communautés villageoises." *Problèmes de Sociologie Congolaise,* no. 1952, March 1961, pp. 157–59.

"Guerre civile." *Afrique Contemporaine,* March/April 1979, pp. 15–17.

"Guerrilla War in Chad: France's Real Interest." *African Communist,* 44, 1971, pp. 76–78.

Gusarov, V. "OAU and the Problem of Settling Conflicts in Chad and on the Horn of Africa." In *Problems of Contemporary Africa.* Rome: Istituto ItaloAfricano, 1984.

Henderson, George. "Qaddafy's Waterloo." *Africa Report,* September/October 1987, pp. 24–27.

"Hissène Habré." *Afrique Contemporain,* September/October 1978.

Hissein Habré. *Citations et pensées.* N'Djamena: Direction de la Presse Présidentielle, 1984.

Hollick, Julian Crandall. "Civil War in Chad, 1978–82." *World Today,* July/August 1982, pp. 297–304.

———. "French Intervention in Africa in 1978." *World Today,* February 1979, pp. 71–80.

Hugot, Pierre. "Les guerres du Tchad." *Etudes,* October 1983.

———. "Une mahdi pour le Tchad." *L'Afrique et l'Asie Modernes,* no. 125, 1980.

———. "Le Tchad entre l'Afrique Blanche et l'Afrique Noire." *Revue Française d'Etudes Politiques Africaines,* no. 1, January 1966, pp. 43–53.

———. "Le vide politique du Tchad musulman." *Revue Française de Sciences Politiques Africaines,* July/August 1979, pp. 27–40.

Hullot, Jean-Bernard. "Tchad: Les difficultés actuelles nécessitent une aide étrangère accrue." *France-Eurafrique,* no. 220, October 1970, pp. 21–22.

Interview de M. François Tombalbaye. *Europe-France-Outremer,* no. 450/451, July/August 1967, pp. 4–6.

Interview de M. François Tombalbaye, Président de la République." *Europe-France-Outremer,* no. 472, May 1969, pp. 14–15.

Issaka-Alamdou, R. *Les relations franco-tchadiennes de la conférence de Berlin à nos jours.* Paris: Imprimerie Daguerre, 1974.

Jacolin, Pierre. "What Do Young People in the Countryside Mean by 'Success'? A View of the Question from Southern Chad." *African Environment.* no. 14–16, 1980, pp. 341–80.

Jalade, Max."Malgré des péripéties, la stabilité du régime est assurée depuis huit ans." *Europe-France-Outremer,* no. 450/451, July/August 1967, pp. 7–9.

————. "Le Parti Progressiste Tchadien." *Communauté France-Eurafrique,* no. 138, January 1963, pp. 11–13.

La Jamahariya et la paix au Tchad. N'Djamena: Establissement Public pour l'Edition, 1982.

Jaulin, Robert. "Eléments et aspects divers de l'organisation civile et pénale des groupes du Moyen-Chari: Groupe Sara Madjingayé et groupe Mbaye." *Bulletin de l'IFAN,* 20, no. 1/2, 1958, pp. 170–90.

Jeannière, Abel. "Le Tchad maintenant." *Projet,* no. 136, June 1979, pp. 748–54.

Joachim, Paulin. "La 'révolution culturelle' Tchadienne." *Europe-France-Outremer,* no. 472, May 1969, pp. 20–21.

Joffe, E.G.H. "Libya and Chad." *Review of African Political Economy,* no. 21, May–September 1981, pp. 84–102.

Jouvé, Edouard. "Le Tchad de Ngarta Tombalbaye au Général Malloum." *Revue Française d'Etudes Politiques Africaines,* no. 146, February 1978, pp. 21–53.

Kelley, Michael P. *A State in Disarray: Conditions of Chad's Survival.* Boulder, CO: Westview Press, 1986.

————. "Weak States and Captured Patrons: French Desire to Disengage from Chad." *Round Table,* no. 296, 1985, pp. 328–38.

Khayar, I. H. *Tchad: Regards sur les élites ouaddaiennes.* Paris: CNRS, 1984.

Kinder, Ahmat. "Les mouvements de population en République du Tchad." *Revue Juridique et Politique,* vol. 34, no. 1, January–March 1980, pp. 218–36.

Kotoko, Ahmed. *Tchad-Cameroun, le destin de Hamai.* Paris: Harmattan, 1989.

Lanne, Bernard. "La chute d'Hissène Habré et le projet de fusion avec la Libye." *Afrique Contemporaine,* January/February 1981, pp. 6–12.

————. "La crise tchadienne." *Mondes et Cultures,* vol. 43, no. 4, 1983, pp. 817–29.

————. "Le deux guerres civiles du Tchad." *Mondes et Cultures,* vol. 40, no. 2, 1980, pp. 425–38.

————. "Les frontières du Tchad et de la Libye." *Revue Juridique et Politique,* vol. 31, no. 3, July–September 1977, pp. 953–66.

————. "Histoire d'une frontière, ou la bande d'Aouzou." *L'Afrique et l'Asie Modernes,* no. 194, 1987, pp. 3–15.

————. *Liste des chefs des unités administratives du Tchad, 1900–1983.* Paris: EHESS, 1983.

————. "Les nouvelles institutions de la République du Tchad." *Revue Juridique et Politique,* vol. 30, no. 2, April–June 1976, pp. 141–73.

————. "Nord et sud dans la vie politique du Tchad." *Revue Française d'Etudes Politiques Africaines,* no. 172/173, April/May 1980, pp. 104–17.

———. "Petit dictionnaire des idées reçus concernant le Tchad." *Le Mois en Afrique,* June/July 1981, pp. 132–142.

———. "Plaidoyer pour Tombalbaye." *Le Mois en Afrique,* vol. 22, no. 251/252, 1986/87, pp. 143–56.

———. "La population du sud du Tchad." *Revue Française d'Etudes Politiques Africaines,* no. 163/164, July/August 1979, pp. 41–81.

———. "Quinze ans d'ouvrages politiques sur le Tchad." *Afrique Contemporaine,* vol. 26, no. 144, 1987, pp. 37–47.

———. "Rébellion et guerre civile au Tchad, 1965–1983." *Cultures et Développement,* vol. 16, no. 3/4, 1984, pp. 757–82.

———. "Le Sud du Tchad dans la guerre civile, 1979–80." *Politique Africaine,* no. 3, September 1981, pp. 75–89.

———. "Le Sud, l'état, et la révolution." *Politique Africaine,* no. 16, 1984.

———. "Tchad: La nécessaire union." *Afrique Contemporaine,* no. 139, July–September 1986, pp. 59–60.

———. *Tchad-Libye: La querelle des frontières* Paris: Karthala, 1982.

La Parole au Peuple. Tchad: Echec au Néo-colonialisme. Paris: Vincennes, n. d.

Laporte, P. Y. "Tchad." In *Année Africaine 1971.* Paris: Editions A. Pedone, 1972, pp. 566–71.

"Lassou, Minister of Foreign Affairs." *Africa Report,* vol. 32, no. 2, 1987, pp. 44–45.

Lavefre, P. "France-Tchad: Coopération et souveraineté." Ph.D. diss. University of Reims, 1972.

Lavroff, D. G. "Les aspects actuels de l'unification de l'Afrique Noire francophone." *Annales Africaines,* 1, 1961, pp. 45–65.

Le Cornec, Jacques. *Les chefferies du Tchad et l'évolution politique.* Paris: Librairie Générale de Droit et de Jurisprudence, 1963.

———. "Les chefferies du Tchad et l'évolution politique." Ph.D. diss., University of Paris, 1961.

———. *Histoire politique du Tchad de 1900 à 1962.* Paris: Librairie Générale de Droit et de Jurisprudence, 1963.

Lefevre, Eric. *Tchad: Opération Manta.* Paris: Lavauzelle, 1984.

Lemarchand, René. "Aux origines de la guerre civile: Les émeutes de Fort-Lamy et Fort-Archambault." *Le Mois en Afrique,* vol. 20, no. 231/232, 1985, pp. 3–15.

———. "Chad: The Misadventures of the North-South Dialectic." *African Studies Review,* vol. 29, no. 3, 1986, pp. 27–41.

———. "Chad: A Precarious Peace Breaks Out." *Africa Report,* March/April 1982, pp. 15–19.

———. "Chad: Putting the Pieces Back Together Again." *Africa Report,* vol. 29, no. 6, November/December 1984, pp. 60–65.

———. "Chad: The Road to Partition." *Current History,* March 1984, pp. 113–16.

———. "Chad: The Roots of Chaos." *Current History,* vol. 80, no. 470, pp. 414–17, 436–38.

———. "The Crisis in Chad." In Gerald J. Bender et al. (eds.), *African Crisis Areas,* Berkeley: University of California Press, 1985, pp. 239–54.

———. "The Politics of Sara Ethnicity: A Note on the Origins of the Chad Civil War." *Cahiers d'Etudes Africaines,* vol. 20, no. 4, 1980, pp. 449–72.

———. "A propos du Tchad: Le Nord face à l'histoire." *Maghreb Review,* vol. 12, no. 1/2, 1987, pp. 18–24.

Lhuisard, A. "La Chine et l'Afrique." *Défense Nationale,* June 1974, pp. 89–105.

"Libya: A Good Year for Qadaffi." *Africa Confidential,* December 21, 1990, pp. 1–2.

"Libyan Interference in Chad." *Department of State Bulletin,* October 1981, pp. 28–30.

Livre Blanc 1963–75. N'Djamena: Service de Presse de la Présidence du Conseil Supérieur Militaire, 1976.

"Le Livre d'Or d'Afrique: Le Tchad." *Afrique,* no. 10, March 1962, pp. 15–65.

Lisette, G. *"Têtes ensemble" pour la décolonisatioin.* Paris: CIEM, 1988.

Lisette, Y., and M. Dumas. *Le RDA et le Tchad.* Paris: Nouvelles Editions Africaines, 1986.

Lofting, Chris. "The French Foreign Legion Rules Again." *Argosy,* no. 371, 1970, pp. 55–77.

"Lol, Choua Mahamat." *Afrique Contemporaine,* May/June 1979.

Lusignan, Guy de. *French-Speaking Africa Since Independence.* New York: Praeger, 1969.

Lycett, Andrew. "Chad's Disastrous War." *Africa Report,* September/October 1978, pp. 4–12.

Madi, Passang. *Retour au Tchad.* N'Djamena: INSH, 1991.

Madjirebayé, Djibangar. "Le rôle des sociétés dans le financement du développement au Tchad." *Revue Juridique et Politique,* vol. 32, no. 1, January–March 1978, pp. 471–84.

Magnant, Jean Pierre. "Peuple, ethnie, et nation: Le cas du Tchad." *Droit et Culture,* no. 8, 1984, pp. 29–50.

———. "Le problème des chefferies pour l'administration du Tchad contemporain." In *Le droit de la fonction publique dans les pays d'Afrique de l'Ouest.* Perpignan: Cahiers de l'Université, no. 6/7, 1989, pp. 269–86.

———. "Quelques grands types de systèmes fonciers traditionnels au Tchad." *Cahiers d'Outre-Mer,* no. 122, April–June 1978, pp. 171–201.

————. "Le Tchad." In C. Conac (ed.), *L'Afrique en transition,* Paris: Economica, 1993.

Mahamat-Saleh, Y. "Les populations musulmanes du Tchad et le pouvoir politique (1946–1975): Contribution à l'étude des problèmes de construction de l'état au Tchad." Ph.D. diss., University of Paris, 1983.

Maikoubou, Dingamtoudji. "Histoire des missions protestantes au Tchad depuis 1920." Ph.D. diss., University of Montpellier, 1988.

Maillard, M. "Les redevances coutumières au Tchad." *Mémoires du CHEAM,* no. 1906, 1951.

Malet, P. "Tchad." In *Année Africaine 1966.* Paris: Editions A. Pedone, 1967, pp. 613–30.

Malloum, Félix. *La politique du Tchad.* N'Djamena: Service de Presse de la Présidence, 1977.

Marinas, L. "La crisis del Chad." *Revista de Politica Internacional* (Madrid), 106, 1969, pp. 143–60.

Marks, T. A. "Lesson Learned in Chad." *Africa Institute Bulletin,* vol. 16, no. 3, 1978, pp. 120–28.

Martin, F. "De l'identité des personnes au Nord Tchad et de quelques problémes juridiques annexes." *Mémoires du CHEAM,* no. 3324, 1960.

Martin, Guy. "Security and Conflict Management of Chad." *Bulletin of Peace Proposals,* March 1990, pp. 37–47.

Masse, Christian. *Rébelles, voyages, et captivité au Lac Thad.* Paris: Editions Magnard, 1979.

Massip, A. "Toubous, qui êtes-vous?" *Afrique Contemporaine,* September/October 1975, pp. 27–30.

Masson, M. "De l'organisation politique de la région du Tchad." Paris: *CHEAM Mémoire,* no. 241, n.d .

May, R. A. "The State of Chad: Political Factions and Political Decay." *Civilisations,* vol. 33, no. 2, 1983, pp. 113–45.

Mayoroum, Youhoudouréou Miayan. *Les relations du Tchad avec les états de l'Afrique centrale de 1956 à 1970.* Paris: Institut Libre d'Etudes des Relations Internationales, 1974.

M'Bokolo, Elikia. "Cultures et ethnies du Tchad: Le divorce colonial." *Demain l'Afrique,* no. 24, April 1974, pp. 31–33.

————. "Forces sociales et idéologies dans la décolonisation de l'AEF." *Journal of African History,* vol. 22, 1981, pp. 393–407.

Mialet, Jean. "L'intervention française au Tchad: L'application d'une politique." *France-Eurafrique,* no. 220, October 1970, pp. 14–20; no. 221, November 1970, pp. 21–26.

Michalon, Thierry. "La Charte Fondamentale et les nouvelles institutions transitoires de l'état tchadien." *Revue Juridique et Politique,* vol. 33, no. 1, Janaury–March 1979, pp. 75–90.

————. "Tchad: Echec d'une constitution ambigué ou effondrement d'un certain type d'état?" *Revue Juridique et Politique,* vol. 33, no. 1, January–March 1979, pp. 75–90.

———. "Le Tchad ou l'Afrique exemplaire." *Projet,* no. 182, 1984, pp. 135–46.

Michalon, Thierry, and A. Moyrand. "Des institutions pour le Tchad: La paix par le droit?" *Revue Juridique et Politique,* vol. 43, no. 2, 1989, pp. 142–63.

Mitchell, C. R. "External Involvement in Civil Strife: The Case of Chad." *The Yearbook of World Affairs,* vol. 26, New York: Praeger, 1972, pp. 152–86.

Mouric, Nelly. "La politique tchadienne de la France sous Valéry d'Estaing: Vers la prise en comte de la rébellion." *Politique Africaine,* no. 16, 1984, pp. 86–101.

Moyrand, Alain. "Déconcentration et décentralisation au Tchad." In *Déconcentration et décentralisation en Afrique francophone,* Paris: Institut International d'Administration Publique, Document No. 4, 1989, pp. 57–114.

———. "Destruction et reconstruction d'un appareil judiciaire: Le cas du Tchad." *Afrique Contemporaine,* no. 156, 1990, pp. 45–50.

———. *La normalisation constitutionnelle du Tchad.* Bordeaux: Centre d'Etude d'Afrique Noire, 1990.

———. "Reflexions sur les incertitudes de l'état du droit au Tchad: Constat et propositions." *Revue Internationale de Droit Comparé,* no. 3, 1989, pp. 595–615.

———. "La responsabilité du fonctionnaire en droit tchadien." *Cahiers de l'Université de Perpignan,* no. 6/7, 1989, pp. 287–321.

———. "Tchad: La crise de la légalité de crise." *Revue du Droit Public,* no. 2, 1988, pp. 381–422.

———. "Les vicissitudes du pouvoir législatif au Tchad." *Revue Africain de Droit International et Comparé,* no. 2, 1989, pp. 206–59.

Moyrand, Alain, and Aché Nabia. "L'organisation judiciaire au Tchad: Commentaire, bilan, et statistique." *Penant,* vol. 98, no. 796, 1988, pp. 75–112.

Muracciole, L. "Les constitutions des états africains d'expression française: La Constitution du 16 Avril 1962 de la République du Tchad." *Revue Juridique et Politique,* April–June 1962, pp. 265–311.

Nabi, D. S. "L'impact de la guerre de libération nationale sur les populations rurales du Guéra: Exemple de Tenki." Thesis, University of N'Djamena, 1986.

Naldi, Gino J. "The Aouzou Strip Dispute: A Legal Analysis." *Journal of African Law,* vol. 33, no. 1, 1989, pp. 72–77.

———. *The OAU: An Analysis of Its Role.* London: Mansell, 1989.

N'Diaye, Jean Pierre. "L'Exemple du Tchad." In *La Jeunesse africaine face à l'impérialisme,* Paris: Maspero, 1972, pp. 27–34.

Ndovi, V. "Chad: Nation-building, Security and OAU Peacekeeping." In S. Wright and J. N. Brownfoot (eds.), *Africa in World Politics: Changing Perspectives,* Basingstoke: Macmillan, 1987, pp. 140–54.

Nemo, J. "Le régime juridique des terres au Hoggar." *Travaux de l'Institut des Recherches Sahariennes,* 22, 1963, pp. 123–44.

Neuberger, Benyamin. *Involvement, Invasion, and Withdrawal: Qadhafi's Libya and Chad, 1969–1981.* Tel Aviv: Tel Aviv University Middle Eastern and African Studies, 1982.

Ngangbet, Michel. *Peut-on encore sauver le Tchad?* Paris: Karthala, 1987.

———. *Tribulations d'un jeune Tchadien: De l'école coloniale à la prison de l'indépendance,* Paris: Harmattan, 1993.

Ngangsop, G. J. *Tchad: Vingt ans de crise.* Paris: Harmattan, 1986.

Ngarbaye, Allaidabaye. "La Cour Suprême du Tchad." in Gérard Conac (ed.), *Les Cours Suprêmes en Afrique,* Paris: Economica, 1988, pp. 351–66.

"Ngarta Tombalbaye-Chad, Survivor of a Record Number of Plots." In A.P.J. Van Rensburg, *Contemporary Leaders of Africa,* Cape Town: Haum, 1975, pp. 55–64.

Nicolas, G. "Crise de l'état et affirmation ethnique en Afrique Noire contemporaine." *Revue Française de Science Politique,* vol. 22, no. 5, October 1972.

Nolutshungu, S. C. "International and Civil Strife in Chad." *Government and Opposition,* vol. 19, no. 3, 1984, pp. 367–77.

———. *Limits of Anarchy: Intervention and State Formation in Chad.* Charlotteville: University Press of Virginia, 1995.

Nomads of the Sahara. London: Minority Rights Group, 1989.

Nouradfine, Delwa K. C. "Problématique de l'administration territoire au Tchad." Ph.D. diss., Montpelier, 1988.

Novicki, Margaret. "Interview: Gouara Lassou, Minister of Foreign Affairs." *Africa Report,* March/April 1987, pp. 44–45.

Nwokedi, Emeka. "Le Nigeria et le conflit tchadien." *Le Mois en Afrique,* June/July 1984, pp. 24–34.

Ofoegbu, Mazi Ray. "Nigeria and Its Neighbors." *Journal of West African Studies,* vol. 12, 1975, pp. 3–24.

Ogunbadejo, Oye. "Qaddafi and Africa's International Relations." *Journal of Modern African Studies,* vol. 24, no. 1, 1986, pp. 33–68.

———. "Qaddafi's North African Design." *International Security,* Summer 1983, pp. 154–78.

Ojo, Olusola. "The OAU and Conflict Management: The Case of Chad." *International Problems* (Tel Aviv), vol. 27, no. 3/4, 1988, pp. 33–47.

"Organisation judiciaire au Tchad." *Penant,* vol. 77, no. 719, January–March 1968, pp. 65–76.

Orobator, S. E. "Chad After the Debacle: Is There a Solution?" *Contemporary Review* (London), vol. 238, no. 1381, February 1981, pp. 86–93.

―――. "Chadian Crisis: The Search for a Solution." *Contemporary Review,* vol. 238, no. 1380, 1981, pp. 1–7.

Otayek, René. "L'intervention du Nigeria dans le conflit tchadien." *Le Mois en Afrique,* vol. 18, no. 209/210, June/July 1983, pp. 51–66.

―――. "La Libye face à la France au Tchad." *Politique Africaine,* no. 16, 1984, pp. 66–85.

Owona, Joseph. "Tchad: L'échec de la Charte Fondamentale du 25 août 1977." *Le Mois en Afrique,* no. 200, September 1982, pp. 16–37.

Pairault, Claude. "Boum après trente ans." *Afrique Contemporaine,* no. 4, 1992, pp. 88–96.

Pittman, D. "The OAU and Chad." In Y. El-Ayouty and I. W. Zartman (eds.), *The OAU after Twenty Years.* New York: Praeger, 1984.

Pledge, Robert. "Chad's Guerilla War." *Africa Report,* November 1969, pp. 10–12.

―――. "France at War in Africa." *Africa Report,* June 1970, pp. 16–19.

―――. "Le Tchad ou la théorie française des dominos africains." *Esprit,* vol. 38, no. 2, no. 389, February 1970, pp. 371–80.

Pouillon, Jean. "Rapport d'enquête au Tchad." *Cahiers d'Etudes Africaines,* no. 3, October 1960, pp. 153–55.

"Présentation du programme tchadien de redressement économique et financière." *Bulletin de l'Afrique Noire,* no. 1427, October 27, 1988, pp. 8–11.

Prevost, Paul Louis. "L'Union Douaniare et Economique de l'Afrique Central." *Revue Française d'Etudes Politiques Africaines,* no. 34, October 1968, pp. 64–93.

"Réconciliation difficile." *Afrique Contemporaine,* November/December 1980, pp. 20–22.

"Les réformes commencent à porter leurs fruits." *Europe-France-Outremer,* April 1969, pp. 29–32.

Renault, C. "Le Tchad en révolte." *Croissance des Jeunes Nations,* February 1970, pp. 19–26.

"République du Tchad. *Année Africaine 1963.* Paris: Pedone, 1965, pp. 455–68.

"République du Tchad." *Année Africaine 1969.* Paris: Pedone 1971, pp. 519–27.

"République du Tchad." *Europe-France-Outremer,* August 1960–August 1987, special annual on all francophone African countries.

Robinson, P. T. "Playing the Arab Card: Niger and Chad's Ambivalent Relations with Libya." In B. E. Arlinghaus (ed.), *African Security Is-*

sues: Sovereignty, Stability, and Solidarity. Boulder, CO: Westview Press, 1984.

Rondos, Alex. "Chad: Conflict, Intervention, and the OAU." In N. O. Obaseki (ed.), Report of the International Peace Academy Workshop, New York, 1983, pp. 46–64.

———. "Civil War and Foreign Intervention in Chad." Current History, May 1985, pp. 209–12.

———. "Why Chad." CSIS Africa Notes, no. 18, 1983.

Rosenkranz, Esther. "Survivances précoloniales: Les problèmes politiques du Kanem." Politique Africaine, no. 33, March 1989, pp. 124–29.

Rousseau, Charles. "France et Tchad. Controverses sur la légalité internationale de l'intervention militaire française au Tchad." Revue Générale de Droit International Publique, vol. 75, 1971, pp. 199–205.

Saint, Louis. "Le Parti Progressiste Tchadien." University of Paris, Mémoire, 1960.

Schweisguth, C. "Sultanat du Ouaddai: Evolution politique, économique, sociale." Mémoire ENFOM, 1957.

Seid, Joseph Brahim. "Les droits fonciers coutumiers au Tchad." Revue Juridique et Politique, vol. 24, no. 4, 1970, pp. 1161–62.

———. "L'expropriation au Tchad." Revue Juridique et Politique, vol. 24, no. 4, 1970, pp. 959–70.

———. "Les modes d'attribution et d'acquisition de la nationalité tchadienne." Revue Juridique et Politique, vol. 25, no. 4, 1971, pp. 565–70.

———. "L'organisation des communes au Tchad." Revue Juridique et Politique, vol. 22, no. 2, 1968, pp. 313–28.

———. "L'organisation judiciaire du Tchad en matière administrative." Revue Juridique et Politique, vol. 23, no. 4, 1969.

———. "L'organisation judiciaire du Tchad en matière civile." Revue Juridique et Politique, vol. 23, no. 4, 1969, pp. 601–4.

———. "Le rôle de la Cour Suprême au Tchad. Revue Juridique et Politique, vol. 23, no. 4, 1969.

Sengbusch, V. von. "Fünf Jahre Republik Tschad." Afrika heute, vol. 4, no. 15, 1966, pp. 46–79.

———. "Le Tchad au centre de l'Afrique." Afrika (Bonn), vol. 8, no. 2, 1967, pp. 4–8.

———. "Der Tschad, Schnittpunkt afrikanischer Geschichte: Von frühen Negerreichen über die Arabisierung und Kolonisierung zum republikanischen Staat." Zeitschrift für Kulturaustausch, no. 16, 1966, pp. 41–45.

———. "Wirtschaftliches Engagement im Tschad." Afrika heute, no. 17, September 15, 1965, pp. 225–32.

Sesay, Amadu. "The OAU Peacekeeping Force in Chad." *Current Research on Peace and Violence,* vol. 12, 1989, pp. 191–200.

"Setback for Chad Liberation Front." *Africa,* August 1978, pp. 41–45.

Siddick, Abba. "Pourquoi combattent les Tchadiens." *Africasia,* no. 15, May 11, 1970, pp. 14–17.

———. "Tchad: Une politique de rechange." *Africasia,* no. 26, 1970, pp. 24–27.

Soffer, Ovadia. *Le diamant noir: Comment on devient ambassadeur d'Israel.* Paris: R. Laffont, 1987.

Solana, G. "La guerre occulta de Chad." *Africa,* no. 338, 1970, pp. 14–16.

Somerville, Keith. "The War in Chad: France and Libya Fight It Out." In *Foreign Military Intervention in Africa,* London: Pinter, 1990, pp. 61–82.

"Le sort des otages français." *Afrique Contemporaine,* May/June 1975, pp. 15–16.

Soudan, François. "Une analyse politique du problème tchadien: Présentation critique des thèses du Dr. Siddick et de son mouvement." *Afrika-Spectrum,* vol. 15, no. 3, 1980, pp. 295–308.

Soulas de Russel, Dominique. "Une analyse politique du problème tchadien: Présentation critique des thèses du Dr. Siddick et de son mouvement." *Afrika-Spectrum,* vol. 15, no. 3, 1980, pp. 295–308.

———. *Tschad-Objekt nationaler und internationaler Machtkampfe.* Hamburg: Institut für Afrika-Kunde, 1981.

———. *Krisen und Konflikte im Tschad.* Hamburg: Institut für Afrika-Kunde, 1982.

Soulie, G. Jean-Louis. "Les événements du Tchad." *L'Afrique et l'Asie,* no. 85/86, 1969, pp. 39–50.

Spartacus. *Les documents secrets: Opération Manta, Tchad 1983–1984.* Paris: Plon, 1985.

"Sudan: The Wild West." *Africa Confidential,* May 27, 1988, pp. 2–4.

Talbot, George T. "Origins, Causes, and Effects of the Tchadian Civil War and the French Interventions, 1968–71." Ph.D. diss. University of Notre Dame, 1974.

Taylor, John. "The Tchad Rebellion." *Contemporary Review,* no. 1267, 1970, pp. 288–89.

Tchad. Paris: Karthala, 1984.

Tchad. Commission d'Enquête Nationale. *Les crimes et détournements de l'ex Président Habré et ses accomplices.* Paris: Harmattan, 1993.

Tchad. Ministère de l'Information. *Les treize préfectures de la République du Tchad.* Fort-Lamy, 1962, 1972.

"Le Tchad." *Actualités Coopération,* no. 16, 1971, pp. 1–5.

"Tchad." *Afrique,* special issue no. 8, 1966, pp. 5–80.

"Tchad." *Afrique 71/72,* annual supplement of *Jeune Afrique,* pp. 423–25.

"Tchad." *Année Africaine 1970.* Paris: Pedone, 1971, pp. 478–82.

"Tchad." In Pierre Biarnes et al. (eds.), *L'Année Politique Africaine 1970.* Dakar: Société Africaine d'Edition.

"Tchad." In D. G. Lavroff and G. Peiser (eds.), *Les Constitutions Africaines.* Paris: Pedone, 1963, pp. 48–63.

"Le Tchad." *Eurafrica,* vol. 9, no. 2/3, 1965, pp. 6–78.

"Tchad: Acte Fondamentale de le République." *Afrique Contemporaine,* January–March 1983, pp. 58–61.

"Tchad: Affaire Claustre." *Afrique Contemporaine,* September/October 1975, pp. 20–21.

"Tchad: Anarchie et confusion." *Afrique Contemporaine,* May/June 1978, pp. 14–16.

"Tchad: Constitution d'un gouvernement d'union nationale." *Afrique Contemporaine,* no. 56, July/August 1971, pp. 19–20.

"Tchad: Départ du Gouverneur Louis." *Revue Française d'Etudes Politiques Africaines,* no. 54, June 1970, pp. 15–18.

"Tchad: Deuxième guerre civile." *Afrique Contemporaine,* May/June 1980, pp. 31–33.

"Tchad: Difficile réconciliation nord-sud." *Afrique Contemporaine,* November/December 1982, pp. 29–30.

"Tchad: Elections présidentielles." Special issue of *Europe-France-Outremer,* no. 472, May 1969, pp. 14–46.

"Le Tchad en révolte." *Croissance des Jeunes Nations,* no. 96, February 1970, pp. 19–26.

"Tchad: La crise s'aggrave." *Afrique Contemporaine,* May/June 1982, pp. 35–36.

"Tchad: La guerre civile." *Afrique Contemporaine,* July/August 1978.

"Tchad: La guerre continue." *Afrique Contemporaine,* July/August 1978.

"Tchad: La réconciliation difficile." *Afrique Contemporaine,* January/February 1980, pp. 20–22.

"Tchad: La réunion de Nairobi." *Afrique Contemporaine,* no. 120, March/April 1982, pp. 23–24.

"Tchad: La situation politique et militaire au 1 mars 1984." *Afrique Contemporaine,* no. 130, April–June 1984, pp. 61–65.

"Tchad: La situation politique au 1 décembre 1984." *Afrique Contemporaine,* no. 133, January–March 1985, pp. 45–51.

"Tchad: Le litige entre le Tchad et la Libye." *Afrique Contemporaine,* September/October 1977, pp. 17–19.

"Tchad: Le rôle de la force interafricaine." *Afrique Contemporaine,* no. 119, January/February 1982, pp. 30–31.

"Tchad: Les accords de Lagos." *Afrique Contemporaine,* September/October 1979, pp. 26–28.

"Tchad: Les Opérations militaires." *Afrique Contemporaine,* no. 46, November/December 1969, pp. 17–20.

"Tchad: Les succès militaires du FROLINAT." *Afrique Contemporaine,* May/June 1978, pp. 15–16.

"Tchad: L'intervention française." *Le Mois en Afrique,* no. 48, December 1969, pp. 20–21.

"Tchad 1970." *Bulletin d'Afrique Noire,* vol. 15, no. 632, 1971, pp. 12762–83.

"Tchad: Retrait du corps expéditionnaire français." *Revue Française d'Etudes Politiques Africaines,* no. 67, July 1971.

"Tchad: Révolution culturelle." *Afrique Contemporaine,* no. 69, September/October 1973.

"Tchad: Tentative de coup d'état." *Afrique Contemporaine,* no. 57, September/October 1971, pp. 14–15.

"Tchad: Visite de M. Chirac." *Afrique Contemporaine,* March/April 1976, pp. 35–36.

Teisserenc, P. "De la communauté ethnique à la communauté nationale: Les lycéens d'Abéché et de Sahr." Ph.D. diss., University of Paris, 1972.

———. "Milieu urbain et recherche d'une identité culturelle: Les lycéens de Fort-Archambault et d'Abéché. *Cahiers d'Etudes Africaines,* no. 51, 1973.

Thibault, Jean. "Tchad: Une année de confusion et d'incertitudes." In Pierre Biarnes, et al. (eds.), *L'Année Politique Africaine 1973,* Dakar: Société Africaine d'Edition, January 1974, pp. 111–16.

———. "Tchad: Vigoreux coup de barre vers le camp arabe." In Pierre Biarnes, et al. (eds.), *L'Année Politique Africaine 1972,* Dakar: Société Africaine d'Edition, January 1973, pp. 111–16.

Thompson, Virginia, and Richard Adloff. *Conflict in Chad.* Berkeley: Institute of International Relations, University of California, 1981.

———. *The Emerging States of French Equatorial Africa.* Stanford: Stanford University Press, 1960.

Tombalbaye, Ngarta (François). "Expression de la civilisation Sara: L'initiation au Yondé mené à Dieu." *France-Eurafrique.* no. 251, November 1974, pp. 25–29.

Touré, M. "Du Contentieux et de la preuve de la nationalité tchadienne." *Revue Juridique et Politique,* vol. 25, no. 4, 1971, pp. 571–76.

Touze, R. L. *370 jours d'un ambassadeur au Tchad.* Paris: France-Empire, 1989.

Trevidic, P. "Tchad." *Année Africaine 1965.* Paris: Pedone, 1966, pp. 485–92.

Triaud, J. L. "Le refus de l'état: L'exemple tchadien." *Esprit,* no. 4, April 1985, pp. 20–26.

Tshunda, Olela. "L'OUA à la question tchadienne." *Africa* (Rome), vol. 44, no. 2, 1989, pp. 263–78.

Tubiana, Marie-José. "Problèmes posés par l'arrivée massive de nomades dans une zone occupée par des sédentaires et par la naissance de groupements d'un type nouveau." In P.T.W. Baxter (ed.), *Property, Poverty, and People: Changing Rights in Property and Problems of Pastoral Development,* Manchester: Manchester University Department of Social Anthropology and International Development Centre, 1989, pp. 217–21.

———. "Tchad 1989: Les changements." *Journal des Africanistes,* vol. 59, no. 1/2, 1989, pp. 185–200.

Tunteng, P. Kivqn. "Coercion, Stability, and National Reconstruction in Chad." *Pan African Journal,* (Nairobi), vol. 5, no. 2, 1972, pp. 109–26.

Udofia, Offiong E. "The Organization of African Unity and Conflicts in Africa: The Chadian Crisis." *Journal of Asian and African Studies,* July 1989, pp. 19–33.

United States. *Area Handbook for Chad;* by Harold D. Nelson et al. Washington, Government Printing Office, 1972. 2nd edition, 1990. By Harold D. Nelson, et al.

United States Congress, House Committee on Foreign Affairs, Subcommittee on Africa. *Libya-Sudan-Chad Triangle.* Washington, Government Printing Office, 1982.

United States Department of State, Bureau of Intelligence and Research. *International Boundary Studies: Chad–Central African Republic* (Series No. 83). Washington: Government Printing Office, 1968.

———. *International Boundary Studies: Chad-Nigeria* (Series No. 90). Washington: Government Printing Office, 1969.

———. *International Boundary Studies: Chad-Sudan* (Series No. 15). Washington: Government Printing Office, 1962.

Urper, S. "Le Tchad en péril. *Cahiers de l'Actualité Religieuse et Sociale,* 507, 1969, pp. 693–98.

Varin, J. "L'enjeu tchadien." *Cahiers du Communisme,* March 1981, pp. 98–105.

Vignès, J. "Tchad: La garde aux portes du Tibesti." *Africasia,* February 21, 1972.

Villeneuve, Robert. "Au Tchad: Unité, tribalisme, et democratie." *Afrique,* vol. 22, March 1963, pp. 19–21.

Vinay, B. "Cooperation intra-africaine et intégration: L'éxperience de l'UDEAC." *Penant,* 81, no. 733, 1971, pp. 313–31.

Whiteman, Kaye. *Chad.* London: Minority Rights Group Report, 1989.

———. "Pompidou and Africa: Gaullism after de Gaulle." *World Today,* vol. 26, no. 6, June 1970, pp. 241–49.

Wirz, Albert. *Krieg in Afrika*. Bonn: Franz Steiner, 1982.

"Wodemi Goukouni." *Afrique Contemporaine,* September/October 1979.

Wright, John. *Libya, Chad, and the Central Sahara*. London: Hurst, 1989.

Yamassoum, Nagoum C. "Les grèves des lycéens de Fort-Lamy en 1971 et 1972." *Le Mois en Afrique,* May/June 1982, pp. 110–24.

Yanoingar, Mairo Salmon. "Le contrat d'entreprise et la livraison d'ouvrage clé main au Tchad." *Revue Juridique et Politique,* vol. 42, no. 2/3, 1988, pp. 477–88.

Yarangar, T. "Existe-t-il un état tchadien?" Ph.D. diss. University of Nice, 1988.

Yewawa, Gbiamango. "Les conflits tchadiens." Ph.D. diss. University of Paris, 1988.

Yost, David S. "French Policy in Chad and the Libyan Challenge." *Orbis,* vol. 26, no. 4, 1983, pp. 965–97.

Youssoubomi, G. "La responsabilité des agents publics au Tchad." *Revue Juridique et Politique,* vol. 27, no. 4, 1973, pp. 909–24.

Zartman, I. William. "What's at Stake in Chad." *Worldview,* November 1983, pp. 4–7.

Zatzfpine, Alexandre. "L'évolution du droit de la nationalité des Républiques francophones d'Afrique et de Madagascar." *Penant,* no. 748, April–June 1975, pp. 147–201; no. 749, July–September 1975, pp. 346–80.

Zeltner, Jean-Claude, and Henry Tourneux. *L'arabe dans le bassin du Tchad*. Paris: Karthala, 1986.

Economics

"L'Afrique Centrale." *Afrique Industrie,* no. 173, November 1978, pp. 144–61.

Agoro, I. O. "The Establishment of the Chad Basin Commission." *International and Comparative Law Quarterly,* vol. 15, 1966.

Alladam, H. "L'attitude des paysans du Moyen Chari vis-à-vis de la culture du coton." *Liaison,* no. 53, 1956, pp. 11–14.

Amady, G. "Le domaine de collectivités publiques tchadiennes." *Revue Juridique et Politique,* no. 4, October 1970, pp. 783–96.

"L'Amélioration des voies du communication du Tchad." *Europe-France-Outremer,* no. 408, January 1964, pp. 43–44.

"Aperçu sur l'économie du Tchad." *Bulletin d'Afrique Noire,* no. 692, May 24, 1972, pp. 13508–25.

"L'arachide au Tchad." *Nations Nouvelles,* September 1966, pp. 17–23.

Autier, P., et al. "The Food and Nutrition Surveillance Systems of Chad and Mali: The 'SAP' after Two Years." *Disasters,* vol. 13, no. 1, 1989, pp. 9–32.

"Autres ressources essentielles: L'élevage et la pêche." *Europe-France-Outremer,* no. 503, December 1971, pp. 53–55.

Aymard, Pierre. "Vers une exploitation rationnelle de la pêche au Tchad." *France-Eurafrique,* 19, no. 189, November 1967, pp. 34–37.

Banque Centrale des Etats de l'Afrique Equatoriale et du Cameroun. "Le Budget du Tchad." *Etudes et Statistiques.* Intermittent publication.

———. "La campagne cotonnière 1967–1968 dans les états producteurs de la zone d'émission." *Etudes et Statistiques,* no. 139, December 1968, pp. 697–705.

———. "Conférence économique de Moundou." *Etudes et Statistiques,* no. 145, June/July 1968, pp. 337–44.

———. "Une expérience de développement régional intégré: L'Opération de développement rural de la vallée du Mandoul." *Etudes et Statistiques,* no. 164, May 1971, pp. 302–17.

———. "L'exploration du Lac Tchad et la mise en valeur du bassin tchadien." *Etudes et Statistiques,* no. 155, June/July 1970, pp. 375–81.

———. "Le Premier Plan quinquennal de développement économique et social du Tchad." *Etudes et Statistiques,* no. 128, November 1967, pp. 1569–88.

———. "République du Tchad: L'Abattoir Frigorifique de Farcha." *Etudes et Statistiques,* no. 159, December 1970, pp. 750–62.

———. "La situation économique et financière du Tchad." *Etudes et Statistiques,* February 1961.

———. "Le Tchad, pays d'élevage et réservoir de viande du centre africain." *Etudes et Statistiques,* February 1959.

Banque des Etats de l'Afrique Centrale. "Le Budget du Tchad." *Etudes et Statistiques.* Intermittent publication.

———. "Le commerce extérieur du Tchad en 1971 et 1972." *Etudes et Statistiques,* no. 10, March 1974, pp. 147–51.

———. "Evolution des budgets des états de la zone d'émission (1964–1974)." *Etudes et Statistiques,* no. 20, March 1975, pp. 152–169.

———. "Les régimes fiscaux comparés des états de la zone d'émission." *Etudes et Statistiques,* no. 7, December 1973, pp. 693–711.

———. "République du Tchad: Indicateurs économiques." *Etudes et Statistiques,* quarterly.

Barnathan, A. "Monographie Cotontchad." In Banque des Etats de l'Afrique Centrale." *Etudes et Statistiques,* no. 14, August/September 1974, pp. 470–90.

Belotteau, Jacques. "Le problème du déficit vivrier au sahel." *Afrique Contemporaine,* October–December 1985, pp. 47–62.

Bernard, Georges. "Un projet commun: Le Bangui-Tchad." *Europe-France-Outremer,* no. 366, May 1960, pp. 18–20.

Bezot, P. "Les recherches rizicoles au Tchad." *L'Agronomie Tropicale,* no. 1, 1966, pp. 70–92.

Biasutt, R. "Reste alter Rassenelemente in den Oasen der Sahara." *Zeitschrift für Rassenkunde,* no. 50, 1935, pp. 68–74.

"Bilan de l'activité de la Caisse Centrale de Coopération Economique en Afrique Noire en 1978." *Bulletin de l'IFAN,* no. 1011, July 1979, pp. 19612–13.

"Bilan du Premier Septennat." *Europe-France-Outremer,* no. 472, May 1969, pp. 16–20.

Billaz, R., and Y. Diawara. *Enquêtes en milieu rural sahélien.* Paris: Presses Universitaires de France, 1981.

Bon, M., and R. Colin. "Les proverbes, facteur de développement [Tchad]." *Développement et Civilisation,* no. 41/42, September–December 1970, pp. 83–123.

Bonfiglio, Angelo Maliki. *Agro-pastoralism in Chad as a Strategy for Survival.* Washington: World Bank, 1993.

Bouquet, Christian. "La culture du blé dans les polders du Lac Tchad." *Les Cahiers d'Outre-Mer,* vol. 22, no. 86, 1969, pp. 203–14.

———. "Les malentendus de l'Opération Polders au Tchad." *Cahiers d'Outre-Mer,* vol. 40, no. 159, 1987, pp. 295–301.

———. "La transformation industrielle des produits de l'agriculture et de l'élevage au Tchad." *L'Information Géographique,* vol. 34, no. 1, January 1970, pp. 13–24.

Bourlet, G. "Malaise et remède de l'agriculture tchadienne." *Liaison,* no. 59, 1957, pp. 23–27; no. 60, 1957, pp. 45–48; no. 61, 1958, pp. 55–58.

Boutrais, Jean (ed.). *Du politique à l'économie: Etudes historiques dans le bassin du Lac Tchad.* Paris: ORSTOM, 1991.

Briey, D. "Industrialization and Social Problems in Central Africa." *International Labour Review,* vol. 43, no. 5, May 1951, pp. 475–506.

British Overseas Trade Board. *Cameroun, Chad, Gabon, CAR, and Equatorial Guinea.* London: The Board, 1975.

Bureau pour le Développment de la Promotion Agricole. *La Culture attelée et la modernisation rural dans le sud du Tchad.* Paris: BDPA, n.d.

———. *Etude agricole de la région du Ouaddai.* 3 vols. Paris: BDPA, 1965. [By J. de La Tour et al.]

———. *La formation des jeunes ruraux au Mandoul.* Paris: BDPA, 1969. [By J. Chevallier and F. Lebouteux.]

———. *Mission de reconnaissance préliminaire à l'étude de la vallée du Mandoul.* 2 vols. Paris: BDPA, 1964. [By P. Geny.]

———. *Opération de modernisation du Centre-East Tchadien: Rapport de fin de campagne.* Paris: BDPA, 1964. [By M. Buisson.]

———. *Projet d'intensification de l'action de modernisation rurale dans le Centre-Est Tchadien.* Paris: BDPA, 1964. [By M. Buisson.]

―――. *Rapport pré-étude pour la réalisation des études socio-économiques intéressant la zone des cuvettes lacustres et ouadis du Lac Tchad.* Paris: BDPA, 1962. [By J. Hautier.]

―――. *République du Tchad: Problèmes sociaux et économiques de l'aménagement des polders de Bol, Bol Guini, et Bol Berin.* 2 vols. Paris: BDPA, 1963. [By M. Jacob.]

―――. *Travaux du groups d'étude sur les effets de l'aide: Etude prospective: Diagnostic et besoins en aide extérieure de la République du Tchad.* Paris: BDPA, 1965, 2 vols.

Cabot, Jean. "La culture du coton du Tchad." *Annales de Géographie,* vol. 66, no. 358, 1957, pp. 499–508.

―――. "Un domaine nouveau de riziculture inondée: Les plaines du Moyen Logone." *Cahiers d'Outre-mer,* vol. 10, no. 38, April–June 1957, pp. 158–73.

―――. "La mise en valeur des régions du Moyen-Logone." *Annales de Géographie,* vol. 64, January/February 1955, pp. 35–46.

―――. "C.E.A.C., une solution aux problèmes de la région." *Le Moniteur Africain,* no. 759, June 1978, pp. 18–28.

―――. "Du mode de production domestique à l'intégration du système capitaliste: Le cas des paysans tchadiens." In C. Coquery-Vidrovitch (ed.), *Sociétés paysannes du Tiers Monde,* Lille: Presses Universitaires de Lille, 1980, pp. 57–65.

Capot-Rey, R. "Borkou et Ounianga: Etude de géographie régionale." Thesis, University of Algiers, 1961.

Carrin, Guy. "Self-financing of Drugs in Developing Countries: The Case of the Public Pharmacy in Fianga, Chad." University of Antwerp, Centre for Development Studies, 1986.

"Chad," In *Surveys of African Economies,* vol. 1, Washington, DC: International Monetary Fund, 1968, pp. 176–227.

Chad: Development Potential and Constraints. Washington, DC: World Bank, 1974.

Chad: Recent Economic Developments. Washington, DC: International Monetary Fund, 1987.

Chambard, Paul, and Géneviève Sigisbert. "L'aide publique bilatérale à l'Afrique francophone." *Europe-Outremer,* no. 564, January 1977, pp. 13–54.

Charrière, G. "La culture attelée: Un progrès dangereux." In J. Peltre-Wurtz (ed.), *Les instruments aratoires en Afrique tropicale,* Paris: ORSTOM, 1984.

Clanet, J. "Les éleveurs de l'Ouest tchadien: La mobilité des éleveurs du Kanem et leur reponses à la crise climatique de 1969–73." Thesis, University of Rouen, 1975.

Clanet, Jean-Charles. "L'insertion des aires pastorales dans les zones sédentaires du Tchad central." *Cahiers d'Outre-mer,* no. 139, July–Sept. 1982, pp. 205–27.

Clement, D. *Pratique d'une opération de développpment agricole: L'opération Mandoul au Tchad.* Toulouse: Mémoire de l'Institut d'Etudes Internationales et des Pays en Voie de Développement, Economie, 1980.

Colin, R. "Mutations sociales et méthodes de développement: Essai sur la dynamique de changement et l'animation en pays Sara du Tchad." Ph.D. diss., University of Paris, 1972.

Copans, Jean. "The 'New' International Division of Labor and the Sahel of the 1970s." In R. E. Boyd (ed.), *International Labour and the Third World,* Aldershot: Avebury, 1987, pp. 179–99.

"Le coton." *Afrique Agriculture,* no. 48, August 1979, pp. 22–43.

"Le coton." *Afrique Agriculture,* no. 57, May 1980, pp. 28–36; no. 93, May 1983, pp. 22–39.

"Le Coton au Tchad." *Nations Nouvelles,* March 1962, pp. 12–21.

"Le Coton au Tchad: Les perspectives restent préoccupantes." *Afrique Contact,* no. 2, July 1969, pp. 21–25.

"Le coton en Afrique de l'Ouest et du Centre." *Afrique Agriculture,* no. 36, August 1978, pp. 24–47.

"Le coton: moteur du développement rural." *Africa,* no. 89, March 1977, pp. 53–90.

Courtin, J. "Engins de pêche du Nord-Tchad." *Travaux de l'Institut de Recherches Sahariennes,* vol. 26, 1967, pp. 103–11.

Couty, P. *Le poisson salé-séché du Lac Tchad et du Bas-Chari: Prix et débouchés,* Dakar: ORSTOM, 1968.

———. *Sur un secteur intermédiaire dans une économie de savane africain: Le natron.* Paris: ORSTOM, 1966.

Couty, P., and P. Duran. *Le commerce du poisson au Tchad.* Paris: ORSTOM, 1968.

Creach, P. V. *Aliments et alimentation des indigènes du Moyen Tchad.* Marseille: M. Leconte, 1941.

———. "La culture vivrière du mil et le problème et la sous-alimentation indigène dans le delta du Chari." *Médecine Tropicale,* vol. 1, no. 3, 1941, pp. 278–88.

Cremona, M. L. "Incontro culturale e ricerca psicologica nel Chad." *Terzo Mondo,* vol. 3, no. 9, 1970, pp. 72–80.

Crouzet, A. "La sécheresse en zone sahélienne." *Notes et Etudes Documentaires,* no. 4216/4217, September 23, 1975.

Damiba, Pierre-Claver, and Paul Schrumpf. *Quel avenir pour le Sahel?* Lausanne: Editions Pierre-Marcel Favre, 1981.

Darambaye, Djibril. "Le Tchad est-il viable?" *France-Eurafrique,* no. 214, February 1970, pp. 36–37.

Darnault, Paul. "Le prolongement du chemin de fer Transcamerounais vers le Tchad méridional." *Europe-France-Outremer,* no. 408, January 1964, pp. 45–47.

Decaluwe, Bernard. "Structures industrielles et pays en voie de développement: Le cas du Tchad." *Canadian Journal of Development Studies,* vol. 2, no. 1, 1980, pp. 242–61.

Defrance, Christian. "L'exploitation du cheptel tchadien et ses perspectives de développement." In Banque Centrale d'Etats d'Afrique Equatoriale et Cameroun, *Etudes et Statistiques,* no. 177, October 1972, pp. 570–88.

Degand, José. "Réflexions sur l'économie du Tchad." *Cultures et Développement,* vol. 4, no. 3 (1972), pp. 565–83.

Delaye, T. *Le coton au Tchad.* Monaco: Paul Bory, 1963.

Delwalle, J. C. "Desertification de l'Afrique au Sud du Sahara." *Bois et Forêts des Tropiques,* no. 149, May/June 1973, pp. 3–20.

Deniau, Jean François. "L'aide française aux pays du Sahel." *Coopération Technique,* no. 73, March 1974, pp. 6–9.

Depierre, D. "Les phacochères au Tchad." *Bois et Forêts des Tropiques,* no. 130, 1970, pp. 3–11.

Depierre, D., and H. Gillet. "Desertification de la zone sahélienne au Tchad." *Bois et Forêts des Tropiques,* no. 139, 1971, pp. 3–25.

———. "Développement de la culture attelée au Tchad." *Europe-France-Outremer,* no. 472, May 1969, pp. 26–27.

Diguimbaye, Georges. "Une experience de développement régional integré: L'opération de développement rural de la vallée du Mandoul (République du Tchad)." In Banque Centrale des Etats de l'Afrique Equatoriale et du Cameroun, *Etudes et Statistiques,* no. 164, 1971, pp. 302–17.

———. "Le Plan de Développement quinquennal 1966–1970: 47 milliards d'investissements prévus." *Europe-France-Outremer,* no. 450/451, July/August 1967, pp. 17–21.

Diguimbaye, Georges, and Robert Langue (eds.). *L'Essor au Tchad.* Paris: Presses Universitaires de France, 1969.

Djibanger, Madjirebayé. "Le rôle des sociétés dans le financement du développement au Tchad." *Revue Juridique et Politique,* vol. 32, no. 1, January–March 1978, pp. 471–83.

Djidingar, Michel. "La promotion du monde rural." *Communauté France-Eurafrique,* no. 138, January 1963, pp. 9–11.

Dossier Sahel. Paris: Ediafric, 1978.

"Douze états d'Afrique Noire de la zone franc en 1977–8." *Bulletin de l'IFAN,* no. 993, February 1979, pp. 19293–306.

Drouhin, M. "La sécheresse, drame de l'Afrique sahélienne." *Industries et Travaux d'Outre-Mer,* no. 236, July 1973, pp. 576–82.

Durand, Jacques-Henri. "A propos de la sécheresse et de ses conséquences au Sahel." *Cahiers d'Outre-Mer,* no. 120, October–December 1977, pp. 383–403.

L'Economie Africaine. Dakar, Société Africaine d'Edition, annual.

"L'économie rurale du Tchad." *Bulletin Afrique Noire,* vol. 16, no. 677, February 2, 1972, pp. 13213–21.

Ediafric. *L'économie des pays de l'Afrique centrale.* Paris, 1971.

Elouard, P. "Quelle aide pour le Sahel?" *Economie et Humanisme,* no. 217, May/June 1974, pp. 70–77.

"Employment Position and Problems in Chad." *International Labour Review,* vol. 85, no. 5, May 1962, pp. 500–7.

Enquête agricole au Tchad, 1960–1961. Paris: INSEE, 1967.

Etude des effets économiques de la diffusion des engrais au Tchad. Paris: SEDES, 1968.

"Faisons le point: Le Tchad sur la voie du redressement." *Marchés Tropicaux et Mediterranéens,* vol. 23, no. 1147, November 4, 1967, pp. 2905–6.

Food and Agriculture Organization. *FAO Africa Survey.* Rome, 1961.

France, Institut National de la Statistique et des Etudes Economiques. *Commerce extérieur des états d'Afrique et de Madagascar, 1949 à 1960: Retrospectif.* Paris, 1962.

France, La Documentation Française. "Le Nord Tchadien: Economie pastorale saharienne." [By H. Berre, and Maillard.] *Notes et Etudes Documentaires,* no. 1730, 1953.

France, Ministère de Coopération. *La Coordination des industries dans la zone Union Douaniaire, Cameroun.* 1963.

———. *Etude du développement régional du Ouaddai.* 1965. [By P. Poyumaillou.]

———. *Etude monographique de trente-et-un pays africains.* 4 vols. Paris, 1965.

———. *République du Tchad: Economie et plan de développement.* 2nd edition. Paris, June 1963.

———. *Situation économique des états africains et de l'Océan Indien.* Paris, 1979.

France, Ministére France Outre-Mer. *Rapport de Mission sur la mise en valeur du Bassin du Logone et du Bas-Chari.* Paris, 1955. [By M. Guillaume.]

———. *Relations avec les états de la Communauté: Economie et plan du développement.* Paris, 1960.

France, Secrétariat d'Etat aux Affaires Etrangères Chargé de la Coopération. *Economie et plan de développement.* Paris, 1968.

———. *Enquête démographique au Tchad, 1964: Résultats définitifs.* Paris, 1966.

———. *Enquête socio-économique au Tchad, 1965.* Paris, 1969.

————. *Plan quinquennal de développement économique et social, 1966–1970.* Vol. 1, *Connaissance du Tchad.* Paris, 1969.

————. *Premier Plan quinquennal de développement économique et social (1966–1970).* Paris, 1967.

France, Secrétariat du comité monétaire de la zone franc. *La zone franc en 1978.* Paris: 1979.

Gaide, M. "Au Tchad: Les transformations subies par l'agriculture traditionnelle sous l'influence de la culture cotonnière." *L'Agronomie Tropicale,* vol. 2, no. 5/6, September/October and November/December 1956, pp. 597–623, 707–31.

Gambarotta, Hector. "The Sahel Region: Splendour Yesterday, Famine Today: What Will Happen Tomorrow?" *Africa Development* (Dakar), vol. 5, no. 1, Janaury–March 1980, pp. 5–38.

Ganay, Solange de, and M. Griaule. "Notes sur les pirogues et le pêche dans la région du Bahr Salamat." *Journal de la Société des Africanistes,* vol. 13, 1943, pp. 187–204.

Garine, I. de, and G. Koppert. "Coping with Seasonal Fluctuations in Food Supply among Savanna Populations: The Massa and Mussey of Chad and Cameroon." In I. de Garine and G. A. Harrison (eds.), *Coping with Uncertainty in Food Supply,* Oxford: Clarendon Press, 1988, pp. 210–59.

Gautier, Julien. "Il faut repenser notre politique agricole en A.E.F." *Marchés coloniaux du Monde,* vol. 7, June 30, 1951, pp. 1753–55, and July 7, 1951, pp. 1813–15.

————. "Le mise en valeur des pays du Logone." *Agronomie Tropicale,* vol. 1, July/August 1946, pp. 339–55.

Gazzo, Y. "La planification au Tchad." Ph.D. diss., University of Paris, 1971.

Gervais, Raymond. "La plus riche des colonies pauvres: La politique monétaire et fiscale de la France au Tchad, 1900–1920. *Canadian Journal of African Studies,* vol. 16, no. 1, 1982, pp. 93–112.

Giffard, Pierre-Louis. "Les gommiers, essences de reboisement pour les régions sahéliens." *Bois et Forêts Tropiques,* no. 161, May/June 1975, pp. 3–21.

Gilg, Jean-Paul. "Culture commerciale et discipline agraire, Dobadéné (Tchad)." *Etudes Rurales,* no. 37–39, January–September 1970, pp. 173–97.

————. "Inventaire et cartographie des faits agraires du Tchad occidental: Note de méthode." *Cahiers d'Etudes Africaines,* vol. 12, no. 3 (no. 47), 1972, pp. 369–441.

————. "Mobilité pastorale au Tchad occidental et central." *Cahiers d'Etudes Africaines,* vol. 12, no. 3, 1963, pp. 491–510.

Gili, L. "Perfectionnement des cadres ruraux au Tchad." *Promotion Rurale,* no. 35, 1970, pp. 31–36.

Gillet, Hubert. "Etude des pâturages du Ranch de l'Ouadi Rime

(Tchad)." *Journal d'Agriculture Tropicale et Botanique Appliquée,* vol. 7, no. 11/12, 1968, pp. 465–528, 615–700.

———. "Une mission scientifique dans l'Ennedi et en Oubangui." *Journal d'Agriculture Tropicale et Botanique Appliquée,* November 1959, pp. 505–73.

———. "Végétation, agriculture, et sol du centre du sud Tchad: Feuilles de Miltou, Dagela, Koumra, Moussafoyo." *Journal d'Agriculture Tropicale et Botanique Appliquée,* vol. 10, no. 1–4, 1963, pp. 53–160.

———. "Végétation, agriculture, et sol du centre Tchad: Feuilles de Mongo-Melfi-Bokoro-Guéra." *Journal d'Agriculture Tropicale et Botanique Appliquée,* vol. 9, no. 11/12, 1962, pp. 451–501.

Gineste, R. "Social and Economic Development Plan for the Republic of Chad." *Community Development Bulletin,* vol. 12, no. 4, September 1961, pp. 670–82.

Guelkodjingar, Daniel N. "Animation Rurale in Chad: Its Contribution to Living Standards and Literacy of Villagers." Ph.D. diss., University of Southern California, 1982.

Heim, P. "Le Tchad: Terre des confins." *Industries,* August 1967, pp. 429–41.

"L'hydraulique agricole: La mise en valeur du bassin du Logone." In *Realités africaines: La mise en valeur de l'A.E.F.* Casablanca: Editions Fontana-Maroc, 1956.

"Les interventions du FAC de 1973 à 1976." *Marchés Tropicaux,* no. 1637, March 1977, pp. 691–93.

Israel, Department of International Cooperation. *Plan fondamental pour la création d'un mouvement de jeunesse pionnière en République du Tchad.* Jerusalem, 1964.

Jacques-Félix, H. *La vie et la mort du Lac Tchad: Rapports avec l'agriculture et l'élevage.* Nogent-sur-Marne, 1947.

Joutel, G. G. "Le chemin de fer Douala-Tchad." *L'Afrique Française,* no. 10, 1933, pp. 572–81.

Julienne, Roland. "Les plans de développement des états de l'Afrique francophone en 1975." *Industries et Travaux d'Outre-Mer,* no. 266, January 1976, pp. 11–18.

———. "Les plans de développement des états de l'Afrique francophone en 1977." *Industries et Travaux d'Outre-Mer,* no. 290, January 1978, pp. 15–25.

Kando-Galhor, Dounia-Atel. "Problématique de la mise en valeur des polders du Lac Tchad." M.A. thesis, University of Laval, 1980.

Kimble, George H. T. *Tropical Africa.* New York: Twentieth Century Fund, 1960.

King, Jack Winfield. "Analysis of Production Potential and Maintenance of Production for Selected Irrigable Soils of the Chari River in Chad." Ph.D. diss., Cornell University, 1980.

Kolingar, A. "Development of Human Resources in Africa: Problems in the Public Sector in Chad." *Cahiers Africains d'Administration Publique,* no. 10, November 1973, pp. 73–75.

Laboubee (Lt.). "Mise en valeur de la palmeraie du Borkou." *Mémoires du CHEAM,* no. 1891, 1951.

———. "Les palmeraies du Borkou." *Mémoires du CHEAM,* no. 1807, 1951.

Lachenman, Gudrun. "Ecology and Structure in the Sahel." *Economics (Tubingen),* no. 32, 1985, pp. 80–106.

Lamana, A. "Chad's Export Policy." *International Trade Forum,* September 1966.

———. "Le coton restera longtemps encoure la première ressource économique du pays." *Les Dossiers de l'Actualité,* no. 2, January 1972.

Lapott, Jacek. "Kadei, das papyrusboot des Tchad-Sees." *Jahrbuch des Museums fur Volkerkunde zu Leipzig,* vol. 37, 1987, pp. 221–40.

Latremolière, Jacques. "Tchad: Le développement économique passe par la paix et l'amité." *France-Eurafrique,* no. 250, October 1974, pp. 20–21.

Lebeuf, A.M.D. "Egrenage de coton au Tchad." *Notes Africaines,* no. 28, October 1945, pp. 14–15.

———. "La Mission Logone–Lac Fitri." *Acta Géographica,* no. 8, January–April 1949, pp. 3–4.

Lefebvre, G. *Etudes de génie rural: Zone Sategui-Deressia.* Paris: BDPA, 1962.

Lefebvre, G., et al. *Etude de génie rural: Zone de Doba.* Paris: BDPA, 1962.

———. *Etude de génie rural: Zone de Eve-Loka.* Paris: BDPA, 1963.

LeHouerou, Henry Noël. *The Grazing Ecosystems of the African Sahel.* Berlin: Springer, 1989.

Levante, M., et al. *Etude des effets économiques de la diffusion engrais au Tchad.* 2 vols. Paris: Secrétariat d'Etat aux Affaires Etrangères, 1968.

Lolito, Gaston. *Sahel: Crises, survie, développement.* Nice: Comité Français pour l'UNICEF, 1987.

Lovejoy, Paul E. "The Borno Salt Industry." *International Journal of African Historical Studies,* vol. 11, no. 4, 1978, pp. 629–68.

Magnen, André. "Le coton dans la région du Logone au Tchad: Son évolution, ses perspectives d'avenir." *Mémoires du CHEAM,* no. 2707, 1957.

Maillard, P. "Les Ouadis à cultures irriguées du Kanem: Leur exploitation et leur organisation coutumière." *Mémoires du CHEAM,* no. 1811, 1951.

Malbrant, René. *L'élevage au Tchad*. Paris: Agence Economique de l'A.E.F., 1931.

Martocq, M. "La 'Cotonfran': Société française d'Outre-Mer." *Liaison,* no. 62, 1958, pp. 51–59.

Massip, J. M. "Inventaire des ressources du Tibesti (Tchad)." Ph.D. diss., University of Paris, 1969.

"Matières premières: Le poids de l'Afrique." *Europe Outre-mer,* no. 531, April 1974, pp. 9–56.

Maton, G. "La mise en valeur des polders du lac Tchad." *Coopération et Développement,* no. 27, September/October 1969, pp. 28–34.

Mear, Adolphe. "L'arachide au Tchad." *Nations Nouvelle,* no. 9, September 1966, pp. 17–23.

Mensching, Horst G. *Die Sahelzone: Naturpotentiel und Probleme seiner Nutzung*. Cologne: Aulis Verlag-Deubner, 1986.

Michon, P. "Les gommiers au Tchad." *Bois et Forêts des Tropiques,* no. 117, 1978, pp. 27–30.

"Les Mines." *Afrique Industrie,* no. 189, July 1979, pp. 35–57.

"Mise en valeur de la vallée du Logone (territoire du Tchad)." *Bulletin de l'Association pour l'Etude des Problèmes de l'Union Française,* vol. 9, August/September 1956, pp. 31–34.

"La modernisation de l'élevage, deuxième richesse du pays." *Europe-France-Outremer,* no. 472, May 1969, pp. 28–30.

Moll. "La mise en valeur du territoire du Tchad." *Renseignements Coloniaux d'Afrique Française,* no. 12, 1912, pp. 391–97.

Muracciole. "Le coton au Tchad." *Mémoires du CHEAM,* no. 2319, 1954.

Mytelka, Lynn Krieger. "Common Market with Some Uncommon Problems." *Africa Report,* vol. 15, no. 7, October 1970, pp. 14–17.

Nendigui, Jean. "Les problèmes des transports au Tchad." In Banque Centrale des Etats de l'Afrique Equatoriale et du Cameroun, *Etudes et Statistiques,* no. 182, March 1973, pp. 151–58.

N'Gangbet, M. "Culture du coton, source de la sous-alimentation Tchadienne." *Liaison,* no. 64, 1958, pp. 28–30.

Nimindé-Dundadengar, Eugène. *Agrarentwicklung und Ernarung in Schwartzafrika das beispiel Tschad*. Gottingen: Herodot, 1982.

"Opération Agriculture." *Marchés Tropicaux et Mediterranéens,* no. 1516, November 29, 1974, pp. 3270–71.

"Paarticipation populaire au développement: Quelques réflexions à partir d'exemples de projets réalisés au Cap Vert, au Niger, en Gambie, et au Tchad." *IFDA Dossiers* (Nyon), no. 62, 1987, pp. 3–15.

Les Paysannats du Tchad. Paris: SEDES, 1965.

Peter, Jean. "Le Fonds Africain de Solidarité." *Revue Juridique et Politique,* no. 1, January–March 1977, pp. 30–42.

"Le Plan de développement Décennal (1971–1980)." *Europe-France-Outremer*, no. 503, December 1971, pp. 47–48.

"Possibilités agricoles du bassin du Logone." *Agronomie Tropicale*, vol. 3, March/April 1948, pp. 115–39.

"Les possibilités d'aménagement hydrauliques dans la région du Logone." *Etudes d'Outre-Mer*, vol. 37, March 1954, pp. 133–36.

"Le Premier Plan quinquennal du Tchad." *Problèmes Economiques* [La Documentation Française], April 27, 1967, pp. 13–25.

Prevost, Paul-Louis. "L'Union Douanière et Economique de l'Afrique Centrale." *Revue Française d'Etudes Politiques Africaines*, no. 34, October 1968, pp. 64–93.

"La production industrielle est en expansion." *Europe-France-Outremer*, no. 472, May 1969, pp. 34–41.

"Production record de Coton." *Europe-France-Outremer*, no. 472, May 1969, pp. 24–25.

"Les projets de mise en valeur régionale. *Europe-France-Outremer*, no. 472, May 1969, pp. 31–34.

Reizler, Stanislas. "La République Centrafricaine et la République du Tchad." *Europe-France-Outremer*, no. 366, May 1960, pp. 52–57.

Renier, P. "Un exemple de coopération interafricaine: La mise en valeur de la cuvette Tchadienne." *Europe-France-Outremer*, no. 408, January 1964, pp. 48–49.

"Republic of Chad: The Work of the BDPA in the Bokoro Area" [by John C. De Wilde, et al.]. In *Experiences with Agricultural Development in Tropical Africa, II: The Case Studies*. Baltimore: Johns Hopkins University Press, 1967, pp. 337–68.

République du Tchad. Paris: Bureau de Liaison des Agents de Coopération Technique, 1971.

"La République du Tchad." *L'Economie* (Paris), no. 814, 1962.

"République du Tchad." *L'Economie Africaine, 1973*. 1974, pp. 88–103.

"La République du Tchad." In "Réalités et grands projets en Afrique equatoriale," special issue of *Perspectives d'Outre-Mer*, no. 40, July 1961.

"République du Tchad." Special issue of *Perspectives d'Outre-Mer*, January/February 1963.

Requin. "Les ressources vivrières du Tibesti et leur répartition." *Journal des Coloniaux et de l'Armée*, no. 725, November 16, 1935, pp. 6–7; no. 727, November 20, 1935, pp. 4–5.

Révére, E. "Les idées italiennes sur le chemin de fer du Tchad." *Afrique Français*, no. 3, 1930, pp. 109–11.

Robson, Peter. "Economic Integration in Equatorial Africa." In Arthur Hazlewood (ed.), *African Integration and Disintegraton: Case Studies in Economic and Political Union*, New York: Oxford University Press, 1967, pp. 27–68.

Rossi, M. "Food Crops and Pre-cooperative Groups: An Experience from Chad." *Journal of Rural Cooperation,* vol. 16, no. 1/2, 1988, pp. 99–110.

"La Sahel et ses problèmes: L'apport de la recherche." *Afrique Contemporaine,* January–March 1984, pp. 11–17.

Le Sahel face aux futurs: Dépendence croissante ou transformation structurelle. Paris: OCDE, 1988.

Sarniguet, J., and J. P. Marty. *Exploitation du cheptel bovin au Tchad.* Vol. 1, *Production, consommation, exploitation.* Vol 2, *Les marchés de la viande en Afrique Centrale.* Paris: Imprimerie Technigraphy, 1968.

Sautter, G. "Le Chemin de fer Bangui-Tchad dans son contexte économique régional." *Institut de Géographie Appliquée de Strasbourg,* 1958.

Seignobos, Christian. "Matiérs prasses, parcs et civilisations agraires Tchad et Nord Cameroun." *Cahiers d'Outre-Mer,* no. 139, July–September 1982, pp. 228–69.

Sigisbert, Géneviève. "Le premier producteur de coton de la zone franc." *Europe-France-Outremer,* no. 503, December 1971, pp. 49–52.

Société d'Etudes pour le Développement Economique et Social. *Perspectives d'industrialisation au Tchad.* Paris, 1962.

Soler, G. "La riziculture au Tchad." *Marchés Coloniaux du Monde,* vol. 8, December 27, 1952, pp. 3304–06.

Somerville, Carolyn M. *Drought and Aid in the Sahel.* Boulder, CO: Westview, 1986.

"Les statistiques du bétail, les produits et sous-produits animaux." *Revue Trimestrielle d'Information Technique et Economique,* no. 14, October–December 1975, pp. 10–19.

Sturzinger, Ulrich. *Der Baumwollanbau im Tschad.* Berlin: Atlantis, 1980.

———. "The Introduction of Cotton Cultivation in Chad: The Role of the Administration, 1920–1936." *African Economic History,* vol. 12, 1983, pp. 213–25.

———. "Tchad: 'Mise en valeur' coton et développement." *Tiers Monde,* July–Sept. 1983, pp. 643–52.

"Tableau des industries textiles en Afrique Noire en 1977." *Bulletin de l'Afrique Noire,* no. 987, January 1979, pp. 19195–210.

Tchad, Chambre de Commerce d'Agriculture et d'Industrie, Fort-Lamy. *La République du Tchad, 1961–1962.* Monaco: Société des Editions Paul Bory, 1962.

Tchad, Ministère de l'Agriculture. *Formation de ressources humaines pour le développement rural du Tchad à l'horizon 2000.* N'Djamena, 1990.

Tchad, Ministère du Plan et de la Coopération. *Connaissance du Tchad.* Paris, 1969.

―――. *Premier Plan quinquennal de développement économique et social, 1966–70.* Paris, 1967.

―――. *Programme d'investissement, 1990–1995.* N'Djamena, 1991.

Tchad, Ministère du Plan et de la Reconstruction. *Tchad: Relance économique en chiffres.* N'Djamena, 1983.

―――. *Projet de Plan intermaire, 1986–88.* N'Djamena, 1986.

Tchad, Service de la Statistique Générale. *La commerce extérieur du Tchad.* Fort-Lamy, 1971.

"Tchad." *L'agriculture africaine.* Paris: Ediafric, 1975.

"Tchad." *L'économie africaine en 1973.* Dakar: Société Africaine d'Edition, 1973, pp. 87–103.

"Tchad." *L'économie africaine en 1975.* Dakar: Société Africaine d'Edition, 1975.

"Tchad." *L'industrie africaine.* Paris: Ediafric, 1975.

"Tchad: Coton et cotonnades." *Afrique '70.* Annual supplement of *Jeune Afrique,* pp. 500–5.

"Tchad: Le lutte contre le sous-développement." *Europe-France-Outremer,* no. 450/451, July/August 1967, pp. 4–59.

"Tchad: Malgré des insuffisances, les resultats du Plan 1966–1970 sont assez encourageants." *Europe-France-Outremer,* no. 495, April 1971, pp. 33–35.

Tchad: Situation économique et priorités. Washington: World Bank, 1987.

Thomson, James T., et al. *Options pour promouvoir le contrôle et la gestion par les renouvelables au Sahel.* Burlington, VT: Associates in Rural Development, 1989.

"Tschad: Transport und Verkehrsprobleme, subregionale Einordnung." *Internationales Afrika Forum,* vol. 8, March 1972, pp. 163–64.

Union of Central African States. *Possibilités d'industrialisation des états africains et malgaches associés.* Brussels: European Economic Community, 1966.

United Nations, Economic Commission for Africa. *Report of the ECA Mission on Economic Cooperation in Central Africa.* New York, 1966.

United States, Bureau of International Programs. *Economic Developments in the Republic of Chad, 1961.* Washington, DC: Government Printing Office, 1962.

United States, Bureau of Labor Statistics, Office of Foreign Labor and Trade. *Labor Conditions in Republic of Chad.* Washington, DC, 1966.

United States, Department of Commerce, Bureau of International Commerce. *Basic Data on the Economy of Chad.* Washington, DC: Government Printing Office, July 1964.

United States, Department of the Interior, Bureau of Mines. *Mineral Industry of Chad.* Washington, DC, 1965.

United States, Department of State. *Newly Independent Nations: Republic of Chad.* Washington, DC, 1963.

Université de Strasbourg, Institut de Géographie Appliquée. *Le chemin de fer Bangui-Tchad dans son contexte économique régional.* Bangui, 1958.

Varin, J. "L'enjeu tchadien." *Cahiers de la Communauté,* March 1981, pp. 98–105.

Verlet, M. *Aspects humains d'utilisation de trois polders de la région du Lac Soro.* 2 vols. Paris: BDPA, 1963.

Verlet, M., et al. *Notes sur les problèmes humains posés par l'exploitation de forages hydrauliques dans la palmeraie du Largeau.* Fort-Lamy: BDPA, 1964.

Vernault, G. "La gomme arabique dans la régions du Tchad." *Agronomie Tropicale,* no. 3/4, 1946, pp. 179–81.

Vinay, B. "L'organisation, les problèmes monétaires, et la politique de crédit dans l'union monétaire d'Afrique centrale." *Revue Juridique et Politique,* vol. 25, no. 3, 1971, pp. 279–96.

Westebbe, R., et al. *Chad Development Potential and Restraints.* Washington, DC: International Bank for Reconstruction and Development, 1974.

World Bank. *Appraisal of Livestock Development Project of Chad.* Report PA-5a, 1972.

Yamoko, Nicolas. "La gomme arabique au Tchad." In Banque Centrale des Etats de l'Afrique Centrale, *Etudes et Statistiques,* no. 153, April 1970, pp. 225–29.

Yantoingar Mairo, Salmon. "Le contrat d'enterprise et la livraison d'ouvrage clé en main au Tchad." *Revue Juridique et Politique,* vol. 42, no. 2/3, March–June 1988, pp. 477–88.

Education

Bhêly-Quénum, Olympe. "Education et culture au Tchad." *France-Eurafrique,* February 1967, pp. 26–28.

Bon, M., and R. Colin. *Les proverbes sara et la pédagogie du développement.* Paris: IRED, 1970.

"Chad." In *World Survey of Education,* Paris: UNESCO, 1966, pp. 311–12; 1971, pp. 287–91.

"Chad." In Helen Kitchen (ed.), *The Educated African,* New York: Praeger, 1962, pp. 420–24.

"Chad: Educational Developments." *International Yearbook of Education,* New York: UNESCO, 1962+.

Clauss, Mechthild. *College in Koyom: Lehren und Lernen in Tschad.* Erlangen: Verlag der Ev. Luther. Mission, 1992.

Colin, R., and M. R. Mercoiret. *Education populaire et développement: Etudes et recherches sur le changement social et les stratégies de l'éducation en République du Tchad.* 6 vols. Paris: Institut d'Enseignement et de Formation pour les Pays en Voie de Développement, 1971.

Coppet, Y. de. *Au pays du Tchad.* Paris: Hachette, 1934.

Coster, S. de, and P. Georis. *Ascension sociale et enseignement dans les états de l'Afrique Moyenne.* Brussels: CEMUBAC, 1963.

Delacroix, M. Y. "L'éducation en milieu tedda: Une étude psychopédagogique." *Dossiers Pédagogiques,* vol. 1, no. 2, 1972, pp. 25–31.

"L'explosion scolaire." *Europe-France-Outremer,* no. 472, May 1969, pp. 22–23.

France, Ministère de la Coopération. *Scolarisation du Tchad.* 1964.

"The Fulani Dilemma: Nomadism and Education." *West Africa,* April 3, 1983, pp. 832–34.

Gardinier, D. E. "L'enseignement colonial français au Tchad, 1900–1960." *L'Afrique et l'Asie Modernes,* no. 161, 1989, pp. 59–71.

Heissler, Nina, P. Lavy, and A. Candela. *Diffusion du livre et développement de la lecture en Afrique (Tchad-Sénégal).* Paris: Culture et Développement, 1965.

Jaulin, Robert. "Les aspirations des écoliers de Fort-Archambault." *Notes Africaines,* no. 80, October 1958, pp. 114–16.

Khayar, Issa. "Education traditionnelle et éducation moderne au Tchad." *Revue Française d'Etudes Africaines Politiques,* July/August 1979, pp. 82–93.

―――. *Le refus de l'école: Contribution à l'étude des problèmes de l'éducation chez les musulmans au Ouadai.* Paris: Adrien Maisonneuve, 1976.

Lebeuf, J. P. "Le Centre Tchadien pour les Sciences Humaines." *Objets et Mondes,* vol. 1, no. 3/4, 1961, pp. 91–93.

―――. "Une école dans la plaine du Tchad." *Notes Africaines,* October 1943.

Mbaisso, Adoum. *L'éducation au Tchad.* Paris: Karthala, 1990.

Mercoiret, Jacques. "L'école et l'éducation traditionnelle dans la société Sara du Mandoul." N'Djamena: IRFED, 1971.

Mercoiret, Jacques, and Marie-Rose Mercoiret. "Les réformes éducatives en Afrique (Sénégal et Tchad)." In A. Bouillon and F. Devalière (eds.), *Introduction à la coopération en Afrique,* Paris: Karthala, 1983, pp. 37–61.

Miaro, Mahamat. "Les déterminations de l'aspiration scolaire et professionnelle chez les éleves de l'enseignement secondaire au Tchad." *Canadian Journal of African Studies,* vol. 8, no. 3, 1974.

Moussy, Bernadette. "Des jardins d'enfants au Togo et au Tchad." *Les Carnets de l'Enfance,* no. 12, January–March 1973, pp. 63–75.

Moyangar, Naideyam. "Les aspects négatifs et les aspects positifs de l'héritage colonial en matières du système éducatif au Tchad." *Afrika Zamani* (Yaoundé), no. 8/9, December 1978, pp. 173–93.

Nomayé, Madana. "Validation du test de Raven au niveau de l'enseignement secondaire au Tchad." Thesis, University of Laval, 1979.

Royal Anthropological Institute. "Creation of the Chad Centre for Social Science." *Man,* vol. 61, no. 169, August 1961.

Sako, Issaka. "La réforme de l'enseignement." *Europe-France-Outremer,* no. 450/451, July/August 1967, pp. 13–16.

Spain, David H. "Achievement Motivation and Modernization in Bornu." Ph.D. diss., Northwestern University, 1969.

Teisserenc, Pierre. "De la communauté ethnique à la communauté nationale: Les lycéens d'Abéché et de Sarh (Tchad)." Ph.D. diss., University of Paris, 1972.

———. "Milieu urbain et recherche d'une identité culturelle: Les lycéens de Fort-Archambault et d'Abéché (Tchad)." *Cahiers d'Etudes Africaines,* vol. 13, no. 4, 1973, no. 51, pp. 511–48.

———. "Les relations de travail et les loisirs des lycéens d'Abéché et de Fort-Archambault." M.A. thesis, University of Paris, 1971.

Togo, Ministère de l'Education Nationale, Direction de la Planification, des Statistiques et de la Conjoncture. *La fille et l'école: Tchad et Togo.* Lomé, 1973.

Traore, Saidou. "L'enseignement arabo-islamique privé et ses conséquences au Ouaddai." Ph.D. diss., University of Lyons, 1989.

Tubiana, Marie-José. "Problèmes de scolarisation dans le nord-est tchadien et perspectives." *Revue Française d'Etudes Politiques Africaines,* no. 178/9, October/November 1980, pp. 128–35.

Science

Afrique Equatoriale Française, Service Géographique. *Carte géologique provisoire du Borkou-Ennedi-Tibesti.* Brazzaville, 1958.

Al-Droubi, Abdullah. *Géochimie des sels et des solutions concentrées.* Strasbourg: Institut de Géologie, University of Louis Pasteur, 1976.

Allan, J. A. (ed.). *The Sahara: Ecological Change and Early History.* London: MENAS, 1981.

André, M., and R. Huet. "Les goitres endémiques au Tchad." *Médicine Tropicale,* vol. 20, no. 3, 1960, pp. 339–48.

Arnaud, E. "Aperçu géographique et géologique de la région ouaddaienne (1910–1911). *Géographie,* vol. 27, 1913, pp. 33–40.

———. "L'Ouaddai et ses confins sahariens." *Dépêche Coloniale Illustrée,* no. 15, August 1912, pp. 181–96.

———. "Les possibilités de rendement du Ouaddai." *Bulletin de la Société de Géographie Commerciale de Paris,* vol. 33, 1912, pp. 536–44.

Assegninou, S. "Notes sur la recherche céréalière au Tchad." *Agronomie Tropicale,* vol. 28, no. 10, 1973, pp. 957–62.

Aubinière."Au Borkou, Ennedi, Tibesti." *Mémoires du CHEAM,* no. 2193, 1952.

Audoin, Antoine Gontran. "Notice hydrographique sur le Lac Tchad." *Géographie,* vol. 12, 1905, pp. 305–20.

Ballion, François. *Chasses et brousse.* Nîmes: Lacour, 1988.

Barbeau, J. *Carte géologigue et notice explicative sur la feuille de Fort-Lamy.* Paris, 1956.

Bardinet, C., and J. Cabot. "Télédiction de paysages par Landsat: Exemple d'utilisation des images numériques de satellites pour l'aménagement en zone tropicale." *Information Géographique,* vol. 49, no. 2, 1985, pp. 45–52.

Billon, B., et al. *Etude hydro-climatologique des polders de la région de Bol.* N'Djamena: ORSTOM, 1963.

Blache, J. *Les poissons du bassin du Tchad et du bassin adjacent du Mayo Kebbi.* Paris: Mémoire ORSTOM, no. 4, 1964.

Blache, J., F. Miton, and A. Stauch. *Premiére contribution à la connaissance de la pêche dans le bassin hydrographique Logone–Chari–Lac Tchad.* Paris: ORSTOM, 1962.

Bocquier, G. *Genèse et évolution de deux toposéquences de sols tropicaux du Tchad: Interprétation biogéodynamique.* Paris: ORSTOM, 1973.

Bouchardeau, A., and R. Lefevre. *Monographie du Lac Tchad.* Paris: ORSTOM, 1957.

Bouchardeau, A. J. Tixier, and M. Beslon. *Monographie du Batha.* Fort-Lamy: ORSTOM, 1959.

Boulnois, J. *La caducée et la symbolique dravidienne indo-mediterranéennes de l'arbre, de la pierre, du serpent, et de la desenere.* Paris: Maisonneuve, 1939.

Bouquet, Christian. *L'homme et les plaines alluviales en milieu tropical: îles et rives du Sud-Kanem.* Bordeaux: Centre d'Etudes de Géographie Tropicale, 1974.

———. *Iles et rives du Sud-Kanem.* Paris: CNRS, 1974.

Bourbon-Parme, S. de. "Exploration du Sahara Oriental." *Terre, Air, Mer,* 1933, pp. 93–108.

———. "Mission de Mgr. le Prince Sixte de Bourbon dans le Sahara."

Bulletin de Musée d'Histoire Naturelle. vol. 4, no. 5, 1932, pp. 465–71.

————. "Première exploration automobile du Tibesti, Borkou, et Ennedi." *Renseignements d'Afrique Française,* no. 10, 1932, pp. 369–78.

Bourgeois, R. "La Mission Tilho au Lac Tchad. *Mouvement Géographique,* no. 28, July 10, 1910, pp. 305–7.

Bruel, G. *Afrique Equatoriale Française.* Paris: Larose, 1918; 1935.

————. "Notes sur la météorologie de la région du Chari." *Annuaire de la Société Météorologique de France,* vol. 53, 1905, pp. 133–51.

————. *Tableau sommaire de l'exploration et de la reconnaisance de l'A.E.F.* Marseille: Sémaphore, 1923.

Bruneau de Laborie, Emile L. B. "Au Lac Tchad, 1920–1921." *La Géographie,* vol. 38, 1922, pp. 137–64, 291–312.

————. "Notes sur le Tibesti et sur l'Ennedi." *Géographie,* no. 1/2, July/August 1928, pp. 66–76.

Buck, Alfred, et al. *Diseases and Infections in the Republic of Chad: A Study of the Ecology of Disease.* Baltimore: Johns Hopkins University Press, 1968.

————. *Health and Disease in Chad.* Baltimore: Johns Hopkins University Press, 1970.

Cabot, Jean. "Au Tchad, le problème des koros, département du Logone: L'exemple du plateau de Sar." *Annales de Géographie,* vol. 70, November/December 1961, pp. 621–33.

————. *Le bassin du Moyen-Logone.* Paris: ORSTOM, 1965.

————. "Un domaine nouveau de riziculture inondée: Les plaines du Moyen Logone." *Cahiers d'Outre-Mer,* vol. 10, no. 38, 1957, pp. 158–73.

————. *Les lits du Logone: Etude géo-morphologique.* Paris: Société d'Edition d'Enseignement Supérier, 1967.

————. "Le Tchad du Nord au Sud." *Raison Présente* (Paris), no. 14, 1970, pp. 15–27.

————. "La vallée du Logone." *Encyclopédie Mensuelle d'Outre-Mer,* no. 70, June 1956, pp. 251–57.

Caix, R. de. "Le problème du Tchad d'après la Mission Tilho." *Renseignements Coloniaux d'Afrique Française,* no. 4, 1912, pp. 133–42.

Capot-Rey, Robert. *Borkou et Ounianga: Etude de géographie régionale.* Algiers: Institut d'Etudes Sahariennes, 1961.

Carmouze, J. P. "Circulation générale des eaux dans le Lac Tchad." *Cahiers ORSTOM,* vol. 5, 1971, pp. 191–212.

————. *La régulation hydrogéochimique du Lac Tchad.* Paris: ORSTOM, 1976.

————. "Sur l'originalité de la régulation saline du Lac Tchad."

Comptes Rendus de l'Académie des Sciences, vol. 275, 1972, pp. 18–71.

Carmouze, J. P., et al. "Contribution à la connaissance du Bassin Tchadien." *Cahiers ORSTOM,* vol. 6, 1972, pp. 103–69.

Carvalho, G., and Giet, H. "Catalogue raisonné et commenté des plantes de l'Ennedi (Tchad septentrional)." *Journal d'Agriculture Tropicale et Botanique Appliquée,* vol. 7, 1960, pp. 49–96, 193–240, 317–78.

Cerf, J. de. *Bahr-el-Ghazal: Terre du Tchad.* Monte Carlo: Regain, 1957.

Chevalier, A. *L'Afrique Centrale Française: Mission Chari–Lac Tchad, 1902–1904.* Paris: Challamel, 1907.

———. "Rapport sur une mission scientifique et économique au Chari–Lac Tchad." *Nouvelles Archives des Missions Scientifiques et Littéraires* (Paris), vol. 13, 1905, pp. 7–52.

Coblentz, A., and H. Pineau. "Toubous et Goranes des confins Nord du Tchad." *Biotypologie,* no. 3/4, 1961.

Compere, P. "Contributions à l'étude des eaux douces de l'Ennedi." *Bulletin de l'IFAN,* vol. 31, 1970, pp. 18–64.

———. "Contribution à la connaissance du bassin tchadien." *Cahiers ORSTOM,* vol. 6, no. 2, 1971, pp. 87–188.

Courtet, H. "Observations géologiques recueillies par la mission Chari–Lac Tchad." *Comptes Rendus de l'Académie des Sciences,* vol. 140, 1905, pp. 160–2.

———. "Le pays Snoussi." *Revue de Troupes Coloniales,* 1904, pp. 493–96.

———. "Les sels de la région du Tchad." *Comptes Rendus de l'Académie des Sciences,* vol. 140, 1905, pp. 316–18.

Cozzi, Paolo. "Le principali popolazioni bovine dell'Africa." *Rivista di Agricoltura Subtropicale e Tropicale,* nos. 1–12, 1973, pp. 24–55.

Cratchley, C. R. "Geophysical and Geological Evidence for the Benue-Chad Basin Cretaceous Rift Valley System and Its Tectonic Implications." *Journal of African Earth Sciences,* vol. 2, no. 2, 1984, pp. 141–50.

Creach, Paul. *Aliments et alimentation des indigènes du Moyen-Chari.* Marseille: Imprimerie de M. Laconte, 1941.

Dabin, B. *Etude générale des conditions d'utilisation des sols de la curvette tchadienne.* Paris: ORSTOM, 1969.

Daget, J. "Introduction à l'étude hydrobiologique du Lac Tchad." *Comptes Rendus Sommaire Séances de la Société du Biogéographie,* no. 350-82, October 1967, pp. 6–10.

Daumont, F. "Visite au massif Saharien de l'Ennedi, frère ignoré du Hoggar et du Tibesti." *Sciences et Voyages,* no. 118, October 1955, pp. 30–32.

De Barry, E. "Eriebtes Leben im Tschadsee-Distrikt." *Neus Afrika,* vol. 7, no. 9, September 1965, pp. 280–83.

Decorse, J. *Chari et Lac Tchad.* Paris: Imprimerie Nationale, 1905.

———. "Médication indigènes." *Revue du Médecine et Hygiène Tropicale,* vol. 4, 1907, pp. 119–28.

Dejoux, Claude. *Synécologie des chironomides du Lac Tchad.* Paris: ORSTOM, 1976.

Deruelle, R. *Carte pédologique du bassin alluvionnaire du Logone et du Chari.* Paris: ORSTOM, 1962.

Desombre, S. *La Guémina: Mission Alger–Lac Tchad, 1937.* Paris: Lesourd, 1945.

Duc, Gérard. "Contribution à la connaissance des teignes de la République du Tchad." Ph.D. diss., University of Lille, 1959.

Dupont, B. "Distribution et nature des fonds du Lac Tchad (nouvelles données)." *Cahiers ORSTOM,* vol. 2, 1970, pp. 9–42.

———. *Etude sédimentologique du Lac Tchad.* N'Djamena: ORSTOM, 1968.

———. *Etudes des formations sédimentaires du Kanem.* N'Djamena: ORSTOM, 1968.

———. *Premières observations sur la physico-chimie du Chari et du Logone.* N'Djamena: ORSTOM, 1968.

Dupont, B., and M. Delaune. "Etudes de quelques coups dans le quaternaire récent du sud du Lac Tchad." *Cahiers ORSTOM,* vol. 2, no. 1, 1970, pp. 49–60.

Dupont, B., and C. Leveque. "Biomasse en mollusques et nature des fonds dans la zone Est du Lac Tchad." *Cahiers ORSTOM,* vol. 2, no. 2, 1968, pp. 113–26.

Dupont, H. "Le cancer chez les Saras." *Journal de la Société des Africanistes,* vol. 12, no. 1/2, 1942, pp. 25–31.

Durand, Jean-René. *Biologie et dynamique des populations d'alestes baremoze du bassin tchadien.* Paris: ORSTOM, 1978.

Durand, Jean-René, and C. Leveque. *Flore et faune aquatique de l'Afrique sahélo-soudannienne.* Paris: ORSTOM, 1980.

Durand, Jean-René, and G. Loubens. *Resultats de pêche au filet maillant et à la senne.* N'Djamena: ORSTOM, 1971.

Dyer, W. Gurnee. "Guelta of the Bleak Sahara: Source of Water Is Mystery in the Tchad." *Natural History,* vol. 74, November 1965, pp. 36–39.

Eickstedt, E. von. "Volker biologische Probleme der Sahara." *Beitrage zur Kolonialforsthung,* 1943, pp. 169–240.

Elliott, C.C.H. "The Harvest Time Method as a Means of Avoiding Guela Damage to Irrigated Rice in Cameroon/Chad." *Journal of Applied Ecology* (Oxford), vol. 16, no. 1, April 1979, pp. 23–35.

Erhart, H., et al. *Etude pédologique du bassin du Moyen Logone.* Paris: ORSTOM, 1952.

Etude d'écoulement en régime sahélien: Massif de l'Ouadai. N'Djamena: ORSTOM, 1959.

Evaluation of Health and Social Situation in the Republic of Chad. Brazzaville: World Health Organization, 1983.

Falvy, A. "Notes sur un voyage aérien aux confins nord du Tchad." *Revue de Troupes Coloniales,* May/June 1935, pp. 241–71.

Faure, H. "Géologie de la cuvette tchadienne." *Cahiers ORSTOM,* vol. 2, no. 1, 1970.

———. "Une hypothèse sur la structure du Ténéré." *Comptes Rendus de l'Académie des Sciences,* vol. 249, no. 23, December 9, 1959, pp. 2591–93.

Ferrandi, J. "Description du Borkou méridional." *Géographie Commerciale de Paris,* vol. 36, 1914, pp. 523–58.

Feyler, L. "Sur le trace de la Vallée du Tafassaset du nord du Grand Erg du Ténéré et la probabilité de son prolongement au sud jusqu'au Tchad." *Comptes Rendus de l'Académie des Sciences,* vol. 200, no. 9, February 25, 1935, pp. 721–34.

Foureau, F. "De Ouargla au Tchad." *Géographie,* vol. 2, 1960, pp. 241–46.

———. *Documents scientifiques de la Mission Saharienne (Mission Foureau-Lamy, 1898–1900).* 3 vols. Paris: Masson et Cie, 1905.

Franz, H. "On the Stratigraphy and Evolution of Climate in the Chad Basin during the Quarternary." In *Background to Evolution in Africa,* Chicago: University of Chicago Press, 1967, pp. 272–83.

Frécaut, René. "Les bilans hydrologiques des lacs." *Annales de Géographie,* vol. 88, no. 485, January/February 1979, pp. 1–15.

Freydenberg, Henri. "Exploration dans le bassin du Tchad." *Géographie,* vol. 15, 1907, pp. 161–70.

———. *Le Tchad et le bassin du Chari.* Paris: F. Schmidt, 1908.

Gabriel, G. "Terrassement-wicklung und vorgeschichtliche Umweltbedingungen im Enneri-Dirennas, Tibesti." *Zeitung für Geomorphologie,* supplement 15, 1972, pp. 113–18.

———. "Zur Vorzietfanna des Tibestigebirges." In E. M. Van Zinderen Bakker (ed.), *Palaeoecology of Africa.* Cape Town: 1972, pp. 161–62.

Gac, J. Y. *Note sur la pluviométrie des hauts bassins du Chari et du Logone.* Bangui: ORSTOM, 1972.

Gama, A. "Mission aérienne au Tibesti." *Revue des Forces Aériennes,* no. 23, June 1931, pp. 690–700.

Gaston, A., and D. Dulieu. *Pâturages naturels du Tchad.* Paris: Maisons Alfort, 1975.

Gauthier-Pilters, H. "Le dromadaire: Faibles et realités." *MIFERMA-Information,* no. 19, December 1970, pp. 47–52.

Gayet, Georges. "L'axe Douala-Tchad." *Connaissance du Monde,* no. 14, January 1960, pp. 73–79.

Gentil, E. "Lettre du 5 Decembre 1897." *Bulletin de la Société de Géographie de Lyons,* vol. 15, 1899, pp. 135–43.

———. "Les territories du Tchad." *Bulletin de la Société de Géographie de Lyons,* vol. 17, 1901, pp. 431–35.

Geyh, M.A. and D. Jakel, "14C-Altersbestimmungen in Rahmen der Forschungsarbeitem der Aussenstelle Bardai-Tibesti." *Pressedienst Wissenschaft F.U. Berlin,* vol. 2, 1975, pp. 107–17.

Gillet, H. *Végétation et sol du Centre Tchad.* N'Djamena: ORSTOM, 1961.

Griaule, M. "Notes biogéographiques sur le Lac Iro." *Comptes Rendus Sommaire des Séances de la Société du Biogéographie,* no. 158/159, 1942, pp. 13–16.

Grove, A. T. "Geomorphology of the Tibesti Region with Special Reference to Western Tibesti." *Geographical Journal,* 1960, pp. 18–31.

———. "Lake Chad." *Geographical Magazine,* vol. 29, no. 3, 1964, pp. 524–37.

Gudbin, C. "Remarques sur quelques techniques de coloration utilisées par les Mbay de Moïssala." *Journal d'Agriculture Tropicale et Botanique Appliquée,* vol. 18, no. 12, 1971, pp. 572–74.

Hagedorn, Horst. "Bau und Bild der Oberglächenformen an der Route Gustav Nachtigals in das Tibesti-Gebirge." *Gedenkschrift Gustav Nachtigal 1874–1974.* Bremen: Ubersee-Museum, 1977, pp. 55–86.

Hallam, W.K.R. "The Chad Basin." *Nigeria Magazine,* no. 91, December 1966, pp. 255–64.

———. "Driving Round the Chad Basin." *Nigerian Field,* vol. 31, no. 3, July 1966, pp. 111–18.

Hepper, F. N. "Plant Life on Sandbanks and Papyrus Swamps." *Geographical Magazine,* vol. 42, 1970, pp. 577–82.

Hilling, D. "Chad-Sea Road." *Geographical Magazine,* vol. 41, 1969.

Hinchungbrooke, John. "Trek to the Tibesti Range." *Geographical Magazine,* vol. 33, no. 2, April 1968, pp. 1025–33.

Iltis, A. "Algues des eaux natronées du Kanem." *Cahiers ORSTOM,* vol. 6, no. 314, 1972, pp. 173–246.

Iltis, A., and S. Riou-Duwat. "Variations saisonnières du peuplement en Rotifères des eaux natronées du Kanem (Tchad)." *Cahiers ORSTOM,* vol. 5, 1971, pp. 101–12.

Jäkel, D. "The Work of the Field Station at Bardai in the Tibesti Mountains." *Geographical Journal,* March 1977, pp. 61–72.

James, P. L. "The Shari Plains." *Journal of Geography,* November 1930, pp. 319–28.

Kanter, H. "Eine Reise in N.O. Tibesti 1958." *Petermans Geografische Mitteilungen,* vol. 107, no. 1, 1960, pp. 21–30.

Kemp, A., and K. L. Durrans. "Expedition to Tibesti." *Weather,* vol. 23, 1968, pp. 331–38.

Kieffer, J. "Le Tchad et son dessèchement." *Bulletin de la Société de Géographie d'Alger et de l'Afrique du Nord,* vol. 10, 1905, pp. 88–102.

Kilian, C. *Quelques observations et découvertes de ma mission de 1927–8 aux confins Imouchar-Teda.* Paris: A. Picard, 1929.

King, Jack Winfield. "Analysis of Production Protential of Selected Irrigable Soils by the Chari River in the Sahel Region of Chad." Ph.D. diss., Cornell University, 1980.

Koechlin, J. *La flore du continent Africain, région du Sud Sahara.* Paris: UNESCO, 1963.

———. "Rapport de mission botanique dans le territoire du Tchad." *Bulletin de l'IEC,* no. 12, 1956, pp. 133–200.

Konate, Ibrahim. "Tchad: Fausse alerte." *Jeune Afrique,* no. 557, September 7, 1971, pp. 28–29.

Kusnir, Imrich. *Géologie, ressources minérales, et ressources en eau du Tchad.* N'Djamena: Centre Nationale d'Appui à la Recherche, 1993.

"Le Lac Tchad à son plus bas niveau le début du siècle." *Afrique Contemporaine,* no. 68, July/August 1973, p. 25.

Lacrouts, M. "Problèmes de commercialisation du bétail en Afrique." *Revue d'Elevage et Médecine Vétérinaire des Pays Tropicaux,* no. 1, 1969, pp. 127–44.

"Lake Chad." In L. C. Beadl. *The Inland Waters of Tropical Africa.* London: Longman, 1974, pp. 160–74.

Launois-Luong, My Hanh, and Michel Launois-Luong. *Catalogue iconographique des principaux acridiens du sahel.* Montpellier: PRIFAS, 1987.

Launois-Luong, Michel. "Les criquets au sahel." *Afrique Contemporaine,* vol. 26, no. 142, 1987, pp. 18–40.

Le Coeur, Charles. *Mission au Tibesti: Carnets de route, 1933–1934.* Paris: Centre National de la Recherche Scientifique, 1969.

Le Dentu, A. "La méningite cérébrospinale en AEF." *Bulletin Mensuel de l'Office d'Hygiène Publique,* no. 31, 1939, pp. 426–51.

Lefranc, J. P. "Reconnaissance automobile aux marchés septentrionales du Tibesti." *Travaux de l'Institut de Recherches Sahariennes,* vol. 11, no. 1, 1954, pp. 95–110.

Le Moigne, J. "Le'élevage des bovides au territoire du Tchad." *Renseignements Coloniales d'Afrique Française,* no. 3, 1917, pp. 69–75.

———. "Les pays conquis de Cameroun." *Renseignements Coloniaux d'Afrique Française,* no. 7/8, 1918, pp. 94–114; no. 9/10, 1918, pp. 130–53.

L'Huillier, P. "Le problème de le désert du Tchad." *Information Géographique,* no. 2, 1957, pp. 62–67.

Loubens, G., and J. Franc. *Etude méthodologique pour la récolte de statistiques de pêche basée sur l'observation des pêcheries d'un bief du delta au Chari.* N'Djamena: ORSTOM, 1972.

Louis, P. *Contribution géophysique à la connaissance géologique du bassin du Lac Tchad.* Paris: ORSTOM, 1970.

Maglione, G. *Géochimie des évaporites: Les depressions interdunaires du Tchad.* Paris: ORSTOM, 1976.

———. *Le gisement dichloro-sulfate sodique de l'île de Napal.* N'Djamena: ORSTOM, 1970.

———. *Premières données sur le régime hydrogéochimique des mares permanentes du Kanem.* N'Djamena: ORSTOM. 1969.

———. *Présence de gaylussite et de trona dans les natronières du Kanem.* N'Djamena: ORSTOM, 1967.

Magnen, André. "La dégradation des sols dans la région du Logone au Tchad." *Mémoires du CHEAM,* no. 2908, 1957.

Maillot, L. "Notice pour la carte chronologique . . . de maladie du sommeil dans les états de l'ancienne fédération d'Afrique Equatoriale Française." *Bulletin de l'Institut de Recherches Scientifiques du Congo,* vol. 1, 1962, pp. 45–54.

Mainguet, M. "La bordure occidentale de l'Ennedi: Etude géomorphologique." *Travaux de l'Institut de Recherches Sahariennes,* vol. 26, 1967, pp. 7–65.

Mainguet, M., and Y. Callot. *L'Erg de Fachi-Bilma.* Paris: CNRS, 1979.

Maire, R. "Etudes sur la flore et la végétation du Sahara central." Paris: Mémoires de la Société Historique de l'Afrique du Nord, 1933.

Maire, R., and T. Monod. *Etudes sur la flore et la végétation du Tibesti.* Paris: Larose, 1950.

Maley, J. "Atlas de pollens du Tchad." *Bulletin du Journal Botanique Nationale Belge,* vol. 40, no. 1, 1970, pp. 29–48.

———. *Etudes palynologiques dans le bassin du Tchad.* Paris: ORSTOM, 1981.

———. "La sédimentation pollinique actuelle dans la zone du Lac Tchad." *Pollen et Spores,* vol. 14, no. 3, 1972, pp. 263–307.

———. "Les variations climatiques dans le bassin du Tchad durant le dernier millénaire: Essai d'interpretation climatique de l'Holocène africain." *Comptes Rendus de l'Académie des Sciences,* no. 276, series D, March 12, 1973, pp. 1673–77.

Maley, J., et al. "Quelques formations lacustres et fluviatiles associées à différentes phases du volcanisme au Tibesti." *Cahiers ORSTOM,* vol. 2, no. 1, 1970, pp. 127–52.

M'Baitoudji, Mathieu Mbaiki. "Lois de répartition, hypothéses de prognostics, et méthodologie de la recherche des gisements de minéraux utiles solides dans la territoire de la République du Tchad." Paris: Centre International pour la Formation et les Echanges Géologiques, 1984.

Meckelein, Wolfgang. *Forschungen in der zentralen Sahara.* Braunschweig: Geo. Westerman Verlag, 1959.

Missions Berliet Ténéré-Tchad: Documents Scientifiques. Paris: Henri J. Hugot, 1962.

Moineau, Jules. "Essai sur la pathologie du territoire du Tchad." Thesis, University of Paris, 1922.

Molinie, C., et al. "Hépatie aigue non-A, non-B épidémique: Etude clinique de 38 cas observés au Tchad." *Gastroentérologie Clinique,* no. 10, 1986, pp. 475–79.

Monod, Théodore. *Rapport sur une mission exécutée dans le nord-est du Tchad en decembre 1966 et janvier 1967.* Fort-Lamy: Institut National Tchadien pour les Sciences Humaines, 1968.

Morris, K.R.S. "The Spread of Sleeping Sickness across Central Africa." *Journal of Tropical Hygiene and Medicine,* no. 66, 1963, pp. 59–76.

Moullet, A., and d'Alberny. "A travers le désert du Tibesti au Hoggar par le Tassili." *Revue de Troupes Coloniales,* vol. 1, 1938, pp. 229–45.

Nebout, M. "Un important foyer d'onchourcose dans le sud du Tchad: Le foyer de Baibokoum." *Médecine Tropicale,* vol. 31, no. 2, 1971, pp. 229–36.

Nzekwo, O. "From Maiduguri to Lake Chad." *Nigeria Magazine,* no. 79, December 1963, pp. 234–47.

Office de la Recherche Scientifique et Technique Outre-Mer. *Liste chronologique des études effectuées par l'ORSTOM en République du Tchad et pour partie dans le Bassin du Lac Tchad.* N'Djamena: ORSTOM, 1974.

Olivier, E. "Le délimitation de la frontière Niger-Tchad." *Revue de la Géographie,* vol. 55, 1905, pp. 52–56.

Pairault, C. "Mission au Tchad." *Cahiers d'Etudes Africaines,* no. 3, 1960, pp. 156–57.

Palayer, Pierre. *Lexique de plantes du pays Sar.* Sarh: CEL, 1978.

Passarge, S. "Zur Oberflachengestaltung von Kanem." *Petermanns Geografische Mitteilungen,* 1904, pp. 210–16.

Pearce, D. "Natural Resource Management and Anti-desertification Policy in the Sahel-Sahara Zone: A Case Study of Gum Arabic." *Geo Journal,* vol. 17, no. 3, 1988, pp. 349–56.

Peignot, A. M. "Notice sur la subdivision de Ziguel." *Bulletin de la Société de Géographie,* vol. 27, no. 5, 1913, pp. 321–30.

Pias, J. *Les formations sédimentaires tertiaires et quaternaires de la cuvette tchadienne et les sols qui en derivent.* Paris: ORSTOM, 1970.

———. *La végétation du Tchad: Ses rapports avec les sols: Variations paléobotaniques au quaternaire.* Paris: ORSTOM, 1970.

Pias, J., and P. Pasot. *Sols de la palmeraie de Largeau.* N'Djamena: ORSTOM, 1962.

Pouillon, J. "Rapport d'enquête au Tchad." *Cahiers d'Etudes Africaines,* no. 3, 1960, pp. 153–55.

Pouyaud, B. *Contribution à l'évaluation de l'évaporation de nappes d'eau libre en climat tropical sec.* Paris: ORSTOM, 1986.

Pouyaud, B., and J. Colombani. "Les variations extrêmes du Lac Tchad." *Annales de Géographie,* no. 545, January/February 1989, pp. 1–23.

Prual, A., et al. "Evaluation of Iron Status in Chadian Pregnant Women: Consequences of Maternal Iron Deficiency on the Status of Newborns." *Tropical and Geographical Medicine,* vol. 40, no. 1, 1988, pp. 1–6.

Pullan, R. A. "Recent Geomorphological Evolution of the Chad Basin." *Journal of the West African Science Association* (Ibadan), vol. 9, 1964, pp. 115–39.

Quezel, P. *La végétation du Sahara.* Stuttgart: Gustav Fischer Verlag, 1965.

Recherches scientifiques au Tchad. Paris: CNRS, 1974.

Riou, C. *Etude de l'évaporation en Afrique Centrale.* Paris: ORSTOM, 1972.

Rioux, J. A. *Mission épidémiologique au Nord-Tchad.* Paris: Arts et Métiers Graphiques, 1960.

Roche, M. A. "Aperçu sur le climat et l'hydrologie du Massif de l'Ennedi et de la Plaine du Mortcha." *Bulletin de Liaison Saharienne,* no. 37, 1960, pp. 41–51.

———. "Evaluation des pertes du Lac Tchad par abandon superficiel et infiltrations marginales." *Cahiers ORSTOM,* vol. 11, 1970, pp. 67–68.

Rosema, A., and J. L. Fisilier. "Meteosat-based Evapotranspiration and Thermal Inertia Mapping in the Lake Chad Region and Niger Delta." *International Journal of Remote Sensing* (London), vol. 11, no. 5, 1990, pp. 741–52.

Rubon, R., and M. Sacx. *Géographie: Le Tchad.* Paris: Istra, 1963.

Sabatier, F. "Les territoires du Lac Tchad." *Bulletin de la Société de Géographie du Marseille,* vol. 24, no. 3, 1905, pp. 295–300.

Sautter, G. "Les liaisons entre le Tchad et la mer: Essai d'analyse géographique d'une situation de concurrence dans le domaine des transports." *Bulletin de l'Association des Géographes Français,* no. 286/287, November/December 1959, pp. 9–17.

Schoep, A. "Quelques considérations sur le bassin du Tchad." *Bulletin de la Société Belge de Géographie,* no. 5, 1905, pp. 350–72.

Servant, M. "Données stratigraphiques sur le quaternaire supérieur et récent au nord-est du Lac Tchad." *Cahiers ORSTOM,* vol. 2, no. 1, 1970, pp. 95–114.

————. *Nouvelles données stratigraphiques sur le quaternaire supérieur et récent au nord-est du Lac Tchad.* Paris: ORSTOM, 1967.

————. *Séquences continentales et variations climatiques: Evolution du bassin du Tchad.* Paris: ORSTOM, 1973.

Servant, M., and S. Servant. "Les formations lacustres et les diatomées du quaternaire récent du fond de la cuvette tchadienne." *Revue de Géographie Physique et de Géologie Dynamique* (Paris), vol. 12, no. 1, 1970, pp. 63–76.

Servant-Vildary, Simone. *Etude des diatomées et paléomnilogie du bassin tchadien.* Paris: ORSTOM, 1978.

Sieffermann, G. "Variations climatiques au quaternaire dans le sudouest de la cuvette tchadienne." *Comptes Rendus du 92ᵉ Congrès National des Sociétés Savantes, Strasbourg 1967,* vol. 11, 1971, pp. 485–94.

Sikes, Sylvia K. *Lake Chad.* London: Methuen, 1972.

Sillans, R. "Sur quelques plantes alimentaires spontanées de l'Afrique centrale." *Bulletin de l'Institut d'Etudes Centrafricaines,* no. 5, 1953, pp. 77–99.

Stanch, A. *Organisation coutumière de la pêche dans le bassin tchadien.* Direction Général Eaux et Forêts, Fort-Lamy, 1960.

————. "La 'seune à bâtonnets.' " In *Service Eaux et Forêts du Tchad,* Fort-Lamy, 1958.

Stemler, A.B.L., et al. "Candatum-Sorghums and Speakers of Chari-Nile Languages in Africa." *Journal of African History,* vol. 16, no. 2, 1975, pp. 161–83.

Talbot, P. A. "Lake Chad." *Geographical Journal,* vol. 38, 1911, pp. 269–78.

Tarrieux, J. "Contribution à l'étude du dattier au Borkou-Ennedi et au Tibesti." *Revue Botanique Appliquée et d'Agronomie Tropicale,* 1930, pp. 922–26.

Terrible, M. "Note sur l'hydrologie de l'Ennedi." *Notes Africaines,* no. 113, January 1967, pp. 8–14.

Tilho, J. *Documents Scientifiques de la Mission Tilho 1906–1909.* 3 vols. Paris: Imprimerie Nationale and Larose, 1910–1914.

————. *Du Lac Tchad aux montagnes du Tibesti.* Paris, 1926.

————. "L'exploration du Sahara oriental: Mission Tilho." *Géo,* vol. 36, 1921, pp. 292–317.

———. *Le Tchad et la capture du Logone par le Niger.* Paris: Gauthier-Villars, 1947.

———. "Variations et disparition possible du Tchad." *Annales de Géographie,* vol. 37, 1928, pp. 238–60.

Touchebeuf de Lussigny, P. *Monographie hydrologique du Lac Tchad.* Paris: ORSTOM, 1969.

Trystram, J. P. *Le régime foncier des Ouaddis du Kanem.* Fort-Lamy: ORSTOM, 1958.

Tubiana, Marie-José. "Stratégies traditionelles et modernes pour une utilisation rationnelle des ressources en eau et en pâturages à nord Darfur." *Revue Française d'Etudes Politiques Africaines,* no. 159, March 1979, pp. 74–97.

United Kingdom, Naval Intelligence Division. *French Equatorial Africa and Cameroons* (Geographical Handbook Series). London, 1942.

Urvoy, Yves F. *Les Bassins du Niger, étude de géographie physique et de paléogéographie.* Paris: Larose, 1942.

Vaillant, A. "La flore méridionale du Lac Tchad." *Bulletin de la Société d'Etudes Camerounaises,* no. 9, March 1945, pp. 13–98.

Vergnes, Henri. "Mission saharienne Ténéré-Tchad." Ph.D. diss., University of Toulouse, 1960.

Vignon, A. "Le réseau hydrographique des pays bas du Tchad." *Afrique Française,* no. 4, 1914, pp. 129–37.

Vincent, Pierre M. *Les volcans tertiaires et quaternaires du Tibesti occidental et central (Sahara du Tchad).* Paris: Editions BRGM, 1963.

Williams, J. J. *South Central Libya and Northern Chad: A Guide-book to Geology and Prehistory.* Tripoli: Petroleum Exploration Society of Libya, 1966.

Ziegert, H. *Gebel ben Ghnema und Nord-Tibesti: Plastozene Klimat und Kulturenfolge in der zentralen Sahara.* Wiesbaden: Franz Steiner Verlag, 1969.

———. "Pleistocene Climatic Changes and Human Industries in the Central Sahara (Eastern Fezzan and Northern Tibesti)." *Actes du Premier Colloque International d'Archéologie Africaine, Fort-Lamy, 1966.* Fort-Lamy: Institut National Tchadien pour les Sciences Humaines, 1969.

Religion

Beyries. "L'Islam au Tchad." *Mémoires du CHEAM,* no. 2934, 1958.

Bezombes. "Le Tchad, centre d'observation sur le monde musulman." *Mémoires du CHEAM,* no. 1536, 1945.

Biobaku, Saburi, and Muhammed al-Hajj. "The Sudanese Mahdiyya and the Niger-Chad Region." In I. M. Lewis (ed.), *Islam in Tropical Africa,* London: Oxofrd University Press, 1966, pp. 408–28.

Boujol, R. "La Senoussiya au Tchad." *Mémoires du CHEAM,* no. 357, 1939.

Cazenave, A. Q. "Les minorités musulmanes du nord-est tchadien." *Mémoires du CHEAM,* no. 1948, 1952.

Chabrélie, Louis. "Notes sur quelques croyances des Sara." *Journal de la Société des Africanistes,* vol. 3, no. 2, 1935, pp. 315–18.

Chèvre, Georges. *Christians in Chad: Responding to God, Responding to War.* Pasadena, CA: Munger Africana Library Notes No. 71, 1983.

Clapham, J. W. *John Olley, Pioneer Missionary to the Chad.* Glasgow: Pickering and Inglis, 1966.

"Collision in Chad." *Christianity Today,* November 8, 1970.

Croquevieille, J. "Histoire de l'islamisation du Tchad." *Tropiques,* vol. 55, no. 393, March 1957.

Dalmais, Paul. "L'avenir religieux du Tchad." *Etudes,* January 1956, pp. 39–51.

———. *L'Islam au Tchad.* Fort-Lamy: 1963.

Dehuz, L. "Au centre du Tchad, à la découverte de la Toute Puissance Margai Tchad, bizarre représentation sur la terre d'une étrange divinité." *Connaissance du Monde,* no. 23, October 1960, pp. 30–38.

Depont, C., and X. Coppolani. *Les confréries religieuses musulmanes.* Algiers: Jourdan, 1897.

Djian. "Notes sur les populations musulmanes du territoire du Tchad au point de vue politico-religieux." *Bulletin de la Société de Recherches Congolaises,* no. 4, 1924, pp. 9–17.

Dumas-Champion, Françoise. "Pouvoir et amertume du fétiche: Deux études de cas, les Koma du Cameroun et les Masa du Tchad," *Systèmes de Pensée en Afrique Noire,* vol. 8, 1985, pp. 141–76.

Duveyrier, H. "La Confrérie Musulmane de Sidi Mohammed Ben Ali es-Senousi et son domaine géographique." *Bulletin de la Société de Géographie de Paris,* vol. 5, 1884, pp. 145–226.

Fedry, Jacques, and Pascal Djiraingue. *Prières traditionnelles du pays Sara.* Sarh: CEL, 1977.

Froelich, Jean Claude. "Islam et culture arabe en Afrique au sud du Sahara." *Revue Française d'Etudes Politiques Africaines,* no. i, January 1966, pp. 54–70.

———. "Relationships between Islam in Africa North and South of the Sahara." *Africa Forum,* vol. 3, no. 2/3, Fall 1967/Winter 1968, pp. 44–57.

Fuchs, Peter. *Kult und Autorietat: Die Religion der Hadjerai.* Berlin: Dietrich Reimer Verlag, 1970.

———. "The Margai Religion of the Hadjerai." *Proceedings of the Eighth International Congress of Anthropological and Ethnological Sciences, 1968.* Tokyo and Kyoto, vol. 3, Tokyo: Science Council of Japan, 1970, pp. 55–56.

———. "Der Synkretismus der Hadjerai (Tschad Sudan)." *Bustan,* no. 3/4, 1968, pp. 63–67.

Fuller, W. H. "Church Crisis in Chad." *Christianity Today,* June 21, 1974, pp. 34–35.

Gibb, H.A.R., and J. H. Kramer. *Shorter Encyclopaedia of Islam.* Ithaca: Cornell University Press, 1953.

Giuntini, A. "Influence de l'Islam dans la région du Logone et du Mayo-Kebbi." *Mémoires du CHEAM,* no. 298, 1947.

Hallaire, Jacques. "Chrétiens africains face à l'initiation ancestrale [Sara, Tchad]." *Etudes,* April 1967, pp. 482–94.

Herse, P. L. "Etude sur les Margayes de Melfi." *Bulletin de l'Institut des Etudes Centrafricaines,* vol. 1, no. 1, 1945, pp. 33–46; vol. 2, no. 1, 1947, pp. 1–97.

———. "Histoire de l'islamisation du Tchad." *Tropiques,* no. 393, March 1957, pp. 9–19.

Huard, Paul, and C. Bacquié. "Un établissement islamique dans le désert tchadien: Ouogayi." *Bulletin de l'IFAN,* vol. 26(B), 1/2, January–April 1964, pp. 6–20.

Hugot, P. "Un mahdi pour le Tchad." *L'Afrique et l'Asie Modernes,* no. 125, 1980.

———. "Tchad et Soudan." *L'Afrique et l'Asie,* no. 37, 1957.

King, A. V. "A Boorii Liturgy from Vatsina." *African Language Studies,* vol. 7, 1966, pp. 105–25.

Kritzeck, James, and W. H. Lewis. *Islam in Africa.* New York: Van Nostrand-Reinhold, 1969.

Labatut, A. "De la confrérie des Senoussya." *Bulletin de la Société Géographique d'Alger,* January–March 1911, pp. 68–81.

Long, David E. *The Hajj Today.* Albany: State University of New York Press, 1979.

Magnant, Jean-Pierre (ed.). *L'Islam au Tchad.* Bordeaux: CEAN, 1992.

Marty, P. *Etudes sur l'Islam et les tribus du Soudan.* 4 vols. Paris: Leroux, 1920.

Masson, A. "Islamisation du Tchad et du Nord-Cameroun." *Mémoires du CHEAM,* no. 265, 1939.

———. "La Senoussiya au Tchad." *Mémoires du CHEAM,* no. 273, 1938.

Moyangar, Bertin. "Le rôle des missions catholiques dans l'histoire du Tchad de 1900 à 1970." Ph.D. diss., University of Paris, 1972.

Nicolas, G. "L'Islam, les confréries chez les Touaregs du Sud." *Mémoires du CHEAM,* no. 792, 1946.

Pascal, Roger. "L'Islam au Tchad." *Mémoires du CHEAM,* no. 4441, 1972.

———. "Les plus jeunes églises d'Afrique: Niger, Tchad." *Missi,* no. 1, 1972, pp. 4–27.

Pouillon, J. "Du sacrifice comme compromise: Note sur le culte dangaléat. In M. Cartry (ed.), *Sous le masque de l'animal: Essais sur le sacrifice en Afrique Noire.* Paris: Presses Universitaires de France, 1987.

Quéchon, M. "Réflexions sur certains aspects du synchrétisme dans l'-Islam ouest-africain." *Cahiers d'Etudes Africaines,* vol. 11, no. 2, 1971, pp. 206–30.

Ruelland, Suzanne. "Des chants pour les dieux: Analyse d'un vocabulaire codé." *Journal des Africanistes,* vol. 57, no. 1/2, 1987, pp. 225–40.

Tomlinson, G.J.F., and G. J. Lethem. *History of Islamic Propaganda in Nigeria.* London: Waterlow and Sons, n.d.

Triaud, Jean-Louis. "Redécouvrir la Sanusiyya: L'étude inédite de l'-interpréte Djian, d'aprés les archives personelles de Muhammad al-Sunni." *Islam et Sociétés au Sud du Sahara,* vol. 5, 1991, pp. 105–8.

———. *Tchad 1900–1902: Une guerre franco-libyenne oubliée? Une confrérie musulmane, la Sanusiyya face à la France.* Paris: Harmattan, 1987.

Trimingham, J. Spencer. *A History of Islam in West Africa.* New York: Oxford University Press, 1962.

———. "The Phases of Islamic Expansion and Islamic Culture Zones in Africa." In I. M. Lewis (ed.), *Islam in Tropical Africa,* London: Oxford University Press, 1966, pp. 127–43.

"Tschad: Kirche in der Wüste." Special issue of *Bethlehem,* May 1972.

Tubiana, Marie-José. *Survivances préislamiques en pays zaghawa.* Paris: Institut d'Ethnologie, 1964.

Vidal, Laurent. *Rituels de possession dans le Sahel.* Paris: Harmattan, 1990.

Vincent, Jeanne Françoise. *Alimentation, vie traditionnelle, et croyances religieuses en pays Hadjerai, Tchad.* Brazzaville: ORSTOM, 1961.

———. "Les Margai du pays Hadjerai: Contribution à l'étude des pratiques religieuses." *Bulletin de l'Institut des Recherches Scientifiques au Congo,* vol. 1, 1962, pp. 63–84.

———. "Techniques divinatoires des Saba." *Journal de la Société des Africanistes,* vol. 36, no. 1, 1966, pp. 45–63.

Weekes, Richard V. (ed.), *Muslim Peoples: A World Ethnographic Survey.* 2nd. ed. 2 vol. Westport, CT: Greenwood Press, 1984.

Zoghby, Samir M. *Islam in Sub-Saharan Africa: A Partially Annotated Guide.* Washington, DC: Library of Congress, 1978.

Literature

Bebnoné, P. *Contes et légendes du Tchad.* Paris: Istra, 1962.
——. "Kaltouma." *Avant-Scène* (Paris), no. 327, pp. 33–39.
Brandily, Monique. "Un chant de Tibesti." *Journal des Africanistes,* vol. 46, no. 1/2, 1976, pp. 127–92.

———. "Mission au Tchad, 1965." *Africa-Tervuren*, vol. 12, no. 3/4, 1966, pp. 100–104.

———. "Les lieux de l'improvisation dans la poésie chantée des Téda." In Bernard Lortat-Jacob (ed.), *L'improvisation dans les musiques de tradition orale*, Paris: SELAF, 1987.

———. "Songs to Birds among the Teda of Chad." *Ethnomusicology*, vol. 26, no. 3, September 1982, pp. 371–90.

Brandily, Monique, and M. Y. Brandily. "Une expédition belge au Tibesti." *Africa-Tervuren*, vol. 8, no. 1/2, 1962, pp. 26–28.

Brench, A. C. *The Novelist's Inheritance in French West Africa: Writers from Senegal to Cameroon*. London: Oxford University Press, 1967.

Bruneau, Xavier. *Roboa-Nat, le sorcier malgré lui*. Yaoundé: Editions C.L.E., 1972.

Caitucoli, Claude. *Douze contes masa*. Berlin: Reimer, 1986.

Caron, Bernard. *Le Coup de Djerba*. Paris: Fleuve Noir, 1978.

Cayrac, Albert, et al. *Contes Sar*. Sarh: CEL, 1978.

Chercheri, Amar. *Reception de la littérature africaine d'expression française jusqu'en 1970*. Paris: Silex, 1982.

Clair, Andrée. *Moudaïha*. Paris: Editions la Farandole, 1973.

———. *Tchindo, la petite soeur de Moudaïha*. Paris: Armand Colin/Bourrelier, 1966.

Dingamoudouel Reoumian, Albert, et al. *Proverbes Ngambay*. Sarh: CEL, 1978.

Ducos, Hélène, and Jean-Jacques Ducos. *Osoko, petite fille du fleuve*. Paris: Rouge et Or, 1972.

Duperray, B. *Contes Ngambayé*. Chantilly, 1954.

Fabre, Paul. *Les Heures d'Abéché*. Marseille: Les Cahiers du Sud, 1935.

———. *La Rondonnée*. Marseille: Les Cahiers du Sud, 1933.

Fortier, Joseph, S.J. *Assimil Mbaye Moïssala*. Chantilly, 1954.

———. *Contes Ngambayé*. Fort-Lamy: Mission Catholique, 1972.

———. *Dragon et sorcières: Contes et moralités du pays Mbaï*. Paris: Armand Colin, 1974.

——— (ed.). *Le mythe et les contes de Sou en pays Mbaï-Moïssala*. Paris: Julliard, 1967.

Fortier, Joseph, S.J., and Yves de la Villéon. *Proverbes Mbay*. Sarh: CEL, 1973.

Heissler, N., et al. *Diffusion du Livre–Développement de la lecture en Afrique: Tchad-Sénégal*. Paris: Culture et Développement, 1965.

Henry, B. "L'hyène et l'écureuil: Conte Sara-Madjingayé." *Liaison*, no. 29/30, November/December 1952, pp. 35–36.

Howard, C. G. *Shuwa Arab Stories*. Oxford: Oxford University Press, 1921.

Jahn, Janheinz, et al. *Who's Who in African Literature.* Tubingen: Erdmann, 1972.

Lukas, J. "Aus der Literatur der Bardai-Kanuri in Bornu." *Zeitschrift für Eingeborenen Sprachen,* vol. 26, no. 1, 1935, pp. 35–56.

McCoy, Andrew. *Lance of God.* London: Secker and Warburg, 1987.

Mayssal, H. "Poésie Massa." *Abbia,* no. 17/18, September 1967, pp. 93–133.

Moussa, R. "Dandé: conte Daï." *Liaison,* no. 32, February 1953, pp. 49–51; no. 33, March 1953, pp. 46–48.

Moustapha, Baba. *Le maître des Djinns.* Yaoundé: CLE, 1977.

N'Garabaye, J. "Un Conte Sara, District de Koumra," *Liaison,* no. 17, November 1951, pp. 27–29.

Polgar, Alfred. *Im Lauf der Zeit.* Hamburg: Rowohlt, 1988.

Regelsperger, G. "Les instruments de musique dans les pays du Chari-Tchad." *La Nature,* 1909, pp. 19–22.

Rey, Gabriel. *Ursu, enfant de la brousse.* Paris, 1961.

Rouch, Alain, and Gérard Clavreuil. *Littératures nationales d'écriture française.* Paris: Bandas, 1986.

Ruelland, Suzanne, and Jean Pierre Caprile. *Contes et récits du Tchad: La femme dans la littérature orale tchadienne.* Paris: EDICEF, 1978.

Sallée, Pierre. "Improvisation et/ou information: Sur trois exemples de polyphones africaines." In Bernard Lortat-Jacob (ed.), *L'improvisation dans les musiques de tradition orale.* Paris: SELAF, 1987.

Seid, Joseph Brahim. *Au Tchad sous les étoiles.* Paris: Présence Africaine, 1962.

———. *Un Enfant du Tchad: Récit.* Paris: SAGEREP–L'Afrique Actuelle, 1967.

———. "Gamar et Guimerie," "Nidjema l'orpheline," and "Le vagabond." *Présence Africaine,* no. 57, 1959, pp. 143–49.

Seydou, Christiane. "Aspects de la littérature péul." In Mahdi Adamu and A.H.M. Kirk-Greene (eds.), *Pastoralists of the African Savanna,* Manchester: Manchester University Press, 1986, pp. 101–112.

Tchoumba-Ngouankeu, I. *Autour du Lac Tchad (contes).* Yaoundé: CLE, 1969.

Valamu, Buna. *Ursu, enfant de la Brousse.* Paris: Alsatia, 1967.

Valtis, Laureine. *Sagaies.* Paris: Editions Saint-Germain-des-Prés, 1979.

Linguistics

Abdoulaye, D., and J. Kelley. "On the 'Compound' Tone in Miagaama." In D. L. Goyvaerts (ed.), *African Linguistics,* Amsterdam: Benjamins, 1985.

Adiwiraah, Eleanore. "A Comparative Analysis of Two Chadic Tales." *Afrika und Übersee,* vol. 74, no. 1, July 1991, pp. 39–48.

"Aires de phonèmes et aires de tons dans les langues d'Afrique centrale." In J.M.C. Thomas and L. Bernot (eds.), *Langues et techniques, nature et société,* vol. 1, *Approche linguistique,* Paris: Klincksieck, 1972, pp. 111–20.

Alexandre, P. *Langues et langage en Afrique Noire.* Paris: Payot, 1967.

Alio, Khalil. "Les classes verbales en bidiya." In Herrmann Jungraithmayr and Henry Tourneux (eds.), *Etudes tchadiques: Classes et extensions verbales,* Paris: Paul Geuthner, 1987, pp. 11–15.

———. *Essai de description de la langue bidiya du Guéra.* Berlin: Reimer, 1986.

———. "Extensions figées et productives en bideya." In Herrmann Jungraithmayr and Henry Tourneux (eds.), *Etudes tchadiques: Classes et extensions verbales,* Paris: Paul Geuthner, 1987, pp. 43–47.

Alio, Khalil, and Herrmann Jungraithmayr. *Lexique bidiya.* Frankfurt: Vittorio Klostermann, 1989.

Angheben, Lino S.J. *Vocabulaire Sara Madjingaye.* Mission de Koumra, 1955.

Barreteau, Daniel, and Herrmann Jungraithmayr. "Le verbe en sibine." In Herrmann Jungraithmayr (ed.), *The Chad Languages in the Hamitosemitic–Nigritic Border Area.* Hamburg: Buske, 1974, pp. 192–229.

Barth, Heinrich. *Collection of Central African Languages.* 2 vols. London: Frank Cass, 1974.

———. "Lettre au Professeur Lepsius au sujet des relations des langues kanuri et Téda." *Zeitschrift der Gesellschaft für Erdkunde zu Berlin,* 2, 1867, pp. 372–74, 384–87.

Bender, M. Lionel (ed.). *Proceedings of the Fourth Nilo-Saharan Conference.* Hamburg: Buske, 1991.

———. *Topics in Nilo-Saharan Linguistics.* Hamburg: Buske, 1989.

Benton, P. A. *The Languages and Peoples of Bornu: Being a Collection of the Writings of P. A. Benton.* 2 vols. London: Frank Cass and Co., 1968.

Blic, A. de. *Premier essai de vocabulaire n'gambayé précedé de notes grammaticales.* Chagoua Mission, 1950.

———. *Proverbes n'gambayé.* Mission de Chagoua, 1951.

Bouquet, C., and J. P. Caprile. "Quelques aspects sociolinguistiques et sociodémographiques de l'extinction d'une langue: Le cas du babalia du Bas-Chari." In L. Bouquiaux (ed.), *Théories et méthodes en linguistique africain,* Paris: Société d'Etudes Linguistiques et Anthropologiques de France, 1976.

Bouquiaux, L. "A propos de la phonologie du sara." *Journal of African Languages,* vol. 3, no. 3, 1964, pp. 260–72.

Boyaldieu, Pascal. *Deux études laal.* Berlin: Reimer, 1982.

———. "La formation du pluriel nominal en kulaal." *Afrika und Übersee,* vol. 69, no. 2, 1986, pp. 209–49.

————. *La langue lua (niellim), groupe Boua.* Cambridge: Cambridge University Press, 1985.

Bynon, James. "Berber and Chadic: The Lexical Evidence." In James Bynon (ed.), *Current Progress in Afro-Asiatic Linguistics,* Amsterdam: Benjamins, 1984, pp. 241–90.

Caitucoli, Claude. *Douze contes Masa: Avec une introduction grammaticale.* Berlin: Reimer, 1986.

————. *Lexique masa: Tchad et Cameroun.* Paris: ACCT, 1983.

Caprile, Jean Pierre. "La dénomination des couleurs chez les Mbay de Moïssala (une ethnie sara du sud du Tchad)." *Bibliothèque de la Société pour l'Etude des Langues Africaines,* vol. 26, 1971, pp. 1–66.

————. *Essai de phonologie du mbay.* Paris: SELAF, 1969.

————. "Essai de phonologie d'un parler mbay." *Bulletin de la Société pour l'Etude des Langues Africaines,* no. 8, October 1968, pp. 1–40.

————. "Etudes et documents Sara-Bongo-Baguirmiens." Ph.D. diss., University of Paris, 1972.

————. *Etudes phonologiques tchadiennes.* Paris: SELAF, 1977.

————. *Lexique tumak-français.* Berlin: Verlag Dietrich Reimer, 1975.

————. *Particularisme du français parlé en Afrique centrale.* Sahr: E.N.A., 1970.

————. "Remarques sur la situation socio-linguistique des confins tchado-oubanguiens et les emprunts à l'arabe dans les langues du 'groupe Sara.' " *Bulletin du SELAF,* vol. 8, October 1968, pp. 41–50.

Caprile, Jean Pierre, and J. Fedry. "Le groupe des langues 'Sara' (République du Tchad)." *Afrique et Langage,* vol. 4, 1970.

Caprile, Jean Pierre, and Herrmann Jungraithmayr. "Inventaire provisoire des langues tchadiques parlées sur le territoire de la République du Tchad." *Africana Marburgensia,* vol. 6, no. 2, 1973.

———— (eds.). *Préalables à la réconstruction du proto-tchadique.* Paris: SELAF, 1978.

————, et al. *Lexique mbai-français.* Lyons: Afrique et Langage, 1970.

Carbou, Henri. *Méthode pratique pour l'étude de l'arabe parlé au Ouadday à l'est du Tchad.* Paris: P. Geuthner, 1913.

Churma, Donald G. "Rule Inversion in Chadic: A Closer Look." *Studies in African Linguistics,* vol. 13, no. i, 1982, pp. 11–29.

Colombel, Veronique de. "Traits chamito-sémitiques de l'uldeme et expansion vocalique." In Herrmann Jungraithmayr and Walter W. Muller (eds.), *Proceedings of the Fourth International Hamito-Semitic Congress,* Amsterdam: Benjamins, 1987.

Coupez, A. "Une leçon de linguistique langue sanga." *Africa Tervuren,* vol. 15, no. 2, 1969, pp. 33–37.

Cyffer, N. "Bibliography of Saharan Languages." *Harsunan Nijeriya* (Kano), no. 6, 1976, pp. 75–93.

Dalgopolsky, Aron B. "On Etymology of Pronouns and Classification of the Chadic Languages." In Yoel L. Arbeitman (ed.), *FUCUS,* Amsterdam: Benjamins, 1988, 201–20.

Dalmais, S. T. *Sondages linguistiques sur différents dialectes du Tchad et du Soudan, apparantes au Sara: Medogo, Kanga, Goula, Mamoun-Kara et Youlou.* Fort-Lamy: Institut National Tchadien des Sciences Humaines, 1961.

Decobert, Christian. *Phonologie arabe du Tchad.* Paris: Librairie Geuthner, 1985.

Derendinger, R. "Contribution à l'étude des langues nègres du centre africain." *Journal de la Société des Africanistes,* vol. 19, no. 2, 1949, pp. 143–194.

———. "Notes sur le dialecte arabe du Tchad. *Revue Africaine,* no. 286, 1912, pp. 1–32.

———. "Traduction d'un texte baghirmien." *Journal de la Société des Africanistes,* vol. 2, no. 2, 1932, pp. 147–151.

———. *Vocabulaire pratique du dialecte arabe centre-africain des rives du Tchad au Ouaddai.* Paris: A. Tournon, 1923.

Duisburg, A. von. "Überreste der Sao-Sprache." *Mitteilungen des Seminars für Orientalische Sprachen zu Berlin,* no. 17, 1914, pp. 39–45.

Duperray, B. *Lexique français-ngambayé.* Chantilly, 1953.

Ebert, Karen H. "Discourse Function of Motion Verbs in Chadic." *Afrikanistische Arbeitspapiere* (Cologne), vol. 10, 1987, pp. 53–71.

———. "Some Aspects of the Kera Verbal System." *Studies in African Linguistics,* vol. 8, December 1977, pp. 33–41.

———. *Sprache und Tradition der Kera.* Berlin: Reimer, 1976.

Ebobisse, Carl. "Ein Teirmärchen aus dem Ost-Dangaleat." *Africana Marbugensia,* vol. 11, no. 1, 1978, pp. 3–18.

———. "L'injonctif en dangléat de l'est." *Africana Marburgensia,* no. 4, 1980, pp. 41–47.

———. *Les verbaux du dangléat de l'est.* Berlin: Reimer, 1987.

Edgar, John Tees. "Allomorphy of the Second Person Singular Prefix in Maba Group Verbs." *Frankfurter afrikanische Blatter,* vol. 3, 1991, pp. 6–13.

———. *A Masalit Grammar.* Berlin: Reimer, 1989.

———. "First Steps toward Proto-Maba." *African Languages and Cultures,* vol. 4, no. 2, 1991, pp. 113–33.

Eguchi, P. K. "Esquises de la langue mambaï." *Kyoto University African Studies,* vol. 6, 1971, pp. 139–94.

Elements pour une orthographe pratique des langues du Tchad. N'Djamena: University of Tchad, 1976.

Etudes tchadiques: Classes et Extensions Verbales. Paris: Geuthner, 1987.

Fedry, Jacques. "Masculin, féminin et collectif en dangaléat (groupe 'Sokoro-Mubi,' Tchad)." *Journal of African Languages,* vol. 10, no. 1, 1971, pp. 34–46.

————. *Phonologie du dangaléat (Tchad).* 2 vols. Lyons: Afrique et Langage, 1971.

————. "Syntagmes de détermination en dangaléat." *Journal of African Languages,* 6, 1, 1969, pp. 5–19.

Fedry, Jacques, and Pascal Djiraingue. *Prières traditionnelles du pays Sara.* Sarh: Collège Charles Lwanga, 1977.

Fellman, Jack. "On the Classification of Chadic as Hamito-Semitic." *Anthropos,* vol. 85, no. 1/3, 1990, pp. 181–189.

Fortier, Joseph S.J. *Dictionnaire mbay-français.* Fort-Archambault: Mission Catholique, 1962.

————. *Grammaire Mbaye-Moïssala (Tchad, groupe Sara).* Lyons: Afrique et Langage, 1971.

Fournier, Maurice. *Introduction phonétique au dialecte des arabes salamat de la région du Lac Tchad.* N'Djamena: CNRS, 1971.

Frajzyngier, Zygmunt. "Borrowed Logophoricity?" *Studies in African Linguistics,* December 1985, pp. 114–18.

————. "'Causative' and 'Benefactive' in Chadic." *Afrika und Übersee,* vol. 68, no. 1, 1985, pp. 23–42.

————. "Encoding Locative in Chadic." *Journal of West African Languages,* vol. 17, no. 1, May 1987, pp. 81–97.

————. "From Proposition to Copula." In Vassiliki Nikiforidou et al. (eds.), *Proceedings of the 12th Annual Meeting of the Berkeley Linguistics Society,* Berkeley, CA: Berkeley Linguistics Society, 1986, pp. 371–86.

————. "On the Intransitive Copy Pronouns in Chadic." *Studies in African Linguistics,* vol. 8, December 1977, pp. 73–84.

————. "On the Proto-Chadic Syntactic Pattern." In James Bynon (ed.), *Current Progress in Afro-Asiatic Linguistics,* Amsterdam: Benjamins, 1984, pp. 139–59.

————. "Lowering Rules in Chadic." *Bulletin of the School of Oriental and African Studies,* vol. 49, no. 2, 1986, pp. 384–85.

————. "The Relative Clause in Proto-Chadic." In Herrmann Jungraithmayr and Walter W. Muller (eds.), *Proceedings of the Fourth International Hamito-Semitic Congress,* Amsterdam: Benjamins, 1987.

————. "Remarques introductives sur l'aoriste et le subjonctif en tchadique." *Africana Marburgensia,* 1980, supp. 4, 5.

————. "Theory and Method of Syntactic Reconstruction: Implications from Chadic." *Linguistische Berichte,* vol. 109, 1987, pp. 184–202.

————. "Ventive and Centrifugal in Chadic." *Afrika und Übersee,* vol. 70, no. i, 1987, pp. 31–47.

Frajzyngier, Zygmunt, and Robert Koops. "Double Epenthesis and N-class in Chadic." In Zygmunt Frajzyngier (ed.), *Current Progress in Chadic Linguistics,* Philadelphia: Benjamins, 1989, pp. 233–50.

Fure, Pierre. *Introduction au parler arabe de l'est du Tchad.* Lyons: Afrique et Langage, 1969.

Furniss, Graham, and Philip J. Jaggar (eds.). *Studies in Hausa Language and Linguistics.* London: Kegan Paul, 1988.

Gaden, H. *Essai de grammaire de la langue baguirmienne.* Paris: Leroux, 1909.

————. "Notes sur le dialecte foul parlé par les Foulbé du Baguirmi." *Journal Asiatique,* vol. 11, 1908, pp. 5–70.

Gaston, A., and G. Fotius. *Lexique de noms vernaculaires de plantes du Tchad.* 2 vols. Fort-Lamy: Laboratoire de Farcha and ORSTOM, 1971.

Gaudiche, A. "La langue boudouma." *Journal de la Société des Africanistes,* vol. 8, no. 1, 1938, pp. 11–32.

Greenberg, Joseph H. "Linguistic Evidence for the Influence of the Kanuri on the Hausa." *Journal of African History,* vol. 1, no. 2, 1960, pp. 205–12.

Guerpillon, L. "Les langages dits 'Kotoko.' " *Etudes Camerounaises,* no. 23/24, September–December 1948, pp. 23–30.

Hagege, Claude. "Description phonologique du Mbum." *Bulletin du SELAF,* vol. 5, no. 2, January 1968, pp. 1–68.

————. *Profil d'un parler arabe du Tchad.* Paris: Geuthner, 1973.

————. "Significance of Central African Languages for Linguistic Theory and Universals." *WORD,* vol. 33, no. 3, 1982, pp. 229–42.

————. "La traduction des écritures en langue mbum." *Bulletin du SELAF,* vol. 5, no. 2, pp. 97–106.

Hair, P.E.H. "Early Kanuri Vocabularies." *Journal of West African Languages,* vol. 6, no. 1, January 1969, pp. 27–30.

Hallaire, Jacques, and Jean Robinne. *Dictionnaire sara-français.* Lyons: Fourvière, 1959.

Hofmann, C. "Ancient Benue-Congo Loans in Chadic?" *Africana Marburgensia,* vol. 3, no. 2, 1970, pp. 3–23.

————. *A Grammar of the Margi Languages.* London: Oxford University Press, 1963.

————. "Provisional Check List of Chadic Languages." *Chadic Newsletter,* January 1971.

Hoskison, James. "Parodies and Verb Stems in Gude." *Linguistics,* no. 141, December 1974, pp. 17–26.

Hunwick, J. O. "The Influence of Arabic in West Africa." *Transactions of the Historical Society of Ghana,* vol. 7, 1964, pp. 13–23.

Ibrishimov, Dimitri. "Z problematyki czadyjsko-kuszyckich prownan leksykalnych." *Przeglad orientalistyczny* (Warsaw), no. 3, 1988, pp. 287–99.

Jouannet, Francis. "Catégories de phonèmes vocaliques sur une base distributionnelle." *Etudes Linguistiques* (Niamey), vol. 1, no. 1, 1979, pp. 105–29.

————. "Prosodie du Kanembou des Ngaldoukou." *Etudes Linguistiques* (Niamey), vol. 1, no. 2, 1979, pp. 71–94.

Jourdan, P. *Notes grammaticales et vocabulaire de la langue Daza.* Chartres: Imprimerie Durand, 1935; and London: K. Paul Trench, 1935.

Jungraithmayr, Herrmann. "Ablaut und Ton im Verbalsystem des Mubi." *Afrika und Übersee,* vol. 61, no. 3/4, November 1978, pp. 312–20.

————. "Apophony and Grammatical Tone in the Afro-Asiatic/Niger-Congo Frontier Area." *Etudes Linguistiques* (Niamey), vol. 1, no. 1, 1979, pp. 130–40.

————. "Apophony and Grammatical Tone in the Tense System of Chadic Languages." *Afrika und Übersee,* vol. 60, 1977, pp. 79–82.

————. "Beobachtungen zur tschadohamitischen Sprache der Jegu (und jonkor) von Abu Telfan (République du Tchad)." *Afrika und Übersee,* vol. 45, 1/2, October 1961, pp. 95–123.

————. "Bericht über eine Forschungsreise nach Darfur und Wadai." *Afrika und Übersee,* vol. 44, no. 2, November 1960, pp. 81–93.

————. "A Brief Note on Certain Characteristics of 'West Chadic' Languages." *Journal of West African Languages,* vol. 4, no. 2, July 1967, pp. 57–58.

———— (ed.). *The Chad Languages in the Hamitosemitic-Nigritic Border Area.* Berlin: Dietrich Reimer, 1982.

————. "Das Verb im Mokulu und das alttschadohamitische Aspektsystem." In J. G. Mohlig Wilhelm et al. (eds.), *Zur Sprachgeschichte und Ethnohistorie in Afrika.* Berlin: Reimer, 1977, pp. 81–90.

————. "Developments in the Study of West African Languages." *Georgetown University Round Table on Languages and Linguistics,* 1986, pp. 64–73.

————. *Die Ron-Sprache.* Gluckstadt: J. J. Augustin, 1970.

————. "La formation des classes verbales en Mokilko et en Mubi." In Herrmann Jungraithmayr and Henry Tourneux (eds.), *Etudes tchadiques: Classes et extensions verbales,* Paris: Paul Geuthner, 1987, pp. 33–40.

————. "Gebrochene Plurale im Mubi." *Zeitschrift der Deutschen Morgenländischen Gesellschaft,* 1980, pp. 456–59.

————. "Grundzüge des Verbalsystems des Mokilko, der Sprache von Mokoulou." *Africana Marburgensia,* vol. 10, no. 2, 1977, pp. 3–12.

————. "Is Hausa an Early or Late Stage Chadic Language?" In Zygmunt Frajzyngier (ed.), *Current Progress in Chadic Linguistics,* Philadelphia: Benjamins, 1989, pp. 251–66.

————. *Lexique Mokilko.* Berlin: Reimer, 1990.

————. "Quelques extensions verbales en mokilko." In Herrmann Jungraithmayr and Henry Tourneux (eds.), *Etudes tchadiques: Classes et extensions verbales,* Paris: Paul Geuthner, 1987, pp. 93–97.

———. "A Tentative Four-Stage Model for the Development of the Chadic Languages." In Pelio Fronzaroli et al. (eds.), *Atti del secondo congresso internazionale di linguistica camito-semitica,* Florence: Instituto di Linguistica, 1978, pp. 381–88.

———. "Über die Mawa: Ethnographische und Linguistische Notizen." In I. Hofmann (ed.), *Festschrift zum 60 Geburtstag von Anton Vorbichler,* Vienna: University of Vienna, 1981, pp. 47–70.

———. "The Zime Dialect Cluster in Southern Chad: Its Verbal Aspect System." *Afrika und Übersee,* vol. 61, no. 1, June 1978, pp. 1–27.

———. "Zur Suffixkonjugation im Osttschadischen." *Afrika und Übersee,* vol. 70, no. 1, 1987, pp. 49–60.

Jungraithmayr, Herrmann, and Al-Amin Abu-Manga. *Einfuhrung in die Ful-Sprache.* Berlin: Reimer, 1989.

Jungraithmayr, Herrmann, and Abakar Adams. *Lexique migama.* Berlin: Reimer, 1992.

Jungraithmayr, Herrmann, and J. P. Caprile. *Cinq textes tchadiques.* Berlin: Reimer, 1978.

Jungraithmayr, Herrmann, and Wilhelm Mohlig. *Einfuhrung in die Hausa-Sprache.* Berlin: Reimer, 1976.

Jungraithmayr, Herrmann, et al. *Chadic Lexical Roots.* Berlin: Reimer, 1981.

Klaproth, J. von. *Essai sur la langue de Bornou suivi des vocabulaires du Baghirmi, du Mandera, et de Tombouctou.* Paris: Decourchant, 1826.

Koelle, S. W. *Grammar of the Bornu or Kanuri Language.* London, 1854.

Laboratoire des langues et civilisations à tradition orale, Groupe d'Etudes Tchadiques. *Etudes tchadiques.* Paris: Geuthner, 1990.

Lacroix, P. F. "Distribution géographique et sociale des parlers péul du Nord Cameroun." *L'Homme,* vol. 2, no. 3, September–December 1962, pp. 75–101.

Lami, P. *Etude succincte de la langue lélé et du dialecte Nantchoa.* Beirut, 1942.

Lange, D. "Un vocabulaire kanuri de la fin du XVIIᵉ siècle." *Cahiers d'Etudes Africaines,* vol. 12, no. 46, 1972, pp. 277–90.

Leben, William E. "Intonation in Chadic: An Overview." In Zygmunt Frajzyngier (ed.), *Current Progress in Chadic Linguistics,* Philadelphia: Benjamins, 1989, pp. 199–217.

Lebeuf, Jean Paul. "Vocabulaire Kotoko: Makari, Goulfeil, Kousseri, Afade." *Bulletin de l'IFAN,* vol. 4, 1942, pp. 160–74.

Le Coeur, Charles. *Dictionnaire ethnographique Téda précedé d'un lexique Français-Téda.* Paris: Larose, 1950.

Le Coeur, Charles, and Marguerite Le Coeur. *Grammaire et textes Téda-Daza.* Dakar: IFAN, 1956.

Lexique thématique de l'Afrique centrale: Tchad: Sara-ngambay. Paris: ACCT, 1985.

Lufaya, Madi Tchazabe. *Contes moundang du Tchad.* Paris: Karthala, 1990.

Lukas, J. "Beiträge zur Kenntnis der Sprachen von Wadai." *Journal de la Société des Africanistes,* vol. 3, no. 1, 1933, pp. 25–55.

———. "Genesis der Verbalformen in Kanuri und Teda." *Wiener Zeitschrift für die Kunde des Morgenlandes,* vol. 34, no. 1/2, 1927, pp. 87–104.

———. "Linguistic Research Between Nile and Lake Chad." *Africa,* vol. 12, no. 3, 1939, pp. 335–49.

———. "The Linguistic Situation in the Lake Chad Area." *Africa,* vol. 9, July 1936, pp. 332–49.

———. *Die Logone Sprache in Zentralen Soudan.* Leipzig: F. A. Brokhaus, 1936.

———. "Mitteilungen über die Stämme und Sprache der östlichen Kanembu." *Afrika und Übersee,* vol. 43, no. 2, July 1959, pp. 106–15.

———. "Parlizipialaspekt und Nominalaspekt in Sprachen des Tschadseegebietes." In H. J. Greschat and H. Jungraithmayr (eds.), *Wort und Religion: Kalima na dini: Studien zur Afrikanistik, Missions wissenschaft Ernest Dammaurr zum 65 Gerbirtstag,* Stuttgart: Evangelischer Missions Verlag, 1969.

———. *Die Sprache der Tebu in der zentralen Sahara.* Berlin: Reimer, 1953.

———. *A Study of the Kanuri Language: Grammar and Vocabulary.* London: Dawsons, 1967.

———."Transition und Intransition im Kanuri." *Wiener Zeitung fur Kunde des Morgenlander,* vol. 35, no. 2–4, 1928, pp. 213–14.

———. "Tschadische Studien." *Afrika und Übersee,* vol. 60, 1977, pp. 192–228.

———. *Zentralsudanische Studien.* Hamburg: De Gruyter Co., 1937.

Manessy, G. "Le français d'Afrique Noire." *Langue Française,* no. 37, February 1978, pp. 91–105.

Mathieu, A. *Vocabulaire du dialecte Diongor de l'Abou Telfan.* N'Djamena: National Archives, 1953.

Migeod, F. W. H. "Ngala and Its Dead Language." *Journal of the Royal Anthropological Institute,* vol. 52, 1922, pp. 230–41.

Mukarovsky, Hans G. "Das Lexem 'Auge' im Tschadischen und im Hamito-Semitischen." *Africana Marburgensia,* vol. 17, no. 1, 1984, pp. 3–12.

———. "Grundzahlworter im Tschadischen, Kuschitischen und Ostischen." In Herrmann Jungraithmayr and Walter W. Muller (eds.), *Pro-*

ceedings of the Fourth International Hamito-Semitic Congress, Amsterdam: Benjamins, 1987.

Muraz, G. *Vocabulaire du patois arabe tchadien et des dialectes Sara-Madjingaye et Sara-M'Baye.* Paris: Lavauzelle, 1931.

Newman, Paul. "A Chadic Language Bibliography (Excluding Hausa)." *Journal of African Languages,* vol. 10, no. 1, 1971, pp. 101–9, 164.

————. "Chado-Hamitic 'Adieu': New Thoughts on Chadic Languages Classifications." In Pelio Fronzaroli et al. (eds.), *Atti del secondo congresso internazionale di linguistica camito-semitica,* Florence: Instituto di Linguistica, 1978, pp. 389–97.

————. "Comparative Chadic." *Journal of African Languages,* vol. 5, no. 3, 1966, pp. 218–51.

————. "The Formation of the Imperfect Verb Stem in Chadic." *Afrika und Übersee,* vol. 60, no. 3, November 1977, pp. 178–92.

————. "Transitive and Intransitive in Chadic Languages." In Veronika Six et al. (eds.), *Afrikanische Sprachen und Kulturen,* Hamburg: Afrika-Kunde, 1989, pp. 188–200.

Newman, Paul, and Roxana Ma. Newman. "Comparative Chadic: Phonology and Lexicon." *Journal of African Languages,* vol. 5, no. 3, 1966, pp. 218–51.

Newman, Roxana Ma. *An English-Hausa Dictionary.* New Haven: Yale University Press, 1990.

Noel, P. *Petit manuel français-kanouri.* Paris: P. Geuthner, 1923.

Nougayrol, Pierre. *La langue des Aiki dits Rounga, Tchad: Equisse descriptive.* Paris: Geuthner, 1989.

————. "Note sur la langue kibet (Tchad)." *Afrikana Marburgensia,* vol. 19, no. 2, 1986, pp. 38–55.

Owens, Jonathan. "Arabic Dialects of Chad and Nigeria." *Zeitschrift fur Arabische Linguistik,* vol. 14, 1985, pp. 45–61.

Pairault, Claude. *Documents du parler d'Iro: Kulaal du Tchad.* Paris: Editions Klincksieck, 1969.

Palayer, Pierre. "La langue sar." Ph.D. diss., University of Toulouse, 1989.

Palayer, P., M. Fournier, and E. Moundo. *Elements de grammaire sar (Tchad).* Lyons: Afrique et Langage, 1970.

Petracek, Karel. "The Ber Group of Saharan Languages." *Archiv Oriental* (Prague), vol. 56, no. 2, 1988, pp. 129–36.

————. "Die Laryngale in den Tschadsprachen." *Africana Marburgensia,* vol. 15, no. 1, 1982, pp. 56–68.

Pilszczikowa, N. "Contribution à l'étude des rapports entre le haoussa et les autres langues du groupe nigéro-tchadien." *Rocznik Orientalistyczny* (Warsaw), vol. 22, no. 2, 1958, pp. 76–99.

Platel, Suzanne. *Esquisse d'une étude du musey.* Paris: SELAF, 1968.

Raymonde, N.D.A. *Vocabulaire français-ngama.* Mission de Maro, 1957.

Reinsch, L. *Der einheitliche Ursprung der Sprachen der alten Welt-nachgewiesen durch Vergleichung der afrikanischen erythraischen und indogermanischen Sprachen mit Zugrundelegung des Teda.* Wiesbaden: M. Sandig, 1968.

Roth, Arlette. *Esquisse grammaticale du parler arabe d'Abéché.* Paris: Geuthner, 1979.

Roth-Laly, A. *Lexique des parlers arabes tchado-soudanais: An Arabic-English-French Lexicon of the Dialects Spoken in Chad-Sudan.* 4 vols. Paris: CNRS, 1969–72.

Ruelland, Suzanne. "Des chants pour des dieux: Analyse d'une vocabulaire codé." *Journal des Africanistes,* vol. 57, no. 1/2, 1987, pp. 225–39.

———. *Dictionnaire tupuri-français-anglais.* Paris: SELAF, 1988.

———. "Rapport préliminaire pour une étude des toponymes du pays tupuri." *Annales de l'Université du Tchad* (N'Djamena), no. 3, 1975, pp. 1–66.

Schuh, Russell G. "Re-employment of Grammatical Morphemes in Chadic." In P. Baldi (ed.), *Linguistic Change and Reconstruction Methodology,* Berlin: Mouton de Gruyter, 1990, pp. 599–618.

———. "Rule Inversion in Chadic." *Studies in African Linguistics,* vol. 3, no. 3, December 1972, pp. 379–97.

Selim, Boukar, and J. P. Caprile. *Lexique thématiques de l'Afrique Centrale.* Paris: ACCT, 1983.

Signate, I. "Promotion de l'arabe au Tchad." *Jeune Afrique,* no. 324, March 26, 1967, pp. 42–43.

Simmons, Pamela. "Né . . . ba Marking in Lélé." *Studies in African Linguistics* (Los Angeles), vol. 13, no. 3, 1982, pp. 217–29.

Solken, H. *Seetzeus Affadeh: Ein Beitrag zur Kotoko-Sprachdokumentation.* Berlin, 1967.

———. "Untersuchungen über die sprachliche Stellung der einstigen So von Bornu." *Anthropos,* vol. 53, 1958, pp. 877–900.

Stevenson, R. C. *Bagirmi Grammar.* Khartoum: University of Khartoum Linguistic Series No. 3, 1969.

———. "Bagirmi Specimen Texts." *Afrika und Übersee,* vol. 40, no. 1, 1956, pp. 45–47.

Thayer, Linda J. *The Deep Structure of the Sentence in Sara-Ngambay Dialogues.* Dallas: University of Texas Press, 1978.

———. "A Reconstructed History of the Chari Languages." Ph.D. diss., University of Illinois, Urbana-Champaign, 1974.

Tinho, J., and M. A. Landermoin. *Grammaire et contes haoussa.* Paris: Imprimerie Nationale, 1909.

Tourneux, Henry. "Une langue tchadique disparue: Le muskfim." *Africana Marburgensia,* vol. 10, no. 2, 1977, pp. 13–34.

————. *Le mulwi ou vulum de Mogroum (Tchad): Phonologie, éléments de grammaire.* Paris: SELAF, 1978.

————. "Nouvelle approche du radical en mulwi (musgu)." *Africana Marburgensia,* vol. 13, no. 1, 1980, pp. 70–76.

————. "Peut-on parler d'extension verbale en munjuk?" In Herrmann Jungraithmayr and Henry Tourneux (eds.), *Etudes tchadiques: Classes et extensions verbales.* Paris: Geuthner, 1987.

Tourneux, Henry, et al. *Les Maba et leur langue.* Paris: SELAF, 1986.

Tran, H. C. "Approche sociolinguistique de l'emprunt français en hausa." *Etudes Linguistiques* (Niamey), vol. 2, no. 1, 1980, pp. 13–51.

Trenga, G. *Le Bura-Mabang du Ouadai: Notes pour servir à l'étude de la langue maba.* Paris: Institut d'Ethnologie, 1947.

Tubiana, Joseph. "A propos d'un dictionnaire mbay-français." *Journal de la Société des Africanistes,* vol. 32, no. 2, 1962, pp. 332–39.

————. "Note sur la langue des Zaghawa." In *Travaux du 25e Congrès International des Orientalistes, Moscou, 9–16 août 1960,* Moscow: Izdatel'stvo vostocnoj Literatury, vol. 5, 1963, pp. 164–219.

Tubiana, Marie-José. "Bouche, voix, langage: La parole chez les Beri." *Journal des Africanistes,* vol. 57, no. 1/2, 1987, pp. 241–55.

Venberg, A. "Phonetic Statement of the Peve Language." *Africana Marburgensia,* vol. 8, no. 1, 1976.

Vine, B. H. "Nasalization in the Sara Languages." *Afrika und Übersee,* vol. 61, no. 2, September 1978, pp. 119–35.

Voigt, Rainer M. "Das Bidiya: Eine neue osttschadische Sprache." *Anthropos,* vol. 83, no. 4–6, 1988, pp. 554–57.

————. "The Two Prefix-Conjugations in East Cushitic, East Semitic, and Chadic." *Bulletin of the School of Oriental and African Studies,* vol. 50, no. 2, 1987, pp. 330–45.

————. "Verbal Conjugation in Proto-Chadic." In Zygmunt Frajzyngier (ed.), *Current Progress in Chadic Linguistics,* Philadelphia: Benjamins, 1989.

Vycichl, Werner. "Etude sur la langue de Ghadames (Sahara)." *Genève-Afrique,* vol. 5, no. 2, 1966, pp. 248–60.

Westermann, Diedrich, and M. A. Bryan. *Handbook of African Languages.* Part 2, *Languages of West Africa.* London: Dawsons, 1970.

Williams, Charles Kinston. "An Alternative Model of Word Order in Proto-Chadic." In Zygmunt Frajzyngier (ed.), *Current Progress in Chadic Linguistics,* Philadelphia: Benjamins, 1989, pp. 111–20.

————. "Chadic Historical Syntax: Reconstructing Word Order in Proto-Chadic." Ph.D. diss., 1990.

Wolff, Ekkehard. "Consonant-tone Interference and Current Theories on Verbal Aspect Systems in Chadic Languages." In Herrmann Jungraithmayr and Walter W. Muller (eds.), *Proceedings of the Fourth International Hamito-Semitic Congress,* Amsterdam: Benjamins, 1987.

————. "New Proposals Concerning the Nature and Development of the Proto-Chadic Tense/Aspect System." In James Bynon (ed.), *Current Progress in Afro-Asiatic Linquistics,* Amsterdam: Benjamins, 1984, pp. 225–39.

————. "Tonogenese in Tschadischen Sprachen." *Afrika und Übersee,* vol. 66, no. 1, 1983, pp. 203–20.

————. "Verb Bases and Stems in Migama." *Afrika und Übersee,* vol. 60, no. 3, November 1977, pp. 163–77.

————. "The Verbal Aspect System in Zime-Mesme." *Afrika und Übersee,* vol. 68, no. 1, 1985, pp. 1–22.

Worbe, A. *Etude de l'arabe parlé au Tchad.* Fort-Lamy: S.N.D., 1962.

Yangontan, Honi, et al. *Conversations et textes ngam.* Sarh: CEL, 1978.

Zeltner, Jean-Claude. *L'Arabe dans le bassin du Tchad.* Paris: Karthala, 1986.

Zima, Petr. "Research in the Territorial and Social Stratification of African Languages." *Zeitschrift für Phonetik,* vol. 28, no. 3/4, 1975, pp. 311–23.

Art

Arkell, A. J. "Beads Made in Darfur and Wadai." *Sudan Notes and Records,* vol. 26, no. 1, 1945, pp. 305–10.

Art ancien du Tchad: Bronzes et céramiques. Paris: Imprimerie Tournon Cie., 1962.

L'Art Sao. Paris: Editions Delroisse, 1972.

Bachy, Victor. "Le cinéma au Tchad." *Revue du Cinéma,* no. 341, 1979, pp. 52–54.

Bailloud, G. "L'Evolution des styles céramiques en Ennedi." *Actes du Premier Colloque d'Archéologie Africaine,* Fort-Lamy, 1969, pp. 31–45.

Bebey, F. *Musique de l'Afrique.* Paris: Horizons de France, 1969.

Brandily, Monique. "Un chant du Tibesti." *Journal des Africanistes,* vol. 46, no. 1/2, 1976, pp. 127–92.

————. *Instruments de musique et musiciens chez les Tedda du Tibesti.* Tervuren: Musée Royal de l'Afrique Centrale, 1974.

————. "Missions au Tchad: Ethno-musicologie." *Africa-Tervuren,* 12, 3/4, 1966, pp. 100–104.

————. "Songs to Birds among the Teda of Chad." *Ethnomusicology,* vol. 26, no. 3, 1982, pp. 371–90.

Brandily, Monique, and M. Y. Brandily. "Une expédition belge au Tibesti." *Africa-Tervuren,* vol. 8, no. 1/2, 1962, pp. 26–28.

Card, Caroline Elizabeth. "Tuareg Music and Social Identity." Ph.D. diss., Indiana University, 1982.

"Une civilisation retrouvée: Les Sao." *Afrique,* December 1961, pp. 53–59.

Dennis, Pierre. "Essai sur l'artisanat tchadien." *Africa-Tervuren,* vol. 13, no. 3/4, 1967, pp. 95–100.

————. *Essai sur les arts plastiques vivants en République du Tchad.* Paris, n.d.

————. "Le tambou de guerre: Sa fabrication chez les Gor." *Notes Africaines de l'IFAN,* no. 105, July 1967, pp. 101–2.

Duvelle, Charles, and Michel Vuylsteke. *Anthologie de la musique du Tchad: Les Sara, le Mayo-Kebbi, populations islamisées.* Paris: Office de la Coopération Radiophonique, 1968.

Foedermayr, Franz. "The Arabian Influence in the Tuareg Music." *African Music,* vol. 4, no. 1, 1966/67, pp. 25–37.

————. "Lieder der Bäle-Bilia." *Mitteilungen der anthropologischen Gesellschaft in Wien,* no. 99, 1969, pp. 64–76.

Ganay, Solonge de. "Le xylophone chez les Sara du Moyen Chari." *Journal de la Société des Africanistes,* vol. 12, 1942, pp. 203–39.

Gauthier, J. G. *Ancient Art of the Northern Cameroon: Sao and Fali.* Oosterhout: Anthropological Publications, 1973.

Gide, André. "Musiques et danses au Tchad." *Revue Musicale,* no. 9, 1927, p. 97.

Heinitz, W. "Eine Melodienprobe von den Sara-Kaba." *Vox Hamburg,* no. 17, 1931, pp. 69–71.

Hottot, R. "Sara-Kabba-jinge Pottery." In *Congrés International des Sciences Anthropologiques et Ethnologiques.* London: Royal Institute of Anthropology, 1934, pp. 254–55.

Lapott, J. "Kedei, das papyrusboot des Tschad-Sees." *Jahrbuch des Museums fur Volkerkunde zu Leipzig,* vol. 37, 1987, pp. 221–40.

Lebeuf, Jean Paul. "L'art du delta du Chari." *Présence Africaine,* no. 10/11, 1951, pp. 96–102.

————. "L'arte degli antiche popoli delle Chari." *Vie Mondo,* April 1952.

————. "Bracelets anthropomorphes de Gawi (Tchad)." *Journal des Africanistes,* vol. 35, no. 1, 1965, pp. 7–10.

————. "Les collections Sao du Musée Leboudy." *Journal de la Société des Africanistes,* vol. 13, 1943, pp. 183–86.

————. "Croquis du Tchad." *Géographie,* no. 1, October 1951, pp. 10–14.

————. "Le Musée National Tchadien, Fort-Lamy." *Museum,* vol. 18, no. 3, 1965, pp. 152–54.

Lebeuf, Jean Paul, and Annie Lebeuf. *Les arts des Sao.* Paris: du Chene, 1977.

Lebeuf, Jean Paul, and A. Masson Detourbet. "L'art ancient du Tchad." *Cahiers d'Art,* vol. 26, 1951, pp. 7–28.

Lortat-Jacob, Bernard. *L'improvisation dans les musiques de tradition orale.* Paris: SELAF, 1987.

Patterson, I. R. *Kanuri Songs.* Lagos: Government Printer, 1926.

Prussin, Labelle. *African Nomadic Architecture.* Herndon, VA: Smithsonian Institution Press, 1995.

Regelsperger, G. "Les instruments de musique dans les pays du Chari-Tchad." *La Nature,* no. 1, 1909, pp. 19–22.

Tubiana, Marie-José. "Danses Zaghawa." *Objets et Mondes,* vol. 6, no. 4, Winter 1966, pp. 279–300.

———. "Hommes sans voix: De l'image que les Beri donnent de leurs forgerons." *Paideuma,* vol. 36, 1990, pp. 335–50.

Tourism

Afrique Centrale: Les Républiques d'expression française. Paris: Hachette, 1962.

Anna, M. "Zakouma, Chad's New National Park." *Animal Life,* no. 42, February 1966, pp. 36–38.

Arthur-Bertrand, H. "Au Tchad les trésors de l'Oued Bahr-el-Ghazal et de la falaise d'Angamma." *France-Eurafrique,* no. 164, July/August 1965, pp. 41–42.

Badel, Gerard. "Le Tchad offre aux touristes des trésors." *France-Eurafrique,* no. 181, February 1967, pp. 29–32.

Biro, Françoise. "L'Ennedi." *France-Eurafrique,* no. 181, February 6, 1967, pp. 35–36.

Blumenthal, Susan. *Bright Continent: A Shoestring Guide to Sub-Saharan Africa.* Garden City, NY: Anchor Press, 1974.

Bohiadi, Bruno. "Tchad: Chasse-Tourisme." *Communauté France-Eurafrique,* no. 138, January 1962, pp. 14–15.

Brydon, David. *Africa Overland: A Route and Planning Guide.* Brentford (UK): Roger Lascelles, 1991.

Buhler, J. *Sur les routes de l'Afrique: De la Mediterranée au Tchad.* Lausanne: Payot, 1948.

"Chad." In Phillip M. Allen and Aaron Segal, *The Traveler's Africa,* New York: Hopkinson and Blake, 1973, pp. 377–91.

"Chad." In Geoff Crowther. *Africa on a Shoestring,* 5th ed., Hawthorne (Australia): Lonely Planet Publications, 1989.

"Chad." In *Travel Guide of Western and Central Africa,* 5th ed., UTA Airlines, Tourist Department, 1989, pp. 36–49.

D'Annelet, André V. J. de Burthe. *A travers l'Afrique française.* 2 vols. Paris: P. Roger, 1932.

Daumont, F. "De Fort-Lamy à Largeau, trois semaines aller en camion, dans les sables, trois heures retour en avion, dans l'azur." *Sciences et Voyages,* no. 109, 1955, pp. 45–51.

Diguen, Abou. *Mon voyage au Soudan tchadien.* Paris: Editions Pierre Roger, 1930.

Dobert, Margarita. "Across Chad for $10." *Africa Report,* vol. 11, June 1966, pp. 46–48.

Eitner, Kurt, and Otto Baedeker. *Afrika: West und Zentralafrika.* Stuttgart: Ernst Klett Verlag, 1971.

Fuchs, Peter. *Ambasira, Land der Damonen.* Vienna: Verlag für Jugend und Volk, 1964.

Gardi, René. *Tschad: Erlebnisse in der unberührten Wildnis um den Tschadsee.* Zurich: Orell Fussli, 1957.

Georges, Louis. *Tchad: Chasses et voyages.* Paris: Boivin, 1951.

Guide Afrique UTA 1984/5. Paris: UTA Airlines, 1984.

Helfritz, Hans. *Schwartze Ritter zwischen Niger und Tschad.* Berlin: Safari Verlag, 1958.

Heseltine, Nigel. *From Libyan Sands to Chad.* London: Museum Press, 1959.

Hudgens, Jim, and Richard Trillo. *West Africa: The Rough Guide.* London: Harrap-Columbus, 1990.

Ichac, P. "Une nouvelle reserve de faune en Afrique: Le Parc National de Zakouma (Tchad)." *Comptes Rendus Sommaires des Séances de la Société de Biogéographie* (Paris), no. 351–355, February 1964, pp. 65–68.

Lorelle, Yves. "Tchad: Une vocation préhistorique et archéologique, une situation touristique exceptionnelle." *France-Eurafrique,* no. 216, April/May 1970, pp. 39–43.

Oberjohann, Heinrich. *Meine Tschadsee Elefanten.* Grenchen: Spaten-Verlag, 1950.

Palleja, Jorge de. *Al Sur del Lago Tchad.* Barcelona: Editorial Juventual, 1968.

"Pierre Ichac connait le Tchad depuis 40 ans." *France-Eurafrique,* no. 248, July 1974, pp. 14–18.

"Les richesses touristiques." *Europe-France-Outremer,* no. 450/451, July/August 1967, pp. 51–53.

Sahara et Sahel Nigérien. Paris: Guides Bleux Hachette, 1977.

Scheid, Teddy. *Journal d'un safari au Tchad.* Brussels: La Renaissance du Livre, 1960.

Tchad, Service de l'Information. *Terre tchadienne.* Fort-Lamy, 1967.

"Tchad." *France-Afrique-Outremer,* no. 387, May 1962, pp. 56–57.

"Tchad." In *Le Moniteur du Tourisme Africain,* Paris: Société Africaine d'Edition, 1971, pp. 189–201.

Le Tchad, son vrai visage. Paris: Editions Delroisse, 1972.

"Tourism in Africa." *Afro-Asian Economic Review,* no. 148/149, January/February 1972, pp. 7–23.

"Un Tourisme original et grandiose." *Eurafrica,* February/March 1965, pp. 54–74.

The Traveler's Guide to Africa. New York: Rand McNally, 1973.

"Tschad." In *Afrika Handbuch,* Hamburg: Übersee-Verlag, 1967, pp. 331–40.

Vaes, A. *Guide du Sahara.* Paris: Hachette, 1988.

Wibberly, Léonard. *Le dernier safari* (novel). Paris: Presses de la Cité, 1973.

Sources and Bibliographies

Africa Confidential. London, fortnightly.

Africa South of the Sahara. London: Europa Publications, 1971+.

Africa South of the Sahara: Index to Periodical Literature. Washington, DC: Library of Congress, Africa and Middle East Division, 1985.

Afrique. Annual publication of *Jeune Afrique.* Paris and Tunis.

Afrique Nouvelle. Dakar.

Alawar, Mohamed A. *A Concise Bibliography of Northern Chad and Fezzan in Southern Libya.* Outwell (UK): Arab Crescent Press, 1983.

Année Africaine. Paris: Pedone, 1963+.

Année Politique Africaine. Dakar: Société Africaine d'Edition, 1966+.

Annuaire Officiel du Tchad. N'Djamena, irregular.

Arbaumont, J. d'. *Bibliographie du domaine Teda-Daza.* Paris: Publications du Centre d'Etudes Asiatiques et Africaines, 1954.

———. "Notes statistiques sur le Tibesti, le Borkou, et l'Ennedi." *Mémoires du CHEAM* (Paris), no. 2356, 1953.

Asamani, J. O. *Index Africanus; catalogue of articles in Western languages published from 1885 to 1965.* Stanford: Hoover Institution Press, 1975.

Ballard, J. A. "Politics and Government in Former French West and Equatorial Africa: A Critical Bibligraphy." *Journal of Modern African Studies,* vol. 3, no. 4, December 1965, pp. 589–605.

Banque Centrale des Etats de l'Afrique Equatoriale et du Cameroun. "Etudes et Statistiques." Monthly.

Baudet, Danièle. *Eléments de bibliographie sur l'art sao, l'archéologie, la paléontologie, la préhistoire, et la proto-histoire du Tchad.* Dakar: IFAN, 1968.

Beadle, L. C. *The Inland Waters of Tropical Africa.* London: Longman, 1974, pp. 324–46.

Bederman, Sanford H. *Africa: A Bibliography of Geography and Related Disciplines.* Atlanta: Georgia State University, 1974.

Belgium, Office de la Coopération au Développement, Service Etudes, Statistiques, et Documentation. *Le République du Tchad.* Brussels, July 1968.

Beriel, Marie-Magdeleine. *Complément à la bibliographie du Tchad (sciences humaines): Etudes et documents tchadiens,* Serie A, 6. Tchad: Institut National des Sciences Humaines, 1974.

Beudot, Françoise. *Elements de bibliographie sur les pays du Sahel.* Paris: OCDE, annual.

————. *Elements de bibliographie sur la sécheresse au Sahel.* Paris: OCDE, 1985.

Biarnes, Pierre, et al. *L'économie africaine.* Dakar: Société Africaine d'Edition, 1970+, annual.

Bibliographie des documents du CILS et le Club du Sahel. Paris: OCDE, 1989.

Bibliographie des travaux en langue française sur l'Afrique au sud du Sahara. Paris: CARDAN, 1982.

Bibliographie ethnographique de l'Afrique Equatoriale Française. Paris: Imprimerie Nationale, 1949.

"Bibliographie touarègue: Langue, culture, et société, 1977–1987." In Salem Chaker (ed.), *Etudes touarègues,* Aix-en-Provence: CNRS, 1988, pp. 92–192.

Bjrkelo, Anders J., and G. E. Wickens. *A Bibliography of the Dar Fur/Wadai Region.* Bergen: University of Bergen, Department of History, 1981.

Blake, David, and Carole Travis. *Periodicals from Africa: A bibliography and Union List of Periodical Publishers in Africa.* Boston: G. K. Hall, 1984.

Blaudin de Thé, B. *Essai de bibliographie du Sahara français et des régions avoisinantes.* Paris: Arts et Métiers Graphiques, 1960.

Bogaert, Jozef. *Sciences humaines en Afrique noire: Guide bibliographique* (1945–1965). Brussels: Centre Documentation Economique et Sociale Africaine, 1966.

Brasseur, P., and J. F. Maurel. *Les sources bibliographiques de l'Afrique de l'Ouest et de l'Afrique Equatoriale d'expression française.* Dakar: Bibliotheque de l'Université, 1970, (1971).

Bruel, Georges. *Bibliographie de l'Afrique Equatoriale Française.* Paris: Larose, 1914.

"Chad." In *African Biographies,* vol. 1, Bonn-Bad Godesberg: Research Institute of the Friedrich-Ebert Stiftung, 1967 (updated September 1974), pp. 1–12.

"Chad." In David Morrison et al., *Black Africa: A Comparative Handbook,* New York: The Free Press, 1972, pp. 204–9.

"Chad." In John Dickie and Alan Rake, *Who's Who in Africa,* London: African Development, 1973, pp. 71–78.

"Chad." In Sean Moroney, *Africa,* vol. 1, New York: Facts on File, pp. 99–112.

Chad: Official Standard Names Approved by the U.S. Board on Geographic Names. Washington, DC: Government Printing Office, 1962.

Chaker, Salem (ed.). *Etudes touarègues.* Aix-en-Provence: CNRS, 1988.

Chapelle, Jean (ed.). *Documents du dépôt officiel d'archives de Fort-Lamy,* 1. Fort-Lamy: Institut National Tchadien pour les Sciences Humaines, 1968.

Chronologie politique africaine. Paris: Fondation Nationale des Sciences Politiques, Centre d'Etudes des Relations Internationales, bimonthly, 1960–1970.

Constitutions of the New African States. Cairo: Egyptian Society of International Law, 1962.

Coulibaly, Siaka. *Eléments de bibliographie sur les pays du Sahel.* Paris: OCDE, 1991.

Dalmais, Paul. *Catalogue Systématique de la Bibliothèque de l'archevêque de N'Djamena.* N'Djamena, 1976.

Darch, Colin, and Alice Nkhoma-Wamunza (eds.), *Africa Index to Continental Periodical Literature,* Munich: Hans Zell Publ, 1984.

Decraene, P. "Tableau des partis politiques de l'Afrique au sud du Sahara." Paris: Fondation Nationale des Sciences Politiques, Centre d'Etudes des Relations Extérieures, 1963, Serie C, Recherches No. 8, 66, pp. 119–20.

"Dépôt National d'Archives du Tchad." *Journal de la Société des Africanistes,* vol. 40, no. 2, 1970.

Deutsche Afrika-Gesellschaft. *Afrikanische Kopfe.* Bonn, 1962+.

Deutsches Institut fur Afrika: Forschung. *Politique, économique, et sociale en Afrique Centrale.* Hamburg, 1974.

Documents du Dépôt National d'Archives de Fort-Lamy. Fort-Lamy: INTSH, 1968.

Duignan, Peter. *Handbook of American Resources for African Studies.* Stanford: Hoover Institution, 1967.

Economist Intelligence Unit. *Country Reports (Chad).* Annual, and quarterly reports.

Ediafric. *L'Afrique Noire de A à Z, 1971.* Paris, 1971.

———. *Les élites africaines.* Paris, 1971.

———. *Gouvernements et cabinets ministériels, partis politiques.* Paris, 1961+.

———. *Hommes et organisations d' Afrique Noire.* Paris: bimonthly.

———. *Personnalités publiques de l'Afrique centrale.* 3rd edition. Paris, 1971.

———. *Répertoire de la diplomatie africaine.* Paris, 1972.

El-Nasri, Abdel Rahman. *A Bibliography of the Sudan, 1938–1958.* London: Oxford University Press, 1962.

Europe-France-Outremer (Paris). Monthly until 1987, including the annual June survey of African states.

France. Ministère de la Coopération. *Etude monographique de trente et un pays africains.* 4 vols. Paris, 1965.

Gaignebet, Wanda. *Inventaire des thèses africanistes de langue française.* Paris: CARDAN, 1975.

———. *Répertoire des thèses africanistes françaises.* Paris: CARDAN, 1982.

Germany, Federal Republic of, Statistisches Bundesamt, Landerberichte Afrikanische Entwicklunrslander. Heft 10: *Tschad.* Wiesbaden: W. Kohlhammer Verlag, 1964.

———. Landerkurzberichte: *Tschad.* (Series Allgemeine Statistik des Auslandes.) Stuttgart/Mainz: W. Kohlhammer Verlag, 1969.

Gorman, G. E, and M. M. Mahoney. *Guide to Current National Bibliographies in the Third World.* Munich: Hans Zell, 1983.

Greenberg, Joseph H. "The Languages of Africa." *International Journal of American Linguistics,* vol. 29, no. 1, January 1963, pp. 1–171.

"A Hausa Bibliography." *Africana Journal,* vol. 6, no. 2, 1975.

Henige, David. *Colonial Governors.* Madison, WI: 1970.

Hertefelt, Marcel d', and Anne Marie Bouttiaux-Ndiaye. *Bibliographie de l'Afrique sud-saharienne: Sciences humaines et sociales, 1986–1987.* Tervuren: Musée Royal de l'Afrique Centrale, 1990.

Hill, Richard (ed.). *A Bibliographic Dictionary of the Sudan.* London: Frank Cass, 1969. Reprint of 1951 edition.

Hoefer, F. *Afrique Australe . . . Afrique Centrale.* Paris: Firmin-Didot, 1848.

Hommes et Destins, vol. 1–4. Paris: Académie des Sciences d'Outre-Mer, 1977+.

Institut Fondamental d'Afrique Noire. *Catalogue des manuscrits de l'-IFAN.* Dakar, 1966.

International African Institute. *Africa.* Quarterly, 1929+, bibliography section.

Jeune Afrique. Paris and Tunis. Weekly.

Joucla, Edmond A. *Bibliographie de l'Afrique occidentale française.* Paris: Société d'Editions Géographiques, Maritimes, et Coloniales, 1937.

Köhler, Jochen. *Deutsche Dissertationen über Afrika: Ein Verzeichnis für die Jahre 1918–1959.* Bonn: K. Schroeder, 1962.

Lanne, Bernard. "Quinze ans d'ouvrages sur le Tchad." *Afrique Contemporaine,* no. 144, October–December 1987, pp. 37–47.

Lebeuf, Jean Paul. "Bibliographie Sao et Kotoko." *Etudes Camerounaises,* June–September 1948, no. 21/22, pp. 121–37.

———. "Le Centre Tchadien pour les Sciences Humaines." *Objets et Mondes,* vol. 1, no. 3/4, 1961, pp. 91–93.

———. "Le Dépôt National d'Archives du Tchad." *Revue Française d'Histoire d'Outre-Mer,* 57, 208, 1970, pp. 297–98.

Lebeuf, Jean Paul, et al. *Bibliographie du Tchad* (sciences humaines). Fort-Lamy: Institut National Tchadien pour les Sciences Humaines, 1968.

Legum, Colin (ed.). *Africa Contemporary Record.* London: Rex Collins, 1968–1987.

Le Rouvreur, A. *Eléments pour un dictionnaire biographique du Tchad et du Niger.* Paris: CNRS, 1978.

Lipschutz, Mark R., and R. Kent Rasmussen. *Dictionary of African Historical Biography.* Berkeley: University of California, 1986.

Malval, Jean. *Essai de chronologie tchadienne, 1707–1940.* Paris: CNRS, 1974.

Le Mois en Afrique: Revue Française d'Etudes Politiques Africaines. Dakar and Paris. Monthly to 1992.

Le Moniteur Africain. Dakar. Weekly.

Moreau, Jacqueline, and Danielle Stordeur. *Bibliographie du Tchad.* Fort-Lamy: Etudes et Documents Tchadiens, Serie A, No. 5, 1970.

Nanda, Bernard, and J. Darnace. "Chad: Bibliographical Services and Related Activities in 1964–1965." *Bibliographie, Documentation, Terminologie,* vol. 7, no. 1, January 1967, pp. 8–9.

OCDE, Centre de Développement. *Bibliographie de documents et rapports sur les pays du Sahel, 1977–1985.* Paris: OCDE, 1989.

OSTROM. *Liste chronologique des études effectuées par l'O.R.S.T.O.M. en République du Tchad et pour partie dans le bassin du Lac Tchad.* N'Djamena: Centre ORSTOM, 1974.

L'Organisation des Recherches de Sciences Humaines du Tchad." *Penant,* vol. 76, no. 711, April–June 1966, pp. 249–62.

"Principales activités de l'Institut National Tchadien pour les Sciences Humaines." *Journal de la Société des Africanistes,* vol. 40, no. 2, 1970, pp. 178–79.

Roubet, C. "Bibliographie Maghreb-Sahara 1967: Anthropologie, préhistoire, ethnographie." *Libyca,* no. 6, 1968, pp. 225–34.

———. "Bibliographie, Maghreb-Sahara, anthropologie, préhistoire, ethnographie, 1968." *Libyca,* no. 17, 1969, pp. 385–93.

Roubet, C., and A. Sayid. "Bibliographie Maghreb-Sahara." *Libyca,* no. 19, 1971, pp. 265–78.

Saix, Etienne. *Bibliographie sur la cuvette du Lac Tchad: Ouvrages publiés et études realisées dans le cadre de la République du Tchad.* Paris: PROHUZA, 1963.

———. *Eléments d'une bibliographie de la cuvette du Lac Tchad.* Paris: PROHUZA, 1962.

Sanner, Pierre. *Bibliographie ethnographique de l'A.E.F., 1914–1948.* Paris: Imprimerie Nationale, 1949.

Scheven, Yvette. *Bibliographies for African Studies, 1970–1986.* London: Hans Zell, 1988.

Seydou, Christiane. *Bibliographie générale du monde peul*. Niamey: IRSH, 1977.

Standing Conference on Library Materials on Africa. *United Kingdom Publications and Theses on Africa*. Cambridge: Heffer, 1963+.

Tchad. *Journal Officiel de l République du Tchad*. Brazzaville and N'-Djamena: Imprimerie Officiel, Semimonthly, 1959+.

Tchad, Ministère de l'Information. *Annuaire Officiel du Tchad*. Paris: Diloutremer, 1970, 1972.

———. *Aperçu sur le Tchad*. Fort-Lamy 1970.

———. *Les moyens d'information au Tchad*. Fort-Lamy, 1968.

———. *Service de la Statistique Générale*. Annuaire statistique du Tchad. Fort-Lamy, 1968.

United States, Board on Geographic Names. *Gazetteer of Chad: Names Approved by the United States Board on Geographic Names*. Washington, DC: Defense Mapping Agency, 1989.

Urvoy, Yves F. "Essai de bibliographie des populations du Soudan central." *Bulletin, Comité d'Etudes Historiques et Scientifiques de l'Afrique Occidentale Française*, vol. 19, 1936, pp. 243–333.

Van Rensburg, A.P.J. *Contemporary Leaders of Africa*. Cape Town: Hann, 1975.

West Africa. London. Weekly.

Westermann, Diedrich, and M. A. Bryan. *Handbook of African Languages*. Part II, *Languages of West Africa*. London: Dawsons, 1970.

Witherell, Julian. *Official Publications of the French Equatorial Africa, French Cameroons, and Togo, 1949–58*. Washington, DC: Library of Congress, 1964.

La zone franc et l'Afrique. Paris: Ediafric, 1981.

About the Author

Samuel Decalo (B.Sc., Ottawa University; M.A. and Ph.D. University of Pennsylvania) is an Israeli citizen, normally resident in the United States. He has taught at various universities, including the University of Rhode Island; Graduate Faculty, New School for Social Research; Emory University; and the University of Florida. He has also taught abroad, at the University of Botswana and at the University of the West Indies, and, is currently professor of political science at the University of Natal in Durban, South Africa.

Professor Decalo has conducted extensive research, including multiple fieldwork visits, in some twenty-five African states, mostly in francophone West and Equatorial Africa. He is the author of sixteen books and sixty articles on Africa and the Middle East, including five of the Scarecrow Press Historical Dictionaries; three in the Clio Press series of "World Bibliographies"; the classic work on African civil-military relations, *Coups and Military Rule in Africa* (Yale University Press, 2nd edition 1990); and *Psychoses of Power: African Personal Dictatorships* (acclaimed by *Choice* as an "Outstanding Book of 1990"). His most recent books are *The Stable Minority: Civilian Rule in Africa, Gabon: Under the Shadow of Big Brother,* and *Israel and Africa: Forty Years, 1956–1996*, all published in 1998 by Florida Academic Press.